CORBA Fundamentals and Programming

Written and Edited by Jon Siegel, Ph.D.

with

Dan Frantz, Ph.D., Digital Equipment Corporation

Hal Mirsky, Expersoft Corporation

Raghu Hudli, Ph.D., IBM Corporation

Peter de Jong, Ph.D., Alan Klein, and Brent Wilkins, Hewlett-Packard, Inc.

Alex Thomas and Wilf Coles, ICL

Sean Baker, Ph.D., Iona Technologies Ltd.

Maurice Balick, SunSoft, Inc.

Wiley Computer Publishing Group

John Wiley & Sons, Inc.

New York • Chichester • Brisbane • Toronto • Singapore

Publisher: Katherine Schowalter
Senior Editor: Robert Elliott
Managing Editor: Micheline Frederick
Text Design & Composition: Integre Technical Publishing Co., Inc.

Designations used by companies to distinguish their products are often claimed as trademarks. In all instances where John Wiley & Sons, Inc. is aware of a claim, the product names appear in initial capital or all capital letters. Readers, however, should contact the appropriate companies for more complete information regarding trademarks and registration.

This text is printed on acid-free paper.

This publication is designed to provide accurate and authoritative information in regard to the subject matter covered. It is sold with the understanding that the publisher is not engaged in rendering legal, accounting, or other professional service. If legal advice or other expert assistance is required, the services of a competent professional person should be sought.

Library of Congress Cataloging-in-Publication Data:
Siegel, Jon.
    CORBA fundamentals and programming / written and edited by Jon
  Siegel.
      p. cm.
    Includes index.
    ISBN 0-471-12148-7 (pbk. : alk. paper)
    1. Object-oriented programming (Computer science) I. Title.
  QA76.64.S52 1996
  005.1—dc20   95-48351
                                            CIP

Printed in the United States of America

10 9 8 7

*To my wife, Nancy, and our sons
Joshua and Adam, for their support.*

Jon Siegel

Trademarks

OMG® and Object Management® are registered trademarks of the Object Management Group. Object World® and the Object World logo are registered trademarks of Object World Corporation. Object Request Broker™, ORB™, CORBA™, OMG IDL™, Information Brokerage™, CORBAservices™ and CORBAfacilities™ are trademarks of the Object Management Group.

Alpha, AXP, DEC, ObjectBroker, OpenVMS, PATHWORKS, ULTRIX, VAX, VMS are registered trademarks of Digital Equipment Corporation.

Expersoft and PowerBroker are trademarks of ExperSoft Corporation.

ParcPlace and VisualWorks are registered trademarks of ParcPlace-Digitalk, Inc.

IBM, SOMobjects, and System Object Model are trademarks of the International Business Machines Corporation.

DAIS and DRS6000 are registered trademarks of International Computers Limited in the United Kingdom and other countries.

Orbix® is a registered trademark of IONA Technologies Ltd.

Sun, Sun Microsystems, the Sun logo, SunSoft, Java, NEO, NEOworks, SPARCworks, SPARCompiler, iMPact, and Solstice are trademarks or registered trademarks of Sun Microsystems, Inc. UNIX and OPEN LOOK are registered trademarks of UNIX System Laboratories, Inc.

All SPARC trademarks are used under license and are trademarks or registered trademarks of SPARC International, Inc. in the United States and other countries. Products bearing SPARC trademarks are based upon an architecture developed by Sun Microsystems, Inc.

About the Authors

Dr. Jon Siegel is Director of Domain Technology for the Object Management Group (OMG) where he has worked since late 1993. At OMG, he chairs the Domain Technology Committee, which sets OMG standards in vertical market areas, and the Liaison Subcommittee, which formalizes relationships with other consortia and sanctioned standards bodies such as ISO. Before joining OMG, Dr. Siegel performed research and development in Computer Science for Shell Oil Company where he championed the use of standards to reduce software development time and cost, and was an early developer of distributed object software. While at Shell, he served as its representative to the Open Software Foundation for four years, and to the Object Management Group for two years. He holds a Ph.D. in Theoretical Chemistry from Boston University.

Dr. Dan Frantz has 15 years of standards experience with CODASYL, ANSI, and ISO. He has been working in the OMG arena for Digital Equipment Corporation since 1994 and currently serves as Digital's representative to OMG's Architecture Board. Dan holds a Ph.D. in Computer Science from the University of Michigan.

Hal Mirsky has been involved in the development of distributed, object-based systems at Logicon Inc. and Expersoft Corporation since 1985. At Expersoft he has managed PowerBroker product development and acts as a mentor on distributed systems development projects.

Dr. Raghu V. Hudli is an Advisory Engineer in the Object Technology group at IBM Austin where he has worked on distributed and object-oriented computing since 1990. His research interests include object-oriented computing, parallel and distributed computing, theory of algorithms, and all aspects of VLSI design automation. He holds a Ph.D. in Computer Science from the University of Nebraska.

Dr. Peter de Jong is an architect for Hewlett-Packard's distributed object program where he has worked on many of HP's submissions to OMG's ORB and Object Services task forces. Before joining HP he worked for IBM on distributed, parallel, and object computing where he created and led the project that produced IBM's first relational database system, Query-by-Example. He holds a Ph.D. in Computer Science from MIT.

Alan Klein is a Usability Engineer at Hewlett-Packard, where he wrote the documentation for Hewlett-Packard Distributed Smalltalk 5.0. He has been promoting OO methods and development since 1988, working within the context of Hewlett-Packard's C++ SoftBench and Distributed Smalltalk.

Brent Wilkins is a software development engineer at Hewlett-Packard in the Distributed Smalltalk project and a key contributor to HP C++ Softbench. He implemented the OMG Interface Repository specification in the current release of HP Distributed Smalltalk.

Alex Thomas has been working with distributed objects since 1987, initially with a large investment bank, then a fine art auction house, and now with ICL. He has contributed to several OMG specifications including CORBA 2.0 Interoperability, the Object Transaction Service, and CORBA Security.

Wilf Coles is a principal software engineer in ICL where he has been working on DAIS Object Request Broker development for the past four years, most recently concentrating on the Object Transaction Service. Prior to that he spent 11 years designing communications and distributed systems.

Dr. Sean Baker is a founding member of IONA Technologies, and is Vice President of Professional Services and lead consultant. He is also responsible for certain product directions including the company's database strategy. Sean holds a Ph.D. in Computer Science from Trinity College, Dublin.

Maurice Balick is a Senior Staff Engineer at SunSoft in its Object Products Division where he was an architect and implementer of NEO's Object Development Framework. Before joining project DOE, Maurice worked for Sun Microsystems' Advanced Development Group on distributed object technologies for window systems.

Acknowledgments

It's not possible to acknowledge all of the people who contributed to this book. It's based on all of the OMG specifications, and hundreds of skilled people from hundreds of companies around the world have participated in their creation. We can't name them all here, but we can at least start by acknowledging our debt to these people for their fine work.

Enthusiastic support from the Object Management Group made this book possible. In particular, we want to thank OMG Vice President Dr. Richard Soley, who provided advice as well as technical review (although Jon Siegel takes full responsibility for any errors or omissions, of course). In addition, thanks to OMG President Chris Stone and Marketing Director Lydia Bennett. OMG supported this effort with network support for electronic mail and file transfer, paid the core costs for our biweekly teleconferences, and most important, granted some time to the principal author.

We also want to give special thanks to all of the contributing companies: Digital Equipment, Expersoft, Hewlett-Packard, IBM, ICL, IONA Technologies, and SunSoft. By making time available for their contributing authors, and giving them encouragement, they made possible the example section. We are not aware of any other standard that is illustrated by a single example worked directly in so many different products, programming languages, and platforms. We are proud to be associated with an effort in which so many competing companies worked so well together for the benefit of their end users and the computing industry as a whole.

The contributing authors worked far beyond the call of duty: Dan Frantz, Hal Mirsky, Raghu Hudli, Peter de Jong, Alan Klein, Brent Wilkins, Alex Thomas, Wilf Coles, Sean Baker, and Maurice Balick. Although we expected that they would work on the book on company time, many additional hours were squeezed in under deadline pressure, and every minute is greatly appreciated.

The crew working on the C implementation consisted of Dan Frantz, Raghu Hudli, Alex Thomas, and Wilf Coles. The C++ crew was Hal Mirsky, Peter de Jong, Sean Baker, and Maurice Balick. Smalltalk was taken care of by Alan Klein and Brent Wilkins. Thanks go to Dan, Raghu, Wilf, Hal, and Sean for work on common sections of the example chapters. Bart Hanlon of HP suggested and outlined the POS example early in our development cycle; we're happy to acknowledge this contribution and sorry that his other duties did not allow him to continue working with us.

As work on the example progressed, Dan Frantz wrote and updated the analysis and design material, and Hal Mirsky did the same for the IDL file—thanks to these two for taking on these crucial tasks. And, while each contributing author helped proofread, Sean Baker took it upon himself to read every page and submit detailed comments, which helped greatly.

We also want to thank these people at the contributing companies for their contributions: at Digital Equipment, John Parodi for his help with the product description; at Expersoft, Susan Carney, Dave Curtis, Joey Garon, Dave Frye, and Jeff Wang; at Hewlett-Packard, thanks to Steve Vinoski, Kevin Chesny, Robert Larson, Lynn Rowley, Stephanie Janowski, Ian Fuller, and Jerry Boortz; at IBM, Raghu Hudli is thankful to F. R. Campagnoni, IBM Austin, for his contributions and help with the IBM SOMobjects sections of the book. He also would like to thank Howard C. Nudd, IBM Austin, for his support. The IBM SOMobjects sections are influenced by the work of the members of the Object Technology Group in IBM Austin. But Raghu claims responsibilities for any inaccuracies and/or inconsistencies in those sections. At IONA Technologies, thanks to Ken Knox and Aidan Hollinshead for their help with coding and writeups, to Cormac ÓFoghlú for support, and Tom Golden for compiling the references. And, at SunSoft, thanks go to Liz Cobo for her assistance and support.

There has been explosive growth in the development of object request brokers since this book has gone to production. We want to thank every ORB vendor for their commitment to CORBA technology, including Postmodern Computing Technologies, Inc., NCR, Fujitsu, Ltd., Hitachi, Ltd., and NEC Corporation. Do not restrict your investigation to the ORB products presented in Chapters 20 through 22; the many other CORBA development environments on the market—including the ones listed above—have much to offer as well. OMG maintains an up-to-date list of ORB vendors; to check it out, see OMG's Web page: http://www.omg.org.

Transaction Processing is a highly specialized topic. For our treatment in this book, we turned to an expert: Edward Cobb of IBM Corporation. Some of the material in Chapter 14 appeared originally in his article, "Objects and Transactions: Together at Last," published in *Object Magazine*, January 1995, and Copyright 1995 by SIGS Publications. We want to thank Mr. Cobb and SIGS Publications for their contribution.

We kept the example moving and synchronized with twice-weekly tele-conferences. With participants spread over eight time zones from the British Isles to California, these teleconferences were not simple to set up or coordinate. We want to acknowledge our teleconference service, Connex International, and especially Wendy and Chris, who provided personalized service setting up our recurring intercontinental conversations.

Since books tend to be written during evening, weekends, and even vacations, authors' families contribute noticeably to the success of a project such as this one. I want to thank my wife Nancy, and our children Joshua and Adam, for their support and patience during the writing and editing of this book. Their help and forbearance made this work possible.

We're sure you'll agree with us, as you read through the example implementation on the eight ORBs, that this is a remarkable book based on a number of remarkable achievements: the shared example presented here and the OMG specifications that make it possible. The cooperative spirit of the OMG carried through our teleconferences into this book where it is on display in every chapter. All of the authors and contributors are proud to be associated with this effort, and hope that it contributes greatly to your understanding of CORBA.

Enjoy!

Jon Siegel

Table of Contents

About the Code

ON PROGRAMMING LANGUAGES AND FONTS

For clarity, we've set off code in the various computer languages, plus commands that you type in, by using the following different fonts:

Helvetica Bold is used exclusively to represent OMG IDL, OMG's language for defining objects' interfaces.

`Courier Bold` represents code in the programming languages C, C++, and Smalltalk. Pay attention to font usage where IDL mappings are discussed; frequently the **IDL** and `programming language` fonts will both appear in the same paragraph when mapping from IDL to that language is being discussed. Courier Bold is also used to represent `commands` that you enter to compile or run the example.

Other special constructs (directories and filenames, for example) are identified by context only, and not represented by any special font.

List of Figures

Introduction

This book presents the Object Management Group's (OMG) Object Management Architecture (OMA): the multivendor standard for object-oriented distributed computing. This includes CORBA—the Common Object Request Broker Architecture—which most people associate with OMG; the CORBAservices and CORBAfacilities are presented here, too.

There are a number of reasons you might be reading this book. For instance, you might be the architect responsible for selecting the interoperability architecture for your enterprise, and someone told you to find out more about CORBA. Or, you might be assigned to a prototype CORBA project, and you need to find out as much as you can about it in order to start your project and evaluation. Or, perhaps your company produces software, and you're considering CORBA as a platform that will let you market on a wide range of networked platforms with minimal porting. Or, there might not be any decision involved: You've been assigned to a CORBA-based development project, and you need a jump-start to find out about CORBA and learn to develop applications that take advantage of the interoperability and portability that the OMA provides.

It turns out that a lot of people need to find out more about CORBA, and there's a lot about CORBA to find out about. We've been writing about this topic in magazines for years and covered a lot of ground, but we really needed a book format to answer the questions people have about such a large topic. This book collects in one place the information you need. Here's how the book is arranged:

The OMG produces *specifications*, but you buy *products*. In order to cover both, we've divided this book into two major sections:

The first section, Chapters 1 through 17, presents the OMG specifications: CORBA, the CORBAservices, and the forthcoming CORBA-facilities. The discussion builds the environment from the architectural foundations of the Interface Definition Language (IDL) and Object Request Broker to the services and facilities that round out the programming and interoperability environment.

The second section, Chapters 18 through 33, presents a single programming example worked in eight ORBs, from seven vendors, in three programming languages. This part of the book answers a definitive "Yes!" to the question, "Is CORBA real?" and gives an example so concrete that you can find the answers to a lot of your implementation questions right here, even before you start to code a prototype yourself.

The discussion of each OMG specification starts from an architectural viewpoint: What does this component do, and how does it contribute to the OMA environment? Then, most topics continue with a more detailed discussion. Usually, this part of the presentation concludes with selected programming details, since we've found that almost everyone wants to see how developers will work with CORBA in real life. Other topics, for example the ORB and interoperability, go into detail because we've found that potential CORBA users want to know how location transparency really works, or how the object invocations are transmitted over the wire from one ORB to another, even though this functionality is automatic and not accessed directly by either end user or programmer. We've put the most detail into topics about which people have been the most curious; if your reaction to a claim is "How do they do that?" you'll probably find the answer later in the chapter where you can either analyze it yourself, or pass the section on to a technical colleague. When you finish reading this part of the book, you'll understand how CORBA and the OMA work together to enable the transparencies that applications need to work in today's networked world: transparencies to programming language, platform, operating system, network protocol, and more.

The products that implement CORBA cover a lot of ground: programming languages from C and C++ to COBOL and Ada; platforms from mainframes to micros to desktops; networks from fiber to satellite links. The tutorial programming example in this book showcases both the diversity and the commonality of the ORBs and CORBA development environments on the market today. It is worked here in eight ORBs, from seven vendors, in the three programming languages C, C++, and Smalltalk. More ORB vendors have worked the example as well; OMG maintains a Web page with pointers to every instance we know about (http://www.omg.org/CORBA_Primer.html). The programmers and authors who wrote the example worked hard to maximize commonality; the analysis and design and the IDL file, are common to *every* implementation; within each language, almost all of the code is as well. Common code is presented only once; ORB-specific sections detail product-specific portions and go on to explain how to use each programming environment to generate your executable objects. When you finish reading about and working the example, you'll have both overview and detailed programming-level knowledge of CORBA products and programming, which spans the range of products on the market today.

Chapter 1 discusses objects, and their benefits, in general. If objects are new to you, this material will help fill in the gaps in your knowledge (and if this isn't enough, check out the references in Appendix A for entire books devoted to this topic). Chapter 2 is a technical overview, covering all of CORBA and the OMA at an architectural level.

Chapters 3 through 9 detail CORBA, and Chapters 10 through 17 detail the rest of the OMA. Chapter 3 is devoted exclusively to OMG's Interface Definition Language (OMG IDL), the cornerstone of interoperability and transparency. We wanted to start out with ORB details—what it does and how it works—but we had to organize this way because all of the ORB interfaces are defined in IDL. If you're never going to program to these interfaces, you can skip most of this chapter and go to the Object Request Broker (ORB) description—Chapter 4—after reading the introductory material (there's a note telling you when to skip ahead). Chapters 4 through 6 describe the ORB, and Chapters 7 through 9 present mappings from IDL to the programming languages C, C++, and Smalltalk. This is where the world of the OMA meets your application code. Chapters 10 through 16 present those CORBAservices that were standardized, or almost complete, when we wrote the book; and Chapter 17 describes the exciting current work at OMG on the higher-level CORBAfacilities.

Each chapter is organized in "drill-down" style—architectural and user-level material toward the front; technical and programming-level details following. If you're not a programmer or a "techie," you can still learn a lot from the first section or two of each chapter up to Chapter 15, and all of Chapters 16 (Security) and 17 (the CORBAfacilities). If you're technically inclined, just read everything straight through. (If you're really technical, of course, you can buy the OMG specifications and read them, or join the OMG and *write* them....)

The rest of the book deals with the programming example. Chapter 18 is the problem statement: We have a retail domain with a depot or warehouse, a store, and a number of point-of-sale (POS) terminals, and our job is to design and implement a distributed computing system to handle sales and inventory. Chapter 19 follows up with a semi-formal object-oriented analysis and design: the objects in our system, what each one does, and which parameters are provided and returned in each invocation. Chapters 20 through 22 describe the ORB products and environments used to work the example in the rest of the book: Chapter 20 for C, 21 for C++, and 22 for Smalltalk. Although the chapters are organized according to the language each ORB uses to work the example here, almost all of the ORBs support multiple programming languages so you should consider all of the ORBs that support your language when you shop for a CORBA environment for your enterprise.

Nor are these the only ORBs on the market; for information on more ORB products (including additional ORBs that implement this example in this book), check out the OMG's Web page listed earlier in this section.

Chapter 23 presents the common IDL file used by every ORB to work the example. Following this, the three modules Depot, Store, and POS Terminal are worked in three-chapter groupings, one chapter each for C, C++, and Smalltalk. There's a roadmap in the beginning of Chapter 18; Figure 18.1 maps the path through the example for each language and ORB. When development is complete, Chapter 33 shows how to fire up your example objects and run your retail empire. The diskette contains the common OMG IDL file, plus all the source code and supplemental files (makefiles or whatever) you need to run the example on all of the listed ORBs. OMG's Web page contains pointers to other ORBs that support the example on-line.

The example here is long on CORBA and short on functionality (although it includes enough to demonstrate that CORBA really does useful work); after all, every reader is interested in CORBA, but only a minority will ever run a retail chain. Most of the code demonstrates how CORBA works and exercises key features that developers need to know to make effective use of object-oriented distributed computing. Objects in the example represent, and work like, objects in the real world, and best-practice programming technique is used throughout (and the text points out places where this makes a difference).

So, how should you read this book? It depends on who you are and what you need to know. If you're an executive more concerned with corporate directions and budget than with electronic plumbing, start by reading Chapters 1 and 2. Then read the beginning few sections of each chapter from 3 through 15, as much as you need of 16 (Security), and all of 17 (the CORBAfacilities). Then skim Chapter 18 (example description) and any other part of the example that interests you. If you're a technical manager or supervisor who will never (or almost never) program a CORBA application yourself, read the first part of the book the same way, but spend more time on the product descriptions and example programming in the second part. If you're on a team evaluating CORBA for your company, you (or someone on the team, anyhow) probably needs to understand almost everything in here. If you're a programmer and you're already sitting at your machine, you can spin the diskette and start at Chapter 18 if you don't mind working ahead of the explanations—the text will guide you through the example whether you understand the overall architecture or not. Then you can read the hows and whys when you're home, away from your machine, or by candlelight during a power failure.

Thanks for picking up this book. The authoring team has done its best to give you everything you need to really understand CORBA, all tucked between two covers. All of us hope you'll like what you find here.

CHAPTER 1

Introducing CORBA

This book contains the information you need to get started with CORBA—the Common Object Request Broker Architecture of the Object Management Group (OMG). *The first third of the book, Chapters 1 through 17, presents and explains CORBA and the Object Management Architecture (OMA).* This chapter is an executive summary, presenting the benefits but only referencing the supporting details. Chapter 2 presents a technical overview, while Chapters 3 through 17 fill in technical details about CORBA, the CORBAservices, and the CORBAfacilities. *Following this, Chapters 18 through 33 present a single tutorial programming example, worked in eight CORBA environments representing three programming languages and seven different vendors.* If you're only interested in programming (unlikely, we presume), you can skip to Chapter 18 right now, fire up one of the CORBA environments on our list, spin the diskette, and start coding; we'll see you here later so you can find out what you've done. But if you want to find out about CORBA first, keep reading here.

Of course, there is more to object-oriented development than CORBA. First, there is a lot more that can be said about the business case for object orientation (OO), and an excellent presentation of this is given in *The Object Revolution* by Michael Guttman and Jason Matthews (see Appendix A for references). Second, many folks recommend a thorough object-oriented analysis and design as the first step for all but the smallest development project. We'll touch on this in Chapter 18 and give references there. In this book, our focus will be on *interoperability* and *implementation*.

1.1 HETEROGENEOUS DISTRIBUTED COMPUTING

Diversity in hardware and software is a fact of life, and our networked computing environment is becoming more diverse, not less, as computers evolve. At the high end, supercomputers working in teams perform complex scientific and engineering calculations, or serve massive databases like airline reservation systems. In the midrange, powerful servers and surprisingly capable desktop machines provide an increasingly complex array of services. And at the low end, embedded systems, which we may not even think of as computers, interact with each other and with conventional systems to provide automation of tasks at home and work: TV sets and VCRs interacting with programming services; thermostats and alarm sensors acting as components of building automation systems; PDAs, pagers, and more. You know from scanning this list that these computers will use a range of operating systems and a number of programming languages. But the need for interoperability spans machine size and type—PDAs and pagers, for instance, are more valuable when they can receive and reply to messages from machines anywhere on the network—not just desktop machines, but also large servers, for example, financial data (a service available today) or airline schedules.

If you're responsible for all or part of the IT in an enterprise, you may have recognized your company's computer and network configuration in that last paragraph—a collection of diverse computers, performing different functions or storing different data in different places, loaded with immovable legacy applications storing legacy data in legacy formats, and hampered from working together by incompatabilities of operating system, network hardware and protocol, thus preventing you from getting your work done. But you know that the computing paradigm has changed: No longer satisfied with using their computers to count their money, companies like yours want to use their computers to *make* money by having them work together to recognize and respond to new opportunities in increasingly rapid and flexible ways.

Let's focus on the problems this environment creates:

- It's difficult to get the hardware—computers and networks—to work together. We need varied types of computer and network hardware and operating systems to get our work done with the price/performance we must have to run our business, but the complexity is difficult to deal with.

- It's even more difficult to get the software to work together. An enterprise today is a collection of diverse parts, (hopefully!) working smoothly together toward a common goal. We need the same attributes in our software, but the different pieces bought by different departments to work on different systems don't speak the same language, and it costs time and money to integrate them.

▪ And, finally, software development takes too long and costs too much. Typically, each project starts from scratch. This approach was acceptable when projects were small and relatively simple, but it will not work for large applications that model the enterprise. We need a way to build all of our software on a common foundation, modeled after the assembly line instead of the craftsman, to cut down time and cost.

Component software is making this possible. Applications are changing; customers are less willing to accept huge, monolithic do-everything applications, and are looking for smaller components that they can combine flexibly and dynamically to create tools focused on their particular business needs. And components will work together only if they have been designed and built on standard interfaces.

Since interoperability must span the enterprise and even go beyond it to customers' and suppliers' systems, these interfaces must be independent of platform, operating system, programming language, even network protocol; anything less will create "islands of interoperability" insulated from each other by arbitrary technological barriers that keep us from realizing the benefits we're entitled from our investment in computing.

1.2 OBJECT TECHNOLOGY

What we need is a new way of looking at the entire problem—from problem statement and analysis through solution design and implementation to deployment, use, maintenance, and extension—which integrates every component and takes us in orderly fashion from each step to the next. *Object technology* is this new way, and in this book, we'll begin to see how.

Since this is too big a topic for a single book, we'll concentrate on the areas concerned with implementation, where OMG's contributions provide the most benefit. In this section, take a look at the concept of object technology and why it has become the new paradigm of computing. But first, a look at how we got here. From the beginning of business computing in the 1950s until desktop computing became well established in the late '80s, computing was such a costly endeavor that programs and systems focused on conserving resources like memory, persistent storage, and input/output. This led to batch-oriented systems that updated periodically instead of continuously, and produced reports perhaps weekly and monthly. In many cases, these reports were out of date before they were printed out.

That is, computing focused on *data*, instead of the uses the data might have, and on *computing procedures*, instead of business processes. Computers, not people, were in the driver's seat, and the people who used computers had to translate data to the program's structure on input, and translate back from the program's structure to their needs when they received the output.

1.2.1 Modeling the Real World

Hardware has changed a lot since the early days; in fact, the rapid pace of change sometimes seems like a problem itself. But there's no denying that abundant computing power, memory, storage, and data communications gives us an environment where we can mold computing to our needs instead of adapting to it.

In a nutshell, object technology means *computing that models the real world*. An object in a computer program corresponds to a real object, both to the programmer when he or she implements it, and to the user when he or she creates, manipulates, and uses it. And, computer objects work together to model the interactions of real-world objects. For instance, a storage tank object in a computer-modeled petroleum refinery might be connected through pipe and valve objects to chemical reactor objects, distiller objects, and other refinery components in an integrated application, which, taken as a whole, simulates refinery operation very closely even though no single part represents the entire system.

1.2.2 Dealing with Complexity

Complexity is the word that best describes the problems we're facing today. The simple computing problems have been solved during the decades already past, and the companies that can't handle the complex problems are going to fall by the wayside during the decades ahead. Fortunately, the tools to work the complex problems are available now, and that's what the rest of this book is about.

Generations of problem-solving experience have shown that the best way of dealing with complexity is to split a huge problem into a number of smaller, more manageable parts. But, we have to be careful how we do this, because the wrong split will make our problem *more* complex instead of simpler. For instance, some approaches split data from functionality; if we started with basically a data problem or a functionality problem, this simplifies our task by letting us focus on the core without distraction from the rest. But if we actually started with an integrated problem, this division leaves us holding only half the clues and half the tools, and still trying to solve the whole thing.

By splitting our computing problem into components that model the real world, we build on things we're all familiar with. Components will be easier for customer, analyst, programmer, and user to grasp, and interactions between objects will appear logical and well-founded.

But object-orientation does more than give us a real-world model. It also helps solve the three major problems of programming:

- *Programs are difficult to change or extend:* When programs are implemented as discrete objects, many changes will turn out to affect only a single object or a small group of related ones. The "house of cards" problem is reduced or eliminated.

- *Programs are difficult to maintain:* Old-paradigm programs scattered related functionality or data throughout a program, almost guaranteeing that maintenance changes would have far-reaching and unanticipated consequences. By basing our programming on modules formulated on real-world objects, we limit the scope of these unwanted effects.

- *Programs take too long to write:* Well-conceived objects invite reuse, making new programs faster and cheaper to write. Sometimes, objects can be reused as written; in other cases, the objects provide a basis that can be extended. Of course, this advantage doesn't happen right away—you need to generate the reusable code before you can benefit from it. But even new project teams benefit from class libraries that provide basic functionality, and more vendor-provided objects are coming on the market every week.

1.3   OBJECT-ORIENTED SOFTWARE INTEGRATION

The next three sections sum up our object-oriented solution to the software integration problem: First, we'll define just what a CORBA object is; second, we'll get a first look at the basic architecture (that is, CORBA), which allows all of the objects on our system to communicate; and third, we'll start examining the higher-level architecture for the objects themselves, which allows *applications* to communicate—OMG's Object Management Architecture or OMA. The rest of the book builds on this introduction: Chapters 2 through 17 give details on all three parts; then the example in Chapters 18 through 33 demonstrates the interoperability solution.

Without a doubt, our ultimate goal is *application integration*. But, in order to get there, OMG had to solve the interoperability problem first, to create a foundation for the work on integration. The interoperability problem is solved: OMG's solution is CORBA, and it's described in Chapter 2 through Chapter 9, and illustrated in the tutorial example. The integration solution is a work in progress: The base layer of CORBAservices is described in Chapter 10 through Chapter 16, but the higher-level CORBAfacilities, which will yield the biggest payoff to developer and end user, are just starting to emerge. We'll summarize the CORBAfacilities in Chapter 17. There is plenty of opportunity to help shape these specifications as they emerge; we'll talk about that too.

1.3.1   What Is an Object?

Objects are discrete software components—they contain data, and can manipulate it (there's a more complete definition in Chapter 2). Usually, they model real-world objects, although sometimes it's useful to create objects specifically for things we want to compute. Other software components send messages to objects with requests; the objects send other messages back with their responses.

In an enterprise, many objects model real-world entities. For example, an oil company's refinery control program might contain a number of Storage Tank objects. Each of these would know what type of liquid it contains (because it had received this information in a message and stored it), how full it was (perhaps by reading a sensor), and how big it was. In response to a request, the tank could respond by telling what it contained—type of liquid and amount. In a modeling calculation, the tank object could "deliver" the liquid to a pipe or valve object by sending it a message, stopping the flow when it became empty, just like a real tank. And it would probably sound an alarm (by sending a message to an alarm system object) if its fill level exceeded a preset safe level.

Usually objects in the computer are created from a template. For our tank object, the template knows all of the properties that a tank might have: a size, location, content type, content amount, connections, and so forth. When we use the template to create a tank object "instance," we place values into the placeholders the template provides in order to make this object represent a *particular* tank. (In object-speak, this template is termed a *class.*)

The template also knows all the things that a tank can do—that is, the messages that we can send it, and ones that it can send to other objects. Each particular tank object instance that we create has the same set of capabilities.

From the template, we can create *as many tank objects as we need or want*. Each one has the *same set of quantities that it can store*, and the *same set of messages that it will respond to*, and *the same set of functions that it can perform*. (What if this template is almost, but not quite, what we need? We can derive a new template from this one using *inheritance*. (For details, look ahead to Section 2.2.2.)

Flexibility is built in, since one of the things an object can do is send messages to other objects. We would expect, for instance, that our tank object would talk to pipe or valve objects, and possibly to sensors that monitor fill level or possibly temperature. Since each tank can connect to its own set of other objects—pipes, valves, sensors—a small set of templates representing these different object types will let us model a refinery of any size and complexity!

A spreadsheet cell is another good example of an object: It contains *data*: probably a numerical value; perhaps instead some text or a formula. It can perform *operations*: It can manipulate the data by displaying them on the screen or a printed page, perhaps in a particular font, size, and format; or by performing calculations; and it can deliver its contents on request (perhaps to a linked document). Like many (but not all) objects, there can be many cells, all identical except for contents and address, and each created from the same template. The spreadsheet program with its loaded spreadsheet data—a collection of objects—is an object itself. The additional operations it can perform include displaying, printing, or formatting ranges of cells, or the entire spreadsheet.

In this book, we won't consider passive collections of data to be objects. That means that your spreadsheet data file, or document data file, are not objects when they're stored on disk. Neither is a CD-ROM disk, nor the files on it. But the spreadsheet data file and document data file become intrinsic parts of objects (or collections of objects) when they are loaded into the programs that manipulate them, and the CD-ROM disk may become the data part of an object when it's loaded into a drive. Why this distinction? Because to us, an object is something that can take part in our component software environment, and that means that an object has to be more than just data.

1.3.2 CORBA: Object Interoperability

In order for objects to plug and play together in a useful way, clients have to know exactly what they can expect from every object they might call upon for a service. In CORBA, the services that an object provides are expressed in a contract that serves as the *interface* between it and the rest of our system. This contract serves two distinct purposes:

- it informs potential clients of the services the object provides, and tells them how to construct a message to invoke the service; and
- it lets the communications infrastructure know the format of all messages the object will receive and send, allowing the infrastructure to translate data formats where necessary to provide transparent connection between sender and receiver.

Each object needs one more thing: a unique handle that a client can pass to the infrastructure to route a message to it. We're deliberately not calling it an address—objects keep the same handle when they move from one location to another. Think of the handle as a kind of address with automatic forwarding.

Now we have a complete conceptual picture of our networked computing environment: Each node is an object with a well-defined interface, identified by a unique handle. Messages pass between a sending object and a target object; the target object is identified by its handle, and the message format is defined in an interface known to the system. This information enables the communications infrastructure to take care of all of the details.

These simple, yet powerful concepts provide the fundamentals for CORBA's component software revolution. The interfaces are expressed in OMG Interface Definition Language—OMG IDL—making them accessible to objects written in virtually any programming language, and the cross-platform communications architecture is the Common Object Request Broker Architecture—CORBA. You'll see for yourself how these principles work when you build and run the example in this book.

1.3.3 The OMA: Application-Level Integration

CORBA is a great accomplishment but it connects only objects, not applications. Enterprise integration requires a lot more than this, and OMG provides it in the Object Management Architecture or OMA (Figure 1.1). Of course, it's based on CORBA, but this is just a starting point.

The Object Management Architecture embodies OMG's vision for the component software environment. One of the organization's earliest products, this architecture shows how standardization of component interfaces will penetrate up to—although not into—application objects in order to create a plug-and-play component software environment based on object technology. Application objects, although not standardized by OMG, will access CORBAservices and CORBAfacilities through standard interfaces to provide benefits to both providers and end users: for providers, lower development costs and an expanded market base; for end users, a lower-cost software environment that can easily be configured to their company's specific needs.

Based on the CORBA architecture we just discussed, the OMA specifies a set of standard interfaces and functions for each component. Different vendors' implementations of the interfaces and their functionality then plug-and-play on customers' networks, allowing integration of additional functionality from purchased modules or in-house development.

The OMA is divided into two major components: lower-level CORBAservices and intermediate-level CORBAfacilities.

The CORBAservices provide basic functionality that almost any object might need: object lifecycle services such as move and copy, naming and directory services, and other basics. Basic does not necessarily mean simple, however; included in this category are object-oriented access to online transaction processing (OLTP, the mainstream application for business

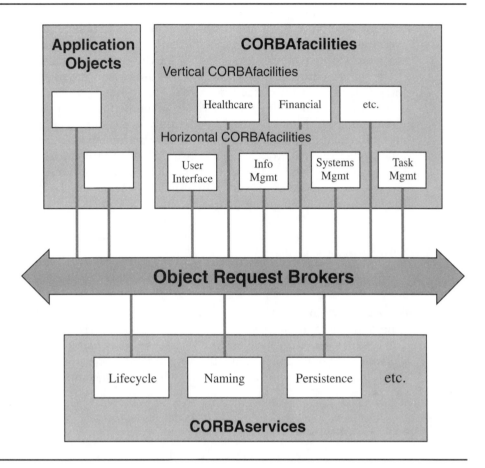

Figure 1.1. OMG's Object Management Architecture. Each service (boxes) is composed of a number of CORBA objects, each accessed by a standard IDL interface. Clients access all services through the Object Request Broker.

accounting) and a sophisticated object Trader service—kind of a "yellow pages" where objects advertise the availability (and price!) of their services. The Trader service has the potential to revolutionize distributed computing. (See Chapter 12 for details.)

Where the CORBAservices provide services for objects, the CORBA-facilities provide services for *applications*. For instance, the Compound Document Mangement CORBAfacility gives applications a standard way to access the components of a compound document. With this in place, a vendor could easily generate a sophisticated set of tools for advanced manipulation of one part of the document—images, say—and market them without having to generate the basic functionality him- or herself. Sophisticated users could upgrade one part of an application suite to a very high level if they require, without having to modify or substitute for the remaining parts.

It is the CORBAfacilities that give meaning to our promise of application integration. The CORBAfacilities architecture has two major components: one, horizontal, including facilities such as compound document services just mentioned, which can be used by virtually every business; and the other, vertical, standardizing management of information specialized to particular industry groups. So large is the scope of this effort that the CORBAfacilities will eventually dwarf CORBA and the CORBAservices in size. OMG does not plan to produce all of the CORBAfacility standards itself, by the way; the organization has put in place procedures to incorporate other consortia standards as CORBAfacilities as long as they conform to the rest of the OMA. Industries such as healthcare, finance, and others are ready to participate; for details, look ahead to Chapter 17.

1.4 CORBA BENEFITS

So, why move to CORBA and the OMA? Here's a summary of the benefits from two points of view: First, for your developers—the people who design and produce your applications; and second, for your users—not just the people who run your applications (and your business!), but also your business itself, for it is a user in its own right, with its own complex set of requirements.

1.4.1 For Your Developers

For developers, there are a large number of reasons to move to CORBA. For example:

- CORBA is the only environment that lets you take advantage of all the tools you've bought, from hardware to development software. There's a reason for all of that diversity in the marketplace (and probably around your company as well)—different tools are tuned for different jobs, and it's not practical to limit your choices in the face of limited budgets, high expectations, and competition hot on your heels. You need an architecture that can run on every hardware platform and network, and an interoperability architecture that links every programming language from C and C++ through Smalltalk and Ada to almost every other, including productivity-building interactive development tools.

- The object-oriented paradigm meshes with software "best practice" from the start of the development cycle to the end: object-oriented analysis and design in the beginning stages, implemented in object-oriented languages and object-oriented databases using object-oriented user interfaces, deployed in a distributed object environment.

▪ Give them an IDL interface and a thin layer of wrapper code, and legacy applications come into the CORBA environment on an equal basis with your new software components. Since you have to keep your business going full speed while you bring in distributed computing and object orientation, this is essential to enabling enterprises to make the transition.

▪ The CORBA/OMA environment maximizes programmer productivity: CORBA provides a sophisticated base, with transparent distribution and easy access to components. The CORBAservices provide the necessary object-oriented foundation, while the CORBAfacilities will standardize management of shared information. Developers create or assemble application objects in this environment, taking advantage of every component.

This standard CORBA/OMA environment helps three ways: Your programmers don't have to build the tools, they're provided for you; the same set of CORBAservices and CORBAfacilities is available with every CORBA environment, so both your applications *and your programmers* port from one platform/ORB to another; and interoperability results because clients on one platform know how to invoke standard operations on objects on any other platform.

▪ Code reuse comes into play two ways: First, components get reused as-is in new or dynamically reconfigured applications; and second, your programmers can build new objects by making incremental modifications to existing ones without having to recode the parts that already work. Since these build on what you already have, the boost from reuse starts out small but snowballs as libraries of components and code accumulate. Experience shows, companies that code for reuse demonstrate savings of 50 to 80 percent after a few projects' library-building.

▪ You can mix and match tools within a project—develop a desktop component using an interactive builder, for instance, while you write its server module in a lower-level language like C++. CORBA will allow the two to interoperate smoothly.

1.4.2 For Your Users, and Your Company

You need to solve the entire integration problem in order to survive, but you also need to devote maximum resources to widening your technological edge in order to compete. There's only one way to do this: Use *industry standards* to get your company onto the playing field the quickest and cheapest way; then devote the resources you saved toward building an edge that beats your competition hands-down.

For your users, *a CORBA/OMA application is a dynamic collection of client and object implementation components, configured and connected at run time to attack the problem at hand.* It may include and integrate:

- components located in different departments or divisions;
- components located both inside and outside your enterprise, including sites of customers, suppliers, and service providers;
- components from multiple software vendors;
- components from both in-house developers and outside vendors;
- components embedded in other elements—automated production facilities or monitoring systems in the enterprise, TVs, VCRs, and alarm systems in the home;
- or more, all working together in an integrated way.

By the time you or your programmers have finished the example in this book, you will (depending on which or how many CORBA environments you complete) be able to demonstrate many of these integration modes and benefits for yourself!

There are many reasons you might have to integrate platforms as diverse as this, some good and some unavoidable. For instance, in most companies, office desktops run PC- or Apple-compatible architectures, while technical and engineering desktops run open-systems workstations; the integration problem from this involves (at least) two or three operating systems and two networks. Many companies are just now trying to integrate equipment acquired by different departments or divisions over the past few decades, chosen with no consideration for ease of possible integration down the road (that is, *now*). And other enterprises have to integrate hardware and software from companies that they acquire during the course of their own business.

You will have to integrate these diverse platforms and systems, because you need them all to run your business at a price you can afford. And you will have to solve the complexity problem in order to survive, because some of your competitors will, and your company's future depends on your doing it better and faster than they do.

1.5   WHAT IS THE OMG?

The Object Management Group is a consortium of computing-involved companies. Its 600-plus members include all of the major vendors of systems and software from around the world, as well as independent software vendors, consulting companies both large and small, and an increasing number of end-user companies primarily involved in setting specifications for the vertical CORBAfacilities. OMG is truly an international organization, with one-third of its members coming from outside the United States, most from Europe, but about 5 percent of the total from other countries, chiefly in the Asian Pacific Rim but also including Australia, Africa, and South America.

Unlike some other consortia, the OMG does not produce software—only specifications. The specifications are freely available for *any* company (OMG member or not) to implement; neither explicit permission nor fee is required. OMG expects that implementations will come from many companies. The numerous ORBs in this book, and even more not included here, demonstrate that this expectation is rapidly becoming reality.

Members of the OMG meet about six times each year to advance the standards process. Task Forces reporting to the OMG TC (Technical Committee) write and issue Requests For Proposals or RFPs, requirements documents for each standard. Responding companies (which must be members of the OMG at the Corporate level) submit the specifications for their software for consideration. A period of time is allowed for revision of submissions; sometimes, revisions target requirements that were not met; other times, different submitters merge proposals where differences were found to be minor or resolvable. A voting process moving successively through the Task Force, Technical Committee, and finally, the OMG Board of Directors declares the successful proposal to be an official OMG specification.

This process is noteworthy because it drives all of the participating companies toward *consensus*. Although submitting companies tend to work individually or in small groups at the beginning of the specification process, by the end, they are typically working in concert, concentrating on the production of a final specification that will withstand the scrutiny of all of their peers in the task force and technical committee. As a result, published OMG specifications tend to bear the names of many submitting companies; for example, the original CORBA specfication was a consensus submission from six companies, and the first set of CORBAservices was cosubmitted by 11.

Companies that submit the successful proposal must market a commercial implementation within a year. This requirement serves both to keep companies' proposals realistic, and to ensure that OMG specifications become reality in the marketplace. In fact, it is market opportunity, and not this requirement, that leads to *many* companies, not just submitters, getting compliant products to market as quickly as they can.

The OMG is an open organization, and welcomes any company to join. Prospective members frequently attend a meeting as guests to find out first-hand about the benefits of membership. For information on how to contact the OMG, look in Appendix A.

CHAPTER 2

Technical Overview

2.1 INTRODUCTION

This chapter introduces all of the important OMA- and CORBA-related concepts, the benefits from each one, and the total benefit that accrues when all work together to provide true intra-enterprise and inter-enterprise distributed computing. The first section presents the big picture, introducing all of the components and how they interconnect. Subsequent sections fill in key details. Although the presentation is more technical than Chapter 1, it does not include programming details. For these, continue with Chapters 3 through 9, which examine the CORBA architecture one component at a time.

2.1.1 CORBA and the OMA

Figure 2.1 shows a request passing from a client to an object implementation in the CORBA architecture. Two aspects of this architecture stand out:

- Both client and object implementation are isolated from the Object Request Broker (ORB) by an IDL interface. *CORBA requires that every object's interface be expressed in OMG IDL. Clients see only the object's interface, never any implementation detail. This guarantees substitutability of the implementation behind the interface—our plug-and-play component software environment.*

- The request does not pass directly from client to object implementation; instead, requests are *always* managed by an ORB. *Every invocation of a CORBA object is passed to the ORB; the form of the invocation is the same whether the target object is local or remote. Distribution details remain in the ORB where they are handled by software you bought, not software you*

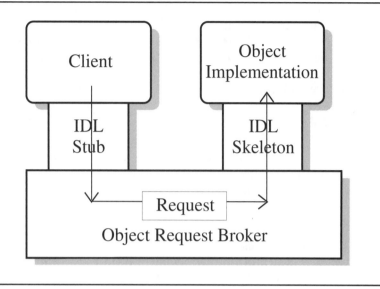

Figure 2.1.   A request passing from client to object implementation.

built. Application code, freed of this adminstrative burden, concentrates on the problem at hand.

It takes more than a flexible request-passing mechanism to build an enterprise-spanning object-based distributed computing system. If, in addition, all components share a common architecture and set of standard IDL interfaces, the resulting system achieves a coherence and synergy that provides many benefits. To the enterprise, the common architecture makes possible a unified enterprise computing environment composed of interoperating components from multiple vendors and in-house developers; to vendors, it provides quick passage from the building of basic components to product differentiation through value-added features and functionality.

OMG's Object Management Architecture (OMA, Figure 1.1) defines this common architecture. The CORBAservices provide system-level services needed by almost any object-based system, while the CORBAfacilities allow standards-based access to common datatypes and functionality needed by enterprise-wide (horizontal) and industry-specific (vertical) application groups.

The first thing we'll detail in this chapter are the characteristics of a CORBA object. Then we'll examine the IDL interface, not only because it enables our component software environment, but also because the ORB uses IDL in its operation. We'll learn details about the ORB next. Then we'll put the two together and see how the combination of IDL interfaces and ORB infrastructure combine to give the benefits of CORBA. With the plumbing in place, we'll cover the Object Management Architecture (OMA) that builds on it, the CORBAservices and CORBAfacilities. By the end of this chapter, we'll understand all of CORBA and the OMA at an architectural level. Chapters 3 through 9 will fill in the programming details.

2.2 WHAT IS A CORBA OBJECT?

In Section 1.3.1 we defined objects in a general way. Here we'll go further, and examine the characteristics that let a software module plug-and-play as an object in the CORBA environment. There are three keys: *encapsulation*, *inheritance*, and *polymorphism*.

2.2.1 Encapsulation

Encapsulation enables plug-and-play software. An encapsulated software module consists of two distinct parts: its *interface*, which the module presents to the outside world, and its *implementation*, which it keeps private. The interface represents a contract or promise by the object: If a client sends the object one of the messages specified in the interface, with the proper input arguments in their agreed-upon formats, the object will provide the response message with the results in their proper places. How the response was calculated or produced and the results placed into their proper places in the return message is of concern only to the object itself; the client is not allowed to examine the process, nor to obtain any additional information.

If we have more than one implementation of an object with the same interface—written in a different programming language, for instance, or using a different database for internal storage—we could substitute one for another on our system and a client would neither know nor care, since the responses to its messages would not change. This substitutability is the key to our component software environment.

Encapsulation also enables CORBA to provide *location transparency*. Clients send the invocation to their local ORB, not to the target object itself; the ORB routes the message to its destination. Applications do not have to be reconfigured when objects move about your enterprise; the ORBs know where they live and automatically route messages to their proper targets. (How does this work? Via the *object reference*, which we'll describe in Section 4.2.2.)

Encapsulation is enough to make our environment componentized, but not object-oriented. We can substitute equivalent implementations, and move them around the network almost at will. But in order to benefit from object-oriented software engineering and development concepts, we also need inheritance and polymorphism.

2.2.2   Inheritance

Sometimes, we can create a new object template more easily by adapting an existing one than by creating it from scratch. For instance, a department manager object is an employee object that knows which department it manages. *Inheritance* is the object-oriented concept that allows us to actually create the manager object template from the employee template in this way.

Inheritance saves designers and programmers a lot of work, since existing object templates can serve as the basis for new ones. It requires forethought, though, since inheritance works better when the fundamental objects are constructed with these extensions in mind. Object-oriented languages like C++ and Smalltalk have inheritance built in, and object-oriented design tools take advantage of it whenever they can, so CORBA includes it too.

2.2.3   Polymorphism

Some operations naturally belong to more than one kind of object. For instance, you would expect to be able to invoke the *draw* operation on just about any graphics object—a square, or circle, or line, or whatever—and have it draw itself on a screen or a printer. But the client invoking the *same* operation on a set of objects actually results in different things happening, since each object has its own methods, which get executed when it receives the order to draw itself. And, if we added a new graphics object to our program—a house, let's say—our client would already know how to draw it: just send it the message *draw*, and it draws itself! This is polymorphism.

These three key components play different roles in CORBA. Encapsulation is the cornerstone. By itself, it enables plug-and-play component software and location transparency. It is also the concept that comes into play when you *wrap* a legacy application in OMG IDL so it can be accessed from your CORBA clients. In contrast, inheritance and polymorphism let CORBA work with object-oriented tools and languages; analysis and design tools use them automatically, as do object-oriented languages like C++ and Smalltalk. So they're built into OMG IDL, but you don't have to use them in order for your software to plug-and-play in the CORBA environment.

2.3   OMG IDL

In CORBA, an object's interface is defined in OMG IDL—Interface Definition Language. The interface definition specifies the operations the object is prepared to perform, the input and output parameters they require, and any exceptions that may be generated along the way. This interface constitutes a contract with clients of the object, who use the *same* interface definition to build and dispatch invocations as the object implementation uses to receive and respond. Client and object implementation are then isolated by at least three components: an IDL stub on the client end, an ORB (or several, as we shall see later, if we are interoperating with a remote system), and a corresponding IDL skeleton on the object implementation end. This isolation provides a great amount of flexibility and many benefits.

Now you can see how CORBA enforces encapsulation: Clients can only access an object as defined by its IDL interface; there is no way in the architecture to get around the interface to access the implementation directly.

Contrast this approach to invocation of objects in programming languages. C++ clients call C++ objects directly: The "interface" consists of C++ statements that invoke methods on the objects. Similarly, Smalltalk clients invoke methods on Smalltalk objects directly through Smalltalk statements. This approach, although straightforward, does not have the flexibility of CORBA: There is no standard way, for example, for a C++ client to invoke a method on a Smalltalk object, or the reverse.

The CORBA architecture separates the interface, written in OMG IDL, from the implementation, which must be written in some programming language. To the client or user, the interface represents a *promise*: When the client sends a proper message to the interface, the response will come back. To the object implementor, the interface represents an *obligation*: He or she must implement, in some programming language, all of the operations specified in the interface. Writing the contract (in OMG IDL) and fulfilling it (in a programming language such as C++, C, or Smalltalk) are usually two separate steps in the writing of a CORBA application, although some ORB environments generate IDL automatically.

2.3.1 Building a CORBA Object

Let's say we're going to build a new CORBA object. The first thing we do is figure out (and write down, if we're following good programming practice) *exactly* what it's going to do. We'll skip that part here, since our object in this chapter is hypothetical, but we do want to point out that analysis and design is a crucial step for the success of your object-oriented project. (To see the results of the analysis and design for the example in this book, take a look at Chapter 19.)

Since this is a CORBA object, the next thing we need to do is define its interface in OMG IDL. The IDL interface specifies all of the operations the object is going to perform, their input and output parameters and return values, and every exception that may be generated. Chapter 3 describes OMG IDL in more detail, including object-oriented aspects such as inheritance. The IDL file for the example worked in this book appears in Chapter 23.

By the way, there wouldn't be much difference if we were building an object from an existing legacy application instead of starting from scratch. Most of our program would already be written; we'd still have to generate an IDL interface to represent the module's functions, and code a thin "wrapper" to connect our IDL layer to the legacy app.

2.3.2 Making Choices

Notice that, even though we have fixed the functionality and syntax for invoking our object, we have *not* fixed any other aspect at this point. Specifically, we have not yet fixed:

- the programming language we will use to implement it;
- the platform or operating system it will run on;
- the ORB it will connect to;
- whether it will run local to its clients or remotely;
- the network hardware or protocol it will use, if remote;
- or other aspects including, for example, security levels and provisions.

The flexibility remaining is a major benefit of the CORBA standard. Standardization allows these important choices to be postponed until later stages of the development process. Although the choice of programming language will happen very early (in fact, that's the next step), the interoperability built in to CORBA allows the selection of local or remote access and network protocol to be postponed until run time. In this chapter, we will point out the decisions that focus on our specific implementation environment.

Even though these important aspects remain undetermined, *we already have all the information we need to construct a client of the object*. In CORBA, all a client developer needs to know is the IDL interface definition and the description of what the object does. This is how CORBA and IDL enable our plug-and-play component software environment. At run time, only one other piece of information will be needed to invoke a method on the object: its object reference (more on this a little later).

2.3.3 Choosing an Implementation Language

As we saw in Figure 2.1, the IDL skeleton connects to our ORB on one end and our object implementation on the other. (There is a similar configuration at the client end as well.) Each connection requires a decision on our part: On the object implementation end, we need to select a programming language; on the other end, we need to select an ORB vendor and product. We'll discuss the language issues first, ORB selection next.

In selecting a programming language, you need to consider two things: *suitability* and *availability*. A programming language is suitable if it can do the things your application needs, using only the computing resources you have available, and if you and your programming team know it or can learn it. At your site, there may be other considerations. For instance, some companies have administrative preferences or restrictions covering certain languages. And for availability, not all ORBs support IDL mappings for every programming language. You will have to check ORBs for availability on the hardware platforms you plan to run on; you will have more freedom (and more decisions to make) if you are able to select hardware platform and ORB software together. Chapter 20 through Chapter 22 introduce the seven ORB products covered in this book, including the platforms covered and languages implemented by each. They're a great place to start your investigation. For pointers to even more ORBs check out the OMG Home Page as referenced in Appendix A.

For every major programming language, an OMG standard *language mapping* specifies how IDL types, method invocations, and other constructs convert into language function calls. This is how the IDL skeleton and the object implementation come together, as shown in Figure 2.2. The IDL compiler uses the mapping specifications to generate a set of function calls from the IDL operations. Your programmer, probably assisted by an automated or semiautomated tool, refers to the IDL file and uses the language mapping to generate the corresponding set of function statements. After compilation and linking, these resolve so that the skeleton makes the right calls to invoke operations on your object implementation.

Since the language mapping is an OMG standard, every vendor's IDL compiler (for a particular language) will generate the *same* set of function calls from a given IDL file. This guarantees that, whichever vendor's ORB you select for a particular language, your object implementation accesses the skeleton using the same syntax. If you deploy on multiple vendors' ORBs, your code will port from one to another. The example presentation in this book brings this out. Thus, you may select a programming language and complete your implementation with the knowledge that you still have freedom to switch ORBs down the road. (Like any standard, there are some details that are not covered. OMG realizes that aspects of the server-side mapping need to be refined, and it has already started a specification effort to increase the portability of code from ORB to ORB; the effort should complete in mid-1996, and compliant products should be available from your favorite vendor about a year later. The example in this book covers the current state of the mapping, including ORB-dependent differences, in detail.)

The current CORBA specification includes standard IDL language mappings for C, C++, and Smalltalk; an Ada mapping is in progress, and a

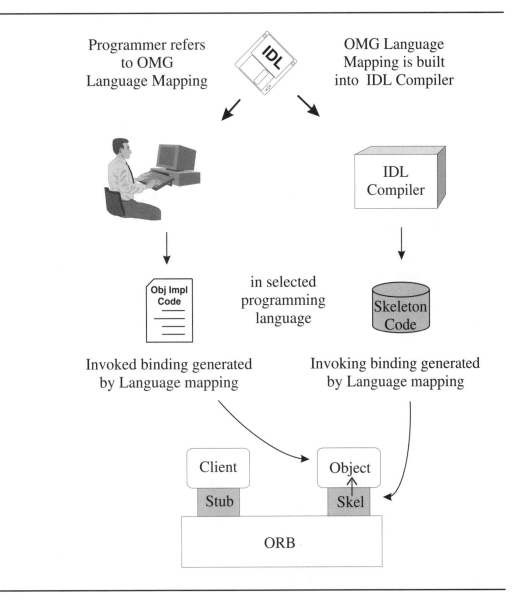

Figure 2.2. Role of the OMG language mapping standard. (Generated components are shown shaded.)

mapping for COBOL is expected to follow. Mappings don't have to be standardized by OMG in order to be useful; nonstandard mappings are available now for objective C and other languages.

2.3.4 Connecting to the ORB

The two ends of the implementation skeleton are truly opposite: The connection to the client, governed by OMG IDL, is standard and provides portability; the connection to the ORB on the other end is proprietary, and this freedom in the specification allows the vendor to implement the connection with the performance characteristics customers demand.

The connections to the ORB, one for each interface in our IDL file, are generated automatically by the IDL compiler. Since the ORB-skeleton interface is proprietary, ORBs and IDL compilers come in matched sets. You must use the IDL compiler with its companion ORB; the skeleton from vendor A will not mate with the ORB from vendor B. Since the language mapping provides a standard junction between object implementation and ORB, and the stubs are generated automatically by the IDL compiler, you can switch ORBs just by recompiling your IDL file and linking with the new stub this produces.

2.3.5 Summary: Object Implementation End

We've covered the complete development process on the object implementation end. Here's a summary of how we narrowed down to our specific ORB and languages environment: We started with an IDL interface definition, which was usable with *any* programming language and ORB (Figure 2.2). We selected a programming language, and, using the OMG standard language mapping, determined the corresponding function calls in that language. Then, using the IDL compiler that came with our ORB, we input the IDL file and generated a skeleton that joins to our chosen ORB. Portability assured by the standard language mapping will allow us to also compile with a different vendor's IDL compiler and generate a skeleton with the *same* function calls, but a stub that connects to the new vendor's ORB.

2.3.6 Client End: Single-ORB Version

Keeping to the spirit of "first things first," in this section, we'll assume that both client and object implementation are written in the same programming language and connected to the same ORB. Soon, in Section 2.5, we'll relax these restrictions and show how client and object implementation can be written in different languages and connected to different ORBs around our network. But first, this important foundation material.

The same execution of the IDL compiler that generated our implementation skeleton also generated a *client stub* (Figure 2.3). Where the skeleton contained function calls, the stub contains function declarations; in our client, we write the corresponding function calls that resolve to the stub. These are the same declarations as on the implementation end, generated

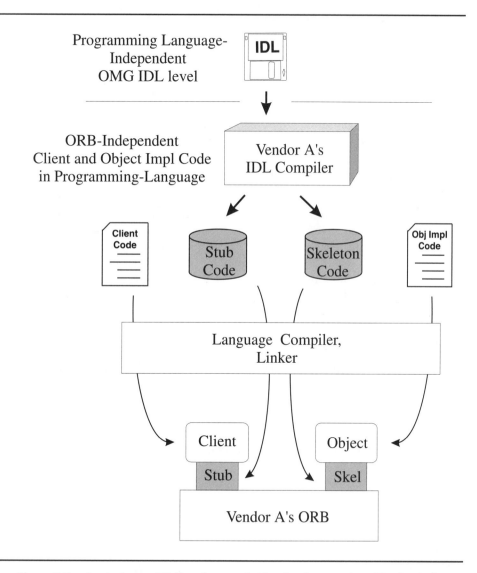

Figure 2.3.   Producing an IDL file, client, and object implementation. (Shading indicates generated components.)

by the standard language mapping. Like our implementation, our client code ports from one ORB to any other that supports the programming language we used. (By the way, this isn't the only way to connect to the ORB. There's also a dynamic connection, which we describe in Section 2.4.4.) And, as you might expect, the stub joins to the ORB with a proprietary interface.

2.3.7   Summary: Both Ends, Single ORB

Now we know all about how CORBA works, at least with a single ORB. It's all summed up in Figure 2.3: We *write* a single IDL file, a client, and an object implementation. The IDL compiler *generates* a stub for the client end, and a skeleton for the object implementation end. Except for some ORB-specific bookkeeping code, our client and implementation port among ORBs using the programming language we chose, so we can recompile with different ORB's IDL compilers to switch from one ORB to another.

2.4   THE OBJECT REQUEST BROKER

If you're familiar with the remote procedure call (RPC) paradigm, you may think we're done. (If you're not, bear with us for a second.) All we would need to do to run this as an RPC would be to establish a network connection between the client stub and the implementation skeleton, and make the call between them. But this would require each stub to resolve individually to its corresponding skeleton, and the CORBA architecture instead resolves *all* of the stubs to the ORB. There are a lot of good reasons for this, and we'll examine them in this section.

2.4.1   Foundations for Interoperability

Our objective is to use a web of ORB-to-ORB communications pathways to enable interoperability among *all* of the CORBA objects on a network. The two problems we have to overcome are *location*—how do we address our invocation to a particular object implementation—and *translation*—how does our invocation get translated to a foreign ORB's data format on the way over, and the response get translated on the way back?

We'll define an *object reference* to solve the first problem. You already know the solution to the second problem: it's IDL. Here's how the object references and IDL work with the ORB to provide the interoperability we promised.

2.4.2   The Object Reference

Some objects in our enterprise will have extremely long lifetimes, and are required to maintain their state persistently from creation to the last day of an enterprise's existence. An example might be the main account object of our accounting system, which keeps track of our enterprise's net worth. Other objects might have intermediate lifetimes, such as a sales transaction object that could be created in response to an actual sale and destroyed after the merchandise was delivered and payment received. And smaller objects might have short, transitory lifetimes, such as a pushbutton on a dialog box that appears only for a single mouse click response.

Every CORBA object in a system, regardless of its lifetime, has its own *object reference*. This is assigned by its ORB at object creation and remains valid until the object is explicitly deleted. Clients obtain object references in various ways, and associate them with the invocation according to the mapping of the language they are using. This association enables the ORB to direct the invocation to the specified target object.

The OMA places certain requirements on the validity of the object reference. For instance, a client is able to store the reference for a particular object in a file or database. When the client retrieves the reference from storage later, the OMA requires that its invocation execute successfully *even if the target object has been moved in the interim* (although not if the target object has been explicitly deleted). This means that the object reference is *not* simply the network or memory address of the object. OMG standards allow each ORB vendor to implement the translation from object reference to actual target object in the way it deems best for its target systems and customer base, as long as these requirements for validity are met.

With the requirement that any ORB understand any object reference at any time, the object reference plays a key role in getting user and resource together in our widespread distributed object system. Object references can be passed around your enterprise—or beyond, to your suppliers, customers, and prospects—using a database, naming or trading service, publicized file location, or any other means. And any application using any ORB on the network can retrieve them and pass them to its own ORB to invoke the object.

Since only ORBs can interpret object references, there's no reason other than curiosity for you to be concerned about their form and how they work. But, since there seems to be a lot of curiosity around, we've put an explanation in Chapter 6 on interoperability.

Since you're in the fortunate position of being an ORB user instead of an ORB builder, the concept of object reference for you is straightforward: You hand the object reference to the ORB, and the ORB gets your invocation to the target object. And, if you're passing it or receiving it as a parameter, the ORB takes care of the details regardless of where, or how far, it's going. It's as simple as that.

2.4.3   IDL and the ORB

If you've ever written a distributed application for a heterogeneous network, you know how much trouble it is to interoperate among a group of platforms with different data formats such as byte ordering. The OMA requires that the ORB take care of these details for you, just as simply as it took care of addressing using the object reference. Fortunately, we've already given it the tool it needs.

That tool, of course, is OMG IDL. The OMG had good reason to make IDL a strongly typed language: Besides using IDL to create the client stub and implementation skeleton, CORBA requires that the Object Request Broker store the IDL definition for all of its objects in an *interface repository* (IR). *This collection of interface definitions is a key resource in the distributed object system.* It must be available, not only to the ORB itself, but also to clients and object implementations, and utilities such as object hierarchy browsers and debuggers. Using IDL interfaces defined by OMG standards, interface definitions can be added to the IR, modified, deleted, or retrieved; the contents of the IR may be searched; and inheritance trees in it may be traced to determine the exact type of an object.

The obvious use of the IR is for interoperability: Knowing the types and order of the arguments in a message enables communicating ORBs to translate byte order and data format wherever necessary. Other potential uses include interface browsing and debugging. The other major use of the IR is in the Dynamic Invocation Interface.

2.4.4   The Dynamic Invocation Interface

If there's any notable limitation of the object architecture we've sketched so far, it would be inflexibility at run time. In order to invoke an operation on an object, a client has to call, and be statically linked to, the corresponding stub. Since the developer determines which stubs a client contains when he or she writes its code, this interface (termed the Static Invocation Interface or SII) *cannot* access new object types that are added to the system later. But sophisticated users of dynamic distributed object systems demand more than this—they want to use new objects as soon as they are added to any ORB on their network, without having to wait for or install a new release of the client software on their desktop.

The Dynamic Invocation Interface (DII) provides this capability, and it's built in to every CORBA-compliant ORB. The DII enables a properly written client at run time to:

- discover new objects;
- discover their interfaces;
- retrieve their interface definitions;

- construct and dispatch invocations; and
- receive the resulting response or exception information

to and from objects whose client stubs are not linked in to its module—for instance, objects that were added to the system after the client was written. The DII is actually an ORB interface defined in OMG IDL (of course!) which includes routines to allow the client and ORB, working together using interface definitions from the IR, to construct and invoke operations on *any* available object.

How does a client figure out which object or interface it wants to retrieve from the IR? This is not the same job as putting together a request. Although a client could browse the IR and select an interface, there are other, more straightforward ways. At installation time, for instance, new objects could create entries in a file known to the client, listing their interface names along with extra information that the client could display in a menu; this would provide the user with the information he or she needs to select the object and the client with the information it needs to retrieve the interface definition from the IR. Standard ways to find out about objects on the system include the Naming and Trader services, discussed in Section 2.7 and Chapter 12.

Systems and network administration tools and desktop managers, which must contend with or manage constantly changing suites of objects, use the DII. Some CORBA application builders prefer the DII because, unlike the SII, it does not create a new stub for each interface a client uses. This allows a smaller ORB memory footprint, although the potential exists for a run-time performance penalty since at least first-time invocations of each interface are, in effect, interpreted at run time as the client and ORB marshal the parameters of the invocation.

Today, statically linked clients provide so much more flexibility than conventional, monolithic applications that dynamic linking seems like a far-off future vision. But it won't be long before users start loading new objects onto the network and accessing them dynamically from some of their familiar desktop apps. (Some lucky users are doing this already!) The first time a user in your organization finds a dynamic client that goes directly to all (or even some) of his or her new objects via the DII, there will be a new standard in your organization for state-of-the-art desktop software—and rightly so. It will be difficult for static clients to compete once dynamic access starts becoming available. For more information on the DII, look ahead to Section 4.3.

2.5 CORBA-BASED INTEROPERABILITY

The section on interoperability in this chapter is short for two reasons: First, we're building on the firm foundation laid in previous sections, and, second, most of the remaining details occur "under the covers" so they are properly postponed until Chapter 6.

2.5.1   Accessing an Object on a Remote ORB

Interoperability in CORBA, as shown in Figure 2.4, is based on ORB-to-ORB communication. The client does *nothing* different for a remote invocation compared to the local case. It passes its usual IDL-based invocation to its local ORB. If the invocation contains the object reference of a local object implementation, the ORB routes it to its target object; if not, the ORB routes the invocation to a remote ORB. The remote ORB then routes the invocation to the target object.

The client cannot tell from either the form of the invocation or the object reference whether the target object is local or remote. The user may be aware that the target is, for instance, an accounting object that resides on a networked mainframe, or a printer on the third floor of an adjoining building, but this does not affect the invocation. *All* details of the invocation are taken care of by the ORB: resolving the object reference to a specific remote ORB and object; translating data byte order and format where necessary; and whatever other chores arise.

Of course, there's a lot going on under the covers. Each ORB is required to maintain at least two (possibly large) databases or directory systems: the IR with its collection of interface definitions, plus an *implementation repository* with information about available object implementations. Communications details must be synchronized as well—ORB network protocols must match, or gateways must translate between them.

However, the CORBA architecture removes this layer from the concern of not only the end user, but from the application programmer as well. The client and object implementation make or receive *only local function calls*, since their communication is through the stub to their local ORB. And OMG

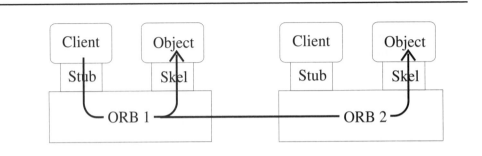

Figure 2.4.   Interoperability uses ORB-to-ORB communication.

standards guarantee that any ORB that bears the CORBA 2.0 brand will interoperate over the network with any other CORBA 2.0-branded ORB.

Implementation details have been taken care of by the ORB implementors. Some protocol-related decisions will affect network administrators—the people at your site who install and configure your networked ORB environment. These people will benefit from the technical details of interoperability presented in Chapter 6.

2.5.2 Integrating a Purchased Object Component

Inter-ORB communication is the key feature that gives CORBA its unparalleled flexibility. Client and object implementation may:

- reside on different vendors' ORBs;
- on different platforms;
- on different operating systems;
- on different networks;
- and be written in different programming languages by programmers who never saw or spoke to each other,

and they will still interoperate perfectly as long as client and object use the same IDL syntax and underlying semantics.

All your programmer needs in order to write a client that accesses a remote object is a copy of its IDL file, the description of what each operation does, and an object reference. This makes it easy to integrate, for example, purchased software components, objects written by other programmers in your company, or objects generated by interactive tools that provide IDL interfaces. Forward-looking companies are widening their competitive advantage by purchasing basic software modules implementing common knowledge in their field, then extending this functionality with modules written in-house. Below shows how to access these objects.

The process is diagrammed in Figure 2.5. When you purchase the software, you will receive both an executable object implementation and an IDL file from the vendor. Install the object on the ORB on the server node where it will reside. The installation process will produce an object reference, which may be automatically placed in a directory or naming service for you, or may be written to a file where you can access it.

Now you're ready to write the client. Move to your development platform. Remember, this does not need to be the same platform or ORB as the one running the object implementation. Load the IDL file, and compile it with the local IDL compiler. *It doesn't matter which language the vendor used to write the object you purchased.* You can write your client in any language you

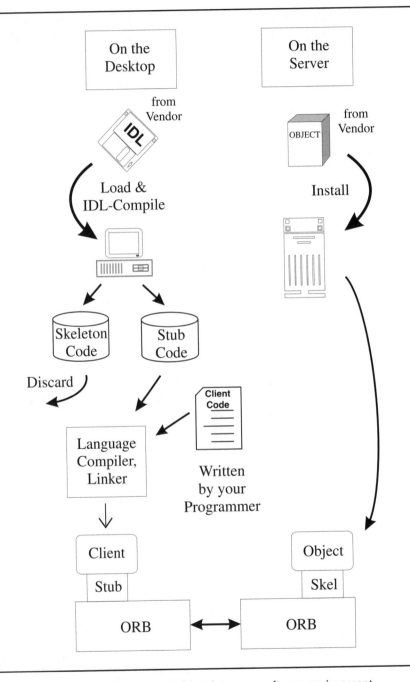

Figure 2.5.   Integrating a purchased object into your software environment.

want, so choose the IDL compiler that supports your desired development environment.

The IDL compilation step will yield both a client stub and an implementation skeleton. *Discard the implementation skeleton.* You don't need it. Use the client stub to access the ORB from your client. In your client code, retrieve the object reference from the naming service or file where it was stored, and use it to invoke operations on the purchased object, wherever it might reside.

2.5.3 Distributing Both Client and Object

It's a simple conceptual jump to go from the process we just described to building a distributed client/object system with different ORBs and platforms for client and object implementation. The client side process would be the same as we showed in Figure 2.5. The object implementation process would be the analog executed on the server development platform, keeping the IDL skeleton and building the code that runs behind it.

When the two components have been completed and registered with their respective ORBs, the client can retrieve the object reference from the naming service or wherever it was stored and invoke operations on the object just by passing an invocation to its local ORB.

This concludes the overview of CORBA. In just a few pages, we've gone from object basics to heterogeneous interoperabilty. But don't think that interoperability—electronic plumbing, really—is all there is to OMG standards. The people who wrote the OMA knew that this was only the beginning. By the time the CORBAservices and CORBAfacilities are fully populated with OMG standards, CORBA will be a small fraction of the whole.

2.6 THE OBJECT MANAGEMENT ARCHITECTURE

If we compare CORBA, with its communications links, to a telephone line, then it's tempting to also think of IDL as a language, but this is not quite right. Instead, IDL plays the role of an *alphabet*: In the same way that different languages use the same alphabet, different applications could all use IDL interfaces but not be able to interoperate if each one created its *own* IDL interface for a particular function.

There must be a common language for all applications, or our vision of plug-and-play component software will not be realized. That common language is the OMG's Object Management Architecture. A foundation of standard services invoked using standard interfaces, the OMA defines an environment where interoperability penetrates upward from the system level into application components.

2.6.1 Structure of the OMA

The structure of the OMA shown in Figure 1.1 didn't just happen—it grew out of a need and a vision, helped along by the efforts of the early architects at the OMG. In their minds, they might have formed a picture that looked something like Figure 2.6. In this figure, we've taken all the software that sits between the user and his or her system and divided it roughly into four layers; the position of each component does not correspond to its connections (since everything connects to the ORB), nor does it correspond exactly to timing (although it does rather roughly). Position here corresponds to how basic or fundamental each component is; the design of the lower layers affects the design of the layers above them, although you don't have to complete all of

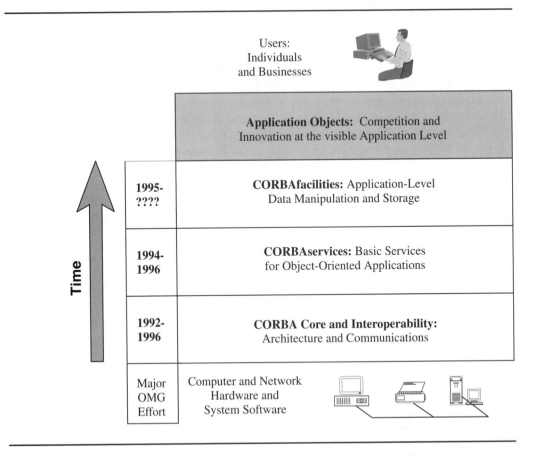

Figure 2.6.   Overview of CORBA and the Object Management Architecture.

the components on any particular layer before you start work on components in the layer above.

Architects' experience plays a role here as well. Without experience building distributed object systems, it's impossible to know what constitutes a great set of basic services, and so on up through the architecture. The designers of OMA components know this, and won't standardize anything before it's ready. This is the reason that OMG standards, and the products that bring them to you, come out at the pace that they do.

The goal of the OMA is simple: When applications provide basic functionality, let them provide it via a standard interface. This enables a component software market both above and below the level of the interface. Below it, multiple implementations of the basic functionality (compound document management, for instance) may still provide differences in performance, price, or adaptation to run on specialized platforms, while above it, specialized components (a sophisticated editor object, perhaps) come to market that can operate on any compound document managed by a component that conforms to the standard interface.

The structure of the OMA, shown in Figure 1.1, was drawn up with this goal in mind. The CORBAservices standardize basic services, which almost every object needs; this component was standardized first and the CORBAfacilities take advantage of much of it. The CORBAfacilities, being standardized now, provide intermediate-level services to applications. Application Objects, at the top, will not, however, be standardized by OMG; this is where vendors compete in innovative ways to provide the best combination of features and value for the customer.

For each component of the OMA, the OMG provides a formal specification—a published document prescribing the syntax (how to invoke each operation on each object) in OMG IDL—and semantics (what each operation does) in text. Vendors of OMA-compliant systems then implement and sell the services (some bundled with the ORB package, others not), where they are accessed via the specified IDL interfaces. Vendors do not have to provide every service, but every service they provide *must* conform to the OMG specifications in order to bear the CORBA brand.

Since each service stands alone and is accessed through standard IDL interfaces, you do not have to obtain all of your services from the same vendor. Standardization enables a high level of mix-and-match. Your enterprise may, for instance, decide to use the same implementation of object services on all platforms and all ORBs to maximize homogeneity. Another enterprise may choose a different vendor for a particular service for another reason—licensing terms, perhaps, or a special compatability with a legacy system or application. However, we notice a trend toward ORB packages offering basic CORBAservices, either bundled or optional. This provides a very easy way to provide your developers with all they need to build CORBA applications.

2.7 THE CORBAservices

The CORBAservices (previously known as the Object Services) provide fundamental, nearly system-level services to OO applications and their components. Eleven CORBAservices have been formally specified so far. They are:

Lifecycle Service

Relationship Service

Naming Service

Persistent Object Service

Externalization Service

Event Service

Object Query Service

Object Properties Service

Object Transaction Service

Concurrency Service

Licensing Service

In addition, five more services specifications are in process, including:

Trader Service

Security Service

Secure Time Service

Object Collection Service

Object Startup Service

If you're interested in the details about any of these services, you'll have to look ahead to Chapters 10 through 16. In this overview chapter, we'll discuss only a few key services that make the biggest contribution to the capabilities of CORBA systems. In particular, we'll discuss the Lifecycle and Relationships services, the Security service, the Transactions and Concurrency services, and the Naming and forthcoming Trader services.

The Lifecycle service provides standard signatures for object Create, Delete, Move, and Copy—fundamental operations for any object system. The Relationship service allows objects to be grouped. Working together, these two services allow groups of objects, such as a compound document, to be manipulated using simple method invocations. Imagine the chaos that would have resulted if every vendor used his or her own IDL signature for these basic operations! No wonder the OMG standardized the Lifecycle Service first.

Security is essential—without it, CORBA would not be usable in areas such as business, commerce, and defense. How do you get end-to-end security in multivendor object networks? What if communications goes over uncontrolled links like commercial phone lines or wireless links? The Security CORBAservice answers a lot of these questions, and ORBs implementing the specification will be available soon.

The Transaction Service, and the Concurrency Service that supports it with file and resource locking, provide CORBA systems with object-oriented access to the mainstream of business accounting systems, OLTP (On-Line Transaction Processing). Developed by a cooperating group that included every major TP vendor, this OMG-standard set of IDL interfaces provides access to all major OLTP systems including IBM CICS, Novell Tuxedo, Transarc Encina, Unisys, Tandem, and others.

How does your application find out whether objects it needs are out on your network, ready to do its work? In the OMA, there are two ways. First is the Naming Service. If you know the name of the object you want, this service will tell you its object reference. It's a simple service, which can also provide access to your local directory system via standard OMG IDL interfaces. Second is the Trader service. This sophisticated service will evolve into the core of the dynamic distributed object environment. It's the one to use when you know pretty closely what you want, but not which object on your system is the best fit, since it contains ancillary data associated with every object. You can ask it for an amortization object to calculate depreciation, or for a printer in your building on the third or fourth floor in an accessible area that prints double-sided sheets faster than 10 pages per minute, and it will return you an object reference. This important service is being standardized by ISO (the International Organization for Standards) in an OMA-compliant way, so the Trader Service that OMG will adopt probably will have the ISO imprimateur right off the bat.

By now, you should be starting to develop a picture in your mind of how this is all going to work together: CORBA and OMG IDL provide the telephone line and alphabet that our apps will use to link up. Then the OMA standardizes the language they use to speak to each other, and provides "matchmaking" services like Naming and Trader to get clients and object implementations together when they need it. When you're ready to use a service, you can find it, you can talk to it, and you can use it.

There's one more layer that we can standardize without penetrating the uppermost reaches where competition adds value and (after all) provides the resource that produces the products we all benefit from. OMG calls this layer the CORBAfacilities.

2.8   THE CORBAfacilities

In order to unify the enterprise, we must be able to share functionality and data. CORBA and the CORBAservices make a great set of pipes, but we need a lot more than plumbing to make good on the promises set out in Chapter 1.

As shown in Figure 2.6, the CORBAfacilities fill in the architecture between the basic CORBAservices and the visible, competitive Application Objects. When the full architecture is realized in off-the-shelf products, you'll be able to share the application-level data and functionality you need to in order to integrate your company's IS. Since top-level Application Objects will not be standardized, the midlevel CORBAfacilities will be accessed either by innovative clients you buy from a competitive software marketplace, or by targeted modules your developers or integrators tailor specifically to your company's needs. And development will be hastened because the basic and intermediate functionality comes from the CORBAservices and CORBA-facilities; only incremental capability and integration need to be provided at the top.

The basic structure of the CORBAfacilities is shown in Figure 1.1. The Horizontal CORBAfacilities, useful for almost every market segment, are composed of four basic categories: user interface, information management, systems management, and task management. The Vertical CORBAfacilities are divided into market segments: Healthcare and Financial Services are two examples; more are working inside OMG. This design was set down by OMG members in the document, *Common Facilities Architecture Guide* issued in late 1995. (Common Facilities and CORBAfacilities refer to the same thing; the first term is used more inside the OMG, while the second is used more outside.)

Unlike basic CORBA and the CORBAservices, which you could buy and use when this book was being written, the CORBAfacilities are work in progress. The architecture guide is complete, and the first specification, Compound Document Management and Display, will be issued in early 1996. The CORBAfacilities promise a revolution in software productivity and capability when they arrive, but it will be a while before the revolution is complete!

There's another difference between this layer and the rest of CORBA and the OMA. Because they handle application-level information (for example, a compound document or a meeting schedule, rather than an object name or reference), the information model adopted by a CORBAfacility will sometimes determine or affect the user's view of the data. OMG members are well aware of this, and are reluctant to impose any standards that have not fully matured. But the discussions at OMG meetings sometimes become intense when a proposed specification gets close to some member's favorite object. This is an area in which many companies will find it worthwhile to participate in OMG standard-setting. The OMG welcomes this; to find how to become involved, see Appendix A.

Don't look for any surprises to come out of OMG in a CORBAfacility specification. OMG policy requires every specification to be based on demonstrable technology, so future output in this category will probably be made up of software you've already seen or used, possibly with new OMG IDL interfaces grafted on to make it conform to the OMA. (There's nothing wrong with this; in fact, the OMA was designed to encourage adaptation of existing good ideas and the software that implements them.)

Let's take a closer look at how the CORBAfacilities are organized, and how the OMG synchronizes this work with existing industry groups that are also engaged in setting standards in their areas.

2.8.1 The Horizontal CORBAfacilities

There are certain functions that "everyone uses"—that have an air of genericity about them. The CORBAfacilities architecture divides these generic functions into the four categories shown in Figure 1.1: user interface, information management, systems management, and task management.

One generic task that "everyone does" is work with compound documents—text, pictures, graphics (possibly live data from spreadsheets), maybe even video and audio, collected into something called a compound document. Presentation of compound documents, whether on a screen or printed on paper, is a user interface CORBAfacility. Interchange of compound documents is an information management CORBAfacility. Why do we need a standard for this? Because there are so many things you can do to (or with) a compound document that no single application could possibly do them all in the best possible way (although some have tried). It's more reasonable to use a generic facility to make the document accessible and displayable, and allow each user to assemble an array of editing tools that focus strength in the specific areas he or she needs.

Task management is an exciting CORBAfacilities area, scoped to include workflow, agents, rule management, and object automation. Since these domains are not nearly as mature as compound documents (or at least some components of compound documents), it will probably be a while before we see OMG specifications along these lines and the products implementing them. Systems management CORBAfacilities try to extract and apply standards that will allow mangement tools to work together.

2.8.2 The Vertical CORBAfacilities

There are a lot of industry groups that can benefit from standards of their own. Some industries have already formed standards consortia, such as the Petrotechnical Open Software Corporation (POSC) and the Workflow Mangement Coalition (WfMC). Other industries haven't formed separate organizations but want to set standards anyhow. Either way, standards can be produced and adopted as vertical CORBAfacilities.

Here's how this works: If an outside organization is producing standards in a CORBAfacilities area, the OMG forms a liaison relationship and helps the organization to express its specifications in OMG IDL in conformance with the OMA. Then the OMG is able to adopt these specifications as the vertical CORBAfacility for that component. Where no recognized outside organization exists, the OMG will establish standards itself.

Within OMG, the group that forms around an industry or vertical CORBAfacility is called a SIG or Special Interest Group. SIGs do not establish OMG specifications themselves; they either work with outside organizations or with the OMG CORBAfacilities Task Force to get that work done. However, a very exciting reorganization taking place within OMG will give the SIGs the central role in establishing standards in their area (and probably a new name as well). Currently, OMG has established SIGs in Healthcare, Financial Services, Telecommunications, Manufacturing, and other industry areas. Since the completion of CORBA and many of the CORBAservices, specification of CORBAfacilities is receiving a lot of attention at OMG and the list of SIGs increases often. Your company can join OMG and participate in the SIG in your area; if there isn't one, you can help one become established. For a complete list of SIGs and OMG liaison relationships, see the OMG's home page on the Web, http://www.omg.org, or contact OMG using the information in Appendix A. In this book, look for more information in Chapter 17.

CHAPTER 3

Introducing OMG IDL

3.1 ABOUT THIS PART OF THE BOOK

There are a number of reasons you might be reading this book. For instance, you might have to help pick an interoperability architecture for your already-networked company, and someone told you to find out more about CORBA. Or, you might be assigned to a prototype CORBA project, and you need to find out as much as you can about every aspect in order to complete the project and evaluation. Or, perhaps your company produces software, and you're considering CORBA as a platform that will let you market on a wide variety of networked platforms with minimal porting.

This means you have to learn enough about every part of CORBA to reach a valid decision, but you're not about to plow through a bunch of highly technical OMG specifications to do it. (And the OMG specs are written for ORB and service implementors anyway, not for users.) If there's a proto-type in your future, you probably want to see how to program for CORBA too, using more than one vendor's ORB since multivendor portability and interoperability are the main reasons you're considering CORBA in the first place.

These are the needs we've taken into account in the rest of this book. Chapters 3 through 9 detail the parts of CORBA and the OMA that have only been summarized so far. How much detail? Certainly enough to let you make your architectural decision with confidence, and enough to give you a concrete idea of what programming for CORBA is like, but probably not enough to get you all the way through your first independent programming project, and certainly not enough to enable you to build your own ORB from scratch. For the programming project, you will at least need the documentation that comes with the ORB product you select (and we recommend a good book or two on OO analysis and design, too); to build an ORB, you will have to refer to the original OMG specifications.

Chapters 10 through 17 detail the rest of the OMA. This chapter is devoted exclusively to OMG's Interface Definition Language (OMG IDL), the cornerstone of interoperability and transparency. We wanted to start out with ORB details—what it does and how it works—but we had to organize this way because all of the ORB interfaces are defined in IDL. If you're never going to program to these interfaces, you can skip most of this chapter and go to the Object Request Broker (ORB) description—Chapter 4—after reading the introductory material (there's a note telling you when to skip ahead). Chapters 4 through 6 describe the ORB, and Chapters 7 through 9 present mappings from IDL to the programming languages C, C++, and Smalltalk. This is where the world of the OMA meets your application code. Chapters 10 through 16 present those CORBAservices that were standardized, or almost complete, when we wrote the book, and Chapter 17 describes the exciting current work at OMG on the higher-level CORBAfacilities.

Each chapter is organized in "drill-down" style—architectural and user-level material toward the front; technical and programming-level details following. If you're not a programmer or a "techie," you can still learn a lot from the first section or two of each chapter up to Chapter 15, and all of Chapters 16 (Security) and 17 (the CORBAfacilities). If you're technically inclined, just read everything straight through. (If you're really technical, of course, you can buy the OMG specifications and read them, or join the OMG and *write* them...)

3.2 CORBA COMPLIANCE

This section gives an overview of how the parts of the CORBA specification fit together, so you can sort through the pieces and make sure you end up with an environment that works the way you planned. We had to use some terms that don't get fully defined until later in the book, but this material is so important it has to be included here. It's a good way to organize the seven chapters that follow.

The CORBA specification is composed of many parts, and most ORB products will not include all of them. Some components, such as the Transaction service, are so specialized and resource-intensive that they will typically be offered separately. Others, such as the three language mappings, form a set of alternatives (although many large enterprises will probably use all three somewhere).

The set of OMG specifications is divided into *compliance points*, strictly defined sets of criteria with which an ORB product must comply in order to be branded CORBA-compliant for that point. There are some optional criteria. These do not have to be included in a product, but if they are, they *must* comply with the OMG specification.

3.2.1 **CORBA Core**

All ORB products must comply with the CORBA Core specification, which includes:

- the CORBA Object Model;
- the CORBA architecture;
- OMG IDL syntax and semantics;

and the following ORB components:

- the Dynamic Invocation Interface (DII);
- the Dynamic Skeleton Interface (DSI);
- the Interface Repository (IR);
- the ORB interface; and
- the Basic Object Adapter.

In addition, the product must support at least

- one Language Mapping.

The product may support any number of additional language mappings.

Each item on this list is described in the OMG CORBA Core specification, which you'll find listed under References in Appendix A.

A compliant ORB product must offer an IDL compiler for at least one programming language. Language mapping standards have been established for C, C++, and Smalltalk; however, some vendors may offer ORB environments for other languages whose mappings have not yet been standardized, such as Ada or COBOL. A vendor is not required to offer a compiler for any particular language; however, the compiler for *every* standardized language *must* comply in order to be branded compliant.

3.2.2 **Additional Compliance Points**

CORBA Interoperability is a separate compliance point—that is, not all ORBs interoperate. To be certified compliant with CORBA Interoperability, an ORB must offer the IIOP protocol, either native or via a half-bridge. (We haven't defined these terms yet; if you're curious, look ahead to Section 6.5.) Additional protocols, including the standardized DCE CIOP, may be offered as well. There is no restriction on the number or format of additional protocols which an ORB may utilize and still be compliant, as long as it can communicate using the IIOP.

Each CORBAservice is a separate compliance point. In principle, vendors may choose individually whether to offer each service, but most vendors are offering a set of CORBAservices, including all of the basics: Lifecycle, Events, Naming, and the Persistent Object Service, and adding Relationships and Externalization (which were standardized later). Transactions and Concurrency, which provide access to OLTP, are typically obtained from the supplier of your OLTP system, which may or may not be the same as your ORB supplier.

The first CORBAfacility, Compound Document Management and Display, has not been specified at this writing, so there is no compliance point for it as yet.

What about testing? There is no CORBA test suite yet, so you'll either have to accept each vendor's word that his or her product complies, or look on a newsstand for a current magazine with an informal test of ORB products. The OMG and X/Open are working together on a comprehensive test suite; prototyping for CORBA Core was completed in early 1995, and the program was on track to proceed to CORBA Interoperability as we wrote this. Watch the OMG home page on the Web for more information on the CORBA testing and branding program.

3.2.3 Specifying Your CORBA Environment

What do you need to specify to have a complete CORBA environment? Because of the way compliance points are specified, you will have to draw up a check-off list. Here are our suggestions for your list:

- CORBA Core. Every ORB has to comply with this.
- At least one language binding. Pick the one or ones you need from
  - C
  - C++
  - Smalltalk
  - Ada (OMG approval nearly complete as of February, 1996)
  - COBOL (not a formal OMG spec yet)
  - or a nonstandardized mapping to another language you prefer.
- CORBA interoperability, including IIOP (required).
- DCE ESIOP, *if* your site plans to use this protocol.
- CORBAservices from this list:
  - Lifecycle
  - Relationships
  - Naming
  - Events
  - Persistent Object Service
  - Externalization

- ◆ Properties
- ◆ Query

- ■ Two important CORBAservices, scheduled for approval by OMG by early 1996:

  - ◆ Trader
  - ◆ Security

- ■ One future CORBAfacility, scheduled for approval by OMG by early 1996:

  - ◆ Compound Document Management and Presentation.

Most of the product summaries in Chapters 20 through 22 include compliance information, at least as of the time the book went to press, along with some vendors' plans for future work. You can check with each vendor for more up-to-date information.

3.3 OMG IDL BY EXAMPLE

The easiest way to learn IDL basics is by working through an example. We'll use a short excerpt from the tutorial example worked in this book. In this section, we're going to focus on the IDL grammar and capabilities, but pay little attention to what these objects actually do; that discussion happens in Chapter 23.

The example concerns a store with point-of-sale (POS) terminals. Here's the interface the POS terminal object uses to communicate with its barcode-reader object, keypad object, and receipt-printer object:

```
//POS Object IDL example
module POS {
        typedef string Barcode;

        interface InputMedia {
            typedef string OperatorCmd;
            void   barcode_input(in Barcode item);
            void   keypad_input(in OperatorCmd cmd);
    };

        interface OutputMedia {
            boolean output_text(in string string_to_print );
    };
```

```
              interface POSTerminal {
                  void  end_of_sale();
                  void  print_POS_sales_summary();
      };
    };
```

(This is where the details start. If you're only looking for a high-level overview, now is the time to skip ahead to Chapter 4 and start looking at the Object Request Broker. You've seen an example, and this will help you figure out whether you need more details about IDL.)

We'll take this example apart, one line at a time. But first, some IDL basics.

3.3.1   IDL Basics

Although IDL interfaces are programming language-independent, the IDL language itself has the appearance (but *not* the semantics) of ANSI C++ in many ways. Notable resemblances include:

- C++-like preprocessing;
- its lexical rules (with new keywords for distribution concepts);
- its grammar, which is a subset of C++ and incorporates syntax for constant, type, and operation declarations; but lacks algorithmic structures and variables.

And many differences:

- the function return type is required (may be void);
- each formal parameter in an operation declaration must have a name;
- and others.

Comments may be placed between /* and */; lines that start with a double-slash (//) also constitute a comment.

Since some programming languages are case-sensitive, while others are not, OMG IDL is restrictive with respect to case: You're not allowed to define two identifiers in the same scope that differ only in case. If you try, they collide and give a compilation error. For example, you can't have a module named MyCompany that contains an operation myCompany.

3.3.2   IDL Modules, Types, and Scoping

OMG IDL is a *strongly typed interface language*; that is, every variable must be declared to be a particular type (but see the next paragraph). This enables ORBs to convert variables from one platform's format to another as they transfer messages around your heterogeneous network. The list of available types is important but boring, so we've relegated it to Appendix B.

IDL provides the **any** type to provide an alternative format to the restrictions that strong typing imposes. (Object purists will insist, correctly it turns out, that there are very few cases where the **any** type is actually required, but we won't get into that here.) A variable of the **any** type may be used anywhere another IDL type would be allowed; since an **any** may represent literally any IDL type, including constructed types and variable-length arrays, and may be cast to any type dynamically at run time, clients and object implementations enjoy the freedom of dynamic typing. Internally, ORBs associate an **any**'s type with its value, allowing them to provide the same level of service for an **any** as they do for all of the other IDL types. On the network, a standard set of typecodes ensures that **any**s passed from any ORB to any other are interpreted correctly.

Definitions of types, constants, exceptions, interfaces, and modules are *scoped*; that is, they are only in effect (and therefore may only be used or referred to) within the section they are defined, unless you use the scoping operator **::** to "import" a definition from an external scope.

In this example, the variables **Barcode** and **POSid** are scoped to the **module POS**. In this module, **Barcode** is used in two interfaces: **Interface InputMedia** and **Interface POSTerminal**. The scoping ensures that the definition is valid (and identical) for both cases. **POSid** is scoped to the module for a different reason; in fact, it is not used here. But it is used later in another module where it is included and referred to as **POS::POSid**. It is proper programming practice to define it in this module, which defines all of the characteristics of the POS terminal object. The external module expects only to use it, not to define it.

Modules aren't the only thing that defines a scope. Interfaces, structs, unions, operations, and exceptions do as well. For instance, in our example, the definition of **OperatorCmd** is restricted in scope to the **interface InputMedia**.

3.3.3   Defining an Interface

Typically, an **interface** construct in an IDL file collects a number of operations that form a natural group. Since many objects bear more than one interface, this is usually not all of the operations of a particular object, but rather some subset. One of the most important aspects of the interface is that it is the unit of inheritance, but we'll postpone this discussion until Section 3.3.9.

The keyword **interface** starts a new scope; inside its curly brackets we get a chance to define yet another set of scoped quantities and finally a set of operations. Of course, this time, the quantities are defined only for the interface.

This example module defines three interfaces: **InputMedia** with two operations, **OutputMedia** with one, and **POSTerminal** with three. **InputMedia** also defines the new type, **OperatorCmd**.

3.3.4 Operations

The format of the operation statement has three required parts, plus another three optional parts, which do not appear in this particular example.

First, the three required components. Look at the operation **output_text** in **interface OutputMedia**. The statement starts by declaring a *return type*. This operation returns a **boolean** (true or false) value; note that most of the other operations in our example return **void**, which is an allowed return type. You can't eliminate the return type declaration just because it's void.

Next is the *operation name*; the IDL compiler will use this name to construct a name for the language mapping. Finally is the *list of parameters*. Each parameter declaration consists of a parameter attribute, which must be either **in**, **out**, or **inout**; a type declaration; and the parameter name. ORBs use these declarations in the operation statements to manipulate data as requests fly about your enterprise.

By the way, the target object reference does not appear in the IDL; binding of invocation to target is handled by each language in the way that fits it most naturally. However, other object references may be included as parameters to operations. The ORBs that transmit the request will recognize these as they pass by; if they are transmitted to a remote ORB, they will first be put into a form that it can recognize and use.

3.3.5 Exceptions

The **exception** is the first optional operation parameter we'll discuss. Operation declarations may optionally contain exceptions. As you might expect, we can scope exception definitions across either our file, module, or interface as we require. (This allows us, for instance, to define one global set of exceptions for our entire "application"—that is, across all of our objects and interfaces—and additional sets of exceptions, which apply only to certain interfaces.) Exceptions are associated with operations using the **raises** expression, and may have one or more values associated with them. For example,

```
exception input_out_of_range { long dummy };
void operation1(in long arg1) raises (input_out_of_range);
```

You can specify multiple exceptions in a list, separated by commas.

There is a set of standard exceptions defined by OMG, which any operation may raise. You don't have to declare these exceptions (in fact, you can't), but your invoking code must be prepared to deal with them after any synchronous invocation.

When an operation raises an exception during its execution, the ORB is responsible for transmitting this information back to the client and notifying it. Notification is accomplished through the language mappings in various ways; we will discuss this in more detail in Chapters 7 through 9 and in the example.

3.3.6 Invocation Semantics and the Oneway Declaration

The second optional operation parameter is the **oneway** declaration. Operations may optionally be declared **oneway** by prepending to their declaration:

oneway void SendMyMessage (in string MyMessage);

A oneway operation must specify a **void** return type; only input parameters are allowed, and no exceptions may be declared. (However, some of the standard exceptions may be raised by an invocation attempt.) Invocation semantics are best-effort by the ORB, which does not guarantee that the invocation will be delivered to the target object. The call returns to the client immediately, and there is no standard way for the client to synchronize with the message delivery to the target object.

Operations *not* declared **oneway** may return results in the return value or **out** or **inout** parameters. You still get a choice of semantics, although discussion is postponed until Section 4.3 since it is provided by the ORB rather than by IDL. For now, we will just point out that CORBA provides both synchronous (blocking) and asynchronous (nonblocking) invocation semantics, plus a unique deferred-synchronous mode.

3.3.7 Context Objects

A **context** object contains a list of name-value pairs called *properties*. Currently, the OMG specification restricts the values to strings, but you can put a number into a string and convert back when you need to, so this isn't a showstopper. There is no limit to the number of pairs a context object may contain, and context objects may be chained together. Context objects are the CORBA equivalent of the environment in UNIX or PC-DOS—a set of user and application preferences, which may or may not affect a particular operation, in a format that a module can scan for items that it needs to take into account. Some environments will have a system context object, a separate context object for each user, and another for each application that requires it. These could be chained together and propagated at run time so that remote executions would occur in the environment you expect.

In IDL, you declare a context for an operation with the expression,

context (context1, context2, ...)

right after the **raises** expression in your operation definition. You add and manipulate context properties using operations addressed to the ORB. Only the ORB can create a context, so there's an operation to do that. Then there are operations to add, set, get, and delete properties, as you might expect.

3.3.8 Attribute Variables

CORBA objects have state—that is, their variables retain the values they're set to, until they are explicitly changed or the object is deleted or destroyed. Consequently, setting and retrieving values of variables is done frequently. To make this easier, OMG IDL provides the **attribute**, a variable with a pair of implicit functions that allow clients to set and retrieve its value. There is also a **readonly attribute**, which lacks the set function. This is handy for variables that are set by the object—perhaps in response to some condition or event—to a value that must then be read by its clients. The accessor functions, implicit in the IDL, are made real by each language mapping. You can read about their form in Chapters 7 through 9.

Here's what an attribute looks like in IDL:

```
interface MyInterface {
    attribute float radius;
};
```

The language mapping for this will be the same as if we had written (still in IDL):

```
interface MyInterface {
    float _get_radius();
    void _set_radius(in float r);
}
```

since accessor function names are generated by prepending **_get_** and **_set_** to the name of the attribute variable. Attributes are just a more convenient way of setting up a variable or struct with a **get/set** operation pair.

3.3.9 Inheritance

Using inheritance, you can derive a new interface from one or more existing interfaces. The derived interface *inherits* all of the elements of the interfaces it is based upon; it then adds whatever new elements (constants, types, attributes, operations, and so forth) that it needs. The new interface starts out with all of the operations of the base interfaces, and adds whichever new ones you want. You are not allowed to redefine the base interfaces, although other base elements may be redefined. This means that a client written originally to invoke the base class is guaranteed to be able to invoke the derived interface, since all of the operations that it expects are included. However, a client written to access the derived interface cannot necessarily work with the base interface, since it may invoke operations that were newly added to the derived interface and do not appear in the base interface.

The syntax for introducing inheritance in IDL is the colon. Here is an example:

```
interface example1 {
    long operation1 (in long arg1);
};

interface example2:example1 {
    void operation2 (in long arg2, out long arg3);
};
```

interface example2 also includes, through inheritance, **operation1**. Even though it does not appear explicitly in the IDL, the language mappings will generate code for it, and the object implementation for **example2** must be prepared to respond to invocations of **operation1** as well as **operation2**. (We use this brief example to illustrate inheritance in each language mapping. Look for it in Chapters 7, 8, and 9.)

Multiple inheritance is allowed. For example, in the interface declaration

```
interface example4:example3, example1 {
    . . .
}
```

interface example4 includes not only all of **example3**, but also **example1**. The language mappings will generate code for all of the operations of both **example3** and **example1** in the stub for **example4**, plus all of its own operations; its object implementation must be prepared to respond to them.

3.3.10 The Object Interface

interface Object defines some operations that are valid on any object. You can think of it as an interface inherited by every object, but that's not how it's implemented—these operations are actually performed by the ORB. This means you don't have to take them into account when you build your object implementation.

In CORBA parlance, these operations are implemented by a *pseudo-object*; that is, not by an actual CORBA object. Their interfaces are defined in OMG IDL, but there are some differences: A pseudo-object may not be specified as a parameter in an operation on an ordinary object, may not be accessed using the DII, and does not have definitions in the interface repository. The IDL that defines them is termed pseudo-IDL or PIDL.

Here's (most of) the PIDL for **interface Object**:

```
interface Object {                          // PIDL
    ImplementationDef get_implementation ();
    InterfaceDef get_interface ();
    Object duplicate ();
    void release ();

    Status create_request (...
    );
};
```

get_implementation returns an object in the implementation repository that describes the implementation of the object, and **get_interface** returns an object in the Interface Repository that provides type information.

duplicate and **release** are operations performed by the ORB on object references because only the ORB is able to do this kind of thing. When your client creates and uses a duplicate object reference, the target object implementation cannot tell past that point whether the original or the copy was used to invoke a request. **release** reclaims storage for the object reference. This operates only on the object reference; the target object is not involved, nor are any other references to that particular target object.

create_request is the operation you perform to start the process of building an invocation for the DII. This operation has a number of parameters, which are defined in Section 4.3.3.

We haven't shown you the entire object interface; there are a few more operations that might help you when you advance to building dynamic invocations in large systems with complex inheritance relationships. But by the time you're ready for them, you won't have any trouble reading about them in either the OMG CORBA Core specification or the documentation that comes with your ORB product. Good luck!

CHAPTER 4

Understanding the ORB, Part 1: Client Side

We've discussed a lot about what the ORB does, but very little about how it does it. In the next three chapters, we'll fill in some of the details. Since the ORB—or, more precisely, our network of intercommunicating ORBs—is the nerve center of our distributed object system, there's a lot to cover.

Fortunately for us, the ORB Core specification is divided into a number of components that we can examine separately. They are:

- the Client Stubs;
- the Dynamic Invocation Interface (DII);
- the ORB Interface and ORB core, including the Interface Repository (IR) and the Implementation Repository;
- the Object Adapter(s);
- the static IDL skeleton(s);
- the Dynamic Skeleton Interface (DSI); and
- the CORBA 2.0 Interoperability specification.

In the first section of this chapter, we'll present an overview of the client side of the ORB. Then, in Sections 4.2 through 4.5 we'll fill in the details, including some of the IDL interfaces of these components. Chapter 5 discusses the object implementation side. CORBA 2.0 Interoperability, a separate OMG standard, is covered in Chapter 6.

4.1   ORB AND CLIENT-SIDE OVERVIEW

Figure 2.1 showed an extremely simplified view of a request passing from a client, through its IDL stub, the ORB, and the target object's skeleton, and finally arriving at the object implementation, where it is executed and the result returned by the corresponding return route. From this, we learned that the definition of all interfaces in OMG IDL allows the ORBs to handle all of the details of request/response passing, including format translation when client and target object reside on different systems; and the client possesses an object reference for each target, and passes it to the ORB in each request to denote the particular object instance that is the target of that request.

It turns out that the two ORB interfaces shown in Figure 2.1 are not sufficient to handle all of the logistics that CORBA users require. A more complete diagram of client, ORB, and object implementation components is shown in Figure 4.1. This figure shows six ORB interfaces and eight ORB components. Two interfaces communicate only with the client, and two oth-

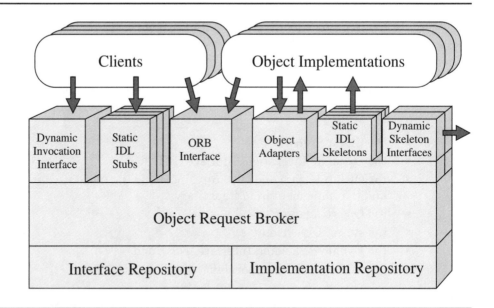

Figure 4.1.   Structure of the Object Request Broker. Interfaces between ORB components and its clients and object implementations (shown by arrows) are expressed in OMG IDL and standardized by the OMG. Interfaces between ORB components (where component boxes abut in the figure) are proprietary.

ers only with the object implementation, while the ORB interface provides services for both. The Dynamic Skeleton Interfaces communicate with remote ORBs. Interface and Implementation Repository services are accessed directly through the ORB interface, and indirectly through method invocations via the SII and DII, which rely on this information in various ways. (We realize that both Interface Repository and Implementation Repository abbreviate to IR. In this book, and almost every other CORBA-related publication, IR refers to the Interface Repository.)

The client initiates requests, which may be passed to the ORB via either a static IDL stub (Static Invocation Interface, SII) or the DII. There are a number of important differences between the SII and the DII; the major one is that the DII lets you postpone selection of object type and operation until run time, while the SII requires this selection to be made at compile time. Formally, we say that the DII allows *dynamic typing* while the SII requires *static typing*. (Both allow dynamic *binding*; that is, you don't have to select the target object *instance* until run time.)

There are additional differences: As a consequence of dynamic binding, the DII cannot check argument type correctness at compile time while the SII can. Structurally, the ORB requires a separate stub for each static interface (generated by the IDL compiler, as we saw in Chapter 2), but only one DII interface that is provided by the ORB itself. While SII invocations are generally synchronous (they block, unless the operation is declared *oneway* in its IDL definition), the DII may be invoked in either synchronous, asynchronous, or deferred synchronous modes.

Since any interface may be invoked via the DII, this means that non-blocking invocation semantics are available for every object on your system. (Why no deferred synchronous static mode? Informal OMG lore says this may be historical: CORBA was created by merging a static ORB specification with only synchronous invocation semantics, and a dynamic ORB specification that had synchronous, asynchronous, and deferred synchronous. The SII folks resisted adding deferred synchronous mode to avoid further growth in the stubs' memory footprint.) There's more on the SII in Section 4.2 and more on the DII (including details on invoking in deferred synchronous mode and polling for results) in Section 4.3.

The ORB interfaces provide access to the Interface and Implementation Repositories, and some operations on object references that only the ORB can perform. These are discussed in Section 4.5.

4.2   CLIENT STRUCTURE AND IDL STUBS

In CORBA, the roles of client and object implementation have meaning only with respect to a particular request; unlike "client/server" architectures, they are not roles to which components commit. A software component that accepts an invocation (that is, an object implementation) may, if its developer wished, turn around and invoke the services of another object (playing the role of client) as part of the processing it does to service the request. Since multiple requests are outstanding, the module is simultaneously client and object implementation; this does not bother the ORB in the slightest. This flexibility allows developers to use the full power of the system and all of the available components to solve their problems and is a major benefit of CORBA.

The role of the client, then, is simply to request services by invoking operations. There are no standard CORBA operations for object implementation management; object activation, deactivation, suspension, and so on are performed either automatically by the ORB or by customized services located *outside* the client, for example in a management tool. Client code deals exclusively with the problem at hand, resulting in maximum portability and interoperability.

The client accesses object implementations through their IDL interfaces, specifying the target object instance via its object reference. The IDL interface isolates the client from the object's implementation details, while the object reference isolates the client from the object's location.

The object reference is neither an address nor a name associated with the object instance. CORBA standardizes only what the object reference does, not how it does it. This allows each ORB designer to optimize or tune object reference handling in the way he or she thinks is best. Some ORBs will be optimized for remote invocations, others will be tuned for quick response from local objects, and still others may compromise or tune for some alternative variable. And performance is one characteristic of an ORB product that you may expect to improve from one release to another. If performance is important to you, look for reviews in recent magazines with performance figures, then confirm in your own environment that the product meets your needs. The CORBA specification gives ORB builders the freedom to design and build implementations to meet your needs, and the resulting products are coming to market with excellent characteristics.

The stub joins to the client at one end and to the ORB at the other. Since the stub is generated by the IDL compiler, and not written by a programmer, it is not necessary for stubs to be interchangeable. (IDL is interchangeable; you run through the IDL compiler to generate the stub you want.)

The client-to-stub interface is defined by the standard OMG language mapping for the programming language you chose. This means that your source code ports from one vendor's ORB to another for the same language, since the bindings generated by your IDL file are defined by this standard rather than by any particular vendor. The example in this book demonstrates this; most of the code is common to every ORB of a particular language and is presented only once in common sections of the example chapters. By the way, OMG knows that source code portability on the server side is more limited than on the client, and is currently working on a standard to remedy this.

Coding to the SII is simple; in addition, this method provides type-checking at compile time, thus avoiding surprises when you run. There are three examples in each language mapping chapter; check out Section 7.2.2 for C, Section 8.2.3 for C++, and Section 9.10.1 for Smalltalk to see how this works.

In contrast to the IDL-defined, standard client-to-stub interface, the stub-to-ORB interface is proprietary. Since standardization is not necessary here, OMG standards allow vendors to construct this junction for performance and reliability. This means that you cannot use stubs from vendor A's IDL compiler with vendor B's ORB. IDL compilers and ORBs come in sets; you cannot mix and match (not that we can think of any benefit from this even if you could).

Invocations via the SII are *synchronous* unless the IDL defines the operation as **oneway**. Synchronous calls block, not returning until the ORB can deliver to the client either the response and result values from the invoked object or an exception. Clients can also invoke operations in deferred synchronous mode but only via the DII, which we cover in the next section.

4.3 THE DYNAMIC INVOCATION INTERFACE

Almost everything in life involves a trade-off. In the DII, you trade off a few more lines of code for each initial object invocation for complete freedom in picking your target object, interface, and operation at run time.

The DII gives a client the capability, at any time, of invoking *any* operation on *any* object that it may access over the network. This includes objects for which the client has no stub—objects newly added to the network or discovered through a Naming or Trading service. (Since this includes every object in your system, you could program exclusively in the DII, something you could not do in the SII without restricting access to new objects.) And, for any object (stub present or not), the DII allows *deferred synchronous*—that is, nonblocking with return result—invocation semantics in addition to the usual synchronous and asynchronous semantics.

Object implementations cannot detect, when they receive an invocation, whether the invocation came into the ORB via the SII or the DII. The ORB is responsible for preparing dynamic requests so that they have exactly the same form as static requests, before it transmits the request to the object implementation. The choice is entirely up to the client, and the work is done by the ORB; object builders have nothing extra to do to prepare for request coming from the DII.

4.3.1 Identifying a Target Object

There are four steps to a dynamic invocation:

1. Identify the object you want to invoke.
2. Retrieve its interface.
3. Construct the invocation.
4. Invoke the request, and receive the results.

In a dynamic distributed object environment, users will probably consult an Object Trading Service to locate object implementations. Described in more detail in Chapter 12, the Trader service is like a combination Yellow Pages and mail-order catalog which lists every available service with ancillary information such as features, location, or cost. Most users will probably access Trader via browsers, clicking through services until they find one they like; additional use will come from programs written to access Trader directly. But there will be no OMG standard for the browser itself; standard Trader interfaces enable browsers to operate interchangeably on different Trader implementations, and OMG expects services like the browser to be produced in a competitive envinronment. On request, the Trader Service furnishes the object reference of the service provider, allowing the client to follow up its successful shopping trip with an immediate use (which might be called a purchase, if the service has an associated cost) of the service.

In this context, the desktop "client" becomes a generic command center, which activates with few (if any) interfaces enabled via static stubs, and proceeds to configure itself to invoke all of the actions its user wants via the DII. This is an extremely powerful concept, relatively unexplored so far in product and prototype even in research, in spite of the availability of the DII in commercial ORBs. Keep an eye on its development; it is a necessary step in the transition from monolithic applications to user-centric distributed computing.

4.3.2 Retrieving the Target Interface

Retrieving the target object's interface is straightforward, although information will have to come from several locations since the primary source, the Interface Repository (see Section 4.4), contains only syntax information. First, using the object reference obtained from the Naming or Trading service, the client invokes the ORB operation **get_interface**. This returns, not the interface itself, but an object reference that returns the top-level components of the interface when passed to the IR. Additional calls return all of the interface's operations (by name), their parameters, and their types.

We'll need more information in order to construct an invocation: what each operation does, the function of each parameter, allowed parameter ranges, allowable sequence of operations, and anything else that might be helpful (or necessary). This won't come from the IR, so it must come from somewhere else; the logical place to look is the Trader, although there is no standard location or format for these data.

4.3.3 Constructing the Invocation

The DII provides standard interfaces for constructing a request. As noted earlier, the request is referred to as a pseudo-object in the OMG specifications, and its interface is described in PIDL or pseudo-IDL. We described PIDL in Section 3.3.10. The interface to create a request is named (of course) **request**.

We've already seen the operation **create_request**; it's part of **interface Object** inherited by every object; it was introduced in Section 3.3.10. The request that is created by this operation will always be directed to the object that was the target of the **create_request**. (What about polymorphism? You can reuse the code you write to create a DII request with the same operation name on a different object, but you cannot reuse the same request object on a series of different targets, even if they all support the same operation with the same signature, because there's no way to change the target object reference on a request object.) Here's the full definition of **create_request**:

```
Typedef unsigned long ORBStatus;

ORBStatus create_request (        // PIDL
    in Context          ctx,       // context object for
                                   // operation
    in Identifier       operation, // intended operation on
                                   // object
    in NVList           arg_list,  // args to operation
    inout NamedValue result,       // operation result
    out Request         request,   // newly created request
    in Flags            req_flags  // request flags
);
```

We already defined **Context** in Section 3.3.7. Here are definitions for the rest.

operation is the same name as the one in the original IDL file used to create the skeleton for the object.

There are two ways to specify the arguments of the operation. You can use either one, but you cannot combine them. Either you pass all of the arguments in **arg_list** when you call **create_request**, or you specify **arg_list** as **null** and use calls to **add_arg** (discussed shortly).

NVList is a list of named values representing the parameter list in our IDL definition; the values in an **NVList** can be of any type. The client invokes an ORB operation to create an **NVList**:

```
ORBStatus create_list (
    in long         count,
    out NVList      new_list
);
```

Each element in the list is a **NamedValue**:

```
typedef unsigned long Flags;

struct NamedValue {
    Identifier      name;           // argument name
    any             argument;       // argument
    long            len;            // length/count of argument
                                    // value
    Flags           arg_modes;      // argument mode flags
};
```

This struct can represent any component of a parameter list.

Flags do just what you think: You can set the flags to `ARG_IN`, `ARG_OUT`, or `ARG_INOUT`.

4.3.4 The Request Interface

Now that we've created a request, there are a number of useful things we can do with (or to) it, all defined in the **request** interface. Even though **request** is a pseudo-object, you map these IDL definitions specifying your request as the target, and the ORB knows exactly what to do.

If you didn't specify values in **arg_list**, you add them to the request with calls to **add_args**, one call per argument:

```
ORBStatus add_arg (
    in Identifier    name,        // argument name
    in TypeCode      arg_type,    // argument datatype
    in void          * value,     // argument value to be added
    in long          len,         // length/count of argument
                                  // value
    in Flags         arg_flags    // argument flags
    );
```

You can delete a request with **ORBStatus delete ()**; ('nuff said...).

4.3.5 Invoking a DII Request, I: Synchronous

Also in the request interface are the operations **invoke**, **send**, and **get_response**:

```
ORBStatus invoke (
    in Flags         invoke_flags    //invocation flags
    );
```

This operation, specified with the **request** as the target, directs the ORB to construct the target request and route it to the object reference, which was the target of the original **create_request** (remember?). **invoke** is the synchronous form; when control returns to your client, **inout** and **out** values will be in their proper places in **arg_list**, and the return value (if any) will be in **result**.

4.3.6 Invoking a DII Request, II: Asynchronous

The operations for asynchronous invocation and result retrieval have two forms, for individual and multiple requests. The individual request forms, **send** and **get_response**, are part of the request interface and are defined in IDL. The multiple forms, which do not have an object as a target, are implemented as ORB calls defined only by their language mappings.

We'll cover the individual forms first. The request is dispatched using:

```
ORBStatus send (
    in Flags         invoke_flags          //invocation flags
    );
```

Control returns to the client immediately, allowing it (and you) to do something productive while the ORB and object implementation work on the request routing and processing. Some standard errors may be raised on in-vocation of **send**, but most will not even be known to the ORB until later when processing has been completed. The OMG specification allows errors to be raised on **send**, but warns that even obvious errors (invalid object reference, for example) may not be raised until you try to **get_response**.

There's only one standard flag defined for send: **INV_NO_RESPONSE**, which indicates that the client will not poll for a response and does not expect any output arguments to be updated. This turns any operation into, effectively, **oneway** even if it was not so declared in the original IDL.

Assuming we did not flag **INV_NO_RESPONSE** and the operation was not declared **oneway** in the IDL, we can poll for the response using:

```
ORBStatus get_response (
     in Flags          response_flags     //response flags
);
```

response_flags lets the client invoke this operation either synchronously or asynchronously. If the flag value is set to **RESP_NO_WAIT**, this call returns immediately. Your client will have to check the **ORBStatus** result to see if the request has completed before attempting to use the result values; if it has not completed, you have to invoke **get_response** again until it does. If your client does not set the flag, then **get_response** blocks (waits) until the invocation has completed before returning with either results or an exception.

send_multiple_requests initiates multiple requests in parallel. Since the request object references are in an array instead of being the target of the operation, **send_multiple_requests** is only defined in each language mapping and not in OMG IDL. In C, it is

```
ORBStatus  send_multiple_requests (          /* C */
     Request           reqs[],      /*array of reqs */
     Environment       *env,
     long              count,       /*number of reqs*/
     Flags             invoke_flags
);
```

The degree of parallelism in both the initiation and execution of the requests is system-dependent, and beyond the control of your client. You may specify **INV_NO_RESPONSE**, but it applies to *every* request in the array.

You can check and retrieve responses using **get_response** if you wish, but **get_response** checks for only the particular request you target, and there is no guarantee that this will be the first one that comes back. (Of course, if it's the first one you want, then this is okay.) If you want whichever one comes back first, you call **get_next_response**, again in C here:

```
ORBStatus get_next_response (        /* C */
    Environment    *env,
    Flags          response_flags,
    Request        *req
);
```

get_next_response, in spite of its name, does not necessarily return requests in the order that they complete nor in the order in which they were called. If multiple requests are queued for return within the ORB, this routine picks one (and you have no way of controlling or predicting which) and returns it. If none has completed, it returns with an **ORBStatus** value of **false** if **RESP_NO_WAIT** is set; otherwise it blocks until a request completes.

This completes the discussion of the SII and DII. Next, we'll take a look at the Interface Repository.

4.4 THE INTERFACE REPOSITORY

The Interface Repository (IR) is crucial to the operation of CORBA. CORBA requires that each ORB bear and implement the IR interface, allowing the IDL definitions for all of the objects it knows about to be stored, modified, and retrieved. These definitions can be used for many different purposes; the CORBA specification manual points out three ways the ORB can use them directly:

- To provide interoperability between different ORB implementations.
- To provide type-checking of request signatures, whether a request was issued through the DII or through a stub.
- To check the correctness of inheritance graphs.

In addition, the information will be helpful for client objects and users. The specification points out a few of the ways they can use the IR:

- To manage installation and distribution of interface definitions around your network.
- During the development process, for instance, to browse or modify interface definitions or other information stored in IDL.
- Language compilers could compile stubs and skeletons directly from the IR instead of from the IDL files (all of the required information is contained in both formats).

4.4.1 Using the IR

There are two basic ways to access the interface repository:

- You can use utilities provided by your ORB vendor.
- You can write code that invokes the standard IR IDL interface mandated by OMG.

The advantage of the IDL interfaces is that they are a standard, allowing the same code to access any compliant IR. The disadvantage, of course, is that you have to write code to use them, while the vendor utilities are useful immediately. (Of course, these utilities use IR APIs, although you can't tell whether they use the standard OMG interfaces or additional ones available only on your particular vendor's ORB. Vendors are expected to extend the OMG basics; the only requirement is that their extensions not break any of the standard mechanisms.)

This means you'll probably start accessing IRs through your vendor's utilities. Each vendor will provide its own way of doing this; most of the ORBs in this book introduce their syntax to store an IDL definition in its section of Chapter 23, and they all provide the remaining details in their documentation. Some ORBs have a command or command-line option for storing an IDL definition; others store automatically when the IDL is compiled. Whatever its form, it's a simple operation for every ORB.

4.4.2 Identifying an Interface Repository

Do not assume that there is a one-to-one correspondence between IRs and ORBs. The OMG specifications are much more flexible than this; the only requirement is that every ORB be able to access at least one IR. So,

- a particular IR may be shared by more than one ORB; and
- an ORB may access more than one IR.

How do ORBs keep track of repositories? Each IR has its own unique RepositoryID. There are several formats for these IDs, appropriate for different situations: Simple formats allow short names to be used on an isolated network or single machine, while a UUID-based format guarantees uniqueness on a network as large as the internet. (UUID stands for Universal, Unique IDentifier. UUIDs originated in OSF DCE, but are now used in non-DCE contexts as well.)

Consequently, your company can maintain a number of IRs simultaneously, for different purposes. Your enterprise-wide production IR can be restricted to interfaces for proven, tested versions of objects both purchased and written in-house, while separate IRs maintain repositories of interfaces for internal development and beta testing of vendor products. In addition, programming groups can maintain private IRs for development and testing.

ORBs will assume that two IRs with the same RepositoryID contain *exactly* the same interface definitions. This will happen automatically if the two ORBs are actually accessing the same repository, but may work through replication instead (which may be either manual or automatic). When you maintain your IRs, make sure you follow this requirement, for a number of reasons: One is because, otherwise, remote invocations could fail due to inconsistent interface definitions at the client and object implementation ends. Another is that developers may retrieve interface definitions from an IR and use them for implementation; to them, the RepositoryID will flag the IR containing the exact version of an interface to which they need to code.

4.4.3   How Do IRs Work?

An implementation of an IR requires some form of persistent object store. For an ORB serving thousands or more different interfaces, regardless of whether their source is local or remote, this can grow to be a substantial component. Fortunately for ORB implementors, the OMG specification allows vendors the freedom to implement the IR in the best way for their target platform and operating system, while the standard set of IDL interfaces maintain interoperability and portability.

For example, an IR may be implemented on top of a database, either written specifically for the ORB or purchased and installed separately. The distribution characteristics of this database will determine how the separate ORBs see their contents. If the database is distributed and replicated, remote ORBs will retrieve interfaces quickly from local copies, but changes will propagate with a latency characteristic of the underlying database implementation.

When you evaluate an ORB product, check out how it manages the information in its IRs. Your needs will differ depending on how much developing and beta testing you plan to do, so beware of blanket recommendations that may assume a set of requirements very different from yours. Scalability is a big factor here; ORB vendors know this and are working hard to provide products that retain both responsiveness and flexibility even when systems grow to thousands of ORBs or more. Clearly, this is an areas where users will benefit in the long run.

4.4.4   Structure of Interface Repositories

OMG specifications do not require IRs to store IDL, although many do. The mandated interfaces treat IR components—modules, interfaces, operations, attributes, parameters, constants, typdefs, exceptions, and contexts—as objects that may contain other objects in this list where appropriate. (For definitions of all of the terms in this list, see Appendix B.) Stored in a hierarchical or nested fashion, this structure allows the original IDL file to be re-created except for comments. Many, perhaps most, IRs store comments as well, allowing the original IDL file to be completely reconstructed.

We're not going to detail the IDL interfaces to the IR because most users will access the IR through their vendors' interfaces, and there isn't a lot of curiosity about how this component works "under the covers" (unlike, for example, interoperability which just about everyone is curious about). But do not underestimate the value of the IR to your enterprise's distributed object environment. Pay attention to the setup of the IR on your network, and leverage it to maximize the interoperability you get from your investment in CORBA.

4.5 THE ORB INTERFACE

interface object (Section 3.3.10) is a part of the ORB interface. We covered it next to the section on inheritance, so we don't have to go over it again here.

The most important part of the ORB interface is the initialization component. There's a part for the client, which we'll cover here, and another for the object implementation, which we'll put off until Chapter 5.

When your first client starts up, it needs object references for its ORB, a Naming service, and the Interface Repository. The OMG felt that these common initialization operations should be standardized since every client has to invoke them, and the format had to allow the client to specify *which* ORB, Naming Service, or Interface Repository it wants since CORBA allows clients to connect to as many of these as they like. The Initialization Specification meets these requirements.

4.5.1 Initializing a Client at Startup

Initialization is defined in pseudo-IDL (PIDL); that is, an operation on the ORB pseudo-object. However, the mappings to C++, C, and Smalltalk do not follow the general principles we'll cover later on, because the normal components of a mapped operation won't be fully defined until we've obtained our first few object references.

Here's the pseudo-IDL invocation to obtain your initial ORB reference:

```
typedef string ORBid;                          //PIDL
typedef sequence <string> arg_list;

ORB ORB_init (inout arg_list argv, in ORBid orb_identifier);
```

Before we explain this, we'll look at the somewhat unconventional language mappings:

```
/* C Language Mapping - Contacting the ORB  */
typedef CORBA_string  CORBA_ORBid;
extern CORBA_ORB CORBA_ORB_init (int *argc,
        char **argv,
        CORBA_ORBid orb_identifier,
        CORBA_Environment *env);
```

and

```
//C++ Language Mapping - Contacting the ORB
namespace CORBA {
    typedef string ORBid;
    ORB_ptr ORB_init (int& argc,
        char** argv,
        ORBid orb_identifier);
}
```

ORBs are identified by strings, typed as **ORBid**. These names will be locally scoped, like filenames; there will not be a formal registry for ORB names. When your site starts to interoperate on a wide scale, someone will appoint an administrator who will register or assign ORB names in a way that avoids collisions between different departments or whatever. Or you can set **ORBid** to **NULL** and pass a parameter pair tagged **ORBid**, which specifies the **ORBid** string (**-ORBid "ORB_depot"**, for example).

The ORB initialization function will remove parameters from the argument list once they are used, in the standard way of C and C++.

The **ORB_init** function may be called multiple times, and will return the same pseudo-object reference if the same parameters are used. This allows, for example, multithreaded applications to access the same ORB from multiple threads, or alternatively, for ORBs to be implemented as a shared library.

Now you can invoke operations on the ORB, but you still need your first object reference in order to do anything useful. The standard way to do this is via the Naming Service, but since the CORBAservices are optional components of the standard, the OMG did not want to mandate including a full-blown service with every ORB just to get things started. (There's a good reason for this. ORBs may be built into just about anything in the future, and some hardware that contains embedded ORBs will be really small—those on wristwatch-sized pagers, for example, or switches in the telephone network. Manufacturers of this equipment want the benefit of an industry standard, but have to keep memory footprint to an absolute minimum. CORBA takes these needs into account in cases like this.)

To meet these requirements, initial object references are provided by the ORB via operations that are modeled after the Naming Service. It's really a mini-Naming Service implemented within the ORB itself, with two operations. The first (**list_initial_services**) returns a list of available service names; you then pass each service name to the next operation (**resolve_initial_references**), and it returns an object reference that gets you started with that service. Currently, the most important two services are all that you can get through this interface: **InterfaceRepository** and **NameService**. OMG manages the list of services available through this interface, since they're implemented within the ORB. The list may grow, but it won't grow very quickly. If a service can be found through the Naming Service, there won't be any reason to add it to this list.

This service is implemented as a pseudo-object—a service provided by the ORB that looks like it's provided by a regular object. And, it's defined in pseudo-IDL:

```
//PIDL Interface to obtain initial services
    typedef string ObjectId;
    typedef sequence <ObectId> ObjectIdList;

    exception InvalidName;

    ObjectIdList list_initial_services ();

    Object resolve_initial_references (in ObjectId identifier)
        raises (InvalidName);
```

Here's how this maps to C and C++:

```
/* C Mapping */
typedef CORBA_string CORBA_ORB_ObjectId;
typedef CORBA_sequence_CORBA_ORB_ObjectId
        CORBA_ORB_ObjectIdList;
typedef struct CORBA_ORB_InvalidName
        CORBA_ORB_InvalidName;

CORBA_ORB_ObjectIdList
        CORBA_ORB_list_initial_services (
        CORBA_ORB orb,
        CORBA_Environment *env);
```

```
CORBA_Object  CORBA_ORB_resolve_initial_references(
       CORBA_ORB orb,
       CORBA_ORB_ObjectId identifier,
       CORBA_Environment *env);
```

and

```
//C++ Language Mapping
namespace CORBA {
    class ORB {
    public:
        typedef String ObjectId;

        class InvalidName {...};

        ObjectIdList_ptr
                list_initial_services();
        Object_ptr resolve_initial_references (
                ObjectId identifier);
    }
}
```

resolve_initial_references operates on the ORB rather than on the Naming Service (which we'll define in Chapter 12) since the service is provided by a pseudo-object. And ObjectId is a string, not a name construct (a sequence of structs containing a string pair for each component of a name, as we'll see in Chapter 12).

In the example in this book, we use **ORB_init** to connect to the ORB but do not need **resolve_initial_references**. This is partly because our store/depot scenario is static rather than dynamic, and the object connections are always the same. Another reason is that the Naming and Initialization Services are so new, as we write this, that not all vendors have them implemented in their ORB products. You should take advantage of the Naming Service as soon as it becomes available; it's designed to store object references for you from session to session and make them available in the most convenient, time-tested way: by name. And, when the Trader service becomes available a bit later in the future, use it even more than you use the Naming Service. The Trader service is the bridge that will let us cross over from statically to dynamically configured object applications—a new, freer way to work.

4.5.2 **Stringifying Object References**

Another part of the CORBA module manipulates object references. This is where you find the operations that convert object references to strings and back. List operations are found here, too:

```
interface ORB {                                          // PIDL
    string  object_to_string (in Object obj);
    Object  string_to_object (in string str);

    Status  create_list (
        in long              count,
        out NVList           new_list
    );
    Status  create_operation_list (
        in OperationDef      oper,
        out NVList           new_list
    );
}
```

If you need to store an object reference yourself—for example, in a flat file or database—you need to convert using **object_to_string** first. After you retrieve it, you need to convert back using **string_to_object**. This is necessary because CORBA only requires the (non-stringified) object reference to remain valid for a particular session—the length of time your client remains active and connected to a particular ORB. The stringified object reference, in contrast, retains its validity across session boundaries, and the operation **string_to_object** returns a standard-format reference, valid in the current session, which refers to the *same* instance as the original reference.

You probably won't be doing this much. The Naming and Trader services (Chapter 12) can give you a valid object reference when you pass them a name, so this is the preferred way to do it. You're going to store a string anyhow; it might as well be a name, which is something you can recognize. If it's a public object, you can find it under its public name. If it's your own private instance, you can store its object reference in your private section of the Naming Service with a name you assign. The Naming Service will take care of session-to-session bookkeeping for you automatically.

We already covered the list operations in Section 4.3.3.

CHAPTER 5

Understanding the ORB, Part 2: Object Implementation Side

5.1 ACTIVATING A SERVER AND INVOKING AN OBJECT IMPLEMENTATION

You can tell from Figure 4.1 that the server side of the ORB is more complicated than the client side. CORBA intentionally keeps the client side as simple as possible. As much of the object management as possible is assigned to the ORB, but the automatic startup that makes the client side so simple and transparent becomes a series of explicit operations on the object implementation. This means that object builders must write code to handshake with the ORB during startup and shutdown, saving and restoring state in the process. None of these steps can be automatic and, as we will see in Section 5.2, these interfaces do not yet benefit from the second pass through the OMG standardization process that neatened up the client side so well.

This requires a structure with many more components and options. Before we dissect it piece by piece, we'll walk through a scenario where an ORB activates and invokes an object in a server. This will clarify the players and their roles, motivating the subsequent presentation of components and interfaces.

The BOA or Basic Object Adapter supports a number of different configurations of server and object implementation. For this first run-through, we'll pick a popular one: a server process distinct from the ORB, within which run a number of distinct object implementations. What's a server? On the client side, we only dealt with Object Implementations, one for each interface in the IDL module, so we never saw a "server." But on the object side, the structure of the implementation is visible, and the BOA is equipped to deal with objects grouped in various ways. In this example, a single process called a server in the OMG specifications is running some number of objects, one for each interface. If you're impatient to see the other server/object configurations the BOA can handle, look ahead to Section 5.6.

Figure 5.1 shows the sequence of operations in our scenario:

1. The ORB receives a request targeting an object in the server. The ORB checks its repository and determines that neither the server nor the object is currently active.
2. The ORB activates the server, using a system-dependent linkage. As part of the activation process, the server is passed the information it

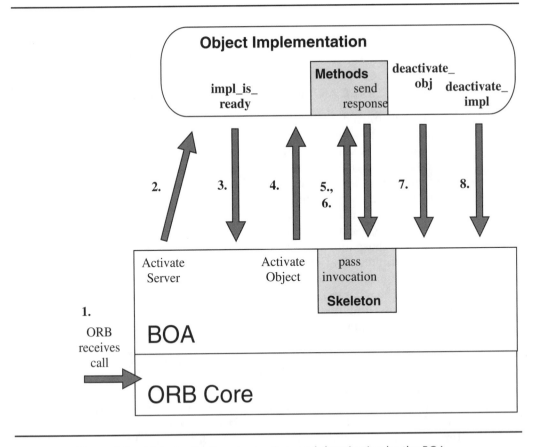

Figure 5.1.   Object activation, invocation, and deactivation by the BOA.

needs to communicate with the BOA. The ORB momentarily holds the original call to the object.

3. The server calls **impl_is_ready**, a call on the BOA, which knows that now the server is ready to activate objects.

4. The BOA calls the server's object activate routine for the target object, passing it the object reference. The server activates the object. If the object had previously been active and stored its state in persistent storage, that information is retrieved and the previous state restored. The key to the persistent store for that object (a filename, database key, or PID for the Persistent Object Service) had been maintained by the BOA, associated with the object reference, and retrieved by the object during startup using **get_id**.

5. The BOA passes the invocation to the object through the skeleton and receives the response, which it routes back to the client.

6. The BOA may receive additional requests on that object, which it passes through the skeleton as in step 5. The BOA may also receive calls for additional objects in the server, which process through steps 4 and then 5 for each new object.

7. The server may, for whatever reason (user request, usage monitoring, and so on) decide to shut down an object. It first calls the BOA routine **deactivate_obj**, specifying the target object, after which the BOA will no longer route calls to that object without reactivating it first. The object saves its state in persistent storage (if it has any such state) before shutting down.

8. Similarly, the server may shut down entirely. It first calls the BOA routine **deactivate_impl**, informing the BOA that it is no longer available to activate objects. On receiving the next request, the BOA will start over at step 1.

5.2 STANDARDIZING THE SERVER SIDE

There may be more than one object adapter; however only one—the BOA or basic object adapter—has been standardized by OMG so far. (See Section 5.5 for more on other object adapters.)

When OMG members wrote the original BOA specification, they envisioned that there would be one or a few ORBs on each system, and that most object invocations would involve interprocess communication (IPC). Since then, lightweight in-process ORBs have become more popular—in fact, all of the ORBs represented in this book reside in-process. This means that the client-ORB connection is *always local*, fast, and efficient; invocations of objects in the same process run at CPU speed, while external invocations are transparently routed to their target via IPC. The combination of speed and flexibility makes it both practical and popular.

This configuration looks a lot like the "library object adapter" mentioned but not standardized in the original CORBA documents. A current OMG effort will almost certainly remedy this; it is expected to produce a standard that benefits from extensive experience with many vendors products sometime late in 1996. But in the meantime, each ORB has a library object adapter that was written independently by its development staff without guidance from any standard.

What does this mean to you and your implementation? Primarily, it means that server-side code, which connects your Object Implementations to the Object Adapter, will not port among different ORBs as cleanly as, for example, code on the client side, which connects to the ORB and retrieves initial object references. (The client side, unlike the server, already benefits from a second round of OMG standardization, which completed in late 1994). Of course, the code generated by the mapping for your programming language ports 100 percent, as does the code for Object Implementation functionality. Differences show up only when we get to functions such as object activation and connection, which are necessarily system- and language-dependent. We'll point out these sections of code as we work the example in the back half of this book.

5.3   SERVER-SIDE COMPONENTS

As the scenario demonstrates, the ORB accepts responsibility for so much object management that, to the client, it looks as though every object is running and active all the time even though it's not. CORBA does not even provide a separate command for a client to start up an object implementation—the client just sends a request, and the ORB does everything else. This does not mean that all of these objects are really running all the time, consuming computing resources. Instead, the interfaces allow enough flexibility that the ORB and your system administrator can manage your objects and resources pretty much the way you need.

Figure 5.2 focuses on the server-side ORB structure. These are the components that we'll go over in this chapter, starting in Section 5.4 with an overview of object implementation structure. Here we'll get our first look at the code in the object implementations, which works with the ORB and Object Adapter to provide the promised management functions.

The Object Adapter provides interfaces between ORB and object, allowing the ORB to prepare the object to receive a request, and allowing objects to notify the ORB that they are ready (or not ready) to process requests. The component of the object adapter between the ORB and the objects is in a

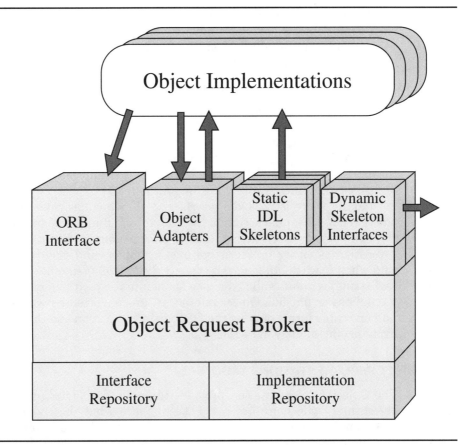

Figure 5.2. Object Request Broker, server side. Object Implementations may invoke ORB operations defined for, say, IR or object reference operations. Object adapters communicate for object activation and deactivation. Static IDL skeletons pass invocations to objects and receive replies. DSI invocations usually pass to another ORB via IPC or over the network, although they may be addressed to objects on this ORB, which supports the DSI.

position to equalize the services provided by various ORBs, allowing the same set of objects to function with ORBs of differing service levels. We'll review general Object Adapter characteristics in Section 5.5, and BOA interfaces in Section 5.6.

Static IDL skeletons are the server-side equivalent of client stubs, created by the IDL compiler to bridge between ORB and object implementation, as we saw in Chapter 2. There will be a skeleton for each object type bound to the ORB. Details are in Section 5.7.

The ORB uses the Dynamic Skeleton Interface or DSI to create a proxy skeleton for objects, typically remote, whose static skeletons are not bound to it. ORBs will typically lack static skeletons for remote invocations, since the installation procedure for an object implementation grafts its skeleton only onto its own ORB and not that of the client. ORBs will then create a dynamic skeleton to pass the invocation to the remote object via its own ORB. Dynamic skeletons can be used for other reasons as well; one frequently mentioned is for local objects created dynamically using scripts or interpreted languages. This component was added to CORBA as part of the interoperability specification, but now forms part of the core CORBA specification. Details are in Section 5.8; some of this information is used in the discussion of interoperability in Chapter 6.

Finally, there is the ORB interface itself, which provides operations on object references, plus access to the interface and implementation repositories. The object reference can take two forms: one is directly usable in an invocation as either target or parameter, but is valid only within the session when it was obtained; the other (called *stringified* since it's actually a text string) remains valid from one session to the next and can be stored in a database or flat file. Object references are converted between stringified and invocable forms only by the ORB, using operations on this interface as explained previously in Section 4.5.

5.4   OBJECT IMPLEMENTATION STRUCTURE

The Object Implementation provides the actual behavior and state of an object, and some more besides. Let's compare what the client sees of the object implementation to what may actually be happening behind the scenes.

The client's view, simply put, is of an object instance that is *always* running, active, and ready to respond to any operation in its IDL interface definition. There is no OMA operation to activate an object instance (although there is an operation to create the instance, by invoking a factory object); the client just sends an invocation and it works. If the client performs an operation that puts the instance into a particular state, that state is preserved unless the object reference is shared and another client modifies the target's state, or the object is explicitly deleted. This state may be preserved for a long time; the client may store an object reference in a Naming Service, database, or disk file and retrieve it months or years later. The client may legitimately expect that an invocation using the retrieved object reference will work—that the object instance will be running, and in the same state as when it was last invoked (assuming that no other client possessing a copy of the object reference has modified or destroyed the object in the meantime). This view, and these requirements, are set out in OMG's Object Model Architecture.

The object implementation's view is not so simple. Except for frequently used servers, most objects are probably *not* running and active all the time, on the off chance that they may be invoked. This would waste too much computing resource to be practical. Instead, the object implementation, the ORB, and CORBAservices such as Persistence work together to activate object instances when needed, and then allow them to store their state and deactivate during periods of nonuse. Subsequent activation restores state before invocations are processed, giving the client the impression that the object instance was running continuously, preserving its state, in the interim.

This behavior is mandated by the OMA. For the client, this simplifies life tremendously—no more worries about saving state. Just hang on to your object reference; when you use it later, everything will be just where you left it. (I wish my workshop at home followed these rules!) But, to the object implementor, this same attribute represents an *obligation*. There is no magic here: When you write an OMA-compliant object, you have to provide a way to save the object's state at shutdown and preferably from time to time "just in case"—checkpointing, so that, if the system goes down for some reason (planned with forewarning or not), the object can come up and restore the state it had when it shut down. And, you have to provide the code to read in the state at startup and put all the values in their proper places. The ORB, BOA, and Persistent Object Service provide some help—they provide a small amount of storage associated with your object reference. Your server can use this to store a key pointing to its persistent storage: a filename, database reference or key, or Persistent Storage ID if you're using the Persistent Object service. Section 5.6 covers the BOA interfaces an object uses to store and retrieve the key to its persistent store.

Who enforces these requirements? There are no "CORBA Police," so no one is going to tap you on the shoulder and remind you to save your object's state in your code. If you are a vendor, you will have to take care of these details before you sell any object implementations with the claim that they are CORBA-compliant; otherwise, your customers will not get what they expect and will complain to you (the first time) and possibly choose a different product (the second time). If you are coding for in-house or personal use, you can choose whether you want to follow this requirement; if your user base is small (one, for example), you may decide to ignore it; but, if your base is potentially large (a large enterprise, perhaps), your company will benefit in the long run if it sets up a formal procedure for verifying that object implementations comply with all of the OMA requirements. OMG and X/Open plan a compliance testing and branding program, but implementation-specific behavior like this is difficult to test using automated procedures. (There's information about this in Section 3.2.)

Don't confuse object *creation* and object *activation*: Objects are created by some program during its normal course of execution; the act of creation yields a new instance and a new object reference, which may be, for example, registered with a Naming or Trading service. If you got your object reference *from* one of these services and used it, you know you didn't create a new object! Objects are activated by the ORB. Well, not all objects, but at least some—objects residing within a server process connected to an adapter like the BOA, which defines operations for object activation and deactivation. This example uses the BOA; other object adapters will vary from this scenario.

What has to happen to create an object in a process separate from the client that initiates the sequence? Let's assume we're connected with a standard BOA. Our client invokes a **create** operation on factory object; the return type for this operation is the object reference of the new object. The factory object first constructs our executable object in whatever form it happens to take, retaining implementation information that will later be passed to the implementation repository. The factory object constructs a key, called an **id**, to the object's future persistent storage (for example, a filename, or PID for the Persistent Object Service, or a database key). Then it either stores the object's interface in the IR and obtains an **InterfaceDef** object reference, or (if the interface was already stored) just retrieves the object reference of the stored interface. Using ORB-dependent operations, the factory creates an entry in the ORB's implementation repository for the object and fills it in, receiving as a result an **ImplementationDef** object reference. The ORB will use this information to activate the object when it receives an invocation. The factory can now call the BOA operation **Object create** with these three quantities—the interface reference, the implementation reference, and the **id**—as input. The BOA and ORB create an object reference associated within the ORB with these three quantities and return it to the factory. The factory returns the object reference to its client, which may use it in future invocations or pass it on to other clients for their use.

You already know that Object Implementations have a component that provides the object's functionality. This part goes into action when the object is called via the language mapping, which we will cover in Chapters 7 through 9. The object can't determine whether the invocation entered through the SII or DII, but it must provide a special interface if it wants to be invoked directly through a DSI.

The DSI is exactly opposite to the DII, where the client knew it was using the DII and the object implementation couldn't tell. Here, the receiver knows whether the invocation is coming in via a static or dynamic skeleton, but the client (caller) does not. We're talking here about a receiver instead of an object implementation because an important use of the DSI is in building bridges between ORBs, where the object implementation is not directly involved. Details appear in the next chapter.

Nevertheless, it is possible for an object to adopt a DSI interface and accept invocations via this route. All the object has to do is register with that interface; whenever invocations come in for that object reference, that object will be invoked via the DSI. Because of the way the DSI works, all of the operations and interfaces supported by that object will come in through a single interface instead of a set of stubs.

5.5   OBJECT ADAPTERS, IN GENERAL

The first few sections of this chapter underscore the reasons to standardize the Object Adapter. The OA is the key to object implementation portability.

In CORBA, the object adapter provides a last chance to "level the playing field" in the ORB-Object interface (Figure 5.3). We need to do this because there is such a variety in the way objects can be provided. Some objects will reside in their own processes, and require activation by the ORB before they can be used; others will coreside in a process with some (but possibly not all) of their clients, and may not be subject to activation; still others may be

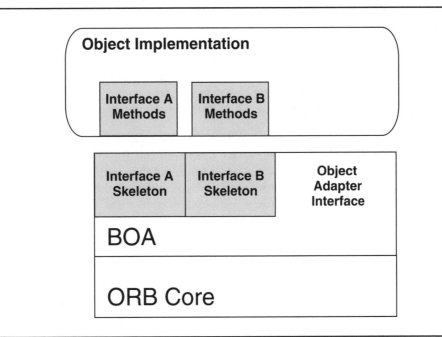

Figure 5.3.   Structure of a typical object adapter. There is one Object Adapter Interface that serves all object implementations. There may be multiple skeletons per Object Implementation and multiple Object Implementations per Object Adapter.

managed by an object-oriented database system and require a different set of services from the invoking ORB. By defining an object adapter for each of these object types, CORBA allows any ORB to operate with the full range of object types.

Object Adapters, such as the BOA, are responsible for:

- registering implementations;
- generating and interpreting object references;
- mapping object references to their corresponding implementations;
- activating and deactivating object implementations;
- invoking methods, via a skeleton or the DSI; and
- coordinating interaction security, in cooperation with the forthcoming Security Object service.

Since most services are accessed through the Object Adapter Interface, ORB builders may locate these services either in the ORB proper or the Object Adapter transparent to the object implementation. Different ORBs may provide different levels of service, with some functions internal and others added by the object adapter. ORBs designed for large-memory systems such as micros and server hardware may, for instance, implement most functionality internally since memory is not a limitation, while ORBs designed for desktop systems may be better implemented "lean and mean" with very little functionality and storage internal to the ORB and most left to the adapter. If objects attach via an adapter tuned to their particular needs, such a multiple-adapter configuration would minimize resource usage on these machines.

OMG documents describe three possible object adapters, although interfaces are standardized for only one, the Basic Object Adapter or BOA. As we've mentioned, this is not enough (although the CORBA specification emphasizes that there should not be a large number of standardized OAs), and more such interfaces are being standardized in a current OMG effort. Here's what OMG has to say about the three OAs.

5.5.1 Basic Object Adapter (BOA)

This is a fairly flexible adapter, designed primarily for servers that reside in their own processes separate from their clients and the ORB. Right now, this is the only object adapter standardized by OMG. The BOA can handle either a program per method, per object, or a shared program for multiple instances of an object type. The BOA provides a small amount of persistent storage for each object, typically used for storing a key to persistent storage, as mentioned. Interfaces for object activation are defined in the specification.

5.5.2 Library Object Adapter

This adapter would be specialized for objects that coreside with accessing clients in a single process. Standardization of this adapter is badly needed, since so many ORBs on the market today (including all in this book) use this configuration. Library objects typically do not require activation or authentication, so these services are not provided. A library object adapter could be designed and tuned for fast performance and small memory footprint.

5.5.3 Object-Oriented Database Adapter

This adapter uses a connection to an object-oriented database to access the objects stored in it. Since the OODB provides the methods and persistent storage, objects may be registered implicitly, and no state is required in the object adapter.

5.6 THE BASIC OBJECT ADAPTER (BOA)

For configurations in which objects reside in processes distinct from the ORB itself, the BOA provides the basic functionality that objects and servers require. The BOA provides:

- generation and interpretation of object references;
- activation and deactivation of object implementations;
- activation and deactivation of individual objects; and
- method invocation via skeletons.

(A service previously assigned to the BOA was Authentication of the Principal making the call. This somewhat nebulous assignment will be refined by the forthcoming Security Service, so we have taken it out of this list.)

The BOA supports object implementations that are constructed from one or more "programs." What's a program? The term encompasses just about anything you can think of that can provide object implementation functionality. In a POSIX-compliant system, it's a process; in other systems, it may be a script or a loadable module. In some operating systems (for example, OS/400 on the IBM AS/400), there is no such thing as a "process"; the operating system provides an ORB-like service for objects, which are registered and may then be invoked at any time. For machines dedicated to a particular database or transaction processing system, the definition of "runnable module" is dictated by that system. The definition of BOA attempts to apply to them all, although systems that deviate substantially from POSIX behavior may very well benefit from more specialized object adapters.

The BOA differentiates between a *server*, which corresponds to an execution unit, and an *object*, which implements a method or interface. Servers may contain multiple objects, although there is a category of server that supports only one.

The BOA interface supports four *activation policies*, covering the different configurations of server and objects. These are illustrated in Figure 5.4, and are:

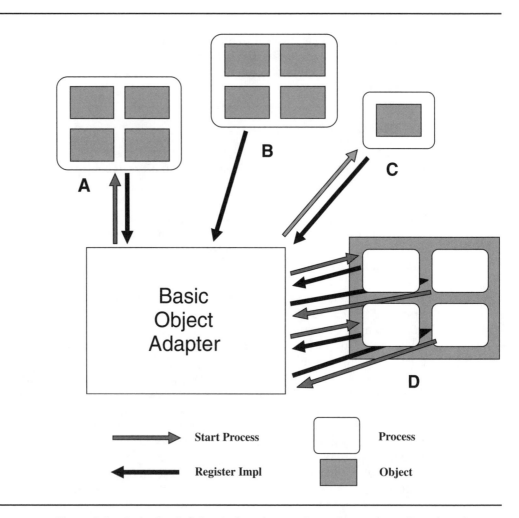

Figure 5.4.   Activation Policies: A, shared server; B, persistent server; C, unshared server; D, server-per-method.

- *Shared server policy:* A server activated by the BOA encompassing multiple active objects.
- *Persistent server policy:* Like the shared server except that the server is activated outside of the BOA and registered in an installation procedure.
- *Unshared server policy:* Only one object of a given implementation at a time can be active on a server.
- *Server-per-method policy:* The BOA starts a separate server for each method invocation; the server fulfills the request and then terminates.

Shared and persistent servers will probably be the most common of these types. A key advantage of the shared server in POSIX-like systems is the reduced process-initiation overhead compared to unshared; a disadvantage is that the operating system is not available to enforce memory and security isolation of one object from another. Persistent servers have the advantage wherever installation and maintenance are so complex that the BOA can't possibly do it all and requires a separate script overseen by a human administrator. Candidates for this position include most transaction processing systems, commercial databases, and some specialized vertical-market support objects. During the installation process, an element in a script can attach the various objects to the BOA or specialized object adapter, register their implementation, and signal the ORB that the objects are ready to process requests.

Unshared servers are appropriate when serving an exclusive resource such as a printer, while server-per-method allows for load balancing or isolation of servers from each other for security or administrative reasons.

The BOA operations used by objects and servers to register activation and deactivation are:

```
void impl_is_ready (in ImplementationDef impl);
void deactivate_impl (in ImplementationDef impl);
void object_is_ready(
    in Object               obj,
    in ImplementationDef  impl
);
void deactivate_object (in Object obj);
```

A shared or shared-persistent server will notify the BOA that it has completed its initialization procedure by calling **impl_is_ready**. The BOA then sends it object activation requests until it calls **deactivate_impl**. The BOA will call the server's object activation routine for an object before making calls to that object, and will assume that the object remains active and ready to respond to invocations until the server calls **deactivate_object** for it.

5.7 THE STATIC IDL SKELETONS

The static IDL skeletons on the server side play the role corresponding to the IDL stubs on the client side. They connect to the server via the mapping for its programming language, and to the OA via a proprietary interface. Invocations pass through the skeletons from the OA to the implementation; requests return by the corresponding return route.

Where object implementations coreside in the same process as their ORB and OA, skeletons may have extremely small footprints and create virtually no noticeable load on the invocation. However, where the server resides in its own process (as in our BOA examples), the skeleton will have to manage IPC communications typically using either shared memory or network communications. Since users expect near instantaneous response even from distributed systems, configurations that place ORB and implementation in the same process tend to dominate in the marketplace.

5.8 THE DYNAMIC SKELETON INTERFACE

Using the DSI, an ORB can deliver requests to any object implementation or proxy it can contact on the network, not just the ones it connects to via static stubs. This capability will be crucial in the dynamic, distributed networks now being built.

The DSI entered the CORBA architecture along with interoperability, and for good reason: It enables two ORBs to construct a bridge that communicates an invocation to the remote object's ORB, and returns the response. Without the DSI, this would be possible only if the invoking ORB had linked a skeleton for the target object, an unlikely case for all of the objects on a dynamic network. Chapter 6 covers interoperability, so we'll postpone coverage of some details until then.

Like many good ideas, the DSI proved valuable for many additional uses not originally intended. These include interactive development tools based on interpreters, debuggers, and monitors that dynamically interpose on objects, and support for dynamically typed languages such as LISP. These uses are so important that the DSI specification is considered part of the CORBA Core and not CORBA Interoperability.

The DSI is implemented via a Dynamic Implementation Routine or DIR. The ORB invokes the *same* routine, the DIR, for *every* DSI request it makes. The target object is specified via the language binding, and the operation is specified as a parameter. DSI invocations do not enter the target via the same language-mapping constructs as the static skeleton; instead, the object implementation is required to support the DIR explicitly (analogous to the support the client gives the DII).

While object implementations are free to support the DSI if they pre-fer, your distributed object environment is much more dependent on all of your ORBs supporting it because the DSI is a key component of CORBA in-teroperability. This specification expects that DSI bridges will form to pass object invocations between ORBs, with one ORB playing the invoker while the other creates a proxy for the target object and becomes the invokee. The initiating ORB makes a standard remote DSI invocation; the target is actu-ally a proxy, but the initiating ORB does not have to make any adjustment for this. The request enters the receiving ORB through the proxy DSI target and is passed through to the target object (and at this stage it does not mat-ter whether the object itself uses SSI or DSI). This is a *request-level bridge*, discussed in Section 6.3.4.

The DSI can be supported by any object adapter, and may include adapter-specific details. Like the static skeleton interface, the DSI is stan-dardized at present only for the BOA. The DSI is specified in terms of pseudo-IDL, pseudo-objects, and directly in terms of the standard mapped languages C, C++, and Smalltalk. All parameters and the return value (if any) are bun-dled up in a single NVList.

We're not going to present the DSI or DIR interfaces here. Although they are a crucial component of CORBA interoperability, you won't have to write to them, and the explanation we've already given is enough to understand how they work.

5.9 ORB SUMMARY

This concludes our discussion of the Object Request Broker. We've described all of the services that your clients and object implementations can expect from their local ORB. In the next chapter, we'll cover interoperability, in-cluding the two protocols—IIOP and DCE CIOP—standardized by the OMG in the CORBA 2.0 specification.

CHAPTER 6

CORBA Interoperability

6.1 WHAT DO YOU NEED TO KNOW ABOUT CORBA INTEROPERABILITY?

There are four CORBA interoperability *user roles*:

- You might use the distributed objects yourself.
- You might select, purchase, install, configure, or maintain the network of distributed objects.
- You might program clients and objects for your system, a customer's system, or the open market.
- You might be an ORB implementor, and actually have to program ORB interoperability.

Each of these roles requires a different amount and type of knowledge of how CORBA interoperability works.

When your company uses CORBA, you will certainly have people playing the first role, and at least one person (hopefully, not many) playing the second. And almost every company wants to know enough about CORBA interoperability to evaluate the third role. The fourth, for most, is a curiosity factor, but there seems to be a lot of curiosity around so we'll have to take it into account in this chapter.

So, instead of just recapping the CORBA interoperability specification from the official documents, we'll start by telling what it means to end users, administrators, and object programmers. Since CORBA takes care of virtually all of the details, this is more a discussion of what you *can* do than what you *have* to do. Then we'll summarize the specifications. We can't include enough detail to let you design and build your own CORBA 2.0 interoperating ORB, but it will be enough to give you a feeling for what's going on "under the covers," so you can be an informed user and purchaser of ORB technology.

6.1.1   For End Users

For end users, CORBA interoperability is a transparent enabling technology. When you run a distributed application, there's nothing on your screen or printout that reveals the interoperability mode or network protocol. (In fact, this makes CORBA interoperability hard to demonstrate: If it's working right, there's nothing special to see!) You may notice the freedom that results from transparent distribution at the application level, but individual applications can provide the same function (albeit with more work by the programmer) using other transports.

For some invocations (where you can tell that there has been an invocation), you may be totally unaware of the location of the target object; where it's important to you, services such as Trader can tell you the physical location of objects such as a printer or scanner when they give you the object reference.

Consequently, if you're a user, you see better and more flexible applications at lower cost, but you can't "see" CORBA interoperability because it's truly under the covers.

6.1.2   For System Administrators and ORB Purchasers

If you're purchasing, installing, configuring, or maintaining ORB environments, you will have to do the same type of analysis and configuration that you would with any other interoperability system. CORBA can take the interoperability headaches out of the application, where they don't belong, but the traffic still appears on the network and you will have to configure for it.

Network protocol will make a difference to you, because you will have to configure your network for the protocols your users run, assuring adequate bandwidth and providing gateways where they turn out to be needed. You will also need to be concerned with security that interacts with the ORB interoperability protocol, and possibly with CORBA access to a transaction processing system. The discussion of CORBA interoperability protocols will be helpful to you, because you will need to take advantage of the possibilities to meet your users' needs.

CORBA-based administration tools are just beginning to be standardized by OMG and X/Open. We talk about the effort in Chapter 17, but we weren't able to discuss the specification itself because it wasn't ready when this book went to press. In the meantime, vendors are providing their own tools. They appreciate the crucial role of systems and network administrators in a distributed environment, and put a lot of effort into the tools and utilities.

6.1.3   For Object Programmers

CORBA interoperability is totally transparent to your application. Once you give an object an OMG IDL interface, its location becomes transparent, and the administrator or installer can site it anywhere on the network.

But you will have to design applications for distribution in order to get the combination of performance and functionality that good programs deliver. The best design leaves room for flexibility at install or run time, allowing the same set of executables to run well at multiple sites with differing requirements and resources. Keep this in mind as you divide your application into objects.

And take advantage of good programming practices that you learned for non-CORBA distributed apps: design to minimize network traffic, cache frequently used data, and use your good sense to ensure good performance and flexibility.

You will learn, as you work the example in the second half of this book, just how easy it is to program objects for distributed systems. CORBA was designed to be the easiest and most flexible distribution system, and OMG's membership believes that it has delivered on this promise.

6.2   ORB-TO-ORB COMMUNICATION

CORBA 2.0 interoperability is based on ORB-to-ORB communication. We've been setting up for this ever since the first page: IDL interfaces, the Interface and Implementation Repositories, and all of the other aspects of CORBA have been designed with interoperability in mind.

Figure 6.1 shows how this works: An invocation from a client of ORB 1 passes through its IDL stub into the ORB core. The ORB examines the object

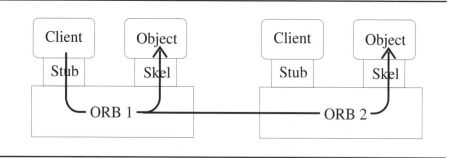

Figure 6.1.   Interoperability via ORB-to-ORB communication. All of the clients connected to ORB 1 can access object implementations in both ORB 1 and ORB 2. The same condition holds for clients connected to ORB 2. The architecture scales to any number of connected ORBs.

reference and looks up the location of the implementation in its implementation repository. If the implementation is local, the ORB passes the invocation through the skeleton to the object for servicing. If the implementation is remote, ORB 1 passes the invocation across the communication pathway to ORB 2, which routes it to the object. Because there is only one form of invocation and the object reference is opaque, the object implementation has no way of knowing (and does not care) whether the client is local or remote.

Because this scenario works regardless of platform, protocol, and format differences that might exist between ORB 1 and ORB 2, it requires both ORBs to know enough about the invocation and response to allow them to translate data where necessary as they transfer the request from Platform 1 to Platform 2 and back.

Notice that *client and object implementation are not involved in the communication step*. In CORBA, the communication always goes from one ORB to another. Granted, the client has specified the object reference of a remote target, but the object reference datatype is opaque to the client so, actually, it either does not know or care whether the target is local or remote. (Of course, the *user* may care, for instance if the remote object is a printer or scanner, but that's not a reason to code location dependence into an application, which will be used by lots of different folks in lots of different configurations.) And object implementations receive almost no information about the invoking client when they receive a request. (Concerned about security? Most likely, requests will clear security within the ORB before they reach their target. For a discussion of CORBA security, see Chapter 16.)

6.2.1 Putting Heterogeneity into Perspective

There are two ways to get ORBs to talk to each other. We can either:

- get all of the ORBs to speak the same protocol, so they can talk to each other directly; or,
- if ORBs speak different protocols, we can install bridges to translate from one protocol to the other.

CORBA 2.0 provides *both* solutions. The first is simple, streamlined, easy to administer, and efficient to use. Every CORBA 2.0-compliant ORB speaks the mandatory protocol IIOP (Section 6.5.4), allowing your enterprise to standardize on it and still choose from almost every ORB on the market with full interoperability. But you may opt for the DCE CIOP (Section 6.6) or a proprietary protocol instead.

But, this solution is *inflexible*. There will be times when a common protocol isn't possible, or isn't desirable for some reason—for example, if you find a product that isn't available on an ORB that speaks your enterprise's common protocol, or if you need to integrate a machine that is special, somehow (a circuit breaker or thermostat, for example, with limited memory and bandwidth). In these cases, *bridging* lets you provide transparent interoperability across domain boundaries. Frequently, hardware bridges are already in place at these boundaries, providing a natural location for a CORBA 2.0 software bridge. The fact is, many (perhaps most) medium- to large-sized companies already use bridging in some form because it provides the flexibility to allow each part of a company to find its most cost-effective computing solution. And, as we'll see, the concept of domains is a general one, which can carry over from CORBA interoperability into other areas such as company organization, network administration, and security.

There is a trade-off here, simplicity versus flexibility, and someone at your company (you, perhaps?) will have to decide how much heterogeneity can be allowed before the costs outweigh the advantages. Or, perhaps your current installed base is *already* heterogeneous, giving you little room to maneuver. In any case, the material in this chapter will help you understand the alternatives, and place them into perspective. With this new knowledge, you will be in a better position to make decisions concerning, or possibly just better understand, this key issue.

6.3 CORBA 2.0 DOMAINS

Let's identify the regions of our enterprise that share a common platform, operating system, network hardware and software, and so forth, and name this type of region a *technology domain*. Is this the only kind of domain we have to consider, or are there others?

It turns out that there are many different types of domains. Some result from technology differences, and others arise from the kind of work people do, the way they work together, and the way their computing resources are purchased and accounted for.

Perhaps you work in a company large enough to have departments, and your department has a number of networked computers, which might include "your" disk servers, "your" compute or database servers, and "your" printers. The money for these machines and their support comes from your department's budget, and you expect other departments in the company to have their own resources and avoid using yours. Your department's equipment constitutes a domain.

On the other hand, if you work for a government or military organization concerned with security, your work might be partitioned into security domains. In this case, you might have one window on your workstation that contains a document classified "Top Secret," while another window displays a document classified "Confidential." Even though both windows display on the same screen and are running on the same workstation, they belong to different security domains. Secure windowed operating systems will not allow a cut-and-paste between two windows that differ in security classification.

These are examples of *administrative* domains. There are also domains imposed by the technology, as we already discussed, and these come in many different varieties. For instance, a domain might share a common platform, network protocol or hardware, or operating system. Data or packet representations will differ across network domain boundaries, while commands will have to be translated across operating system boundaries.

The CORBA 2.0 specification lists technology domains, administrative domains, and policy domains as just some of the different types that have to be taken into account.

We can draw some generalizations about domains:

- *They exist for a reason.* For instance, there are people who are very concerned about the boundaries of a departmental domain, or the different security domains. While the reason for technical domains may not be as logical ("The Turbocooled 986 Multiprocessor Server had better price/performance, but it's little endian."), they're important enough to keep the domains distinct. Our interoperability solution must take this into account.

- *Applications and data will, in general, be shared across domain boundaries.* We can make life simpler by keeping applications and data domain-independent, and providing domain-related services in an infrastructure layer. For example, a security attribute may restrict data to a particular security domain, but this is a property of the particular data and not something that should be coded into an application, where we would have to deal with it whether the dataset is marked secure or not. The CORBA architecture is a good start on this task.

- *If every quantity in one domain has a corresponding quantity in another domain (that is, the quantities "map" from one domain to the other), then we can render the boundary transparent by providing a bridge to perform translations where necessary.* However, if a quantity or service that exists on one side has no equivalent on the other, then some aspect of the boundary will be apparent to the user under at least some circumstance no matter what we do in the bridge.

- *ORB boundaries define only a small fraction of the domains in a system.* However, the ORB infrastructure is the best place to deal with almost all of the boundaries as enablers of interoperability.

Taking these factors into consideration, the framers of CORBA 2.0 interoperability based it on a concept of bridging far more general than inter-ORB communications. To get a general idea of what the specification is talking about and what it will let us do, we'll first present two different kinds of bridging, and then two kinds of bridges. The two kinds of bridging are *technological* and *policy-mediated* bridging. The two kinds of bridges are *immediate* and *mediated* bridges.

6.3.1   Technological and Policy-Mediated Bridging

There is a tendency to assume that domain boundaries should be rendered transparent everywhere, but this is strictly true only for technological boundaries—network protocol or data formats, for instance, or ORB platforms. Where technical differences like these prevent direct interoperation, bridges can map quantities on one side to those on the other and remove the barriers, keeping in mind that differences in service level can create boundaries where total interoperability is just not possible. Where the boundary is purely technological, this will (almost always) be fine with everyone.

However, some boundaries are administrative rather than technological. Administrative domain boundaries separate organizations with different policies, goals, or resources. While some degree of interoperability may be desirable across these boundaries, the participants require *control* over the data flow for many important (at least to them) reasons. Bridging these domains requires *policy mediation*—that is, traffic across the boundaries must be monitored and controlled in ways that depend on content. You're familiar with this type of control if your company uses a firewall to separate your corporate network from the external network; make the firewall concept object-oriented, and it becomes policy-mediated CORBA 2.0 bridging. In fact, since policy-mediated bridging requires that the bridge understand the traffic across the boundary, CORBA provides an ideal infrastructure for providing this type of control.

6.3.2   Immediate and Mediated Bridges

Now let's talk about different ways to build a bridge. The two major approaches are *immediate bridging* and *mediated bridging*. Figure 6.2 shows how each of these works.

The CORBA 2.0 specification discusses bridging in very general terms, and ends up so abstract that it's difficult to form a mental picture unless you already know what it's talking about. In order to be more concrete, we'll talk specifically about bridging between different network protocols here; if you're interested in bridging something else (data format, let's say) then just substitute that in your mind as you read through the section.

In immediate bridging, two domains talk directly to each other over a single bridge that translates whatever parts of the message require it, as shown in Figure 6.2. Immediate bridging is a two-domain concept; the generalization of Figure 6.2 to multiple domains just contains many copies of the two-domain linkage, one for each connected domain pair.

This is fast and efficient, since each bridge can be designed specifically for the domain pair it serves. On the other hand, this approach is inflexible and may require a lot of bridges since the number required increases rapidly—as $(n^2 - n)/2$, actually—with the number of domains. Figure 6.3 shows immediate bridging for an installation with four domains; this requires *six* bridges. Increasing the number of domains to six raises the number of bridges required to 15! In a few paragraphs we'll show how much simpler this is with mediated bridging.

Immediate-mode bridging is the preferred approach for policy-only bridging, since messages do not require translation. The bridge is actually a firewall, examining message contents to determine if they may pass through its barrier. If a bridge's policy is configurable, a single bridge type may be

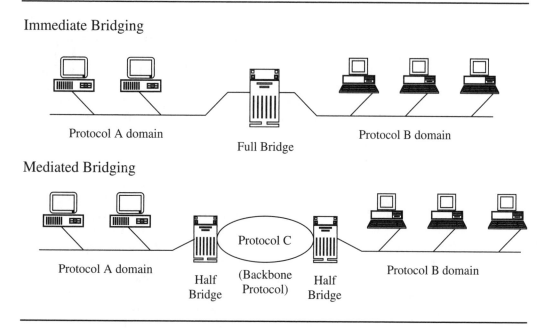

Immediate Bridging

Protocol A domain

Full Bridge

Protocol B domain

Mediated Bridging

Protocol A domain

Half Bridge

Protocol C

(Backbone Protocol)

Half Bridge

Protocol B domain

Figure 6.2.   Immediate and mediated bridging.

installed at various places around an enterprise to enforce any number of security policies and their domains. For more details, see Chapter 16 on Security.

In mediated bridging, all domains bridge to a single common protocol (that is, for protocol domains. Remember, we might be bridging something else). When a message passes over the first bridge from its originating domain, the parts that require it are translated into the common protocol. When the message passes from the common region into the destination domain, a second bridge translates it into the destination protocol.

The big advantage of mediated bridging is that the number of bridge types only grows as fast as the number of different domains (Figure 6.3), avoiding the exponential increase seen with immediate bridging. Another advantage is that this conforms to the backbone configuration of most large, multiprotocol networks; mediated bridging configures naturally in these networks since CORBA bridges will probably locate in the same position at which protocol bridges already exist. In an open market situation, if every vendor of an interoperability product makes available a bridge to an agreed-upon common protocol, customers can buy any of these products and know that the protocol will interoperate with every other one. This (by clever coincidence) is how CORBA 2.0 guarantees out-of-the-box interoperability; the common protocol is the IIOP discussed in Section 6.5.4.

Disadvantages are first, that it isn't as efficient for small numbers of domains (for instance, two, as shown in Figure 6.2); in this case, you would be better off using an immediate bridge. Second, almost every message gets translated twice. Why almost all, and not every one? Because messages to or from a domain that uses the same protocol as the common region will need to be translated only once. You can overcome this disadvantage by putting high-traffic services on domains that use the same protocol as the backbone, or by adding direct bridges for high-demand services that can't use that trick.

The mediated bridging (a backbone) configuration with four domains, shown in Figure 6.3, requires only three bridges: Three domains require bridging to the backbone; one uses the backbone mode natively and does not require a bridge (this trick may not always be possible). Immediate bridging requires six bridges. The number of immediate-mode bridges increases as $(n^2 - n)/2$ with the number of domains; 6 domains would require 15 immediate bridges compared to only 5 in the mediated configuration.

The CORBA 2.0 specification discusses bridges, gateways, and domains the way we covered it here, and in more detail in some areas. But not all of the discussion leads to implementable specifications. For instance, administrative and security domains are only discussed and not specified; the plus is that the specification is architected in a way that makes it practical to implement these domains. We can anticipate that the forthcoming OMG

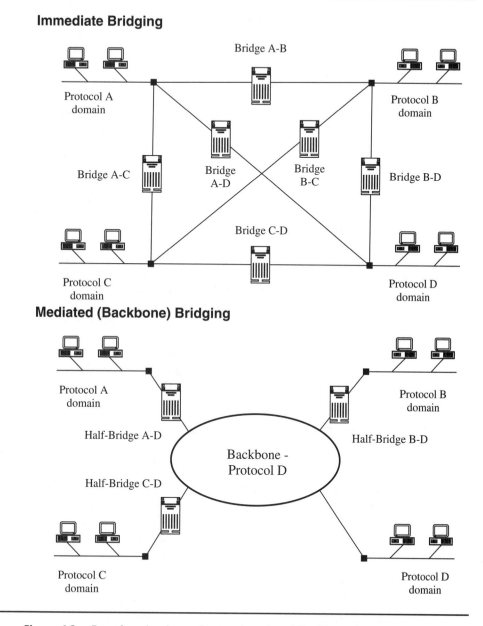

Figure 6.3.   Four domains, immediate and mediated (backbone) bridging. The immediate bridging configuration requires six bridges, while the mediated (backbone) bridging configuration requires only three. The difference becomes proportionately greater as the number of domains increases.

security specification will take advantage of these concepts, but this decision is currently in the hands of the OMG members. The only part of the actual specification that uses this discussion as a basis is the half-bridge concept, which provides interoperability between protocol domains, as we'll see in the next section.

What's the difference between a half-bridge and a full bridge? Take another look at Figure 6.3, and trace the path from domain B to domain C in the mediated bridge configuration. It passes through two bridge components; each is a *half-bridge*, since you need both to handle the general case of transmission from any one protocol to any other protocol. In the immediate bridge configuration, the path from domain E to F (or any other domain pair, for that matter) passes through only one bridge: a *full bridge*, of course.

This explains the terminology of the CORBA 2.0 compliance statement in Section 3.2. IIOP (see Section 6.5.4) is the name of the single protocol with which every ORB *must* communicate in order to be considered CORBA 2.0-compliant. But, first, an ORB does *not* need to implement this protocol internally; and second, an ORB is allowed to implement any number of additional protocols as well. So, any distributed ORB, with any native non-IIOP protocol, can be made CORBA 2.0-compliant by providing a half-bridge that connects its native protocol to the IIOP backbone. In the mediated configuration, this gives its domain immediate access to every other ORB on the network.

Note that there are no degrees of compliance with CORBA 2.0. An ORB that uses another procotol and provides a half-bridge to IIOP is *just as compliant* as an ORB that implements IIOP as its native protocol.

6.3.3   Interoperable Object References (IORs)

Yes, Virginia, there really is a standard form for the object reference. Clients, object implementations, and their users may think it's like Santa Claus because they can never hold one or see one. It's not even used internally for single-ORB request routing and is never passed to a client or object implementation, so you shouldn't expect to examine an object reference in your code and find that it looks anything like this. It's used only in inter-ORB invocations, so it's emitted and accepted by ORBs speaking to the network, and used by the bridges between them. It's called an *interoperable object reference* or IOR.

The information in the IOR lets invocations pass from one vendor's ORB to another's. This requires the following information:

- *What type is the object?* ORBs may have to know the object's type in order to preserve the integrity of its type system.

- *What protocols may the invoking ORB use?* This is not as straightforward as you might think at first. As it leaves the originating ORB, the IOR lists the protocol or protocols accepted by that ORB. But as it crosses a bridge, it becomes invokable only by protocols accepted by the bridge. This requires bridges to recognize IORs and update this information as they pass across. Remember, IORs are not just targets, they may be passed as parameters also. Every one needs to be recognized and updated.

- *What ORB services are available?* The invocation may involve extended ORB services; OMG specifications already allow these for invocations within a transaction, and will soon add security. By putting this information into the IOR, we can eliminate ORB-to-ORB negotiation of the context information.

- *Is the object reference null?* (That is, a special object reference signifying no object.) By recognizing nulls in advance, the bridge can avoid a lot of unnecessary work.

The IOR specified by OMG to meet these requirements consists of a type ID (the same one defined in the Interface Repository chapter), followed by one or more *tagged profiles*.

Each protocol usable for CORBA 2.0 ORB-to-ORB communications has a *tag* and a *profile*. The tag is a 4-byte quantity, registered by OMG so ORB builders can avoid duplicate entries. Any company can register a protocol with OMG and receive a tag by sending email to *tag-request@omg.org*; there are no requirements and no charge. This does not make the protocol an OMG standard; it justs ensures that other ORB vendors will not accidentally use the same tag.

The profile contains all the information a remote ORB needs to perform an invocation using the protocol. Profiles come in two forms, single- or multiple-component. Single-component profiles have a profile ID (like the IIOP, just mentioned). Multiple-component profiles have a component ID for each part. They provide kind of a "smorgasbord" of protocol components, which an ORB can use to construct an invocation. The profile ID for a multi-component protocol is 1 (one); then each component has its own component ID as well.

Some protocols are special: they are official OMG standards. So far there are two, which we'll cover later in this chapter: the IIOP, and the DCE-ESIOP. The tag for the IIOP is 0 (zero). The DCE ESIOP has a multicomponent profile; each component is registered, and we'll cover them in Section 6.6.

The format of a profile is defined by the implementor or group that registered the tag. (The only requirement, after all, is that all users of the tag agree on the contents of the profile.) The implementor does not need to divulge the format and contents of the profile in order to register, but OMG will accept and make public the definition if it is given. Just as for the tag, registration does not make the profile an OMG standard; it only provides a convenient reference point for profile definitions.

Figure 6.4 shows how IORs provide interoperability across a domain boundary. We'll use actual CORBA protocol names even though we won't

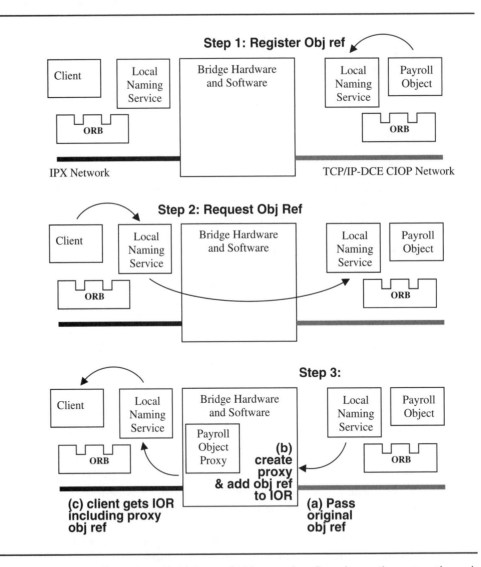

Figure 6.4. Illustration of bridging and IOR operation. Every invocation passes through an ORB (or more than one), although this part of the path is omitted for clarity.

define them formally until later in the chapter; we think this sounds more realistic than "protocol A" and "protocol B." You can substitute your favorite protocol or domain attribute pair and things will fit together just about the same way.

We've drawn an enterprise with two network domains; suppose that one is TCP/IP and the other is Novell IPX. Each domain consists of several vendors' ORBs; suppose that all of the ORBs in the TCP/IP domain use the DCE CIOP inter-ORB protocol and the ones in the Novell domain use GIOP over IPX. To keep things simple, suppose the two domains are joined by a single immediate bridge. (This example would be even more fun with an IIOP backbone and two half-bridges. Try working this out for yourself.) Although each domain has its own Naming Service implementation, all of the information in each of them is accessible from the other. In our example, the system adminstrator set up the root of our *naming context* hierarchy (a kind of subdirectory of object names, defined in Chapter 12) with names that point to each of our domains: IPX, TCPIP, and so on. Using the CORBA IOR as a pointer, the Naming Service will automatically resolve any name to its proper domain.

What happens when we retrieve an object reference from a foreign domain and invoke an operation on the object? Let's install a server object named Payroll in the TCP/IP domain and register it with the Naming Service (step 1). Of course, this places our DCE CIOP IOR in the Naming Service in that domain. Name structure is hierarchical in the CORBA Naming Service, so let's suppose the full name of the object is /uObject/TCPIP/DCE-CIOP/Accounting/PayrollObject. This is English, more or less (although it does show a touch of computerese), so it's easy to pass around to our friends anywhere in our enterprise, including other domains. (Don't assume that the CORBA Naming Service uses slashes to separate name components; actually, it's name syntax-independent. But we had to use something here to show the separation, so we picked slashes. We'll fill in the details in Chapter 12.)

In step 2, a client in the IPX domain passes the full name of the payroll object to its local Naming Service in a request for its object reference. As the Naming Service unravels the hierarchical name, the invocation passes automatically from the IPX domain where it started to the TCP/IP domain where the object is registered. (For details of the **resolve** operation, see Chapter 12.) The object reference of the Payroll object is the return value of this invocation.

The object reference passes back over the bridge to the IPX domain in step 3. The bridge knows that this return value is an object reference from the operation signature, which it retrieved from its interface repository. The bridge must pass a usable object reference back to the client, and IPX clients cannot invoke operations directly on TCP/IP DCE CIOP objects. So the bridge constructs a proxy skeleton using the Dynamic Skeleton Interface and adds its reference to the IOR. It doesn't need to remove the original reference; the IOR may be passed on to a domain where it will be valid, so it stays.

The object reference that the client just received is just an opaque pointer, of course; only the ORB knows that this is an IOR and not a local reference. Neither the client nor the ORB is aware that the IOR refers to a proxy, nor is it necessary for them to know. The client constructs an invocation for Payroll and passes it to its local ORB. The ORB examines the IOR and determines that the only IOR component that the ORB can communicate with is the IPX component, which happens to be the proxy on the bridge, so it addresses the invocation there. The proxy and bridge translate the invocation from GIOP/IPX to DCE CIOP and route the invocation onto the DCE CIOP domain network to Payroll's ORB.

This concludes the example. We'll just point out here, for the technically inclined, that it is not necessarily the end of the route for the invocation; if the Payroll object has moved, then the invocation may yet bounce back to the bridge with a **LOCATION_FORWARD** return status and be automatically rerouted to Payroll's new location. We also realize that this discussion (and the specification itself) raise a few more questions than they answer, for example about proxy lifetimes and housekeeping. At the current level of specification, these are considered implementation details. When we wrote this part of the book, there were no commercial CORBA 2.0 bridge or gateway products on the market so we can't talk about how these details were worked out in practice. Parameters such as the ones we mentioned will surely need to be tuned for different network and application configurations. Ask your ORB vendor, or check the computer magazines, to follow this part of the story as products emerge and mature.

The CORBA 2.0 specification discusses "stringifying" an IOR. Ideally, you could stringify an IOR, save it on an external medium, and use it on another system. This trick would work only if the systems were connected by a network, security constraints allowed the interoperation, and all identifers embedded in the reference could be resolved properly in the foreign domain. It will not work if you carry the stringified object reference across a domain boundary, which can only be crossed using a proxy object.

Thus it's a lot easier to pass the object reference as a parameter from one system to the other and let the ORBs do the work. Naming and Trading services do this automatically; but if you're writing both ends of the application yourself, you can always pass the object reference as a parameter in a call.

We think the CORBA 2.0 stringified object reference format is primarily a tool for builders of ORBs and bridges. For one thing, there is no standard API for retrieving the IOR from a client or server, so ORBs and bridges are the only components that can use this part of the specification.

Before we leave this section, there's one more part of the IOR we need to cover. Some services require the cooperation of the ORB to pass information that is not included in the IDL definition. The first OMG standard service to require this is the Transaction Service: every invocation between an **open transaction** call and its corresponding **commit** is part of a particular transaction. However, the Transaction Service may be taking care of operations for other clients at the same time, so the ORB ends up responsible for keeping track of a transaction identifier and passing it to the service with every invocation. This is certainly not in the IDL; the client is not even aware that his or her transaction *has* an identifier.

Consequently, CORBA 2.0 defines a Service Context and a corresponding service context ID for this. OMG specifies context IDs for services it standardizes; the Transaction Service got the first one, and its serviceID = 0 (zero). The Security Service will surely get its own service context ID. Implementors may register their own service context IDs with OMG the same way they register a profile or component ID.

6.3.4   In-Line and Request-Level Bridging

If you think about it, you realize that nothing prevents ORB-to-ORB interoperability even without an OMG standard. Check out Figure 6.5: Anyone with two ORBs and their IDL compilers can build a bridge that includes the skeleton from one ORB and the stub from the other, and pass a request through. Split the bridge into two parts connected over the network and you're distributed, to boot. (In fact, this is such an appealing concept that an OMG member once suggested that no interoperability standard was necessary; vendors or users could just build bridges for objects that needed to interoperate. Fortunately, more practical heads prevailed, so we didn't end

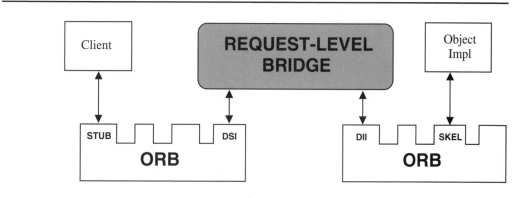

Figure 6.5.   Request-level bridges are built using public ORB APIs.

up with a network filled with thousands of do-it-yourself bridges, and ORBs spiked with stubs and skeletons for every interface type on the Internet, just in case.)

Figure 6.5 shows a *request-level bridge*, which is built using public ORB APIs; CORBA provides a number of APIs that are used in these bridges, including one, the DSI, that was standardized specifically for use here (although it has a number of other important uses). APIs and CORBA components useful or essential for bridging are the DII, the DSI, Interface Repositories, Object Adapters including the BOA, and object references including IORs.

The alternative to the request-level bridge is the *in-line bridge* (Figure 6.6). This is the bridge you would build if you needed the most streamlined possible implementation and you had the builders of both ORBs participating in the effort. In an in-line bridge, code inside the ORBs perform the translations and mappings to go from one to the other, and there is no public API. Many vendors talk from one instance to another of their own ORBs using in-line bridges; typically, this interaction is invisible to the user and programmer. Since all internal representations are identical, this can be very efficient.

The fact is, you can't tell by using it whether an ORB employs a request-level bridge or an in-line bridge. The difference only has to do with the connection between the bridge and the ORB, and not with the message format or protocol that is output to the network—that is, either form of bridge could communicate using either a standard or proprietary protocol. In general, request-level bridges will be easier to build, while in-line bridges will

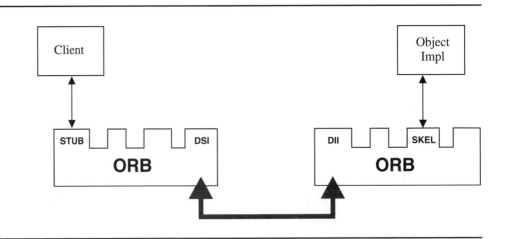

Figure 6.6. In-line bridges are built using ORB-internal APIs.

be more efficient, although clever design can minimize the penalty associated with the request-level bridge. For now, we'll just note that in-line bridging provides ORB implementors with a known way to improve performance, always a worthy goal.

6.3.5 Interface-Specific and Generic Request-Level Bridges

Request-level bridges may be either:

- *Interface-specific:* Built using IDL compiler-generated stubs and skeletons, this type of bridge supports only interfaces that were incorporated into the bridge when it was constructed.
- *Generic:* Taking full advantage of the DII, DSI, and interface repository, this type of bridge supports every interface known to the system.

Lack of flexibility is a notable disadvantage for the interface-specific bridge. Since stubs and skeletons must be built in, you must either replace or augment the interface-specific bridges in your system every time you add an object with a new interface. But this bridge type compensates with a performance advantage over the generic bridge since it does not have to construct any components "on the fly." However, cleverly built generic bridges may construct and save stubs similar in function to those provided by the IDL compiler so this penalty may be lessened in the future.

6.4 STRUCTURE OF THE INTEROPERABILITY SPECIFICATION

Figure 6.7 shows the structure of the CORBA 2.0 Interoperability Specification. In this section, we'll take a look at what's in each box and how they fit together; the next two sections will take a closer look at the most interesting boxes, the ones that are already being turned into products that you can buy from your vendors.

We've emphasized the CORBA 1.2 API in the figure on purpose. *There is no publicly available API for CORBA 2.0 interoperability:* If your target object reference is a local object, your invocation stays local; if it's remote, then your invocation goes remote. If your ORB uses CORBA 2.0 for interoperability, then that's what you get; if it doesn't, then you don't. That's because clients and object implementations talk to ORBs, and not to the network. All of the network communication is one ORB talking to another. That's the way CORBA works.

So, on to the boxes: The box labelled CORBA 2.0 contains most of what we've covered so far: the basic architecture built on bridging; the Interoperable Object Reference with its protocol profiles and components; the

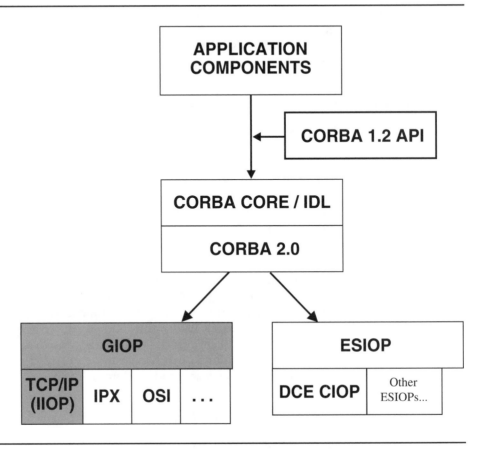

Figure 6.7. Structure of the CORBA 2.0 interoperability specification. Shaded components are mandatory for CORBA 2.0 compliance.

interoperability interfaces including the DSI; and the provisions for context-specific services.

GIOP, or General Inter-ORB Protocol, contains the specifications for the general, CORBA-2.0 mandated inter-ORB messaging protocol, which has been designed to be implemented on any reliable transport. In this box are the Common Data Representation, the seven GIOP messages and their formats, and a set of transport assumptions.

Underneath the GIOP box are a set of boxes representing reliable protocols. The first, TCP/IP, is mandatory. The others are easily implementable; it's very likely that implementations will be out by the time you read this.

ESIOP (pronounced Aesop) stands for Environment-Specific Inter-ORB Protocol. There isn't much in the box marked ESIOP; every ESIOP gets to define its protocol independently as long as it meets the requirements for ORB-to-ORB communication of object requests and responses.

The DCE ESIOP specifies ORB-to-ORB communication based on DCE RPC invocations and responses. It adopts the same Common Data Representation as the GIOP, but replaces the seven messages of the GIOP with two DCE RPC operations, *locate* and *invoke*. For this ESIOP, the invocation contents not only maps to IIOP, it's identical. But, the messaging semantics and location mechanisms are completely different. At least the DCE ESIOP domains will be relatively easy to bridge to IIOP.

There is only one OMG-standard ESIOP right now—the DCE CIOP. (The DCE ESIOP is officially designated the DCE Common Inter-ORB Protocol or DCE-CIOP in the OMG specification.) But ORBs can also communicate using proprietary protocols. There's nothing wrong with this; it may be the only way to achieve a necessary performance characteristic or cram functionality into a small or embedded system. But proprietary protocols should stick as closely as possible to the GIOP structure to allow bridging to the standard IIOP and other GIOP-based protocols, as well as provide a bridge to the IIOP so that they can bear the CORBA 2.0 compliance brand and interoperate with other standard CORBA implementations.

6.5 GENERAL INTER-ORB PROTOCOL (GIOP) AND INTERNET INTER-ORB PROTOCOL (IIOP)

IIOP, which is the GIOP over TCP/IP, is the one protocol *mandatory* for CORBA 2.0 compliance. The GIOP/IIOP specification was designed to meet these goals:

- *Widest possible availability:* The IIOP is based on TCP/IP, the most widely used and flexible communications transport mechanism available, and defines only the minimum additional layers to transfer CORBA requests between ORBs.

- *Simplicity:* Working within the other necessary goals, the GIOP was kept as simple as possible.

- *Scalability:* It is designed to scale to the size of today's Internet, and beyond.

- *Low cost:* Both ORB reengineering at implementation, and run-time support costs, were minimized as much as possible.

- *Generality:* The GIOP was designed for implementation on any reliable, connection-oriented protocol, not just TCP/IP.

- *Architectural neutrality:* GIOP makes minimal assumptions about the architecture and implementation of the ORBs and bridges that support it.

The GIOP consists of three specifications:

- The Common Data Representation (CDR) definition;
- GIOP message formats; and
- GIOP transport assumptions.

The IIOP specification adds

- Internet IOP message transport.

The IIOP is not a separate specification; it is a mapping of the GIOP to the specific transport TCP/IP (Figure 6.7). Other mappings are possible; mappings to Novell Netware's IPX and OSI are already underway.

6.5.1   Common Data Representation (CDR)

The CDR defines representations for all OMG IDL datatypes, including type codes and constructed types such as **struct**, **sequence**, and **enum**.

The specification takes into account byte ordering and alignment. *Receiver-makes-right* semantics avoids unnecessary translation of messages between machines of the same byte order.

We're not going to list any of the representations—there's nothing you can do with them unless you're building your own ORB; and if you are, then you need a copy of the spec and not just this book.

The point of the CDR is that all GIOPs share a common data representation, so bridging this part of the message should be easy.

6.5.2   GIOP Message Formats

GIOP defines seven distinct messages for ORB-to-ORB communications. These carry requests, locate object implementations, and manage communication channels. They support all of the functions and behavior required by CORBA, including exception reporting, passing of operation context, and following of objects that dynamically relocate or migrate.

These seven messages, and the accompanying list of message transfer characteristics, meet the needs of the object-oriented CORBA semantics in the most efficient way possible. A frequent comment about this mechanism is that it's "just another RPC," but, in fact, these seven messages with their associated characteristics are quite different from an RPC. You can program to these messages only if you build your own ORB. We're including this information because of the widespread curiosity about how remote CORBA invocations compare to an RPC mechanism. If you're still curious, keep reading here; if your curiosity was satisfied by these comments, feel free to skip ahead to Section 6.5.3.

The seven messages simplify communications. Binding and format agreement are accomplished without negotiation. In most cases, messages from client ORB to object ORB can be sent as soon as a connection is established. Some characteristics of message transfer are:

- *The connection is asymmetric:* Client and server roles are distinct, assigned at connection. The client originates the connection, and may send requests but not replies. The server accepts the connection, and may send replies but not requests. This simplifies the specification, and avoids some race conditions that might otherwise arise.

- *Requests may be multiplexed:* That is, multiple clients within an originating ORB may share a connection to a remote ORB. Information in the request differentiates it from others on the same connection.

- *Requests may overlap:* If asynchronous, any order of requests and replies is supported through request/reply identifiers.

Of the seven messages, three may be sent by the client: Request, CancelRequest, and LocateRequest. Three may be sent only by the server: Reply, LocateReply, and CloseConnection. Both may send MessageError.

All GIOP messages start with a GIOP header. It's simple enough, so here it is in IDL:

```
struct MessageHeader {
    char            magic[4];
    Version         GIOP_version;
    boolean         byte_order;
    octet           message_type;
    unsigned long   message_size;
};
```

The magic number is GIOP encoded in ISO Latin-1; no surprise here. There's only one version so far, and it's 1.0. The byte order is specified next, and then the message type, which must be one of the seven we just listed. Finally, comes the message size in octets.

Here are brief descriptions of the seven GIOP messages:

Request message: The request message consists of the GIOP header, a request header, and a request body. The header contains the service context, a request ID, object identifier, operation, and some other information. The request body contains all of the **in** and **inout** parameters.

Reply message: The reply message consists of the GIOP header, a reply header, and a reply body. The reply header contains a service context, the same request ID as the request, and a status code. If the status code contains **no_exception**, then the reply body contains the return value, if any, followed by all of the **inout** and **out** parameters. If the status code is **USER_EXCEPTION** or **SYSTEM_EXCEPTION**, the body contains encoded exception information. And finally, if the status code is **LOCATION_FORWARD**, the body contains an IOR to which the originating ORB should redirect the original request. This resending takes place without the knowledge of the originating client.

CancelRequest: CancelRequest messages contain the usual GIOP header followed by a CancelRequest header with the request ID. This message notifies a server that the client is no longer expecting a reply for the specified pending Request or LocateRequest message.

LocateRequest: LocateRequest messages are sent by a client to a server to determine whether a particular object reference is valid; whether the current server is capable of servicing requests; or, if not, a new address for requests for that object reference. LocateRequest provides a way to get the same information as a LocationForward reply from a Request, without having to transmit potentially large amounts of data.

LocateReply: This is the server's reply to a LocateRequest message. It contains, besides the usual GIOP header, a LocateReply header with the request ID and a status value, and a LocateReply body that contains, if applicable, the IOR of the new target.

CloseConnection: These messages are sent by servers to inform clients (or, more precisely, their ORBs) that the server intends to close the connection and will not provide further responses. The server is only allowed to send this when there are no pending requests, although requests may be received during the interval between the sending of CloseConnection and its acknowledgment at the receiving ORB. This also informs the ORBs that they will not receive replies to requests pending on that connection, and that these may safely be reissued on another connection. The ORB will send a **COMM_FAILURE** exception to the clients, with a completion status of **COMPLETED_MAYBE**. The CloseConnection message consists of only the GIOP header; the message type value says it all.

MessageError: These messages are sent in response to any GIOP message that is, for some reason, uninterpretable. For example, the magic number may be wrong, or the version number unrecognized. This message consists of only the GIOP header as well; the sender is supposed to know what it did wrong.

Those are the seven messages. We've treated them summarily because you'll never need them unless you build your own ORB, and this is definitely not the book for that task. But these couple of pages let you know basically what's going on under the covers, and reassures you that there is, for instance, a version number in every message so that progress won't find your ORB totally unprepared.

6.5.3 GIOP Message Transport Requirements

GIOP message transport requirements were chosen specifically to map to TCP/IP, the most prevalent transport, as well as the widely used Novell IPX and OSI. Basically, GIOP requires:

- a connection-oriented protocol;
- reliable delivery (byte order must be preserved, and acknowledgment of delivery must be available);
- participants must be notified of disorderly connection loss; and
- the model for initiating a connection must meet certain requirements (modeled after TCP/IP; no surprise here).

This concludes the description of the GIOP. Analogous to the way OMG IDL maps to various programming languages, the GIOP is not directly usable but becomes so when mapped to one of many possible transports, such as TCP/IP.

6.5.4 Internet Inter-ORB Protocol (IIOP)

The mapping of the GIOP onto TCP/IP is so straightforward that this section of the specification is extremely brief. It consists primarily of the specification for the IIOP IOR, which contains the hostname and port that listens for the client-initiated connection. If you're an ORB builder, chances are good that you already know exactly what to do.

6.6 ENVIRONMENT-SPECIFIC INTER-ORB PROTOCOLS (ESIOPs), INCLUDING THE DCE CIOP

A non-GIOP protocol is an ESIOP if it's based on CORBA 2.0; that is, the basic architecture including domains and bridging, the IOR, and the interoperability interfaces including the DSI. Not every inter-ORB protocol is an

ESIOP; it is certainly possible to construct a proprietary protocol that does not include the CORBA 2.0 components. In some demanding environments, this may be the only way to meet requirements for such specialized applications as guaranteed real-time response as in a fly-by-wire control system or control system for a nuclear power plant.

The DCE-based protocol adopted by OMG as part of CORBA 2.0 is an ESIOP. It conforms to all of the CORBA 2.0 requirements that we listed; in addition, it uses the same CDR as the GIOP, a characteristic that will facilitate bridging between it and GIOP domains. It is every bit an OMG standard; even though it is not mandatory for all ORBs, it is the *only* compliant way to implement a DCE-based protocol in CORBA 2.0. That is, you don't *have* to do DCE, but if you do, you *have* to do it *this way* if you want to be branded CORBA 2.0-compliant.

In the specification, the name of the protocol is DCE Common Inter-ORB Protocol, abbreviated DCE-CIOP, so that's how we'll refer to it.

DCE-CIOP replaces the functionality of the seven GIOP messages with two DCE RPC calls, *locate* and *invoke*. And it replaces the GIOP transport assumptions with a reliance on the DCE RPC service to handle these two calls.

6.6.1 The Role of DCE in the DCE-CIOP

Since the initials DCE figure so prominently in the name of this protocol, some people have misinterpreted the role of the DCE RPC in CORBA 2.0 communications. If you're sure you understand how DCE plays the role of a protocol in ORB-to-ORB communications, you can skip to the next section. Otherwise, read on.

The DCE-CIOP is a protocol for ORB-to-ORB communications, where it plays the same role as the IIOP. Client and object implementation still interact only with their local ORBs, and the fact that an invocation may have to go over the network is still hidden from them. In fact, there is no CORBA facility that allows a client to determine the protocol used by any request it makes.

The RPCs used by the DCE-CIOP have been chosen specifically for ORB-to-ORB communications, and they are not related to the operation specified by any particular client. Regardless of the number and variety of objects and operations in your interface, only two DCE RPC operations are ever invoked by the DCE-CIOP: *locate* and *invoke*. Your client's requested operation is a parameter of the *invoke* RPC call, as we will see shortly.

This means that the DCE-CIOP does not make your DCE servers automatically accessible to CORBA clients, nor are DCE clients automatically able to invoke operations on CORBA object implementations. CORBA is a world for ORBs only; ORBs contain too much functionality for the casual programmer to build their equivalent into a DCE-based client or server.

Why use DCE-CIOP, then? There are a lot of good reasons, especially if you're part of a large enterprise: If your enterprise network is already configured for DCE, then you have the best reason: you've already made the investment in the protocol—software purchase, installation and configuration, and staff training. You can avoid duplicating these steps for yet another protocol by purchasing DCE-CIOP ORBs. At the same time, you may take advantage of DCE network administration, Naming and Directory services, and possibly DCE security, depending on what comes out of the current OMG security standardization effort.

And for the ORB builder, the DCE runtime provides many of the services he or she would otherwise have to build him- or herself as part of the system. DCE code and services have been developing for years before CORBA, and now constitute a code base well suited for the next generation of distributed computing. Users of DCE-CIOP-based ORBs benefit automatically from all of this previous work.

6.6.2 Structure of the DCE-CIOP Specification

The DCE-CIOP runs over an RPC that is interoperable with the DCE protocols specified in a number of places, including readily available OSF and X/Open documents. (See the References in Appendix A for details.) The DCE RPC:

- defines both connection-oriented and connectionless protocols;
- supports multiple underlying transport protocols, including TCP/IP;
- supports multiple outstanding requests to multiple CORBA objects over the same connection; and
- supports fragmentation of messages, an advantage for large requests and responses.

Each interaction between ORBs occurs as a remote procedure call on one of the two DCE RPC interfaces defined in the specification: *locate* and *invoke*. Each of these is a synchronous DCE RPC, consisting of both a request and response. Asynchronous CORBA invocations are implemented internal to the ORB using DCE threads.

Two DCE RPC interfaces are defined. One transmits messages as pipes of uninterpreted bytes; the other transmits as conformant arrays of uninterpreted bytes. Of these, the pipe-based form has a number of implementation and performance advantages and is used whenever possible. (Of course, this choice is made by the ORBs based on mutual availability of the preferred interface; client and object implementation are not aware of any difference through their interfaces or parameters.)

DCE-CIOP uses the same CDR as GIOP, and DCE-ESIOP message headers are also specified as OMG IDL types.

The IOR uses the **TAG_MULTIPLE_COMPONENTS** profile designation, and contains six components which:

- identify a server process via a DCE string binding;
- identify a server process via the DCE name service;
- identify the target object when a request message is sent to a server;
- enable a DCE-CIOP client to recognize objects that share an endpoint;
- indicate whether the client should send a locate or request message; and
- indicate when the pipe-based interface is not available.

Two DCE-CIOP interfaces defined in DCE IDL are **dce_ciop_pipe** and **dce_ciop_array**. Each defines two operations as we said before, **locate** and **invoke**. ORB builders access these interfaces in the same way that DCE client and server builders would access DCE stubs in their work. We will not go over these interfaces here, since they're internal to the ORB. If you're building an ORB and want to use DCE CIOP, you'll have to get your own copy of the OMG specification for a reference. The message contents are similar enough to those of the GIOP that we won't detail them either; the material so far covers both the similarities and differences well enough for our purposes here.

6.7 ONE LAST WORD ON INTEROPERABILITY

We've devoted a lot of space to interoperability, especially considering that all of the interfaces covered in this chapter are not available to client and object programmers. But interoperability is serious business—our component software environment is based on it, so we have a lot of concern for what's going on under the covers when our objects get together over the network.

But it's important to keep everything in perspective, and OMG has a good idea where the payoffs lie for both user and software vendor. In OMG's picture, the payoffs are in:

- a *common architecture* with common interface specifications and protocol (whether direct or bridged), a necessary enabling component;
- a set of *common interfaces* to low- and intermediate-level components (the CORBAservices and, even more important, the CORBAfacilities) which enable the big payoff; and
- the jump from the static distributed environment—today's CORBA—to a *dynamic distributed environment*, supported by the forthcoming Trader

specification, in conjunction with the DII and DSI, which is necessary to obtain the full return from the equipment and software infrastructure we're installing and paying for even today.

In this picture, the protocol lies hidden in the infrastructure. The reason CORBA 2.0 was such big news wasn't because it was such a great achievement; it was because it was a workable solution to a huge problem we created ourselves in the first place.

What's the best protocol? It depends on circumstances. You can't use the same protocol in a miniature, wireless hand-held as you would in a powerful workstation, and even the workstation may need a protocol change if it moves from a five-unit isolated LAN to a million-unit multinational enterprise. The framers of CORBA knew this; that's why the specification allows full compliance whether IIOP is implemented natively or via a half-bridge. There are no degrees of compliance; any ORB that provides interoperability with IIOP *either way* is *fully compliant*.

What should you look for in an interoperable ORB product? First, make sure that it conforms to the OMG specifications. Beyond that, there are a number of things to look for: reliability, robustness, scalability (how many ORBs, workstations, servers, etc. will you be running?), security, administrability, vendor company characteristics, and so on. You will not need the same ORB profile vis-a-vis these criteria as another company, so do your own evaluation, and make up your own mind.

CHAPTER 7

Language Mappings, Part 1: C

7.1 ROLE OF A LANGUAGE MAPPING

So far, we've only seen how to write our CORBA interface definitions in OMG IDL. Since these definitions are programming language-independent, how are we going to access these interfaces from our code?

Programming language mappings "map," that is, define, one-to-one correspondences from OMG IDL constructs to programming language constructs. These constructs tell client and object-implementation writers what to write to invoke an operation on a CORBA object. In a nonobject-oriented language like C, invocations typically map to function calls; in object-oriented languages like C++ and Smalltalk, mappings try to make CORBA invocations look like language-object invocations.

It would be really nice if we could go the other way as well, and generate the IDL automatically from either the client or object implementation source code. You can, and some products already do it. However, they cannot take advantage of everything that IDL has to offer: oneway invocations; attributes including read-only and read-write; DII invocations including asynchronous, deferred synchronous, and multiple deferred synchronous modes; and the other special IDL features that become important as your distributed system grows in complexity. So, while this feature will save a lot of time for a lot of programmers, the best of the bunch will still code IDL by hand where its advanced properties let them tune their distributed system and make it sing.

This part of the chapter, through Section 7.1.1, summarizes aspects common to all language mappings. The remainder of the chapter covers the C language mapping, followed by Chapter 8 on C++ and Chapter 9 on Smalltalk.

What about other languages? Languages with pointers, structures, and dynamic memory allocation support IDL mappings most easily, but languages without them (FORTRAN, for example) support mappings as well. An Ada mapping has been submitted for standardization; contact OMG for a copy of the specification if you're interested. There is current work on a COBOL binding as well.

7.1.1 Language Mapping Functions

A language mapping has a lot to do. First, it has to express all of the constructs of IDL including:

- basic and constructed data types, constants, and objects;
- operation invocations, including parameter passing;
- setting and retrieving attribute values; and
- raising exceptions and handling exception conditions.

To ensure interoperability, *every* language mapping must provide a mapping for *every* IDL datatype. If some IDL datatypes were not supported by every language, operation signatures that used them would not interoperate everywhere.

There is also a converse problem, that of language datatypes that do not map directly to IDL datatypes. For example, COBOL includes PIC 99 and VSAM record types, which do not correspond to any current IDL type. In late 1995, OMG members were evaluating possible extensions to the current roster of IDL types; candidate specifications would provide more natural mappings to datatypes found in COBOL and Ada, as well as various international character sets. But, since interoperability does not require that every language datatype have a corresponding IDL type, we expect that many unusual language types will continue to lack IDL types even after this effort concludes. For up-to-date information on this, contact OMG or your ORB vendor.

There must be a datatype to represent the object reference. This representation is opaque; that is, the datatype is represented by a language-specific datatype, but the program does not (and, generally, cannot) interpret the value that the type contains. Object references may be passed as parameters or return values in invocations, and may be passed to ORB and BOA operations.

Object invocations are mapped in various ways. In C, the static invocation interface mapping requires the client to insert an object reference into the mapped function call to specify the target. In C++ and Smalltalk, both object-oriented languages, a CORBA invocation looks like a C++ or Smalltalk object invocation.

For the DII, mappings vary. In C, the mapping follows the normal definitions even though the target is a pseudo-object. In C++, attribute operations replace **add_argument**. The CORBA 2.0 specification speculates that a mapping for a dynamic language like LISP could make a dynamic invocation look like an invocation of a language object. Unfortunately, no such mapping exists today (at least that we know about).

The mapping must also provide access to ORB and BOA functionality, which, although expressed in PIDL, is not always accessed as the call that would be constructed from it. In fact, some of the PIDL definitions are left incomplete, to be fully defined only in the various language mappings. Similarly, the mappings provide access to the DII, including the various deferred invocation modes and the DSI for the server side.

The last thing the language mapping does is fix responsibility for memory allocation and freeing among the client, the stub, and the ORB. We'll point out how this happens in the various languages as we work our way through the next three chapters.

And, finally, remember that C and C++ are both generated by the same compiler. Some ORB vendors required mappings for those two languages that coincided in the various functional areas, including memory management. This requirement, in the end, resulted in some changes in an older version of the C mapping being required by the C++ mapping. All of the products represented in this book use the current mappings.

We admit in advance that the simple examples we'll use to illustrate the three mappings are rather dry. We've done this on purpose: Since the second half of the book contains realistic examples worked in detail in all three language mappings, the illustrations in this part have been kept as simple as possible to make the principles clear. For each language, we'll show an interface and invocation, an inheritance example, an attribute, and an exception. We'll also discuss how memory management is handled for each.

7.2 C MAPPING FUNDAMENTALS

7.2.1 Mapping to Types

In order to preserve system independence, CORBA sets down strict definitions of types such as long, short, and float. Since C compilers may differ in their own definitions of these types, the C mapping does *not* map IDL types directly to C types in spite of the similarity of their names. Instead, the IDL compiler maps, for example,

- IDL **long**   to C `CORBA_long`;
- IDL **short**   to C `CORBA_short`;
- IDL **float**   to C `CORBA_float`;
- IDL **double** to C `CORBA_double`

and so on. A header file assures that, on any system, **CORBA_long** always maps to a 32-bit integer; a **CORBA_float** always maps to an IEEE 32-bit floating point number, and on through the list. We won't print the whole list of basic types here; you'll get it with your IDL compiler documentation, and it's basically what you expect.

IDL structured types may be fixed-length or variable-length; mapping varies depending on which of these your IDL variable is. We won't get into details here; suffice it to say that OMG specifies both mapping and memory allocation responsibilities (caller or callee) for all of these types, allowing use of all IDL types, including variable-length structured types, as **in**, **out**, and **inout** parameters of CORBA invocations. We used structs in the example, so you can examine one or two mappings there. For more detail, check out the documentation that came with your IDL compiler, or read the OMG C Mapping specification.

7.2.2 Mapping an Operation

Here is the simple single-operation interface we'll use for our basic example:

```
interface example1 {
    long op1 (in long arg1);
}
```

This example generates the C declarations:

```
typedef CORBA_Object example1;
extern CORBA_long example1_op1 (
    example1 o,
    CORBA_long arg1,
    CORBA_Environment *ev
);
```

example1 is of type **CORBA_Object**; that is, it's an object reference. It's an opaque type, meaning that your code can't do anything internally with it, and even close examination of its contents won't reveal anything useful. But your code can pass a **CORBA_Object** back and forth to the ORB as either target, argument, or return type of a call. The next fragment will show this, but first we need to take a closer look at the rest of these declarations.

In C, operation names are constructed by concatenating the names of the interface and the operation separated by an underscore; here we get **example1_op1**. Parameter names carry over without change; in our example we get **arg1**.

For **out** and **inout** parameters except arrays, the client must pass the address of a variable of that type. For arrays, pass the address of the first element.

For **in** parameters, pass the value of the parameter for basic types, enumeration types, and object references. For arrays, pass the address of the first element. For other structured types, pass the address of a variable of that type. For strings, pass a **char ***.

inout parameters work as follows: For basic types, enumeration types, object references, and structured types, pass the address of a variable of the correct type. For strings, pass the address as a **char ***. And for arrays, pass the address of the first element.

C identifier names are constructed by replacing the IDL double-colon separator (::) with an underscore; therefore a name collision will occur if you (for example) string together the name of your interface and operation separated by an underscore, and assign this name to a IDL identifier. Many other IDL constructs can bring on this same problem. Since this collision does not occur in the C++ and Smalltalk mappings, if you're working in one of those languages and don't test-compile your IDL in C also, you can accidentally create an IDL file that won't interoperate between languages. OMG recommends that you avoid indiscriminate underscores in your IDL for this reason. We've avoided all underscores in our IDL file for maximum portability among C, C++, and Smalltalk; this demonstrates best programming practice for writing of portable IDL.

The final point from this example is the specifying of the target object and the environment. Our single-parameter IDL operation adds two parameters when it moves to C: the target object reference is added at the front, and the environment at the rear. In C, the same object reference can be both passed and used to specify a target. In object-oriented languages, this is not the case: invocations of CORBA objects resemble invocations of language objects. We'll see this in C++ and Smalltalk in the next two chapters. The environment is used to return exception information.

7.2.3 Passing an Object Reference

Next, an example of passing an object reference. We can build on **example1** to show this. Consider the following:

```
#include "example1.idl"
interface example2 {
    example1 op2 ( ) ;
};
```

op2 is an operation with no input parameters that returns the object reference to an **example1** object. Don't think that this is an esoteric construct; actually, this is pretty close to the way your client code will be passed *all* of its object references. **op2** may be, for example, an analog of the Naming or Trader Service invocation, with its arguments omitted for clarity.

Here are the C declarations that result from the mapping:

```
#include "example1.h"
typedef CORBA_Object example2;
extern example1 example2_op2 (
    example2 o,
    CORBA_Environment  *ev
);
```

and here's how you would use it:

```
#include "example2.h"
example1 ex1;
example2 ex2;
CORBA_Environment  ev;

/* Code to bind ex2 to an actual object  */
/* reference goes here.  */

ex1 = example2_op2 (ex2, &ev);
```

By the way, the **CORBA_Environment** parameter is used for exception handling and explained in Section 7.4.

7.2.4 Inheritance

We were introduced to the IDL for our inheritance example back in Section 3.3.9. Here it is again. We'll inherit from **example1**, as follows:

```
#include "example1.idl"
interface example3:example1 {
    void op3 (in long arg3, out long arg4);
}
```

which generates the following C declarations:

```
typedef CORBA_Object example3;
extern CORBA_long example3_op1 (
    example3 o,
    CORBA_long arg1,
    CORBA_Environment *ev
    );
extern void example3_op3 (
    example3 o,
    CORBA_long arg3,
```

```
CORBA_long *arg4,
CORBA_Environment *ev
);
```

As a result of the inheritance from **interface example1**, **interface example3** includes operation **op1**. A client could invoke **op1** equivalently on either **example1** (as `example1_op1`) or **example3** (as `example3_op1`). And, the client could invoke `example1_op1` using an object of type `example3` as well.

7.3 MAPPING FOR ATTRIBUTES

We've already seen that each IDL attribute declaration generates a pair of implicit **_set_** and **_get_** functions for the attribute, unless a **readonly** declaration eliminates the **_set_** function. The C mapping for these functions follows the implicit IDL. That is, the IDL declaration:

```
interface example4 {
    attribute float radius
}
```

which is equivalent to the following (illegal if you wrote it, since IDL identifiers cannot start with an underscore) IDL:

```
interface example4 {
    float _get_radius:
    void _set_radius (in float r);
}
```

maps to

```
extern CORBA_float example4__get_radius (
    example4 o,
    CORBA_Environment *ev
    );
extern void example4__set_radius (
    example4 o,
    CORBA_float r,
    CORBA_Environment *ev
    );
```

Yes, those really are two consecutive underscores separating the name of the interface from the **get** and **set** in the names of the functions.

7.4 MAPPING AND HANDLING EXCEPTIONS

Two types are involved in raising and handling an exception. First there's the exception that we declared in our IDL. For instance, the exception that we considered in Section 3.3.5:

exception input_out_of_range { long dummy };

would produce the following C declarations:

```
typedef struct input_out_of_range {
    CORBA_long   dummy;
} input_out_of_range;
#define  ex_input_out_of_range <unique id>
```

where **<unique_id>** is an identifier that uniquely identifies the exception type.

Second, the C mapping uses the **CORBA_Environment** type to pass exception information back to the client. The **CORBA_Environment** typedef specifies the relevant exception types, including at least:

```
typedef struct CORBA_Environment {
    CORBA_exception_type   _major;
    ...
}  CORBA_Environment;
```

where **_major** may take one of the values:

```
CORBA_NO_EXCEPTION,
CORBA_USER_EXCEPTION, or
CORBA_SYSTEM_EXCEPTION.
```

If the value of **_major** signals an exception condition, then exception information will be present in **CORBA_Environment** and may be accessed using three functions defined specifically for this purpose. We will spare you the details in this chapter; you'll find out more in Chapter 24 where the example includes an exception. And if you want all the details, check out the documentation that came with your ORB environment.

7.5 MEMORY ALLOCATION AND DEALLOCATION

Memory allocation for **in** parameters is simple: the client is responsible for providing and freeing all storage for **in** parameters.

Unfortunately, the world of **out** and **inout** parameters is not so simple. The writers of the mapping specification have managed to cram 20 parameter types into six parameter passing cases. In the simplest of the six cases, for fixed-length parameters including structs, the caller allocates and deallocates all storage except for any that may be encapsulated within the parameter itself.

Object references are almost as simple, making the caller responsible for allocating storage. But you have to be careful if the parameter is an **inout**: the object implementation will invoke **CORBA_Object_release** on the original input value in order to reassign the parameter. This means that you need to create a duplicate using **CORBA_duplicate** *before* you make the call with the **inout** parameter in order to avoid releasing the object reference completely.

inout strings are an interesting case. The object implementation may deallocate the input string and reassign the `char*` to point to the new storage holding the output string. This allows the output string to be longer than the input. The client is ultimately responsible for freeing the storage. The object implementation is not allowed to return a null pointer.

There are three additional cases, covering primarily what is done when variable-length types are passed as **out** or **inout** parameters. In these cases, memory must be allocated by the object implementation, but deallocated by the client. Strict rules attempt (and do it well) to avoid both conflict and memory leaks, but the programmer (you, perhaps) is responsible for memorizing the rules and freeing memory when it is no longer needed. The consequence may be minor for a small test program that runs only for a brief interval and is then killed, but will be serious for large servers that run continuously for days, weeks, or months serving many users with mission-critical functionality. In such programs, memory leaks can accumulate over time and degrade performance if the programmer does not observe these rules carefully!

Memory management, like method invocation, varies greatly from one language mapping to another. Keep these principles in mind as we proceed to C++.

CHAPTER 8

Language Mappings, Part 2: C++

C++ and Smalltalk, unlike C, are object-oriented languages. Both languages include constructs to define objects and invoke operations on them. The OMG language mappings for C++ and Smalltalk take advantage of these constructs, and purposely make CORBA objects look as much like language objects as possible. This capability marks the first of a number of differences between the C language mapping we've just examined and the ones we're about to cover.

A second difference between the C and C++ mappings arises from the differing states of the two languages. C++ lacks both the maturity and stability of C; there is currently no official standard for the language, although one is rapidly approaching its final form. OMG members found it difficult to write a standard mapping to a language that was not itself standardized. (They found it even more difficult to *implement* a mapping to a language that was not yet standardized, as we'll see later in this book.) The state of C++ consists of a standard that is rapidly approaching stability, surrounded by a number of compiler implementations that approximate the standard to varying degrees. This fluidity, which results in a mapping standard with several options presented in various appendices, marks the second difference between the C++ mapping and the C mapping we just examined.

There's a third difference. C++ applications vary widely. On one axis of variability, we can imagine, at one end, applications consisting of relatively few, coarse-grained objects with simple relationships and calling sequences. On the other end of the axis, we can picture applications with thousands (or more) of fine-grained objects, whose calling sequences interlock and intertwine as references to multiple objects and groups are passed through a sequence of intermediate objects and are not called until the end of the chain. Both styles are important; the first one corresponds most closely with many business applications including the example in this book, while the second might include spreadsheets or user-interface class libraries. It turns out that the first class of applications benefits from automatic memory handling in the C++ mapping, while the latter with its thousands of fine-grained objects may suffer severe performance penalties as automatic compiler procedures create unnecessary copies of objects as their references pass from one routine to another. So the C++ mapping provides two different types of object references, one for each of these styles. We'll point them out in Section 8.2.3.

Summing up, in the C++ mapping you can expect

- an object-oriented mapping,
- with some options that allow for variability in compilers, and
- other options that allow for variations in coding purpose and style.

8.1 C++ MAPPING AND YOUR C++ COMPILER

The OMG mapping is based on the C++ environment defined by the ANSI/ISO C++ standardization committee, which in turn is based on *The Annotated C++ Reference Manual* by Ellis and Stroustrop. Some components of the environment vary from one compiler to another; you may have selected your compiler because of its maturity and features compared to alternative products. You are not the only one affected by this; the writers of the OMG C++ Mapping specification and every ORB implementor are affected as well. Mentioned in the OMG document are:

Exception handling: A fully compliant implementation requires exception handling as specified in the C++ manual. Unfortunately, not all compilers support this, so some mappings have been forced to use an alternative. Note that this is not the fault of the ORB vendor; ORB environments typically use C++ compilers that already exist on the target platform. An appendix to the OMG specification defines a way to use an environment struct to pass exception information.

The `namespace` construct: The mapping relies on the **`namespace`** construct. This feature was almost impossible to resist, since it corresponds so closely with OMG IDL's scoping of names to file, module, interface, and so on. Let's hope that this feature gets into C++ compilers quickly.

Templates: Citing the variability in template capability among compilers, the specification avoids requiring them. Use of templates is allowed, but they do not appear in the specification itself.

C and C++ compatibility: The OMG C++ Mapping specification mentions compatibility of the C and C++ mappings, specifically in call parameter memory management, as a feature. This is more important for ORB vendors than end users—it's almost impossible for you to notice whether your C and C++ code perform invocations use the same stub or different stubs. There are two advantages for coders, so we'll mention them briefly: First, memory management for call parameters in the C mapping was improved markedly (okay, okay, some less-than-perfect decisions in the original mapping were fixed up); and second, since types are handled identically in C and C++, once you've learned memory management for one language, you automatically know the other one.

8.2   C++ MAPPING FUNDAMENTALS

8.2.1   Mapping for Basic Datatypes

Before we can do anything, we have to know how the defined IDL types (Appendix B) map to C++ types. Because the IDL types are defined in a system-independent way, they cannot map directly to C++ types such as **long**, **short**, or **float**, which may be defined differently on different systems. Therefore, the C++ mapping, like the C mapping, defines them in terms of **CORBA_long**, **CORBA_short**, and so on which are defined in a system-specific header file that ensures that the CORBA requirements are met.

The header file then maps, for example,

- IDL **long** to C++ **CORBA::long**;
- IDL **short** to C++ **CORBA::short**;
- IDL **float** to C++ **CORBA::float**;
- IDL **double** to C++ **CORBA::double**.

and so on. A header file assures that, on any system, **CORBA::long** always maps to a 32-bit integer; a **CORBA::float** always maps to an IEEE 32-bit floating point number, and so on through the list.

8.2.2   Mapping for Other Types

The IDL provides mappings for string types, structured types (struct, union, and sequence), and arrays. It also discusses use of **Typedefs**, and mapping for the **any** type. Although we will not go into the details in this chapter, the tutorial example deliberately includes a **struct**, a **sequence**, and an **enum** to illustrate their mapping.

T_var Types   The C++ mapping provides a **_var** type for almost every type that automates memory management. Termed **T_var** types, their names are constructed by adding **_var** to the name of the type. Most helpful for variable-length structured types, **T_var** types are also defined for fixed-length structured types to allow a more consistent programming style. Thus, you can code in terms of **T_vars** for structured types uniformly, regardless of whether the underlying types are fixed- or variable-length. **T_vars** are designed specifically for allocation on the stack; when used this way, all storage used by the type is automatically freed when the variable goes out of scope.

One instance where the **T_var** type shows its benefit is the change of length of a variable-length type. This is helpful, for example, when simply copying a longer string into an existing string, but it really shows its worth when used for **out** and **inout** variables, which change size during a CORBA invocation. Here, the automatic memory management provided by the **_var** type allows the client, the ORB, and the object implementation to work together to deallocate memory used by the **inout** and **out** parameters at the start of the call, and allocate exactly the memory required by the returning values for all of these types. (Although **out** parameters are not read by the object implementation before being set, they may contain values—and therefore occupy memory—left over from a previous call.) Without the help provided by the **_var** class, you would have to keep track of this memory, and perform at least some of this deallocation yourself.

An object of type **T_var** behaves similarly to the structured type **T**, except that members must be accessed indirectly. For a struct, this means using an arrow (**->**) instead of a dot (**.**).

```
// IDL
struct S { string name; float age; };
void f(out S p);
```

```
// C++
S a;
S_var b;
f(b);
a = b; // deep-copy
cout << "names " << a.name << ", " << b->name << endl;
```

T_var types are extremely helpful in the right places. But where should you avoid using **T_var** types? Keep in mind that **T_vars** are deallocated automatically when they go out of scope. If you're writing fine-grained code that passes through scope after scope, creating and destroying millions of **T_vars** along the way, you will probably pay a price in performance. Use conventional types for this style of code, allocating memory with **new**

so it sticks around until you're ready to let it go. But use good coding practice to keep track of all of your allocated memory, and free it when you're done.

In our programming example in the second half of this book, watch for the use of types **string_var** in several places, and **_var** structured types in the POS modules in Chapter 31.

8.2.3   Mapping an Operation

Remember the simple interface we used in the C example? It was:

```
interface example1 {
    long op1 (in long arg1);
}
```

In C, this example generated about five lines of declarations, which told us how to invoke **op1** on an **example1** object. Recall we had to specify the object reference and the environment explicitly. In C++, the invocation looks object-oriented:

```
// C++
// Declare object reference:
    example1_var    myex1;
    CORBA::long     mylongin, mylongout;

// code to retrieve a reference to an
// example1 object and bind it to myex1  . . .

    mylongout = myex1->op1 ( mylongin );
```

The CORBA object reference in C++ can take one of two forms: pointer (**_ptr**) or variable (**_var**); the **_var** form is memory-managed automatically, analogous to the **T_var** structured variable types we just mentioned. If you're building relatively coarse-grained objects, the kind most applications end up distributing around the network, you should use the **_var** form because **_var** object references are automatically destroyed when they go out of scope. But if you're building an application with many fine-grained objects (and using CORBA to ensure interlanguage portability, for example), you may have to use the **_ptr** form to avoid memory management operations that may hamper performance by occurring at inopportune moments. The cost of using **_ptr** object references is that you have to keep track of them, and free their memory yourself to avoid memory leaks.

8.2.4 Using Interface Class Members

An interface maps to a C++ class that contains public definitions of the types, constants, operations, and exceptions defined in the interface. C++ classes produced from your IDL are special. You can do many useful things with them, but some uses are forbidden. You *cannot*:

- create or hold an instance of an interface class (automatic when you obtain an object reference);
- derive from an interface class (derive in your IDL file instead); or
- use a pointer (**A***) or a reference (**A&**) to an interface class (use **_var** or **_ptr** instead).

Of course, you can declare and use variables declared in the interface in the normal way.

These restrictions allow for a wide variety of implementations of the language mapping. For instance, they ensure that interface classes can be implemented as abstract base classes. Keep in mind that an IDL compiler must produce, and we must use, a number of distinct classes in order to provide all of the CORBA functionality we've gone over so far. So, before we're done, we'll have at least a stub class, a skeleton class, a server class, and possibly an implementation class for each interface. By deriving all of these from an abstract base class, the IDL compiler automatically creates a consistency among all of these different components, which really helps when it comes time to code them up.

The C++ mapping results in portable C++ code (especially on the client side, at least for now). But if you ever compare the **.h** files produced by the same IDL from two different C++ IDL compilers, you'll find that they surely differ, possibly quite a bit in places. That's because the C++ mapping specification was deliberately written in a way that leaves flexibility to implementors to allow them to accommodate different C++ compilers, for instance, or derive from their own base class and have every object inherit functionality useful on their particular system. But this does not affect the client; your client code will port among all of these different compiled IDL stubs with little, if any, modification.

8.2.5 Passing an Object Reference

Next, an example of passing an object reference. This is the same example we used in the last chapter on the C mapping:

```
#include "example1.idl"
interface example2 {
    example1 op2 ( ) ;
};
```

op2 is an operation with no input parameters, which returns the object reference to an **example1** object. This is pretty close to the way your client code will be passed *all* of its object references. In the example later, we'll write what we call a PseudoNameService that works just like this. The C++ looks like this:

```
// C++
// Declare object references:
    example1_var    myex1;
    example2_var    myex2;

// code to retrieve a reference to an
// example2 object and bind it to myex2  . . .

    myex1 = myex2->op2 ( );

// now we have an example1 object reference
// bound to myex1
```

8.2.6 Mapping for Inheritance

Here, once more, is the three-line inheritance example from back in Section 3.3.9. It inherits from **example1**, as follows:

```
#include "example1.idl"
interface example3:example1 {
    void op3 (in long arg3, out long arg4);
}
```

which we can use in C++ as follows:

```
// C++
// Declare object reference:
    example3_var    myex3;
    CORBA::long     mylongin, mylongout;

// code to retrieve a reference to an
// example3 object and bind it to myex3  . . .

// now we can invoke not only . . .
```

```
      void = myex3->op3 ( mylongin, mylongout );

   // but also, through inheritance,

      mylongout = myex3->op1 ( mylongin );
```

8.3 MAPPING FOR ATTRIBUTES

Each read-write attribute maps to a pair of overloaded C++ functions, one to set the attribute's value and the other to get it. The **set** function takes a parameter with the same type as the attribute, while the **get** function takes no parameters but returns the same type as the attribute. If your attribute is declared **readonly** in its IDL, the compiler generates only the **get** function.

So, our attribute example:

```
interface example4 {
    attribute float radius
}
```

would be used like this:

```
// C++
// Declare object reference:
   example4_var    myex4;
   CORBA::float    myfloatout;

// code to retrieve a reference to an
// example4 object and bind it to myex4  . . .

// set:
   example4->radius(3.14159);

// get:
   myfloatout = example4->radius();
```

8.4 MAPPING AND HANDLING EXCEPTIONS

We'll use the IDL from the example later in this book to illustrate basic exception handling. The IDL defines the exception **BarcodeNotFound** in **module AStore**:

```
module AStore {
    . . .
    exception BarcodeNotFound {POS::Barcode item;};
    . . .
}
```

It's actually used in the depot module, in the following C++ code:

```
void Depot_i::FindItemInfo
                ( AStore::AStoreId StoreId,
                  const char* Item,
                  CORBA::Long Quantity,
                  AStore::ItemInfo*& IInfo) {
    IInfo = new AStore::ItemInfo;
    if (m_items.Locate(Item,*IInfo)) {
    }
    else {
      // Raise the exception here
      throw(AStore::BarcodeNotFound(Item));
    }
}
```

This is about as simple as it gets, at least for the programmer. Behind the scenes, the exception maps to a C++ class defined in the **CORBA** module and is a variable-length struct that self-manages its storage. Declarations are in the **.h** file, so you don't have to declare the exception type in your code.

Recall that we have defined both systems exceptions and user exceptions in CORBA. There is a base **Exception** class, defined in the **CORBA** module. The **SystemException** and **UserException** classes both derive from this, and each specific system exception derives from **SystemException**. This hierarchy allows any exception to be caught simply by catching the **Exception** type:

```
//C++
try {
. . .
} catch (const Exception &exc) {
. . .
}
```

This approach looks simple so far, but you have to narrow to either **UserException** or **SystemException**. Alternatively, all user exceptions can be caught by catching the **UserException** type, and all system exceptions by catching the **SystemException** type:

```
//C++
try {
. . .
} catch (const UserException &ue) { . . . }
} catch (const SystemException &se) { . . . }
}
```

8.4.1   Without C++ Exception Handling

ORB vendors and users alike benefit when an ORB environment can be used on many different C++ compilers. Users are more likely to find an ORB environment that works with their chosen C++ compiler (which is frequently not supplied by the ORB vendor); vendors can sell into more companies. But, at least in the present state of C++ language evolution, many C++ compilers do not yet support native exception handling. To accommodate these compilers, the C++ mapping provides an alternative way to handle exceptions.

In nonexception handling environments, an **Environment** parameter passed to each operation is used to convey exception information to the caller. Exceptions are still created using the same hierarchy, so narrowing is used to determine the exception type. There's an example of this in Chapter 28.

8.5   SERVER-SIDE MAPPING

When you write your server, you will be implementing a class that executes the methods you wrote in your IDL file.

However, this class cannot have the same name as the interface, because the interface class is an abstract base class that cannot be realized (Section 8.2.4). Implementation classes are created in different ways by different ORBs; the most common methods are inheritance from the abstract base class, or from some other class related somehow, and delegation.

The server-side mapping provides two functions that are accessible from within the body of a member function: **_this()** and **_boa()**. The **_this()** function returns an object reference (**T_ptr**) for the target object. The **_boa()** function returns a **BOA_ptr** to the appropriate BOA object. You may not assume where the **_boa()** function is defined, only that it is available within the member function. The **_boa()** function could be a member function, a static member function, or a static function defined in a namespace that is accessible from the member functions of the implementation.

8.5.1   Using C++ Inheritance for Interface Implementation

Each IDL compiler creates its implementation classes in its own way, optimizing differently for the platforms, C++ compilers, and markets that the company targets. Many—most, perhaps, at least now—derive implementation classes by inheritance, although the base class choice varies widely. (Some use delegation instead of inheritance; other methods are possible too.)

We'll go through a basic example here so that you know what to expect when you code your server side, but we caution you that details will definitely differ from what you see here.

For our example, we'll look at an implementation class derived from a generated base class founded on the OMG IDL interface definition. The generated base classes are known as *skeleton classes*, and the derived classes are known as *implementation classes*. Each operation of the interface has a corresponding virtual member function declared in the skeleton class. The signature of the member function is identical to that of the generated client stub class. The implementation class provides implementations for these member functions. The BOA invokes the methods via calls to the skeleton class's virtual functions.

We'll use this IDL interface for the example in this section:

```
// IDL
interface A
{
    short op1();
    void op2(in long l);
};
```

Suppose our (hypothetical) IDL compiler generates an interface class **A** for this interface. This class contains the C++ definitions for the typedefs, constants, exceptions, attributes, and operations in the OMG IDL interface. It will have a form similar to the following:

```
// C++
class A : public virtual CORBA::Object
{
  public:
    virtual Short op1() = 0;
    virtual void op2(Long l) = 0;
    ...
};
```

Some ORB implementations might not use public virtual inheritance from **CORBA::Object**, and might not make the operations pure virtual, but the signatures of the operations will be the same.

On the server side, the IDL compiler will generate a skeleton class. This class is partially opaque to the programmer, though it will contain a member function corresponding to each operation in the interface.

```
// C++
class _sk_A : public A
{
  public:
    // ...server-side implementation-specific
    //  detail goes here...
    virtual Short op1() = 0;
    virtual void op2(Long 1) = 0;
    ...
};
```

To implement this interface, you must derive from this skeleton class and implement each of the operations in the OMG IDL interface. An implementation class declaration for interface **A** could take the form:

```
// C++
class A_impl : public _sk_A
{
  public:
    Short op1();
    void op2(Long 1);
    ...
};
```

8.6 C++ MAPPING SUMMARY

That's all we're going to say here about the C++ mapping. We've covered the basics—mapping to types, interfaces, operations, exceptions, and a bit about mapping to the server side. To add the next level of detail would suddenly expand this chapter to five times its size, so we'll leave that step to the vendors who provide manuals for IDL-to-C++ compilers. (You could check out the specification in OMG's CORBA manual if you wanted, but you'd find that it was written for IDL compiler *writers*, and not compiler users!)

Notice how IDL can map naturally to an object-oriented language like C++. One reason is that the operation syntax and format maps naturally; another is that the object-oriented nature of C++ allows the mapping to do a lot of work behind the scenes. The OMG mapping document is a long one, full of detail telling the compiler writer how to generate classes "under the covers" which do the work that lets you work with such short declarations in your own code.

In the next chapter, we'll cover the Smalltalk mapping. Smalltalk, like C++, is an object-oriented language. But unlike either C or C++, Smalltalk brings with it an entire execution environment.

CHAPTER 9

Language Mappings, Part 3: Smalltalk

9.1 SMALLTALK MAPPING FUNDAMENTALS

So far we've looked at two language mappings: C, and C++. Since these two languages are closely related, there were obvious similarities between their mappings, mostly in the area of type declarations and memory management. But, since C++ is an object-oriented language where C is not, there were also obvious differences. For one thing, in C++, a CORBA invocation looks like a language object invocation; in C there is no such thing as a language object, and the invocation format could be called, charitably, awkward at best.

Like C++, Smalltalk is an object-oriented language. Unlike both C and C++, Smalltalk is not statically typed; look for differences in the way types are handled at the boundary between IDL and Smalltalk, especially for structured types. Keep in mind that dynamic typing is an advantage for variable-length structured types. Another major difference is that Smalltalk development exists within an image that handles object creation and destruction, eliminating the need for Basic Object Adapter (BOA) objects.

Another issue with Smalltalk is that standardization of the language itself has not been finalized, but the fact that most of the popular Smalltalk implementations are similar at the base level gives the language a common ground for the mappings. Refer to the design goals of the mapping that follows for guidelines.

In general, IDL-specific pragmas may appear anywhere in a specification, although in real life, a particular implementation may constrain their location.

9.1.1   Design Goals of the Mapping

The Smalltalk Mapping had a number of specific goals:

- Whenever possible, IDL types are mapped directly to existing, portable Smalltalk classes.
- The Smalltalk mapping only describes the public (client) interface to Smalltalk classes and objects supporting IDL. Individual IDL compilers or CORBA implementations might define additional private interfaces.
- The implementation of IDL interfaces is left unspecified. Implementations may choose to either map each IDL interface to a separate Smalltalk class, provide one Smalltalk class to map all IDL interfaces, or allow arbitrary Smalltalk classes to map IDL interfaces.
- Because of the dynamic nature of Smalltalk, the mapping of the **any** and **union** types is such that an explicit mapping is unnecessary. Instead, the value of the **any** and **union** types can be passed directly. In the case of the **any** type, the Smalltalk mapping will derive a **TypeCode**, which can be used to represent the value. In the case of the **union** type, the Smalltalk mapping will derive a discriminator, which can be used to represent the value.
- The explicit passing of environment and context values on operations is not required.
- Except in the case of object references, no memory management is required for data parameters and return results from operations. All such Smalltalk objects reside within Smalltalk memory, and garbage collection will reclaim their storage when they are no longer used.

9.1.2   Smalltalk Implementation Requirements

The following list provides a brief description of the mapping of IDL elements to the Smalltalk language.

IDL Element	Smalltalk Language
object references	Smalltalk objects that represent CORBA objects. The Smalltalk objects must respond to all messages defined by the CORBA objects' interface.
interfaces	A set of messages to which Smalltalk objects that represent object references must respond. The set of messages corresponds to the attributes and operations defined in the interface and inherited interfaces.
operations	Smalltalk messages.
attributes	Smalltalk messages.

constants	Smalltalk objects available in **CORBAConstants** dictionary.
integral types	Smalltalk objects that conform to the **Integer** class.
floating point type	Smalltalk objects that conform to the **Float** class.
boolean type	Smalltalk **true** or **false** objects.
enumeration types	Smalltalk objects that conform to the **CORBAEnum** protocol.
any type	Smalltalk objects that can be mapped into an IDL type.
structure types	Smalltalk objects that conform to the **Dictionary** class.
union types	Smalltalk objects that map to the possible value types of the IDL **union**, or that conform to the **CORBAUnion** protocol.
sequence type	Smalltalk objects that conform to the **Ordered-Collection** class.
string type	Smalltalk objects that conform to the **String** class.
array type	Smalltalk objects that conform to the **Array** class.
exception type	Smalltalk objects that conform to the **Dictionary** class.

9.1.3 Smalltalk Annotation Conventions

Inside the Smalltalk implementation, the initial capitalization of a protocol indicates a corresponding set of IDL operations. For example, the **Depot** class has the Depot protocol that maps to the IDL operations for the **Depot** interface. This is not a mandatory convention; however, it enhances the readability and usability of the code.

Smalltalk implementations generally require that class names and global variables have an uppercase first letter, while other names have a lowercase first letter.

9.1.4 Conversion of Names to Smalltalk Identifiers

The use of underscore characters in IDL identifiers is not allowed in all Smalltalk language implementations. Thus, a conversion algorithm is required to convert names used in IDL to valid Smalltalk identifiers.

To convert an IDL identifier to a Smalltalk identifier, remove each underscore and capitalize the following letter (if it exists). For instance,

add_to_copy_map

becomes the Smalltalk identifier

addToCopyMap

In order to eliminate possible ambiguities that may result from these conventions, an explicit naming mechanism must also be provided by the implementation. For example, compiler **pragmas** could be used to specify individual names.

One aspect of the language mapping can cause an IDL compiler to map incorrectly to Smalltalk code, resulting in namespace collisions. Because Smalltalk implementations generally support only a global namespace, and disallow underscore characters in identifiers, the mapping of identifiers used in IDL to Smalltalk identifiers can result in a name collision. As an example, consider the following IDL declaration:

```
interface Example {
        void sample_op ();
        void sampleOp ();
};
```

Both of these operations map to the Smalltalk selector **sampleOp**. In order to prevent name collision problems, each implementation of the IDL language binding must support an explicit naming mechanism, which can be used to map an IDL identifier into an arbitrary Smalltalk identifier. For example, HP Distributed Smalltalk uses **#pragma** as the mechanism.

9.1.5   Mapping for Basic Datatypes

The basic datatypes are mapped as follows:

IDL Type	Smalltalk Representation
short	an instance of an appropriate integral class
long	an instance of an appropriate integral class
unsigned short	an instance of an appropriate integral class
unsigned long	an instance of an appropriate integral class
float	an instance of an appropriate floating point class
double	an instance of an appropriate floating point class
char	an instance of the **Character** class
boolean	the value **true** or **false**
octet	an instance of an appropriate integral class with a value in the range [0, 255]

The template datatypes (sequences, strings, arrays) are mapped as follows:

IDL Type	Smalltalk Representation
sequence	an instance of the **OrderedCollection** class
string	an instance of the **String** class
array	an instance of the **Array** class

9.2 MAPPING FOR THE ANY TYPE

Due to the dynamic nature of Smalltalk, where the class of objects can be determined at run time, an explicit mapping of the **any** type to a particular Smalltalk class is not required. Instead, wherever an **any** is required, the user may pass any Smalltalk object that can be mapped into an IDL type. For instance, if an IDL **struct** type is defined in an interface, a **Dictionary** for that structure type will be mapped. Instances of this class can be used wherever an **any** is expected, since that Smalltalk object can be mapped to the IDL structure.

Likewise, when an **any** is returned as the result of an operation, the actual Smalltalk object that represents the value of the **any** data structure will be returned.

9.3 MAPPING FOR ENUMS

IDL enumerators are stored in a dictionary named **CORBAConstants** under the fully qualified name of the enumerator, not subject to the name conversion algorithm. The enumerators are accessed by sending the **at:** message to the dictionary with an instance of a **String** whose value is the fully qualified name.

These enumerator Smalltalk objects must support the **CORBAEnum** protocol, to allow enumerators of the same type to be compared. The order in which the enumerators are named in the specification of an enumeration defines the relative order of the enumerators. The protocol must support the following instance methods:

< aCORBAEnum

Answers **true** if the receiver is less than **aCORBAEnum**; otherwise, answers **false**.

<= aCORBAEnum

Answers **true** if the receiver is less than or equal to **aCORBAEnum**; otherwise, answers **false**.

= aCORBAEnum

Answers **true** if the receiver is equal to **aCORBAEnum**; otherwise, answers **false**.

> aCORBAEnum

Answers **true** if the receiver is greater than **aCORBAEnum**; otherwise, answers **false**.

>= aCORBAEnum

Answers **true** if the receiver is greater than or equal to **aCORBAEnum**; otherwise, answers **false**.

For example, given the following IDL specification,

```
module Graphics {
    enum ChartStyle {lineChart,
                     barChart,
                     stackedBarChart,
                     pieChart};
};
```

the **Graphics::lineChart** enumeration value can be accessed with the following Smalltalk code:

```
value := CORBAConstants at: '::Graphics::lineChart'.
```

After this call, the **value** variable is assigned to a Smalltalk object that can be compared with other enumeration values.

9.4 MAPPING FOR STRUCT TYPES

An IDL **struct** is mapped to an instance of the **Dictionary** class. The key for each IDL struct member is an instance of **Symbol** whose value is the name of the element converted according to the algorithm (see section 9.1.4, Conversion of Names to Smalltalk Identifiers) given earlier. For example, a structure with a field of **my_field** would be accessed by sending the **at:** message with the key **#myField**. For example, given the following IDL declaration:

```
struct Binding {
    Name binding_name;
    BindingType binding_type;
};
```

the **binding_name** element can be accessed as follows:

```
aBindingStruct at: #bindingName
```

and set as follows:

```
aBindingStruct at: #bindingName put: aName
```

9.5   MAPPING FOR UNION TYPES

For IDL union types, two binding mechanisms are provided: an *implicit* binding and an *explicit* binding. Although not required, implementations may choose to provide both implicit and explicit mappings for other IDL types, such as structs and sequences. In the explicit mapping, the IDL type is mapped to a user-specified Smalltalk class. The implicit binding takes maximum advantage of the dynamic nature of Smalltalk and is the least intrusive binding for the Smalltalk programmer. The explicit binding retains the value of the discriminator and provides greater control for the programmer.

Although the particular mechanism for choosing implicit versus explicit binding semantics is implementation-specific, all implementations must provide both mechanisms. Binding semantics are expected to be specifiable on a per-union declaration basis; for example, using compiler pragmas.

9.5.1   Implicit Binding

Wherever a union is required, the user may pass any Smalltalk object that can be mapped to an IDL type, and whose type matches one of the types of the values in the union. Consider the following example:

```
struct S { long x; long y; };

union U switch (short) {
    case 1: S s;
    case 2: long l;
    default: char c;
};
```

Here, a **Dictionary** for structure **S** will be mapped. Instances of **Dictionary** with run-time elements as defined in structure **S**, integral numbers, or characters can be used wherever a union of type **U** is expected. In this example, instances of these classes can be mapped into one of the **S**, **long**, or **char** types, and an appropriate discriminator value can be determined at run time.

Likewise, when a union is returned as the result of an operation, the actual Smalltalk object that represents the value of the union will be returned.

9.5.2   Explicit Binding

Use of the explicit binding will result in specific Smalltalk classes being accepted and returned by the ORB. Each union object must conform to the **CORBAUnion** protocol. This protocol must support the following instance methods:

discriminator

Answers the discriminator associated with the instance.

discriminator: anObject

Sets the discriminator associated with the instance.

value

Answers the value associated with the instance.

value: anObject

Sets the value associated with the instance.

To create an object that supports the **CORBAUnion** protocol, the instance method **asCORBAUnion: aDiscriminator** can be invoked by any Smalltalk object. This method will return a Smalltalk object conforming to the **CORBAUnion** protocol, whose discriminator will be set to **aDiscriminator** and whose value will be set to the receiver of the message.

9.6   MAPPING OF ARRAY TYPES

Instances of the Smalltalk **Array** class are used to represent IDL elements with the **array** type.

9.7   MAPPING FOR SEQUENCE TYPES

Instances of the **OrderedCollection** class are used to represent IDL elements with the **sequence** type. A sequence is a one-dimensional array with two characteristics: a subtype and an optional maximum size. Use a < > combination to specify the type of data that belongs in a sequence and, optionally, the upper limit of elements, as shown in the following list.

Example		Comment
`sequence<string>`	`elements;`	The sequence elements' members will be of type `string`.
`sequence<NameComponent>`	`Name;`	The sequence Name's members will be of the type **NameComponent**.
`sequence<char , 2048 >`	`TextBuffer;`	The sequence **TextBuffer** will have a maximum number of 2048 members, all of which will be characters.

9.8 MAPPING OF STRING TYPES

Instances of the Smalltalk **String** class are used to represent IDL elements with the **string** type. Smalltalk strings and their subclasses may be passed and will be returned by IDL operations involving **string** arguments. A string can be unbounded or have a maximum size (specified via the **< >** combination), as in these samples.

Example		Comment
`string`	`username;`	The string **username** is unbounded.
`string<25>`	`ChartLabel;`	The string **ChartLabel** may be no longer than 25 characters.

9.9 MAPPING AN INTERFACE

Each IDL interface defines the operations that object references with that interface must support. In Smalltalk, each IDL interface defines the methods to which object references with that interface must respond.

Implementations are free to map each IDL interface to a separate Smalltalk class, map all IDL interfaces to a single Smalltalk class, or map arbitrary Smalltalk classes to IDL interfaces.

9.10 MAPPING AN INTERFACE

A CORBA object is represented in Smalltalk as a Smalltalk object called an object reference. The object reference must respond to all messages defined by that CORBA object's interface.

An object reference can have a value that indicates that it does not represent a CORBA object. This value is the standard Smalltalk value **nil**.

9.10.1 Invocation of Operations

IDL and Smalltalk message syntaxes both allow zero or more input parameters to be supplied in a request. For return values, Smalltalk methods yield a single result object, whereas IDL allows an optional result and zero or more **out** or **inout** parameters to be returned from an invocation. In this binding, the nonvoid result of an operation is returned as the result of the corresponding Smalltalk method, whereas **out** and **inout** parameters are to be communicated back to the caller via instances of a class conforming to the **CORBAParameter** protocol, passed as explicit parameters.

For example, the following operations:

boolean definesProperty (in string key);
void defines_property (
                     in string key,
                     out boolean is_defined);

are used as follows:

```
aBool := self definesProperty: aString.
self
        definesProperty: aString
        isDefined: (aBool := nil asCORBAParameter).
```

As another example, the operations:

boolean has_property_protection(in string key,
                     out Protection pval);

ORBStatus create_request (in Context ctx,
                     in Identifier operation,
                     in NVList arg_list,
                     inout DynamicInvocation::NamedValue result,
                     out Request request,
                     in Flags reg_flags);

would be invoked as:

```
aBool := self
        hasPropertyProtection: aString
        pval: (protection := nil asCORBAParameter).
aStatus := ORBObject
        createRequest: aContext
        operation: anIdentifier
```

```
argList: anNVList
result: (result := aNamedValue asCORBAParameter)
request: (request := nil asCORBAParameter)
reqFlags: aFlags.
```

The return value of IDL operations that are specified with a **void** return type is undefined.

9.11 MAPPING AN OPERATION

IDL operations having zero parameters map directly to Smalltalk unary messages, while IDL operations having one or more parameters correspond to Smalltalk keyword messages. To determine the default selector for such an operation, begin with the IDL operation identifier and concatenate the parameter name of each parameter, followed by a colon, ignoring the first parameter. The mapped selector is subject to the identifier conversion algorithm.

For example, the following IDL operation:

```
void find_item_info (
                    in AStore::AStoreId store_id,
                    in POS::Barcode item,
                    in long quantity,
                    out AStore::ItemInfo item_info)
                raises (AStore::BarcodeNotFound);
    };
```

maps to the following Smalltalk selector:

```
findItemInfo:item:quantity:itemInfo:
```

9.11.1 Implicit Arguments/Passing an Object Reference

Unlike the C mapping, where an object reference, environment, and optional context must be passed as parameters to each operation, the Smalltalk mapping does not require these parameters to be passed to each operation.

The object reference is provided in the client code as the receiver of a message. So, although it is not a parameter on the operation, it is a required part of the operation invocation.

This mapping defines the **CORBAexceptionEvent** protocol to convey exception information in place of the environment used in the C mapping. This protocol can either be mapped into native Smalltalk exceptions or used in cases where native Smalltalk exception handling is unavailable.

A context expression can be associated with the current Smalltalk process by sending the message **corbaContext:** to the current process, along with a valid context parameter. The current context can be retrieved by sending the **corbaContext** message to the current process.

The current process may be obtained by sending the message **activeProcess** to the Smalltalk global variable named **Processor**.

9.11.2 Argument Passing Considerations

All parameters passed into and returned from the Smalltalk methods used to invoke operations are allocated in memory maintained by the Smalltalk virtual machine. Thus, explicit **free()**ing of the memory is not required. The memory will be garbage collected when it is no longer referenced.

The only exceptions are object references. Since object references may contain pointers to memory allocated by the operating system, it is necessary for the user to explicitly free them when no longer needed. This is accomplished by using the operation **release** of the **CORBA::Object** interface.

9.11.3 Inheritance

We were introduced to the IDL for our inheritance example back in Section 3.3.9. Here it is again, slightly modified:

```
interface example1 {
    long operation1 (in long arg1);
};

interface example2:example1 {
    void operation2 (in long arg1, out long arg2);
};
```

As a result of the inheritance from **interface example1**, **interface example2** includes operation **operation1**. The following two Smalltalk classes correctly implement the example IDL. **Example1**:

```
Superclass: Object

Protocol: operations

operation1: arg
    "Do whatever operation1 does."
```

Example2:

```
Superclass: Example1

Protocol: operations

operation2: firstArg arg2: secondArg
    "Do whatever operation2 does."
```

Notice that **Example1** inherits from **Object**; **Example2** inherits from **Example1**.

IDL also supports multiple inheritance; however, Smalltalk (most implementations) supports only single inheritance. Thus, mapping an IDL interface with multiple inheritance to a Smalltalk implementation requires that the multiple inheritance structure be "flattened" into a single inheritance structure.

9.12   MAPPING FOR ATTRIBUTES

IDL attribute declarations are a shorthand mechanism to define pairs of simple accessing operations; one to get the value of the attribute and one to set it. Such accessing methods are common in Smalltalk programs as well; thus, attribute declarations are mapped to standard methods to get and set the named attribute value, respectively. For example:

```
attribute string title;
readonly attribute string my_name;
```

means that Smalltalk programmers can expect to use title and title: methods to get and set the title attribute of the CORBA object, and the **myName** method to retrieve the **my_name** attribute.

9.13   MAPPING FOR CONSTANTS

IDL allows constant expressions to be declared globally as well as in interface and module definitions. IDL constant values are stored in a dictionary named **CORBAConstants** under the fully qualified name of the constant, not subject to the name conversion algorithm. The constants are accessed by sending the **at:** message to the dictionary with an instance of a **String** whose value is the fully qualified name.

For example, given the following IDL specification:

```
module ApplicationBasics {
    const CopyDepth shallow_cpy = 4;
};
```

the **ApplicationBasics::shallow_cpy** constant can be accessed with the following Smalltalk code:

```
value := CORBAConstants at:
        '::ApplicationBasics::shallow_cpy'.
```

After this call, the value variable will contain the integral value 4.

9.14 MAPPING FOR EXCEPTION TYPES

Each defined exception type is mapped to an instance of the **Dictionary** class. Exception handling is implemented using the normal Smalltalk exception handling mechanisms. Thus, to raise an exception, the programmer can merely invoke **#error:**.

Since IDL exceptions are allowed to have arbitrary structured values returned with the exception, the programmer needs a way to specify this information as well. Fortunately, Smalltalk is up to the task. Consider the example Smalltalk fragment that raises the **BAD_INV_ORDER** exception (one of the standard exceptions defined in interface **Object**):

```
^(self standardExceptions at: #BAD_INV_ORDER) errorSignal

    raiseWith: (Dictionary with: #minor -> minor

        with: #completed -> #COMPLETED_NO)
```

In order to allow the ORB to correctly return the error result structure to the sender of the method, an array must be returned as the parameter of the error. Here, the symbolic name of the event is provided in an array, along with the type-structure representation of the required error result values. These values will be marshalled by the ORB to ensure that the same exception can be raised in the context of the client of the remote operation.

As with normal Smalltalk exceptions, a **#handle:do:** recovery block may be used to catch and recover from these exceptions. The main difference is that the ORB call context will have already unwound to the site of the remote call before the exception is raised. This greatly limits the extent to which recovery can be accomplished.

For example, the **NamingContext** interface declares these exceptions:

```
interface NamingContext {
...
enum NotFoundReason {missing_node, not_context, not_object};

exception NotFound {NotFoundReason why; Name rest_of_name; };
exception CannotProceed {NamingContext cxt; Name rest_of_name; };
exception InvalidName {};
exception AlreadyBound {};
exception NotEmpty {};
...
};
```

For exceptions declared with empty braces, no additional information is available to the client code when the exception is raised.

Exceptions can be declared anywhere within an IDL module. Exceptions declared at the beginning of the module apply to the module as a whole; exceptions declared within an interface apply to that interface only.

9.15 HANDLING EXCEPTIONS

IDL allows each operation definition to include information about the kinds of run-time errors that may be encountered. These are specified in an exception definition that declares an optional error structure, which will be returned by the operation should an error be detected. Since Smalltalk exception handling classes are not yet standardized between existing implementations, a generalized mapping is provided.

In this binding, the IDL compiler creates exception objects and populates the **CORBAConstants** dictionary. These exception objects are accessed from the **CORBAConstants** dictionary by sending the **at:** message with an instance of a **String** whose value is the fully qualified name. Each exception object must conform to the **CORBAExceptionEvent** protocol. This protocol must support the following instance methods:

corbaHandle: aHandlerBlock do: aBlock

Exceptions may be handled by sending an exception object the message **corbaHandle:do:** with appropriate handler and scoping blocks as parameters. The **aBlock** parameter is the Smalltalk block to evaluate. It is passed no parameters. The **aHandlerBlock** parameter is a block to evaluate when an exception occurs. It has one parameter: a Smalltalk object that conforms to the **CORBAExceptionValue** protocol.

corbaRaise

Exceptions may be raised by sending an exception object the message **corbaRaise**.

corbaRaiseWith: aDictionary

Exceptions may be raised by sending an exception object the message **corbaRaiseWith:**. The parameter is expected to be an instance of the Smalltalk **Dictionary** class, as described here.

For example, given the following IDL specification:

```
interface NamingContext {
            ...
            exception NotEmpty {};
            void destroy ()
                        raises (NotEmpty);
            ...
};
```

the **NamingContext::NotEmpty** exception can be raised as follows:

```
(CORBAConstants at: '::NamingContext::NotEmpty')
    corbaRaise.
```

The exception can be handled as follows:

```
(CORBAConstants at: '::NamingContext::NotEmpty')
    corbaHandle: [:ev | "error handling logic here"]
    do: [aNamingContext destroy].
```

9.15.1 Exception Values

CORBA IDL allows values to be returned as part of the exception. Exception values are constructed using instances of the Smalltalk **Dictionary** class. The keys of the dictionary are the names of the elements of the exception, the names of which are converted using the name conversion algorithm. The following example illustrates how exception values are used:

```
interface NamingContext {
        ...
        exception CannotProceed {
            NamingContext cxt;
```

```
        Name rest_of_name;
    };
    Object resolve (in Name n)
            raises (CannotProceed);

    ...
};
```

would be raised as follows:

```
(CORBAConstants at: '::NamingContext::CannotProceed')
    corbaRaiseWith: (Dictionary
        with: (Association key: #cxt value: aNamingContext)
        with: (Association key: #restOfName value: aName)).
```

9.15.2 The CORBAExceptionValue Protocol

When an exception is raised, the exception block is evaluated, passing it one argument, which conforms to the **CORBAExceptionValue** protocol. This protocol must support the following instance message:

corbaExceptionValue

Answers the **Dictionary** the exception was raised with.

Given the **NamingContext** interface just defined, the following code illustrates how exceptions are handled:

```
(CORBAConstants at: '::NamingContext::NotEmpty')
    corbaHandle: [:ev |
        cxt := ev corbaExceptionValue at: #cxt.
        restOfName := ev corbaExceptionValue at: #restOfName]
    do: [aNamingContext destroy].
```

In this example, the **cxt** and **restOfName** variables will be set to the respective values from the exception structure, if the exception is raised.

9.16 MEMORY ALLOCATION AND DEALLOCATION

One of the design goals is to make every Smalltalk object used in the mapping a pure Smalltalk object: namely, datatypes used in mappings do not point to operating system-defined memory. This permits the mapping and users of the mapping to ignore memory management issues, since Smalltalk handles this itself (via garbage collection). Smalltalk objects that are used as object references may contain pointers to operating system memory, and so must be freed in an explicit manner.

Except in the case of object references, no memory management is required for data parameters and return results from operations. All such Smalltalk objects reside within Smalltalk memory, and so garbage collection will reclaim their storage when they are no longer used.

## CHAPTER 10

CORBAservices, Part 1: Lifecycle and Relationship Services

10.1 ABOUT THE CORBAservices AND CORBAfacilities

If the OMG had planned to stop after producing an object-oriented substitute for the remote procedure call, the technical summary part of this book would be over and we'd be starting the example here.

Of course, we would also miss out on the real benefits and savings of the component software revolution, because it's going to take a lot more than electronic plumbing to fulfill the promises we made in Chapters 1 and 2. As we pointed out in those chapters, the Object Management Architecture or OMA is the part of the OMG specifications aimed at making applications work together above the plumbing level, and this is where the *real* payoff lies for end-user companies adopting OMG technology.

This chapter starts a new and different part of this book. Until now, we've been talking about plumbing—*how* our software components talk to each other. Starting now, we'll be talking about the standardized components themselves. If you're interested in architecture and not so concerned with protocols, you may have even skipped over some of the intervening chapters to get here. That's okay; we've arranged the book to make it easy for you to get the architectural overview that you need. You'll find that the first part of each CORBAservice presentation is an architectural and functional view. This is followed by IDL and semantic descriptions of key interfaces. Coders will want to concentrate on these sections; architects can skip on to the next service.

Chapters 10 through 17 cover the OMA. Most of the space is spent on the CORBAservices, but only because there is more to talk about; in fact, the CORBAfacilities are the components that will be most visible to you because they address application-level functionality. Your applications will use and rely on the CORBAservices, to be sure, but most of these are so basic that you won't really be paying attention. But it's a fact of life that there's more completed on the CORBAservices because they are used by the CORBAfacilities as well as by application clients directly, so they had to be worked on first. (Without them, the CORBAfacilities would have to create redundant versions of the basic service interfaces they provide.)

As a result, the CORBAservices provide material for Chapters 10 through 16, while the CORBAfacilities have to be content with just Chapter 17. You can expect this to change quickly; OMG's members are working hard to establish standards in areas from compound document management to finance to healthcare. If your company has something to contribute, you should contact OMG to see how to help out. Check out Chapter 17 first, and then look in Appendix A for contact information.

Don't get the impression that the OMA is a layered model, because it's not: *Every* service is directly accessible from every client, and basic CORBAservices such as Object Lifecycle, Naming, Events, Transaction, and the rest are used on the same basis by application objects as by the CORBAfacilities.

10.1.1 Building Applications from Software Components

The Object Management Architecture (Figure 10.1) embodies OMG's vision for the component software environment. One of the organization's earliest products, this architecture shows how standardization of component interfaces will penetrate up to—although not into—application objects in order to create a plug-and-play component software environment based on object technology. Application objects, although not standardized by OMG, will access CORBAservices and CORBAfacilities through standard interfaces to provide benefits to both providers and end users: for providers, lower development costs and an expanded market base; for end users, a lower-cost software environment, which can easily be configured to their companies' specific needs.

For each service and facility, OMG standardizes a service definition: interfaces defined in OMG IDL, and the accompanying semantics (functionality) defined clearly in text. As with CORBA, the implementation itself is *not* standardized. This enables competition both among providers of a facility and among independent providers of clients that use it. For the facility, meaningful competitive differentiators include (for example) platform availability, performance, resource utilization, and price; the irrelevant dif-

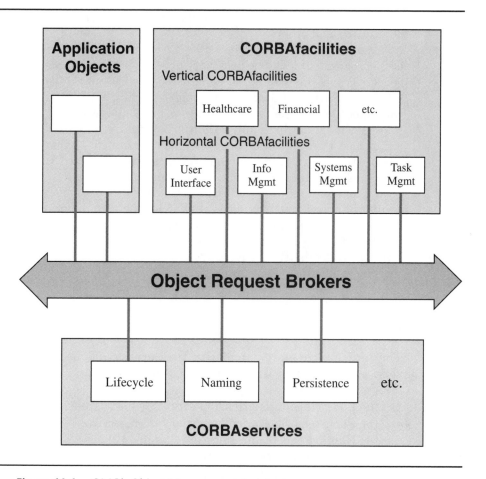

Figure 10.1. OMG's Object Management Architecture.

ferentiators of vendor-specific interface and data-file format are no longer a factor. Vendor-supplied clients that use the facility can differentiate on features, sophistication, ease of use, price, or other aspects; providers of these clients benefit from an expanded market base since any user running a standard facility can buy and use any vendor's standard client to access it.

There's a lot that OMG can standardize here. The CORBAservices provide basic functionality, which virtually every object-oriented program will need. The horizontal CORBAfacilities add application-level functionality with near-universal utility, such as compound document management and presentation and help facilities. Finally, the vertical market CORBAfacilities provide standard ways to access and manipulate data and functions, which span applications within specific industry groups such as financial services, healthcare, and others.

Application writing will be very different in an OMA environment. Little or no programming will be necessary to access or manipulate your industry-specific data—this will all be done using vertical market-specific CORBA-facilities. With data available through standard CORBA invocations, you can expect data presentation facilities to be available as well, although these may be nonstandardized application objects rather than CORBAfacilities. In either case, the application developer benefits from not having to write these parts of the program him- or herself. The new part of a particular application may consist of an experimental algorithm built into a new CORBA object or just incorporated into a "breadboard" object that provides such a testing facility, or a well-tested analysis applied to a new combination of data taken from spread-out parts of a large corporation, or computer support for a new product or service. In any case, the transparent data access and manipulation provided by the CORBAservices and CORBAfacilities will minimize the time and effort spent on infrastructure and allow your programmer to concentrate on problems in your immediate business domain.

10.1.2   The CORBAservices

The next six chapters summarize the current and near-future CORBA-services. The specific services described in this book are, by chapter,

- the Lifecycle and Relationship services (this chapter);
- the Persistent Object and Externalization services (Chapter 11);
- the Naming and Trader services (Chapter 12);
- the Event Service (Chapter 13);
- the Transaction and Concurrency services (Chapter 14);
- the Property and Query services (Chapter 15); and, finally,
- the Security and Licensing services (Chapter 16).

Beyond these, OMG members are also working on specifications for an Object Startup Service, which will primarily benefit the Transaction Service, but will be general enough to be useful to any object that needs to initialize in a special way when the ORB or systems first starts up (whether normally or after a crash); and an Object Collection Service, which will standardize such constructs as set and bag, replacing the temporary definition provided by the Object Query Service.

In this book, we will describe the services in enough detail to let you figure out how these services fit into your component software environment, and how some of their key interfaces are defined in OMG IDL. We'll use examples wherever we can to bring out how services work not only by themselves but together with other services to help you get your work done. Remember that many of the services were designed to work together in this way. Space does not permit a complete description of every service; the CORBAservices specification is about as long as this entire book so you know that we've had to leave something out. Start out with the material here; if you think you need more detail when you're finished with this book, you can either buy the specification from the OMG or read about it in the documentation to your CORBAservices package.

The CORBAservices specifications are a relatively recent development, in spite of the volume of detail incorporated here. In fact, they're so new that versions were not available to the people who programmed the example in the second half of this book. That's one of the reasons that the example does not use the services; the other reason is that we needed to limit the amount of new material in the example in order to keep it learnable, and all of the authors agreed that we had reached that limit without including any CORBAservices. In a CORBA environment, good programming practice requires you to reuse code whenever you can, instead of developing from scratch, and this means use of CORBAservices and CORBAfacilities wherever you can. Your next step, after you finish the example in this book, should be to rework it using the services, then apply the lessons you learn doing this to every CORBA application you design and implement in the future.

10.2 THE OBJECT LIFECYCLE SERVICE

The Lifecycle Service defines services and conventions for creating, deleting, copying, and moving objects. The conventions allow clients to perform lifecycle operations on objects in different locations, and to specify target locations where necesary, using standard interfaces and without violating the principal of location transparency built into CORBA. As you can imagine, this requires a number of new concepts. We'll present them in as logical an order as we can.

10.2.1 Factory Objects

In order to create an object using a CORBA invocation, a client must have a reference for an object where it can send the command—that is, a factory object; no reference, no new object. Where did the factory object come from? It must have come from somewhere, because magic is not part of the CORBA architecture.

No, we haven't solved the general chicken-and-egg problem, and we only know of two ways for objects to be created: The first objects in your system are created and started from a command-line prompt (or script, which is basically the same thing). If you started the right ones, they can in turn create and run additional objects.

This means you won't need a factory for every object on your sytem. Objects that are "one-of-a-kind"—your accounting system or object-oriented database, for example—do not need a factory because they're started during an installation procedure. (You might say that there's a factory working in the procedure, but this is moot because no client will ever have to call it.) And objects that work together in your desktop application don't need factories because they all come into existence together when you start it up.

So what kind of objects might need to be created by a factory object? Most likely, objects that are useful in multiple instances or copies; or objects that need to be moved from place to place; or objects that are created, pass through a work stage where they accomplish something useful, and then are archived, and the working copy deleted when they are done.

So you might find a factory object very useful to create compound document objects if your job is to create reports. Or, you might use an object to represent an order for equipment at your plant: you invoke the factory object to create an order object each time a salesperson turns in a signed contract. If you're an engineer designing a simulator for an oil refinery, your builder program might well call a factory each time you press a menu button for a new object, whether it's a storage tank, distiller, valve, or whatever.

Don't get the impression that an object that creates other objects is special somehow because it's called a factory. *Any* object that creates another object is a factory, and object creation is an integral part of distributed object computing. You still create objects in the most natural way in your particular object environment—for example, some ORBs let you use the normal programming-language mechanisms to create a CORBA object that resides in your same process. All we've done here is give the object-creating object (or module) a name: factory object.

There are a lot of things a factory object has to do, and some are more useful, although the creation process can occur without them. The "have to's" include:

- determine the location for the new object;
- assemble the resources (memory, permanent storage, system-dependent resources, etc.) that the object needs;
- register with the BOA for an object reference and pointer to permanent storage;
- create the object using the resources just collected;
- signal the BOA that the object is ready for activation; and
- return the object reference to the calling client.

The useful other things include

- registering the object with a Naming or Trading service so other clients can access it, if that's proper for this object.

As this description makes clear, there is no such thing as a generic factory object. And if there can be no standard factory, then there is no standard interface for object creation either. (There is, however, a standard for specifying resources that may be needed in object creation, but we won't get to it in this book.)

10.2.2 Move, Copy, and Delete

Where the Lifecycle specifies standard interfaces is, rather, for

- moving an object;
- copying an object; and
- deleting an object.

If the object paradigm is new to you, these may not turn out to be the "services" you expected.

If you're the client programmer, things work as you would expect. You invoke **move**, **copy**, or **remove** on the affected object; in effect, ordering it to move, copy, or delete itself, and the object does it.

But what if you're the object implementation programmer? These invocations, suddenly, are coming right at you. *To the object implementation programmer, the Lifecycle operations* **move***,* **copy***, and* **remove** *are not a "service" but an obligation.* Let's take a closer look at how this works.

10.2.3 Object and Interface Categories

The objects that bear CORBAservices interfaces divide into two distinct categories, and the types of interfaces themselves divide into three. For the objects, the categories are:

- *Specific objects:* These bear the interface as their primary purpose (as the Name Service bears the interface that resolves names).
- *Generic objects:* These bear a CORBAservices interface incidentally (like a compound document object that bears the Lifecycle interface, although Move, Copy, and Delete are certainly *not* its primary purpose).

The three types of interfaces are:

- *Functional interfaces:* These actually provide the service (including the Name Service interface just mentioned as an example).
- *Participant interfaces:* Born (and usually inherited by) generic objects participating in the service in some way, not usually as the primary provider.
- *Administrative interfaces:* Used to administer the service in some way.

We will see examples of all of these interface categories in the CORBA-services.

For Lifecycle, the **move**, **copy**, and **remove** interfaces are participant interfaces born by generic objects. These CORBAservices were not standardized so that ORB environments could provide Lifecycle services; rather, they standardize the interfaces that clients use to invoke Lifecycle services on generic objects—objects you build or buy, which need to be moved, copied, or deleted.

Typically, these objects will inherit the Lifecycle module as a component of their interface. Inheritance provides an easy way for an object to acquire interface components. Programmers should remember that, when an object inherits an interface, the programmer has an obligation to provide the functionality behind that interface.

The OMG membership recognized that these operations would be extremely implementation-dependent, and did not attempt to provide anything more than an interface signature for them. **remove** involves a complete cleanup of all allocated resources; **copy** requires externalization of the object's state at the source, followed by creation of a new instance at the destination location, which initializes using that state; and **move** can be pictured as a **copy** followed by a **remove** of the original object.

Here's how to get the maximum benefit from the Lifecycle CORBA-service: When you buy an object-oriented product with objects that must be created, moved, copied, or deleted, make sure the objects bear the standard Lifecycle interfaces. And if you build an application with objects like this, make sure they inherit the Lifecycle module and that you program the behavior this requires. When your network grows to tens of thousands of nodes and your system administrator discovers one day that he or she has to clean up one million objects, you'll really appreciate having every one of them respond to the same operation for **remove**.

10.2.4 Location: Factory Finders

What do we really mean by location transparency? Typically, we mean that we've divided our environment into an application layer and an infrastructure level, and that all location dependencies are confined to the infrastructure level. We want location-transparent applications so that we only need to buy and install one version that will run anywhere; not because we don't care where a particular instance is running, because frequently we *do* care.

There are lots of reasons to care about an object's location. Your accounting system object may work just fine on your mainframe or server, but not on Suzy's laptop, which lacks the horsepower and connectivity for that kind of application. And Suzy's compound document report object will be much more useful on her laptop than on her desktop machine during her three-week sales trip to Australia.

To express the concept of location in an interface-independent way, the Lifecycle Service defines the *factory finder* object. We'll use Suzy's report to illustrate how factory finders work.

Just before she takes off for her Australia sales trip, Suzy wants to copy her report object onto her laptop. (Suzy appreciates the value of a backup copy, so she plans to leave the original on her desktop machine.) Of course, Suzy isn't a programmer, so she isn't going to code up a quick utility to move the object. Instead, she benefits from the standard environment that CORBA makes possible, including handy utilities like this one, which her system administrator provides for every desktop.

Using a graphical user interface, Suzy selects the report object on her desktop machine and asks for a copy. The utility gives her a choice of locations, including her laptop and possibly a tape backup unit. The list includes all of the locations represented by factory finder objects set up by Suzy's system administrator. Note that even the concept of location is context-dependent, and that the factory finder interface does not attempt to categorize what it means. This allows each application to set up factory finders that represent the important aspects of location for its own purpose.

Suzy selects her laptop from the list on her screen. The utility invokes the Lifecycle operation **copy** on her report, specifying the factory finder object representing her laptop as a parameter. Here's the IDL the utility uses:

```
interface LifeCycleObject {
    LifeCycleObject copy (
            in FactoryFinder there,
            in Criteria the_criteria)
        raises (NoFactory, NotCopyable,
            InvalidCriteria,
            CannotMeetCriteria);
}
```

Notice how generic this invocation is. Nothing in it refers specifically to a report, allowing the same interface to move any object from a scroll bar to a nuclear power plant. (Okay, okay, an OO representation of a nuclear power plant. And this probably requires the relationship service also, coming up in the next section.)

The target of the request is the original object. This way, the request always goes to an object that knows everything that has to be done to accomplish the copy. The return value is the object reference of the copy, which is returned to the utility. We expect that the utility will register the copy with a Naming Service, or represent it as an icon on the laptop's desktop, when the operation is complete. **Criteria** represent constraints on the creation process, described in the specification.

Do not assume that the factory finder object actually resides on Suzy's laptop. The specification only requires that the factory finder *represent* that location; its implementation may do this any way it likes. For example, the factory finder object may simply retrieve a pointer to Suzy's laptop from a database of location information. The report object invokes the **find_factories** operation on the factory finder object reference it received in the **copy** invocation:

```
Factories find_factories (
    in Key factory_key
    )
    raises (no_factory);
```

The **factory_key** is a name, as defined by the Naming Service (Chapter 12). Note that it is supplied by the report object rather than the client, to keep the invocation as generic as possible. The report object supplies the name that represents its object type when it makes the invocation. When the operation completes, the report object receives as a return value the object reference of a document factory, which will create a document on Suzy's laptop. The IDL allows the factory finder to return a list of factories in case there are more than one in its location, but in this example, we'll presume there is only one.

Again, do not assume that the document factory object is on Suzy's laptop. Our only requirement was that the report object copy reside on the laptop, and that is the only thing we know for sure. For all we know, the factory may execute on the desktop machine while it creates the copy on the laptop's hard disk. (It's probably a good bet that there is a document factory object on Suzy's laptop so she can create new documents during her 17-hour flight, when she recovers from the free champagne and gets bored with the third movie. But this does not mean that this is the one that the utility uses.)

The report object and the factory object now work together to create a new document object on Suzy's laptop, and duplicate the contents of the original report in the new instance. There is no standard interface for this part of the operation, since it is totally application-dependent. In fact, it is not even required to be object-oriented or expressed in OMG IDL, although we expect this would have a lot of advantages.

10.2.5 Deleting or Moving an Object

Here is the IDL that Lifecycle objects inherit to allow deletion or moving:

```
void remove ()
    raises (NotRemovable);
void move (
        in FactoryFinder there,
        in Criteria the_criteria)
    raises (NoFactory, NotMovable,
        InvalidCriteria, CannotMeetCriteria);
```

The target of **remove** is the object itself; it is expected to clean up all of its mess before it goes away. If you are the programmer who built this object and allocated its resources, then you are expected to release them when you execute a **remove**. The client will not help you out here, so any memory leaks are your responsibility.

Of course, some objects are not removable, or at least not removable by just anybody. Your company would be in trouble if anyone on the network could kill the main accounting system just by dragging its icon over to the nearest trash can. For these objects, programmers have two choices: The objects can either not bear the Lifecycle interface, so that invocations return the standard exception **BAD_OPERATION** signalling an unsupported operation, or they can bear the interface but return the exception **NotRemovable**. A well-written client will check for both. Some objects may check the privileges of the invoker to determine whether a remove request is valid; the standard exception **NO_PERMISSION** is provided for this instance.

move is basically a **copy** followed by a **remove**, and its signature reflects this.

10.3 THE RELATIONSHIP SERVICE

That's all we're going to say about the simple view of object Lifecycle. Now it's time for a small dose of reality.

Suzy's report is actually a compound document. She's been working on it for a few weeks already, and so far it's composed of four chapter objects that contain a total of six graph objects, three spreadsheet objects, one embedded bitmap, and an embedded audio clip annotation from her boss about a change he wants. And one of the graphs is linked to a spreadsheet, which updates automatically from the daily sales report object generated by the accounting department.

The components, all distinct objects, are connected by *relationships*. Not only will the copy operation have to take these relationships into account, it may also have to differentiate between a "shallow" copy, which duplicates the core object and copies the relationships, and a "deep" copy, which duplicates the core object, all participants, and makes a new set of relationships connecting the new objects. Life is starting to get a little complicated.

10.3.1   Relationships and Roles

We're using objects in our computing because they're the best way to represent things in the real world, and things in the real world relate to each other in lots of different ways. For instance,

- A person *owns* a car.
- A person *is employed by* a company.
- A person *checks out* a book from a library.
- Suzy's report *contains* four chapters.
- Chapter 1 *contains* a graphic logo.
- Chapter 2 *references* a graph.
- The graph *references* the regional sales data spreadsheet.

Each of these bulleted items represents a relationship. Applications can use these relationships in many different ways, and just about any object you can think of may be involved in a relationship at some time or other. The OMG members wanted a single service specification to meet needs for relationships wherever they were needed. The way they accomplished this affects your view of the relationship service, whether you're an architect or a programmer.

There wasn't any problem making the service generally applicable— all they had to do was represent the role and relationship information as settable attributes. The service does a good job at this, and we'll go over enough examples to show you how this works.

You might expect an object to be involved in its relationships somehow. If this were a romance novel, it would be, but this is a computer book, so it isn't. Instead of involving the objects themselves, the Relationship Service creates Role and Node Objects, which serve as proxies, representing objects in their various relationships. (I know someone who tried to set up his marriage this way, but it didn't last long.)

This arrangement has at least two advantages compared to the alternative, where objects represent themselves: First, it allows *immutable* objects—that is, objects that are not "relationship-ready"—to be related by the service. Second, it allows relationships to be traced and traversed without involving the objects themselves. If the objects are large or difficult to access (for instance, due to security constraints) this can be a big plus. In the extreme case, role and relationship objects could sit on desktop machines for fast access while their related brethren reside on the mainframe.

There is one slight disadvantage, or at least something that both programmer and architect should be aware of: There is no standard way for a client to go from an object to its roles or relationships, although going the other way (from a role or node to its related object) is easy. This means that clients holding a reference to an object will have to find out about its relationships in other ways. Since upper-level clients will tend to work with relationships—that is, role and node objects—more than the objects they represent anyhow, this will rarely be a problem. For example, Suzy's compound document report is represented as a node object, as we'll see in Section 10.3.3. The compound document editor traces relationships out to their roles and the related objects they represent—a chapter, for instance—when Suzy requests a component be put into edit mode on her screen.

There are lots of ways to find out about an object's relationships. If you're a user or administrator, you can look in your Naming service. If you're the programmer of the object, you can inherit the **node** interface as we'll describe shortly; this allows your object to point directly to its relationships. And immutable objects can be given a pointer to their node object as a property using the new OMG Property service (described in Chapter 15), although this has a chicken/egg problem of its own.

So, more about relationships. We can characterize relationships by:

Type: Both the related objects and the relationships themselves are typed. *Employment* is a relationship between a person and a company, for example, while *ownership* relates a person and a car.

Roles: The relationship defines the roles that the related objects may assume. In the *employment* relationship, the company assumes the role of *employer* and the person assumes the role of *employee*. An object may simultaneously assume different roles in distinct relationships. For instance, Robert may be an *employee* of Objectifed Software Inc. and the *owner* of a 1988 Yugo.

Degree: Relationships are characterized by the number of required roles. *Employment* has two: *employer* and *employee*. Checking out, as a book from a library, has three: *checker*, the person; *checkee*, the book; and *agent*, the library. This is distinct from a relationship's cardinality, which is next:

Cardinality: The maximum number of relationships that may involve a particular role. For example, the *employer* role of our company may be involved in *employee* relationships with many people.

Semantics: Semantics may define relationship-specific attributes and operations. Examples include *job title*, an attribute of the employment relationship, and *due date*, an attribute of the checkout relationship. Note that due date is neither an attribute of the book, nor the library, nor the borrower; it is distinctly an attribute of the relationship that connects all three.

10.3.2 Basic Relationship Service: Roles and Relationships

The Relationship Service definition provides three separate levels or compliance points for implementations.

The basic level defines only roles and relationships. To represent, for example, the relationship between Robert and his Yugo, the relationship service creates an object that represents Robert in his role as *owner*, and another that represents the car in its role as *owned thing*. It then creates a relationship object that joins the two roles. This is shown pictorially in Figure 10.2.

We started with two objects: a person object whose instance is Robert, and a car object whose instance is Yugo. Using a relationship factory, we created two role objects: an *owner* role for Robert, and an *owned thing* role

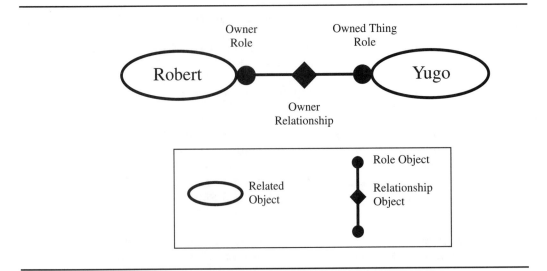

Figure 10.2. Relationship between Robert and his Yugo.

for the Yugo. Then we created an *owns* relationship object, which relates Robert and the Yugo. The role objects can tell us the object they represent and the relationship they're involved in. This lets us navigate from one role object to the other roles involved in this relationship. And the *owns* relationship object will only accept an *owner* and an *owned thing* object in its relationship; an attempt to register roles of different types than this will return an error.

But there are also a few things we can't do. First, we can't navigate from Robert to his role as owner using a relationship service interface or operations since the Robert object exists outside of the relationship service. (If an object is expected to participate in relationships, then it would be logical to have it inherit the node interface, which would support this. But this is not part of the base level of the Relationship Service.) And second, we can't navigate from Robert's *owner* role with the Yugo to his *employee* role with Objectified Software, Inc. since these two relationships do not share roles. This navigation requires the next level of the Relationship service, which adds the **Node** object and the **Traversal** interface.

10.3.3   Second Level: Graphs of Related Objects

The second level of the Relationship Service adds support for graphs of related objects through the **Node** and **Traversal** interfaces. The **Node** interface collects all of the roles a related object is involved in. The **Traversal** interface provides an operation that traverses the graph—that is, it follows all of the relationships, visiting each related object exactly once. This is useful when we attach an operation to a traversal, such as **move** or **copy**.

Remember Suzy's report? Let's concentrate on just a few components and see how these two levels of the Relationship Service keep them together. They're shown in Figure 10.3. At this level, each object is represented by a single node object, regardless of the number of roles it assumes and the relationships they participate in. The node will be a separate object when it represents an immutable object, but it can be an interface inherited by the object itself if the object was programmed to be "relationship-ready."

So the document object is a node that collects references to the object it represents (the document) and all of the roles that it assumes in all of its relationships. We've shown container roles for only two of the chapter objects in the figure to keep things simple; we already said that the report had four chapters so far and may grow even bigger. One of the chapters contains a graph, which references a spreadsheet. The other contains a graphic logo. Our compound document is well-represented here.

In our distributed object-oriented environment, these are all active objects, which may have been created by totally independent programs. In

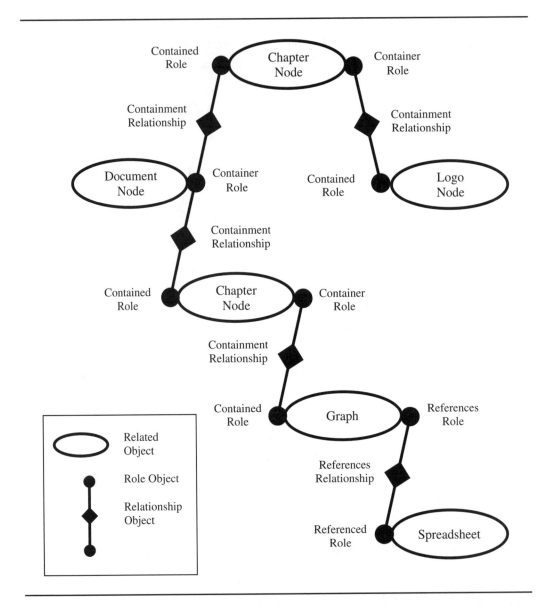

Figure 10.3. Related components of Suzy's compound document report. One of the chapters contains a graph that references a spreadsheet. The other contains a graphic logo.

principle, the only thing that holds them together is the document node object that we created. (This is just an example, of course. Your site may choose to purchase all of its software modules from a single company, while another site may decide to enhance support for one component—graphics or video, for example—by purchasing a special module from a vendor who specializes in that area.) The Relationship Service does not care where the objects' software came from—it can relate anything that has an object reference and meets the type criteria for the relationship.

The **Traversal** interface provides an operation that, for this example, would start at the document node and visit each node in the report exactly once. We'll discuss traversal in Section 10.4.4, although not in detail.

10.3.4 Third Level: The Specific Relationships Containment and Reference

Containment and Reference are two important relationship types that are singled out by the Relationship service for special treatment: their IDL is specified as Level 3 of the Relationship service. We won't get to this level in this book; once you understand the second level and know that these two key relationships are standardized, you won't need any more details until you actually get ready to use the service in your application, and by that time you'll have your vendor's doc set.

10.3.5 Object Identity

The concept of object identity is a tough one, especially if you get into it a bit. At first glance, it may seem easy—either two objects are identical or they're not. But a lot of things can happen in a distributed environment. Remember how we created a proxy object in our bridge in Chapter 6 and gave it an entry in the IOR? If you invoke an operation on the proxy and on the actual object, you get the same answer. If you try to determine state, it's the same. But one object reference refers to the bridge, while the other refers to the actual object. Are these the same or not?

The best answer to this question is, it depends. That is, it depends on who's asking the question, and why he or she wants to know. If you're configuring the network and tracing protocols, for instance, the proxy on the bridge and the actual object are different, but if you just want to invoke an operation and get the response, they're the same. This can get even more subtle when you install a proxy object for debugging, tracing, or security purposes.

So CORBA did not provide for object identity in the basic architecture specification. This is appropriate for CORBA, but the Relationship Service must implement traversal and it needs some notion of object identity in order to figure out what it is doing and when it is done.

So the Relationship Service defines an Object Identity module that supports enough of a concept of object identity to enable relationship and compound object operations without requiring that a universal object identity be supported by every object. Objects that must participate in relationships or compound lifecycle operations must support the **IdentifiableObject** interface. Any other object that wants to be identifiable for any reason may inherit and support the interface as well.

The interface has two components. First, a **readonly attribute Object-Identifier** returns a random self-chosen ID, which a client can compare to the ID of another **IdentifiableObject**. If the two differ, the objects are guaranteed to be different; if they are the same, the objects may be the same or it may be a coincidence. This method of checking identity is okay if you want to know only whether two objects are different, and for this it is very quick. You can use this method in a traversal *if* you first check that every object has a unique ID. If the check comes out okay, go ahead and traverse. If it doesn't, you may need to switch to code that uses the other component of **IdentifiableObject**.

The second component is the **is_identical** operation. You target this to the object in question, and pass it the object reference of the object you want to check for equality. The operation returns *true* if the passed object reference refers to the same object as the target; otherwise it returns *false*. The object has to implement this check itself, and the service definition doesn't give any help here.

10.3.6   The Compound Lifecycle Module

The Relationship Service was adopted by OMG after the Lifecycle Service; with its adoption, OMG had the tools it needed to specify Lifecycle operations on compound objects. The Compound Lifecycle Module, adopted simultaneously with the Relationship Service, contains the merged module for this service.

The Compound Lifecycle interface defines an **Operations** interface, which defines lifecycle operations on the graphs of related objects provided by the relationship service. Here's how it works. When Suzy's utility invokes the Lifecycle **copy** operation on the document node object, the node realizes that this request wants a copy of the entire graph. So it creates an object that supports the **CosCompoundLifeCycle::Operations** interface and invokes the **copy** operation on it, specifying itself as the starting node in the graph of connected objects to be copied.

The operations object starts by traversing the graph. The traversal object does not visit every object, however: instead, it gets a propagation value from each node's roles. Traversal criteria may take one of the values *deep*, *shallow*, *inhibit*, or *none*. There is a separate traversal criterion value for each Lifecycle operation: **copy**, **move**, **delete**.

deep: Specifies that the operation be applied to the node, the relationship, and the related objects.

shallow: Specifies that the operation be applied to the relationship, but not to the related objects. If the operation were a *copy*, for example, the original object would be copied, and the relationship would be copied, but the new relationship object would point to the new original object on one end, but to the *original* related object on the other end.

none: Means that the operation has no effect on the relationship or related objects. In this case, the traversal object would not visit the related objects and no lifecycle operations would be performed on them.

inhibit: This value goes farther than *none*. It specifies that the operation should not propagate to the designated node via any role, not just the designated role. That is, it protects the node from the operation. This is particularly useful as a propagation mode for the **remove** operation, since it ensures the node's continued existence.

The traversal produces a list of objects, nodes, roles, and relationships that need to be copied. The operations object reviews the list and, among other things, removes duplicate references to objects that were visited more than once due to multiple references in the graph. It then copies the objects first, roles next, and then creates and establishes relationships so that the new graph has the desired correspondence to the original.

The Compound Lifecycle operations are probably the best example of different objects from different sources working smoothly together via OMG specifications. Role, relationship, and node objects are *specific* objects (Section 10.2.3); the implementations for these objects was provided to you as part of the Lifecycle and Relationship services. The Compound Lifecycle Operations object probably came to you the same way. But the various objects they relate, and the real target of your copy invocation, are objects that came from diverse sources: chapters, graphs, figures, either purchased implementations or possibly objects your staff coded in-house; and all of these objects participate in Compound Lifecycle operations through their inheritance and use of standard Lifecycle operations for individual objects.

These diverse objects work together like this because the operations object, when it gets done with list-making and settles down to business, can invoke the Lifecycle operations **move**, **copy**, or **remove** on these objects, knowing that they will respond to the standard invocation. And it assumes that they all have a factory in the range of the factory finder you provide.

This is one good reason to have your programming staff equip every object they implement, if there's any chance it will ever need to be moved or copied, with the standard Lifecycle interface from the CORBAservices.

This completes our description of the Relationship service and the Compound Lifecycle addition. We'll finish up this chapter by going over the IDL for the **Role**, **Relationship**, and **Node** interfaces, to make completely clear for the technical folk how these objects are defined and how they connect to the objects they relate. If you're interested in more detail on Traversal and Compound Lifecycle, you'll have to check either the documentation that came with your Lifecycle service or the specification, which you can get directly from OMG.

10.4   ROLE AND RELATIONSHIP IDL

10.4.1   RoleFactory and Role Object IDL

Role objects are created by RoleFactory objects. Here's a summary of the IDL for the RoleFactory object:

```
interface RoleFactory {
    exception . . .;
    readonly attribute InterfacedDef role_type;
    . . .
    Role create_role (
        in RelatedObject related_object
        )
        raises (NilRelatedObject, RelatedObjectTypeError);
}
```

Each RoleFactory object only creates Role objects of a single type, so you need an array of factories if you plan to produce an assortment of objects of different roles. (Using our examples, we'd have separate factories for Owner role objects, Owned Thing role objects, ContainedIn role objects, ContainedBy role objects. . . .) By making the Role the actual type of the Role object, the Relationship service gets to take advantage of the object type system for consistency checking later on when relationships are formed. The RoleFactory makes the type information available as a **readonly** attribute, in case a client wants to check that it has the object reference for the right factory type.

And the object instance that the Role object represents—what we've been calling the Related object—is assigned when the Role object is created. This allows the RoleFactory to check that the type of the Related object is one that is allowed to assume that role.

Here is a summary of the IDL for the Role object. We've cut it down to the essentials for clarity; you won't need more than we've presented in this book unless you plan to implement the service yourself. To see all of the IDL, you can either consult the documentation that you got from your Relationship service vendor or check out the standard specification available from the OMG.

```
interface Role {
    exception . . . ;
    readonly attribute RelatedObject related_object;
    RelatedObject get_other_related_object (
        in RelationshipHandle Rel,
        in RoleName target_name)
        raises ( . . . );
    Role get_other_role (
        in RelationshipHandle rel,
        in RoleName target_name)
        raises ( . . . );
    void get_relationships (
        in unsigned long how_many,
        out RelationshipHandles rels,
        out RelationshipIterator iterator );
    void link (
        in RelationshipHandle rel,
        in NamedRoles named_roles)
        raises ( . . . );
    void unlink (
        in RelationshipHandle rel )
        raises ( . . . );
}
```

The **RelatedObject** was assigned when the Role object was created; now its object reference is a **readonly attribute**, which can be retrieved by any client. Once the Role object becomes involved in a relationship, a client can retrieve either the other Role object or its related object using the operations **get_other_role** and **get_other_related_object**. Since a Role object could be involved in a number of relationships (the Container role, for example), there is also an operation to **get_relationships**, which can return any number of relationships.

We'll cover the **link** and **unlink** operations in the next few paragraphs, which discuss the **Relationship Factory** interface.

10.4.2 Relationship Factory and Relationship Object IDL

Relationship objects are created by Relationship Factories, and there's a separate factory for each relationship object type. This truly is an assembly-line factory operation with "just-in-time" component delivery. You feed roles in one end with the **create** invocation, and a complete Relationship object, with roles designated, emerges from the other end:

```
struct NamedRole (Rolename name; Role aRole);
typedef sequence<NamedRole> NamedRoles;

interface RelationshipFactory {
    struct NamedRoleType {
        RoleName name;
        InterfaceDef named_role_type;
    }
    typedef sequence<NamedRoleType>
        NamedRoleTypes;
    readonly attribute InterfaceDef relationship_type;
    readonly attribute unsigned short degree;
    readonly attribute NamedRoleTypes named_role_types;
    exception ( . . . );

    Relationship create (
        in NamedRoles named_roles
        )
        raises (
            RoleTypeError,
            MaxCardinalityExceeded,
            DegreeError,
            DuplicateRoleName,
            UnknownRoleName
        )
}
```

Roles are handed to the Relationship Factory in the struct **NamedRole**, where each one has a name. The IDL sets this up, and then defines enough

readonly attributes so that a client can confirm all of the things he or she should already know about the factory—which relationship it creates, which role types it accepts, and so on.

Finally, we get to the **Relationship create** operation, which is just as advertised. Feed it the roles (with their names), and out comes a relationship.

Remember the **link** and **unlink** operations of our Role object? They're not for use by your clients. The **link** operation is intended only for use by **RelationshipFactory** objects during creation. Before it returns, the **RelationshipFactory** uses the **link** operation to inform the roles that they are now involved in a relationship. The Relationship object itself uses **unlink**, as described in the next few paragraphs.

Here's the IDL for the Relationship object we just created:

```
interface Relationship : IdentifiableObject {
    . . .
    readonly attribute NamedRoles named_roles;
    void destroy ( ) raises (CannotUnlink);
}
```

This is pretty simple. You can get back the sequence of **NamedRoles**, and you can try to destroy the relationship. From the **NamedRoles**, you can get to the related objects, so the chain is complete, at least as far as this relationship is concerned. The **destroy** operation will invoke **unlink** on the Role objects involved in the relationship. Remember that we still need the Node object to link relationships of a common related object, so we'll cover that next.

10.4.3   IDL for Graphs of Related Objects: The Node

Nodes are identifiable objects that support the **Node** interface. They collect roles of a related object and the related object itself. The Node object enables traversals of a graph of related objects by supporting:

- a readonly attribute, which returns all of its roles;
- an operation that returns all roles of a particular type; and
- operations to add and remove roles from its list.

There is also an attribute that returns the related object. This is not used in traversals, but is the essential connection to go from the results of the traversal to an actual operation on the related objects such as a **copy** or **move**.

The **node interface** can be used in two ways: An object that is "relationship-aware" can inherit the interface, or a separate node object can be instantiated and used as a proxy for the related object. We've gone over the advantages and disadvantages already; briefly, the first case ensures that every client that has a reference to the object also has the reference to the node, while the second case allows two things: involvement of immutable objects, and traversal of graphs without activating the objects themselves.

The Node object is created by a NodeFactory. Its IDL interface is straight-forward:

```
interface NodeFactory {
    Node create_node (
        in Object related_object
        )
}
```

As you might expect, the Related object is assigned at creation. There is only one type of Node object, so there is only one NodeFactory (unlike roles and relationships). This is logical; a node could conceivably participate in just about any relationship from just about any point of view, and we want to be able to represent this easily. For example, Robert may simultaneously be an employee of Objectified Software, Inc. (he works for the company), an owner of Objectified Software, Inc. (he owns stock in the company), and the owner of a 1988 Yugo (he owns the car). (Presumably, when he sells his stock in Objectified Software, Inc., he will be able to buy a better car.) Robert's Node object would collect all of these roles.

Here's a summary of the **Node** object's interface:

```
interface Node : IdentifiableObject {
    typedef sequence<role> Roles;
    exception ( . . .);

    readonly attribute RelatedObject related_object;
    readonly attribute Roles roles_of_node;
    Roles roles_of_type (
        in InterfaceDef role_type
        )
    void add_role (in Role a_role)
        raises (DuplicateRoleType);
    void remove_role (in InterfaceDef of_type)
        raises (NoSuchRole);
}
```

As promised, the **RelatedObject** and **Roles** are easily retrieved as **readonly attributes**, as are the roles of a particular type. These aren't actually roles of the same type; this is forbidden by the **DuplicateRoleType** exception of the **add_role** operation. But a node can have multiple roles with a common supertype, which would be returned by **roles_of_type**. This restriction guarantees that cardinality constraints, enforced at the Role level, cannot be inadvertently violated at the Node level instead.

10.4.4 Traversing a Graph of Related Objects

By enabling traversal of the graph of related objects via this interface, the Node object is the key to group operations. We're not going to cover traversal in detail here for two reasons: First, the traversal object will be provided as part of the Relationship Service, so you and your programmers won't be programming to its interfaces, and you'll receive a detailed explanation of how it works in your Relationship service documentation; and second, we believe that it's one step beyond the level of technical detail that most readers expect from this book. If you're really interested in programming to the traversal object interface, you should buy the CORBAservices specification from the OMG; see Appendix A for details.

This completes our discussion of the Lifecycle and Relationship services, including the Compound Lifecycle service, which operates on a graph of related objects. Now we know how to create, move, copy, and delete both individual and groups of related objects, and we also know how to start applying an arbitrary operation on a group of related objects. These are powerful concepts, and a good start to our exploration of the total capabilities of the OMA.

## CHAPTER 11

CORBAservices, Part 2: Persistent Object and Externalization Services

The OMA specifies rules about certain aspects of objects' behavior. This way, your client knows in advance what to expect from the remote objects on your network, even ones that were designed and written completely independently. You can think of this part of the OMA as a kind of "object etiquette"; if every object obeys it, interactions will proceed smoothly, and no one will be surprised by anything that happens. Perhaps the most important part of this prescribed interaction involves objects' persistent state.

The OMA says that every object's state (for objects that maintain internal state) must remain unchanged from one invocation to the next. Since CORBA allows an object reference to be stored during one session and retrieved during a later one, this means that state must be preserved even over these arbitrarily long intervals. If your client creates an object during a session, then your client can reasonably expect that the object will always reflect the state that you set in it unless either: **1.** you shared the object with other clients, for example by registering its object reference with the naming service or actually sending the object reference to another object in an operation; or **2.** a client holding a copy of the object reference has deleted the object. In the first case, the state of the object may be changed by any client holding the reference; in the second, references after the deletion will fail, and there is no such concept as persistent state for an object that no longer exists. If an object does not have internal state—that is, if all output depends only on the input parameters and not on the result of any previous invocation—this requirement does not apply, of course.

Persistence is a really simple concept, at least as far as the client is concerned. (Remember this sentence; 5 or 10 pages further on, you may no longer think of anything about the Persistent Object Service as "simple.") From the client's point of view, an object instance is *always* running and, therefore, *always* preserves its state. You don't have to start it up, or shut it down, or save it, or restore it; it's just *there*. From the client's point of view, this part of the OMA represents a *service*.

Now suppose you're the person *writing* the object implementation, instead of the one using it. (Okay, maybe you're writing it and using it both. Same difference.) What does this requirement for persistent state mean to you? It no longer represents a service; instead it represents an *obligation*: You must include, in your implementation, some way for your object to keep its state persistent over time from the moment it is created until the moment it is destroyed. And you have to do it by coding; remember that magic is not a part of the OMA specification!

Of course, there are a lot of different ways you can do this. The easiest, perhaps, is to just stay active in memory all the time. This may be an acceptable solution for objects that come and go quickly, or small objects that don't consume a lot of resource. But some objects occupy a lot of memory, or are expected to preserve state across sessions, shutdowns, or system crashes. For these, you need a way to preserve state on persistent storage.

But there are a lot of persistent storage methods around, and new ones have a tendency to show up from time to time. Relational databases and flat files are well established and enjoy widespread use. Record-oriented file systems augment the flat file model with additional features, and other systems, including object-oriented databases, fit into this scenario as well. In addition, some systems provide persistent storage as part of their paradigm and don't even have a syntax for specifying the operation, "store." (UNIX folks may find this hard to picture, but AS/400 users know what we're talking about.) Different objects will need different storage methods. Some will use a particular method because it fits the best out of the available choices; others may use a method because it was the only one available to the implementor when he or she was writing it. For instance, an employee object in a Human Resources object collection may store easily as either a row in a relational table or a record in a VSAM file, while a raster graphics object, which would choke on either of these alternatives, can slip naturally onto a flat file, at least on most systems.

But wait, there's more—or at least one more thing. For some objects, it's logical to allow clients to specify when they store and restore their state. When you edit a document or spreadsheet, for example, you assume you're editing a copy of the version on persistent storage. When you complete an edit that you like, you store to disk to preserve your work in case of a power glitch or application freeze-up. (At least we'll assume that you do, since we assume that all readers of this book are supremely knowledgeable computer users. We will also point out here that this part of preserving state, at least, could be automated.) When you complete an edit you don't like, on the other hand, you may request the application to revert your work copy to the previous stored version. We admit that this example is based on a semantic confusion of the distinct operations "store" (which could and should be fully automatic) and "checkpoint" (which requires some user input). But it at least points up the need for some client input into the **store** and **restore** operations of some object implementations, a need that must be taken into account in our Persistent Object Service.

The OMA provides the Persistent Object Service or POS the means by which to standardize this process, as much as it can. (We confess at this point to an unfortunate acronym collision. Through Chapter 17, POS stands for Persistent Object Service. After that, in the example chapters, it stands for point of sale as in POS terminal. Sorry! There weren't enough letters to go around, and besides we didn't get to pick either one of these.) It is the job of the POS to standardize an object's storage and retrieval of its persistent state:

- whether the storage is controlled automatically or explicitly by the client;
- whether control is over the state of a single object or a graph of related objects;
- regardless of which of a number of persistent storage methods is being used;
- over a wide range of granularities of storage operations and stored entities.

In the face of all of these alternatives, the POS still attempts to provide an object-oriented persistent object service with standard IDL interfaces. How well does it do? We'll leave the verdict to you and the rest of the market. We'll also point out that you don't have to use the POS; you can use any persistent storage method you choose. The POS should be available, in reasonably portable format, on just about every platform you run an ORB on, but some alternative methods, including object-oriented databases (OODBs), may make persistence nearly automatic. If one of these methods is available on all of the platforms you will port to, the POS won't have much more to offer you.

11.1 ARCHITECTURE OF THE POS

In order to provide flexibility and standardization with the same service, the architects divided the POS up in to a number of components, as shown in Figure 11.1. They are:

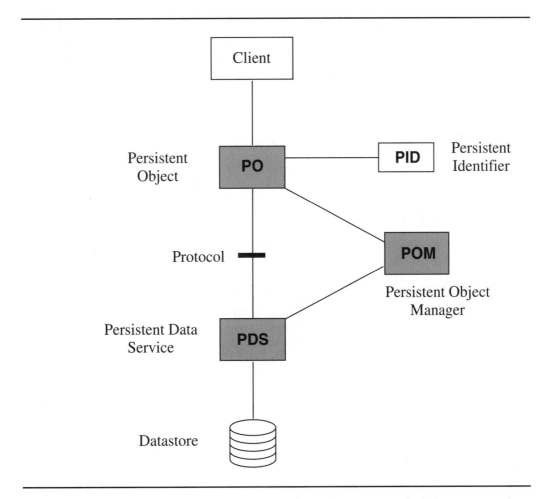

Figure 11.1. Components of the Persistent Object Service. Shaded components bear the five-operation interface described in the text for control of persistence via either **connect** or **store/restore**.

The Persistent Object: As we hinted earlier, some objects control their persistence themselves while others expose this function to their clients. The term "persistent object," abbreviated PO, refers to both types. An object supports client control of persistence by inheriting and implementing the PO interface, which we'll describe shortly.

The PID: Yet another identifier for our object. Sure to be confused with the object reference, the PID or Persistent Identifier actually identifies the PO's state data within the persistent storage. Like the Object Reference, the PID can be stringified for storage and used in a later session. Unlike the Object Reference, the PID cannot be used as a target for an invocation; it can only be used in the context of the POS.

The Client: If the PO inherits and implements the PO interface, then the client may play a role in the working of the POS. We'll show how in this chapter.

The Persistent Object Manager: This is where the decisions get made. It looks simple in Figure 11.1, but in reality we have multiple PDSs, datastores, and protocols. The Persistent Object Manager or POM gets to sort all this out, as we'll show soon.

The Persistent Data Service and the Protocol: The Persistent Data Service or PDS is the component that implements the Protocol interface and coordinates the actual persistence operations.

The Datastore: This may be as simple as a flat file, or as complicated as a database (possibly incorporating transactional semantics). Since many datastores are passive, the datastore needs a PDS to initiate storage and retrieval operations.

To keep things simple in spite of having so many components, the POS uses the same set of operations (with almost the same set of parameters) for the PO, POM, and PDS interfaces. The set of operations follows:

11.1.1   Controlling Persistence

The POS provides two alternative ways to control an object's persistence: Connection, and Store/Restore.

- **Connection** establishes a relationship between the object's dynamic state data and its persistent data. While the connection is established, the data may be viewed as the same; after the connection is ended, the persistent data keep the values they had upon disconnection. Connection operations are **connect** and **disconnect**.
- **Store/Restore** allows client or object control of data movement between persistent storage and dynamic use. Its operations are, logically enough, **store** and **restore**.

There is also a **delete** method, which deletes the PID. As shown by shading in Figure 11.1, this five-operation interface is borne by the Persistent object as **interface PO**; the POM as **interface POM**; and the PDS as **interface PDS**. This enables implementations of the POS to be simpler than the multi-component structure suggests, since the request that starts out at the client may simply be passed through the PO to the POM, which actually does the work to initiate the persistent storage.

11.2 POS EXAMPLE

To see how this works, let's follow the steps as a client asks the POS to store a simple document object. We've purposely avoided the complications of storing a compound document using the Relationship Service to join its components; although this is a good combined use of the two services, it would get in the way of our description of persistence if we tried it on the first go-around here.

We'll presume that our client object already has the PID of the document. We may have used it to retrieve the previously stored version, or perhaps just created the PID using the PID factory object, or stored the PID in the Naming Service along with the document object reference. CORBA provides a number of ways to do this, depending on how we go about it and where we are in our document editing process.

Our document object, when it was written, inherited the PO interface so we can invoke **store** from our client. The document is the target of the operation, and the document's PID is the only parameter.

The PO, in turn, invokes **store** on the Persistent Object Manager. The operation has an additional parameter:

void store (in Object obj, in PID p);

The document inserts its own object reference as the first parameter. This will be passed through to the PDS, which needs to know which object to store. But first the POM has some preparation to do.

The POM gets the **datastore_type** attribute from the PID. For the next step, the POM needs to know which PDS and protocol combination to use. This isn't standardized yet, so the POM will have to use nonstandard operations (presumably implemented in OMG IDL) to find out which protocol(s) and PDS(s) our document PO can work with. This means that POs may work with only one or a few versions of POM, at least until the OMG comes up with a revised and more specific version of the POS. The OMG members who wrote the standard knew that you would want this more specific version now, but felt strongly (and say so in the specification) that it was way too early to fix this, due to lack of commercial experience in producing robust, flexible persistent object service. We expect this to get fixed quickly, although "quickly" may be a year or more in this arena. In the meantime, see your supplier's documentation for this step.

So, using the vendor-supplied methods, the POM finds the PDS and protocol that go with our object type (document) and its PID. It then invokes the **store** operation on the PDS, which will actually do the work. Remember, there are lots of PDSs around; it was the POM that determined which one we needed and retrieved its object reference so the **store** operation could be targeted correctly. The **store** operation includes the PO's object reference here as well:

void store (in Object obj, in PID p);

The PO and the PDS share a **protocol**. There are a number of established protocols, and one of the jobs of the POM is to select a PDS that shares a protocol with the PO we're working with. Using the protocol, the PDS requests the PO to send its data. The PDS accepts the data and routes it to the persistent storage medium, whatever it happens to be.

11.3 PROTOCOLS

The POS describes three specific protocols, admitting that many others are possible. We'll describe those three here, briefly, and finish up with a list of other protocols that might be implemented.

11.3.1 The Direct Access Protocol

The most direct way to set and get values associated with an object is through attributes. The Direct Access or DA protocol builds on this, providing a way for the programmer to create a data object in the PDS whose attributes are maintained persistent by the service. The specification is admirably complete, including DA-specific interfaces for the PID, PO, PDS, and protocol. We admit that the specification marks some interfaces as optional, allowing certain systems to implement the service in a more natural way.

Using the DA protocol, you set and get attributes on your persistent object in the normal way using IDL operations; the difference is that the service maintains the values persistent. The use of an established IDL paradigm makes the service almost as easy to use as it is to explain.

Extensions to the specification allow dynamic access to persistent attributes, and allow clustering of data objects for group operations.

11.3.2 The ODMG-93 Protocol

The ODMG-93 protocol builds on the Object Database Management Group's 1993 specification for object databases (see the reference in Appendix A). It's a superset of the DA protocol; if you're already using (or contemplate using) an OODB that conforms to ODMG-93, then you can benefit from using this protocol, since your data will pass straight through the PDS to the datastore with no conversion taking place.

We won't dwell on the ODMG-93 protocol in this book since the ODMG folks are already hard at work explaining and popularizing their work and its benefits. There are pointers to references in Appendix A; follow them up for details.

11.3.3 The Dynamic Data Object Protocol

The Dynamic Data Object or DDO protocol is a datastore-neutral representation of an object's persistent data. Using the DDO, you can refer to all of the persistent data for an object with a single PID. This is handy if you have a number of data items to store and retrieve together; less so if you have a single large item such as a bitmap or whatever.

11.3.4 Other Protocols

Some protocols are "already defined" and well established; all we need to do is point out here that they're available. POSIX files are the best example; the protocol consists of file read and write operations.

Specialized protocols can take advantage of particular environments. For example, a service could effectively create a single-level store (that is, values that you set and get are automatically persistent) in a LISP environment, or on a specialized machine like the AS/400.

11.4 DATASTORES

There's only one component we haven't covered—the datastore. A number of datastore interfaces can be defined; others do not need to be defined because they correspond to protocols. For example, if your datastore is an ODMG database and your object uses the ODMG-93 protocol, the PDS does not need to do any reformatting of the data that can pass through it and go directly into the OODB.

The POS defines the DS_CLI module with its collection of IDL interfaces primarily to standardize the storage layer used with the DDO PDS. CLI stands for Call Level Interface; in full, it is referred to as the X/Open Data Management Call Level Interface, an X/Open standard designed for record database and file systems. It works well with, for example, relational databases and VSAM file systems that support user sessions, connections, transactions, and scanning using cursors.

This interface is standardized for the benefit of companies that either implement the POS themselves, or provide a datastore that can be used by another vendor's POS. This means that we don't need to cover it in detail here. As a user and architect, you just need to remember that the POS can use relational tables or VSAM files as one of its storage options, so if this alternative fits your data, look for this component in the POS implementation that you get from your vendor.

11.5   THE EXTERNALIZATION SERVICE

Externalization has similarities with so many of the other CORBAservices that it's kind of hard to explain, but here we go anyhow. The Externalization Service (ES) defines interfaces, protocols, and conventions for recording and playing back an object's state as a standardized stream of data that can be either captured on a suitable recording medium or sent over the network.

Externalization is like persistence, because the state is permanently recorded. Unlike the POS, however, the ES does not provide a mode where changes to individual variables in an object are immediately made persistent. Since this would require a full recording of the object's state for every small change to any component, the ES is a poor general substitute for the POS.

Externalization is like a move or a copy, in that an object's state is externalized at one location and internalized at another, remote location. Three significant differences are: first, there's no way to specify the destination when you initiate the operation (**move** and **copy** are single operations; the ES uses the pair **externalize** and **internalize**); second, with the ES, it is possible to internalize at a location not connected to the original via any network; and third, the internalization may be delayed by any length of time, unlike a copy that is presumed to take place at the speed of light. (The next time your overloaded network takes an hour to move your report from your workstation to your boss's laptop, think of this sentence . . . .)

The ES uses the Relationship Service to externalize groups of related objects, and ES operations on compound (that is, related) objects purposely resemble their lifecycle counterparts. The service is built on a **Stream** object. There are three views of externalization, each with its own interface standardized by the service. They are the client's view, the externalized object's view, and the stream's view.

The client always invokes operations on the **Stream** object; never on the object being externalized or internalized. On externalization, the stream records the object's type. On internalization, the **Stream** object reads the type from the recording and invokes a factory object for that type to create an uninitialized instance, which then accepts the rest of the stream data. There is also a way to internalize state to a previously created object.

This means that, in order to be externalizable and internalizable, an object type must inherit and support the following interfaces, which are invoked by the **Stream** object:

- the Lifecycle Service (and must have a factory available to the **Stream** object);
- the **identifiable object** interface of the Relationship service; and
- the **streamable** interface, and the **StreamIO** interface, which it invokes on the stream object.

This is an example of good architecture: instead of reinventing interfaces and operations, the ES builds on CORBAservices that were already defined. This makes the ES specification easier to understand because it builds on things we already know, quicker to implement because common components don't have to be recoded, and shorter to document because references are shorter than text.

When you purchase an implementation of the ES, you get Stream, StreamFactory, and StreamIO object implementations from your vendor. (There is some "service" in the CORBAservices after all!) There will probably be many Stream and StreamIO instances in your system, since each represents a particular external representation of an object or group of related objects. If you are also building externalizable objects, you will have to inherit several interfaces and build implementations into your code. We'll go over these interfaces soon.

11.5.1 Stream Format

There is a standard stream format, which makes it possible to externalize an object on one system and know for sure that you can internalize on *any* other system that can run your object type. It also makes it possible to wait for a long time while your system byte-swaps data needlessly if you specify standard format on the wrong system when you don't really need it. So you're better off if you understand something about the standard format and when to use it.

The standard format specifies a set of storage formats for basic data-types. For integers, the standard is big-endian format; for floats it's IEEE 754 format in either single or double precision depending on the data. If your machine uses these formats for its native representation, go ahead and specify standard format for all of your externalizations because it won't cost you anything—you're already there so no translation will be performed.

If your machine is little-endian or uses non-IEEE floats, and you're sure you will *only* want to internalize on your same machine type, you can save some time by allowing externalization to use your native format, especially if your object is huge. Full-screen bitmaps and large binary datasets fit this description; if you're only externalizing a couple of bytes of personnel data or an 80-character string, then you might as well use standard format because the delay will not be noticeable. (This remark does not apply if you're externalizing a billion small objects at once!)

Remember that use of native format means you *cannot* internalize on a machine with a different byte order or floating point format; if you're internalizing on a different machine, then you need to use standard format and pay the price to byte-swap here. To specify standard format, you put the string literal **StandardExternalizationFormat** into the **NameComponent::id** of its key. Since the key is a name, we'll talk more about how to do this under the Naming Service in Chapter 12.

11.5.2 Externalization Interfaces

In this section we'll go over the first two steps of externalization, including the client's initialization step and the target's connection to the **Stream** object.

There are two **StreamFactory** interfaces. A simple factory interface specifies no details about the **Stream** object:

```
interface StreamFactory {
    Stream create();
}
```

while an alternative form lets you specify a file to receive the stream output:

```
interface FileStreamFactory {
    Stream create (
        in string theFileName)
        raises ( InvalidFileNameError);
}
```

Additional characteristics of **Stream** objects will be system-dependent: common targets for externalization will include floppy disks, various tape formats typically including cartridges of different sizes and types, network devices, and more. Interfaces for these **StreamFactory** objects can easily be constructed by inheriting from the basic standard interfaces. These extensions are not standardized yet; there are too many, and it is too early to make this practical. Watch for the market to settle on standard formats for common target devices on popular operating systems, and for the OMG to bless these invocations a year or three down the road.

The **Stream** object you create with one of these invocations becomes the target of your externalize request. The reference of the object you want to externalize is the input parameter:

void externalize (in Streamable theObject);

Note that the argument type is not **Object**; it's **Streamable**, which is a sub-type. Remember, in order to be externalizable, the target object had to inherit the **Streamable** interface and implement its functions. This means that every externalizable object is of type **Streamable**, so the standard invocation makes sure that we can only attempt externalization on objects that are ready for us.

The first thing **externalize** does is write enough implementation-dependent information to the record to enable it to re-create the object and internalize its state later. Then the stream object invokes **externalize_to_stream** on the target object. Here's how that works.

The **Streamable** interface is inherited and implemented by externalizable objects, and includes the operations invoked by the **Stream** object that trigger externalization and internalization. If you're building a externalizable object, you need to inherit this interface and build this behavior in. The **Stream** object, which you buy, expects your object to support this in order to be externalizable:

```
interface Streamable::IdentifiableObject {
    readonly attribute Key external_form_id;
    void externalize_to_stream (
        in StreamIO targetStreamIO);
    void internalize_from_stream (
        in StreamIO SourceStreamIO,
        in FactoryFinder there)
        raises ( . . .);
}
```

The **Streamable** object inherits from **IdentifiableObject** in order to support externalization of groups of related objects. We're not going to cover externalization of groups in any more detail in this book; for more information, check the documentation that comes with your CORBAservices product or buy the specification from the OMG.

The **externalize_to_stream** invocation is your object's cue to output all of its state to the stream by making calls on the **StreamIO** object it received as a parameter. We're not going to cover the **StreamIO** interface in detail; it defines separate read and write operations for each primitive OMG IDL datatype. When you're done, you call **flush** to ensure that all data get written to the medium on your external device.

internalize_from_stream works basically the same way, in reverse. The standard invocation creates an uninitialized instance of the object using its factory as a first step, and internalizes the state next. An alternative invocation uses an existing object instance as the target.

This concludes our discussion of persistence and externalization. Using only services covered so far, we can create, move, copy, and delete both single objects and groups of related objects. We can do this in a single step over the network using the Lifecycle Service, and in two steps without a network using externalization. This not only helps us get a lot of our own work done, it also lets us share it with others using standardized operations and interfaces. And, the services covered so far also illustrate the way objects and interfaces can work together to extend each others' capabilities. Pay attention to the way the interfaces use inheritance, and how the objects and services use each other, to maximize the contribution of each component and minimize the number of distinct interfaces and lines of code. Try to model your own applications using the best points you can learn from these services and the rest yet to come.

## CHAPTER 12

CORBAservices, Part 3: Naming and Trader Services

If your boss challenged you to sum up, in one word, what makes distributed object systems unique and worthwhile, you might say *sharing*. It's the sharing of information, resource, and analysis that brings about the synergy that magnifies the efforts of the people who work together, leveraging your investment in both technology and people, and creating value for the enterprise.

And, if sharing is the key concept in distributed object systems, then this chapter is the key to the entire book because the two services described here, Naming and Trader, are the components that open up the environment to sharing.

Naming is so basic that it's the service mentioned first in the Initialization Service: as soon as a client connects to the ORB, it can invoke a standard call to retrieve the object reference for the Naming Service, because from that it can get references to objects to do anything else that's available on the system. This makes the Naming Service the one place that everyone knows how to get to, which makes it a great place for objects to meet.

But the Naming Service, for all of its basic virtues, is limited in what it can do. You can associate a name, or a hierarchy of names, with an object reference, but you can't store extra information such as syntax or specifications for what the object does, how much it costs to run, the room where you pick up the output from the printer object (or, perhaps, the *city* where you pick up the output from the printer object!). To do this, you need the

Trader. Trader is like an electronic combination of a mail order catalog and the Yellow Pages, where you can look up any service you want, from every provider available. When you find one you like, Trader gives you the object reference and away you go. (Where do you get the object reference for the Trader? From the Naming Service, of course! So it's important for the Trader object to go by a well-known name.)

Here's our prediction. (It's dangerous to predict in a book like this; someone might take out a copy a few years down the road, check things out, and point out to the world whether we were right or wrong. But we'll go ahead anyhow.) For the next few years of distributed object computing, most clients will rely on the Naming service to find their objects, and use static IDL stubs to access them. This environment is a lot more open than one without distributed objects because an application may spread out over the entire network, but it is not completely free because each client is limited to the predetermined set of objects bound with static IDL stubs. But, gradually (and this has already started at some lucky advanced sites), a new generation of clients will be delivered to the market that will be more dynamic: Clients will access the Trader service to let users find new object-implemented services, and these objects will be accessible from those clients immediately via the DII. Applications will be assembled and modified on-the-fly by end users to take advantage of new objects, which they find by browsing the Trader, and utilize by accessing via these DII-enabled clients. This paradigm switch will require a maturation of both client and user, but the enterprise that adopts it early will have a significant advantage in processing power. After the first few popular applications demonstrate the power of dynamic object discovery typing and binding, there will be a mad rush by everyone else to catch up, or at least not to be left out.

The Trader Service is so crucial to the dynamic environment that we've included it in this chapter even though its standard has yet to be fixed by the OMG. In Section 12.3, we review key parts of the ISO Trader Standard, which is the requirements section of the OMG Trader RFP, and speculate on what kind of environment might result.

But first we discuss the Naming Service, starting in the next section.

By the way: If the Naming Service is so important, why didn't we use it in the worked example in the second half of this book? It's so new, most of the ORBs didn't have working services at the time we wrote the code. But we needed one, so we wrote a pseudo-name service and everyone used that, including the ORB vendors who actually had a working service, so that all of the implementations would be the same in this respect. After you get the example working with the pseudo-name service, do an exercise to convert it over to the real service when your ORB vendor provides one (which might be today). This will get you started coding on your own, and accomplish something useful, in the same exercise.

12.1 ACCESSING NAMES

The IDL API, which we present in Section 12.2, is a mighty dry way of looking at the Naming Service (which we will abbreviate NS). If this book were only for programmers, then it would be the only one we'd present (like the CORBAservices specification published by OMG); however, this book is for both programmers and users—anyone who wants to benefit from distributed objects—so it's fitting to present here a few alternative and more reasonable ways of looking at the Naming Service.

Users will access names either as icons or via browsers, or through the clients they run that utilize the NS under the covers as they play traffic cop for all of the objects they invoke. Users will drag and drop icons representing objects, activating or linking objects with mouse clicks in the next few years and (hopefully) something more sophisticated like voice commands in the years to come.

The important thing about the NS isn't how its IDL works; it's that the NS *enables* these browsers and icons that make objects directly accessible to the user, and simultaneously give the client and object programmer a means to pass object references around the enterprise. NS interoperability is the key to success here, because objects in one domain will have to resolve names of objects in other domains in order to invoke operations on them. So the OMG NS specification allows services to *federate*, or share, their name databases so that all of the objects in remote name services can appear in results returned by your name service. If you're an end user or an architect, and you realize that names and object references will be provided all over your enterprise (and beyond, if you want) by the NS, and that browsers and icons will make NS queries and display the results, then you can skip all of the IDL and go straight to Trader in Section 12.3.

12.2 REPRESENTING NAMES

A wag once said, "One good thing about standards is there are so many to choose from!" He was probably talking about naming standards. Every operating system has a naming convention for its file system, and there are other naming systems (X.500, for example) besides. In UNIX, we have a hierarchy separated by slashes, with name components separated by dots; names can be almost as long as you want, and no spaces allowed. In DOS and Windows (pre Windows-95, anyhow), components are separated by backslashes, length is "8 dot 3" characters, and no spaces are allowed. X.500 establishes a "flat" namespace (more or less), with named components instead of a hierarchy; components are separated by commas, and spaces *are* allowed. Yikes!

The folks at OMG know that enough is enough, and wisely declined the opportunity to establish yet another naming convention. Instead, the

Naming Service is designed around a syntax-independent, in-memory hierarchical name structure that can be used with *any* of the established naming conventions, including the ones we named and many, many more besides. The NS delivers the multilevel name structure to the requesting client, which is responsible for putting in the separating slashes, or backslashes, or whatever, before displaying the compound name in a browser. It would be easy to write an object that converts a NS name struct into a displayable string; you may get one from your NS provider even though it's not part of the standard service.

Here's the IDL for a name in the service. **Istring** is a placeholder for a future internationalized IDL string type:

```
typedef string Istring
struct NameComponent {
    Istring id;
    Istring kind;
};

typedef sequence <NameComponent> Name;
```

So, a **Name** is a sequence of **NameComponents**. All but the last component are bound to Naming Contexts (described in the next paragraph); the last one is bound to an object reference. If the sequence has more than one component (the only interesting case) then it is termed a *compound name*; you can pass a compound name to the service anywhere a name is called for, and the service will resolve all of the levels automatically.

Don't let Naming Context throw you. If we were only naming files, we could use the words directory and subdirectory here and you'd know what's going on. A Naming Context is basically a directory for objects. By the way, the Naming Context is an object and it has a name; the name is bound to the object by the service in the same way any other name is bound. There's nothing special about the name of a naming context; the difference is in the type of object it's bound to.

You bind a name to an object using this IDL:

```
void bind (in Name n, in Object obj);
```

This operation establishes a correspondence in the NS between the **Name n** and the **Object obj**. If you pass in a compound name, then all components except the last are resolved before the last one is bound to the object. This means that each call to bind can bind only one component of a compound name. If you have a five-component compound name, and none of the components has been bound, you'll make five calls before you're done. But this won't happen often; mostly you'll be adding components one or a few layers at a time, so you'll only have to make one call per new name.

There's a special operation to bind a name to a Naming Context so that it can be resolved by the service:

void bind_context (in Name n, in NamingContext nc);

The **resolve** operation retrieves the object reference that we—or, more likely, someone else—bound to the name with a prior **bind**. If we pass in a compound name, it must match the bound name exactly in order for the operation to succeed:

Object resolve (in name n);

There are a few more operations in the standard: **rebind**, **rebind_context**, **unbind**; create a new context with **new_context** or create and bind in one operation with **bind_new_context**. These complete the programmer's tool chest. We won't cover them in this book; when you need them, see the documentation that came with your NS software product.

12.3 TRADER SERVICE

Telephone books provide us with a good analogy for the Naming and Trader services. When you know whom you want to call, you use the White Pages and look the person or company up by name: Peter Smith on Elm Street, or The Cracker Barrel on Route 117. But if you just know that you want a store that sells dishwashers, the White Pages aren't much help because they list by name, and you want to search by category. Fortunately, there is a category listing of telephone customers called the Yellow Pages; you'll find most of the stores that sell dishwashers listed together under Appliances (sorry, not under dishwashers). Add a mail order catalog to the Yellow Pages and you have, in concept at least, the Object Trader Service. Since the basis for the Trader requirements document is an ISO standard written by a committee that works very closely with the OMG, we can make some educated predictions about what the final specification might look like. But, because no specification is fixed until the final vote by the OMG members, we advise you to wait for the actual OMG specification before you do your final coding.

The Trader Service will let you go "object shopping" on-line. As we've already pointed out, if you combine the Trader Service with a DII client you can invoke an object you like as soon as you discover it. Without the DII, when you discover an object you want to try out, you'll have to access it through a client that has its interface in a stub. This means either reprogramming the client you're using, or buying (or writing, or whatever) a client with the interface and stub programmed and linked in. Since the premise of distributed objects is that end users will be able to get their work done without programming, we're definitely plugging for the DII environment, at least eventually. (There is one way you can take advantage of Trader without the DII: you may use the Trader to discover an alternate provider of the *same* service you're already using, with the same interface. You could easily switch a client at run time to invoke an operation onto a different target instance that implements the same interface.)

12.3.1 Accessing the Trader Service

As with the Naming Service, we don't want to give the impression here that everyone will need to program to the Trader API in order to use the service. Most users will access the Trader through a browser, and never look at the API. Since the browsers will be objects that you will buy, you probably won't use the API yourself even if you're a programmer. You'll just invoke an operation to display the browser on your user's screen, and the browser will return the object reference of the selected server when the user clicks the OK button.

So users will probably get their Trader results back in some visual object—an icon, usually, or an indication that the selected service provider object has been accessed. Drag and drop or clicking in these primitive times, presumably to be replaced by voice or gesture command later, is a lot easier for regular folks to access Trader than by coding to the API in IDL and some mapped programming language such as C++.

12.3.2 How the Trader Will Work

From the requirements listed in the OMG Trader RFP, we can make some predictions about how the Trader Service will work. Server objects will register *service offers* with their local trader. The ISO standard calls this operation *export*. Along with their object reference, they will register various pieces of information about what they do, how and where they do it, how much it costs, where to pick up output, and so on, termed *offer properties*. Don't look to the ISO standard for an official "property list"; it only standardizes the general framework for the service and leaves the particulars—including what's actually on this list—to the implementors. On the one hand, this is fitting because different trading domains will need different lists, and the expertise to draw up the list lives in the domains. On the other hand, without consensus about what's on the list, you don't know what to ask the Trader for, and a severe mismatch can render the Trader nearly useless. We think that the Trader property list needs some time to evolve, especially for widely used domains like the Internet, and that neither ISO nor OMG is the place for this to happen. Watch for this to be standardized by convention, rather than by explicit action by some standards body.

Since a Trader listing is very different from an object reference, it's okay for an object to list information such as its location and machine type here. This may be important to the user (who may want to run his or her linear regression on a turbo-cooled Mach 16 quad-processor Octavium Super-Server, or whatever). We kept location and platform information out of our applications when we designed and wrote them, but now that it's time to run them, this information is rightly very important to us! In fact, one reason we have the freedom to execute or access objects wherever we want at run time is because we kept these dependencies out of them during implementation.

The Trader, if it follows the ISO standard, will store service and offer properties, and search its database for you based on matching criteria and preference criteria that you specify for each request. Search results will meet all of the matching criteria, and be ranked according to how well they met the preference criteria. This makes it easy for a browser to let you specify what you require in some fields, and what you want in others, and display the results in (more or less) the order that you're interested in, since this corresponds to a basic Trader function that will be provided by every standard implementation.

Traders may *federate* all, or some, of the offers they contain. That is, they may combine their information so that a client inquiring of any one of a set of linked traders has access to the offers contained in all of them. Not necessarily all of the offers, however; servers may place limits on how far away their offer may be extended when they register with the Trader. They may also modify these limits, or other characteristics of their offer, anytime they want.

That's about all we can say about Trader until it becomes an official OMG specification. We hope that this presentation has made you excited about the possibilities, and anxious to see the specification and the Trader software objects that implement it.

## CHAPTER 13

CORBAservices, Part 4: Event Service

CORBA object invocations are just what we need when a client wants to invoke an operation on an object it knows about, but sometimes we need communication that just doesn't fit this model. Here's an example that we see in object linking and embedding: Say we've got a spreadsheet cell that contains this year's after-tax profit. This is a pretty important number, so it's referenced in many places: for example, it's printed in the table of financial results in a report to the board of directors, it appears as a bar in a graph in the annual report, it's used in an HR report on company contributions to the health insurance plan, and in a confidential memo that has something to do with union negotiations.

One more thing: the accounting isn't final, so the number is going to change. Of course, every object that uses the value wants to be notified if it changes, and the cell itself doesn't know (or care) where these objects are or what they're doing. Its value is an attribute, which the other objects fetch when they need it.

It turns out that this is an example of a general problem: Objects will need to be notified when something happens to another object. Typically, more than one object will need to be notified, and the list of interested objects may change any time. The object that originates the notification is probably a sophisticated object in its own right, and it's not appropriate for us to burden it with responsibility for the complex list maintenance and multiple invocations required by event handling. But the semantics of notification differ enough from CORBA invocation that the ORB is not a suitable candidate for the job, either.

The communication semantics we need are provided by the Event service (ES), which we cover in this chapter. But before we do, we'll briefly touch on a few other communication semantics that may be provided in future object services, or may be available from other sources.

13.1 COMMUNICATION SEMANTICS

The ORB gives us three distinct communication semantics. The most basic is *synchronous* invocation: the sender specifies the receiver; the message is transmitted without delay; the sender waits for the reply (thus the term "synchronous"), which is required; and the message is known to be successfully sent when the reply is received. SII invocations can be declared "oneway" which renders them *asynchronous*. CORBA specifies that oneway invocations are processed by the ORB and network as "best effort"; transmission is *not* guaranteed, and no error is returned even if the effort fails. More interesting are the *deferred-synchronous* modes of the DII, which allow the sender to continue processing while its remote invocations are serviced elsewhere.

By the way, one important characteristic of an invocation is that it is transmitted *at-most-once*. Some operations are *idempotent*: the end state is the same no matter how many times they are sent and executed; for example, "delete the file *myletter.doc*," or "set *count* equal to *35*." Others are definitely *not* idempotent; for example "subtract $10 from my bank account balance." In some systems (but not CORBA), *all* operations are required to be idempotent. This is handy in distributed systems, since you can send another copy of a command if you're not sure that the first got through. If a system is not idempotent, a good semantic (specified by CORBA for *every* invocation) is *at-most-once*, as you can tell from the bank balance example.

For all ORB communications, regardless of mode, three conditions always hold:

- The sender always selects the receiver.
- There is always a single receiver.
- There is no queue; if the receiver is not available, the communication attempt fails.

But what about communication semantics where one or more of these conditions does not hold?

By turning off one or two of these conditions, we define additional communication semantics that are useful under certain circumstances. Even more interesting, some of these can be implemented using CORBA as the basic transport, so we can define them as CORBAservices.

If we turn off the first two, we get OMG's Event Service. (In fact, some modes of the Event Service turn off the third condition as well.) Interested recipients register their interest in receiving events, and the sender has no way of finding out where the events are going; multiple receivers may independently register to receive notification of the same event; and in "pull" mode, the event waits in a queue for the recipient to notify the service that it is ready.

If we turn off the third condition, we get messaging semantics. Like CORBA, the sender knows the recipient, and the relationship is one-to-one, but the queuing behavior is different: a messaging service delivers every message to its target's *message queue* where it waits to be retrieved. Delivery to the queue is "guaranteed." (That is, a minimum quality-of-service level is specified. Purists will argue, plausibly, that it is not possible to truly guarantee delivery.) Objects retrieve their messages at their leisure, but every message is guaranteed, subject to whatever constraints, to be placed on the queue. You can think of messaging as "email for objects." OMG is considering a messaging service specification, but there was no official schedule when this book was written. You can check the OMG Web page for recent developments.

The final semantic we'll discuss is broadcast. In all of the previous three cases, messages were addressed to the specific recipient. In broadcast, a message is sent to a group of objects, and each one decides for itself whether it's interested in the contents. The semantic doesn't distinguish whether each object intercepts the same copy of the message, or a separate copy is sent to each recipient; from the point of view of the objects, these two cases are the same (although, from the point of view of your network administrator, they are definitely *not* the same!). If you're really sending the same copy to every object, broadcast is useful because it decreases network traffic. Diskless workstations use broadcast messages for another reason: they don't know who the recipient is! They broadcast a "boot me" message containing their workstation ID; their server responds to it while all of the other workstations ignore it. We are not aware of any immediate plans in OMG to standardize a service based on broadcast, but we could think of a couple of uses for it, especially for some really popular Web sites and Web events.

So the real significance of the ES is that it lets CORBA handle situations that require decoupled communication semantics in a natural way, applying them to linking, embedding, and similar situations. The message service, should it be adopted by OMG, will extend the semantics even further. Broadcast semantics are farther out in the future, since there are no plans for them at present, but we can see eventual consideration for such a service, which may be well used to disseminate popular information over highly populated media such as the Internet.

13.2 EVENT SERVICE ARCHITECTURE

The Event Service standard uses inheritance to build up from the simplest case of two objects trading events, through an event channel that decouples the interactions, and finally to a typed event channel that translates the generic **any** event data into your specific datatype before delivery. There are so many options that we can't possibly cover them all here (otherwise this would turn into the Event Service book). We'll cover the event channel, which is the simplest part of the service that is truly useful, and we'll briefly discuss the impact of typed event channels on your architecture, but we will not present their IDL interfaces or programming details.

The Event Service supports several options at each end of the event channel. The object that supplies the event is called the *supplier* (no surprise here); the objects that receive the event are called the *consumers*.

The event channel object decouples communication between suppliers and consumers. To suppliers, it is a consumer; to consumers, it is a supplier. It accepts connections from one or many suppliers, and one or many consumers, as shown in Figure 13.1. An event received from any one of the suppliers is transmitted to every consumer. You can have as many event channel objects as you want, each working independently of the others. This keeps objects from being interrupted by events that don't concern them. Events include a piece of data, type **any**, so you can inform the receiver of the reason for the event. Since the **any** could be a struct or string, for instance, you can send a lot of information; but remember, there's usually a price to be paid in performance for large data transfers so you don't want to be too casual about sending large structs around with your events unless you're working with a department of desktop Crays connected with fiber links. Well, you know what we mean.

The ES supports both a *push* model and a *pull* model for events independently *at both ends* of the channel. A push supplier sends an event to the channel whenever it wants by invoking a **push** operation; the channel must accept it. A pull supplier supports a **pull** *server* interface; the channel plays the role of client and solicits an event at the channel's discretion. (When,

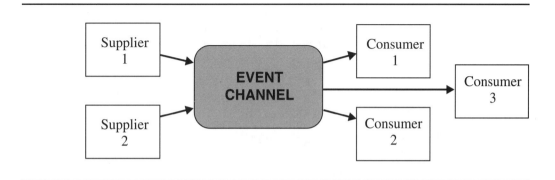

Figure 13.1. An event channel with multiple suppliers and consumers.

exactly? Perhaps when it receives a pull from a client at the far end of the channel, or at timed intervals. The service specification does not fix this.) At the consumer end, a push consumer supports the **push** server interface which is invoked by the channel client, while a pull consumer invokes the **pull** operation on the channel that responds with the event if there is one on the queue. The pull operation comes in two flavors: **pull** blocks until an event is received, while **try_pull** returns immediately with a **boolean** that tells whether an event was returned.

One interesting architectural aspect of this channel definition is the store-and-deliver behavior. The channel is obligated to store an event for some length of time if the supplier is using **push** mode and at least one consumer is using **pull**. If this were a true messaging service, there would be an explicit requirement for how long the message had to be maintained on the queue: "forever" (which would actually be determined by some administrative tool, we imagine). But it's not, and there is no required length of time for event storage before the channel is allowed to remove the event from the queue. The service specification allows the implementer to define the performance limits of the function under the umbrella of "quality of service." As a result, one compliant implementation of the service may deliver events only to objects that are connected and registered when the events come in, while another compliant implementation may store events for a week, delivering the entire queue to any new object that registers before the queue is purged.

So, in order to make successful use of the Event Service, keep in mind that it is only intended to be an event service and not a messaging service under a pseudonym. Don't push the storage time and capacity limits of the queue, unless your service provider tells you in the documentation that it's okay. And, if you do, don't expect your implementation to port to every other platform because another event service may not have interpreted the specification as liberally as yours.

Queue storage time and capacity are not the only aspects of quality of service that are of concern to the Event Service. Central to its serviceability are both speed of delivery and capacity, as measured in, for example, total events per second per channel or per ORB. In an actual installation, these performance benchmarks will vary with a number of factors including hardware configuration and loading, process prioritization, and software characteristics. Requirements will vary as well: If you are updating a document that prints overnight, delays of a few hundred milliseconds during editing will not concern you most of the time. (They might, if they occur just before printing!) But if you are adjusting the rudder of a guided missile during flight, you will probably consider these delays unacceptable. To OMG, these quality-of-service factors are implementation details to be worked out between supplier and consumer. There is some good justification for this: While you're specifying your real-time operating system, low-latency network, high-performance CPUs, and prioritizing job scheduler, you can probably remember to specify an event service with the performance characteristics you need without OMG having to write these characteristics into a specification.

With all of these variables affecting quality of service, does it belong in the interface definition? Some people still think it does, at least as an optional parameter or attribute that could be used where the environment supports it. This sophisticated market will probably produce examples of the ES extended to support quality-of-service selection or monitoring. If they prove useful, OMG may standardize them in a later version of the CORBAservices.

13.3   EVENT SERVICE INTERFACES

We're going to go over an example of an event channel with a single push-supplier object and two consumer objects, one in **push** mode and the other in **pull**. This will accomplish two things: First, it will fill in some details for readers who plan to program with the ES, and second, it will clarify the concepts of push, pull, and channel, even for those who never plan to program but still want to be clear on what's going on.

First let's go over what happens as an event is transmitted from the supplier to both consumers. This is diagrammed in Figure 13.2. Here are the steps:

A. First, the supplier object sends the event to the channel object. Here, the supplier object is the client, and invokes the **push** operation on the channel that is the server.

When the same event is being sent to multiple objects, the ES does not specify the order in which it is sent, or how much time is allowed to elapse between the first notification and the last. These quality of service factors are considered to be implementation details, as we just pointed out. So the next two steps actually occur in indeterminate order, at least as far as the users of the service are concerned.

B. One is the **push** to the **push_consumer** object. The push consumer object must support (that is, inherit and implement) the **push_consumer** interface. This makes the object a *server*, to which the channel plays *client*. When the channel receives an event, it invokes the **push** operation on the consumer. The invocation mode is not specified, but you can bet that it was invoked **oneway** to prevent the client from blocking execution of this channel thread by failing to return from the invocation immediately.

C. The other thing that happens is the channel object places the event on a queue where it waits for the **pull_consumer** object, which is a *client*

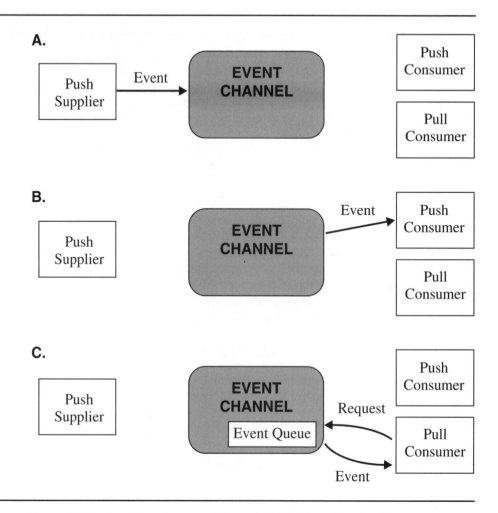

Figure 13.2.   Operation of an event channel with both push and pull consumers.

here, to invoke the **pull** operation on the channel that is the *server*. How long does the event wait on the queue? As we pointed out a few pages back, the ES doesn't say. Look in the documentation for your ES to find out how long your events will last. And, by the way, how many events can fit in the queue? Don't presume that event queues will always be small. Suppose your programmer set up a single channel for all of the events from a spreadsheet, and a user set it up for 1024 × 2048 cells and linked to every cell. Then he or she looped through 1,000 different values for cell C3, recalculating the whole sheet with every iteration. You can multiply out how many events this generates, if you're curious—it's a whole bunch. And if one of the receivers of these events registered to use the **pull** interface, and is iconified and fast asleep, every one of these events is accumulating on a queue in a channel somewhere and may stay there until the user turns off his or her machine to go home that evening. I know power users who do calculations like this five times before morning coffee. Check the documentation for your ES to make sure it can handle the load that some users provide without even thinking.

Here are the interfaces the objects use. We have two **PushConsumer** objects: the event channel, and the first true consumer object. They both support the **PushConsumer** interface:

```
interface PushConsumer {
    void push (in any data) raises (Disconnected);
    void disconnect_push_consumer ();
}
```

The channel implements this interface to allow it to receive events from the supplier object as a server. The consumer object, in order to receive push events from the channel, also has to inherit and implement this interface. This makes the object a server in the eyes of the ES, of course.

The **PushSupplier** object also supports an interface:

```
interface PushSupplier {
    void disconnect_push_supplier ();
}
```

The symmetric disconnect operations allow either side to shut down communications. Since some configurations of ES implementations may include independent objects that may shut down arbitrarily, for instance when a user quits his spreadsheet, this capability is a necessary part of the specification. Well-behaved objects will not shut down at times that will place an unnecessary burden on any user, of course.

The channel supports the **PullSupplier** interface invoked by the **PullConsumer** object:

```
interface PullSupplier {
    any pull () raises (disconnected);
    any try_pull ( out Boolean has_event)
        raises (disconnected);
```

```
        void disconnect_pull_supplier ();
}
```

This interface dishes out events stored on the queue we've been talking about. If there is an event on the queue, **pull** returns right away; otherwise, it blocks until an event is received by the channel and made available on the queue. **try_pull** returns immediately in either case. If there is an event, **has_event** will be **true** and the event value will be placed in the **any**; if not, **has_event** will be **false**.

13.3.1 Registering for Events on a Channel

There's a sophisticated set of interfaces for registering to send or receive events. The object that creates an event channel gets to control what gets to register as event supplier and consumer. This way, for instance, an object can ensure that it is the only one that can send events on a channel, while it makes the consumer end of the channel public so that any number of objects can receive events. Or, an object that creates a number of objects can also create a private event channel to connect them.

For details on registration interfaces, see either the OMG specification for the ES or the documentation that came with your ES implementation.

13.3.2 Typed Event Channels

All of the events we've passed so far include only an **any** datatype. What if you want to pass some particular piece of data in your events?

You can do this using the ES as specified, but you have to create a specialized version of the channel and the objects that access it. The specification tells what to do, and what the interfaces will look like when you're done (with your particular datatypes inserted, of course).

Since the ES passes an **any**, all this saves you is the translation step from your **any** to the **struct** that you actually passed. And the spec even includes an implementation suggestion that just puts a translation object between the event supplier and the channel on one end, and the channel and consumer on the other, so you're not even saving overhead. But this may make your code less complicated, or enable substitution of more sophisticated implementations later, so if you're building a system that passes lots of events with sophisticated structs, you might consider building a special typed event channel for them.

## CHAPTER 14

CORBAservices, Part 5: Transaction and Concurrency Services

On-line Transaction Processing (OLTP) is the foundation of the world's business computing. It is the system that ensures that the last 100 widgets are promised to only one customer; that the last two seats on flight 423 to Hawaii are assigned, together, to a honeymooning couple; that the balance printed on your ATM ticket in Taipei exactly matches the balance in the bank's central datastore in New York City. And, OLTP accomplishes this *reliably*, even in the face of (noncatastrophic) failure of hardware and software around the system.

In this chapter, we'll look at OLTP and OMG's Transaction Processing (TP) specification. First we'll summarize the business problem, and see how *transactional semantics* require that all of the parties involved in a transaction be prepared before allowing it to be *committed*; if any one of the parties cannot complete its part of the transaction, the entire transaction is *rolled back*. Then we'll review flat and nested transactions, and, finally, summarize the TP specification itself.

The Object Transaction Service extends transactional semantics to distributed, object-oriented applications. Using the service, our applications will have the reliability and robustness that business requires, in an environment where multiuser data access comes naturally. And keep in mind that transactional access can be appropriate for nonbusiness data too; record-keeping is done in many contexts, and a TP system is almost always easier and less expensive in the long run than trying to code up equivalent reliability in-house.

And a final benefit of the service is *legacy systems integration*. Key provisions of the service allow smooth integration of object and nonobject TP-systems, on one or several ORBs or just out there on the network. These provisions allow your distributed, object-oriented TP clients and applications to integrate smoothly with your existing TP mainframes, providing a smooth transition from one world to the other. We'll give some details later, plus pointers to more information in some OMG references.

14.1   THE BUSINESS PROBLEM

OLTP refers to a class of applications critical to the operational needs of many businesses. OLTP systems control day-to-day activities—taking orders, operating production lines, transferring funds. It applies to all industries—private as well as the public sector.

The first OLTP applications were deployed to reduce costs by automating clerical tasks. As applications matured, they encompassed more business rules, becoming increasingly critical to daily operations so that, today, most businesses cannot operate without them. Their databases not only support operational applications, but also form the foundation for strategic decision-making.

OLTP applications inherently deal with shared data. For example:

- Accepted orders reduce product inventory, causing fewer items to be available for subsequent orders.
- Credit card payments reduce balances, enabling subsequent charges to be accepted.

Even when data are not updated, multiple users may read it and act on its contents. For example:

- When inventory falls below 100, order 1,000 more from the wholesaler.
- When credit limit is exceeded, send collection notice.

Allowing multiple users to read and update the same data requires a mechanism to protect its integrity. This mechanism must ensure that:

- Only one application can update the data at a time. This guarantees that the persistent copy reflects all activities that operate against it.
- Data seen by an application is consistent with the current state of the business. This guarantees that applications will follow business rules (for instance, taking orders only when there is sufficient inventory).

- Changes made to the data persist. This prevents decisions from being made with incorrect information (such as using last week's inventory rather than today's).

The mechanism that provides these guarantees is the *transaction*.

14.2 TRANSACTION CONCEPTS

The transaction concept is an important programming paradigm for simplifying the construction of reliable business applications. Initially deployed in commercial applications to protect data in centralized databases, it is being extended to the broader context of distributed computation. Today, transactions are considered the key to constructing reliable distributed applications.

Transaction semantics define the conditions that guarantee, for a sequence of operations, that the result *always* meets TP requirements. These requirements have become known by the acronym ACID, for Atomicity, Consistency, Isolation, and Durability. The transaction as a whole must demonstrate:

atomicity: All changes are either completely done—*committed*—or completely undone—*rolled back*. Recoverable data change uniformly and only at transaction boundaries (the beginning and end of a transaction).

consistency: The effects of a transaction preserve invariant properties of your system. When you transfer funds at an ATM, your checking account is credited and your savings account debited *simultaneously*. Recoverable data are visible to other applications only when committed.

isolation: Intermediate states are not visible to other transactions. The two sides of your double-entry bookkeeping system change together, and never get out of synchronization. Transactions appear to execute serially, even if performed concurrently.

durability: The effects of a completed transaction are persistent. Changes are never lost except for catastrophic failure.

Transaction semantics can be defined as part of any object that provides ACID properties. Examples are OODBMS and persistent objects. The value of a separate transaction service is that it allows:

- transactions that include multiple, separately defined ACID objects; and
- transactions that combine objects and nonobject resources.

14.3   OTS FEATURES

OMG required the writers of the OTS to meet a number of requirements targeted especially at the integration of legacy TP systems and simultaneous execution of parts of a single transaction on multiple TP systems. Legacy systems integration, especially, is crucial; if this had not been accomplished, businesses would not have a feasible pathway to move to object-oriented TP systems.

Here is a rundown of some of the features of the TP specification.

14.3.1   Support for Multiple Transaction Models

As we will describe in detail in Section 14.5, the OTS supports both the flat and nested transaction models. The flat transaction model, which is widely supported in the industry today, must be provided by every OTS supplier. The nested transaction model, which provides finer granularity isolation and facilitates object reuse in a transactional environment, is optional. The chained transaction model is not supported.

14.3.2   Evolutionary Deployment

The ability to wrap and integrate existing TP systems is a key feature of the OTS. OMG members knew that object technology would penetrate business computing much quicker if it could happen without disturbing current systems.

14.3.3   Model Interoperability

Especially during the transition from existing procedural TP systems to object-oriented systems, businesses need to make the two work together. So, the OTS was designed to accommodate:

- a single transaction that includes ORB and non-ORB applications and resources;
- interoperability between the object transaction service model and the X/Open Distributed Transaction Processing (DTP) model;
- access to existing (nonobject) programs and resource managers by objects;
- access to objects by existing programs and resource managers;
- coordination by a single transaction service of the activities of both object and nonobject resource managers; and
- the network case—a single transaction, distributed between an object and nonobject system, each of which has its own transaction service.

14.3.4   Network Interoperability

Businesses need to interoperate between systems offered by multiple vendors under a variety of conditions including:

- *Single transaction service, single ORB:* It must be possible for a single transaction service to interoperate with itself using a single ORB.
- *Multiple transaction services, single ORB:* It must be possible for one transaction service to interoperate with a cooperating transaction service using a single ORB.
- *Single transaction service, multiple ORBs:* It must be possible for a single transaction service to interoperate with itself using different ORBs.
- *Multiple transaction services, multiple ORBs:* It must be possible for one transaction service to interoperate with a cooperating transaction service using different ORBs.

The OTS specifies all of the interactions required between cooperating transaction service implementations to support single-ORB interoperability. It relies on CORBA 2.0 interoperability to provide transaction service interaction between ORBs.

14.3.5   Flexible Transaction Propagation Control

Both client and object implementations can control transaction propagation:

- A client controls whether its transaction is propagated with an operation.
- A client can invoke operations on objects with transactional behavior and objects without transactional behavior within the execution of a single transaction.
- An object can specify transactional behavior for its interfaces.

The OTS supports both implicit (system managed) propagation and explicit (application managed) propagation, as described in Section 14.4.1. With implicit propagation, transactional behavior is not specified in the operation's signature. With explicit propagation, applications define their own mechanisms for sharing a common transaction.

14.3.6   Support for TP Monitors

Businesses deploy mission-critical applications on commercial transaction processing systems that use a TP monitor to provide both efficient scheduling and resource sharing for a large number of users. The OTS includes:

- the ability to execute multiple transactions concurrently;
- the ability to execute clients, servers, and transaction services in separate processes;

and can be used in a TP monitor environment.

14.3.7 Support for Existing TP Standards

The OTS uses a model similar to that of both the X/Open DTP model and the OSI TP protocol. This makes possible a mapping to the following established TP standards or specfications (For full references, see Appendix A):

the X/Open TX interface

the X/Open XA interface

the OSI TP protocol

LU 6.2 protocol

Mapping is not supported where these TP systems use chained transactions, which are not part of the OTS specification.

14.4 OTS COMPONENTS

Basically, here's how the OTS works: You can invoke any operation on any object during a transaction, but the object must be either *transactional* or *recoverable* for that operation to display transaction semantics.

A *recoverable object* is an object whose data are affected by the committing or rolling back of a transaction. The recoverable object owns the data, and implements a failure-recovery mechanism. Typically, the object places data into stable storage during the transaction. If failure occurs during the transaction, then during the restart procedure, the transactional object reads its saved state data from stable storage, discovers that a transaction was in process, and participates in a commit/rollback protocol with the Transaction service. The recoverable object must be prepared to deal with messages from the transaction manager to commit or roll back the current transaction.

A *transactional object* is any object whose behavior is affected by being in the scope of the transaction. It may behave this way because it is itself a recoverable object (since all recoverable objects are transactional), or because it refers to data stored in recoverable objects. Like the recoverable object, the transactional object must be prepared to deal with messages from the transaction manager to commit or roll back the current transaction.

Transactions are started and ended by declaration of an initiating client. Between the start and end, certain operations by that client and other clients will be handled by the transaction manager and acquire the four properties of transactions just listed. Needless to say, these operations must all be invoked on transactional or recoverable objects in order for this to work. When the client declares the end of the transaction, the transaction manager asks all of the objects involved if they are ready to commit. If they all respond yes, the transaction manager gives the word to commit; if no, the manager gives the command to roll back, and the *entire* transaction fails.

This process is termed *two-phase commit*. It's invisible to the client, which just invokes a commit operation; the two-phase commit is carried out under the covers by the TP system itself. In case you're curious, we've exposed some of the interface to this in Section 14.8.

At any time before the final *commit*, any participant in a transaction can force the transaction to be rolled back (eventually). If a transaction is rolled back, all participants roll back their changes. Typically, a participant will request the rollback of the current transaction after encountering a failure. It is implementation-specific whether the Transaction Service itself monitors the participants in a transaction for failures or inactivity.

Where do transactional and recoverable objects come from? Recoverable objects, the ones that actually store the transactional data, usually come from software suppliers; frequently, databases will have transactional modes, and some TP systems come with an integral datastore. Transactional objects—the modules that tell the database what to do—are usually written by your staff or integrator, since they deal with your business' unique schema. These objects are transactional rather than recoverable since they aren't affected by commit or rollback; the database owns the data and takes care of the two-phase commit/rollback procedure. There may be other objects involved behind the scenes, but these are the ones you will be most concerned about, at least at first. By the way, the OTS opens up your system and increases your options. If you discover an opportunity to use a recoverable object that you can write yourself, the interfaces are available for you to integrate it into your system.

14.4.1 Transaction Context

There's a well-established programming convention in TP that says that every operation executed between a begin transaction statement and an end transaction statement is part of the transaction, and that no explicit transactional declaration is required on the individual operations. Besides making for cleaner code, this allows functions that have no explicit transactional declarations to be executed in the scope of a transaction.

The OMG went to great lengths to preserve this environment in the OTS. Basically, it required the ORB to become "transaction-aware." If you'll think back on what you've read so far, you'll realize that this is the *first* time the ORB has ever become involved in any communication beyond just passing it through. This is an indication of just how important the OMG believes OLTP is to the success of CORBA and the OMA. The operation to begin a transaction is actually executed by a pseudo-object located in the ORB (where every pseudo-object is located, of course). It sets up a *transaction context*, which the ORB automatically inserts as a parameter to every invocation in the scope of the transaction until the client invokes the corresponding end transaction operation. This is termed *implicit transaction propagation*. Transactional and recoverable objects look for the transaction context to determine whether a request is part of a transaction and, if so, which one. If you plan to use the OTS, check with your ORB vendor to ensure that the ORB you buy will support the service. You don't have to buy the OTS from the same vendor as your ORB, but there is a component of ORB support that must be in there or else *no* OTS will work.

By the way, there is also a CORBA mode that supports *explicit* passing of the transaction context. This allows the originating client, or any other object that receives the context from that object, to extend the bounds of the transaction explicitly.

Believe it or not, we have passed over some of the details: how the initiating client can delegate authority to end the transaction; how other clients can perform operations in an implicitly propagated transaction; and how to tell which operations are transactional. Some of the answers will come out in the rest of the chapter. If TP is new to you and this introduction piques your interest, you can follow up with the references to this chapter listed in Appendix A.

Now that we've covered the basics, we'll go over the two types of transactions covered by the service, see how the service fits together, look at a brief example, and finish up with a sample of OTS IDL.

14.5 FLAT TRANSACTIONS

We'll deal with only two basic types of transactions: flat, and nested. There is also a chained transaction type, which is not supported by the OTS. We've just described a flat transaction; it has a single start and end, and a single level.

The flat transaction model is widely supported in the industry today in transaction processing systems such as IBM's CICS and Transarc's ENCINA as well as database systems from IBM, Oracle, and Sybase. It is the basis for the X/Open Distributed Transaction Processing model and the ISO OSI-TP standard.

14.6 NESTED TRANSACTIONS

Nested transactions permit creation of transactions embedded within an existing transaction to form a transaction hierarchy (Figure 14.1). The existing transaction is called the *parent* of the embedded transaction. The embedded transaction is a *subtransaction* and is called a *child* of the parent transaction.

Subtransactions can be embedded in other subtransactions to any level of nesting. The *ancestors* of a transaction are the parents of the subtransaction and the parents of its ancestors. The *descendants* of a transaction are the children of the transaction and the children of its descendants. Subtransactions are strictly nested. A transaction cannot commit unless all of its children have completed. When a transaction is rolled back, all of its children are rolled back.

A *top-level* transaction is a transaction without a parent. A flat transaction can be modeled as a top-level transaction without children. A top-level transaction and all of its descendants are called a *transaction family*.

Subtransactions are atomic; however, when a subtransaction commits, its changes remain pending until commitment of all its ancestors. Thus, subtransactions are not durable—only top-level transactions are durable.

Isolation also applies to subtransactions. When a transaction has multiple children, a child appears to execute serially to other siblings, even if they execute concurrently.

A subtransaction can fail without causing the entire transaction family to fail. This *failure granularity* aligns nicely with the partitioning of application function provided by encapsulation.

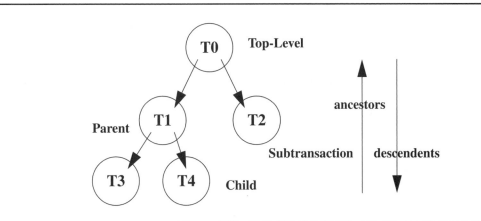

Figure 14.1. A transaction hierarchy.

14.7 OMG'S OBJECT TRANSACTION SERVICE

Figure 14.2 shows the components of the OTS, and how they work together to execute a transaction. A *transactional client* makes requests (1) of the OTS to define the boundaries of a series of operations that constitute a transaction. It then invokes *transactional operations* (2) on *transactional objects*. During the transaction, requests can also be made (3) on *recoverable objects*.

Transactional objects are used to implement two types of application servers—*transactional* and *recoverable*.

- A *transactional server* is a collection of objects whose behavior is affected by the transaction, but has no recoverable state of its own. It implements recoverable changes using other objects. It does not participate in transaction completion, but may force transaction rollback.

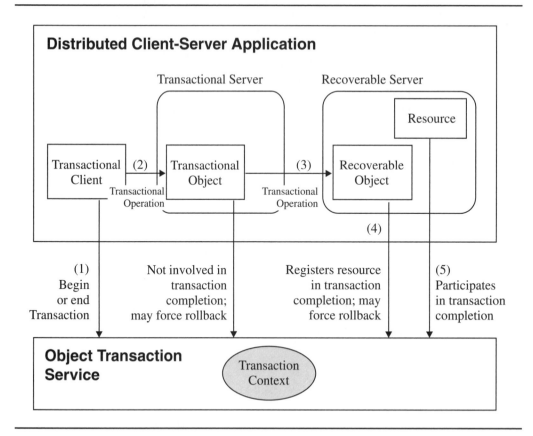

Figure 14.2.   Object Transaction Service overview.

▪ A *recoverable server* is a collection of objects, at least one of which has recoverable state. It participates in transaction completion by registering (4) *Resource* objects. The *Resource* implements *transaction completion* by participating (5) in two-phase commit.

For each active transaction, OTS maintains a *transaction context* that it associates with transactional operations. The transaction context is an *implicit parameter* of transactional operations and is transferred by the ORB along with the operation, as we pointed out in Section 14.4.1.

14.8 TRANSACTION SERVICE EXAMPLE

Our goal here is to cover enough of the OTS to give you a basic understanding of what it can do, and perhaps some of how it works, so that you can decide if you're interested in buying and using it, and know enough to figure out what people tell you about various OTS implementations and programs. It's a complex service with many parts, and we don't have the space to cover all of them in enough detail to make sense. So, we'll cover the service by presenting an example and showing the parts of the OTS that come into play as the different stages of the example execute.

The client code following this paragraph implements an order entry application. It's shown in pseudo-code—operations are only shown if they are part of the flow; exception checking is omitted as are most declarations; and coding is, at best, imprecise. The inventory and the purchase order are implemented as objects—**Inventory** and **Purchase**. The transaction consists of a **reduce** operation on **Inventory** followed by an **add** operation on **Purchase**. If sufficient inventory is not available, the transaction is rolled back.

```
//  Transaction Example  --  pseudocode
Boolean OrderEntry ( Amount quantity ){

   Inventory   theInventory;
   Purchase    thePurchaseOrder;

   Current     theCurrentTransaction;

   theCurrentTransaction.begin();
     Amount balance = theInventory.query();
     if (balance > quantity)
       { theInventory.reduce( quantity );
         thePurchaseOrder.add( quantity );
         theCurrentTransaction.commit();
         return True;}
```

```
          else
          { theCurrentTransaction.rollback();
            return False; }
      }
```

From the client's perspective, **Inventory** and **Purchase** implement the transactional guarantees. **Inventory** may rely on these features in a database management system, rather than implement them itself. Such an object would be a *transactional server*—it has no recoverable state of its own, but needs to be part of the transaction so that the object with recoverable state (the database) can participate in transaction completion.

The type **Current** represents a pseudo-object; the code here looks like a conventional CORBA object invocation on **theCurrentTransaction**, but the operation is actually executed by a pseudo-object located within the ORB (conceptually, at least; remember that the boundaries of the ORB are frequently difficult to trace). Invoking **begin** on **theCurrent-Transaction** creates a transaction context that is added by the ORB to every invocation signature until we invoke either **commit** or **rollback** on **theCurrentTransaction**.

While we're looking at **Current**, let's go over its IDL:

```
interface Current {
    void begin()
        raises( . . . );
    void commit(in boolean report_heuristics)
        raises( . . . );
    void rollback()
        raises( . . . );
    void rollback_only()
        raises( . . . );

    Status get_status();
    string get_transaction_name();
    void set_timeout(in unsigned long seconds);

    Control get_control();
    Control suspend();
    void resume(in Control which)
        raises( . . . );
};
```

As we just pointed out, **begin** creates a new transaction, and its transaction context is associated with the client thread of control. If there already is a current transaction, the new transaction becomes a subtransaction of it. **commit** and **rollback** do what we said; note that the originating client controls access to the object reference to **current**, which is the target of the **commit** and **rollback** operations.

rollback_only sets the transaction status so that **rollback** is the only possible outcome, without forcing the rollback to occur immediately. **rollback_only**, **get_status**, and **get_transaction_name** are operations used internally by the TP system to stay organized; we're not going to describe them here. **get_control** and **suspend** return a control object that, when passed to **resume**, associates this transaction's context with our thread of execution. **suspend** also ceases the assocation of any context with our thread. That is, between a **suspend** and the **resume** with that same Control object as an argument, invocations we make are not part of any transaction; with the **resume** invocation, the transaction resumes.

Continuing with our example: We first query inventory to see if we have enough widgets, or whatever. If we do, we issue invocations to reduce the quantity in inventory and add that same quantity to the purchase order. On `commit`, the two operations update "simultaneously," assuming that no exceptions are raised by objects `theInventory` and `thePurchaseOrder`.

If inventory is not sufficient, our example code does not try to fill the purchase order, and instead invokes `rollback` to terminate the transaction. We admit, we hadn't done anything to change the state of any transactional object so there isn't really anything to roll back, but imagine that we were filling orders for widgets and handles, and we had already added 2,000 widgets to the order and discovered we didn't have any handles, so we invoked `rollback` to cancel everything, widgets and handles together.

Current is associated with implicit propagation; there is another set of interfaces that you use if you require explicit control, but we won't detail them here.

We will spare you the details of most of the interfaces used by objects participating in the service, since you're probably going to be a user and not an implementor of the service. There is one, however, that reveals succinctly some key information on how the two-phase commit protocol works under the covers, so we'll go over it here. It is the **Resource** interface:

```
interface Resource {
    Vote prepare();
    void rollback()
        raises( ... );
    void commit()
        raises( ... );
    void commit_one_phase()
```

```
        raises( . . . );
    void forget();
};
```

prepare is invoked to begin the two-phase commit protocol on the resource. The resource responds with its vote on how to end the transaction: If no persistent data have been modified by the transaction, the resource returns **VoteReadOnly**. The transaction service will then ignore this resource for the rest of the processing of this transaction, and the resource can forget about the transaction. If the resource is prepared to commit—that is, the persistent data have already been written to stable storage (although they probably have not been made visible to the outside world)—it returns **VoteCommit**. The resource must still be prepared to roll back, however, since one of the other resources in the transaction may not have done so well with its own processing. And, if the resource is not prepared to commit, or if it has no knowledge of the transaction (it should assume that the knowledge was lost in a system crash, for instance), it returns **VoteRollback**. Like **VoteReadOnly**, this response relieves the resource of further responsibility for this transaction and it can forget that it ever existed.

In the event of failure, the OTS will attempt to continue the two-phase commit protocol. This requires recoverable servers to remember transaction state and be able to restore the proper copy of recoverable state from information recorded during **prepare**.

rollback and **commit** do what you think. **commit** raises a **NotPrepared** exception if the prepare operation didn't come first. **commit_one_phase** is like **commit** except it doesn't require a prior prepare; the resource can raise the **TransactionRolledBack** standard exception if it receives a **commit_one_phase** request and can't do it. **forget** is used to clean up after certain exception conditions.

This concludes our discussion of the Object Transaction Service. But before we leave this topic entirely, we'll briefly skim the Concurrency Control Service, which supports the OTS with resource locks.

14.9   CONCURRENCY CONTROL SERVICE

Frequently, a database will have to ensure that only one client at a time gets access to a record; or a file system will have to restrict write access to a file in order to prevent conflicting edits. This need is common enough that OMG established the Concurrency Control Service (CCS) to help take care of it. The service was designed specifically to service the OTS so it understands the transaction context, but the locking concept is general and the CCS can be useful in a more general way. If you are creating resources somewhere in your architecture and need to regulate access to them, the CCS may be just what you need. However, it's more likely (assuming that you're an end-user company, and not a database vendor) that you will buy a facility like a database or file system and find that a locking facility is already part of it.

That's because the CCS isn't a concurrency control service at all; it's really a lock managing facility. Control is provided by the facility that uses the CCS such as a database, TP system, or file system, and these are typically items that end users buy rather than write.

Here's an analogy that might help: Imagine you're back in high school, and it's the first day of gym class. The locker room is lined with lockers (of course), all without locks—this represents your DB system without the CCS. The gym teacher comes in with a box full of locks—this represents the CCS by itself: a bunch of locks in a box, which you could lock and unlock all day and never make any difference to anything. So you hang one lock on each locker, and suddenly things get useful, at least under the circumstances. Analogous to the locks in this story, the locks managed by the CCS are useful only when they're hung on an electronic "locker" with the right hooks, such as a database or TP system.

This means, for one thing, that if you want to add concurrency control to a system you already own and use (like a UNIX file system, for instance), the CCS is not going to help you out (unless you plan to rewrite the internal file system code yourself). Using our analogy, the file system doesn't have anyplace for you to hang the locks, so you'd have to code that part—the entire resource control system—yourself.

The CCS is a well-designed and written facility, with five lock levels to enable fine-grained locking without undue overhead. If you're building a datastore facility and need to regulate access, this is the facility you should use for lock management. But if you're planning to buy your database and TP system from an outside vendor, you'll access the CCS indirectly and never program to it. So, we're not going to describe it here. If you need to use the CCS, we're sure you won't have any trouble figuring it out from the OMG specifications or the doc set that comes with your vendor's implementation.

## CHAPTER 15

CORBAservices, Part 6: Property and Query Services

If your system only has a few objects, they will be easy to keep track of, and life will be simple. Unfortunately, life isn't like this. A few objects are not enough to keep most systems going, so a small object system will likely either grow or die. Being die-hard optimists (we have to be, in this business), we'll assume that your system is going to grow, and that sooner or later, you'll have thousands, or hundreds of thousands, or maybe even gazillions of objects. And when you do, you'll have to keep track of them, sort them, organize them, and retrieve them. The Relationship service will only go so far. Granted, it keeps our compound document in one piece no matter how complicated it gets. But an organization can have a whole bunch of documents. Consider the U.S. Congress, for example. Or maybe we'd better not. That belongs in a different book, by a different author. Stephen King, perhaps.

In this chapter, we'll consider two CORBAservices designed to help cope with large numbers of objects. There's a third service involved here implicitly—the Collection Service—which was entering the earliest stages of the OMG standardization process as we wrote this, and which will work very closely with the Query Service. We'll include a few sentences about it in Section 15.3.4.

The Object Property Service (OPS) lets you assign properties to an object. A property is like an attribute, except it's defined dynamically by the client instead of statically in the IDL defining the object's type by your object provider. For instance, you can assign a property to each of your documents that records how important the document is to you. Or your network adminstration tool can assign a property to each object it manages, recording information about its registration status with the tool. These properties are clearly associated with the object, but not part of the object's type.

But it's the possibilities opened up by the Object Query Service (OQS) that are the most exciting. The OQS unifies your CORBA objects, OO databases, and relational databases into a single query target. It does this just the way you expect, by specifying a common interface to a set of OQS objects that query these different systems. Any information stored with an OQS front end can participate; OMG expects that most database vendors will supply their own OQS objects, but these can also be built and supplied by outsiders for any system with a public interface. Since the information in their databases is a key business asset, the OQS is certain to become a cornerstone of many businesses' IS installation.

In this chapter, we'll take a look at the capabilities of the OPS and OQS, and some of the basic interfaces that your programmers will use to invoke them. This will give you a good idea of how these services will allow you to organize your objects. These services are the most recent of all the ones described in this book, adopted during the third quarter of 1995 and published later in the year. Check the CORBA products directory on the OMG home page (*http://www.omg.org*) for up-to-date information on availability of OPS and OQS products for your favorite ORB.

15.1 THE PROPERTY SERVICE

Before we discuss properties, let's review attributes for a second. An attribute is a variable defined in an object's IDL, containing a value that is permanently associated with an object. Good design practice dictates that an object's type definitions be kept as simple as possible, so IDL files tend to assign attributes to objects only where the attribute reflects a value intrinsic to the object and useful to (virtually) every instance.

But sometimes we need to add an attribute-like element to an object whose IDL is already completely defined—objects we've purchased, or that were written by someone else, perhaps; or a personal label that few (or no) other users will ever need. We've given several examples already—the documents that we've labelled "very important" or "not very important," or network control objects that are labelled by our network management system. These are just specific examples of a much more general problem. The point is, sometimes clients need to be able to *add* a label to an object, and being able to read or write the value of attributes already provided is just not enough.

The Object Property Service extends the OMA, giving clients the ability to hang *properties* on objects. Each **property** has a name and a value;

the value is typed as an **any**, allowing anything the client wants (including **structs**) to be stored and retrieved. More precisely, clients can dynamically create and delete properties, and get and set their values. Properties may be manipulated individually, or in batches using a special interface defined by the specification. An additional interface allows *modes* of properties to be set: **normal**, **readonly**, **fixed_normal** (cannot be deleted), and **fixed_readonly** (cannot be deleted or changed). An object can define **readonly** or **fixed_readonly** properties upon creation, and be assured that they will remain unchanged as long as the object exists.

One last thing: How are properties associated with objects? If the object was built after the property service was created, all it has to do is inherit the **PropertySet** or **PropertySetDef** interface and implement its functionality. But what if it doesn't—that is, what if we have an immutable object? The service specification says, with characteristic precision, that "the association of properties with an object is considered an implementation detail." The Relationship Service (Chapter 15) solved a similar problem by creating the role object that embodies the role and contains a pointer to the related object—a proxy object that represents the actual object in the service. A similar proxy could serve here as well; in fact, an augmented role object could conceivably serve both purposes. But this is an implementation detail, of course.

15.1.1   Basic Property Service IDL

A **property** is a two-tuple of **<property_name, property_value>**.

property_name is a string that names the property; it is *not* a name as defined by the Naming Service. **property_value** is of type **any** and contains the value assigned to the property. If we don't need to define modes (**readonly** or whatever) for a property, this is the struct we use to define it. **Properties** is defined as **sequence<Property>**, and will let us perform operations on more than one property at a time.

If we do want to assign modes, then we use the **PropertyDef**: a three-tuple of **<property_name, property_value, property_mode>**. Recall that **property_mode** can take the string values **normal**, **readonly**, **fixed_normal**, and **fixed_readonly**. **readonly** properties cannot be set, **fixed_normal** properties cannot be deleted, and **fixed_readonly** properties can neither be set nor deleted. You're right, a client could delete a **readonly** property and redefine a property with the same name but a different value; presumably, the definers of the service had a reason for providing such a nonrobust mode and there's a use for it somewhere. We recommend you avoid the **readonly** mode and use **fixed_readonly** instead. There's actually a fifth value, **undefined**. You can't set a property to have an **undefined** mode, but you can get this mode back from a **get_mode** request. And, as you might expect, **Property-Defs** is defined as **sequence<PropertyDef>** to handle groups of properties with modes.

There is an extensive set of exceptions defined by the service to handle just about all of the situations that might arise when a client tries to set or get a property value, or define a new property, and something goes wrong. We won't list them all here; your vendor will give you a list when you get an implementation of the service so you'll have it when you need it.

Here's the **PropertySet** interface, in four different pieces:

15.1.2 Defining and Modifying Properties

These operations in the **PropertySet** interface let a client define or change the value of a property:

```
void define_property (
    in PropertyName property_name,
    in any property_value)
raises ( . . . );

void define_properties (
    in properties nproperties )
raises ( MultipleExceptions);
```

If the property already exists, the service checks the property type (the **any** typecode). If the new value has a different type, the attempt will fail; you have to delete the old property first using **delete_property** before you redefine it.

15.1.3 Listing and Getting Properties

Here's how we retrieve the values we set, or get a list of all property names if we don't remember the ones we set or need to know which properties were defined on an object by everyone else:

```
unsigned long get_number_of_properties ( );

void get_all_property_names (
    in unsigned long how_many,
    out PropertyNames property_names,
    out PropertyNamesIterator rest );
```

```
any get_property_value (
    in PropertyName property_name,
raises ( . . . );

boolean get_properties (
    in PropertyNames property_names,
    out Properties nProperties );

void get_all_properties (
    in unsigned long how_many,
    out Properties nproperties,
    out PropertiesIterator rest );
```

get_number_of_properties returns the number of properties in this **PropertySet**.

get_all_property_names returns all of the property names defined in the **PropertySet**. If there are more than **how_many**, the remainder are put into a **PropertyNamesIterator**. The iterator lets the client retrieve the rest of the names; we won't give details here.

get_property_value returns the value of the property you ask for, of course, assuming that it's there. **get_properties** returns values for all of the properties listed in **property_names** and sets the **boolean** flag to **true**. If retrieval fails for some of the properties, the **boolean** flag is set to **false**. In this case, you'll have to retrieve each property individually; this operation does not return mixed results.

get_all_properties returns all of the properties defined in the **PropertySet**; excess greater than **how_many** are returned in the iterator.

15.1.4 Deleting Properties

Here are the operations a client uses to delete one or more properties:

```
void delete_property (
    in PropertyName property_name)
raises ( . . . );

void delete_properties (
    in PropertyNames property_names )
raises ( MultipleExceptions );

boolean delete_all_properties ( ) ;
```

They work just the way you expect. **delete_all_properties** will not delete fixed properties; if deletion fails, the client can invoke **get_number_of_**

properties or **get_all_property_names** to find out how many and which ones survived the attempted purge. There is no iterator for exceptions here!

15.1.5 Determining Whether a Property Is Defined

is_property_defined returns **true** if it is, and **false** if it's not:

```
boolean is_property_defined (
     in PropertyName property_name )
raises ( . . . );
```

15.2 GETTING AND SETTING PROPERTY MODES

There's a whole set of interfaces for getting and setting property modes. We've already talked about what the modes are and how they work; we're not going to include interface details here because there's little to be gained—when you're ready to code a client to manipulate property modes, you'll have the doc set for the service you're using and it will include all of these interface definitions.

There is one architectural issue: What about changing **fixed** mode properties? Does a property have an "owner" who can manipulate **fixed** mode properties when everyone else can't? What if there isn't, and you make a mistake when you set it on initialization? Is it frozen in place until the end of time (which, for most computers, is the next time the local power company decides to switch mains and send you a one- or two-second outage as a byproduct)?

Perhaps you've already guessed the answer: The service says that this is an "implementation issue." The good news is that most implementations of the property service that you buy should provide a way to do this; the bad news is that it's not standardized, and code you write to manipulate fixed properties using one service may not port to another. This may be the best the service definers thought they could do at the time; without a formal security service defined by OMG, there was no reliable way to determine the owner of an object or a property. Look for a revised version of the Property Service specification that includes these interfaces, sometime in the future. But don't expect it until after the Security Service settles in.

15.3 THE OBJECT QUERY SERVICE

A powerful implementation of the Object Query Service can, conceivably, merge all of your CORBA objects, plus your OO databases, your relational databases, and even files on your system, into a database that you can search with a single query invocation. (The OQS doesn't actually merge the datastores, of course; it does the usual OMG thing and puts a standard interface layer on top of each one, so they look the same to a client. That way, the service can transmit a single query through to all of them at once.)

If your query requirements are more modest, you will be pleased to know that a smaller and cheaper implementation of the OQS will still be capable of conducting queries of your set of CORBA objects. Or, perhaps, an OQS add-on to your OO database could add this capability and let you search through your CORBA objects, plus the objects in this one database.

The OQS specifies an extremely flexible service, which can be implemented in a range of capabilities and scopes. This has an advantage: You can expect to be able to select from a range of products and select one that fits your needs and budget (with an implicit assumption here that your budget is tuned to the market, more or less). It has a corresponding responsibility: You will have to educate yourself on the capabilities of the service and of each product you consider. You will also have to determine your needs, and ensure that the product you select will do what you expect. This will be your responsibility; like databases, OQSs will come in a wide range of prices and capabilities, and no one knows your requirements (and budget) as well as you (and your accountant).

In this part of the chapter we will investigate the components of the OQS that provide the capabilities you might need. Hopefully, when we're done, you will be in a position to be an intelligent purchaser and user of the service.

By the way, the reason that we're using future tense in this section is because the OQS is a very recent addition to the CORBAservices. Adopted in August 1995, the ink on the specification was barely dry when we wrote this chapter and no vendor implementations had hit the market. But the specification was written by vendors who intend to market compliant products, so we turned to them for information, and that's what we're presenting here. We know from reading the specification that everything we say here is possible, but no one can say for sure what will actually be implemented, prove practical, and finish the journey to the marketplace. So keep in touch with your favorite vendors, and stay flexible until products take final shape.

15.3.1   OQS Building Blocks

It turns out that we need only a few basic building blocks to construct a Query Service:

- First, we need a standard query language so that all of the objects in the system can both service your query and pass it on to additional objects or components.

- Second, we need a standard interface so that an object that holds a query can pass it to an independently built object for invocation.

- Third, we need to be able to construct collections of CORBA objects so that we can query them.

- Fourth, we need query managers, which bear the standard interface we just mentioned, to perform and/or pass on the query. There will be a number of types of query managers.

The diagram in Figure 15.1 shows a large-scale OQS installation that simultaneously queries a collection of CORBA objects, an OODB, and a relational DB. The query in the diagram is not an object; it's a string in the query language (more on this coming up) that gets passed from QE (query evaluator) to QE. There is a query object, but it's only used by service implementors so we won't mention it here except to warn you not to be confused by it if you read the OMG specification later. The dark bar at the top of each QE symbolizes the standard interface we mentioned in the second bullet in the preceding list.

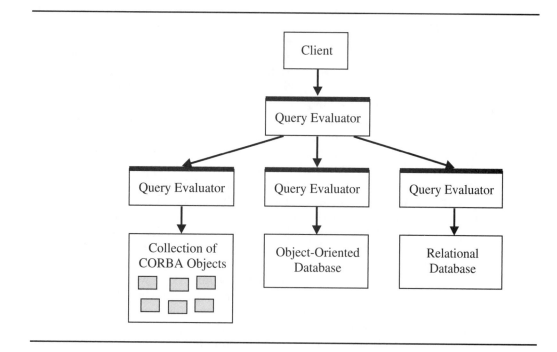

Figure 15.1. Nesting and federation of query evaluators.

Next we'll discuss each of the four standard building blocks in turn. When we're done, we still won't have enough to build our integrated system so we'll see what else we have to add. Here we go.

15.3.2   Standardized Query Language

Choosing a query language for the OQS was an extremely difficult task; in fact, several standards committees have been working far longer than the OMG members on this problem, and may be still working as you read this. But the OMG adoption procedure does not have a "wait for the standards committees to finish" mode and it does have a deadline, so the OMG adopters had to pick something. They actually picked two things, and they are (see Appendix A for full references):

- SQL-92 Query, the subset of SQL-92, which deals directly with query (that is, no schema, session, diagnostics, etc.), and
- OQL-93, an adaptation of SQL-92 Query to cover all objects in the object model defined by the ODMG (Object Database Management Group).

They had to pick two because there is no single query language that provides full query capability for all of the world's databases and is object-oriented and thus capable of queries that scope to CORBA and OODB objects. But the specification recognizes that standards in this area are progressing, and that there should ultimately be only one standard query language in the OQS. We will not discuss the issues here; they change rapidly and are more appropriately aired in a magazine or over electronic mail.

In order to comply with the OQS specification, an implementation must support either one or the other of these query languages. Of course, this means that compliant implementations of the OQS will divide into two families: those that support SQL Query, and those that support OQL. The relationship between the two languages is subtle; OQL-93 contains almost (but not quite) SQL-92 Query as a subset. If your domain is either purely object or purely relational, you will have no problem choosing (unless you plan a migration from relational to object and want your OQS rollout to coincide with the switch). But if you have both, you will have to investigate the consequences, and possibly implement large-scope queries in both languages.

SQL-92 is the most widely used query language, with more products and trained practitioners than any other. OQS products that implement SQL Query can fit into many sites without the disorientation of database changes or staff retraining.

OQL is a fully object-oriented query language that extends query capability to any object in the ODMG object model and, thereby, to the OMG object model. Queries can traverse object inheritance hierarchies, invoke interobject relationships, and query over arbitrary collections, as well as invoke operations on objects. OQL had to be included in the specification to meet the requirement of the OMG members for an object-oriented service capable of invocation on collections of CORBA objects. And, as we just pointed out, it almost includes SQL Query as a subset.

OQL is specified by the ODMG, an independent consortium of OODB vendors devoted to creation and promulgation of standards related to OODBs. Their specification, presented in *The Object Database Standard: ODMG-93 v1.2*, sets the industry standard for object-oriented database modeling and query. There's a full reference in Appendix A; to find out more, get a copy of the ODMG book and study it.

15.3.3 Standardized Interface

In order to pass a query from one QE to another, especially if the QEs are implemented independently by different vendors, they have to share a common interface. Of course, this is CORBA's strong point, so the interface is expressed in OMG IDL. It is:

```
interface QueryEvaluator {
    readonly attribute sequence<QLType> ql_types;
    readonly attribute QLType default_ql_type;

    any evaluate (
        in string query,
        in QLType ql_type,
        in parameterlist params )
        raises ( . . . );
}
```

Looks simple, right? Of course, the devil is in the details, but we won't get to them in this book. A client can read the attribute **default_ql_type** to find the default query language for the QE, or the other attribute **ql_types** for a list of all of its other supported query languages. Then you just construct your query as a string in your chosen supported query language and pass it to the QE, specifying the language and a list of parameters, which are (you guessed it) implementation-specific. When the query either completes or encounters an error, you get back either an **any** or an exception. The **any** type specification provides generality; the most common return type will probably be a collection of objects or records, but may differ for particular queries.

15.3.4   Standardized Collections

If you're familiar with collections of objects, then you're already familiar with the terms *set* and *bag*, for example. If you're not, wait a couple of years, buy a copy of the second edition of this book, and look up the Collection Service, because that's where it's going to appear. The OMG members prioritized the Query Service ahead of the Collection Service, so they standardized it first. But since Query uses Collections, the authors of the OQS had to provide a "stand-in" collection interface that will be used only during the brief interval between the issuance of the OQS and the Collection Service, expected to last about a year. One of the requirements on the future standalone Collection Service specification is that it work with the OQS, so you can rest assured that whatever results from the RFP will be compatible.

We're not going to devote a lot of space to the temporary collection interfaces for obvious reasons, but we do have to talk about how they fit into the OQS structure.

If you want to query a collection of CORBA objects, you need to buy a **QueryableCollection** object implementation from your OQS vendor. This object inherits, and supports, both the **QueryEvaluator** and **Collection** interfaces. Your client invokes the **Collection** interfaces to construct the group of objects you want to query, and then invokes the **QueryEvaluator** interface to execute the query.

15.3.5   Query Evaluators/Managers

What about the objects that actually execute your query? All we've said about them so far is that they bear the **QueryEvaluator** interface, and that some instances also bear the **Collection** interfaces, and you want to buy them and not build them yourself. But there's a lot more to it than this, especially if you want to construct a system that looks anything like Figure 15.1.

These are the things you buy, or already own, that actually make up the OQS. In Figure 15.1, consider the Query Evaluator (QE) on the right along with the native query system just below it. What's a native query system? One example is a database, and you know how huge they can be. Consider this QE to be a front end to all of the query and processing power of your corporate database. You might also have one (or a hundred) smaller QEs front-ending a collection of personal databases.

This is a really powerful concept: *any* database or datastore can be integrated into your OQS. All it needs is a QE object with the **QueryEvaluator** interface on the top end and an interface into the database or datastore on the bottom. The QE object doesn't have to be supplied by the database vendor, although that is a logical first place to look for one. (Presumably, database vendors will see an advantage in having their products integrate into an enterprise's data storage this way.) By the way, the OQS writers were fully aware of this, and wrote the specification to take advantage of caching, indexing, and internal optimization mechanisms present in some native query systems.

In this architecture, the QE plays the role of *integrator*. It takes in a standardized query, through a standardized interface, and executes it on a particular domain with a particular query system. You'll need a different QE for each database type that you want to involve, plus a **QueryableCollection** QE for your CORBA objects, all responding to the same standard query language, but once you have all of these you'll be able to start a single query with a single invocation and have it passed to every database in your domain, just as Figure 15.1 illustrates.

Almost. You need one other thing, and that's the QE at the top that takes in the original query and passes it to all of the other QEs. Of course, it bears the **QueryEvaluator** interface to take in the query, and invokes the **QueryEvaluator** interface to pass it on.

The only slight catch here—and it is slight—is that the interfaces that let you connect the QEs like this and scope a query to a particular set of QEs are not part of the OQS standard. In just about all of the services we've described to now, the scope or target of an operation was the object we invoked, but this is not the case here. This is a reasonable limitation for the standard; each installation will be unique, and the value of a standard is limited in this case. The general cases are covered: objects in relational or OO databases, which are already set up, and CORBA objects in collections, which are included in the OQS specification. But the programming interface you use to tell your upper-level QE that the target of the next query is whatever, is not part of the OMG OQS specification. How will you do this? Perhaps through a GUI that lets you check or uncheck a box for each potential target, or drag a database onto the query object icon, if you're a user. If you're a programmer, the provider will give you an API for this. But don't look in the OMG OQS specification for it.

Like the Object Transaction Service, the OQS is targeted directly at a mainstream need of business computer users. Simultaneously, it merges legacy systems and data, and reaches to the future to encompass object-oriented storage of new and larger data types and formats. OMG and its members expect the OQS to be a major factor in the embracing of distributed object technology by business around the world.

## CHAPTER 16

CORBAservices, Part 7: Security and Licensing Services

16.1 INTRODUCTION

Why are we devoting a chapter to security when it isn't even an OMG specification yet? (OK, two things here: First, by the time you read this, there almost certainly will be an OMG Security service specification, but there wasn't when we wrote it. Second, yes, the Licensing Service is official but we won't devote much space to it because it's a little too specialized even for this book. We expect many more people to *buy* applications with license management than to *write* them.)

We're doing it because security is an essential part of a networked computing system. And security in heterogeneous, multivendor, distributed object systems is a new field without a large experience base. And finally, we have a lot of worthwhile information on distributed object security to tell you about.

For about a year ending in mid-1994, a working group of security specialists coalesced at OMG and wrote a document entitled *The OMG Security White Paper*. Knowing that this document would form the basis for the OMG Security RFP, the group concentrated on stating the distributed security problem as precisely and completely as possible, as well as listing the requirements for distributed security, without prescribing any particular solution or even a security architecture. The paper has been widely recognized as an excellent piece of work.

Even though the OMG Security Specification was not complete when we wrote this, the Security White Paper lets us paint a pretty good picture of the services it will provide and the security environment you will be able to establish, although we can't say for sure which interfaces you will use or what the security products will look like. This chapter is based on the *Security White Paper*. If it whets your appetite, you should ask the OMG for a copy of the paper (this one is free of charge); see Appendix A for details.

16.2 SECURITY OVERVIEW

The *Security White Paper* talks about security *functions*, *mechanisms*, *services*, *policies*, and *threats*:

- A security function is, basically, a description of a single element of a security service—a security building block.
- A security mechanism is the implementation of one (or sometimes more than one) security function. Then you build up a security service by combining security mechanisms and putting a user interface on top. This is usually done by security-knowledgeable staff—even using building blocks, security is best left to the experts.
- The white paper assumes that your security policy is separate from your security mechanisms. Even more important, it requires that the security service be able to support a range of security policies, so that all different types of installations—from small business sites to large commercial installations to sensitive military and government users—can configure the security they need, for a price they can afford, consuming only the staff and hardware resources justified by the level of protection they need.
- A threat is a potential violation of security. No surprise here.

Everyone—users and suppliers alike—is very concerned with potential costs. And money is not the only potential cost. Security can also cost time for programmers, administrators, and users; it can require additional equipment; or it can slow system performance. One key requirement is the minimizing of all of these costs. We'll talk more about this later on.

16.3 TRUST IN DISTRIBUTED OBJECT SYSTEMS

Security is an important issue in any distributed system, as information in transit is more vulnerable, and use of multiple machines introduces issues of trust and consistency between them. Distributed object systems are generally more complex than some traditional client/server systems, and the security issues can be more subtle.

Distributed object systems can be unlimited in scale and may be continually evolving. This means systems that:

- have many components,
- have rich interactions between components, and
- can introduce intricate boundaries of trust.

Distributed object systems have many components. One of the key goals of OMG is to make it possible (in fact, easy) to build complex software systems from a set of CORBA objects. The components that a user or application programmer uses directly when interacting with a software system may only be the tip of the iceberg, with many more underlying objects in the distributed system coming into play through delegation. Also, because of subclassing, inheritance, or customization, the implementations of objects may change over time, often without the user or programmer knowing or caring.

There are rich interactions between components. Simple client/server architectures have straightforward interactions between components, which are usually well understood by users and programmers. In distributed object systems, the distinction between clients and servers is no longer a clear one—a server that implements a CORBA object might also act as a client of another object. Some objects may be implemented by delegating part of their implementation to another object, or (more generally) by using a set of objects connected in some arbitrary graph.

Users and programmers do not always understand—or even care about—all of the interactions that take place between objects that they invoke. Encapsulation hides the details of an object's implementation, including which method of implementation is selected in response to a particular invocation. So the proper use and understanding of a security architecture should not have to depend upon a full understanding of how objects interact "behind the scenes."

Boundaries of trust are more intricate. In a simple client/server system with relatively few components connected in straightforward ways, it is usually clear which of these components are trusted and by whom. For example, clients of a network file system will typically trust the server, but not vice versa.

With distributed object systems, however, things can be more complicated. The "natural" boundaries between objects provided by encapsulation may not always be the right ones to respect, as object boundaries are not always supported by underlying security protection mechanisms. So a user may trust an object with confidential data, for example, when its implementation runs on his or her local machine, but not if it is running on some unknown machine. Even if the implementation is running on a trusted machine, it may use other objects that run elsewhere or are not known to keep data confidential. CORBA-compliant systems have the flexibility to introduce and/or replace large numbers of components, and this very property risks leaving them vulnerable to Trojan horses.

In an environment where users and programmers may not be aware of all the objects with which they are interacting, which objects (or collections of objects) can they trust? Similarly, where object implementations (or the CORBA implementation supporting them) make decisions about security, which other objects should they trust? An OMA security architecture should allow for environments where mistrust between objects is ubiquitous.

The trust that users and programmers have in objects and that object implementations have in each other also depends on the trust in the CORBA implementation and the boundary of trust between object implementations and CORBA implementation. Moving some security into the CORBA implementation could mean little trust is needed in most object implementations. Also, use of trusted tools to generate objects, or moving some security into run-time libraries, can reduce the trust needed in the part of the object implementation written by the application developer.

16.4 DISTRIBUTED SECURITY REQUIREMENTS

The *Security White Paper* identifies a set of General Requirements and a set of Functional Requirements that are common to most commercial and governmental installations, although it points out that some military or governmental sites will have additional, stricter requirements.

Here is the full list of General Requirements. We'll concentrate on about seven of them in the next sections; if you're interested in details about the rest, get a free copy of the *Security White Paper* from OMG.

Consistency

Scalability

Availability

Business Requirements

Regulatory Requirements

Enforceability

Portability

Usability

Evaluation Criteria

Performance

Flexibility

Adherance to Standards

Mechanism Independence

CORBA Interoperability

16.4.1 Consistency

The security model must offer a consistent and standard approach that enables portability across all platforms, and encompasses both legacy and new system applications. This includes:

- *Support for the use of common policies:* For instance, who should be able to access what sort of information within a domain that includes heterogeneous machines.
- *Compatibility with existing permission mechanisms:* The model should function as a means of enhancing these mechanisms.
- *Fit with existing environments:* For example, the ability to provide end-to-end security even over inherently insecure communication services.
- *Fit with existing logons:* Extra logons are not needed.
- *Fit with existing user databases:* Additional user administration is not needed.

16.4.2 Scalability

It must be possible to provide security for a range of systems from small, local systems to large intra- and inter-enterprise ones. For larger systems, it should be possible:

- To base access controls on the privilege attributes of users such as roles or groups (rather than individual identities) to reduce administrative costs.
- To have a number of security domains that enforce different security policy details, but support interworking between them consistent with their mutual trust.
- To manage securely the distribution of cryptographic keys across large networks, without undue administrative overheads; for example, by using public key technology.

There are real differences between governmental and business needs for computer security. A government should be willing to invest a large amount of time and money to prevent a security breach that might expose a large city to risk of terrorist attack, while a business would only consider investing a small amount to prevent a breach that puts at risk a contract bid that might net at most a few thousands, or perhaps tens of thousands, of dollars (or francs, or pesos, or whatever).

There's no doubt that many advances in computer security have been funded by the substantial amounts that governments around the world spend to protect data connected with their national defense. But the computer industry has not always been quick to turn these advances into reasonably priced security mechanisms for business use. The white paper and RFP specifically mention costs associated with business security. End users from the business community will play a prominent role on the evaluation task force.

16.4.3   Regulatory Requirements

This is not the same as evaluation criteria. We'll get to the orange book and ITSEC stuff in a few minutes. The security model must conform to government regulations on the use of security mechanisms (cryptography, for example). There are several types of controls, including:

- controls on what can be exported;
- deployment and use controls, such as limitations on confidentiality (for instance, use of encryption is controlled in France); and
- privacy controls.

Details vary between countries; examples of requirements to satisfy a number of these are:

- to allow customization to permit the use of different cryptographic algorithms
- to keep the amount of information encrypted for confidentiality to a minimum
- to use anonymous identities for auditing, required in Germany

16.4.4   Enforceability

Enforceability is a problem within the OMA. Trojan horses, for example, are even easier to substitute in a dynamic, distributed environment than in the more familiar world of single executable images. But the advantages of the transparencies are a powerful motivator, and security providers believe that this problem can be overcome. The white paper and RFP make this a requirement.

16.4.5 Usability

Poor usability is probably responsible for more security risks than any other factor. We've all seen screens and ATM cards bearing passwords or PINs inscribed with magic marker; this is at least not surprising on networked systems that require a number of passwords for access to all their services. You might question the need to inscribe a single password, especially if it's the name of the user's kid, or dog, or whatever.

- *Usability for end users:* For example, users should need to log on to the distributed system only once to access object systems and other IT services. This requirement restates the "single system logon" mentioned in many previous security requirements documents. The Aerospace Industry Association, for instance, has an entire paper devoted to just this subject.

- *Usability for administrators:* The administrative model should be simple and unambiguous, and represented intuitively at its user interface. Most controls should be assigned to groups; it should not be necessary for an administrator to specify controls for individual objects or individual users of an object (except where security policy or specialized function requires it).

- *Usability for programmers:* There are two possible models for security at the programmer level. Either the programmer is responsible for ensuring that his or her object conforms to the security model or the system is. If the programmer is responsible, then every programmer must learn secure programming techniques, and every object must pass a formal evaluation before it can be deployed in a secure environment. The disadvantages of this model are obvious. In the alternative model, the system provides and assures security for any object developed by any programmer when it is registered with the ORB. This requires sophisticated development tools and run-time libraries, but it has the potential to protect against Trojan horses in addition to providing security assurance for both in-house developed and purchased objects.

So, the white paper and RFP do not require that object developers need to understand security to fit with the security policy (unless a particular object needs special protection for its own functions and data).

16.4.6 Evaluation Criteria

This is the orange book stuff. There must be a law somewhere that you have to refer to the orange book if you're talking about computer security, so here it is. Since OMG is an international organization, we are equally concerned with ITSEC requirements.

A secure product must meet appropriate assurance criteria, to give the required level of confidence in the correctness and effectiveness of the security functionality. There are international criteria for assurance (as well as security functionality), such as the US TCSEC and the European ITSEC criteria, though Common Criteria are now being produced which should replace these. Formal evaluation may not be needed for many commercial systems, though an object system vendor may have to show sound development and quality assurance processes.

16.5 SECURITY FUNCTIONALITY

Security functionality includes:

- *Identification and authentication of principals:* For human users and objects that need to operate under their own rights to verify they are who they claim to be.

- *Authentication of each user of the system:* This may be done using a security service, but it must also be possible to acquire credentials of users who have been authenticated outside the object system so that the number of user logons is not increased. User authentication should be possible using different methods such as passwords, smart cards or thumb print readers. Authentication of other objects may also be needed when these act as principals with their own identities and rights.

- *Authorization and access control:* Deciding whether a principal can access an object, normally using the identity and/or other privilege attributes of the principal (such as role, groups, security clearance) and the control attributes of the target object (saying which principals, or principals with which attributes) can access it. Finer granularity of privileges can reduce the amount of damage any one principal can do. It should be possible to assign such access privileges to any user or object on the system or network. Authorization for each application object must be manageable separately, and at varying levels.

- *Security auditing to make users accountable for their security related actions:* It is normally the human user who should be made accountable. Auditing mechanisms should be able to identify him or her correctly, even after a chain of calls between objects. The audit functionality required may be dictated by criteria such as the TCSEC and ITSEC. Audit trails should be protected so that unauthorized users cannot modify or delete audit information. In a distributed object system, audit information from a number of machines is likely to need collecting more centrally.

- *Secure communication between objects:* To protect both systems data (e.g. security attributes of principals) and business data in transit between objects, which is often over insecure communications pathways.

  Distributed systems are vulnerable to attack when information is in transit. Information must be sent to the correct place and protected against corruption and replay; it may also need to be confidential. Systems data as well as application data needs protecting. Security of communications should be end to end, not relying on (though able to exploit) security in the communications services, and able to work between domains in large systems.

  The communication facility used by the security model must be capable of supporting a variety of authentication protocols or algorithms and be capable of extending the set of protocols supported as new ones are developed.

- *Cryptography:* Is used in support of many of the other functions. It is rarely visible directly outside the security services, except to provide encryption of data under direct object control.

- *Administrative tools:* Administration of security information about principals, server objects, and security policy configuration options is also needed.

16.6 COMPONENTS IN THE SECURITY SERVICE

Figure 16.1 is about as close as the white paper comes to suggesting a security architecture. It doesn't really constrain how security is to be implemented; it just indicates that there will have to be security components that present their services to the OMA via interfaces—and remember, standardization of interfaces is what OMG is all about. (Interfaces 'R' Us.) Under the covers—that is, below the line in the figure—the security services will have the structure and architecture the submitters specify in their RFP response. In fact, the documents anticipate that some portion of the security specification will involve the ORB, the object adapter, and possibly other OMA components.

The *Security White Paper* uses the diagram in Figure 16.1 to describe how security components work together in a typical session involving a user logon and invocation of several remote objects on systems with differing levels of security. If you're interested in the details, you'll have to request the paper—we're not going to go into that fine a level of detail in this book.

16.6.1 Trusted Computing Base (TCB)

Figure 16.1 also suggests the next concept—the Trusted Computing Base or TCB. This consists of the trusted core software components, which cannot be bypassed in operation. It isn't just the stuff below the line—portions of the

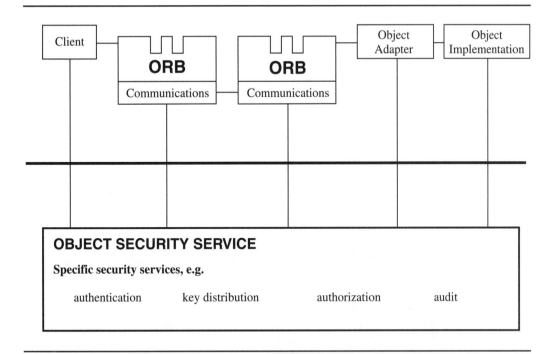

Figure 16.1.   General architecture of the Object Security Service.

ORB, Object Adapters, and some other components may have to be trusted as well. Imagine a thin layer at the bottom of the boxes—ORBs and adapters, for instance—as part of the TCB in addition to the software below the line.

This organization of the Trusted Computing Base has a number of benefits:

- It prevents (collections of) object implementations from interfering with each other and gaining unauthorized access to each other's data.
- It reduces the amount of software that is responsible for enforcing the security of the system and must therefore be trusted (and, for more secure systems, evaluated).
- It minimizes the security functionality needed in clients and object implementations, and, therefore, the security skills needed by their developers.
- It allows a consistent security policy to be enforced across the system.

The TCB should be kept to a minimum, but is likely to contain operating systems, communications software, ORBs, object adapters, security services, and other object services called upon during a security-relevant operation.

(Note that integrity and confidentiality protection of data in transit is often imposed above the communications layer.)

Elements of the TCB will be distributed across the network, and not all parts will be equally trusted. For example, an ORB on a machine that uses a B1 secure operating system may be more trusted than an identical one that runs on a system that has not been evaluated. Recall that the boundary of trust between objects is affected by the trust in the environments in which they run—CORBA as well as the underlying system. The establishment of trust between different parts of a distributed secure object system should normally be done between parts of the distributed TCB. However, it should also be possible for object implementations to establish their own level of mutual trust.

16.7   SECURITY SUMMARY

With most services, you have to implement the service before you can do the things it enables. For example, we had to implement the Lifecycle service before we could move objects around, at least using a standard interface.

But with security, we can't really do anything more with it than we could without it. (In fact, you might be able to do less.) But you can do things securely, which means you can do them longer, or cheaper, or safer. This is why we have been able to experiment with CORBA for so long without a formal security service specification.

Now, both implementors and users of CORBA have finished experimenting, and are starting to use distributed objects for mission-critical applications and data. And obvious advantages of distributed objects for network-based commerce like the WWW add to the reasons to push for a formal security specification.

We'll report on the security specification in the next edition of this book. If you want to find out about it before then, you can either contact OMG directly, or ask your CORBA vendor about his or her security service plans.

16.8   THE LICENSING SERVICE

There are a lot of licensing models out there. The simplest is single-user licensing, but this is extended to concurrent-user, charge-per-hour, and many other models. And there are already a number of licensing software products on the marketplace. So, following the example set by a number of other services (including the Naming Service, for example), the OMG did not establish yet another licensing model with this service.

Instead, the service provides a generic set of interfaces that can be used by virtually any vendor to provide access to his or her licensing software product regardless of its licensing model. Several major licensing software companies contributed to the specification, and all agreed that the interfaces met their needs.

We've bundled licensing into this chapter because of its obvious tie-in with, and use of, security.

One school of thought holds that licensing must be in place in order for software vending to be economic, especially in the distributed object environment where per-unit revenues may be small. OMG therefore prioritized this service in the early stages of CORBA development so that it could serve as such an enabler. If you are an end user, the message to you is that CORBA supports an environment where software diversity is encouraged because developers can be fairly compensated for what they produce. And if you are a software provider, you should be encouraged to produce objects for this environment for the same reason.

If you're an end user, there's almost no reason for you to need details of the standard because you won't ever write software to it or deal with it directly. You'll either register using standard scripts, or dialog boxes, or by calling the vendor to put "money in the meter" (or whatever licensing mode you and your software employ). If you're a provider of licensed software, you'll get all the information you need from the documentation that came with the licensing software package you bought. And, finally, if you're a provider of licensing software, you'll need a copy of the actual specification, and you get that from OMG directly. See Appendix A for contact information.

## CHAPTER 17

The CORBAfacilities

17.1 WHERE WE ARE, AND WHERE WE'RE GOING

If you're a programmer, by the time you've read through to here, you're probably really impressed with the CORBA/OMA environment. You've been given a rich toolkit: CORBA provides a base architecture and interoperability, and the CORBAservices built upon it are accumulating to form an increasingly comprehensive support base. The Lifecycle, Relationship, Naming, Event, and Persistent Object services support basic OO operations; Trader opens up the system to dynamic object discovery and binding; Transaction and Query services provide OO access to basic business functions, and the Licensing service adds ISV support.

But if you're an end user, you might not be quite as impressed. Where, for example, does your spreadsheet or your formatted document fit into the architecture? After you've updated and queried your datastore, how do you create and distribute your report? What about standard objects for your specialized domain, such as Healthcare, Telecommunications, Financial Services?

The good news is, they're in there. The reality is, however, that the OMA is not complete yet, and the CORBAfacilities that will provide these services is very much a work in progress.

The CORBAfacilities architecture divides them into a horizontal component and a vertical component. Horizontal facilities are usable by nearly everyone: compound documents, help facilities, and system administration, for example. Vertical facilities are those shared by a number of different applications *within a specialized market area* such as Healthcare, Telecommunications, and Financial Services, as we just mentioned.

The most exciting news is that a recent reorganization of the OMG's specification-setting member committees has just established the Domain

Technical Committee (DTC) with the authority to establish OMG specifications in vertical market software. Tailored to the needs of these vertical markets, the committee combines domain ISVs and end-user companies with their involvement, experience, and expertise in each area, with the system and ORB vendors who bring valuable CORBA experience, into vertical market task forces which use the established OMG process to set software standards in their domain. Only a few months old when this book went to print in early 1996, the DTC and its first task forces have the excitement and enthusiasm of the early pioneers, and are eagerly seeking more companies—both ISVs and end users—to join and help them out.

In this final chapter on the OMA, we'll take a look at both parts of the CORBAfacilities: Horizontal and Vertical. The CORBAfacilities Task Force has signalled its intended direction in architecture and roadmap documents; these will let us examine its probable direction, even though no official CORBAfacility specifications have emerged as yet. And the OMG reorganization document lets us anticipate the directions the organization will take in vertical markets.

By the way, the OMG is an open organization, which actively seeks out new members to broaden the base of participants in the process. A multilevel membership structure, coupled with a revenue-based fee schedule, allows small and emerging companies to participate at the same level as their bigger cousins for a price most can genuinely afford. OMG hopes that the information in this book, and in this chapter in particular, will motivate your company to join and participate in the OMG process. To contact OMG, see Appendix A.

17.2 THE HORIZONTAL CORBAfacilities

We introduced the CORBAfacilities in Section 1.3.3 and Section 2.6, where we covered the purpose of, and motivation for, the facilities. In this chapter, we'll complement that introduction with an architectural viewpoint.

The horizontal CORBAfacilities are divided into these four basic areas:

User interface: Facilities that make an information system accessible to its users and responsive to their needs. For example, the Compound Presentation facility requested in CF RFP1 falls in this category.

Information management: Facilities for modeling, defining, storing, retrieving, managing, and interchanging information. For example, the Compound Interchange facility requested in CF RFP1 falls in this category.

Systems management: Facilities for the management of complex, multivendor information systems.

Task management: Facilities to automate work processes, including both user and system processes.

Let's take a closer look at each of these categories. First, we'll consider the functionality that falls inside each one; when we're done, we'll look at how they combine to cover the total application space, and what a computing environment will look like as the CORBAfacilities work completes.

17.2.1   User Interface

The User Interface component, according to the architecture document, encompasses the major categories of *user interface enablers*, such as window managers and terminal emulator programs, and class libraries of UI objects; a *work management system*, which manages the session and visualizes the desktop; and *task and process automation*, which enables automation through scripting and interactive recording of macros.

That is, these functions form the layer between the application on the one hand and the hardware and display software on the other. With these facilities in place, applications can be written to take advantage of a user interface object layer, which interacts, in turn, with native window systems and hardware.

The CORBAfacilities architecture document lists these components under User Interface:

Rendering management: General purpose presentation of objects on screen, hard copy, or other media.

Compound presentation management: Requested in the first CORBAfacilities RFP, currently in process at OMG, this facility supports presentation on screen or hard copy of compound documents.

User support: This facility covers common run-time application features including help, and spell and grammar checking.

Desktop management: Facilities for the end-user desktop.

Scripting: Interactive creation of automatic scripts.

Of these, the first and last are general, while the middle three specialize the user interface to particular domains. We could think of more: spreadsheets and map data would be examples in the general category, plus there are hundreds of datatypes used in specialized vertical markets. The CORBAfacilities task force has shown good sense in limiting the number of items on its first list; the architecture allows for additional services, and we'll look for them as the facilities accumulate.

A Compound Presentation Facility specification is underway as CF RFP 1; details are in Section 17.4. The Roadmap indicates that Desktop, Help, and Text Checking won't happen until after the five RFPs in Section 17.3.

17.2.2 Information Management

This category looks like it brings in all of IS, but fortunately the architecture document shows that isn't quite what the OMG task force had in mind (well, except for Data Interchange perhaps). Here are the components listed in the write-up:

Information modeling facility: Creation of information models and schemas.

Information storage and retrieval facility: Persistent storage and retrieval of information.

Compound interchange facility: Interchange of data in compound documents.

Data interchange facility: General interchange of data, including format conversion.

Information exchange facility: Supports the interchange of information.

Data encoding and representation facility: Data format encodings and translations.

Time operations facility: Manipulation of time and calendar data.

The Information Modeling facility is targeted specifically at OMA-based schemas. It envisions a standard set of services to manipulate these schemas, including graphical editors, browsers, repositories, reporting system, and more. In general, the requirements envision a sophisticated data handling facility for the OMG object model.

Many CORBAfacilities consist, in whole or in part, of wrappers around established CORBAservices. The Information Storage and Retrieval facility is an example. It is slated to provide wrappers around the Persistent Object Service for initialization, search and retrieval, access control, and a repository with version and configuration management, metadata and model management, change notification, and other features.

The Compound Interchange facility covers storage and retrieval of compound documents. For this section, it's a pretty specialized service.

The Data Interchange facility is just the opposite: It looks like a general filtering and conversion facility, and the write-up covers so much ground that it's impossible to tell which direction this one is going to head.

Information exchange refers to generalized semantic exchanges; remember we've got OMA objects interoperating already. The write-up discusses standardization of a language at a high enough level to express agent programs and protocol descriptions; plus vocabulary and communication service and interaction control.

Data encoding is not the same as data interchange; here we're talking about compression and decompression, and conversion between internal machine representation and some canonical representation.

Time operations specify a number of sophisticated operations in what is, in present company, a specialized category.

If these categories seem huge and poorly defined, reconsider them in light of OMG's requirement that specifications be based on actual running computer progams and marketable software products. No groundbreaking, precedent-setting technology is ever going to come from a specification process with these ground rules. Compound interchange, data encoding, and time management look like good candidates for the OMG process right now; in fact, compound interchange is almost complete, and time is proceeding nicely. Information modeling could be ready next, while the others will probably have to get done in parts. We'll talk more about the CORBAfacilities schedule, which is called the roadmap, in Section 17.3.

17.2.3 Systems Management

One interesting aspect of Systems Management CORBAfacilities is where the specification is coming from, and how it's being introduced into the OMG process. The RFP process is only one way for specifications to be brought in; the other way is via *fast track* where an OMG corporate member company submits a specification that it believes is ready for standardization *without modification*. Why the strict requirement? Because there is no provision in the fast track process for revision of the submission to take others' objections into account. (Of course, the submitter can always modify in light of comments and restart the fast track process from the beginning.)

X/Open's SYSMAN group has been working on CORBA-based systems management facilities for some time, and has informed OMG that they intend to submit their specifications as candidates under the Systems Management CORBAfacility when they are ready. OMG and X/Open have a long history of close cooperative work, and OMG has said, explicitly in fact, that this area belongs to X/Open, and OMG will wait for them to submit. There's nothing wrong with this; X/Open has committed to meeting all of OMG's requirements, and the RFC submission still has to be accepted by the OMG members by the same vote as an RFP submission would. In fact, there's an additional requirement for *industry* (not just OMG member) comment, which makes an RFC more difficult to pass than the usual RFP. A number of OMG member companies are co-submitters with X/Open on the SYSMAN RFC: AT&T GIS, Bull, Digital Equipment, IBM, Sun, Tandem, and Tivoli.

X/Open has presented OMG with a presubmission draft of its expected RFC submission. A summary on the cover page gives its goal and scope:

> This specification describes an approach to the development of standards-based, open system adminstration applications, using common management facilities. It defines a framework (Object Request Broker and management facilities) to allow the development of applications that will significantly decrease the effort required to adminster distributed systems. The framework is based upon the CORBA and CORBAservices specifications.
>
> In addition, a set of management facilities are defined that allow management-specific interfaces to be common across environments, allowing the development of heterogeneous, interoperable applications.

We won't go over SYSMAN details here; there's too much of it, and even a brief architectural view would be a whole chapter. Documents describing it are available from X/Open, and during the RFC evaluation process, members may obtain them for free from the OMG.

The good news about this part of the CORBAfacilities is that a good bunch of people are working on a difficult problem, and think they have it just about solved, at least for the first go-around. Although we'll have to wait a while for the specification to work its way through the OMG process, we can figure that this important part of our IS installation can be based upon a standard service soon enough.

17.2.4   Task Management

Task Management covers automation and execution of user tasks, under a number of different disguises. The architecture document divides this category into:

Workflow: Objects that automate a work process, whether structured or ad hoc.

Agents: These may be static or mobile. There has been a lot of speculation and experimental implementation of agents, and a lot of people expect agents to solve their problems, especially dealing with information overload.

Rule management: Declarative event-condition-action rule specification and processing. Obviously, this requires a rule specification language and a rule execution engine.

Automation facility: Conventions and interfaces that allow access to the functionality of one object from another through scripts and macros.

Although broad, this area at least has a focus that we can grasp easily. Some of the items on this list are well defined and will be easy to specify using current technology; others seem wishful and futuristic.

OMG maintains a liaison relationship with the Workflow Management Coalition (WfMC), a roughly similar consortium concentrating on workflow technology. With the WfMC starting to work in CORBA, IDL, and the OMA, it's likely that candidate technology in the first category will emerge from its members over the next few years.

Many members of the CORBAfacilities task force want to work on agent technology right away; it combines a method to solve a pressing problem with an intrinsic high-tech appeal. Other members of the OMG want to wait, feeling that the technology needs to mature. In the next section, we'll look at the CORBAfacilities roadmap and see when it might come up.

17.3   CORBAfacilities ROADMAP

The CORBAfacilities roadmap is a rough schedule of when the different categories of facilities might come up for RFP. Here's a look at the first five planned RFPs. The first two are already working, and we'll cover them in the next two sections.

Possible Start	RFP Number: Topics	Projected Finish
Oct. 94	RFP1: Compound Presentation and Interchange	Oct. 95–Feb. 96
Mar. 95	RFP2: Time Operations, Internationalization	Mar. 96
Sep. 95	RFP3: Data Interchange, Automation	Sep. 96
Sep. 95	RFP4: Scripting, Agent Facility, Rule Management	Sep. 96
Feb. 96	RFP5: Information Exchange	Feb. 97

Do not make plans based on this schedule! For one thing, it's not a promise. (OMG committees can't make promises anyhow, since nothing is certain until the members vote to make it happen, and every vote is truly at each member's discretion.) And the dates are just projections; the TF hoped to meet these dates when the roadmap was drawn up, but no RFP can start until two things happen. First, the TF has to decide that it has the resources available to do the work, and second, the TF has to draft a set of requirements that pass votes in both the TF itself and the OMG TC.

In light of this, we have to point out that in late 1995, the TF's workload was substantial: It was working simultaneously on the Compound Presentation and Interchange RFP, the Time and Internationalization RFP, and the X/Open SYSMAN RFC at the time that it was scheduled to issue RFPs for the substantial and broadly scoped technologies in RFP3 and RFP4. The task force is staffed and run by volunteers, and we expect that even their best effort and most talented work will result in substantial delays from this schedule.

Nevertheless, the task force is doing very well indeed. RFP1 resulted in the submission of OpenDoc by Component Integration Laboratories; we'll discuss this in the next section. And the second RFP resulted in a high-quality submission from a number of OMG member companies.

What this does tell us is that the task force members have prioritized data and information interchange and various forms of automation very highly indeed. The user-visible items Desktop Management, Help Facility, and Text Checking come right after the items in the table. As the roadmap points out, there are a number of factors involved in the prioritization including need and impact, and technology readiness, and we can't really be sure which of these factors the members believed was more pressing when they ordered the list. In any case, even incremental progress on these important problems will give us a far richer OMA environment than we would have otherwise.

17.4 CORBAfacilities RFP 1

CORBAfacilities RFP 1, for Compound Presentation and Interchange, was issued in October 1994, and is expected to complete during the first half of 1996. The task force was fortunate to receive the OpenDoc compound document management facility as a candidate, along with the Fresco user interface management system.

Both of these facilities were originally built using CORBA and OMG IDL, and thus met the most basic requirement in the RFP. They also bene-fited from years of development and had acquired, especially in the case of OpenDoc, the aura of a de facto standard already by virtue of the companies that participated in the development and pledged to support the format once it completes.

OpenDoc is a product of Component Integration Laboratories, originally founded by IBM, Apple Computer, and Novell. Adobe Systems, Inc. has since joined at sponsor level, and the roster of full members includes Taligent, Oracle, and OMG. IBM contributed SOM, ensuring that the foundation of

OpenDoc would be CORBA-compliant, while Apple contributed the Bento compartmentalized storage format. Because OpenDoc, like the X/Open SYS-MAN, was not an adopted OMG technology when we wrote this chapter, we will not present a summary here; there are numerous articles and papers on OpenDoc, and we have included pointers to several in the reference section, Appendix A.

17.5 CORBAfacilities RFP 2

CORBAfacilities RFP 2, for Internationalization and Time Operation facilities, was issued in March 1995.

The Internationalization portion requested a sophisticated combination of internationalization and localization services including, for example, control over formats for currency, decimal and thousands points, rendering including arabic and oriental character sets, and more. There are two good reasons for this facility to come up early in the sequence: First, OMG is very much an international organization and represents the interests of its member companies, which come from all parts of the world; and second, internationalized products have a broader potential market so every member can benefit by considering the export market for their software.

The Time Operations portion requested an equally sophisticated set of time and date operations. This facility apparently was not basic enough for the CORBAservices task force, so they let it be worked here. But it seems anomalously plain compared to some of the other services we've considered in this chapter.

17.6 VERTICAL MARKET CORBAfacilities

OMG wants this to be the "audience participation" part of the book, with good reason. With the electronic plumbing nearly complete, a good CORBA-services foundation well underway, the horizontal CORBAfacilities getting started, and high-quality commercial ORBs coming to market from multiple vendors, many industry segments are starting to see the value in establishing standard objects in their domain, with interfaces written in OMG IDL and architecture based on CORBA and the OMA.

As we pointed out earlier in this chapter, a recent reorganization of OMG's Technical Committee now allows members to form Task Forces specialized around vertical markets and work directly on these standards. Before the reorganization, work within specialized markets was done by SIGs (Special Interest Groups), which were not empowered to work directly on establishing OMG specifications.

Some of this work will be done within OMG task forces, with the rest done in outside consortia and trade organizations, and brought into the OMG through both the RFC and RFP processes. One convenient route would have specifications from an outside consortium introduced into the OMG process by a task force representing that industry. This would ensure that the technology got the skilled attention it required, but still avoid duplicating the outside organization's work.

Here are some of the ways this process could work. The simplest scenario involves an industry where no trade group is working on software standards. A number of companies in that industry join OMG and form a SIG where they discuss the benefits of standard objects. Realizing the need for more members to spread the workload and achieve industry consensus, the group "spreads the word" and recruits additional member companies. An industry trade organization, if it exists, may become involved at this point also. When the SIG feels that is has reached "critical mass," it writes a mission statement and petitions the Domain Technical Committee to become a Task Force or TF. As a TF, the group is empowered to conduct the steps leading to selection of technologies, which become OMG specifications by vote of the DTC and OMG board of directors.

An alternative scenario starts with an industry trade organization that decides to set software standards based on CORBA and the OMA. (This has happened several times already; in telecommunications, DAVIC and TINA-C consortia have done this; in workflow, the Workflow Management Coalition.) OMG members recognize and acknowledge this outside effort, and a close working relationship grows between the two organizations. Companies that belong to both the organization and the OMG petition the DTC to be recognized as a TF, which can then support the adoption of these specifications by the OMG through either RFP or RFC.

The OMG process aims for a broad-based standard that will achieve wide industry acceptance. The DTC is unlikely to recognize a SIG's petition to become a TF until the SIG either demonstrates broad industry membership, or has the support of a major industry trade organization. OMG itself, through its staff, will support recruitment in an industry that shows promise in forming a SIG and advancing to TF. The technology adoption process itself requires effort; it will take more than a few companies to produce and select a specification that will survive the scrutiny of the DTC and board of directors.

As this book was written, the OMG had Domain Task Forces active in these vertical markets:

- Healthcare
- Telecommunications
- Financial services
- Manufacturing
- Business Objects

The Manufacturing SIG is interesting in part because, due to its general nature, it can serve as a nucleus for standardization efforts in a range of manufacturing industries.

We're going to close this section here. We've already presented OMG's reasons for doing this, in fact twice, if you count both Chapter 2 and the introduction to this chapter. This section is supposed to be for architectural details, and there aren't many because the new organization was just getting started as we finished this part of the book.

You can find out if a task force is working in your vertical market area by contacting OMG using the pointers in Appendix A. If they're already working on your area, you might want to join and help out, or at least find out what's going on. And if they're not, you might want to join and get something started. For one thing, do you know anyone who can do a better job than you? And for another, if you don't do it, your competitors will do it without you!

17.7   THE OMG ARCHITECTURE BOARD

There's another part of the OMG reorganization that is worth mentioning—in fact, it will play a key role in maintaining consistency in the far-flung components of the OMA.

The OMG Architecture Board (AB) is a newly formed body charged not only with maintaining, but also enforcing, the OMA on the various technologies adopted by OMG. Led by the Director of Architecture for the OMG, a neutral staff member, the board also includes 10 representatives from member companies: five from the Platform Technical Committee, the TC that originally produced CORBA and the OMA, and the remaining five from the Domain Technical Committee.

Among other things, the AB must approve every RFP before it is issued, and every submission before it is adopted. It will look for consistent adherence to the OMA; for example, a service that provides its own persistent storage will be sent back to be modified to use the Persistent Object CORBAservice.

Without the AB, inconsistencies could reduce the interoperability or integration of applications built up from OMA components. With the AB now in place, users of OMG technology can have a lot more confidence in the robustness of the architecture and its future growth.

17.8   OMA SUMMARY

This section brings to a close the architecture and specification part of the book. So far, we've talked only about specifications, not products; you may have started to get a feeling that things somehow weren't quite real, and this last chapter about future technologies probably gave that feeling another boost. But rest assured, things will get a lot more concrete when you turn the page and start coding the tutorial example program!

But, before you turn the page, take a moment to review everything you've read here. Details are important, and we hope you remember them, but we're really talking about the big picture, and how every component we've described is designed to fit into a coherent whole and interoperate smoothly with other components, regardless of source, as long as they adhere to OMG's architecture and specifications.

Consider the synergy: how the software elements of CORBA and the OMA make the most of the networked computer resource already spread around your enterprise. The coherent architecture was specified from the beginning; all of the parts fit together because they were designed to. They work on every platform, because they were produced by a talented multi-vendor collaborative effort. And the benefits accrue to architect, developer, and end user alike.

OMG was fortunate in two respects. First, it was formed before there was enough of an "object legacy" to hinder the acceptance of a coherent architecture, and second, its founders had the vision to establish an architecture that extended from the basic messaging and protocol level through the system-like CORBAservices to the CORBAfacilities with their close connection to the application level itself. Remember, this is not a layered architecture; since every client and object communicates through the ORB, every service is accessible to every object on the system.

And with this image, we conclude our look into the future. Reality hits on the next page where we start the tutorial example: Real ORBs. Real code. Real data. Really working, today, on a computer near you. So turn the page, and let's get started!

## CHAPTER 18

The Tutorial Example: Overview and Scenario

In at least one respect, CORBA programming is like mountain climbing, or skiing, or playing the guitar—no matter how much you read about it, you can't really appreciate it until you've actually done it. Even the detailed description you find in a technical specification can only carry you so far. To really understand CORBA, you'll have to write and compile some code, link and run some modules, and finally connect all of your distributed objects and get them to work together.

So, the rest of this book is devoted to a tutorial example of CORBA programming. We hope you'll spin the diskette that comes with the book (or, even better, work the example by typing code in yourself) and work along with us, but you're free to just read along and assume that everything "really works" if that suits you better. But if you actually work the example, when you've finished you'll not only be in a better position to decide if CORBA is the architecture for your enterprise, you'll also be ready to start work on your first project.

The authors have chosen this example with care. The scenario models a distributed environment, and demonstrates CORBA interoperability in a natural way. The example is close enough to real life that we were able to create computer objects that model real-world objects. And we've tried to use "best-practice" wherever we could: commenting our code, indenting to show modularization, and so on.

But we have deliberately kept our solution as simple as possible, because the objective of the exercise is to teach you CORBA programming and the advantages of object-oriented architecture within the OMA. So the objects and interfaces are real and fully developed, but the functionality within them is only a shell or model, and is usually implemented in only a few lines of code. This way, as you work the exercise, you'll spend almost all of your time working on the things that this book is really supposed to be about. It would take a lot of programming time to turn the example code into a real-life application, and you wouldn't learn any more about CORBA by doing it. (You'd probably learn less, since you'd be concentrating on side issues. You would learn a lot about retailing, but that's a different book by an entirely different set of authors.) There's a partial list of things we left out in Section 18.2.2.

This chapter poses a simple client/server problem, and Chapter 19 performs a first-level Object-Oriented Analysis and Design (OOA&D) on it. Neither chapter discusses any CORBA aspects, coding conventions, data typing, or language issues. These "implementation details" have been left to the next steps, as they would be in a real-life programming exercise.

Do not assume that the problem statement, OOA&D, and coding were produced by the authoring team on the first pass. The truth is far from this; instead of using the older "waterfall" approach where each level is analyzed in excruciating detail and frozen before progressing to the next, we used an iterative procedure. After we stated the problem as well as we could at first, we started design and found that we had forgotten some details in the statement or found we wanted something different. Similarly, after doing some coding, we found we wanted to change some design, which in turn, led us to change the problem statement a slight bit. Since you only get to see our final product, you may get the impression that this is the first version we came up with, but please take our word that this is far from the case. Of course, after the first two iterations, smaller and smaller changes were made, but you should be just as prepared to deal with this "spiral" type of development as we were. This OOA&D, of course, has little to do with CORBA as such, but it is a normal part of any object-oriented system. This chapter didn't spring full-blown into our heads, and you shouldn't expect the same for your own problems.

18.1   EXAMPLE ROADMAP

We figured that if all you wanted was a single-platform, single-language development environment, you'd probably be reading a different book. Instead, you're reading this book to find out about how CORBA ORBs and objects work, and how all of the CORBA components fit together. You want the answers to the questions that are hard, or sometimes impossible, to answer without firing up the development environment and ORB and getting your hands on the code: Which code is common to *every* environment and product? Which code is common to *every* ORB product that implements C++, or C, or Smalltalk? Which parts of your code port easily, and which require more effort?

So we structured this half of the book to bring these answers out into the open. We admit, this means you'll have to put out a little more effort to trace your way through the example, but the advantage is worthwhile. Common code is presented only once, isolated in its own sections of the book, for everyone to read and study together. These sections are followed by shorter sections for each product, where the differences (and advantages!) of each product are brought out.

Figure 18.1 is a map of the rest of the book. It shows, by the splitting and rejoining of the paths, which sections are common and which are language- or product-specific. A description with a little more detail follows.

The IDL is common to *every* implementation:

- The code that is determined by the language mapping and may be produced by an IDL compiler is common to all implementations in each programming language.
- The code that implements the functionality set down in the analysis and design is also common to all implementations in each programming language.
- Only the code that takes care of details such as connecting an object to the ORB and object initialization is different for each ORB. (Remember, this is one part that is not yet standardized by OMG. But the standard is in progress right now, and the second edition of this book should show a big improvement here!)

This book is arranged to take advantage of all of this commonality. Here's how to go through the example:

Everyone should read Chapter 18 (this chapter), Chapter 19 (Analysis and Design), Chapters 20 through 22 (product descriptions), and Chapter 23 (Coding and Compiling the IDL). The material here applies equally to *every* ORB and programming language: it's where we divide the problem into objects, assign each one its jobs to do, and set down the OMG IDL interfaces for each one.

At this point, we're almost ready to split by programming language, but not quite. When you read the A&D in Chapter 19, you'll discover that it's very clear *what* the objects do, but not *how* they do it. There's good reason for this; the A&D is concerned with the *problem* space, while algorithms and methods belong in the *solution* space. But, since algorithms and methods are mostly language-independent, we still need to set them down before we get into the language-dependent sections, and we chose to use the first section of each C chapter (the first of the language-specific chapters) for each

	C			C++				Smalltalk
Starting Up	Chapter 18: Scenario							
	Chapter 19: Analysis and Design							
	Chapters 20, 21, and 22: ORBs supporting C, C++, Smalltalk, and other languages							
	Chapter 23: Writing and Compiling the IDL							
	23.8: Obj Broker	23.9: SOM	23.10: DAIS	23.11: PwrBrkr	23.12: ORB+	23.13: Orbix	23.14: NEO	23.15: Distributed Smalltalk
The Depot	Section 24.1: Language-Independent Overview							
	Section 24.2: C Mapping Code			Section 25.1: C++ Mapping Code				Section 26.1: Getting Started
	Section 24.3: Coding Functionality in C			Section 25.2: Coding Functionality in C++				Section 26.2: Coding Funct. in Smalltalk
	24.5: Obj Broker	24.6: SOM	24.7: DAIS	25.6: PwrBrkr	25.7: ORB+	25.8: Orbix	25.9: NEO	26.4: Distributed Smalltalk
The Store	Section 27.1: Language-Independent Overview							
	Section 74.2: C Mapping Code			Section 28.1: C++ Mapping Code				Section 96.1: Getting Started
	Section 27.3: Coding Functionality in C			Section 28.2: Coding Functionality in C++				Section 96.2: Coding Funct. in Smalltalk
	27.5: Obj Broker	27.6: SOM	27.7: DAIS	28.4: PwrBrkr	28.5: ORB+	28.6: Orbix	28.7: NEO	29.3: Distributed Smalltalk
The POS	Section 30.1: Language-Independent Overview							
	Section 30.2: C Mapping Code			Section 31.1: C++ Mapping Code				Section 32.1: Getting Started
	Section 30.3: Coding Functionality in C			Section 31.2: Coding Functionality in C++				Section 32.2: Coding Funct. in Smalltalk
	30.5: Obj Broker	30.6: SOM	30.7: DAIS	31.4: PwrBrkr	31.5: ORB+	31.6: Orbix	31.7: NEO	32.4: Distributed Smalltalk
Run	33.2: Obj Broker	33.3: SOM	33.4: DAIS	33.5: PwrBrkr	33.6: ORB+	33.7: Orbix	33.8: NEO	33.9: Distributed Smalltalk

Figure 18.1. Example roadmap. Use this to plot your path through the example, based on the programming language and specific ORB you choose. Because of the way CORBA works, the planning, analysis and design, and IDL coding are common to all languages, and most of the coding is language-specific but not ORB-specific. Only the last part of each module—Depot, Store, and POS—includes ORB-specific code and procedures.

module. So, for each component (Depot, Store, and POS), there's an overview section covering its functionality and coding, which applies regardless of language. For the Depot, it's Section 24.1; for the Store, it's Section 27.1; and for the POS, it's Section 30.1. Read this just before you dive into the coding sections.

Now we split things up by programming language. (You don't have to work or read just a single language! You can learn a lot about the suitabilities of a particular language by comparing it to other languages working the same problem. This book gives you a great opportunity to compare three languages side-by-side without having to do all of the work yourself.)

Each language starts with two sections common to all of its ORBs, and concludes with individual sections for each ORB environment.

So if you're working in C, regardless of ORB, you work through Section 24.2 where you write or import the C code generated by the language mapping, which is common to all ORBs, and Section 24.3, where you write the code implementing the functionality dictated by the A&D, which is also common. Then you skip to the one section in the back half of the chapter that discusses the ORB you've chosen, to add the ORB-specific code and learn how to compile, link, and activate your object.

If you're working in C++, from Section 24.1 (the Depot overview), you skip to Section 25.1 to write or import the code generated by the C++ mapping and IDL compiler, and Section 25.2 to write the code implementing the functionality dictated by the A&D. Then you skip to the one section in the back half of the chapter that discusses the ORB you've chosen, to add the ORB-specific code and learn how to compile, link, and activate your object.

If you're working in Smalltalk, from Section 24.1 (the Depot overview) you skip to Section 26.1 and work your way straight through the chapter because we have only one Smalltalk implementation in this book. But it is arranged in about the same way as the others, so you can make some comparisons to the other languages.

At this point, regardless of ORB, you have the Depot code completed and running and it's time to start on the Store object.

Chapters 27, 28, and 29 discuss the Store object coding using a structure that exactly parallels the treatment of the Depot.

Chapters 30, 31, and 32 do the same for the POS and its associated objects.

Finally (whew!), we're ready to fire up all the objects and run our retail domain. This is covered in a single chapter, Chapter 33, with a section for each ORB.

What if you're using an ORB that isn't covered in this book? That's okay; there are lots of great ORBs, and we can't possibly cover all of them, even in 700 pages. If you're using C, C++, or Smalltalk, you can still use all of the common components before you either start out on your own or look around for help.

If you're using a different language entirely—Ada, perhaps, or COBOL (an appropriate choice for a retailing application!)—you need somewhere to go for more information and we have just the place.

OMG has set up a home page on the Web for information about this book and example. All ORB vendors that have implemented the example, whether they're included in this book or not, can post its implementation on the Web and give the OMG a URL to point to. Information about the book itself, about the example in general, or about interoperability among the different ORBs is available, too, probably on the OMG's own pages (but you'll have to examine the URLs to see where each page actually is). Find the book home page at *http://www.omg.org/CORBAprinciples.book.html*.

What about running a Depot and Store using one ORB, and a POS from another? All you need to do this, in principle, is a pair of CORBA 2.0-compliant ORBs; work up the example using them, and the sets of objects should work together almost right away. But products that do this were not shipping when we wrote this book, so we can't describe any special parts of the process here. But we can tell you that it should work, using exactly the same code, when the products do come out. You can either try to figure out how to run it yourself using the documentation that comes with these future products, or you can surf to the book's home page on the Web for directions and hints when the products become available.

18.2 PROBLEM OVERVIEW

A chain of grocery stores is changing its information handling. It is installing intelligent cash registers, called Point-of-Sale (POS) terminals, with bar-code readers and receipt printers. These POS terminals are all connected to a single store computer that contains information common to all POSs in the store but potentially different from information in other stores (such as markup, tax policy, and store totals). The store computer answers requests and stores summary data for the POS terminals. All store computers for stores in the chain are, in turn, connected to the central office's depot, which supplies item information to the store such as cost before markup and descriptive information to be printed on receipts. The depot also keeps track of each store's inventory and will, eventually, schedule deliveries to the store based on the inventory.

To expand on this description, we will first give a detailed set of tasks that will be performed by the overall system and its parts. We then specify what is explicitly excluded from the problem. After these detailed parts, we specify a set of objects along with some "desk-checking" information to convince ourselves that we understand the problem.

18.2.1   Detailed Problem Statement

Here is a "management level" problem statement, stating the rough information flow as a series of tasks.

A. A chain food store has several POS stations connected to a store computer. A cashier turns on the POS station and logs in to the store computer stating that the POS system is ready for business—the store computer obviously performs some security checks to make sure the POS station and the cashier are who they say they are. The store computer runs continuously and is connected to a continuously running central depot computer. It is the job of the depot to keep track of all inventory and to respond to requests with the chain's cost for each item, as well as the taxable status for an item (food, clothes, other). All taxation is calculated at the local store.

B. Each POS station is connected to a bar-code scanner and keypad. The bar-code scanner outputs a number to the POS station. The keypad can transmit one of five choices to the POS station:

1. Log in a new cashier.
2. Print a slip showing the total sales for this POS station since the last login.
3. Print a slip showing the total sales for the entire store since the store computer started.
4. Indicate a quantity that applies to the next scanned item. Two or more of these in a row without intervening bar-code input are resolved by forgetting all but the last quantity. Once a bar code is input, the quantity for the next item is automatically set to 1; that is, if any bar code comes in without a preceding quantity, its quantity is 1.
5. Total a sale (a series of one or more grocery items). [Note, once a sale has started (either a quantity or bar code entered), the only legal input is another quantity or the Total choice. Reports or logins are disabled.]

C. The store has multiple items, each of which has a bar code. A customer brings a basket of items to a cashier at one of the POS stations. The cashier, who runs each item over a bar-code scanner, may enter a quantity greater than 1 via the keyboard for each bar-coded item when more than one of the same item is being purchased. (That is, duplicate items do not necessarily pass under the scanner.) The POS station then prints the sum of all sales to finish the sales slip. The cashier rips off the printed sales slip and gives it to the customer. The cashier bags the order, collects the money, and tells the customer to have a happy day, whether the customer is smiling or not.

D. In order to print each line of the sales slip and to tell the central depot about its inventory, each POS station sends bar-code number and quantity to the store computer, which passes them on to the central depot, getting back at least the chain's cost for the item, the tax type for the item, and the item name. The store computer then adds on a store-specific constant percentage markup for an individual item, which is then reported back to the POS station and printed as the customer's per-item price for the sales slip. The store computer also returns the taxable price for each item to the POS so that it can figure out the tax at the end. The POS station calculates the amount of the (possibly) multiple items for a single line of the sales slip. A single line printed on the sales slip has the bar code, the item name, the sales price for each item, the quantity of each item and the total sales price for the line.

E. The store computer keeps track of the total amount of sales during the day. From any POS station, the store manager can ask for a daily report. The POS station reports the total sales since the store computer started. (There is no special console for the store computer; any POS can get the store totals.)

F. The POS station keeps a running tally of all its sales since its login time. The cashier can ask for this running total at any time except during a sale.

G. The taxes are calculated at the store level to allow for varying jurisdictions' policies. The chain management provides a standard tax object that calculates a flat tax for everything that is taxable. In the example, the total taxable amount is calculated by adding up the individual taxable amounts per item. The taxable amount per item is either 0 or the full value of the item. The taxes are always calculated on a final taxable sales total, not on an item-by-item basis, to avoid cumulative rounding errors.

H. For the purpose of this example, an item is either taxable or not taxable, and the sum of all taxable items is multiplied by a constant percentage to arrive at the tax. This is very simplistic but will do for the example. In real life, each store may have a different tax object that inherits from the basic object but that calculates taxes in a different way. The reason for calculating taxes on the total instead of each item is that rounding of individual items to the penny might lead to a different result from the rounding of the total sales. Again, a simplification for the sake of the example.

18.2.2 Problem Issues Explicitly Ignored

Here are some of the scenarios and issues that were explicitly left out of the problem statement but would probably be accounted for in any real application. You can probably think of more.

A. Customer returns an item.

B. Customer takes a previously scanned item out of the sale.

C. Customer decides to abort entire sales transaction.

D. Accounting periods—totals by day aren't kept, dates aren't printed, summations are never zeroed except for POS total when a new cashier logs in (which implies that another cashier is logging out). Similarly, the running store totals are not kept persistently since the beginning of time or ever reset except at store computer start-up.

E. The depot does not yet automatically schedule a delivery when the store's inventory for a given item falls below the low-water-mark.

F. Communications lines and computers never go down. In particular, a store never releases a StoreAccess object servicing any POS station that has called in since the beginning of the store computer's startup.

G. The store does not cache its own inventory or the price of items.

H. Shutting down the store or depot.

I. Arithmetic overflow on the running sums.

J. No optimization done on store and item cost/quantity database.

K. The POS station does not keep track of multiple items in case there is a sale of "n-items/currency-price" that is different from individual item price.

L. Does not deal with amount tendered nor calculate change. The sociological implications may be profound, but let's pretend we live in an era when knowing how to calculate change was a requirement for being a cashier, instead of (perhaps) a requirement for being a manager.

M. Cashiers are not identified by numbers, and security when a new cashier logs in is ignored (but a comment shows where it might be placed).

N. All bar codes will eventually be scanned correctly, and no price will have to be entered by hand. [This would require a completely parallel path to set price, taxes, sums, etc. This would double the amount of code, without teaching anything more about CORBA.]

O. Inventory count going negative in the depot is ignored. In real life, it would not be ignored.

P. At the depot in the current state of development, the store ID is ignored, and all stores are serviced from a single database—in real life, each store would have its own database at the depot.

18.2.3 Use-Cases

Use-cases are a technique used in OOA&D to help determine whether the design is complete. They are analogous to "walk-through" design techniques of the past. Another way of defining a use-case is as a "business rule"—it states what will happen in the business. In particular, use-cases identify specific actions that start the "system" working.

If everything is specified properly in the objects, you should be able to "desk-check" the working of the system for each use-case by looking at the objects defined here and walking through the implementation specified. This is not a foolproof method, but it does turn up a lot of design flaws before you get to the coding stages.

Initialization Here are three similar initialization use-cases that cover the functionality we're interested in:

1. Turn on a POS station.
2. Turn on a store computer.
3. Turn on the depot computer.

Each of these starts up the related object and calls its "initialize" operation in some system-dependent manner.

Login-to-POS

1. A new cashier comes to a running POS station and types L on the (simulated) keypad.
2. The keypad calls the "login" operation of the related POS station.

Request-a-report (two types)

1. A person types P or S on the keypad at a legal time.
2. The keypad calls the **print_POS_sales_summary** or **print_store_sales_summary** operation on the related POS station.

Perform-a-sale

1. (Optional) the operator enters Qn on the keypad, indicating a request for multiple items for the next bar code. The keypad calls the **item_quantity** operation on the POSTerminal object with input argument n.

2. The operator runs a grocery item over the bar-code scanner. The (simulated) scanner calls operation **send_barcode** on the POSTerminal object with input argument the number from the scanner. Much happiness ensues while objects call other objects. Two possible outcomes:

   - Bar code not recognized—scan ignored, cashier tries again. [For the sake of simplicity, we assume success eventually.]
   - Bar code recognized. All the correct calculations ensue, and a line of a sales slip is printed. If this is the first line, print out the name of the store.

3. Repeat 1 and 2 until cashier enters T at the keypad, at which time the keypad calls the **end_sale** operation on the POSTerminal object with no arguments. It enjoys itself updating all the numbers, printing out extra lines at the end of the sales slip, including subtotal, taxes, and grand total.

18.2.4 Deployment

When the system is finally deployed, we expect the following configuration:

> Each POS station is a separate computer in a LAN within the store. It contains the POSTerminal object, the InputMedia and the OutputMedia objects. The Store object, the StoreAccess objects it creates, and the Tax object reside on a separate computer in the same LAN, but on a different computer from the POS stations. The depot is on a separate computer reachable by WAN.

Of course, you'll be able to test your prototype on a single computer, and the instructions in Chapter 33 will tell you how. But you will also be able to try out a distributed environment, albeit with only one vendor's ORB at a time, at least until CORBA 2.0-enabled ORBs appear on the market.

## CHAPTER 19

The Tutorial Example: Analysis and Design

This chapter presents a somewhat more formal object-oriented analysis and design for the problem statement in Chapter 18. We didn't use a formal OOA&D methodology for this, nor did we use any computerized tool except our word processor, but we did have a lot of experience to draw upon. We strongly recommend that you pick a methodology before designing your first OO project, and probably a computerized tool as well, although we are not going to give you any advice here on which one to pick.

As you read the object descriptions in this chapter, you will see the many places where neither the problem statement nor the design are completely realistic. We intended them only to be evocative of real-world problems that have distributed components. We have designed input and output objects, for example, that are extremely simple, since making them realistic would not teach you anything more about CORBA. We likewise made the tax objects very simple, intending only to show how CORBA objects might be used; they are not intended to be realistic for any application, because a realistic set of tax objects would probably be larger than the entire rest of this simple application and would have little to do with CORBA.

This level of design defines some local variables (objects' state) and enough implementation discussion to reassure ourselves that we have indeed captured all the information processing needs of the system. Specifically, we have provided enough information to show that the points in the detailed object descriptions yield the desired results without too much arm-waving.

This level of design also intentionally has few explicit references to CORBA, although it does identify which state variables are IDL attributes (that is, variables that are publicly available through CORBA _get_ and _set_ interfaces, obviating the need to explicitly state operations [methods] that access these variables). This kind of design recognizes that the resulting system will likely be distributed. That fact subtly influences the selection of objects. For example, the particular object selections tend to minimize the network traffic. As with all distributed applications, this aspect should not be over- or underemphasized since the particular deployment of objects tends to change over time and early decisions may well be changed, yielding performance that may be subaverage, much less suboptimal.

We made one other concession to CORBA in this otherwise general object-oriented design: naming conventions. In converting this design to IDL in Section 23.1, to avoid confusion we used, where possible, the same names used in this chapter. To do this, we had to anticipate some naming recommendations for using IDL. One of recommendations states that, since the translation of IDL to a language binding often introduces underscores, you are advised to avoid possible conflicts by not using underscores in your IDL names. In order to follow that recommendation and to enhance readability without underscores, we use a different naming convention. Each word in a variable name begins with a capital letter. IDL pays no attention to case of names, but it does insist that it be consistent, because some of the language binding are case-dependent. Thus, for variables we identify as IDL attributes and for IDL interfaces and operations, we use this convention. Otherwise, in this chapter, we use some local variable names with underscores.

In Chapter 23, we will start implementation by extracting distributed aspects into a set of CORBA interfaces expressed in IDL. The IDL will not have many of the local variables or local operations needed to express a complete system design. The IDL will contain only those object interfaces, attributes, and datatypes that need to be public in a distributed environment.

Finally, talking about datatypes, this level of design does not specify datatypes except in general terms such as "reference to", "list of", "structure containing", and so forth, vaguely at that. All details of that sort are left to the IDL chapter and individual language mappings. Some of the "local variables" mentioned in the analysis might be turned into IDL datatypes and have their names changed to satisfy those conventions (as mentioned), but we don't consider that here.

19.1 OBJECT DEFINITIONS

One thing we needed to do was to divide our problem space into a number of objects. In keeping with the principles of object orientation, we wanted them to correspond as much as possible to real-life objects; this also helps us divide the functionality in a natural way. The major objects were easy to determine, but it took our programmers and designers a few iterations before the objects supporting the POS were fully stable. The objects in the final design are:

InputMedia Object

OutputMedia Object

POSTerminal Object

Store Object

StoreAccess Object

Tax Object

Depot Object

PseudoNameService Object

Figure 19.1 shows how these objects connect to make everything work. Every object accesses the PseudoNameService (PNS). In the figure, we show only one store connected to the depot; the example could easily be extended to more but we haven't taken the time or space to do this. It is possible to run more than one POS using the example code presented here.

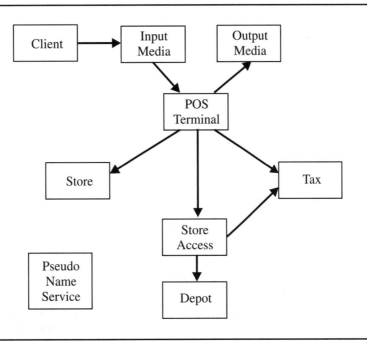

Figure 19.1. Objects in the POS example problem. Arrows indicate direction of an invocation. Every object calls the PseudoNameService.

The full definition of each object is given in the rest of this chapter. Each following subsection gives one object definition. Each has a short glossary definition, a list of state variables (some identified as CORBA attributes), a list of operations (also called methods), and implementation details for each operation.

19.1.1 InputMedia Object

Glossary

InputMedia simulates a keypad device and a bar-code reader device for the purpose of the demo only. Those devices are simulated by a single keyboard that routes its output to either "BarcodeInput" (when the line is all numeric, simulating a bar-code scanner) or to "KeypadInput" (line starts with a letter).

State Variables

POSRef:	Reference to the POSTerminal object that this input device services.
(local):	Local variables to help scanning input line from the terminal that is simulating the input devices.

Operations

Initialization

Parameters:	None; no return.
Description:	Start up the device at system start-up time, but only after starting the POSTerminal object.

Implementation:

1. Find the POSTerminal object reference, POSRef.

Called from:	Start-up.

BarcodeInput

Parameters:	Input "Item" (a string representing the bar code); no return.
Description:	A simulated bar-code reader—it presents the scanned bar code.

Implementation:

1. Simulated by input from a line-oriented input device. Any number followed by a return is treated as coming from a bar-code reader. It calls operation "SendBarcode" on the POSTerminal object with input argument the bar-code string from the scanner.

Called from: Start-up.

KeypadInput

Parameters: Input "Cmd" (a string representing input from a POS's keypad); no return.

Description: A simulated keypad reader—it presents input from a clerk.

Implementation:

1. Simulated by input from a line-oriented input device. Any line beginning with the following letters and ending with return have the following meaning and call the appropriate operation on its POS reference. Other keypad input is ignored.

   L Login a new cashier—Call "Login" operation of the POS-Terminal object with no arguments.

   P Print a POSTerminal sales total (i.e., sum of all sales since last login)—Call "PrintPOSSalesSummary" operation on the POSTerminal object with no arguments.

   S Print a store sales total (i.e., sum of all sales in entire store since the computer was turned on)—Call "PrintStore-SalesSummary" operation on the POSTerminal object, no arguments.

   Qn (That is, a Q followed by a number) The next bar code scanned is to be replicated this many times—Call the "Item-Quantity" operation on the POSTerminal object with input argument n.

   T End of sale, calculate subtotals, taxes, grand total—Call the "EndSale" operation on the POSTerminal object with no arguments.

2. After calling the operation, wait for return, then read a new line, starting from step 1. (Must wait since we are using simulated input = simulated output device. The simulation wouldn't need to wait if the devices were real and separate.)

Called from: InputMedia client.

19.1.2 OutputMedia Object

Glossary

OutputMedia simulates the existence of a sales tape printer and/or a screen showing current status of a transaction. The output device is simulated by simple, line-oriented output to a console terminal. A more realistic UI object might have multiple methods with multiple parameters given different meanings, but that is not deemed necessary for the purpose of the example.

State Variables

None

Operations

OutputText

Parameters:	Input "StringToPrint"; no return.
Description:	Output the "StringToPrint" to the media.
Implementation:	Like the description says, man!
Called from:	POSTerminal operations: "PrintPOSSalesSummary", "PrintStoreSalesSummary", "SendBarcode", "EndSale".

19.1.3 POSTerminal Object

Glossary

POS handles interaction with the media devices (InputMedia and OutputMedia objects), remembers the state of ongoing sales calculations, allows new cashiers to log in, and delivers reports about the POS station or the store.

State Variables

storeRef:	Reference to the Store object.
storeAccessRef:	Reference to the StoreAccess object.
outputMediaRef:	Reference to the OutputMedia object connected to the POSTerminal.
taxRef:	Reference to the tax calculator object.
POSid:	Identification of this POSTerminal.
itemBarcode:	From bar-code scanner.
itemQuantity:	From keypad; one (1) otherwise.
item_info:	A structure returned from the depot via the find_price operation, containing at least the following:
item	Should be the same as itemBarcode.
itemtype	The tax type of the item for use by the Tax object.
item_cost	Wholesale cost before markup.
name	Text description of the item suitable for printing on a receipt.

quantity	Remaining quantity in the store's inventory (should match what's on the store's shelves).
item_price	Price to customer, including store's markup; set by operation find_price.
item_tax_price	Amount of this item that is taxable; set by operation find_price.
itemExtension:	Calculated internally from quantity times price.
saleSubtotal:	Running total of itemExtension.
taxableSubtotal:	Running total of taxable itemExtension.
saleTotal:	Sum of final saleSubtotal + tax.
saleTax:	Tax on this sale.
POSlist:	Sequence of structures representing all POS-Terminals and their totals.

Operations

Initialization

| Parameters: | None |
| Description: | Start up the POSTerminal. |

Implementation:

   1. Find storeRef, outputMediaRef, taxRef, and POSId.

| Called from: | Start-up. |

Login

| Parameters: | None; no return. |
| Description: | Tell the POSTerminal object and thus the Store object that a new cashier is starting; retrieve reference to a StoreAccess object for use by the POS later. |

Implementation:

   1. Set itemQuantity to 1, all other values to 0.

   2. Register new POS/cashier by calling "Login" operation on storeRef object with input parameter POSId. (Since there is no security for this demo, there are no security parameters or failure returns.) This operation returns a reference to a StoreAccess object to be used by this POS.

| Called from: | InputMedia operation "KeypadInput". |

PrintPOSSalesSummary

| Parameters: | None; no return. |
| Description: | Tell the POSTerminal object to print a slip of its POSTotal and POSTaxTotal. |

Implementation:

1. Ignore this command if itemBarcode or saleSubtotal is nonzero, since that means the POS station is in the middle of a sale.

2. Obtain this POS's "Total" and "TaxTotal" by calling the Store operation "GetPOSTotals", getting a sequence of all the store's POSes and then selecting the POS information for this POS's POSid. (We recognize that this is a relatively poor use of object-oriented methods—encapsulation, in particular—because we are obtaining from the store much information we don't need, and we have to search through that information to find the information pertaining to us. We decided to leave the design at this level because we wanted to stop adding more methods in order to keep the example simpler.)

3. Format "Total" and "TaxTotal" and call the "OutputText" operation on the outputMediaRef object with the formatted string being an input argument.

Called from: InputMedia operation "KeypadInput".

PrintStoreSalesSummary

Parameters: None; no return.

Description: Tell the POSTerminal object to print a slip of the store's total, and the store's tax total, and the similar totals for each POS station in the store since each POS station logged in.

Implementation:

1. Ignore this command if itemBarcode or saleSubtotal is nonzero, since that means the POSTerminal is in the middle of a sale.

2. Call "_get__Totals" operations on storeRef object to get the store's total and tax total.

3. Format the store's total and tax total and call "OutputText" operation on outputMediaRef object, with the formatted string being an input argument.

4. Call operation "GetPOSTotals" of the storeRef object to get a sequence of structures, POSlist, about all the POS stations in the store.

5. For each structure in the sequence (representing a POS), format the POS's id, POS's total sales, and POS's total taxes; use that formatted string as an input argument on a call on the "OutputText" operation on outputMediaRef object.

Called from: InputMedia operation "KeypadInput".

ItemQuantity

Parameter: Input "Quantity"; no return.

Description: Sets the quantity to be applied to the next barcode message. Note that successive calls to this operation overwrites the previous call. Also, the local variable itemQuantity is reset to 1 after a bar code is read and processed so that the next bar code will be processed with quantity 1.

Implementation:

1. Set itemQuantity to "Quantity".

SendBarcode

Parameters: Input "Item"; no return.

Description: Informs POSTerminal of a grocery item scanned by the bar-code scanner. The POSTerminal object then sends messages to the StoreAccess object (which sends to the Depot object) about the inventory reductions and to get retail and taxable price as well as information to complete the sales receipt.

Implementation:

1. Copy "Item" to local itemBarcode.

2. Call "FindPrice" operation on storeAccessRef object with input arguments itemQuantity and itemBarcode; and output arguments item_price, item_tax_price, and structure item_info.

3. If return from 2 is the exception BarcodeNotFound, zero out itemBarcode, set itemQuantity to 1, and return. (Thereby requiring operator to rescan. The operator only notices this when the receipt maker doesn't go ka-chunk. Very annoying. In future versions, we should add a beep for error.) If there is no exception, continue.

4. Calculate itemExtension from item_price and itemQuantity, then accumulate into saleSubtotal.

5. Call "OutputText" operation of the outputMediaRef object with input argument of a formatted string including itemBarcode, item_info.name, itemQuantity, item_price, and itemExtension, putting asterisk after bar code if item is taxable (i.e., item_tax_price not 0).

6. Accumulate product of item_tax_price and itemQuantity into taxableSubtotal.

7. Set itemQuantity to 1.

Called from: InputMedia operation "BarcodeInput".

EndSale

Parameters: None; no return.

Description: Tell the POSTerminal object to complete the sale by calculating tax on taxable items, completing the printing of the sales slip, reporting the sale to the store, and preparing for new command.

Implementation:

1. Call "OutputText" operation of outputMediaRef object with input argument a formatted string of taxableSubtotal.

2. Call "CalculateTax" operation of taxRef object with input arguments taxableSubtotal; returns saleTax.

3. Call "OutputText" operation of outputMediaRef object with input argument a formatted string of saleTax.

4. Calculate saleTotal as sum of saleSubtotal and saleTax.

5. Call "OutputText" operation of outputMediaRef object with input argument a formatted string of saleTotal.

6. Call operation "UpdateStoreTotals" of storeRef object with input arguments saleTotal, saleTax, and POSId.

7. Set to 0: itemBarcode, saleSubtotal, saleTaxableSubtotal.

8. Set itemQuantity to 1.

Called from: InputMedia operation "KeypadInput".

19.1.4   Store Object

Glossary

The Store handles multiple POSes, logging them in, keeping track of their sales, and reporting totals on the store and the POSes.

State Variables

Totals: (CORBA Attribute, read-only) a structure consisting of two numbers collected since the store computer last started:

StoreTotal   Running sum of total sales (including taxes) for all POSes.

StoreTaxTotal   Running sum of total taxes for all POSes.

POSlist: A sequence of structures about POSTerminal objects that have logged into the store. Each structure contains the id of the POSTerminal, the total sales reported by that POSTerminal since last login, and the total taxes collected by that POSTerminal since last login.

Operations

Initialization

Parameters: None; no return.

Description: Start up the store when the store computer starts.

Implementation:

1. Set StoreTotal and StoreTaxTotal to 0.
2. Set POSlist sequence to indicate no logged in POSes.

Called from: Start-up.

Login

Parameters: Input "Id" (i.e. POS id); return reference to StoreAccess object.

Description: Register a new cashier/POS with the store and start keeping track of sales and tax totals for that POSTerminal. (Note: this is also where security would go if there were any.) Create a StoreAccess object and return its reference.

Implementation:

1. If there is no POSTerminal with "Id" already in the sequence,

   - Create a StoreAccess object.
   - Add another POSInfo structure to the POSlist sequence, setting its POSId, zeroing the totals, and setting its StoreAccess reference.

2. If there is already a POSTerminal in the sequence with POSId the same as "Id", just zero out the totals.
3. Return the StoreAccess object reference.

Called from: POSTerminal operation "Login".

GetPOSTotals

Parameters: Output "POSData"; no return.

Description: Return, in the output parameter, the state of the store's current knowledge of the registered POSTerminals (POSlist).

Implementation:

    1. Set POSData values to current values in POSlist.

Called from:	POSTerminal operations "PrintPOSSalesSummary", "PrintStoreSalesSummary".
Comment:	A better encapsulation-design would be to return just a list of POS totals rather than the POSlist which contains a lot of other information. We didn't do that because we wanted to keep the number of methods down for this example.

UpdateStoreTotals

Parameters:	Input "Id" (i.e., id of POS caller), "Price", "Taxes"; no return.
Definition:	Accumulate the parameters into the store state and into the POS state kept by the store.

Implementation:

    1. Search POSlist sequence for structure containing a POS id equal to parameter "Id".

- If not found, there is a major inconsistency in the operation of the entire system. (Notify MIS manager by beeper—not implemented in demo.) The demo dies.
- If found, add "Price" and "Taxes" to corresponding fields in the structure found.

    2. Add "Price" to StoreTotal and add "Taxes" to StoreTaxTotal.

Called from:	POSTerminal operation "EndSale".

_get__Totals

Parameters:	None; returns the structure "Totals".
Called from:	POSTerminal operation "PrintStoreSalesSummary".

Implementation:

    1. Note: This is automatically generated for the Store object by IDL compilers since it refers to an IDL attribute. It is declared read-only, so only the store can set it.

19.1.5 StoreAccess Object

Glossary

StoreAccess Object is the intermediary between the POS and the central depot concerning access to the grocery item database. One such object is created for each POS that logs in to the Store.

State Variables

depotRef:	Reference to chain's depot object.
taxRef:	Reference to local tax calculation object.
storeMarkup:	Percentage markup (Note: this is constant for all items in the store. This is quite unrealistic, but to do otherwise would require a local database for all items with markup for each, or at least a designator from the depot as to loss-leader, small, medium, high, or something like that. Definitely not needed for this CORBA demo.)
store_id:	Store identification number, used to identify self to central office depot.

Operations

Initialization

Parameters:	None; no return.
Description:	Start up StoreAccess object.
Implementation:	

   1. Set depotRef, taxRef, and storeMarkup.

Called from:	Store operation "Login".

FindPrice

Parameters:	Input "Item" (a bar code), and "Quantity"; output "ItemPrice", "ItemTaxPrice", and "IInfo"; no return value.
Exception:	BarcodeNotFound.
Description:	Given input parameters, tell depot about inventory reduction and ask it for IInfo (the information about the bar code in the database). Calculate the output parameters from IInfo's cost, markup, and ItemType (the tax type), the latter using the taxRef object.

Implementation:

   1. Call "FindItemInfo" operation of depotRef object with input arguments local variable "store_id", passing through received arguments "Item", and "Quantity"; output argument is passed through argument "IInfo" which returns (among other things) the item's cost and item's type.

   2. If 1 yields BarcodeNotFound exception, raise exception BarcodeNotFound and quit. Else (i.e., bar code was found), continue.

   3. Calculate "ItemPrice" as item's cost times storeMarkup.

   4. Call "FindTaxablePrice" operation on taxRef object with input arguments "ItemPrice" and the item's type, receiving back output argument "ItemTaxPrice".

Called from: POSTerminal operation "SendBarcode".

19.1.6 Tax Object

Glossary

Performs tax services such as determining whether an item is taxable and calculating taxes. For the purposes of the demo, it implements a flat tax method, where clothes and food are not taxable but everything else is taxed via a straight percentage of sales price.

State Variables

Rate: Percentage charged.

Operations

Initialization

Parameters: None; no return.

Description: Start-up when store system starts.

Implementation:

   1. Set Rate.

Called from: Start-up.

CalculateTax

Parameters: Input "TaxableAmount"; returns tax on that amount.

Description: Calculate tax on parameter amount and return as result.

Implementation:

   1. Multiply "TaxableAmount" by Rate, round it, return it.

Called from: POSTerminal operation "EndSale".

FindTaxablePrice

Parameters: Input "ItemPrice", "ItemType"; return taxable price.

Description: Determine how much, if any, of "ItemPrice" is taxable in this jurisdiction. In this case, food and clothes are not taxable, but everything else is 100% taxable.

Implementation:

    1. If "ItemType" is "food" or "clothes", return 0.

    2. Else return "ItemPrice".

Called from: StoreAccess operation "FindPrice".

19.1.7 Depot Object

Glossary

The Depot object is the inventory controller for the grocery store chain and source of information about items for sale in all the stores. It currently only responds to queries. (For future editions, it might print out a reorder slip.)

State Variables

(Ideally: Multiple stores, each with its own database; practically for this example, each store uses the same database.)

Database contains multiple items, each with structure:

    barcodeKey

    itemName

    inventoryCount

    itemCost

    taxType

Operations

Initialization

Description: Started after system boot time at corporate headquarters.

Implementation:

    1. Initialize access to database (perhaps read it all into memory).

Called from: Start-up.

FindItemInfo

Parameters: Input "StoreId", "Item" (a bar code), "Quantity"; output parameter "IInfo", a structure containing the database information about the grocery item corresponding to the bar code in "Item".

Exception: BarcodeNotFound.

Description: Look up the information and return the values asked for. If the "Item" (bar code) is not found in the database, raise an exception.

Implementation:

1. Ideally, look up a different database for each "StoreId". For the sake of the example's simplicity, all stores use the same database.

2. Search for key "Item". If not found, raise exception BarcodeNot-Found and quit. Else, continue.

3. Reduce database quantity for "Item" by "Quantity".

4. From database, set values in output parameter "IInfo", a structure.

Called from: StoreAccess operation "FindPrice".

19.1.8 PseudoNameService Object

When we started implementing this example, we came across an issue that affects everyone who uses a distributed implementation: how to get access to another object. In CORBA, this comes down to "how do I get an object reference?" OMG has defined a name service as explained in the first part of this book, but that name service was not available for all the implementations at the time the book was written.

We decided to provide a super-simple version of the name service, and we call it the PseudoNameService. In general, it is intended to make it easier for the other seven, application-oriented objects to cooperate. It is a CORBA object just like any other object, containing two interfaces. To maintain consistency in the discussion of this example, we now describe this object at the same level we described the other objects.

In defining this PseudoNameService (often called PNS in the following sections), we've actually only put off the problem a little. The various pieces of our applications still have a need to find the PNS object itself. We hide this in a subroutine that isn't properly part of the PNS object. Details of the initial access are explained more fully in the introductory sections for each language binding. For now, we just define the PNS object. (The OMG has defined an Initialization Specification just to get around this chicken-and-egg problem: It allows a client to query the ORB for the name service object reference with a standard call. Unfortunately, we weren't able to use it because the specification was so new that many—in fact, most—ORBs didn't have it when we wrote the example.)

Glossary

Performs the naming services of binding a textual name to an object reference and finding an object reference given a textual name.

State Variables

name_list: A list of structures, each containing a name (in character format) and the object reference corresponding to that name.

Operations

Initialization

Parameters: None; no return.

Description: First routine started for the entire store system.

Implementation:

1. Set the list of known names to null.

2. Make available a file containing a reference to the PNS.

Called from: Start-up.

BindName

Parameters: Input "ObjectName" (a string specifying the name of the object); input "ObjectRef" (a reference to the object); no return value—assume success (not realistic since the PNS might get overloaded with names).

Description: Enter the association into the PNS.

Implementation:

1. To the existing name_list, add another structure containing ObjectName and ObjectRef.

Called from: All objects that "advertise" their services to clients.

ResolveName

Parameters: Input "ObjectName" (a string); return value is an object reference.

Description: Find an object reference, given its name.

Implementation:

1. If "ObjectName" is found in "name_list", return the associated object reference.

2. Else return a null object reference, indicating an error.

Called from: All objects needing access to objects in the remainder of the application.

## CHAPTER 20

ORB Products: C Language Mapping

20.1 ORB PRODUCTS OVERVIEW

Right here, we start a very different part of the book. We're finished with the general, specification-level discussion; everything from here on deals with real products and real code—products you can buy and load, IDL and programming language code you can write and compile, ORBs you can connect to (and connect to each other!), and clients and object implementations you can run.

The example we presented in the last two chapters is worked in the rest of this book in three programming languages, using a grand total of eight ORB environments from seven vendors. Each ORB and environment has been tuned by its vendor and technical team to be the best it can be for the users they have targeted. As you will see in the next three chapters, this can lead to products that differ markedly yet still conform completely to the OMG specifications and interoperate fully over the network.

20.1.1 ORBs and Language Support

Most ORBs support more than one programming language, but we can only put each description into a single chapter. So we've divided the sections into chapters according to the language that each ORB uses to work the example in this book. But you shouldn't assume that the ORBs are restricted to that language; for example, at press time, the following ORBs supported, or planned to support, these languages:

- C++: All of the ORBs in this book except HP Distributed Smalltalk (ORB Plus is HP's C++ ORB);

- C: NEO, plus the ORBs listed in this chapter;
- Smalltalk: PowerBroker, SOMObjects, Orbix, and NEO, in addition to Distributed Smalltalk;
- OLE: PowerBroker, DAIS, Orbix, and ObjectBroker all provide some level of integration with OLE;
- Other languages: Sun and Orbix for JAVA, Orbix for Ada, and DAIS for COBOL;
- Other ORBs: Contact OMG for pointers to many more ORB vendors and products supporting these languages and more. See Section 20.1.3 for details.

20.1.2   ORB Features and the Programming Example

One important feature of an ORB development environment is its ability to automate parts of the development process and to hide details of, for example, how objects connect and work together. For the typical development tool, the more automation and simplification, the better.

Unfortunately, though, it's really hard to learn the details about something when everything is hidden under the covers. Since the differences in the products appear on the surface, and the similarities that enable integration are sometimes hidden, when we work the example we're going to dig under the surface layer of these ORB environments in order to teach you how CORBA works. This way, you'll be in a better position to take advantage of CORBA *everywhere* it fits into your enterprise; in addition, you'll be much less likely to get into trouble from misunderstanding what CORBA can and cannot do.

So, all of the companies and developers who helped write this book agreed to make the example *heuristic*, that is, to expose the OMG-standardized components of CORBA that enable objects to work together: IDL interfaces, language mappings, where objects reside and run, how they connect. And, for every ORB, these components are brought out into the open *even though they are handled automatically in various ways by the products in this book and many other ORB products on the market*. This presentation starts in Chapter 23 and continues through the end of this book. If the working of the example seems primitive, that's because it was made so deliberately, just this once, for your benefit. Learn the details this time through, and then let your ORB environment handle them for you and your development staff as you apply CORBA to real-world problems and projects.

20.1.3   Advanced ORB Product Features

The advanced features of ORBs and their development environments are crucial, too, because they determine the usability of the product and the productivity of the programmers and users who depend on it. The designers of the CORBA specification knew this; that's why CORBA specifies the interface and protocol layers very tightly while saying virtually nothing about the development layer above them. This allows development environments the freedom to flourish *without* spoiling the interoperability the standard confers. There's no reference implementation for CORBA. Instead, *all* of the products you see here, and many others besides, are fully conformant implementations of the specification, and are still able to offer a wide range of development and run-time enhancements.

In the next three chapters, the vendors of these ORBs present details of their products. This is the one place in this book where you can learn what these products can do when they're not in "teaching mode." It's a great place to start an investigation leading to the purchase of one—or more!—ORBs and programming environments for your company. All of the ORBs support the OMG specifications for CORBA and will incorporate CORBAservices and CORBAfacilities as they become available, but some may meet your company's needs or wants better than others. And there's a good possibility that different groups in your company—engineering, R&D, finance—may benefit from different ORBs and environments. Finally, with CORBA, you can allow them this freedom without sacrificing interoperability!

These are not the only ORBs available, of course—many other vendors offer ORBs and development environments that conform to the OMG specifications and have the potential to fit well in your enterprise. We're limited to eight ORBs mostly by space and time restrictions; don't overlook a good product just because it's not included in this book. OMG offers several easy ways to find out about additional ORBs. You can either contact OMG directly (see Appendix A) and ask for the CORBA products directory, or you can surf to the OMG home page (*http://www.omg.org*) which has two places to look: either the CORBA products directory online, or the *CORBA Principles and Programming* pages with pointers to updated versions of example code and advice for every ORB vendor who has notified OMG that he or she has working example code on the Web (including all seven vendors in this book, plus many more).

Products are divided into chapters by the programming language they use to work the example in this book: Chapter 20 for C; Chapter 21 for C++; and Chapter 22 for Smalltalk. Remember, these are not the only languages these ORBs support! Within each chapter, presentations are arranged alphabetically by company name. (Hey, we had to decide somehow.)

20.2   DIGITAL EQUIPMENT CORPORATION: OBJECTBROKER

ObjectBroker is Digital Equipment Corporation's implementation of the CORBA specification. ObjectBroker also implements features beyond the CORBA specification, features that result from years of experience in delivering distributed object systems, from steady product improvement based on customer feedback and from engineering innovation. A conceptual illustration of ObjectBroker functions is shown in Figure 20.1.

In 1991, ObjectBroker became the first commercially available ORB. Today it has the largest installed customer base and, with implementations on 21 platforms, it also has the broadest coverage of heterogeneous, multivendor platforms. It provides both CORBA V1.2 C bindings and CORBA V2 C++ bindings. ObjectBroker's other technical strong points include:

PC integration

wrapping tools and technology

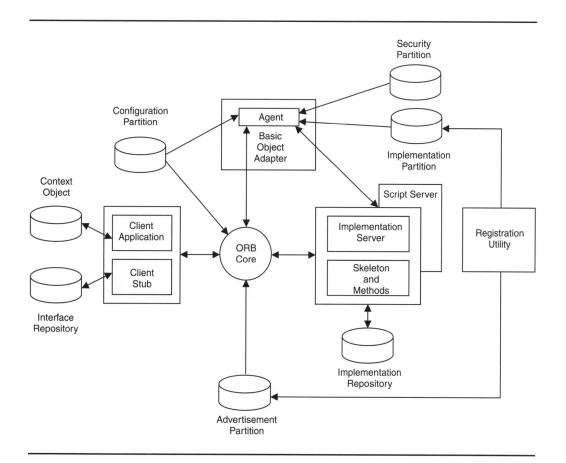

Figure 20.1. ObjectBroker architecture.

brokering

brokering control mechanisms

ease of use

security

These features are described in detail shortly. Their common theme is the total integration of enterprise-level computing infrastructure, including desktop systems, back-room servers, and legacy systems and applications.

An object-oriented approach to that integration presents the opportunity to hide the differences and underlying complexities of such a heterogeneous environment. Thus, the OO paradigm provides a golden opportunity to achieve integration of the distributed computing infrastructure, and an ORB like ObjectBroker lets you take advantage of this opportunity. From the desktop to the datacenter, ObjectBroker provides interconnectivity that counts.

20.2.1 PC Integration

PCs make up the majority of desktop systems in the enterprise. Integrating these desktops as clients in the distributed computing system is a critical concern for many of Digital's customers. ObjectBroker's PC integration features include:

- Implementation of ObjectBroker on Windows, Windows95, and Windows NT platforms, which means that any PC can be a first-class participant in a distributed object system.
- DDE support for interapplication data transfer.
- The OLE Network Portal, which allows unmodified, off-the-shelf PC applications to access remote objects via OLE interfaces.
- Visual Basic support, which provides a familiar tool for Rapid Application Development.
- Second-generation connectivity to Microsoft desktops.

ObjectBroker works cooperatively with Microsoft's OLE and DDE capabilities to allow shrink-wrapped applications running locally on PCs to exchange information with applications running on UNIX, OpenVMS, and Windows NT systems. For example, a Microsoft Excel spreadsheet can access a financial application or database on a UNIX, OpenVMS, or MVS server and return that data for use in the spreadsheet. The interfaces to Microsoft's

Object Linking and Embedding (OLE) and Dynamic Data Exchange (DDE) are included in ObjectBroker, allowing users of shrink-wrapped software to reach out into the network in a familiar manner.

ObjectBroker's OLE Network Portal provides Microsoft's Object Linking and Embedding (OLE) functions for data objects stored on non-Microsoft platforms. The portal enables OLE-supporting applications (current versions of Microsoft Word and Excel, Lotus 1-2-3, AmiPro,and so on) to link and/or embed OLE data objects that reside on UNIX and OpenVMS servers.

The Network Portal intercepts relevant OLE calls on the PC and maps them to ObjectBroker messages, which are sent to an appropriate server. From the application user's perspective, the process is transparent; the object behaves as though it were stored locally on the PC. Within an OLE application, the ObjectBroker portal appears to be a local OLE V2 server application. In this way, information from sources across the network can be dynamically linked into desktop applications. Making such distributed information available to desktop applications increases the return on all software investments.

ObjectBroker also provides an interface to Microsoft's Visual Basic (VB) so that you can make direct calls to ObjectBroker from within the familiar VB development environment. This feature facilitates the rapid development of graphical client/server applications, and allows the users of desktop tools to extend their capabilities to information residing on server systems anywhere on the network. This Visual Basic language binding allows PC users to manipulate and invoke CORBA objects through the Dynamic Invocation Interface.

ObjectBroker V2.6 provides second-generation connectivity to Microsoft desktop systems, allowing you to use CORBA objects in the same way you now use OLE objects on the local PC. In addition to the DDE Listener and OLE Network Portal capabilities provided in Version 2.5, V2.6 allows an unmodified CORBA object server to be accessed via OLE Automation and OLE custom interfaces.

Remote CORBA objects can be dragged and dropped and linked among unmodified Microsoft desktop applications. ObjectBroker automatically provides OLE automation access to a CORBA object's methods, as well as a local desktop rendering of the object for drag and drop and embedding operations. In addition, a remote object's local appearance and its automation interfaces can be customized.

Though much work remains to be done in the area of interoperability between CORBA systems and Microsoft desktop platforms, Digital provides extremely useful PC integration today, and provides assurance of a clear upgrade path. Digital fully supports the OMG process for achieving standardized CORBA/OLE interoperation in the future.

20.2.2 **Wrapping of Legacy Systems/Applications**

Digital believes that the *wrapping* of legacy systems and applications—that is, the ability to put an object-oriented veneer around a customer's existing software systems—is vitally important. Wrapping lets customers preserve the immense investment that has been made in such software, by enabling the inclusion of these systems as objects in a modern distributed computing infrastructure.

ObjectBroker provides three mechanisms that let you encapsulate existing legacy applications and data, without modifying source code, thus facilitating the integration of existing applications into new client/server architectures. ObjectBroker supports:

- a scripting mechanism;
- the CORBA-defined mechanism for creating a server skeleton (API wrapping); and
- built-in client-side servers.

ObjectBroker's scripting feature allows applications that were not designed for direct program access (those that have no callable API) to be encapsulated and accessed as a collection of methods. The script is a command-line interface (CLI) program such as a UNIX shell script or an OpenVMS DCL command procedure; it invokes the application via command line and captures its output. Thus the script server can be used to issue SQL or ODBC commands for data access.

ObjectBroker's implementation of the CORBA-defined mechanism for creating a server skeleton allows legacy applications that have callable APIs to behave as CORBA servers. The skeleton runs as a result of a request for an operation. The skeleton implements the methods that perform the operation (by calling the legacy application) and performs other support tasks as needed.

ObjectBroker's built-in client-side server feature lets an implementor use the same code to build a server as a separate executable, a static link library, or a dynamic link library. This feature provides support for clients that may request an in-process server for reasons of efficiency (this feature can be used on non-PC platforms as well).

All three approaches can be used in combination with ObjectBroker's Visual Basic support. This lets programmers and system integrators quickly build graphical desktop interfaces to servers that encapsulate unmodified legacy applications written in any language. The result is an ability to move rapidly to a client/server architecture that provides easy end-user access to remote applications and data.

20.2.3 Brokering

The two essential aspects of distributed objects are the object-orientation of the software itself, and the *brokering* function. Brokering is the notion of a software layer that translates abstract requests sent to an object into actions by specific pieces of software, regardless of where that software happens to reside.

The sophistication of ObjectBroker's brokering function is most evident when CORBA's dynamic invocation interface (DII) is used. The DII lets ObjectBroker choose among multiple implementations of a given object method based on characteristics associated with the request (such as location of client, security mechanism, and more) and with the user (identity, preferences, corporate role).

ObjectBroker provides three mechanisms in support of attribute-based brokering:

context object

attributes

multiple implementations

A context object contains information about the client, the environment, or the characteristics of a request. It is used by ObjectBroker during method resolution to identify user preferences for the selection of a server. The context object provides a way to specify request characteristics that are difficult to pass as parameters.

ObjectBroker provides a GUI interface and a context object language for customer-defined attributes; it provides predefined attributes as well. For example, ObjectBroker defines the OBB_DEFAULT_NODES attribute, which indicates the nodes on which an object can run. Customers can define any number of additional attributes in a context object, and context objects can be defined and shared at the user, group, or system level.

ObjectBroker provides several language mechanisms that help you control the brokering of multiple implementations of a method or server. These language mechanisms are described in the following section.

20.2.4 Brokering Control Mechanisms

ObjectBroker supports OMG Interface Definition Language (IDL), the language that lets you define an object's interface. ObjectBroker also provides three language extension features that aid in describing, structuring, and generating a distributed application:

Implementation Mapping Language (IML)

Method Mapping Language (MML)

Code Generation Facilities

In essence, IML lets you capture the characteristics of a particular server or method implementation. MML lets you specify the rules and conditions that ObjectBroker uses to decide which server or method implementation best satisfies a client's request.

The purpose of segmenting information about interfaces, implementations, and methods is to make it easier to understand and manage the brokering function of an ORB. These different pieces of system information are viewed by different audiences who need to do—and to understand—different things.

IML lets the server implementor (who clearly knows more than anyone else about the implementation) describe the characteristics of the implementation for each interface, including the OS-specific information used for invocation, the methods that make up the implementation, and the attributes used for method selection. For example, the IML file can specify things such as server activation policy (that is, persistence, and whether the server is shared), event notification policy, context object attributes allowed, script usage (for legacy applications), and so forth. IML also allows custom characteristics, such as a different security mechanism, to be specified.

MML is used to create a structure for method resolution when there is more than one active implementation for a given interface. Thus MML lets a system administrator or architect specify the characteristics, rules, and conditions that control the selection of a method implementation.

ObjectBroker generates default IML and MML files from IDL. Default values can be accepted, or the files can be modified as required. There is no reason to burden the interface designer (the author of the IDL) with the information specified in IML, nor to burden the implementor with the information specified in the MML. The three-way segmentation means that you can target your training efforts more precisely and limit the distribution of this information to the appropriate recipients.

20.2.5 Ease of Use

In addition to generating default IML and MML files from IDL input, Object-Broker has a QuickStart mechanism for code generation. This mechanism allows a user or product evaluator to go from IDL to running client and server executables in 10 minutes. Starting with OMG IDL, the QuickStart mechanism:

- creates skeleton code for clients, servers, and methods, including header and include files;
- inserts dummy values for the parameter datatypes specified in the IDL file;
- creates client and server makefiles; and
- creates client and server executables.

These executables simply exercise the methods sequentially, passing and displaying dummy parameter values and then terminating execution. The QuickStart feature lets evaluators see immediately what ObjectBroker can do. It provides boilerplate code for those developing applications, and serves as an example/tutorial on the subjects of parameter passing and memory management.

The programmer then modifies the QuickStart-generated skeleton code to include real application logic. At the programmer's option, code is preserved over iterations of the generation process as new source files and makefiles are created.

20.2.6 Security

ObjectBroker V2.6 provides Kerberos DCE authentication via DCE's Generic Security Services interface (GSSAPI). Thus, ObjectBroker provides customers with the ability to use an open, industrial-strength security mechanism that is both robust and scalable across large, multivendor distributed systems.

Kerberos provides authentication, mutual authentication, and protection against replay and sequencing attacks. And, by implementing these security enhancements through GSSAPI, ObjectBroker gives customers more options in choosing and integrating third-party authentication packages, as they become available. In addition, support for DCE Security facilitates integration with DCE-based software systems.

20.2.7 ObjectBroker Future

Beyond ObjectBroker V2.6, Digital will implement CORBA V2 interoperability via both the IIOP and DCE-CIOP protocols, as well as additional CORBAservices beyond the Naming service available in V2.6. Over time, several trends will drive the inclusion of new capabilities in ObjectBroker.

The scope and complexity of the business solutions implemented with ORB technology is steadily increasing. The first customer pilot projects, which are now in production deployment, focused on application integration problems. These projects typically used object wrappers to encapsulate existing applications, often running on legacy systems, with complementary or overlapping functions at times provided by different systems. New solution components—such as an innovative new user interface or business delivery system—were then built to integrate data and application logic from disparate sources.

Increasingly, our customers want to use popular PC desktop tools—as well as more sophisticated OO design and analysis approaches—for rapid application prototyping and development. Security becomes more of a customer concern as the use of distributed systems grows. Customers want to add transaction semantics in order to more fully integrate production applications with newer business systems. Customers need queuing and reliable messaging technology to integrate applications that either cannot use a request/response communication style, or need to be distributed in time as well as geographically. And, as application integration expands, customers want to add workflow control so that business policies can be systematically applied in the reengineering of business processes.

The ObjectBroker vision is to provide ever-increasing enterprise-level integration, while continuously improving scalability, reliability, ease of use, and performance. ObjectBroker will also add advanced capabilities in the areas of:

- Microsoft OLE integration;
- simplified development, including the integration of leading third-party OO development tools;
- transactional semantics;
- queuing semantics and asynchronous behaviors;
- workflow semantics;
- application management via leading third-party system and network management tools.

Digital is targeting these areas for two reasons. The first is that our major customers are already proceeding along these dimensions and have requested these capabilities. As ObjectBroker customers succeed in integrating their current heterogeneous environments, they naturally want to extend these capabilities to more types of services and many more client interfaces.

The second reason is that Digital already has a great deal of experience in delivering mission-critical capabilities in other software products and in our service offerings. Thus it makes sense to incorporate them in our strategic object-based offerings as we help customers move to three-tier client/server approaches to solve the next generation of business problems.

20.2.8 Summary

ObjectBroker is an excellent implementation of the CORBA specification. It provides additional features over and above those in the CORBA specification in the areas of PC integration, legacy system wrapping, and security. ObjectBroker also provides sophisticated and flexible control over the brokering of multiple implementations. All these features are aimed at providing useful integration of the distributed hardware and software infrastructure found in a typical large enterprise.

20.3 IBM: SOMobjects

Object-oriented programming (or OOP) is an important new programming technology that offers expanded opportunities for software reuse and extensibility. Object-oriented programming shifts the emphasis of software development away from functional decomposition and toward the recognition of units (called *objects*) that encapsulate both code and data. As a result, programs become easier to maintain and enhance. Object-oriented programs are typically more impervious to the "ripple effects" of subsequent design changes than their nonobject-oriented counterparts. This, in turn, leads to improvements in programmer productivity.

Despite its promise, penetration of object-oriented technology to major commercial software products has progressed slowly because of certain obstacles. This is particularly true of products that offer only a binary programming interface to their internal object classes (that is, products that do not allow access to source code).

The first obstacle that developers must confront is the choice of an object-oriented programming language. So-called "pure" object-oriented languages (such as Smalltalk) presume a complete run-time environment (sometimes known as a *virtual machine*), because their semantics represent a major departure from traditional, procedure-oriented system architectures. As long as the developer works within the supplied environment, everything works smoothly and consistently. When the need arises to interact with foreign environments, however (for example, to make an external procedure call), the pure-object paradigm ends, and objects must be reduced to data structures for external manipulation. Unfortunately, data structures do not retain the advantages that objects offer with regard to encapsulation and code reuse. "Hybrid" languages such as C++, on the other hand, require less run-time support, but sometimes result in tight bindings between programs that implement objects (called *class libraries*) and their clients (the programs that use them). That is, implementation detail is often unavoidably compiled into the client programs. Tight binding between class libraries and their clients means that client programs often must be recompiled whenever simple changes are made in the library. Furthermore, no binary standard exists for C++ objects, so the C++ class libraries produced by one C++ compiler cannot (in general) be used from C++ programs built with a different C++ compiler.

The second obstacle developers of object-oriented software must confront is that, because different object-oriented languages and toolkits embrace incompatible models of what objects are and how they work, software developed using a particular language or toolkit is naturally limited in scope. Classes implemented in one language cannot be readily used from another. A C++ programmer, for example, cannot easily use classes developed in Smalltalk, nor can a Smalltalk programmer make effective use of C++ classes. Object-oriented language and toolkit boundaries become, in effect, barriers to interoperability. Ironically, no such barrier exists for ordinary procedure libraries. Software developers routinely construct procedure libraries that can be shared across a variety of languages, by adhering to standard linkage conventions. Object-oriented class libraries are inherently different in that no binary standards or conventions exist to derive a new class from an existing one, or even to invoke a method in a standard way. Procedure libraries also enjoy the benefit that their implementations can be freely changed without requiring client programs to be recompiled, unlike the situation for C++ class libraries.

For developers who need to provide binary class libraries, these are serious obstacles. In an era of open systems and heterogeneous networking, a single-language solution is frequently not broad enough. Certainly, mandating a specific compiler from a specific vendor in order to use a class library might be grounds not to include the class library with an operating system or other general-purpose product. *The System Object Model (SOM) is IBM's solution to these problems.*

20.3.1 Introducing SOM and the SOMobjects Toolkit

The System Object Model (SOM) is a new object-oriented programming technology for building, packaging, and manipulating binary class libraries.

- With SOM, class implementors describe the interface for a class of objects (names of the methods it supports, the return types, parameter types, and so forth) in a standard language called the Interface Definition Language, or IDL.

- They then implement methods in their preferred programming language (which may be either an object-oriented programming language or a procedural language such as C).

This means that programmers can begin using SOM quickly, and also extends the advantages of OOP to programmers who use non-object-oriented programming languages.

A principal benefit of using SOM is that it accommodates changes in implementation details and even in certain facets of a class's interface, without breaking the binary interface to a class library and without requiring recompilation of client programs. As a rule of thumb, if changes to a SOM class do not require source code changes in client programs, then those client programs will not need to be recompiled. This is not true of many object-oriented languages, and it is one of the chief benefits of using SOM. For instance, SOM classes can undergo structural changes such as the following, yet retain full backward, binary compatibility:

- adding new methods,
- changing the size of an object by adding or deleting instance variables,
- inserting new parent (base) classes above a class in the inheritance hierarchy, and
- relocating methods upward in the class hierarchy.

In short, implementors can make the typical kinds of changes to an implementation and its interfaces that evolving software systems experience over time.

Unlike the object models found in formal object-oriented programming languages, SOM is *language-neutral*. It preserves the key OOP characteristics of encapsulation, inheritance, and polymorphism, without requiring that the user of a SOM class and the implementor of a SOM class use the same programming language. SOM is said to be language-neutral for four reasons:

- All SOM interactions consist of standard procedure calls. On systems that have a standard linkage convention for system calls, SOM interactions conform to those conventions. Thus, most programming languages that can make external procedure calls can use SOM.
- The form of the SOM Application Programming Interface, or API (the way that programmers invoke methods, create objects, and so on) can vary widely from language to language, as a benefit of the SOM bindings. Bindings are a set of macros and procedure calls that make implementing and using SOM classes more convenient by tailoring the interface to a particular programming language.
- SOM supports several mechanisms for method resolution that can be readily mapped into the semantics of a wide range of object-oriented programming languages. Thus, SOM class libraries can be shared across object-

oriented languages that have differing object models. A SOM object can potentially be accessed with three different forms of method resolution:

- *Offset resolution:* Roughly equivalent to the C++ "virtual function" concept. Offset resolution implies a static scheme for typing objects, with polymorphism based strictly on class derivation. It offers the best performance characteristics for SOM method resolution. Methods accessible through offset resolution are called static methods, because they are considered a fixed aspect of an object's interface.

- *Name-lookup resolution:* Similar to that employed by Objective-C and Smalltalk. Name resolution supports untyped (sometimes called dynamically typed) access to objects, with polymorphism based on the actual protocols that objects honor. Name resolution offers the opportunity to write code to manipulate objects with little or no awareness of the type or shape of the object when the code is compiled.

- *Dispatch-function resolution:* A unique feature of SOM that permits method resolution based on arbitrary rules known only in the domain of the receiving object. Languages that require special entry or exit sequences or local objects that represent distributed object domains are good candidates for using dispatch-function resolution. This technique offers the highest degree of encapsulation for the implementation of an object, with some cost in performance.

- SOM conforms fully with the Object Management Group's (OMG) Common Object Request Broker Architecture (CORBA) standards. Interfaces to SOM classes are described in CORBA's Interface Definition Language, IDL, and the entire SOMobjects Toolkit supports all CORBA-defined data types. The SOM bindings for the C language are compatible with the C bindings prescribed by CORBA. All information about the interface to a SOM class is available at run time through a CORBA-defined Interface Repository.

SOM is not intended to replace existing object-oriented languages. Rather, it is intended to complement them so that application programs written in different programming languages can share common SOM class libraries. For example, SOM can be used with C++ to:

- Provide upwardly compatible class libraries, so that when a new version of a SOM class is released, client code needn't be recompiled, as long as no changes to the client's source code are required.

- Allow other language users (and other C++ compiler users) to use SOM classes implemented in C++.

- Allow C++ programs to use SOM classes implemented using other languages.

▪ Allow other language users to implement SOM classes derived from SOM classes implemented in C++.

▪ Allow C++ programmers to implement SOM classes derived from SOM classes implemented using other languages.

▪ Allow encapsulation (implementation hiding) so that SOM class libraries can be shared without exposing private instance variables and methods.

▪ Allow dynamic (run-time) method resolution in addition to static (compile-time) method resolution (on SOM objects).

▪ Allow information about classes to be obtained and updated at run time. (C++ classes are compile-time structures that have no properties at run time.)

20.3.2   The SOM Compiler

The *SOMobjects Toolkit* contains a tool called the *SOM Compiler* that helps implementors build classes in which *interface and implementation are decoupled*. The SOM Compiler reads the IDL definition of a class interface and generates an implementation skeleton for the class. It also generates implementation and usage bindings for class implementors and clients.

Bindings are language-specific macros and procedures that make implementing and using SOM classes more convenient. These bindings offer a convenient interface to SOM that is tailored to a particular programming language. For instance, C programmers can invoke methods in the same way they make ordinary procedure calls. The C++ bindings "wrap" SOM objects as C++ objects, so that C++ programmers can invoke methods on SOM objects in the same way they invoke methods on C++ objects. In addition, SOM objects receive full C++ typechecking, just as C++ objects do. Currently, the SOM Compiler can generate both C and C++ language bindings for a class. The C and C++ bindings will work with a variety of commercial products available from IBM and others. In addition, SOM Smalltalk bindings are available from IBM and ParcPlace, and SOM COBOL bindings are available from MicroFocus. Vendors of other programming languages may also offer SOM bindings. Check with your language vendor about possible SOM support.

20.3.3   The SOM Run-Time Library

In addition to the SOM Compiler, SOM includes a *run-time library*. This library provides, among other things, a set of *classes, methods, and procedures used to create objects and invoke methods* on them. The library allows any programming language to use SOM classes (classes developed using SOM) if that language can:

- call external procedures,
- store a pointer to a procedure and subsequently invoke that procedure, and
- map IDL types onto the programming language's native types.

Thus, the user of a SOM class and the implementor of a SOM class need not use the same programming language, and neither is required to use an object-oriented language. The independence of client language and implementation language also extends to subclassing: a SOM class can be derived from other SOM classes, and the subclass may or may not be implemented in the same language as the parent class(es). Moreover, SOM's run-time environment allows applications to access information about classes dynamically (at run time).

20.3.4 Frameworks Provided in the SOMobjects Toolkit

In addition to SOM itself (the SOM Compiler and the SOM run-time library), the SOMobjects Developer Toolkit also provides a set of *frameworks* (class libraries) that can be used in developing object-oriented applications. These include Distributed SOM, the Interface Repository Framework, the Persistence Framework, and the Emitter Framework, described below.

Distributed SOM framework (or DSOM) allows application programs *to access SOM objects across address spaces*. That is, application programs can access objects in other processes, even on different machines. DSOM provides this transparent access to remote objects through its Object Request Broker (ORB): the location and implementation of the object are hidden from the client, and the client accesses the object as if it were local. The DSOM framework simplifies server-side programming in most cases by providing a simple "generic" server program that users can use. All the server programmer needs to provide are the application class libraries that the implementor wants to distribute. Applications that require additional flexibility or functionality than what is provided by the generic server can use application-specific server programs. The current release of DSOM supports distribution of objects among processes within a workstation, and across a local area network consisting of IBM OS/2 systems, IBM AIX systems, and Microsoft Windows 3.1. Future releases will support additional platforms including IBM OS/400 and IBM MVS. Multiple transport protocols are supported for communication between clients and servers. Future releases will also support enterprise-wide distribution of objects.

The *interface repository* is a database, optionally created and maintained by the SOM Compiler, that holds all the information contained in the IDL description of a class of objects. The Interface Repository Framework provides run-time access to all information contained in the IDL description of a class of objects. Type information is available as *TypeCodes*—a CORBA-defined way of encoding the complete description of any data type that can be constructed in IDL.

The *Persistence framework* is a collection of SOM classes that provide methods for saving objects (either in a file or in a more specialized repository) and later restoring them. This means that the state of an object can be preserved beyond the termination of the process that creates it. This facility is useful for constructing object-oriented databases, spreadsheets, and so forth. Objects can be stored singly or in groups. They can be stored in default formats or in specially designed formats. Furthermore, objects of arbitrary complexity can be saved and restored.

The *Emitter framework* is a collection of SOM classes that allows programmers *to write their own emitters. Emitter* is a general term used to  back-end output component of the SOM Compiler. Each emitter information about an interface, generated by the SOM Compiler ses an IDL specification, and produces output organized in a different mat. SOM provides a set of emitters that generate the binding files C++ programming (header files and implementation templates). n, users may wish to write their own special-purpose emitters. For an implementor could write an emitter to produce documentation inding files for programming languages other than C or C++.

Metaclass framework* is a collection of SOM metaclasses that provide functionality that may be useful to SOM class designers for modifying the default semantics of method invocation and object creation. A set of metaclasses are provided with the SOMobjects Toolkit. Users can create additional metaclasses.

20.3.5   Concepts of the System Object Model (SOM)

The *System Object Model* (SOM), provided by the *SOMobjects Developer Toolkit*, is a set of libraries, utilities, and conventions used to create binary class libraries that can be used by application programs written in various object-oriented programming languages, such as C++ and Smalltalk, or in traditional procedural languages, such as C and COBOL. The following paragraphs introduce some of the basic terminology used when creating classes in SOM:

- An *object* is an OOP entity that has *behavior* (its methods or operations) and *state* (its data values). In SOM, an object is a run-time entity with a specific set of methods and instance variables. The methods are used by a client programmer to make the object exhibit behavior (that is, to do something), and the instance variables are used by the object to store its state. (The state of an object can change over time, which allows the object's behavior to change.) When a method is invoked on an object, the object is said to be the *receiver* or *target* of the method call.

▪   An object's *implementation* is determined by the procedures that execute its methods, and by the type and layout of its instance variables. The procedures and instance variables that implement an object are normally *encapsulated* (hidden from the caller), so a program can use the object's methods without knowing anything about how those methods are implemented. Instead, a user is given access to the object's methods through its *interface* (a description of the methods in terms of the data elements required as input and the type of value each method returns).

▪   An interface through which an object may be manipulated is represented by an *object type*. That is, by declaring a type for an object variable, a programmer specifies the interface that is intended to be used to access that object. *SOM IDL* (the SOM Interface Definition Language) is used to define object interfaces. The *interface names* used in these IDL definitions are also the type names used by programmers when typing SOM object variables.

▪   In SOM, as in most approaches to object-oriented programming, a *class* defines the implementation of objects. That is, the implementation of any SOM object (as well as its interface) is defined by some specific SOM class. A class definition begins with an IDL specification of the interface to its objects, and the name of this interface is used as the class name as well. Each object of a given class may also be called an *instance* of the class, or an *instantiation* of the class.

▪   *Inheritance*, or *class derivation*, is a technique for developing new classes from existing classes. The original class is called the *base* class, or the *parent* class, or sometimes the direct *ancestor* class. The derived class is called a *child* class or a *subclass*. The primary advantage of inheritance is that a derived class inherits all of its parent's methods and instance variables. Also, through inheritance, a new class can *override* (or redefine) methods of its parent, in order to provide enhanced functionality as needed. In addition, a derived class can introduce new methods of its own. If a class results from several generations of successive class derivation, that class "knows" all of its ancestors' methods (whether overridden or not), and an object (or instance) of that class can execute any of those methods.

▪   SOM classes can also take advantage of *multiple inheritance*, which means that a new class is jointly derived from two or more parent classes. In this case, the derived class inherits methods from all of its parents (and all of its ancestors), giving it greatly expanded capabilities. In the event that different parents have methods of the same name that execute differently, SOM provides ways for avoiding conflicts.

▪   In the SOM run time, classes are themselves objects. That is, classes have their own methods and interfaces, and are themselves defined by other classes. For this reason, a class is often called a *class object*. Likewise, the terms *class methods* and *class variables* are used to distinguish between the methods/variables of a class object versus those of its instances. (Note that the type of an object is *not* the same as the type of its class, which as a class object has its own type.)

▪   A class that defines the implementation of class objects is called a *metaclass*. Just as an instance of a class is an object, so an instance of a metaclass is a class object. Moreover, just as an ordinary class defines methods that its objects respond to, so a metaclass defines methods that a class object responds to. For example, such methods might involve operations that execute when a class (that is, a class object) is creating an instance of itself (an object). Just as classes are derived from parent classes, so metaclasses can be derived from parent metaclasses, in order to define new functionality for class objects.

▪   The SOM system contains three primitive classes that are the basis for all subsequent classes:

◆   SOMObject, the root ancestor class for all SOM classes;

◆   SOMClass, the root ancestor class for all SOM metaclasses; and

◆   SOMClassMgr, the class of the SOMClassMgrObject, an object created automatically during SOM initialization to maintain a registry of existing classes and to assist in dynamic class loading/unloading.

SOMClass is defined as a subclass (or child) of SOMObject and inherits all generic object methods; this is why instances of a metaclass are class *objects* (rather than simply classes) in the SOM run time.

As stated earlier, SOM classes are designed to be language neutral. They can be implemented in one programming language and used in programs of another language. To achieve language neutrality, the *interface* for a class of objects must be defined separately from its *implementation*. That is, defining interface and implementation requires two completely separate steps (plus an intervening compile), as follows:

▪   An interface is the information that a program must know in order to use an object of a particular class. This interface is described in an interface definition (which is also the class definition), using a formal language whose syntax is independent of the programming language used to implement the class's methods. For SOM classes, this is the SOM Interface Definition

Language (SOM IDL). The interface is defined in a file known as the *IDL source file* (or, using its extension, this is often called the *.idl file*).

An interface definition is specified within the *interface declaration* (or *interface statement*) of the .idl file, which includes: the interface name (or class name) and the name(s) of the class's parent(s), and the names of the class's attributes and the signatures of its new methods. (Recall that the complete set of available methods also includes all inherited methods.)

Each *method signature* includes the method name, and the type and order of its arguments, as well as the type of its return value (if any). *Attributes* are instance variables for which *set* and *get* methods will automatically be defined, for use by the application program. (By contrast, instance variables that are not attributes are hidden from the user.)

■ Once the IDL source file is complete, the SOM Compiler is used to analyze the .idl file and create the *implementation template file*, within which the class implementation will be defined. Before issuing the SOM Compiler command, **sc**, the class implementor can set an environment variable that determines which emitters (output-generating programs) the SOM Compiler will call and, consequently, which programming language and operating system the resulting *binding files* will relate to. (Alternatively, this emitter information can be placed on the command line for **sc**.) In addition to the implementation template file itself, the binding files include two language-specific header files that will be #included in the implementation template file and in application program files. The header files define many useful SOM macros, functions, and procedures that can be invoked from the files that include the header files.

■ The implementation of a class is done by the class implementor in the *implementation template file* (often called just the *implementation file* or the *template file*). As produced by the SOM Compiler, the template file contains *stub procedures* for each method of the class. These are incomplete method procedures that the class implementor uses as a basis for implementing the class by writing the corresponding code in the programming language of choice.

In summary, the process of implementing a SOM class includes using the SOM IDL syntax to create an IDL source file that specifies the interface to a class of objects—that is, the methods and attributes that a program can use to manipulate an object of that class. The SOM Compiler is then run to produce an implementation template file and two binding (header) files that are specific to the designated programming language and operating system. Finally, the class implementor writes language-specific code in the template file to implement the method procedures.

At this point, the next step is to write the application (or client) program(s) that use the objects and methods of the newly implemented class.

(Observe, here, that a programmer could write an application program using a class implemented entirely by someone else.) If not done previously, the SOM Compiler is run to generate usage bindings for the new class, as appropriate for the language used by the client program (which may be different from the language in which the class was implemented). After the client program is finished, the programmer compiles and links it using a language-specific compiler, and then executes the program. (Notice again, the client program can invoke methods on objects of the SOM class without knowing how those methods are implemented.)

For a more detailed description of the SOMobjects Toolkit, refer to other publications devoted exclusively to SOMobjects (see Appendix A for references). Or visit the SOM World Wide Web page *http://www.austin.ibm.com/developer/objects/som1.html*. The Web page contains up-to-date information about the SOMobjects product and its features.

20.4   ICL: DAIS

20.4.1   20.4.1: Introduction

The DAIS product set is designed to simplify the development, deployment and operation of large-scale, mission-critical distributed computing in heterogeneous environments. Targeted at enterprise-level computing, the product offers extensive run-time management features that permit the very best performance to be obtained from a wide variety of host platforms and networks.

Originating from the ANSA research program, which had significant influence on both the OMG architecture and the ISO Open Distributed Processing Reference Model, DAIS was launched in October 1993, and is now used across a wide spectrum of enterprises, including major utilities, telecommunications organizations, financial institutions, manufacturers, universities and government agencies.

Recognizing that few developments actually involve starting from scratch and that CORBA represents an ideal way of integrating existing applications, options for DAIS include tools for accessing existing systems through integration at the database level and also through "screen-scraping" using a script-driven virtual terminal facility for driving traditional, mainframe-based transaction processing applications.

20.4.2   Architecture

The DAIS ORB is a realization of the Open Distributed Processing Reference Model populated with OMG-defined CORBA component specifications.

The ODP Reference Model provides a formal framework that has been standardized by both ISO and ITU-T (formerly CCITT), addressing particularly the manageability and scalability issues found in large-scale distrbuted systems. Some of the important ODP concepts, now realized in DAIS, are described in the following subsections.

Transparencies, Interceptors, and Binding   In DAIS, the mechanisms implementing remote invocations, transaction coordination, authorization checking, and so forth are referred to as *transparencies*. The ORB can be thought of as simply a stack of transparency mechanisms that support the high-level application environment. Because not all objects and configurations require the use of the same mechanisms, a client and target object go through a process called *binding* during which the requirements and capabilities of each side are matched and the resources necessary for them to talk to one another identified.

Further transparencies can be added by implementing them as *interceptors*. Each interceptor is an object that is called by the ORB and has an interface similar to the CORBA Dynamic Skeleton Interface used for ORB bridges. The ORB calls the interceptors according to the binding established between the client and target objects and passes the current request as a parameter. The interceptors can perform any function needed to progress the request, including making other invocations such as authenticating the target.

Concurrency and Threads   Many aspects of distributed systems imply that the ORB must be able to support concurrency:

▪   When either a *oneway* (asynchronous) request is made or a normal synchronous request is invoked using the DII's *send_deferred* call, the client and target can proceed concurrently. If concurrency support is not intrinsic to the ORB and the ORB is forced to process requests sequentially, distribution transparency is compromised since the objects must be carefully mapped to processes so that the required concurrency is available. The maximum potential concurrency of an application is often difficult to predict, but if the developer's estimate is wrong, the application will deadlock.

▪   As more sophisticated transparencies are developed—for example, supporting particular flavors of authentication, coordination or resilience protocols—the interactions visible at the application level no longer have a simple correspondence to the messages that might be passed over the network. DAIS permits this lower-level activity to be optimized by performing it concurrently where possible, so even where concurrency is not used by the application, its presence in the ORB still delivers important benefits.

Having concurrency available in the user environment is particularly useful. On a workstation running MS Windows, for example, client functions such as forms-based order processing can execute alongside server functions such as receiving and displaying stock prices.

Domains and Federation   To ensure scalability and help keep a large distributed system manageable, DAIS employs the concept of groups of objects called *domains*. Domains represent a common characteristic or dependency, such as the ability to support a particular communications protocol or the sharing of a particular security policy. The ORB uses domains to determine whether particular optimizations are possible, such as using UNIX interprocess communication calls for local objects.

Domains also are used to enable interworking with foreign systems, where *bridges* are employed to translate between different ORBs or similar systems. Domain structures will be employed extensively by the forthcoming DAIS Security facility, both to simplify administration and to ensure that the implementation can scale to large systems while still behaving optimally in the local case. Here, a development of the interdomain bridge is to implement a kind of firewall between differently administered systems, permitting each system to operate autonomously as far as possible by enforcing checks at the boundary between the two.

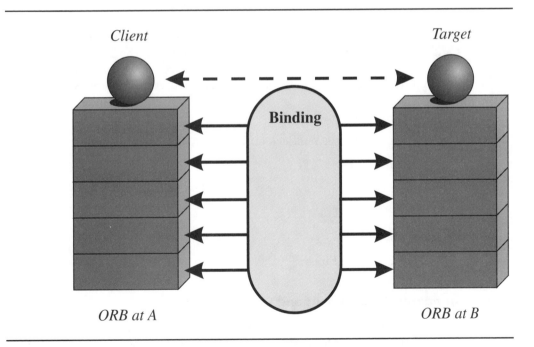

Figure 20.2.   DAIS transparency mechanisms.

20.4.3 The DAIS Core

A DAIS *Capsule* is a unit of resources, and is the environment in which objects are instantiated and executed. In general, a capsule has an independent address space and supports multiple threads of execution. In POSIX systems, a capsule usually corresponds to a process.

Distributed Execution Service   At the heart of the capsule is the Distributed Execution Service, which provides:

- integrated scheduling of processing and communications resources among objects within the capsule;
- fragmentation and reordering of large messages where the underlying protocol has transmission size limits;
- ability to monitor and tune the low-level comms activity to ensure optimum data throughput;
- support for concurrent use of multiple protocols within a DAIS capsule, allowing servers or clients to communicate concurrently using different protocols;
- reliable communication over unreliable protocols, such as UDP using low-level error checking time-outs and retransmission techniques.

Message Passing Services   The Message Passing Services consist of send and receive functions for each supported protocol. As the MPSs are modular components, capsules can be built with support for the protocols required and multiple protocols can be used simultaneously. MPSs are available for:

TCP and UDP via Sockets

TCP and UDP via WinSock on Windows platforms

TCP and UDP via XTI

TCP via TLI

Novell IPX via TLI

OSI via XTI

IPC via Nested Pipes

20.4.4 Standards Development and Conformance

OMG specifications provide the means of protecting customers' investment in applications development for DAIS, or indeed for other ORBs, by ensuring that software components remain portable and can interoperate.

ICL's strategy for DAIS is to maintain conformance with OMG specifications and to proactively contribute toward the definition of new specifications, always within the coherent ODP reference model. For example, DAIS technology has been proposed and incorporated into the CORBA specifications for:

CORBA 2.0 core

Lifecycle, Event, and Naming Services

Transaction management

20.4.5 Language Mappings

DAIS supports the OMG C and C++ language bindings. A language binding for COBOL is also available, and support for Object COBOL (aligned with the proposed COBOL '97 standard) will also be provided.

Bindings and tooling for supporting popular application builders including Gupta SQL Windows and Borland Delphi are also being developed.

20.4.6 Visual Basic and OLE/COM Integration

DAIS can generate code from an IDL description to provide a Microsoft OLE server supporting the automation, linking, or embedding APIs. Such "proxy servers" can be accessed from Visual Basic and other environments and represent CORBA object implementations.

It is expected that a low-level bridge to Microsoft COM domains will be available in the near future, and will reflect the OMG's COM/CORBA specifications.

20.4.7 Interface Repository

ICL is developing a comprehensive repository for use during development and optionally at run time. The repository will be remotely accessible and may federate to synchronize information across an enterprise.

The repository contains both interface and implementation information and can be populated by the IDL compiler or a CASE tool. The repository can generate static stubs and skeletons at build time or be used dynamically at run time.

20.4.8 Interoperability

DAIS provides native (nongatewayed) support for the CORBA GIOP over Internet (IIOP) interoperability protocol for interworking with ORBs and related systems.

20.4.9   DAIS Services

Trader   The Trader is a service that allows clients to look for objects satisfying particular criteria. For example, a client could ask a Trader to find "a color printer in my company that costs less than $1 per page." The DAIS Trader is an intercept of the ODP Trader standard on which the OMG Object Trader Service specification is expected to be based.

People tend to talk about finding or locating objects when they are actually seeking a particular type of service. It is important to distinguish this form of location (matching given criteria) from physical location (routing a message). Once the Trader has found an object matching the stated requirement, its reference is returned to the client, and operations may be invoked on the object in the normal way. The Trader does not involve itself in subsequent invocations between the client and the target object. In this scheme, an object reference always corresponds to a definite target object, not to any one of a number of possible candidates, so no communications overheads are incurred in further resolution of the object's location.

Trader databases are organized into domains, and objects wishing to advertise themselves do so by registering "offers" with the local Trader. An object is registered according to its (interface) type, the name it uses, and a list of properties expressed as name/value pairs.

Clients trying to locate specific services can constrain their requirements by adding a predicate to their lookup request. For example, there might be several printers within one department all under the context Legal, one a high-speed, color laser device, and another a monochrome, draft-quality printer. Clients could predicate their selection using "PrinterType=='LASER' && Capability=='COLOR'", which would refine the lookup process to those printers with those capabilities within the target context. If successful, the Trader will return an object reference or a set of references to the client.

Lifecycle Service   The generic factory interface of the Lifecycle Service is implemented using a resource management component called the Node Manager and a local creation component called simply the Factory.

Alert Service   The Alert Service is used for propagating system- and application-generated events, and performs some of the functions of the OMG Event Service.

Naming/Integrated Directory Service   An OMG Naming Service implementation is available, and gateways between this and other directory systems including X.500 are planned.

Concurrency Service   The Concurrency Service interfaces permit concurrent access to any object to be controlled using shared and exclusive locks.

Object Transaction Service A Transaction service conformant to the OMG OTS specification is also planned to be available in the near future. DAIS/OTS will be capable of coordinating transactions across all DAIS platforms, allowing, for example, a Windows-based application to initiate and commit transactions across remote machines. The DAIS/OTS builds on experience gained in developing a distributed transaction processing monitor for relational databases.

Security A security option, known as DAIS/SE, is in development at the time of writing. DAIS/SE is based on the ECMA SESAME protocol, a comprehensive set of security services covering access control (based on roles, groups, or other privileges), sophisticated delegation control, a nonrepudiation facility and (replaceable) shared and public key cryptography. It permits security controls to be applied and enforced transparently to application invocations.

20.4.10 Legacy System Integration

DAIS Information System The Information System (DAIS/IS) provides powerful facilities to support access to distributed heterogenous databases. It provides distribution transparency for large volumes of data and conceals from application programs the complexity and variability of data storage structures and the methods of access to their content. DAIS/IS supports Oracle, Sybase, Ingres, and IDMS databases on a variety of platforms.

DAIS/TI The DAIS/TI option is a script-driven terminal session emulator for encapsulating transaction processing applications on ICL VME mainframes.

20.4.11 GUI Integration

The X Window System can be used directly with DAIS since DAIS provides a means of coordinating DAIS MPS communications with X (or similar systems) in a single POSIX process.

DAIS ports are available for Microsoft Windows environments.

The Visix *Galaxy* cross-platform GUI is also an example of an object-oriented product that is being used with DAIS.

20.4.12 Workflow

ICL's *RoleModel* is a distributed workflow infrastructure built using DAIS. The product supports the intelligent routing and transformation of information between users and applications. Different "business process domains" can be integrated to provide enterprise-wide workflow capabilities.

ICL's *Processwise Workbench* complements RoleModel by providing process modelling capabilities and generation of workflow rules that drive RoleModel.

20.4.13 Platforms

DAIS is currently available on (and interoperates across) the following platforms:

Digital Alpha/OSF/1

Digital Alpha/Open VMS

Digital VAX/OpenVMS

Hewlett Packard HP9000/HP-UX

ICL SPARC Servers/DRS/NX

ICL Multiprocessing Servers/DRS/NX 7MP

ICL Series 39/OpenVME

IBM PC/MS Windows 3.11

IBM PC/MS Windows 95

IBM PC/MS Windows/NT 3.5

IBM PC/OS/2 Warp

IBM PC/SCO Unix 3.2

IBM PC/UnixWare 2.1

IBM PC/Netware 4.1

NEC EWS 4800/Unix SVR4

Pyramid Nile/DC/OSx

Sun SPARC/Solaris 2

Sun SPARC/SunOS

The list of supported operating systems and platforms is being extended. For availability details, consult the product description.

20.4.14 Product Packaging

DAIS is packaged into a Software Development Kit and Run-Time Library, plus optional DAIS Services (DAIS/TI, DAIS/OTS, and so on). With some

23,000 employees and operations in 80 countries, ICL is able to offer a range of training, implementation, support, planning, and other professional services to complement the software.

The ICL-developed **OPEN**_framework_ provides a powerful overall approach for analysis of requirements, quantification of benefits, and specification of technological components for complex system developments.

Together, these elements provide a complete package for DAIS customers whatever the level of support required.

20.4.15 Further Information

For up-to-date information on DAIS features and options, consult the product descriptions, summaries of which may be found on the World Wide Web (_http://www.icl.com_).

CHAPTER 21

ORB Products: C++ Language Mapping

21.1 PRODUCTS SUPPORTING C++

Did you skip right to here because you're interested only in C++? There are a few good reasons why you should read Chapter 20 first: Its introduction contains some general information about ORB products and the descriptions in this book; all of the ORBs described in that chapter support, or plan to support, the C++ language mapping so you should consider them as additional candidates for a C++ ORB; and finally, Chapter 20 contains a pointer to OMG for information about many additional ORB products that support C++ and additional languages.

As we described in the introduction to Chapter 20, many of the products described in this chapter support, or plan to support, languages besides C++. They're grouped here because they work the example in C++ in this book. A description of each one follows.

21.2 EXPERSOFT: POWERBROKER

PowerBroker is an environment for building, deploying, and managing distributed object systems. Its foundation, the PowerBroker ORB, complies fully with all CORBA 2.0 specification requirements. In addition, PowerBroker includes a comprehensive set of CORBA-compliant Object Services that are integrated to form a powerful, federated, distributed computing environment.

314

PowerBroker ORB extends the CORBA specification to support asynchronous method invocation, passing objects by value, and other features required for robust applications. PowerBroker Object Services also extend the capabilities defined in CORBAservices specifications (formerly called Common Object Services) to provide a unified framework for building applications and systems. The utility of object services is highly dependent on their implementations, and on the extent to which they cooperate and build on each other's functions. Together, PowerBroker object services constitute a cohesive architecture for distributed object management, aimed at simplifying and reducing the amount of code that must be written for a robust, fully functional application.

PowerBroker supports both the CORBA IDL C++ Language Mapping and the CORBA Smalltalk Language Mapping. Applications written in both C++ and Smalltalk share all of PowerBroker's capabilities and object services, and can transparently invoke methods on objects implemented in the other language. In addition to C++ and Smalltalk, PowerBroker can automatically generate OLE Automation interfaces to CORBA objects, giving Microsoft Visual Basic programmers transparent access to PowerBroker distributed CORBA objects and services.

21.2.1 PowerBroker IDL Compiler and Interface Repository

Under CORBA 1, ORB-related development activities centered on compilers that directly generate stubs and skeletons target languages from IDL files. This approach was necessary under CORBA 1, since the Interface Repository (IR) did not contain all of the information described in the corresponding IDL. Under CORBA 2.0, however, the extended IR preserves all of the information from IDL, and also supports a standard interface for writing into the repository. Consequently, the IR (rather than IDL files) becomes the primary medium of interface expression and focus of CORBA-related development activity. PowerBroker CORBAplus provides a dynamic IR engine, with an accompanying graphical tool for browsing, editing, and interactive interface creation. (See Figure 21.1.)

IDL source files are compiled into the Interface Repository. Alternatively, the repository can be populated interactively with the IFR graphical tool, which supports dialogs for composing new interfaces without writing IDL. Components that generate programming interfaces (such as client stubs and skeletons) in specific languages work directly from the IR contents. PowerBroker CORBAplus has generators for C++ and OLE Automation interfaces. PowerBroker Smalltalk users can browse the IR directly from the Smalltalk environment, and invoke built-in generators to bind Smalltalk classes to CORBA interfaces.

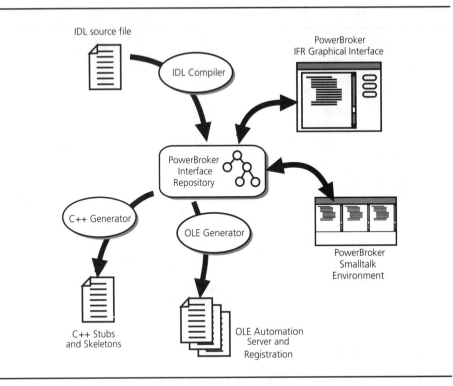

Figure 21.1.   PowerBroker interface repository and code generation.

21.2.2   PowerBroker ORB Core

At the core of PowerBroker's run-time architecture is an efficient, light-weight, user-modifiable distribution engine written in C++. This engine constitutes a distributed virtual machine, providing a uniform platform for message management, parameter marshaling, object location, and protocol management across a broad range of hardware platforms, operating systems, and network protocols.

The PowerBroker core takes the form of a design pattern—a template of cooperating components (classes) that captures the essential "shape" of a solution to a general design problem (in this case, communication between distributed objects), which can be customized to a variety of specific contexts. As is the case with successful, reusable design patterns in general, the PowerBroker ORB Core pattern has evolved over time, factored from Expersoft's extensive experience in building successful distributed object systems.

Expersoft offers an optional development kit that gives advanced Power-Broker users direct access to the ORB Core pattern and components. With this development kit, users can modify and extend fundamental, internal behaviors of the ORB core. Figure 21.2 illustrates the key components of the ORB core.

The PowerBroker core design pattern centers around a component type called Message Conduit. Message Conduits export the same interface that they consume, so that conduits can be assembled into a stack at run time. In general, Message Conduits exchange and transform fragmentary message buffers that form object requests and their corresponding replies. The Message Conduit interface constitutes an abstract protocol between conduits that allows each conduit in a stack to perform an independent, orthogonal transformation or operation on object request and reply messages. At the bottom, conduit stacks are terminated by Transport Adapters, which provide a normalized interface to different network transport layers, so that a variety of communication architectures and protocols may be interchangeably "plugged" into the stack at run time. Stacks may manage multiple concurrent requests through a Request Multiplexer component that arbitrates the use of lower, shared conduit stack elements. The Binder dynamically configures conduit stacks to satisfy the requirements of individual client-object associations.

The core design pattern is completely open and accessible to Power-Broker users. All of these component types can be modified, extended, or reimplemented, creating custom message-handling components to facilitate message spooling, message tracing and debugging, integrating new transport protocols, encryption, custom data marshaling, and so on. The implementations of PowerBroker standard core components are extremely lightweight and efficient. These features of PowerBroker makes it particularly suitable for embedding in vertical applications.

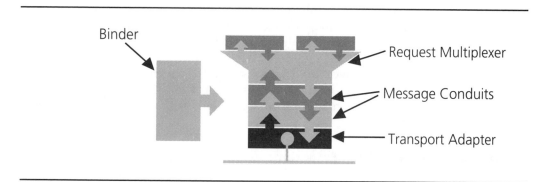

Figure 21.2. PowerBroker configurable ORB Core.

21.2.3   **PowerBroker Object Services**

While a well-architected ORB is necessary for successful distributed object systems, it is not in itself sufficient for most applications. Other components in the PowerBroker product suite are extended, integrated implementations of CORBAservices (formerly known as Common Object Services). CORBA Object Service Specifications, in their raw form, are somewhat disjointed and vague in places, leaving implements with wide latitude for design choices. With this latitude comes the challenge of constructing a cohesive object service architecture whose elements form an integrated design model well-suited to application requirements.

PowerBroker CORBAplus Object Services include implementations of the following CORBAservices:

Naming

Persistence

Lifecycle

Event

Externalization

Other service implementations (including Relationships, Transactions, and Security) are in progress or planned. All of these implementations are fully compliant with their respective CORBA specifications.

Beyond mere compliance, however, Expersoft has specifically constructed PowerBroker Object Services to provide users with a well-integrated service architecture that takes maximum advantage of synergy between services. For example, PowerBroker Lifecycle services are designed to use (by default) Externalization and Persistent Object services to perform object copy and migration operations. In addition, PowerBroker ORB extensions will automatically generate externalization and storage methods for user-defined objects. As a result, users can achieve powerful object behaviors (such as object migration, storage, dynamic recoverability) automatically, without having to explicitly design or code these behaviors in application objects.

PowerBroker object services can support large run-time systems by organizing services into localized domains called cells. PowerBroker cells can be federated into large system configurations without suffering from centralized bottlenecks.

21.2.4   **PowerBroker CORBA Extensions**

PowerBroker supports several useful extensions to the CORBA object model. Though the discussion of all of these extensions is beyond the present scope, we will describe two examples—*asynchronous method invocation* and *passing object parameters by value.*

Asynchronous Invocations   CORBA supports deferred synchronous invocations in the Dynamic Invocation Interface. This programming interface, however, is unsuitably clumsy for many application purposes, and does not permit full asynchronous behavior (such as a callback mechanism). Power-Broker provides two extensions to simplify deferred synchronous programming, and to enable asynchronous programming.

The first mechanism, called Futures, allows programmers to make non-blocking method invocations with nearly complete transparency. Nonblocking PowerBroker invocations have the same form and syntax as normal synchronous invocations. This is achieved through the use of data types called Futures that wrap out parameters and return values, hiding synchronization primitives. Assume the following interface in IDL:

```
interface A // IDL
{
    struct S { long l; string str; };
    float op1( in boolean flag, out S s);
};
```

If requested, the PowerBroker C++ code generator will produce a client-side stub with Future parameters:

```
class A // C++
{
    struct S { ... };
    virtual future<CORBA::Float>
        op1(
            CORBA::Boolean flag,
            future<S>& s);
};
```

Note that the operation result and the **out** parameter are not mapped as usual for C++, but are mapped to a parameterized type **future<X>**, where X is the parameter's original type. The operation may be invoked as follows:

```
future<CORBA::Float> f;
future<A::S> s;
A_ptr ap;
...
f = ap->op1(CORBA::True, s);
```

```
// op1 invocation returns immediately
...
cout << s->str ...
// usage will block if not complete
```

When the deferred synchronous method is invoked, the client program returns immediately, without waiting for completion of the remote operation. Opaque placeholder values are assigned to the future objects, and they are set to the unresolved state. When the operation completes and sends a reply to the client, the futures are assigned the actual result values and set to the resolved state. The future template overloads cast operators and member dereference operators so that the future objects syntactically appear to be identical to their target types. If the client attempts to access a result value before the remote operation completes, the client will block at the point at which the value was used.

PowerBroker provides an alternative mechanism that modifies the operation's signature to allow the operation caller to provide a local callback object. When the operation completes, the PowerBroker will asynchronously call the user-provided callback, supplying all of the operation results.

Both of these techniques have the advantage of being handled completely with client-side language mapping extensions. The object implementation and ORB communication layers need not be aware of the synchronization properties of the invocation or be explicitly designed to support asynchronous calls.

Object Value Parameters CORBA objects may only be passed by reference as parameters in other object requests. While this provides simple semantics, it has proven to be a limitation in several application domains, creating programming inconveniences as users attempt to devise "workarounds." PowerBroker extends CORBA request semantics to support object value parameters in invocations. When an object is passed by value, the parameter receiver (either server or client, depending on whether the parameter was in or out) is passed a new copy of the object, with a new identity. The copy is local to the receiving context, and is independent of the original parameter owned by the sender. In order to achieve this, PowerBroker requires the following properties and behaviors for the object type:

- In order to be marshaled, the object's abstract state must either be known by the ORB, or the object must be capable of producing its abstract state in a canonical, encapsulated form.
- The receiving context must support an implementation of the object type that is known to be equivalent to the type being sent. (PowerBroker provides programmers with mechanisms for declaring implementation equivalency.)

PowerBroker provides automated support for generating methods required to enable object value parameters.

21.2.5 Summary

- PowerBroker is a complete distributed computing environment.
- PowerBroker fully complies with CORBA 2.0 ORB and CORBAservices Specifications, but also provides powerful extensions.
- PowerBroker's core engine is open and user-modifiable.
- PowerBroker's scalable architecture has been proven in large-scale deployed systems in a wide range of application domains, including finance, telecommunications, transportation, and manufacturing.
- PowerBroker represents several years of practice and evolution in distributed object computing systems.
- PowerBroker provides choice of object models, languages, and platforms.

21.3 IONA TECHNOLOGIES: ORBIX

Orbix, from IONA Technologies, was the first ORB to fully support the CORBA standard and the first to support C++. Initially, Orbix supported the C++ language, and support has since been added for other languages and programming environments, including Smalltalk, Ada, and OLE. Orbix is a mature ORB that implements all of the elements of CORBA 2.0, including the stub approach (Static Invocation Interface or SII), the Dynamic Invocation Interface (DII), the Implementation Repository (including all of the specified activation modes) and the Interface Repository. It also provides some Orbix-specific enhancements, aimed mainly at allowing application programmers to extend the functionality of the ORB itself, as we will see later.

The three main aims of Orbix can be summarized as follows:

- *To be easy to use:* CORBA, and distributed programming in general, have been made easy to use by adopting the programming conventions of the chosen language or environment. Hence, components of the system can communicate with each other with the same ease that a program can call one of its own procedures or functions. This simplifies the construction of new applications and the building of systems from existing applications. Feedback from many real projects has shown that this ease of use has been achieved.

- *To be flexible:* Orbix has an open architecture that allows programmers access to a wide variety of hooks. One advantage of this is that Orbix can be integrated with a wide variety of other technologies used to construct real systems.

- *To be lightweight:* Versions of Orbix run on real-time operating systems and therefore Orbix must be lightweight and efficient. All versions of Orbix benefit because its central core is a straightforward efficient implementation of CORBA.

An important component of Orbix is its compiler technology, which translates CORBA IDL into programming language code (for example C++) that performs remote calls. The generated code is sufficiently sophisticated so that programmers are not burdened with extra programming steps.

Orbix is available on more than 20 operating systems, including a dozen versions of UNIX, 16-bit Windows 3.1, Windows for Workgroups 3.11, Windows 95, Windows NT, OS/2, MVS, VMS, and Macintosh. The UNIX support includes Solaris, HP/UX, AIX, IRIX, OSF/1, SunOS, Solaris x86, UnixWare, SCO, Sinix, and Ultrix. Both client and server sides are supported on all platforms (including Windows), and full interoperability is provided between all of these.

Real-time versions of Orbix are available on VxWorks, QNX, and LynxOS, with others planned. This wide availability of Orbix enables high-level integration between embedded systems and the management layers that surround them.

The following CORBAservices can optionally be used to help construct Orbix applications, and others (including security services) will be implemented as they are specified by OMG:

Naming Service

Event Service

Object Transaction Service

Initialization Service

Lifecycle Service

Persistence

IONA's view of CORBA is that it is suitable for two distinct but related activities:

- Writing a distributed system using conventional programming languages, such as C++ and Smalltalk. The requirements here are that the objects of the system can communicate with each other easily; that is, with high *transparency*. By transparency we mean that objects can communicate without considering difficult issues such as network protocols, byte streams, network addresses, data representation conversions, (and, as we will see later) object persistence and replication.

▪ Application integration, for both new and existing applications. Applications can provide a number of IDL interfaces and make these available to the overall system. This allows new applications to be written by combining the facilities of existing applications. Since the components of the system are objects whose internals are hidden from their clients, these objects can interface to legacy systems. This support for legacy systems is crucial for some applications.

IONA Technologies was formed in March 1991 primarily as a result of experience gained from various research projects during the period 1985–91. These projects focused on issues such as C++ distributed programming, distributed object-oriented operating systems (on UNIX, micro-kernels, and as standalone kernels), and transparent persistence for objects. IONA realized that the lessons from these projects could be used to build, from scratch, an elegant implementation of CORBA; rather than suffering the disadvantages of retrofitting CORBA into an existing system.

The rest of this section is structured as follows. Section 21.3.1 gives an overview of the run-time actions of Orbix; Section 21.3.2 discusses the openness of the system, showing how Orbix can be extended by programmers; Section 21.3.3 presents the CORBA OLE integration; Section 21.3.4 presents IONA's third-party product integration program, which is a very important aspect of the product; and Section 21.3.5 gives an overview of the implementation of Orbix.

21.3.1 Run-time View of Orbix

Figure 21.3 provides a summary of the automatic steps carried out by Orbix when an operation call is made on a remote object. The calling object in the client has a pointer to a *proxy* object (sometimes called a *surrogate*) in its address space. The proxy has the same interface as the target object, and the code to implement the proxy is generated automatically by the IDL compiler. When an operation is invoked on the proxy, it uses the Orbix *run-time* layer and *communications facility* to transmit the request to the target object. On the server side, the request is received by the Orbix run-time layer, and the target object is located within the server's address space.

Clients can use synchronous or asynchronous communications. The former is by far the most commonly required mode; with it, the caller is blocked for the duration of the call. Asynchronous calls, in which the caller is not blocked, are more difficult for applications to manage, but worthwhile in

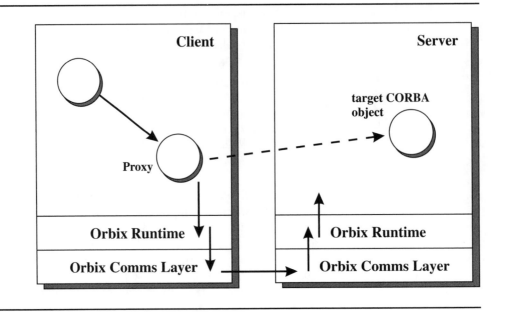

Figure 21.3.   Run-time structure of Orbix.

some circumstances. Many potential uses of asynchronous communication can be programmed more efficiently using multithreaded servers.

Orbix provides status information on the servers that are registered and those that are running, as well as the ability to log individual operation calls.

21.3.2 Openness of Orbix

In designing Orbix, IONA was aware that application writers across various domains would need various extensions to be made to the system and would need to use the system in conjunction with other subsystems. It is the explicit aim of Orbix to provide both of these flexibilities. An example extension is a specialized security mechanism; example integrations include the Isis fault-tolerant distributed systems toolkit. These and other examples will be discussed in Section 21.3.4.

To facilitate these extensions and integrations, Orbix provides a number of tools that benefit from the object-oriented implementation of the system. These include Filters, Smart Proxies, Loaders, and Locators. These facilities add significantly to the flexibility of Orbix, but remember that they are optional—most programmers can use the system without being aware of them. Each will be discussed in turn in the following subsections, and others will be briefly mentioned at the end of this section.

Filters   A client or server programmer can define a filter class and create an instance of this. This object may be invoked when the process makes a remote call, when a server receives a call, when the server replies, and when the client receives this reply. Typical usages of filters include the following:

- monitoring and maintenance of audit trails;
- addition of specialist authentication information when a client makes a call to a remote server (examples of this include transmission of Kerberos authentication tickets);
- encryption of the request buffer (but special support is also provided for this);
- provision of specialist security checks in a server (a filter can reject a call if the security checks are not successful);
- control of database management system transactions when requests arrive at a server;
- creation of threads in a server so that each current request is assigned to a separate thread. Such filters are provided by Orbix, but they can be changed to suit specialist needs. Threads increase throughput, decrease latency, and reduce the difficulty of providing deadlock free software.

Smart Proxies   Referring again to Figure 21.3, the default action of the generated stubs of each IDL class is to forward each request to the correct remote object. These stubs are the methods of the proxy objects. An Orbix programmer can, however, change this default. Using inheritance, the generated proxy code can be redefined in a derived class, which can use application-specific rules to optimize access to the remote target object. Instances of such derived classes are termed *smart proxies*. The simplest example of this is a smart proxy that caches values from the target object, so that subsequent operation calls from a calling object can be handled completely within the smart proxy.

Smart proxy support is typically transparent to an Orbix client programmer; a server programmer will provide a library with which the clients can link in order to include the smart proxy code.

As stated before, a commonly presented example of smart proxies is when a server programmer wishes to allow his or her clients to cache state from the target objects; this improves performance (both by increasing the responsiveness to clients and by enabling the server to handle more clients) and reduces the number of remote calls. Where necessary, the server holding the real object can make calls to the smart proxy to notify it of changes to the state of the object. There are many other uses of smart proxies, but we will mention just two here:

- Fault tolerance, where the smart proxy can rebind to an alternative remote server when the original server fails (because, for example, its machine fails).

- Load balancing, where the smart proxy can, on each request, decide to which one of a set of servers it will forward a call. Standard load balancing techniques can be used to choose a lightly loaded server.

Loaders   When a request arrives at a server, Orbix searches for the target object within that server. If this simple search fails, Orbix returns an exception to the client. However, if the server has created one or more *loader* objects, then Orbix will give these a chance to load the required object. A loader object therefore provides the crucial low-level facilities needed to support persistent objects. Loaders can be written by any Orbix programmer, or they can be provided "off the shelf" through cooperative agreements between IONA and DBMS vendors.

Locators   It is unlikely that a single mechanism for locating servers in a distributed system will suffice in all possible domains and environments. Orbix allows system-level programmers to write a *locator* object. This has a single function, `lookUp()`, which returns a list of hostnames on which the server can be found. The implementation of this may, for example, use *trading* techniques (as specified in the Open Distributed Processing Standard) to match a requester's requirements with the set of property values specified for a given server.

Other Open Features   A *protocol switch* has been incorporated into the communications layer of Orbix to make it easy to add different communication protocols. Orbix has a number of such protocols available, including IIOP (the CORBA interoperability protocol), direct layering on TCP/IP, use of the Isis protocols (see Section 21.3.4), and the NEO/Talk protocol supported by SUN. This list can be extended by using the protocol switch. Orbix will choose the most appropriate protocol to use in each case.

As well as transmitting object references as operation parameters and return values, Orbix allows applications to specify that the value of an object is to be transmitted instead. This allows the receiving process to access the object's data without further remote calls. The actual values to transmit can be controlled by the programmer.

21.3.3 CORBA OLE Integration

CORBA and OLE (Object Linking and Embedding, from Microsoft) are the two leading technologies for enabling application integration. Although both are object-oriented, they have different origins: OLE has arisen because of the need to integrate desktop applications such as word processors and spreadsheets; CORBA has started by providing a general purpose messaging system between applications (or components) of a distributed system.

Orbix for Windows has provided the vehicle for our integration of the two systems. Windows-based distributed applications can be written in conventional programming languages, such as C++, using the CORBA programming paradigm. In addition, OLE-based programming systems, such as Visual Basic, can transparently access distributed CORBA services. Further, Orbix is fully integrated with OCXs. This allows customers to implement CORBA interfaces in a variety of languages on Windows, including Visual Basic and Delphi.

The COM (Component Object Model) layer of OLE is similar to the base CORBA standard in that it provides a communications mechanism between objects. OLE also provides an Automation layer, which runs on top of COM. Developers of Windows applications can provide an Automation server that provides an interface, which is then accessible from local programs such as those written in Visual Basic. Automation was designed as a generic mechanism to support multiple scripting languages; products such as Visual Basic, PowerBuilder, and FoxPro all include sophisticated Automation support.

The Orbix IDL compiler has been extended to automatically generate Automation interfaces from IDL definitions. Once these Automation interfaces are available, OLE-based languages can easily make CORBA calls to objects on any machine.

To show how simply this can be done, let us assume that we have two IDL interfaces, **Bank** and **Account**; and that the **Bank** interface defines an operation called **NewAccount()**, which takes the name of the new account holder (as a string) and returns an **account** object reference. It would be normal in Visual Basic to have the account owner's name typed into a text box on the screen (we'll assume this box is called **owner**). The following (standard) Visual Basic code makes a remote call to a CORBA **Bank** object anywhere in the system:

```
Set  acc =   b.NewAccount(owner.Text)
```

At the start of the statement, the variable **b** references a remote bank object, which provides the **NewAccount()** operation. The parameter to the call is **owner.Text**, which reads the string from the text box. Afterward, calls can be made on the variable **acc**, to deposit money or carry out other actions.

Orbix's OLE-CORBA support provides a two-way connection between OLE and CORBA. Just as OLE clients can call CORBA objects, CORBA clients can make CORBA calls to OLE servers without being aware of the translation.

As an example of OLE and CORBA integration, IONA has provided a Visual Basic graphical user interface for the example in the second half of this book. This simple interface replaces the **InputMedia**, **OutputMedia**, and **POSTerminal** objects with a single user interface. To reflect a real system, there are separate areas of the screen for the keypad, the bar-code reader and the receipt output, but these are controlled by the one Visual Basic program. Space restrictions prevent us from presenting the code for the interface in the book, but it can be loaded from the IONA ftp and WWW sites. (See Appendix A for access information.) Also on these sites is a supplement to Chapter 31 that shows the user interface, and explains its features and the most important parts of the Visual Basic code that controls it.

21.3.4 Orbix and Third-Party Product Integration Program

Applications that use an ORB typically employ other technology as well, such as databases, transaction monitors, graphical user interfaces, class libraries, and so on. Applications should not be constrained in their choice of these technologies because of their use of an ORB. At the very least, there should be no barrier to the use of different technologies in the one system. However, tighter integration is frequently of great benefit; that is, integration in which one or both of the technologies are aware of the other. In this regard, an active partners' program has been built up through which various technologies have already been integrated with Orbix, and some of these are outlined here.

Orbix+Isis Fault-Tolerant Computing Isis is a toolkit for writing distributed fault-tolerant programs. It provides an *automatic broadcast* facility that enables a programmer to write servers that act as server groups. A request can be handled as long as any one of the members of the target group can be accessed.

Orbix+Isis is a CORBA-compliant system that supports *object groups*: A CORBA client can successfully invoke an operation as long as there is one server available that contains a member of the required object group. The combination of Orbix and Isis provides the developer with a powerful tool for building distributed systems: the easy-to-use C++ Orbix environment layered on top of the Isis availability and reliability primitives. It automatically handles such complex issues as ensuring that each member of an object group processes the request messages for the group in the same order.

Clients are normally coded in the same manner as normal Orbix clients, but there are a range of options available to sophisticated clients. For example, a client may wish to receive more than one reply if each available member of the group carries out some of the requested work. This facility is integrated with the Orbix smart proxy support so that the complexity of, say, a client receiving several replies can be handled by a smart proxy and hence hidden from most client programmers.

Servers can also be programmed in the same manner as normal Orbix servers; in particular, the coding steps are the same as those in normal Orbix, and members of object groups are normal C++ objects. Objects remain lightweight and, therefore, a server can contain many objects (normally these objects would be members of different object groups).

As with clients, there is a range of possibilities for enhancing servers. Instead of having all of the members of an object group handle a message, a scheme called *client-choice* can be used in which a single member is chosen to handle a call. The members of an object group can also be programmed so that they all receive a request, but only one of them, the *coordinator*, carries it out. The others, the *cohorts*, automatically monitor the coordinator, and one of them will take over immediately if the coordinator fails. This *coordinator-cohorts* style is very useful if the cost of executing an operation is expensive (only one of the members of the object group will execute each operation), and it also allows members of an object group to share the load generated by a set of clients.

A second form of object group is provided in which a client's operation call is (transparently) routed to an *Event Stream*, which forwards the calls to any number of *Event Receivers*. This scheme decouples clients and servers, and appears like a publish and subscribe system. In particular, clients do not need to know the identity of the receivers, so new receivers can be added easily. Second, Event Streams store requests, allowing clients to make operation calls even if there are currently no receivers. The system can also scale well, because the receivers need not be aware of each other.

Orbix NEO/Talk   Orbix has been fully integrated with the NEO system, SunSoft's implementation of CORBA. This allows a deep level of interworking between the two systems.

Orbix and Databases   Orbix can be used with any RDBMS and a growing number of OODBMSs. As an example of this, Orbix has been integrated with the ObjectStore OODBMS. The dual aims of this are:

- To allow Orbix objects to be stored in ObjectStore (such objects are called Orbix+ObjectStore objects).
- To allow ObjectStore objects to be invoked by CORBA clients/servers.

Although Orbix provides a simple mechanism for supporting persistent objects, DBMSs offer a great deal more, such as queries and on-line back-ups. On the other hand, Orbix provides a more flexible distribution model than DBMSs, and hence there is natural scope for integration. For example, an Orbix application can contain Orbix+ObjectStore objects, normal Orbix objects, normal ObjectStore objects, and also normal programming language (C++) level objects. A very high degree of transparency is provided when programming and accessing these objects. A combination of Orbix loaders and filters is used to implement integrations with OODBMSs, and it is provided as a library known as an *adapter*.

The integration also allows servers to control the boundaries of the transactions; that is to say that they can control when the DBMS commits or aborts transactions. (These choices can be "exported" to clients by providing simple IDL calls to an object within the server.) A number of different styles are provided, allowing a single operation or a group of operations to be within a transaction.

Orbix and GUIs   C++ and Visual Basic are just two of the languages that can be used to write graphical user interfaces on Windows. On UNIX, the X Windows System's event loop has been integrated with Orbix, so that any X Windows GUI can be used. In addition, Orbix has been integrated with the UIM/X and Galaxy GUI builders.

Real-Time Orbix   Real-time Orbix is a full but streamlined version of Orbix for systems such as VxWorks, QNX, and LynxOS. The challenges in producing these systems have included low memory availability, high-performance requirements (including special intra-machine communications) and catering for diskless machines (without access to any file system).

Orbix and Transactions   The CORBA Object Transaction Service has been implemented on Orbix. This allows transactions in multiple databases to be committed atomically.

Other Programming Languages   Orbix supports the following languages: C++, Java, Ada, Smalltalk, Visual Basic, and many other Windows languages. An integration with Tcl has been carried out, and is available from IONA.

21.3.5   Implementation of Orbix

The CORBA specification is relatively free of implementation stipulations. An ORB mediates between clients and implementations (of application objects) and must provide a standard interface to such clients, and another to such implementations. So what, in practice, is the ORB? CORBA does not specify whether it is a set of run-time libraries, a set of daemon processes, a server machine, or part of an operating system; it can be any of these.

Orbix is implemented as a pair of libraries—one for client applications and one for servers—and the **orbixd** activation daemon. **orbixd** need only be present at nodes running CORBA servers, and it is responsible for (re-) launching server processes dynamically as required. Nondistributed client and server applications in the same process address space can be built using the server library alone. In this case, references from one object to another are direct (for example, they are direct pointers in C++, and operation invocations are simple C++ virtual function calls).

Where is the Orbix ORB? Because of its library implementation, the Orbix ORB is conceptually omnipresent: there is no distinct component that can be identified and stated as encapsulating the entire ORB. There is no central component through which all object requests must pass; instead, object requests are passed directly from the client code to the invoked object implementation.

The role of **orbixd** is to connect clients and servers for the first time. **orbixd** uses a simple database, the Implementation Repository, to obtain activation information for its servers; for each server, the information includes the appropriate CORBA activation mode, the name of the associated executable image and any command-line parameters.

21.4 HEWLETT-PACKARD: ORB PLUS

HP ORB Plus is an implementation of the CORBA 2.0 specification and supports distributed C++ applications. This software provides a lightweight, fast ORB with a small memory footprint that scales depending on the features chosen and the application's requirements. HP ORB Plus can be readily embedded in distributed applications requiring a fast response cycle and a lightweight distributed communications infrastructure.

The HP ORB Plus software is a flexible framework that allows application developers to select the features they need. HP ORB Plus supports the CORBA 2.0 communication protocols and can support domain specific custom protocols. It also allows for multiple simultaneous communication protocols. HP also provides a larger distributed object framework into which HP ORB Plus fits, including the user environment, network and system management, and software development.

Developing applications in HP ORB Plus is natural for C++ programmers. HP ORB Plus provides a Simplified Object Adapter (SOA). The IDL compiler accepts standard CORBA IDL files with no need for modification. Programming can be done using HP SoftBench, which provides a sophisticated, easy-to-use software development environment. HP ORB Plus is distributed with tutorials and sample applications, which progress in complexity from CORBA basics to advanced topics.

The major components of HP ORB Plus are the:

- efficient ORB with a minimal memory allocation;
- SOA, a lightweight, simplified object adapter;
- IDL compiler and CORBA-compliant C++ mapping;
- multiple transport layer support;
- transport-independent locator;
- Dynamic Invocation Interface support;
- enterprise-wide object services;
- progressive sample application.

HP ORB Plus also plans to support the

- Dynamic Skeleton Interface;
- Interface Repository.

21.4.1 Interoperability

HP ORB Plus supports the CORBA 2.0 standard, including both the IIOP and DCE CIOP communication protocols. Thus, the ORB will be able to operate efficiently in both DCE environments (using DCE CIOP), as well as non-DCE environments (using IIOP).

The HP ORB Plus framework provides a modular connection to different transport layers. The same ORB can simultaneously access both IIOP and DCE CIOP protocols.

For requests between a client and server in the same process, HP ORB Plus bypasses the transport stack, resulting in a very fast round-trip time, on the same order as a local C++ object invocation. HP ORB Plus will automatically choose the fastest of the available transports when handling a request.

A design goal for HP ORB Plus is transport independence. In addition to the CORBA 2.0 standard transports, customer specific transports can be developed and used.

A Locator provides object references for registered server objects running on a network. The Locator is used to locate the process where an object resides. When a server process starts up, it registers the process with the Locator. When a client makes a first request to a server object and cannot determine the location of the server object, it asks the Locator to find the location of the process associated with the object reference. The client will then use this information to route the request to the object in the server process. The Locator can activate server processes (and objects) if required.

HP also offers a CORBA-compliant implementation for Smalltalk programmers in HP Distributed Smalltalk (Chapter 22). Developers can develop mixed applications using both HP ORB Plus and HP Distributed Smalltalk objects that interoperate.

21.4.2 Enterprise Object Services

HP ORB Plus supports Events, Naming, and Lifecycle object services, based on the OMG standard, and intends to support additional object services. In line with the framework approach, the application developer is not required to use any object services but can select the ones needed.

The object service strategy is to provide federated enterprise-wide object services that support enterprise-wide distributed applications. A federated object service can respond locally to a request if appropriate, thus avoiding unnecessary remote requests that can be costly in a wide-area enterprise environment. The object service may also provide interfaces for batch operations to decrease the number of individual requests.

The object services fit into a distributed object framework between the ORB and the user environment. The application developer takes advantage of this larger framework to construct a distributed application utilizing a lightweight ORB connected to the one (or more) transport layers needed, selected object services, and appropriate parts of the user environment.

21.4.3 Application Development

HP ORB Plus provides an Interface Definition Language (IDL) compiler that compiles CORBA IDL files into stub and skeleton C++ code that conforms to the OMG C++ mapping. The IDL compiler provides a number of options typical of most language compilers and can be used directly in makefiles. The compiler generates a number of C++ files that declare interface classes and types, server base classes, and server skeleton types. The compiler also provides C++ definition files that define interface classes and types, server base classes, and server skeleton types. The ORB uses these files to ensure that a request from a client is matched with the appropriate interface when the server object receives it.

Application development is based on standard C++ programming and does not require any specific software development tool or application development environment. For example, the developer can use the programming tools available in the HP-UX environment. The developer may also use other application development environments that HP may make available in the future.

HP intends to integrate HP ORB Plus with HP SoftBench, which is an integrated set of window-based programming tools and a framework for integrating other tools. HP SoftBench has a graphical user interface with its own interactive on-line help system. It provides communication between different development tools (such as editors, program builders, debuggers, and file managers). HP SoftBench also provides support for both distributed and local tool execution and data accessing.

HP ORB Plus provides a set of sample applications demonstrating basic CORBA programming as well as more advanced topics, such as object services programming for those services that are available. A progressive set of sample applications takes the programmer from simple usage of the SOA to complex scenarios involving object services. The basic application shows a simple sample application demonstrating basic concepts in CORBA programming. The same application is then developed and expanded to show greater complexity. New programmers can thus follow a gentle learning curve in understanding this new technology. Programmers can progress at their own pace to the more advanced sample applications. Since they are already familiar with the core of the application, they can readily identify and assimilate new concepts and code. The developer can access on-line help that explains the sample applications.

21.4.4 Network and System Management

HP provides network and system management tools as part of the overall distributed object framework. The System Administration Management (SAM) tool provides a window-based GUI that helps administrators accomplish tasks without having to know the specific HP-UX commands and options. Administrators can easily set up and configure computers using SAM. On-line help explains the menu options and tasks that can be performed.

If developers are using DCE as the transport layer for HP ORB Plus, the HP DCE/9000 product provides administrative tools to configure and administer computers running HP DCE/9000.

The HP OpenView product also provides support for network and system management.

21.4.5 Conclusion

HP ORB Plus provides a CORBA 2.0-compliant ORB in a distributed object framework, including the areas of software development and network and system management. HP ORB Plus itself follows a framework approach that allows developers to select the components needed to make their distributed application operate most effectively and efficiently.

21.5 SUNSOFT, INC. NEO PRODUCT FAMILY

The NEO product family results from a long-term effort by SunSoft to produce a comprehensive set of tools and frameworks working in concert to provide developers, system administrators, and end users the necessary environment to develop, integrate, administer, and run distributed object applications.

Originally known as Project DOE, NEO started in 1989 when Sun cofounded the OMG. It immediately benefited from the lessons learned with Spring OS, a research operating system based entirely on distributed objects, and developed at the time by Sun Microsystems Laboratories.

From the start, it was decided that NEO should be able to generate and support systems with the following properties:

- *Low administration cost:* As applications built with NEO get deployed over large numbers of nodes, maybe over large enterprise networks, their cost of ownership should not rise exponentially.

- *Scalable systems in several dimensions:* This comprises granularity (size of each object), cardinality (number of objects and servers), space (area of distribution), and time (implementations and interfaces evolution).

- *Reliable systems:* Persistent objects (both object references and object states) allow systems to fail without any permanent impact on the distributed applications.

After a brief overview of the NEO product family, we will take a closer look at NEOworks, a comprehensive set of development tools and frameworks designed to enhance the productivity of distributed object developers.

21.5.1 Product Overview

NEO contains the following major components:

- *Operating environment—SolarisNEO:* A high-performance operating environment, SolarisNEO, is an extension to Solaris 2.4, SunSoft's networked operating environment. Solaris provides a solid foundation of capabilities to ensure that object-based applications are powerful, scalable, easy to administer, and reliable. SolarisNEO adds to this the tools to administer and manage networked objects and object-based applications:

- ◆ NEOnet: a CORBA-compliant distributed object broker infrastructure
- ◆ NEOshare: a CORBA-based service that finds, manages, and shares services over the network
- ◆ NEOdesktop: a desktop environment based on OpenStep

▪ *Development tools for distributed objects—WorkShopNEO:* SunSoft has invested heavily in robust, market-tested tools to develop and deploy networked object applications that minimize programming, improve the ability of engineers to create applications that exactly meet requirements, enhance creativity while upholding corporate standards, and support the creation of large programs by teams of developers.

SunSoft's development environment is based on the proven WorkShop technology and NEXTSTEP, the most advanced GUI development and deployment environment in the industry. WorkShopNEO includes:

- ◆ OpenStep Developer: easy-to-use, object-oriented tools for graphically assembling three-tiered applications from prebuilt, reusable objects
- ◆ NEOworks: a comprehensive set of tools to develop CORBA-compliant, networked object applications
- ◆ SPARCworks: a suite of intuitive software productivity tools designed to increase developer productivity and software quality

▪ *Administration Tools—SolsticeNEO:* Administration is a significant cost for enterprise computing environments. To ensure that the economies of NEO extend to systems management, SunSoft has created powerful tools to ensure positive control over every facet of NEO administration:

- ◆ NEO installation and management
- ◆ application and object installation and management
- ◆ workgroup management

▪ *Connectivity with legacy systems, data, and desktops:* Little commercial software is built in a vacuum, completely removed from legacy data, existing applications, or heterogenous platforms. SunSoft has crafted the necessary procedures, tools, and guidelines to make coexistence with these environments straightforward and trouble-free. They also have tools and techniques to support NEO connectivity to mainframe databases, Windows applications running on personal computers, World Wide Web browsers and object environments from other vendors.

21.5.2 World Wide Web Connection: Java

In addition to traditional implementation languages such as C, C++, and Objective-C, WorkShopNEO also supports Java, the object-oriented language for interactive Web-based applications.

Java client *applets* make it possible for Java-enabled Web browsers such as Sun's HotJava or Netscape's Navigator to access NEO applications from anywhere on the World Wide Web without requiring any special code, drivers, or anything else to be preinstalled on the client machines.

21.5.3 NEOworks

CORBA enables the creation of powerful applications. However, the merging of various advanced concepts such as OO, distributed computing, persistence, and multithreading can make the development of serious CORBA applications quite challenging.

One of the goals of NEO is to make developers more productive and to reduce development cycles. Something had to be done to simplify the development process of CORBA applications. This is accomplished by NEOworks.

NEOworks enables the developer to focus on the application code (that is, filling in the "body" of methods). To this end, NEOworks provides the following:

- *Object Server Language (OSL), compiler and maker:* Given IDL interfaces and a few customization parameters, these tools generate entire object servers—albeit with empty methods. Once a server template is generated, the developer only has to fill in the body of the methods.

- *Transparent persistence mechanism:* Using a subset of IDL called Data Definition Language (DDL), a developer can describe the persistent state of an object and have all of the code related to persistence generated by the Object Server Maker. The developer will then be able to access the persistent state of the object as local member variables from within the object's methods.

- *Service registration and resolution:* SolarisNEO comes bundled with NEOshare, a COSS naming service. The COSS specifies little semantics or topology for the Naming Service. NEOworks provides a small set of routines that add a simple distributed topology and clear semantics on top of the Naming Service.

  These routines can be used to automatically register (and later find) new services in NEOshare. They also allow services under development to coexist *safely* with deployed services and even to share some resources without having the development services endangering the deployed services.

- *A distributed debugger and powerful tracing facilities:* Even the simplest program once distributed can become very difficult to debug. WorkshopNEO's debugger goes a long way toward solving that problem by allowing its users to "single-step" into methods implemented in other processes and even on other machines than the client code on which the debugging session was started.

This tool becomes invaluable in large complex applications where a client often hangs, not because of a local implementation problem, but because some remote service fails to perform properly.

In some cases, particularly intermittent bugs, even a distributed debugger is not enough, and one must use "tracing statements" (glorified **printf()**). But, once again, working in a distributed environment can make tracing very difficult. For example, it is meaningless to print an error message on the console of some server far removed from the user simply because that's where an error was detected.

The tracing tools provided with NEOworks are both powerful and efficient; tracing behavior inside a running server can be customized without disturbing the server's execution.

21.5.4 System Administration

The system administration costs of large distributed applications can easily grow exponentially with the number of nodes and services provided. A major goal of NEO is to provide tools that will keep the system administration costs down by allowing distributed control of the services deployed.

Commands to the object administration tool, NEOadmin, perform basic system management tasks such as starting and stopping ORBs, controlling and displaying the status of object servers and processes, redirecting the output of tracing and logging facilities, and managing workgroups.

In addition to a rich set of basic commands, NEOadmin has a built-in Tcl interpreter, which allows arbitrarily complex scripts to perform large, repetitive actions with a single command. NEOadmin can be run either interactively or take command line arguments. The latter is useful in makefiles and other automated administration applications.

NEOadmin can control and customize NEO object servers wherever they are installed because of a small CORBA object inserted in each server built with NEOworks. In effect, this small NEOadmin surrogate makes each object server itself a first-class distributed object with an interface defined in IDL, and accessible from remote clients such as NEOadmin.

21.5.5 Developing a Distributed Object Application with NEOworks

As with any feature-rich environment, it can take a while to discover all the details of NEO. But developing a straightforward object server can be very simple indeed. Attendees of an introductory seminar on NEO development build their first server and client during the afternoon of the first day.

Viewed as a simple recipe, building a NEO server implementing an arbitrary interface called Foo can be done by following these steps diagrammed in Figure 21.4:

1. Obtain the IDL file describing the interface to implement; let's call it Foo.idl.
2. (Optional) Describe the persistent state of your objects using the Data Definition Language (DDL) in a file called Foo.ddl.
3. Make some implementation choices such as multithreading, time-outs before objects and/or servers are deactivated, service's name in the Naming Service, and so on. and describe them using the Object Server Language (OSL) in a file called Foo.impl.
4. Get the OSL compiler to generate a sample server implementation in FooImpl.cc and FooImpl.hh. You can actually build and install a Foo server using the code generated by the OSL compiler, but the body of each method simply raises the CORBA::NO_IMPLEMENT exception.
5. Fill in (at least a few of) the methods of the implementation class by replacing the code that raises the NO_IMPLEMENT exception.

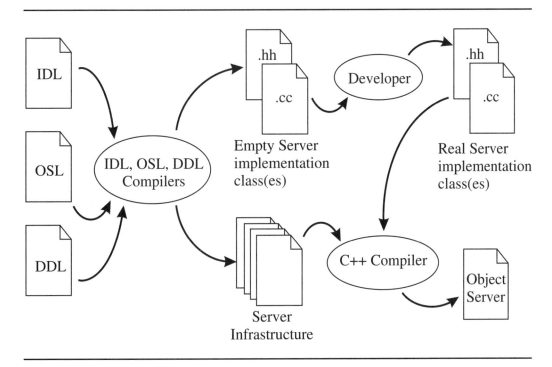

Figure 21.4. The flow of information from IDL to an object server.

6. Compile and link the server. (Each of the code generation, compilation, and linking steps can be executed with a single command from a customized Makefile generated by NEOworks for your particular development project).
7. (Optional) Make an SVR4 package that will install the server and register its service(s) in the Naming Service. (This too can be done in one step from the NEOworks-generated Makefile).
8. Install the package using standard UNIX tools on any server where it needs to be installed.

21.5.6 Further Information

You can get the latest information about the entire NEO product family on the World Wide Web at *http://www.sun.com/sunsoft/neo*, or by calling Sun at (800) USA-4SUN.

## CHAPTER 22

ORB Product: Smalltalk Language Mapping

22.1 INTRODUCTION TO SMALLTALK ORBS

As a language designed to be object-oriented from its beginnings, Smalltalk has a lot going for it as a vehicle for CORBA. Formerly viewed as a specialized vehicle for teaching OO concepts and small projects, it is now moving its way into mainstream business applications. In addition to the one product described here, the PowerBroker, SOMObjects, and ORBIX products support, or plan to support, Smalltalk. These are not the only ORBs with Smalltalk support; for more, contact the OMG using the pointers in Section 20.1.3.

22.2 USING HP DISTRIBUTED SMALLTALK

HP Distributed Smalltalk is an integrated set of frameworks that provides an advanced object-oriented environment for rapid development and deployment of CORBA-compliant applications allowing both Smalltalk and C++ objects to interoperate with each other. Introduced in early 1993, and now in its fifth major release, HP Distributed Smalltalk leverages the ParcPlace Smalltalk language and the VisualWorks development environment. The major components of HP Distributed Smalltalk are:

- *The HP Distributed Smalltalk ORB:* A full Smalltalk implementation of CORBA 2.0 that provides interoperability between different ORBs from different vendors, written in different languages and running on different platforms.

- *Remote Procedure Call (RPC) communication:* Supports efficient and reliable transfer of messages between systems with simultaneous protocol support for NCS and IIOP.
- *HP Distributed Smalltalk object services:* Basic CORBAservices and HP Distributed Smalltalk specific services.
- *Multiplatform support:* HP Distributed Smalltalk applications that run on one platform (hardware and operating system combination) can run, without porting, on any other supported platform.
- *OODBMS and RDBMS access:* HP Distributed Smalltalk provides database access via VisualWorks to Sybase, Oracle, and DB2, and access to OO databases through their Smalltalk interfaces.
- *HP Distributed Smalltalk developer tools and services:* Provide support specifically designed for developing, testing, tuning, and delivering distributed applications. These tools are incorporated in the ParcPlace Smalltalk language environment.
- *HP Distributed Smalltalk user environment and services:* Include a reusable demonstration user interface and desktop environment support for users' work sessions and normal desktop activity.
- *HP Distributed Smalltalk sample application objects:* Provide developers with example code that can be reused or extended, or can provide a source of ideas for developing alternate applications.

22.2.1 Supported CORBAservices and Policies

The supported CORBAservices are:

Initialization

Naming

Lifecycle

Event Notification

Concurrency Control

Transactions

The HP Distributed Smalltalk specific policies are:

Compound Lifecycle: Compound objects, built from simple objects, can include application components, anything that appears on a user's desktop (such as a document, a mail handler, or a graphics toolbox), and complete applications.

Relationships—Containment and links: Links allow networked relationships among objects. Objects can be linked with various levels of referential integrity (determining how to handle situations when one of the parties to the link is deleted), and in one-to-one, one-to-many, and many-to-many relationships.

Together with links, containment establishes and maintains relationships between objects. Each object has a specific location within some container. Containers are related hierarchically. Programmers can use these objects to build specific implementations such as a bill of sale (containing information about items in a shipment) with minimal extra programming.

Properties and property management: Properties are part of an object's external interface (owner, creation date, modification date, version, access control list, and so on). They are a dynamic version of attributes.

Application Objects and their Assistants: Application objects are relatively large-grained compound objects that end users deal with (such as a file folder or an order entry form). Application assistants are lightweight objects that implement most of the policies and participate in most of the services that desktop objects need to participate in.

Presentation/semantic split: A logical split between distributed objects, the presentation/semantic split provides an efficient architecture for dis-

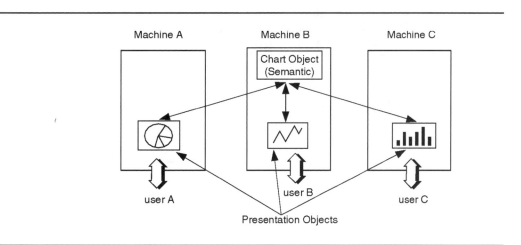

Figure 22.1.   The bulk of user interaction is with local presentation objects, minimizing the need to propagate semantically relevant changes over the network. Here, for example, a user might choose to look at a chart (semantic object) as a pie, line, or bar chart presentation object.

tributed applications. Local presentation objects handle the bulk of user interaction, while a semantic object (which can be anywhere on the network) holds a shared persistent state of the object (see Figure 22.1).

22.2.2 Developer and User Services

HP Distributed Smalltalk Launcher A modified VisualWorks Launcher (see Figure 22.2) launches HP Distributed Smalltalk. A Request Broker, Interface Repository and Sample Applications icon and an **HPDST** menu category provide quick access to functionality.

Configuration Notebook   Choosing **HPDST: Settings** brings up the settings notebook for establishing the initial references. It (Figure 22.3) contains the following:

- *TI (Transport Independent) Locator:* This service helps images find the initial references to the shared repository, Naming Service, and security.
- *Adapter id:* This is a unique identifier used to identify images in some domain (some set of systems). The Adapter id can be used to configure the TI Locator, Naming service, repository, and security.

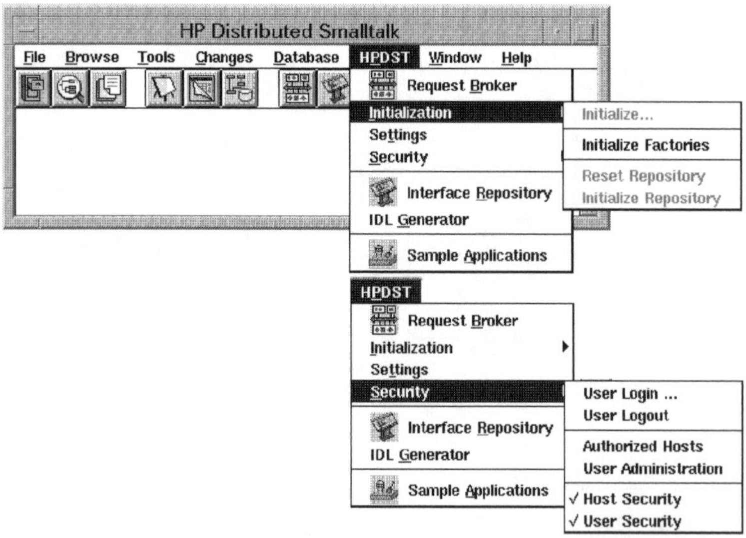

Figure 22.2.   The HP Distributed Smalltalk Launcher.

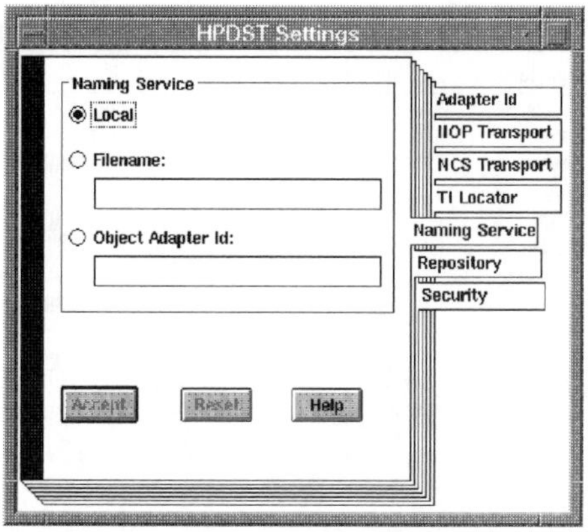

Figure 22.3.   The HP Distributed Smalltalk Configuration notebook.

- *IIOP Transport:* Internet Inter-ORB protocol that enables objects and applications to interoperate over a network with other OMG CORBA applications.
- *NCS Transport:* RPC (NCS 1.5.1) conversations and packet transfer for communication from HP Distributed Smalltalk to HP Distributed Smalltalk only.
- *Repository:* A service used to share the interface repository on a remote system.
- *Security:* The user security database for user-level access control.
- *Naming Service:* This service supports naming to help locate local and remote objects.

Security   Developers can use or extend HP Distributed Smalltalk's access control services in the applications they build, setting controls for host systems, users, or both. Host system access control lets developers determine whether an image can receive messages from another system. User-level access control lets a developer determine whether a given user has any one of several kinds of privileges (such as read or write privilege) for a given object. Developers can administer access control programmatically or from the default user interface.

Request Broker Panel   The technical user interface to HP Distributed Smalltalk for administrators and developers is invaluable for testing and maintenance (Figure 22.5). The control panel provides:

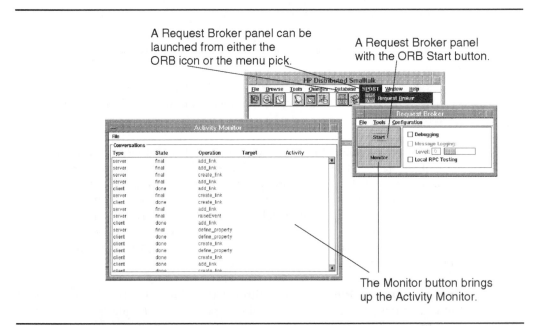

Figure 22.4. The HP Distributed Smalltalk access control service.

A Request Broker panel can be launched from either the ORB icon or the menu pick.

A Request Broker panel with the ORB Start button.

The Monitor button brings up the Activity Monitor.

Figure 22.5. The HP Distributed Smalltalk Request Broker Panel and Activity Monitor.

- controls to start and stop the system cleanly;
- support for local RPC testing (simulated distribution);
- tracing facilities to log network conversations between objects;
- performance monitoring.

Interface Repository Browser and Editor The interface repository browser provides an iconic view of the contents of the interface repository where publicly available interfaces are specified (see Figure 22.6). It is organized hierarchically so that developers can explore and edit interfaces.

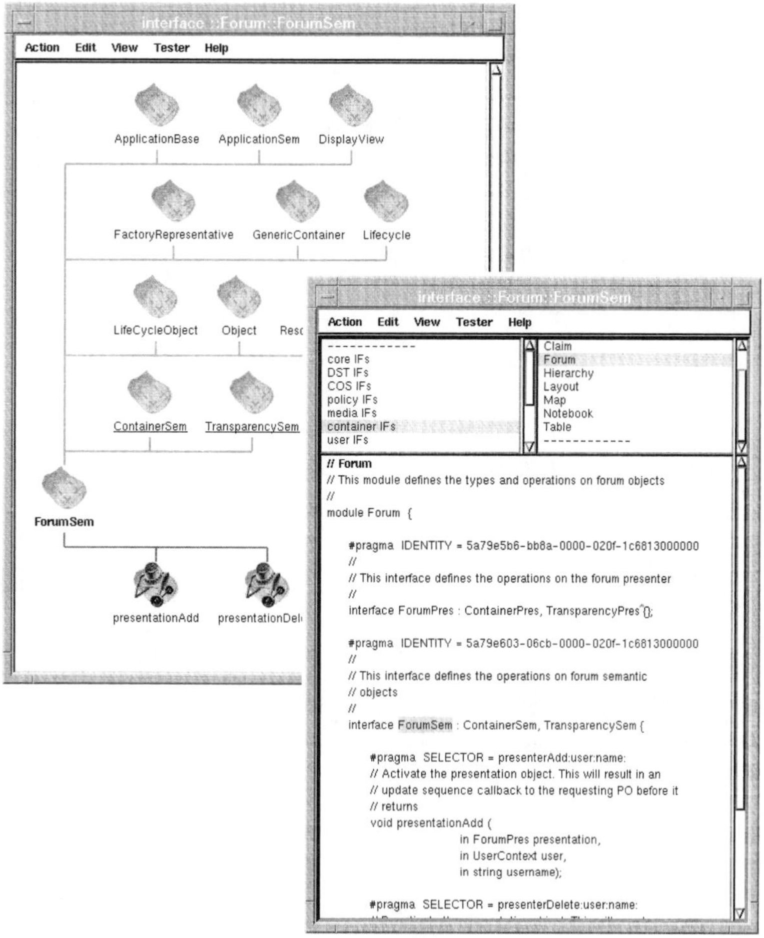

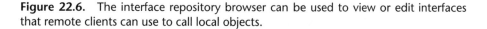

Figure 22.6. The interface repository browser can be used to view or edit interfaces that remote clients can use to call local objects.

Shared Interface Repository   In HP Distributed Smalltalk, users can share an interface repository on a remote system so they do not have the overhead of keeping a copy of all of the interfaces on every system. The product also supports version management of interfaces, which is very important in large-scale, evolving distributed systems.

Remote Context Inspector and Debugger   This service is an extension that allows debugging on remote images when appropriate. It supports object inspection and debugging for the entire distributed execution context, including communication between images. Figure 22.7 shows using the debugger to step through code and inspect objects that might be located anywhere in a distributed environment.

IDL Generator   The IDL Generator allows the programmer to select items from a menu to create IDL modules rather than having to write the code.

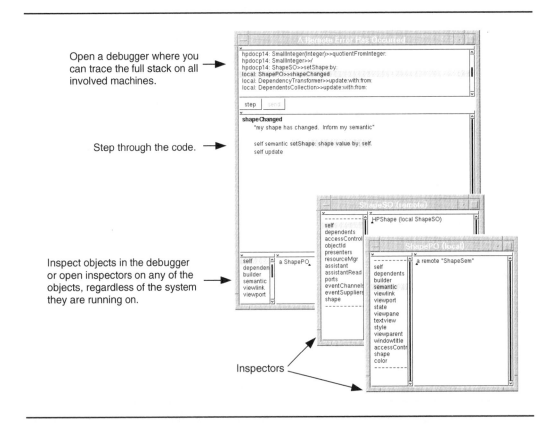

Figure 22.7.   Screens associated with a remote debugger.

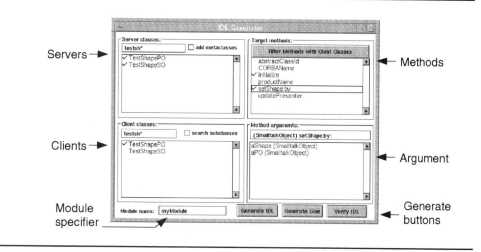

Figure 22.8.   Interface for the HP Distributed SmalltalkIDL Generator.

The IDL Generator appears as a multipane window in which the user makes selections and then clicks the Generate IDL button. A consistency checker is included that highlights any errors in the consistency of types, operations, and interfaces between Smalltalk and IDL (see Figure 22.8).

Stripping Tool   To prepare an application for delivery, developers use the HP Distributed Smalltalk stripping tool to remove unneeded classes and interfaces and seal source code when application development is complete. The stripping tool's user interface suggests likely items for removal (see Figure 22.9).

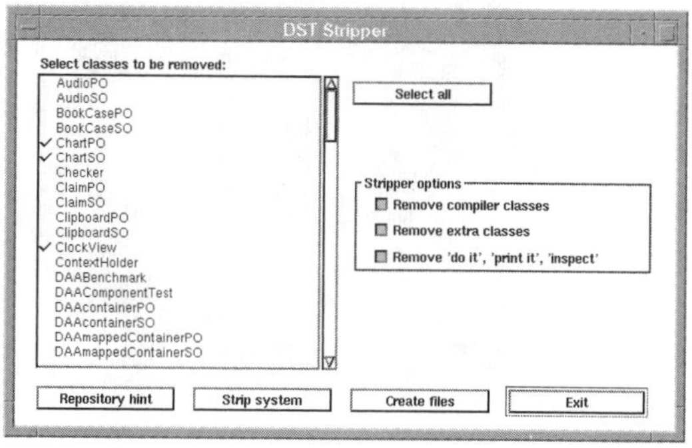

Figure 22.9.   Interface for the HP Distributed Smalltalk stripping tool.

22.2.3 Example Code

All HP Distributed Smalltalk code is available to read, reuse, or extend, but the default user interface and certain sample applications may be the best place to start. In the default user interface, all the objects a user works with locally (folders, file cabinets, documents, and so on) are contained in an office. All offices in the same domain are in the same building. Users can navigate between buildings to access objects in other offices (Figure 22.10).

Sample applications illustrate the use of distributed objects. For example, the Forum (Figure 22.11) provides a shared window in which several users can view and annotate a picture or document.

Users can also build their own objects from any of the sample objects available, including a table, chart, input field, picture, and text window. The sample applications can be extended and customized to create a variety of simple distributed applications.

22.2.4 Creating Applications

HP Distributed Smalltalk allows VisualWorks programmers to create distributed applications quickly and easily. Like any Smalltalk application,

Figure 22.10.   The screen for presenting the office metaphor and some typical objects in an office.

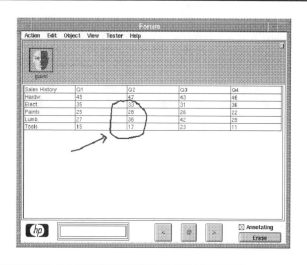

Figure 22.11.   User interfaces to the sample applications Forum and Notebook.

the distributed development process is iterative and designed for dynamic refinement.

Development   Distributed application development is a four-step process:

1. Design and test the application objects locally.
2. Define the object interfaces and register them in the interface repository.
3. Use HP Distributed Smalltalk's simulated remote testing tools (which actually use the ORB to marshall and unmarshall object requests) to verify the interfaces specified in the interface repository.
4. Track messages and tune performance.

Distribution   Once an application is developed, tested, and tuned locally, it is easy to set it up for distributed use:

1. Copy the application classes to the Smalltalk images they will run on.
2. Update the interface repositories in these images.

The application can then run in the fully distributed environment without further change. Except for actual packet transfer, the distributed application is identical to the simulated remote application developed, tuned, and tested during development.

Delivery   Once the application is tested, developers can deliver it to their users by stripping the environment of unneeded objects and tools. Once stripped, the application looks exactly the same as applications developed in other languages, and thus can be executed on any supported platform, including: HP-UX, SunOS/Solaris, IBM AIX, Microsoft Windows, Microsoft Windows NT, or IBM OS/2. Support for these platforms is available under a run-time license from Hewlett-Packard.

## CHAPTER 23

Coding and Compiling the IDL

23.1 CODING THE IDL

If you're serious about working the example, now is the time to sit down at your computer. In the first half of this chapter, we start with the Analysis and Design (A&D) developed in Chapters 18 and 19 and generate the OMG IDL file containing all of our objects' interfaces. In the second half, we compile it into client stubs and object skeletons using the IDL compiler that comes with your chosen ORB product.

In some sense, this chapter is the "answer book" for the problem given in Chapters 18 and 19. If you enjoy a challenge, you might want to try generating an IDL file yourself from those chapters, and comparing the results to what we present here. (You may want to switch to our version of the file before continuing on, to get operation and parameter names into synch.) If this is all new to you, just follow along one section at a time.

Regardless of how you do it, you'll need all of the IDL stored as files in order to compile it in the last half of the chapter. If you're working along, you should type it in by hand as you work your way through the example. Or, if you prefer, just read the IDL file off of the diskette. But we recommend that you study the chapter even so, since real-life problems usually don't come with an answer-diskette in the back.

Ready to start typing? Here we go....

23.2 INTRODUCTION

The A&D gives a lot of guidance in writing the IDL. We did this on purpose; we knew during the design phase what the next step would be. Because the A&D specifically states object, attribute, and operation names, the main things we need to do here are to translate the A&D constructs to IDL, and define the modularity of the components.

Here are the assumptions that were "built in" to the A&D as we wrote it, to enable easy transformation into IDL:

1. Each object defined in the A&D will be defined as an IDL interface.
2. State variables are assumed to be implementation details and will not be part of the IDL unless the A&D states they are attributes.
3. To help illustrate IDL syntax, we will use a variety of IDL constructs to specify our objects.
4. We will use capital letters to separate words in identifiers rather than underscores. (Underscores, although legal IDL characters, can cause compilation and portability problems with both C and Smalltalk.)

First, let us consider how to best modularize the IDL that represents these objects. We define each object as an IDL interface and group logically related interfaces within IDL modules. In creating these groupings, we have made some assumptions on how the system will be deployed. We know from the A&D that object instances will exist on separate computers:

Each POS station is a separate computer in a LAN within the store. It contains the POS object, the InputMedia and the OutputMedia objects.

The Store object, the StoreAccess objects it creates, and the Tax object reside on a separate computer in the same LAN, but on a different computer from the POS stations.

The depot is on a separate computer reachable by WAN.

This deployment strategy suggests that we create three modules, one for each computer system. The analysis suggests these three:

```
module POS
{
    interface POSTerminal;
    interface InputMedia;
    interface OutputMedia;
};
```

```
module AStore
{
    interface Store;
    interface StoreAccess;
    interface Tax;
};

module CentralOffice
{
    interface Depot;
};
```

The last object to define in IDL is the PseudoName Service. It will be accessed by all the above modules, so it is declared separately as:

```
interface PseudoNameService
{
    void        BindName(
                    in string ObjectName,
                    in Object ObjectRef);
    Object      ResolveName(
                    in string ObjectName);
};
```

The next step in completing the IDL is to add the operations and supporting datatypes to each module. We will address each module in turn, filling in the details of the IDL as we go.

23.3 POS MODULE

The POS module is composed of three interfaces and several data types. Together, these components make up the point-of-sale terminal software. The objects are discussed in the following three sections, and the complete POS module is shown in Section 23.3.4.

23.3.1 InputMedia Object

The InputMedia object is described in the A&D in Section 19.1.1 in enough detail to define almost completely the IDL file we're about to generate. We won't reprint the A&D here; it's close at hand, and we have to conserve paper someplace. Be sure you flip back to Section 19.1.1 and compare the A&D to the IDL here.

The A&D defines three operations for InputMedia:

Initialization
KeypadInput
BarcodeInput

As described, the **Initialization** operation is not invoked by other components in the system, so it need not be part of InputMedia's public IDL interface. **KeypadInput** and **BarcodeInput** are, however, both invoked by a client. They will be part of the InputMedia interface.

The A&D states that the operation **BarcodeInput** takes one input parameter, item, which represents the scanned bar code. IDL has a typedef construct for defining synonyms to existing types, allowing us to define a datatype, **Barcode**, to represent the bar code. The bar-code type is used by both the **POS** and **InputMedia** interfaces so we will define it outside the scope of InputMedia. The IDL for **Barcode** is:

typedef string Barcode;

KeypadInput also has a single input parameter; in this case, "a string representing input from the POS's keypad." The IDL string type is used for both barcodes and keypad input. Neither **KeypadInput** nor **BarcodeInput** returns a value, so the IDL must declare their return value void.

InputMedia does not contain any attributes so the POS module is now:

```
module POS
{
    typedef string Barcode;
    interface InputMedia
    {
        typedef string OperatorCmd;

        void    BarcodeInput(in Barcode Item);
        void    KeypadInput(in OperatorCmd Cmd);
    };
};
```

23.3.2 OutputMedia Object

As stated in the A&D, Section 19.1.2, OutputMedia has a single operation and no attributes. The operation, **OutputText**, has one input argument. This argument is a string to be printed, and it is represented with CORBA's **string** type. Here is the complete IDL for the OutputMedia interface:

```
interface OutputMedia {

    boolean    OutputText(in string StringToPrint);

};
```

23.3.3 POSTerminal Object

The A&D for the POSTerminal object, Section 19.1.3, defines several operations including an Initialization method. As with the InputMedia, we do not anticipate remote invocations of this operation so it will not be defined in the IDL. Each of the other operations is invoked by InputMedia based on specific user inputs. The implementation discussions do not specify a need for any attributes, so the POSTerminal IDL shown here contains only the following operations:

Login
PrintPOSSalesSummary
PrintStoreSalesSummary
SendBarcode
ItemQuantity
EndOfSale

23.3.4 The Complete POS Module

This module completely defines the POS in IDL. Note that we have added the type **POSId**; it is used by the operation **Login** in the **Store** interface:

```
module POS
{
    typedef long POSId;
    typedef string Barcode;
    interface InputMedia
    {
        typedef string OperatorCmd;

        void    BarcodeInput(in Barcode Item);
        void    KeypadInput(in OperatorCmd Cmd);
    };

    interface OutputMedia {

        boolean    OutputText(in string StringToPrint);
```

```
    };

    interface POSTerminal {

        void Login();
        void PrintPOSSalesSummary();
        void PrintStoreSalesSummary();
        void SendBarcode(in Barcode Item);
        void ItemQuantity (in long Quantity);
        void EndOfSale();
    };

};
```

23.4   ASTORE MODULE

The IDL for the AStore module is derived from the A&D for the Store (Section 19.1.4), StoreAccess (Section 19.1.5), and Tax (Section 19.1.6) objects. The IDL for each interface is presented in segments in the next three sections and the completed module is shown in Section 23.4.4.

23.4.1   Store Object

The Store handles messages to Initialize, login a POS, and to report totals, but once again the A&D operation "Initialize" will not be represented in IDL. The A&D further specifies that the Store will track running totals from all POSTerminals and will contain an attribute that contains these totals.

We used a single struct attribute, instead of two independent attributes, to avoid possible inconsistencies. This is an example of a problem that comes up frequently in the design of distributed systems, where multiple clients can access a single server for both update and retrieval, so we'll point it out here. Consider the following scenario:

1. POS 1 calls the **get** operation for the store total.
2. POS 2 calls **UpdateStoreTotals**, which changes both the store total and the store tax total.
3. POS 1 calls the **get** operation for the store tax total.

Even if POS 1 calls the **get** operation for the store tax total immediately after the **get** for the store total, there can be no guarantee that the totals are consistent, because POS 2 is an independent object and can submit an update at any time. Granted, the probability is slight under light load conditions as we have in this example, but accounting systems are not supposed to report inconsistent results under any conditions.

To avoid this problem, we define a struct with two fields, the store total and store tax total, and a single IDL attribute of the struct type:

```
struct StoreTotals {
    float    StoreTotal;
    float    StoreTaxTotal;
};
readonly attribute StoreTotals Totals;
```

By combining the two values into a single struct, which is retrieved via a single operation, the A&D guarantees that the result will be consistent for *single-threaded servers* (which cannot execute multiple requests simultaneously). Extending this guarantee to multithreaded servers requires thread control via locks and semaphores, which we will neither define nor explain here. They are extremely useful tools for distributed applications, but we're afraid they just won't fit into this book.

POSTerminals invoke Store's operation **Login** to start a session with the store. **Login** assigns a StoreAccess object to the POS and returns a reference to the StoreAccess object. This can be expressed in IDL as:

```
StoreAccess Login(in POS::POSId Id);
```

Note that **Login**'s return type is the reference to the **StoreAccess** object. CORBA semantics dictate that **Login** return an object reference, not a copy of the actual object implementation. We will see in later chapters how this is accomplished in C, C++, and Smalltalk.

To complete the **Store** IDL, we create definitions for the **StoreId** attribute and the operation **GetPOSTotals**, which reports store totals. From the A&D, **GetPOSTotals** returns "the state of the store's current knowledge of all of the registered POS stations."

To support this requirement, we define a structure that represents the state of a **POS** object and a sequence type of these structures. We do not know, nor do we wish to hard code, the maximum number of **POS** objects that can use a **Store** object, so an IDL "unbounded" sequence type (an unbounded sequence can dynamically change size at run time) is used.

```
struct POSInfo {
    POS::POSId    Id;
    StoreAccess   StoreAccessReference;
    float         TotalSales;
```

```
        float           TotalTaxes;
};


typedef sequence <POSInfo> POSList;
```

The **POSInfo** struct was defined to contain all information that the **Store** maintains about each **POSTerminal**, including a reference to the **POS**'s **StoreAccess** object. **POSInfo** is defined in the **AStore** module as shown in Section 23.4.4.

The last step is to add **UpdateStoreTotals**, which completes the IDL for the **Store**:

```
interface Store {
    struct StoreTotals {
        float    StoreTotal;
        float    StoreTaxTotal;
    };

    readonly attribute AStoreId StoreId;

    readonly attribute StoreTotals Totals;

    StoreAccess Login(in POS::POSId Id);
    void    GetPOSTotals(out POSList POSData);
    void    UpdateStoreTotals(
            in POS::POSId Id,
            in float    Price,
            in float    Taxes);
};
```

23.4.2 StoreAccess Object

The **StoreAccess** object is, from the A&D Section 19.1.5, "the intermediary between the POS and the central depot concerning access to the grocery item data base. One such object is created for each POS that logs in to the Store." The A&D indicates that **StoreAccess** has two operations and several state variables. None of the state variables was specified as an attribute. Of the operations, only **FindPrice** needs to be part of the IDL interface, because it is the only operation invoked by remote clients.

The A&D states that **FindPrice** accepts inputs to specify the item and outputs the price, taxable price, and an "item info." It also must raise an exception, **BarcodeNotFound**, if it cannot locate the item in the database.

We discussed IDL exceptions in Section 3.3.5; now (finally!), we'll use one. We'll define **BarcodeNotFound**, in the AStore module, to contain the offending bar code as follows:

```
exception BarcodeNotFound {POS::Barcode item;};
```

FindPrice also has an output parameter of type **ItemInfo**, defined in the A&D as "a structure containing at least ItemInfo.item, ItemInfo.ItemType, ItemInfo.ItemCost, and ItemInfo.Name." These types are used by several interfaces, so we will put the following declaration in the **AStore** module.

```
enum ItemTypes {food, clothes, other};
struct ItemInfo {
    POS::Barcode Item;
    ItemTypes     Itemtype;
    float         Itemcost;
    string        Name;
    long          Quantity;
};
```

ItemTypes is expressed as an IDL enumerated list. Its three identifiers represent the set of item types carried by stores in our system (as defined in the A&D, of course). **ItemInfo** is defined as stated in the A&D, plus an additional member, which contains the quantity in inventory for the item (bar code).

FindPrice can now be defined as follows:

```
void    FindPrice(
            in POS::Barcode Item,
            in long              Quantity,
            out float            ItemPrice,
            out float            ItemTaxPrice,
            out ItemInfo         IInfo)
        raises (BarcodeNotFound);
```

The IDL interface StoreAccess is therefore:

```
interface StoreAccess {

    void    FindPrice(
            in POS::Barcode Item,
            in long         Quantity,
            out float       ItemPrice,
            out float       ItemTaxPrice,
```

```
              out ItemInfo      IInfo)
        raises (BarcodeNotFound);

    };
```

23.4.3 Tax Object

The Tax object performs tax services for the **Store** object. The A&D Section 19.1.6 states that it contains the operations:

```
Initialize
CalculateTax
FindTaxablePrice
```

Two state variables are defined in the A&D but, because they are not attributes, they do not appear in the IDL. And, as usual, Initialize will not be part of the IDL.

Both IDL operations return floating point numbers that represent the tax and taxable price for an item respectively. The IDL for the Tax object is:

```
interface Tax {

    float CalculateTax(in float TaxableAmount);

    float FindTaxablePrice(
                in float          ItemPrice,
                in ItemTypes    ItemType);

    };
```

23.4.4 Complete AStore Module

The completed IDL for the module **AStore** is:

```
module AStore {

    enum ItemTypes {food, clothes, other};
    typedef long AStoreId;

    struct ItemInfo {
        POS::Barcode Item;
        ItemTypes       Itemtype;
```

```
    float        Itemcost;
    string       Name;
    long         Quantity;
};

exception BarcodeNotFound {POS::Barcode item;};

interface StoreAccess; // forward reference

struct POSInfo {
    POS::POSId   Id;
    StoreAccess  StoreAccessReference;
    float        TotalSales;
    float        TotalTaxes;
};

typedef sequence <POSInfo> POSList;

interface Tax {

    float CalculateTax(in float      TaxableAmount);

    float FindTaxablePrice(
            in float        ItemPrice,
            in ItemTypes    ItemType);

};

interface Store {

    struct StoreTotals {
        float   StoreTotal;
        float   StoreTaxTotal;
    };

    readonly attribute AStoreId StoreId;

    readonly attribute StoreTotals Totals;

    StoreAccess Login(in POS::POSId Id);
    void    GetPOSTotals(out POSList POSData);
    void    UpdateStoreTotals(
```

```
                    in POS::POSId      Id,
                    in float           Price,
                    in float           Taxes);
        };

        interface StoreAccess {

            void    FindPrice(
                    in POS::Barcode    Item,
                    in long            Quantity,
                    out float          ItemPrice,
                    out float          ItemTaxPrice,
                    out ItemInfo       IInfo)
                raises (BarcodeNotFound);

        };

    };
```

23.5   CENTRALOFFICE MODULE

The **CentralOffice** module contains the single interface **Depot**. **Depot** has a single operation, **FindItemInfo**, which selects and returns an **ItemInfo** structure based on three input arguments. Note that **FindItemInfo** uses types defined in the **AStore** and **POS** modules so we must scope references to the type names as shown here. The A&D, in Section 19.1.7, also states that **FindItemInfo** raises the exception **BarcodeNotFound** when given an invalid bar code (formal argument **item**). Based on these observations, the complete IDL declaration for **CentralOffice** is as follows:

```
    module CentralOffice {

        interface Depot {
            void FindItemInfo(
                in AStore::AStoreId   StoreId,
                in POS::Barcode       Item,
                in long               Quantity,
                out AStore::ItemInfo  IInfo)
            raises (AStore::BarcodeNotFound);
        };
    };
```

23.6   **THE IDL FILES**

In preparation for compiling the IDL, we must partition it into one or more source files. IDL source files are typically named with the sufix .idl, although this may vary between IDL compilers. We'll put the IDL for each module into a single file, since we have only a few dependencies. (If we had an object that was inherited by a number of different modules, we might put its IDL into a file by itself for easier inclusion.)

Here is the skeleton of each file. If you've been typing in the IDL as we went along, edit your files to reflect this structure:

File POS.idl

```
#ifndef POS_IDL
#define POS_IDL

module POS {
...
};

#endif
```

File Store.idl

```
#ifndef STORE_IDL
#define STORE_IDL

#include "pos.idl"

module AStore {
...
};

#endif
```

File Central.idl

```
#ifndef CENTRAL_IDL
#define CENTRAL_IDL
#include "pos.idl"
#include "store.idl"
```

```
module CentralOffice {
...
};

#endif
```

File PNS.idl

```
#ifndef PNS_IDL
#define PNS_IDL

interface PseudoNameService
{
...
};

#endif
```

The IDL compiler supports C++ style preprocessing so we use "cpp" conditional, define, and include directives. Each file is bracketed by the lines:

```
#ifndef name
#define name

#endif
```

where name is replaced by a, hopefully, unique string derived from the filename. For example, POS_IDL, is used in the file POS.idl. These three lines protect against multiple-declaration errors.

Notice also that Central.idl and Store.idl use the cpp include statement so the IDL compiler will know of constructs from the other modules.

If your files contain the IDL given at the end of each module section in this chapter, bracketed by the structure we just presented, then you're ready to compile your stubs and skeletons starting in the next section.

23.7 COMPILING THE IDL

The IDL files that we've just completed represent the fulfillment of the promise we made at the beginning of this book: They completely specify the interfaces of all of the objects in our system, and can (and will!) be implemented in several programming languages, on a wide variety of platforms.

And, when CORBA 2.0-compliant ORBs become available sometime in the very near future, objects from any one implementation will interoperate with objects from any other, transparent to differences in programming language, platform, or other component.

Now it's time to compile these IDL files into client stubs and object implementation skeletons. Many IDL compilers generate various header files and "starter" files for your client and object implementation code, in addition to stubs and skeletons. Your ORB vendor will tell you, in the next half of this chapter and in your documentation, which files are output by the IDL compiler and what you're supposed to do with them.

In case you skipped Chapters 20 through 22, here is a listing of the programming language that each ORB uses to work the example and the section in this chapter where its IDL compiler is presented; keep in mind that almost all of these ORBs actually implement multiple languages: ORBs working the example in C are Object Broker (Section 23.8), SOMobjects (Section 23.9), and DAIS (Section 23.10); ORBs working in C++ are Powerbroker (Section 23.11), Orbix (Section 23.12), ORB Plus (Section 23.13), and NEO (Section 23.14); and the ORB working in Smalltalk is Distributed Smalltalk (Section 23.15).

Skip ahead to the section on your ORB and IDL compiler. Follow the instructions it gives you to compile the IDL. Some compilers add **#pragma** directives as IDL comments; these give the compiler additional information it needs without spoiling the "standardness" of the IDL; the **#pragma**s are ignored by other compilers so you still end up with a standard file that can be compiled by any standard IDL compiler.

When you've finished compiling the IDL, turn to Chapter 24 where we'll start coding the **Depot** object.

23.8 OBJECTBROKER

ObjectBroker is Digital Equipment Corporation's CORBA-compliant ORB. It has language bindings for both C and C++, but this example will show only the C bindings since they are the oldest bindings in OMG, and this book needed some balance. Using C, you are exposed to quite a bit more of the mechanics of what an ORB must do. You can enviously look at the simpler C++ code of the other vendors and feel confident that Digital's C++ implementation will be just as simple and conformant as they are. All of the upcoming steps are true for the C++ bindings as well as for the C bindings— the client calls and server methods are just a lot easier to read, understand, and code. C, however, is where *real programmers* start.

The method of creating the sample application shown here is not the easiest method available in ObjectBroker. ObjectBroker has available a

QuickStart facility that takes IDL files and automatically produces completely working applications based only on those IDL files (although they pass only empty messages). QuickStart provides complete outlines for you, and bypasses your need to use the utilities shown here. In this book, however, since there is a set of routines that all vendors are using to show OMA commonality, we will not use QuickStart, but will instead perform the same functions that QuickStart would do for you (as a matter of fact, we stole some QuickStart-generated code). Again, you can feel like a hunter on the veldt, or whatever primitive image appeals to you, as a *real programmer*.

Starting the coding from scratch, we have four IDL files, containing eight interfaces that cumulatively have 17 explicit methods (plus several implicit methods due to IDL attributes). The configuration for our system will have five "processes," each of which can run on separate computers. Each of the processes contains a main program and some supporting subroutines. Some of the processes are pure clients, some pure servers, but most are a combination of both.

Some of the interfaces from a module (an IDL file) will run in a single process and some will run in separate processes. Most of the methods will be called through the auspices of a BOA (meaning that they might be on separate computers) but, in one case, two of the methods will be "lightweight" or "built-in," meaning that they are called from the same process as their client, essentially using an optimized BOA for efficiency sake.

An ORB must be prepared to deal with all these possibilities, so it has these and other options, many more than we are going to use. Clearly, we had better have a good idea of where we're going before we start using some of the options of any ORB, especially one as rich in functionality as ObjectBroker. Fortunately, as complicated as it may seem, this example is still simple compared to most real world examples! Right. A little like telling a prisoner that he should be happy Alcatraz is not Devil's Island.

Figure 23.1 shows the end result that we are seeking. It shows the IDL files contributing to the five different "processes," which interfaces are where, and where communications take place.

23.8.1   IDL

ObjectBroker coding starts out by taking the OMG-specified, 100%-compliant IDL from this chapter as-is, requiring no manual changes. One useful modification made to each IDL file is done automatically for you by the ObjectBroker IDL compiler—it adds a pragma containing a UUID (Universal, Unique IDentifier) for each piece of information that might be needed by another IDL file, client, or server. (This includes repository_id's of various

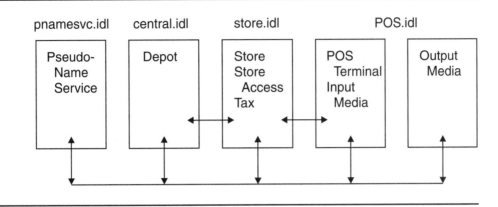

Figure 23.1. ObjectBroker processes, interfaces, and communications pathways.

sorts, but, thank goodness, you don't have to worry about the details of what those mean.)

The first thing you should do whenever you start working with an IDL file is to annotate that IDL by generating the UUIDs. This will guarantee that the names you assign are never confused with other names throughout the Milky Way galaxy (that's how universal UUIDs are). To assign the pragma UUIDs to the Central.idl file, for example, simply type:

```
> obbgen -u -f Central.idl
```

After this command, the end of the IDL file will contain pragmas uniquely identifying all the important parts of the IDL file. You do the same for the other files. You don't have to worry about accidentally adding pragmas a second time; ObjectBroker is smart enough to notice they're already there if you issue this command a second time.

(Since ObjectBroker runs on many platforms with different command lines, this book will show how to run the example for UNIX-based platforms (practically identical with Windows NT). This command line varies greatly from some of the proprietary platforms, so check the ObjectBroker documentation on how to do the same thing elsewhere. For UNIX, we will write the command with an angle bracket (>) to indicate the UNIX prompt and the rest of it in bold to indicate what you type.)

23.8.2 Initializing the Interface Repository

Whenever you deal with more than one or two interfaces, it is usually a good idea to store them in an interface repository (IR, discussed initially in

Section 4.4). This helps keep the information together and makes certain options easier later on.

When you are just developing your application, you want to make sure that you don't interfere with any ongoing production applications. (Just ask your boss...) ObjectBroker gives you that capability through the use of private IRs at several different levels. There are many ways of dealing with private IRs, but the easiest one is to define it in a *context object* private to the user.

A context object contains properties and values that can be accessed directly by programs or through command lines. ObjectBroker will allow you to create a private context object that makes it easy for you to develop and debug your application before moving to production. Two of the most important properties that can be defined in a context object are the location of the IR and the list of computers that are searched for objects in a distributed environment. For now, we'll deal only with the first property and mention the second later when we're done debugging.

ObjectBroker starts you with a default context object that you can easily modify for your needs. To change properties in the context object without writing C programs, Digital has devised a simple language called COL (for Context Object Language) that is manipulated from the command line. It describes the properties and values that are to be stored in your context object. For example, the following file, primer.col, declares the location of the IR and states that all processes can be found on the local computer—a good idea while debugging.

```
ContextObject
    Table OBB_DEFAULT_TABLE
        OBB_REPOSITORY: OBB_STRING
          ="obb/primer.ir";
        OBB_DEFAULT_NODES: OBB_STRING = OBB_LOCAL;
    End Table
End ContextObject
```

The only new (as opposed to the ObjectBroker-supplied default) part of this .col file is the line in bold, the location of the private IR.

Thus, your second step (after adding UUIDs to the IDL files) is to create this file and then load it into your private context object by issuing the command:

```
> obbldctx -c -U primer.col
```

The **-c** modifier here tells ObjectBroker to create a new context; **-U** says to define it at the "user" level. (Be careful with case on the modifiers of the UNIX commands; they are significant.) After this, every time you issue a command referring to the IR, you will be referring to your private IR, primer.ir.

Now that your private IR's location has been specified, this is a good time to load all the IDL files into it by issuing the command:

```
> obbldrep -c POS.idl Store.idl Central.idl \
                    PNS.idl
```

(The notation here of a backslash at the end of the line indicates a continuation of the command.) The **-c** modifier again tells ObjectBroker to create a new object, this time a new IR.

If you wish, you can check that the IR indeed has loaded your IDL by checking with the command:

```
> obbshrep
```

This utility will show you the current contents of the IR; now it is just the IDL, with comments stripped out.

23.8.3 ObjectBroker's IML and MML Languages

Because of the many ways you might wish to organize your system, any ORB must provide a method of allowing you to describe an object's implementation. As you will see in the rest of this book, CORBA allows many ways of doing that. Digital provides two simple languages that let you define aspects of the configuration. Don't let additional languages scare you. If you are a beginner, ObjectBroker will provide you with a default set of definition files (MML, or Method Mapping Language, and IML, or Implementation Mapping Language files). These languages are easy to deal with because they are similar in syntax to that used by OMG IDL.

Your next step is to generate these MML and IML files. For the depot, it is done simply by:

```
> obbgen -i central.iml CentralOffice::Depot
> obbgen -m central.mml CentralOffice::Depot
```

These two commands tell ObjectBroker to use the information stored in the IR to give you default IML and MML files for the Depot interface in the CentralOffice module. As an example of what is produced, central.iml is:

```
// OBB Default IML file
// --------------------
/ Use this file as a base for your additional IML
// definitions.

implementation DepotImpl
    {
    activation_type ( program );
    activation_policy ( shared );
    activation_string ( "<tba> - command to run
        implementation" );
    implementation_identifier (
        "7049337f74c8.0c.bb.09.00.00.00.00.00" );
    registration_attribute string
        Implementation Name = "DepotImpl";
    method_dispatcher_routine
        DepotImpl__dispatch();
    registration_routine DepotImpl__register ();
    deactivate_impl_routine DepotImpl__notify ();
    FindItemInfo ( ) implements
            ( CentralOffice::Depot::FindItemInfo )
        invoke_builtin ("DepotImpl_FindItemInfo");
    };
```

The details of this implementation mapping file are mostly unimportant at this level, and you can usually ignore this file until you get deeply into the options. The one line that affects us later is activation_type. Here it means that the Depot implementation runs in a process and is activated by the BOA—that is, it stands on its own. We'll change this only for methods that sit in the same process as their clients (upcoming). All the other names and attributes of the IML will work in concert with other ObjectBroker generated routines, as we'll see.

The corresponding MML file is even simpler:

```
// OBB Default MML file
// --------------------
//
// Use this file as a base for your additional MML
// definitions.

method_map DepotMap
    interface CentralOffice::Depot
    {
    FindItemInfo :
```

```
    {
    default :
        select_implementation
            by_name ( DepotImpl )
            by_identifier (
      "7049337f74c8.0c.bb.09.00.00.00.00.00" )
        ;
    };
  };
```

The interesting thing about MML files is that they allow you to affect the selection policies of a method according to some attributes that may be important to you—distance, loading factor, or whatever. These are fairly advanced options in ObjectBroker. We won't modify the default generated MML files for this example.

Once we've generated and possibly modified the MML and IML files for a particular interface, we put them into the IR by:

> **obbldrep central.iml central.mml**

Again, putting them into the IR centralizes ObjectBroker's knowledge about your choices.

The examples of IML and MML just shown work for all the interfaces in our four IDLs, except two. (You can check out the detailed instructions on the floppy provided with the book to double-check which commands you must execute—they're just variations on the theme shown here.)

Recall from Figure 23.1 that we saw that one of the "processes" was going to contain POSTerminal and InputMedia methods along with their clients. These are called "built-in" or "lightweight" methods, since the ORB doesn't have to bother looking for the methods in another process on this computer or as a process on another computer entirely. In order to tell the ORB that you're going to organize your program this way, you change the IML files for POSTerminal and InputMedia. You change the line that says:

```
activation_type ( program );
```

to:

```
activation_type ( static_load );
```

and then you delete the line that starts with:

```
activation_string ...
```

Together, these two actions tell ObjectBroker that POSTerminal and InputMedia will be in the same address space as the client. ObjectBroker also supports the ability to dynamically load the implementation, but this feature will not be used in this example. ObjectBroker will invoke the methods for these objects much more efficiently since it won't have to search for them. After you've made the changes to these two IML files, put them into the IR also.

At this point, you have your private IR loaded with the IDL, IML, and MML files for all the interfaces you need. From this point on, the IR is frozen, and you use it only to generate stubs, skeletons, and dispatch routines.

23.8.4 Client/Server Communication in ObjectBroker

The essence of any ORB is that it satisfies a client's request by calling an operation (or method) on an object regardless of whether it is in the same or in a different address space. (That address space may also be on another computer and in a different hardware architecture, but that is secondary to the address space consideration.) Any ORB must perform certain functions to complete the mapping of the client's request to the method, and then return information from the method back to the server.

In ObjectBroker's ORB, the resulting organization of programs looks something like that in Figure 23.2. In the client process, there must be stubs

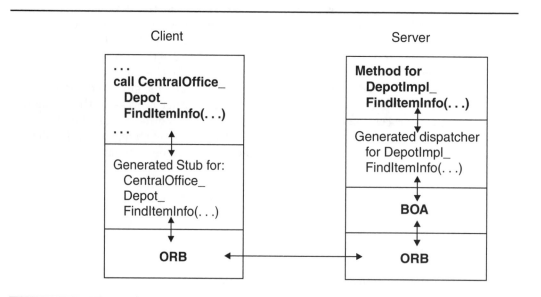

Figure 23.2. ObjectBroker example components.

that receive actual transfer of control on the client computer. These stubs contain "magic code," not to be read by us mortals. (As a matter of fact, Digital puts a disclaimer in the generated code stating that if you change it, Digital is not responsible for problems. All ORBs perform similar magic.) Stubs are generated by ObjectBroker to match the IDL, MML, and IML specified in the IR. They work in conjunction with the BOA, which uses dispatchers (also magic code generated by ObjectBroker) and methods in the servers. The client code and the methods in the servers are the only code you have to write as a client/server programmer, out of all the parts shown in Figure 23.2. The remainder are either library routines for the ORB or are generated from what you've put into the IR.

23.8.5   Stubs

Stubs are the easiest part of any client/server system to understand. They merely receive a call, bundle up its parts, and pass it onto the ORB. Every C-mapping stub is called according to rules in the CORBA spec. You must generate two files to be able to call a stub:

- An include file (.h) that describes the signature of the methods of the object and the datatypes included in the IDL for the interface. You use this include file in any client call you make to ensure that you have the right name and the right signature for the subroutine.
- Code that gains control, does the bundling, and passes control on to the ORB, which supports the specified C binding.

To create the stubs for the depot interface, for example, you say:

```
> obbgen -lc -c centstb.c -B central.h -ps \
    CentralOffice::Depot
```

Remember, whenever you issue an **obbgen** command (and most other **obb** commands), you are referring to information you put in the IR. In this case, -c says you want client stubs for the CentralOffice::Depot interface to be generated into the file censtb.c. The -lc indicates that C language bindings should be used (output to .c and .h files). The include file (option -B) is to be written to central.h. The -ps option states that the stubs should be generated using a "static" method map routine, which means that the stubs have information built into them at the time of generation instead of looking up information in the IR at run time; this is by far the most efficient method of doing lookup.

You perform the same procedure for each interface. In some cases, you can ask for stubs for several interfaces to be generated in the same file, as for the Store module, which has three interfaces. It makes no difference whether methods will be in different processes or computers, the stubs are always generated the same.

```
> obbgen -lc -c stostb.c -B astore.h -ps \
    AStore::Store AStore::StoreAccess AStore::Tax
```

23.8.6   Dispatch and Method Routines

Generating dispatch routines and method skeletons is just as easy as stubs, although there are usually at least three files generated:

■   A server-side or implementation include file (.imh) that describes the signature of the server-side methods of the object and the datatypes included in the IDL for the interface. You use this include file in any server calls you make among each other to ensure that you have the right name and the right signature for the subroutine.
■   Dispatch code that gains control from the BOA, does the unbundling, and passes control on to the server method.
■   A skeleton for the server of the interface named. This file has all methods for the interface specified as proper routine headers and empty bodies. Your job is to fill in the methods.

For example, for the Depot:

```
> obbgen -lc -d centdsp.c -B central DepotImpl
> obbgen -lc -t central.c -B central DepotImpl
```

An interesting distinction is that the code you are generating is server-side or implementation code rather than interface signatures; hence the use of the name DepotImpl rather than CentralOffice::Depot. The first command creates a dispatch routine that will cooperate with the BOA; again, you never have to touch it.

The second command yields the method skeletons, which you then fill in. An extremely convenient feature of ObjectBroker's skeleton generation is that it allows you to keep filled-in methods, even if you regenerate the method skeleton with new IDL. Two other convenient routines are generated as part of the method skeleton: a registration routine and a routine to help with rundown of an executable image due to a management command (to stop a server, for example). The first of these routines is normally called by a server's main program as part of startup. The second is usually ignored except for very specialized uses.

Most of the servers are generated similar to the preceding. ObjectBroker also allows you to put multiple interfaces into the same dispatch file and multiple method groupings into the method skeleton file. An interesting variation occurs when a module has several interfaces. They all need access to all the data definitions, but you may well want to put them into different processes as part of your client/server setup. The POS module is an example of this—two of the interfaces go in one process but a third goes into a second. The sequence of commands to separate the methods might be:

```
> obbgen -t posterm.c    POSTerminalImpl
> obbgen -t im.c         InputMediaImpl
> obbgen -t om.c         OutputMediaImpl
```

ObjectBroker creates three separate method templates, and you can put them into any process you wish. In our case, we'll include both posterm.c and im.c in one process and om.c in another.

When we split the methods like this, we must also separate the dispatch routines since they call on the methods and are thus put into the same process the method goes into. Since we're only creating two processes, we can create just two dispatchers instead of three as we did previously with templates. (We could have done the same with templates—we just wanted to show you that ObjectBroker lets you do things in many different ways).

```
> obbgen -lc -d postidsp.c -B pos POSTerminalImpl \
      InputMediaImpl
> obbgen -lc -d omdsp.c -B OutputMediaImpl
```

The routine postidsp.c will be included in the process containing the methods for the POSTerminal and the InputMedia. The routine omdsp.c will be included in the process for the OutputMedia.

Finally, all the templates and dispatchers will want to have a file that contains data structures and definitions for the implementations, no matter where they are. The easiest way to do this is:

```
> obbgen -lc -d posdsp.c -B pos \
  POSTerminalImpl InputMediaImpl OutputMediaImpl
```

The -B modifier tells ObjectBroker to put implementation definitions for all POS interfaces into a single file, pos.imh, so that it can be included by any of the dispatchers or methods at compilation time, no matter where they go. In order to get this file, we created the file posdsp.c, which we can just throw away since we don't plan on including all three interfaces in a single process at this time.

23.9   DEVELOPING SOMobjects APPLICATIONS

This section is a brief overview of the development of applications using the SOMobjects Toolkit. A comprehensive description of SOMobjects application development can be found in the *SOMobjects Toolkit User's Guide* (see Appendix A for references). The makefiles included with the point-of-sale example source code are also a source of information about the specific commands and modifiers required to generate the header and template files, compile and build the classes into dynamic link libraries, and register the servers. A makefile has been included for building the application on both AIX and OS/2 using the SOMobjects Toolkit version 2.1. The most up-to-date source code for the latest version of the SOMobjects toolkit can be found at the Web site: *http://www.austin.ibm.com/developer/objects/som1.html*.

There are two major ways to build SOM applications. One is to use a language compiler with direct-to-SOM capabilities, and the other is to specify the application objects first using IDL and implement the objects via the templates produced by the SOM compiler. The latter process can be used with any ANSI C compiler and almost all C++ compilers. Currently, direct-to-SOM C++ compilers are available from IBM and Metaware. IBM also has a direct-to-SOM object-oriented COBOL compiler.

Using a direct-to-SOM compiler, the programmer bypasses the IDL definition step entirely and directly implements an application using the standard constructs of the C++ or OO COBOL language. Under the covers, however, the language run time is actually the SOM run time, and the objects themselves are actually SOM objects. When needed, direct-to-SOM compilers can generate the IDL definition files from the application objects.

The dynamic link libraries produced using direct-to-SOM compilers have the same characteristics as any other SOM class library; that is, they can be accessed across languages, they can be used and subclassed in binary form, and they provide for release-to-release binary compatibility.

The more traditional (if it is possible for CORBA programming to have a tradition yet) way to build SOM applications is to begin by creating the IDL definitions of the object classes. This process is the focus of the remainder of this section, and consists of the following steps:

1. Define the object interfaces in IDL.
2. Use the SOM compiler to generate the header files and object templates from the IDL.
3. Code the method implementations in the object templates.
4. Implement the client code that uses the classes.
5. Compile and link the classes into dynamic link libraries and compile and link the client code with the libraries.
6. Register the servers in the implementation repository.

23.9.1 Defining SOM Classes Using IDL

The interface and datatype definitions for SOM classes are defined in standard CORBA IDL with one extension; all objects must be derived from the base class SOMObject. This may be done directly or as a result of derivation from a class that has SOMObject at the root of its class hierarchy. Now is a good time to note the difference between SOMobjects and SOMObject. The former is the product name of the IBM product that supports distributed object programming accross address spaces and platforms (and architectures), while the latter is an object type. The difference in the names is in the case of the letter o in object. Similarly, a collection of instances of SOMObject would be SOMObjects, not to be confused with the product SOMobjects toolkit. Finally, when we say SOM objects, these are objects that are in the SOM runtime.

In order to provide an implementation template, the SOM compiler needs additional information about the class implementation that is not included in IDL, which is exclusively concerned with the object interface. SOM uses a number of implementaton annotations to control the form of the implementation templates for classes.

These implementation annotations are typically enclosed in

```
#ifdef __SOMIDL__
.........
.........
#endif
```

statements so that the same IDL specification can be used with any CORBA IDL compiler, but the implementation annotations will only be processed by the SOM IDL compiler.

23.9.2 Generating the Header Files and Object Templates from the IDL

Using the IDL definition of the object classes, the SOM compiler can be used to generate the appropriate language-specific bindings for the class implementations. There are two types of binding files produced by the SOM compiler; usage bindings (header files) included by a client, which allow the client to access the class, and implementation bindings (object templates), into which the developer places the implementation code for the methods defined on the class.

The SOM compiler accepts a number of modifiers to specify the kind of files to be produced and the language for which to produce the files. For a ficticious sample.idl file, the command line to generate the C binding files on AIX and OS/2 might look like the following:

```
sc -u s"c;h;ih" sample.idl
```

sc: The SOM compiler command. The **-s"c;h;ih;ir"** option tells the compiler to generate the following files from the sample.idl file:

sample.c: The object template (called implementation bindings) into which the programmer will put the method implementations for the objects defined in the sample IDL file. The template consists of the function stubs representing the methods on the object(s) defined in sample.idl.

sample.h: The header file (called usage bindings) that clients of objects include in their code to create and use the object(s) in sample.idl.

sample.ih: The header file that is included with the sample.c implementation file.

In addition, the **ir** option along with **-u** tells the compiler to update the SOM interface repository with the interface information for the object(s) in sample.idl.

For the POS example IDL files, typing the following command will generate the C binding files and register the object interfaces in the SOM Interface Repository:

```
sc -u -s"c;h;ih;ir" POS.idl Central.idl PNS.idl Store.idl
```

23.9.3 Customizing the Object Implementation Templates

SOM is foremost a class library packaging technology for the construction of reusable *binary* components. These components can be combined into applications in a single address space or distributed across address spaces on the same or different computers on a network. SOM predates the CORBA specification and was originally implemented to serve the role of what CORBA defines as a "library-based" object request broker. As a result, some of the code automatically generated by the SOM compiler may seem a bit strange unless you consider its role in providing cross-language interoperability for binary objects both within and across address spaces.

However, the programmer does not need to be concerned with this compiler-generated code, and implements the object methods using standard language constructs and the appropriate CORBA language bindings. For the point-of-sale example, the implementation language is C.

23.9.4 Implementing the Client Code Using SOM Classes

The client code accesses SOM classes using the appropriate CORBA language bindings. In the point-of-sale example presented in this book, the objects are accessed using the C language bindings. If a programmer wanted to use C++ instead, he or she could use the SOM compiler to produce C++ usage bindings (header file) from the IDL definitions of the objects. Client-side programming is fairly straightforward in SOMobjects. Clients find servers by their names (called aliases in SOMobjects) and create an object reference for the servers. They could then ask the server to create (remote) instances of objects of specific classes. Alternatively, the clients may have a string form of an object reference that they obtained from a nameserver or by other means (such as the result of a remote method invocation). The clients can then convert the string form to an object reference.

23.9.5 Registering the Servers in the Implementation Repository

Server-side programming is quite simple in most cases, thanks to the default server program somdsvr that is provided with the toolkit. In most cases, all that is needed is implementation of the SOM objects. These implementations now need to be served by a server. The association of these implementations with servers is created using a tool called regimpl. A repository called Implementation Repository is used by regimpl to create and update server registration information. Using regimpl, the administrator registers the server and its properties for use by client programs. Some of the properties specified are the classes the server supports, the server class itself, the name of the machine on which the server can be activated, and so on. Most of the properties have default values. For example, the server class would be **SOMDServer**, and the hostname would be local host. An example of regimpl usage is given in Section 24.6. In cases where the generic somdsvr program is not adequate, users can implement customized server programs. somdsvr takes the server alias as a command-line argument, and activates the server with that alias (as specified in the implementation repository).

23.9.6 Compiling and Linking the Classes and Client Code into Dynamic Link Libraries

The SOM class and client code are compiled and linked using standard platform specific compilers and linkers. An important part of SOM, and fundamental to supporting binary reuse, is the packaging of classes as dynamically loaded libraries (DLL). This allows the class implementations to be updated without having to relink the client code. All SOM class implementations are therefore packaged as DLLs. This also gives SOM the ability to dynamically load classes and create instances of objects. The interface repostitory (into which the IDL file has been compiled) has the information that is required by the SOM runtime to load the DLL for a particular interface. This is exactly how the generic somdsvr program is able to support user-defined server implementations. The somdsvr program looks at the implementation repository to find out which classes the server with the given alias supports, then consults the interface repository to find the DLL name, and then loads the DLL for the classes the server supports.

23.9.7 The CentralOffice and PseudoNameService IDL Definitions

As mentioned previously, SOM adds some information to the IDL specification to control the implementation files generated by the compiler. As a matter of programming practice, all SOM-specific annotations are bracketed by **#ifdef __SOMIDL__**, **#endif** directives. This ensures that IDL definitions produced for SOM can be used with any CORBA-compliant IDL compiler; the implementation annotations will be ignored by other compilers.

Here is the SOM IDL file for the CentralOffice module and for the PseuoNameService class:

```
#ifdef __SOMIDL__
#include <somdserv.idl>
#endif

// Include interface definition for store and POS objects.
#include "pos.idl"
#include "store.idl"

module CentralOffice {

#ifdef __SOMIDL__
  interface Depot : SOMDServer {
#else
  interface Depot {
#endif
    void FindItemInfo (
            in   AStore::AStoreId StoreId
            ,in POS::Barcode    Item
            ,in long            Quantity
            ,out AStore::ItemInfo IInfo)
        raises (AStore::BarcodeNotFound);
```

```
#ifdef __SOMIDL__
    implementation {
        releaseorder:FindItemInfo;
        override:somDefaultInit, somDestruct;
        somToken ostate;
        dllname = "dobjs.dll";
    };
#endif
  };
};
#endif


#ifndef PNAMESVC_IDL
#define PNAMESVC_IDL

#ifdef __SOMIDL__
#include <somdserv.idl>
interface PseudoNameService : SOMDServer
#else
interface PseudoNameService
#endif

{
  void    BindName(in string ObjectName
#ifdef __SOMIDL__
          ,in SOMObject ObjectRef);

  SOMObject ResolveName(in string ObjectName);
#else
          ,in Object ObjectRef);

  Object ResolveName(in string ObjectName);
#endif

#ifdef __SOMIDL__

        implementation {
        releaseorder:BindName,
                ResolveName;
        override:somDefaultInit,
                somDestruct;
```

```
            somToken ostate;
            dllname = "dobjs.dll";



        };

    #endif
    };


    #endif
```

As mentioned previously, all SOM objects must be directly or indirectly derived from SOMObject. Both Depot and PseudoNameService classes are derived from a SOM system object called SOMDServer (which is, in turn, derived from SOMObject). As a result, the Depot and PseudoNameService classes inherit the necessary data and behavior to serve as the distinguished "server" object that exists in every SOM server process. For a simple application such as the point-of-sale example, this allows deployment of the Depot and PseudoNameService as servers without any additional programming. The programmer implements the class like any other SOM class. At deployment time, the class is registered in the SOM Implementation Repository as the server class to be created in the generic server process executable shipped with the SOMobjects Toolkit. At execution time, the server object is automatically created by the generic server process when the server is activated.

Each interface includes an **implementation** statement. This statement begins with the keyword **implementation** and contains a set of SOM modifiers, directives, and declarations that control the implementation files generated by the SOM compiler.

releaseorder: A modifier that specifies the methods that comprise the interface to an object. This is used by the SOM compiler to maintain release-to-release binary compatibility when methods are added to a class. The names of methods added to a class are appended to the end of the release order list. It is important to maintain the order. Even if methods are deleted or migrated, the release order should not be changed by implementations that wish to maintain release-to-release binary compatibility.

override: A modifier that specifies methods in the parent class that are to be overridden in the derived class. This causes the SOM compiler to produce a stub routine in the object implementation template for the overridden methods, in addition to those introduced by the class itself. **somDefaultInit** and **somDestruct** are the default constructor and destructor methods introduced by the parent class SOMobject. The **somDefaultInit** method is where the class-specific initialization and startup activities for the Depot and Pseudo-NameService objects are performed. The **somDestruct** method is where any class-specific destruction operations are performed, such as releasing allocated memory. For performance reasons, the **somDestruct** methods are overridden in derived classes even though no changes will be made to the existing routines. This ensures backward compatibility for preexisting applications, but allows the compiler to optimize object destruction for new classes.

somToken ostate: A declaration of an instance variable. Instance variables can be declared as any CORBA type. The use of **somToken** in this particular case designates **ostate** to be of a type defined elsewhere in the implementation. In this case, it references the structure for the simple database (defined in db.c) that the Depot object uses to store and access information about the products, and that the PseudoNameService object uses to store and access object references. Instance variables can be accessed in two ways: either using a macro that SOM creates for each instance variable that is defined as the variable name with an underscore prepended (**_ostate**), or by using the **somThis** pointer that is initialized in each method to point to the instance data for that object instance (**somThis->ostate**). Both methods of manipulating instance data are used in the SOM POS example code.

dllname: specifies the file from which the class implementation is to be loaded by the SOM run time during application execution.

23.9.8 AStore Module IDL Definitions

In general, the SOM annotations in Store.idl are similar to those described for Central.idl and PNS.idl. One notable addition is the specification of the **storeInit** method in the **StoreAccess** class definition. This method was defined to allow values to be passed into the **StoreAccess** constructor method. The default constructor routine generated by the SOM compiler, **somDefaultInit**, does not take any arguments. In order to provide a constructor that accepts arguments, the method was defined and annotated as storeInit: init in the SOM implementation statement. This annotation directs the SOM compiler to generate the appropriate constructor method stub for the **storeInit** method. Here is the SOM IDL file for the AStore module.

```
#ifndef _STORE_IDL
#define _STORE_IDL
```

```
#ifdef __SOMIDL__
#include <somdserv.idl>
#include <somobj.idl>
#endif

// include interface definition for Point Of Sale objects

#include "POS.idl"

module AStore {

  enum ItemTypes {food, clothes, other};
  typedef long AStoreId;


  struct ItemInfo {
    POS::Barcode    Item;
    ItemTypes       Itemtype;
    float           Itemcost;
    string          Name;
    long            Quantity;
  };

  // The barcodeNotFound exception indicates that the
  // input barcode does not match to any known item.
  exception BarcodeNotFound { POS::Barcode item; };

  interface StoreAccess; // /forward reference

  struct POSInfo {
    POS::POSId    Id;
    StoreAccess   StoreAccessReference;
    float         TotalSales;
    float         TotalTaxes;
  };

  typedef sequence <POSInfo> POSList;

#ifdef __SOMIDL__
  interface Tax : SOMObject {
#else
  interface Tax {
#endif
```

```
        float CalculateTax(in float          TaxableAmount);
        float FindTaxablePrice(in float      ItemPrice
                        ,in ItemTypes      ItemType);

#ifdef __SOMIDL__
    implementation {
        releaseorder:CalculateTax,
                FindTaxablePrice;
        somToken ostate;
        override:somDefaultInit, somDestruct;
        dllname = "dobjs.dll";


    };
#endif
  };

#ifdef __SOMIDL__
  interface Store : SOMDServer {
#else
  interface Store {
#endif
    struct StoreTotals {
      float    StoreTotal;
      float    StoreTaxTotal;
    };

    readonly attribute AStoreId StoreId;
    readonly attribute StoreTotals Totals;

    StoreAccess Login(in POS::POSId Id);
    void  GetPOSTotals(out POSList POSData);
    void  UpdateStoreTotals(
        in POS::POSId   Id
        ,in float          Price
        ,in float          Taxes);
#ifdef __SOMIDL__
    implementation {
        releaseorder: Login, GetPOSTotals, UpdateStoreTotals,
                _get_StoreId, _get_Totals;
        override: somDefaultInit, somDestruct;
        dllname = "dobjs.dll";
```

```
// instance data
        somToken ostate;
    };
#endif


    };

#ifdef __SOMIDL__
  interface StoreAccess : SOMObject {
#else
  interface StoreAccess {
#endif

    // itemtaxprice is 0 or return value of FindTaxablePrice()
    void    FindPrice(
            in POS::Barcode   Item
            ,in long          Quantity
            ,out float        ItemPrice
            ,out float        ItemTaxPrice
            ,out ItemInfo     IInfo)
        raises (BarcodeNotFound);

#ifdef __SOMIDL__

    /* constructor for creating StoreAccess instances with initialization
    parameters */
    void storeInit(
            inout somInitCtrl   ctrl
            ,in SOMObject       taxref
            ,in SOMObject       depotref
            ,in float           markup
            ,in long            storeid);

    implementation {

        releaseorder: FindPrice, storeInit;
        storeInit: init;
        override: somDefaultInit, somDestruct;
        somToken ostate;
        dllname = "dobjs.dll";
    };
#endif
```

```
      };

   };
   #endif
```

23.9.9   POS Module IDL Definitions

Here is the SOM POS module definition:

```
#ifndef _POS_IDL
#define _POS_IDL

#ifdef __SOMIDL__
#include <somdserv.idl>
#endif

module POS {

   typedef long    POSId;
   typedef string  Barcode;

#ifdef __SOMIDL__
   interface InputMedia : SOMObject {
#else
   interface InputMedia {
#endif

      typedef string OperatorCmd;

      void      BarcodeInput(in Barcode Item);
      void      KeypadInput(in OperatorCmd Cmd);

#ifdef __SOMIDL__
      implementation {
         releaseorder:  BarcodeInput, KeypadInput;
         override:      somDefaultInit, somDestruct;
         somToken       ostate;

         dllname = "dobjs.dll";
      };
#endif
```

```
    };

#ifdef __SOMIDL__
  interface OutputMedia : SOMDServer {
#else
  interface OutputMedia {
#endif

    boolean    OutputText(in string StringToPrint);
#ifdef __SOMIDL__
    implementation {
        releaseorder :  OutputText;
        override:        somDefaultInit, somDestruct;
        somToken        ostate;
        dllname = "dobjs.dll";
    };
#endif
  };


#ifdef __SOMIDL__
  interface POSTerminal : SOMObject {
#else
  interface POSTerminal {
#endif

    void Login();
    void PrintPOSSalesSummary();
    void PrintStoreSalesSummary();
    void SendBarcode(in Barcode Item);
    void ItemQuantity (in long Qty);
    void EndOfSale();

#ifdef __SOMIDL__
    implementation {
        releaseorder: Login, PrintPOSSalesSummary,
                PrintStoreSalesSummary,
                SendBarcode, ItemQuantity,
                EndOfSale;
        override: somDefaultInit, somDestruct;
        somToken ostate;
```

```
            dllname = "dobjs.dll";
    };
#endif
  };

};
#endif
```

The SOM annotations for the POS module are similar to those described for the previous IDL files. Note that all the interfaces have the same dllname modifier. For this book example, to keep things simple, all interfaces are packed in the same DLL. This is not required by the SOMobjects Toolkit. In practice, all interfaces are rarely packaged in the same DLL.

23.10 COMPILING THE IDL WITH DAIS

DAIS is the CORBA conformant ORB offered by ICL. Although it has language bindings for both C and C++ (with others currently in development) we will only show the C bindings in this example since it allows us to contrast and compare implementations in a number of languages from a number of vendors.

The first thing that we need to do when building an application is to generate the header files and stub code from the IDL that enable the application to service or invoke objects with those interfaces. As DAIS IDL is 100 percent compatible with CORBA IDL, we don't require any modifications to the IDL that we have designed in the common part of this chapter. Normally, this stage would be performed as part of a make file or similar building process (an example is on the diskette), but we'll do it manually for now to see how it works.

The commands we're using are for a generic SVR4.2 UNIX machine such as a Sun running Solaris 2.x or an ICL DRS6000. If you are using DAIS on platforms such as VMS or Windows, you will need to use different C compiler flags and system libraries.

One of our objectives for the example is to demonstrate just how similar application implementations can be across the different vendors' ORB implementations. Many ORB implementations have vendor-specific extensions that make your job easier when writing an application, and DAIS is no exception. These extensions aren't yet covered by the OMG standardization effort though, so rather than rely on them, we have coded using the basic CORBA environment. Although this is slightly more long-winded, it means that the code will work on all compliant ORB implementations with only minimal changes.

In this stage of the example, we assume that we want to generate code in the current directory but that the IDL is in another directory. This reflects typical usage where the IDL may be shared between application implementations. In order to make things a little easier, we'll assign environment variables defining the locations of the example IDL and the installation point for DAIS. For the Bourne shell we would do this as follows:

```
DAIS_ROOT=/dais          # dais installation point
export DAIS_ROOT

PRIMER_IDL=/primer/IDL # example IDL directory
export PRIMER_IDL
```

If you are using another shell, you may have to do this differently or explicitly state the directories in the following commands.

To begin with, we'll generate the stub and template code for the Central-Office component and explain everything in detail. The command

```
stubgen -s -lc -t -I$PRIMER_IDL Central.idl
```

reads in the IDL definitions and generates the corresponding C code.

The **-s** flag forces strict CORBA conformance with regard to mixed-case identifiers (no case differences are significant) and numeric types in expressions (integers and floating point numbers cannot be mixed).

The **-lc** flag specifies that output is to be generated in C. DAIS supports other languages, but for the purposes of the example we are just doing C here.

The **-t** flag says that we want a server template to be generated that contains an empty function definition for each server method.

The **-I** flag can be used to specify alternative directories in which to search for IDL files. We can use it to specify the location of both the original source IDL files and any IDL files that are **#include**'d. We can repeat the flag on the command line to specify a number of IDL directories that will be searched in the specified order just like a C compiler. We're using it here to allow the IDL to be located in another directory while generating output in the current directory.

The last argument is the name of the IDL file itself.

Provided that the IDL syntax is correct and no other problems were encountered, we will find a number of C source files in the current directory. These are:

- *central.h:* The header file to be **#include**'d by any client or server application using interfaces defined in central.idl.

- *c_central.c:* The stub routines corresponding to IDL operations for clients to invoke.
- *s_central.c:* The "skeletons" or stubs for the server side. The ORB calls these routines, and they in turn call the operation implementation provided by the developer.
- *m_central.c:* This file contains code optimized for marshalling any complex argument types used by the interface.
- *centralSrv.c:* This file contains template function definitions for the operations defined in central.idl. This is the starter file that is used when coding the application; we won't be using it yet, but we will later.

The following two files are automatically included by central.h— applications do not have to include them explicitly, but you will see that they have been generated, and because we don't want you to delete them, we'll tell you what they're for!

- *m_central.h:* Contains prototypes and macros for marshalling functions.
- *t_central.h:* Provides C equivalents of the IDL datatypes used in the interface.

We can now generate the stubs, skeletons, and templates for the other interfaces in the same way as for CentralOffice:

```
stubgen -s -lc -t -I$PRIMER_IDL PNS.idl
stubgen -s -lc -t -I$PRIMER_IDL POS.idl
stubgen -s -lc -t -I$PRIMER_IDL Store.idl
```

We must then compile all this code. Again, most systems will have utilities to automate this part, but, ultimately, the compiler will perform something like the following:

```
cc -c -I. -I$DAIS_ROOT/include c_central.c
cc -c -I. -I$DAIS_ROOT/include m_central.c
cc -c -I. -I$DAIS_ROOT/include s_central.c
cc -c -I. -I$DAIS_ROOT/include c_pnamesvc.c
cc -c -I. -I$DAIS_ROOT/include m_pnamesvc.c
cc -c -I. -I$DAIS_ROOT/include s_pnamesvc.c
cc -c -I. -I$DAIS_ROOT/include c_store.c
cc -c -I. -I$DAIS_ROOT/include m_store.c
cc -c -I. -I$DAIS_ROOT/include s_store.c
cc -c -I. -I$DAIS_ROOT/include c_pos.c
cc -c -I. -I$DAIS_ROOT/include m_pos.c
cc -c -I. -I$DAIS_ROOT/include s_pos.c
```

The C compiler flags we use are **-c** to specify output as an object file for later linking with other object files, and **-I** to specify the directories containing the header files. Here, the directories we need to specify are the current directory for the generated header files and the directory where the DAIS orb.h file is held.

At this point, we've prepared all the application-specific code that allows the application to use the ORB. Now we are ready to start coding the application itself.

23.11   COMPILING THE IDL WITH POWERBROKER

This section introduces the PowerBroker IDL compiler, idlc. It describes how to run the compiler and the steps necessary to code the generated "implementation" class. PowerBroker also contains a dynamic interface repository engine and an accompanying graphical tool for browsing interfaces, editing IDL, and running C++ or OLE code generators. The graphical tool is available for UNIX (Motif) and Windows. However, to allow us to focus on the primary goal of translating our IDL to C++, we will base our discussion on using the command-line program idlc.

If you need more detailed information on idlc's command syntax and file-name conventions, look at the README file on the accompanying diskette.

23.11.1   Idlc Tutorial

This tutorial has been written for the Solaris 2.4 operating system. Where applicable, usage differences between Solaris and other environments, such as Windows NT, are noted. Before proceeding, you must install PowerBroker on your computer using the PowerBroker Installation Guide. The environment variable PBHOME is used to specify the PowerBroker installation directory.

The tutorial walks us through the process of compiling the POS IDL file. You will need to repeat these steps to compile the Store and Depot.

Idlc accepts your IDL files and produces several header and implementation files. These files contain the CORBA 2.0 C++ language mapping for the IDL constructs found in your IDL specification. For example, given the POS IDL specification file POS.idl, idlc generates the files:

POS.h

POS.C

POS_s.h

POS_s.C

POS.model

The header file POS.h declares the C++ types associated with the IDL defined in the IDL specification. POS.h declares a C++ class for every interface construct in the IDL specification. The C++ types in these header files can be used by client programs and object implementations. For clients, POS.h provides remote access to objects through stubs that correspond to the IDL-defined interfaces. A PowerBroker client program includes this header file and makes a request by calling one of the stub routines on an object reference.

For object implementations, the header file POS_s.h provides a C++ base object implementation class for every interface construct in the IDL specification. A PowerBroker object implementation class is then derived from this base class. You should add application logic in the derived implementation class.

The implementation file POS.C contains client-side and shared implementations of the types declared in POS.h, including interface stub classes used by a PowerBroker client program.

The implementation file POS_s.C contains the implementations of operation dispatch methods required by object implementations.

Idlc can also optionally produce a "model" of a PowerBroker object implementation class (in file POS.model in the list) from the IDL specification. This file is intended as a "bootstrap" for your implementation class.

On a Windows NT platform, idlc can generate DOS-compatible filenames as shown here. For example, given an IDL specification file called example.idl, idlc generates the files:

example.h

example.c

exampl_s.c

example.mod

Note the difference between the names of the files generated for a Windows NT platform and the names of the files generated for a UNIX platform where filenames are truncated to eight characters followed by an extension.

The PowerBroker IDL compiler can also generate alternative PowerBroker C++ interface stubs and implementation skeletons for C++ dialects that do not support C++ exceptions. This alternative mapping uses CORBA's Environment class to communicate exception information.

Here is a detailed look at the steps you should take to build PowerBroker applications for the POS:

1. Write your IDL specification in the file POS.idl.
2. Compile your IDL specification using idlc, by typing the following command:

```
%idlc -I. -I$PBHOME/include POS.idl
```

If there were no syntax errors, idlc generated the following files:

POS.h

POS.C

POS_s.h

POS_s.C

The header file contains the C++ types that correspond to the IDL constructs found in pos.idl. Client and server programs that use these types must include the .h or _s.h file. The file POS.C implements client-side and shared functions for the classes in POS.h. You must compile this file and link it in with your client application. The file POS_s.C implements operation dispatch methods required by object implementations. You should not edit these files, but simply compile and link POS.o in the client executable and both POS.o and POS_s.o in the server executable.

3. Once your IDL compiles, generate an object implementation model using idlc. You can use the **-Wb,generate_model** command line option with idlc to generate the file POS.model, which serves as a model of your object implementation. It defines a C++ class for every interface construct in your IDL specification file. This class inherits from a parent class (the base object implementation class defined in the .h file) that has the same name as the interface name with the string _base_impl appended to it.

   Type the following command to generate the model (and .h and .C files) file:

```
%idlc -Wb,generate_model -I. -I$PBHOME/include POS.idl
```

4. For the POS, POS.model contains starting points for the implementation classes for the POSTerminal, InputMedia, and OutputMedia interfaces. The following list shows the header files you should create for the POS.

FILE	IMPL CLASS	BASE CLASS
POS_Ter.h	`POSTerminal_i`	`POS::POSTerminal_base_impl`
POS_IM.h	`InputMedia_i`	`POS::InputMedia_base_impl`
POS_OM.h	`OutputMedia_i`	`POS::OutputMedia_base_impl`

The three base classes are in the file POS.h.

Consider the following example, where the template for the "impl class" are copied from POS.model to the corresponding file as shown. For example, for POSTerminal, POS_Ter.h is:

```
// file POS_Ter.h

#include <pos.h>

class POSTerminal_i : public POS::POSTerminal_base_impl {
public:
    // ...
};
```

23.12 COMPILING THE IDL IN ORBIX

The standard IDL files can be used with Orbix without any modification. This and other features make Orbix very easy to use. In addition, the programmer needs to write only IDL and the chosen programming language code; no other code or configuration files are required. This section discusses the Orbix C++ support; other languages are handled with equal simplicity.

Each IDL file must be compiled, both to check the syntax and to map it into C++ so that it can be used by clients and implemented at the server side. The Orbix IDL compiler can be run from the command line as follows. However, before doing so you must ensure that Orbix can find its configuration file. If the file **Orbix.cfg** has been installed in the system's **/etc** directory on Unix, or **\orbix** directory on Windows, then you need take no further action. If, however, it is not installed there, then you must set the environment variable **IT_CONFIG_PATH** to point to it.

```
idl -B Pos.idl
idl -B Store.idl
idl -B Central.idl
idl -B PNS.idl
```

On Windows, a graphical tool can alternatively be used to run the IDL compiler.

The IDL compiler produces C++ code to suit the chosen C++ compiler. For example, it will use C++ exceptions where these are supported, or it will use a standard workaround where they are not supported.

The Orbix IDL compiler produces three output files for each IDL file. From the file Store.idl, it produces the following files:

Filename	Contents
Store.hh	Header file containing the C++ translation of the IDL. This is included (using #include in the normal way) by both the client and the server C++ code.
StoreC.cc	Client stub code. This is compiled and linked with the client.
StoreC.cc	Client skeleton code. This is compiled and linked with the server.

Note, the code extensions are generated to suit the chosen C++ compiler. In addition, other filename roots can be specified via a switch to the IDL compiler. These files contain automatically generated code and need not be edited by the programmer. They contain all of the code required to make CORBA-compliant remote invocations, including all of the necessary marshalling, unmarshalling, and dispatching code. They can be compiled using the chosen C++ compiler; for example:

```
CC  -I<include_dir>   -c StoreC.cc
CC  -I<include_dir>   -c StoreS.cc
```

Normal CC switches include the **-I** switch to indicate the location of the standard include files (typically the Orbix **include** directory). The resulting file **StoreC.o** must be linked with any client that uses the Store IDL definitions; and the file **StoreS.o** must be linked with the Store server. Example Makefiles will be shown later.

The IDL compiler itself takes a set of switches that can be used to control its actions. The most commonly used switch, **-S**, instructs the IDL compiler to produce a starting point for the C++ class that is to be written to implement an interface. The result is a pair of files containing the implementation class definition and the definition of its member functions. The server programmer need add only member variables (and optionally other functions) and then code the bodies of the member functions.

For example, to code the Store IDL interface, a programmer would add member variables and possibly a constructor and destructor to the following code (by convention, interface Store is implemented by class Store_i):

```
class Store_i : public StoreBOAImpl {
public:
    // (automatically generated) declaration
    // of each member function
};
```

The definition of each member function is also automatically generated, with a null body that can be filled in by the programmer (naturally, during early development, a programmer may decide to fill in only a subset of the function bodies).

Another switch, **-R**, is used to register the IDL definitions in the Interface Repository.

23.13   ORB PLUS

The IDL compiler for ORB Plus is called cidl. The following statement would compile the Central.idl file.

```
cidl Central.idl
```

The compiler produces the following declarations and definitions for the client and server portions of the applications:

- Client-side C++ declarations

    centralTypes.hh

- Client-side C++ definitions

    centralTypes.cc

- Server-side C++ declarations

    centralServer.hh

- Server-side C++ definitions

    centralServer.cc

Before parsing the IDL declarations, cidl runs its input through the C++ preprocessor, thus allowing the use of preprocessor directives such as **#include**, **#ifdef**, and **#define**.

You need to compile the store and POS idl files in the same way you just compiled Central.idl. ORB Plus compiles the IDL file in the example without the need to add pragmas.

23.14 NEO

Once the IDL files have been written, NEOworks requires very little work before a *dummy-server* can be produced. All the client stubs, server skeletons, and accompanying header files can be automatically generated and compiled into libraries by executing a single **make** command. In fact, an entire working dummy-server can be generated with a single **make** command, and this is the more usual development path: IDL → dummy-server → fully implemented server. But, given the pedagogical purpose of this book, we will break down the process into smaller steps.

The Makefile needed for this work is, itself, generated from an Imakefile using an ODF utility derived from X Windows' imake. Here is the Imakefile used to generate the IDL's Makefile:

```
# interfaces/Imakefile

# a few directives specifying where to look
# for various includes directories
PARAM_ODF_DIR=/opt/SUNWdoe/include/odf
include $(PARAM_ODF_DIR)/Makefiles/Makefile.odf
IDLSRC = $(PWD)/../interfaces
INCLUDES += -I$(IDLSRC) -I$(IDLSRC)/odf_output

# actual directives to generate skeletons and
# IFR information for the interfaces described in
# various IDL source files
IDL_Library(PNS)
IDL_Library(POS)
IDL_Library(Store)
IDL_Library(Central)
```

First a custom Makefile has to be generated for this particular platform:

```
% odfimake
```

And now simply running make for the default rule in the generated Makefile will generate the C++ client stubs, server skeletons, and headers, and compile everything into a set of dynamically loadable libraries:

```
% make
```

Given the large number of stub and skeleton source and object files, all the generated code, except for the final libraries, is written in a subdirectory of the current directory called odf_output. For example, if you wish to see the actual skeleton source code generated for store.idl, you should look at odf_output/storeCode.cc.

The Makefiles for the various object servers will simply point at this directory in order to find the header files and libraries necessary to use a given IDL interface; therefore, store.hh is included in, and libstore.so is linked with, any piece of code accessing an AStore object.

23.15 HP DISTRIBUTED SMALLTALK

Smalltalk has some real differences from the other languages in this book. For instance, it's dynamically typed, and everything in Smalltalk is an object. Since there's no such thing as "compiling" in Smalltalk, you can expect some differences in how we present our counterpart to the compilation steps in the chapters written by our friends working in C and C++.

Nevertheless, we stayed within the constraints of the demo application as much as we could. This gives you a good view of the way Smalltalk implements CORBA, and shows you just what happens to some parts that would otherwise be hidden under the covers. Like a few of the other ORBs, we've used the example's PseudoNameService even though our Naming CORBA-service is complete. In addition to the Naming service, the Basic Lifecyle Service and the Presentation/Semantic Split policy would have been more optimum for this example.

In this section, we'll prepare the IDL for HP Distributed Smalltalk and register our IDL interfaces with the Interface Repository (IR) Browser. When we're done, we'll be ready to implement the methods in code in Chapters 26, 29, and 32 in parallel with the other languages.

23.15.1 Preparing the HP Distributed Smalltalk Image to Accept IDL

Before you load the IDL, you must make sure the interface repository is initialized. There are two ways to do this:

- Choose the menu option, **HPDST: Initialization: Initialize**, which initializes the IR without starting the request broker.

- Choose the menu option, **HPDST: Request Broker**, which brings up the Request Broker panel. Pressing the Start button will start the ORB and initialize the IR.

23.15.2 Importing IDL Files

Normally, you would develop your IDL within HP Distributed Smalltalk's IR browser, but since the IDL for this example is generated outside of the HP Distributed Smalltalk environment, you use an import mechanism to bring the IDL files into the IR. There are two ways to import IDL files. First, you can use an ANSI C++ preprocessor to preprocess the IDL file:

1. Preprocess the IDL using an ANSI C++ preprocessor that is available on your system and capture the output into a file (example.idl).
2. Import the preprocessed IDL file (example.idl) into HP Distributed Smalltalk by executing:

```
IDLCompiler importIDLFile: 'example.idl' category:
'OMG Primer Example'
```

The first argument is the name of the preprocessed IDL file. The second argument is the name under which the contents of the IDL file will appear in the IR browser.

Or use the VisualWorks DLL and C Connect preprocessor (CPreprocessor):

1. If you have purchased the VisualWorks DLL and C Connect package, you can use the C preprocessor that comes with this package. Even though this preprocessor is not ANSI C++-compliant, it will work in most cases. Load the DLL/C connect package according to VisualWorks installation instructions.
2. Modify the **IDLCompiler class>>preprocess:** method to work with **CPreprocessor**. By default, the method does nothing (just returns its argument). Make:

```
^CPreprocessor preprocess: aStream
```

the body of the method.
3. Import the IDL file into HP Distributed Smalltalk by executing:

```
IDLCompiler importIDLFile: 'example.idl' category:
'OMG Primer Example'
```

The first argument is the name of the IDL file. The second argument is the name under which the contents of the IDL file will appear in the IR browser.

At this point, the example IDL is compiled and loaded into the IR.

Note that **DSTRepository**, in class category **CORBA-Repository**, is the HP Distributed Smalltalk implementation of the CORBA Interface Repository. Interfaces to all publicly available objects (including all messages that can be sent between images) are registered here.

23.15.3 Using the Interface Repository Browser for Editing IDL

In order to verify that the IDL was properly preprocessed, compiled, and stored in the IR, you need to open the HP Distributed Smalltalk IR browser. The IR browser gives you protected access to the contents of both local and remote repositories (IDL). It is the best and most convenient tool to use when you want to explore or edit IDL.

You open the IR Browser by choosing the menu option, **HPDST: Interface Repository**, which brings up the IR browser shown in Figure 23.3. Once the IR browser is ready, you can browse and edit your IDL.

23.15.4 Customizing the IDL for HP Distributed Smalltalk

With the IDL in the IR, you can start developing your implementation. However, for illustration purposes we will add IDL compiler pragmas that will override the default (implicit) binding, making the IDL more convenient for Smalltalk. The pragmas discussed in this section can be added to your IDL via the IR browser discussed above.

Of the several pragmas recognized by the HP Distributed Smalltalk IDL compiler we will discuss only two: **selector** and **class**. Remember that pragmas are entirely optional. You will normally find IDL annotated with pragmas in order to make some IDL constructs more convenient or natural in the Smalltalk environment.

The first pragma that we will use is the **selector** pragma. The selector pragma is used to override the default conversion of IDL operation signatures to Smalltalk selector names (see Chapter 9). In simpler terms, the **selector** pragma specifies which Smalltalk selector or message the IDL operation will map to. The syntax of a selector pragma is:

```
#pragma selector <IDL operation name> <Smalltalk selector>
```

Here's an example taken from the CentralOffice module:

```
#pragma selector FindItemInfo findItemInfo:barCode:quantity:itemInfo:
void FindItemInfo (
                in AStore::AStoreId StoreId,
                in POS::Barcode Item,
```

Choose
Edit menu: **Definition**
to get a browser
window like this,
where you can modify
the definition.

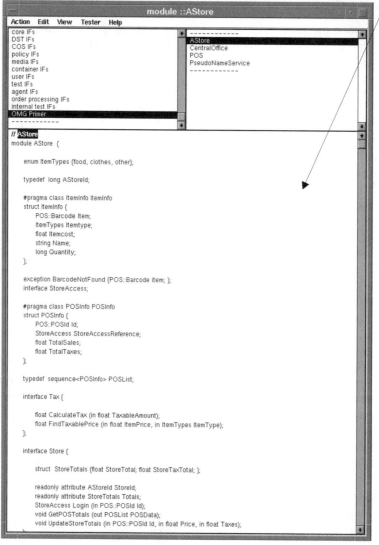

Figure 23.3. Module ASTORE in Smalltalk Edit window.

```
            in long Quantity,
            out AStore::ItemInfo iInfo)
            raises (AStore::BarcodeNotFound);
```

Without the selector pragma, the corresponding (default) Smalltalk selector generated by the IDL compiler would be:

findItemInfo:item:quantity:iInfo:

With the selector pragma, the IDL operation is mapped to the Smalltalk selector:

findItemInfo:barCode:quantity:itemInfo:

The second pragma we will use in this example is the **class** pragma. Again, this pragma is totally optional. A **class** pragma is recommended for all data declarations, including structs and unions. The **class** pragma controls how the datatype is passed out (marshalled) and passed in (unmarshalled) from/to Smalltalk. It also controls how the datatype is handled when the datatype is passed as an IDL type **any**. The syntax of a class pragma is:

#pragma class <IDL type> <Smalltalk className>

Here's an example taken from the AStore module:

```
#pragma class ItemInfo ItemInfo
struct ItemInfo {
        POS::Barcode Item;
        ItemTypes Itemtype;
        float Itemcost;
        string Name;
        long Quantity;
    };
```

Without the class pragma, the **ItemInfo** struct will map to a Smalltalk **Dictionary** whose keys are the names of the structure fields (item, itemType, itemCost, name, and quantity) and whose corresponding values are the respective field values. With the **class** pragma specified, Smalltalk can treat the structure as an instance of the **ItemInfo** class. Methods can be added to the **ItemInfo** class to make it more convenient for Smalltalk to manipulate the data. But when the ItemInfo instance is passed as a parameter to an IDL operation, the data will be converted back into the IDL structure.

All pragmas in the IDL for this example are discussed in detail in the respective coding chapters.

23.15.5 AStore Module IDL Definitions

Here is the HP Distributed Smalltalk IDL AStore module definition that is contained in the IR. The only change from the common IDL is the preprocessing and the addition of the **class** pragma on the **ItemInfo** structure. The **class** pragma is not required and was added for illustration purposes only.

```
module AStore {

    enum ItemTypes {food, clothes, other};

    typedef long AStoreId;

    #pragma class ItemInfo ItemInfo
    struct ItemInfo {
        POS::Barcode Item;
        ItemTypes Itemtype;
        float Itemcost;
        string Name;
        long Quantity;
    };

    exception BarcodeNotFound {POS::Barcode item; };
    interface StoreAccess;

    struct POSInfo {
        POS::POSId Id;
        StoreAccess StoreAccessReference;
        float TotalSales;
        float TotalTaxes;
    };

    typedef sequence<POSInfo> POSList;

    interface Tax {

        float CalculateTax (in float TaxableAmount);
        float FindTaxablePrice (in float ItemPrice, in ItemTypes ItemType);
    };
```

```
interface Store {

    struct StoreTotals {float StoreTotal; float StoreTaxTotal; };

    readonly attribute AStoreId StoreId;
    readonly attribute StoreTotals Totals;
    StoreAccess Login (in POS::POSId Id);
    void GetPOSTotals (out POSList POSData);
    void UpdateStoreTotals (in POS::POSId Id, in float Price, in float Taxes);
    };

interface StoreAccess {

    void FindPrice (
            in POS::Barcode Item,
            in long Quantity,
            out float ItemPrice,
            out float ItemTaxPrice,
            out ItemInfo IInfo)
        raises (BarcodeNotFound);
        };
};
#endif
```

23.15.6 CentralOffice Module IDL Definitions

Here is the HP Distributed Smalltalk CentralOffice IDL module definition that is contained in the IR. The only change from the common IDL is the preprocessing and the addition of the selector pragma on the **FindItemInfo** operation. The selector pragma is not required and was added for illustration purposes only.

```
module CentralOffice {

interface Depot {
    #pragma selector FindItemInfo findItemInfo:barCode:quantity:itemInfo:
    void FindItemInfo (
                in AStore::AStoreId StoreId,
                in POS::Barcode Item,
                in long Quantity,
                out AStore::ItemInfo IInfo)
            raises (AStore::BarcodeNotFound);
```

```
        };
};
```

23.15.7 POS Module IDL Definitions

Here is the HP Distributed Smalltalk **POS** IDL module definition. There are no changes from the common IDL other than preprocessing.

```
module POS {

    typedef long POSId;

    typedef string Barcode;

    interface InputMedia {

        typedef string OperatorCmd;

        void BarcodeInput (in Barcode Item);
        void KeypadInput (in OperatorCmd Cmd);
    };

    interface OutputMedia {

        boolean OutputText (in string StringToPrint);
    };

    interface POSTerminal {

        void Login ();
        void PrintPOSSalesSummary ();
        void PrintStoreSalesSummary ();
        void SendBarcode (in Barcode Item);
        void ItemQuantity (in long Quantity);
        void EndOfSale ();
    };
};
```

23.15.8 PseudoNameService Module IDL Definitions

Here is the HP Distributed Smalltalk **PseudoNameService** IDL module definition. There are no changes from the common IDL other than preprocessing.

```
interface PseudoNameService {

    void BindName (in string ObjectName,
        in Object ObjectRef);
    Object ResolveName (in string ObjectName);
};
```

23.15.9 Smalltalk IDL Summary

With these steps accomplished, your IDL file is registered in the HP Distributed Smalltalk System, and each interface is registered in the Interface Repository. The IDL has been checked for consistency, and is free from syntax errors and ready to go to work. The first step in coding the example is to review Depot implementation details in Section 24.1, so turn the page and we'll get started.

## CHAPTER 24

Coding the Depot: Overview and C Language Coding

24.1 LANGUAGE-INDEPENDENT OVERVIEW: DEPOT IMPLEMENTATION

This section is for everyone, regardless of which programming language you're using. It adds implementation detail to the requirements set out in the A&D, which we left out on purpose when we were writing it; at that point, we were primarily concerned with analyzing and stating the *problem*, and implementation details would have been an unnecessary and annoying distraction. Now, with the problem thoroughly analyzed (keeping in mind that, for any real-life problem, we would actually iterate through the entire A&D implementation procedure a number of times, spiraling in on an optimal solution), we are free to concentrate on the *solution*, and it is appropriate for us to focus now on algorithms, data flow, file formats, and other implementation details.

Of course, the Depot object has to execute the functionality prescribed in our A&D in every language, so we'll work out the language-independent details in this section—algorithms, file formats, data flow details—and then split into language-specific chapters. The Store and POS chapters are organized just like this one. Figure 18.1 shows this organization in some detail.

Before we head into the Depot, we'll review how the rest of the next nine chapters are organized. We've divided the code for each module into three parts, based on what it does and where it comes from:

- Code generated from the IDL by the language mapping. For each language, this code is common to all ORBs because the language mapping is an OMG standard.

- Code that executes the functionality of the module. For each language, this code is common to all ORBs because we've used good programming practice to write portable code.

- Code that takes care of system and ORB-dependent details. This is the only code that differs, for a given language, from one ORB to another.

To emphasize commonality of the different CORBA implementations in this book, the common code from the first two parts is presented only once, in its own sections. Chapters presenting C language coding start with the language-independent overview, and the common code is presented in the sections 2 and 3 of those chapters. C++ and Smalltalk chapters start right out with common code in sections 1 and 2.

The implementors have done their best to maximize the amount of common code, and minimize the amount of ORB-specific code. Recall, however, that the current OMG standards effort on server-side portability will reduce the amount of ORB-specific code even further. But, for now, you can use the division of code among the different sections to judge how portable an application can be in CORBA when written by experienced programmers who have portability as a specific goal.

Since we need the Pseudo-Name Service right away, we've put its explanation in this chapter as well. So read on to learn how these objects work. At the end of this section, C programmers will continue on, while C++ and Smalltalk programmers will be sent off to Chapters 25 and 26, respectively.

24.1.1   Language-Independent Depot Implementation Details

We've purposely structured this example to illustrate as many facets of CORBA as we could, in a reasonably realistic way. Look for these CORBA features in the Depot and PNS:

- passing of object references between objects;
- stringifying/destringifying of an object reference for external storage/ retrieval;
- use of **in** and **out** parameters (sorry; we don't have an **inout** parameter); and
- raising of a CORBA exception.

The depot component is implemented as a server called **CentralSrv**. This server creates a single CORBA object of interface **Depot**, which is then registered with the Pseudo-Name server using the name **Depot**.

The **Depot** interface defines just one operation:

```
void FindItemInfo(
    in AStore::AStoreId StoreId
    ,in POS::Barcode Item
    ,in long Quantity
    ,out AStore::ItemInfo IInfo)
    raises (AStore::BarcodeNotFound);
```

Using an **out** parameter called **IInfo**, **FindItemInfo()** returns the **ItemInfo** (that is, item type, item cost, item name, and so on) of the item specified by the **Item** parameter. To fulfill this requirement, the depot needs to have a database giving the following data for each item type handled by the depot:

barcode   item_name   item_quantity   item_cost   item_type

For simplicity, this data is stored in a text file called depot.dat. In a full commercial implementation of the Depot, this data would almost certainly be stored by a database management system. An example line of this data file is:

102345   Pasta   77   12.38   Food

When the depot is started, it reads this file and stores the data in an in-memory search structure. The details of this search structure (and in particular its efficiency) need not concern us here since this is straightforward programming that is independent of any CORBA concerns. It could be a binary search tree, or a simple linear list. In fact, the different language implementations presented in this book use totally different algorithms for the search, thus demonstrating the isolation of interface and implementation that we have been emphasizing. You'll find details of each algorithm in the language-specific sections of this and the next two chapters.

The actions of the operation **FindItemInfo()** can be summarized as follows:

▪ Take the **Item** parameter (of type **POS::Barcode**) and use it to look up the search structure for the **ItemInfo** record. If the item cannot be found in the search structure, return immediately with an exception of type **AStore::BarcodeNotFound**.

▪ Use the **StoreId** parameter of the call to update statistics for the specified store.

▪ Use the **Quantity** parameter of the call to reduce the count of the chosen item held in stock by the depot. For simplicity, this updating has *not* been carried out in the sample code.

The code for **FindItemInfo()** can be written without using any special CORBAfacilities, and in particular, without invoking on any other CORBA objects in the network.

24.1.2 Language-Independent Pseudo-Name Service Implementation Details

The Name Service is fundamental in a distributed object system—that's why its object reference is the first one returned by the initialization service on client startup, and why it was standardized in the first group of CORBA-services by the OMG. But, because this example was written shortly after the publication of the CORBA Naming Service Specification, many ORBs lacked compliant implementations of the service. The Pseudo-Name Service is an extremely lightweight substitute for the CORBA Naming Service which provides the naming functions necessary for the example. To maintain uniformity throughout this book, even the ORBs which were shipping CORBA Naming Service implementations use the Pseudo-Naming Service for the example.

The Pseudo-Name Service allows the components of our example to find the other objects they need to communicate with. It is implemented as a server called **PNS**, which contains a single CORBA object of interface **PseudoNameService**. This interface defines the following IDL operations:

> **void BindName (in string ObjectName, in Object ObjectRef);**
> **Object ResolveName (in string ObjectName);**

Each call to **BindName()** requests the name service to associate the object reference **ObjectRef** with the name **ObjectName**. Each call to **ResolveName()** requests the name service to look up the specified name (**ObjectName**) and return the corresponding object reference (or return nil if the specified name is not known to the name service).

The IDL interface **PNS** must be implemented in the chosen programming language. To maintain the necessary associations between names and object references, the name service object must use a nonpersistent search structure. As with the depot, the nature of this search structure is not of great concern to us here (typically in the implementations in this book, the same form of data structure is used by the depot and the name service).

The actions of the operation **BindName()** can be summarized as follows:

- Take the **ObjectName** parameter (of type **string**) and use it to update the search structure; that is, to associate that name with the object reference passed as parameter **ObjectRef**.

The actions of the operation **ResolveName()** can be summarized as follows:

- Take the **ObjectName** parameter (of type **string**) and use it to find the search structure for the associated object reference. Return this reference; or the CORBA nil value if the specified name is unknown to the name service.

24.1.3 Finding the Pseudo-Name Service

Since the role of the Pseudo-Name Service is to assist objects in finding other objects, the question naturally arises as to how the Pseudo-Name Service itself is found. We chose to create a text file that contains the stringified object reference for the **PseudoNameService** object in the **PNS** server. The name of the text file, PNS.dat, is the common factor which enables initialization. At startup each component that needs to use the Pseudo-Name Service reads the text file PNS.dat given to it, and translates the stringified object reference into a reference that can be used to invoke the **BindName()** and **ResolveName()** operations.

On startup, the Psuedo-Name Service server outputs the stringified object reference of its PseudoNameService object into a file named PNS.dat. You will have to copy this output file to each of the directories containing the other clients and servers.

This concludes the language-independent discussion of the Depot and PNS implementations, and now it's time to start coding. If you're working the example in C, continue with the next section. If you're working in C++, skip to the start of Chapter 25. And if you're working in Smalltalk, skip to the start of Chapter 26.

24.2 C MAPPING COMPONENT

This section, and the one that follows, present C language code common to every C language ORB. If you're working the example in ObjectBroker, SOM-Objects, or DAIS, you need to read both of these sections before skipping to the section specific to your ORB. Don't try to skip this part; there's relatively little ORB-specific code and all of the important stuff (like the interfaces and the functionality!) is worked in common code.

We summarized the OMG IDL-C Language Mapping in Chapter 7 and will take advantage of the details we presented there. We will also fill in some details that we skipped, when we need them here.

The IDL interfaces define, via the language mapping, the C language API for all of our objects. The original CORBA concept assumed that the programmer would generate C code APIs by hand from the IDL, but clever work and good sense by ORB implementors has automated most of this work. But, you still need to know how the transformation occurs since it defines the starting point for your coding project, and that's what we'll cover in this section.

The declarations that we present in this section are part of your first C language file, central.c. If you're working the example by typing it in yourself, you'll need to type them in as you read along. If you plan on using the starter files produced by your ORB, grab them from the IDL compiler output—we listed the names in Chapter 23. They'll contain the declarations we present here, and possibly some additional code that your system will need later.

The CORBA C mapping states that types, constants, exceptions, and operations are identified by their global name. The names are derived from IDL scoped names—types, constants, exceptions, and operations are scoped by the module name and interface name. The C global name corresponding to an IDL global name is derived by converting occurrences of the scoping operator "::" to "_" (an underscore) and eliminating the leading underscore. The prototype for the C language stub mapping of an IDL operation looks like:

```
ModuleName_InterfaceName_OperationName(
    CORBA_Object targetObject,
    CORBA_Environment env,
    [CORBA_Context cxt,]
    arguments ...);
```

The module name, if any, appears first, followed by the interface name and then by the operation name each separated by an underscore.The remainder of the mapping looks like a standard C function call with at least two, and potentially three, implicit arguments; the target object reference always appears first and is followed by the Environment argument. If there is a Context clause in the IDL definition, then the third argument is the Context object reference. The explicit arguments follow in the order they are specified in the IDL definition. The C mapping also has to generate pointer arguments based on the type of the parameter and also the "direction of flow of value" of the argument in, out, inout. In general inout and out arguments are pointer types in C. structs, and sequences are passed as pointer arguments regardless of the "direction of flow of value."

Specifically, the C mapping for the types defined in Central.idl and imported from POS.idl and Store.idl are given below.

IDL Type	C Type
AStore::ItemTypes	`AStore_ItemTypes`
AStore::AStoreId	`AStore_AStoreId`
AStore::ItemInfo	`AStore_ItemInfo`
CentralOffice::Depot	`CentralOffice_Depot`

The operations defined on the Depot and Pseudo-Name Service objects have the following C language stub mapping:

```
void CentralOffice_Depot_FindItemInfo(
          CORBA_Object      depotObject,
          CORBA_Environment *env,
          AStore_StoreId    StoreId,
          POS_Barcode       Item,
          CORBA_long        Quantity,
          AStore_ItemInfo   *IInfo);
```

There are two arguments in the C function prototype that were implicit in the IDL operation declaration. They are the target object (depotObject) which is of type **CORBA_Object** and the Environment parameter of type **CORBA_Environment**. Also, note that **POS::Barcode** is mapped to **POS_Barcode**.

The Pseudo-Name Service interface has two methods—**BindName** and **ResolveName**. The bind method defines an association of a name with an object reference. The resolve method "resolves" the name by returning the associated object reference. Since the Pseudo-Name Service is not defined within the scope of any module, the module qualifier is absent in the C mapping for the methods.

```
void   PseudoNameService_BindName(
          CORBA_Object       pNameServObject,
          CORBA_Environment *env,
          CORBA_string       ObjectName,
          CORBA_Object       ObjectRef);

CORBA_Object PseudoNameService_ResolveName(
          CORBA_Object       pNameServObject,
          CORBA_Environment *env,
          CORBA_string       Objectname);
```

This completes the C declarations generated by the IDL. Since the depot object is a server, we need to implement the functionality of these interfaces. We'll do that in the next section.

24.3   CODING THE DEPOT AND PNS COMMON FUNCTIONALITY IN C

Now we need to code the functionality of the Depot object and the Pseudo-Name Service object. There's almost nothing ORB-specific about this, so we'll do it all in this section. If you're working the example by hand, you'll need to type all of this code into your .c file as we go along. At the end of this section, we'll send you off to the section on your specific ORB for final coding, compilation, and linking.

In the common code sections in this chapter and the other C-bindings chapters, the methods for the objects have their function names and first two parameter names listed in *italics*. This indicates that these names are not specified by CORBA and each vendor has chosen a different naming convention for its product. Here's why:

Although the stub name called by the client is specified precisely by the C-mapping rules and the client call is portable, the function name of a method that services that stub can't be the same as the client name for two very good reasons:

1. the stub and the client might be in the same process and you can't have two routines with the same name using most linkers; and
2. there may be multiple implementations for a given method and they must have different names.

This forces ORB vendors to choose their own names for the object function, without guidance (yet) from OMG.

And, about those parameter names: The first parameter to a method is specified by CORBA to be a reference to the object for the method and the second is a pointer to the environment; however, CORBA doesn't specify the names for these parameters. These names are referenced in the body of the method and must be specified in the function header. Since these are, in a sense, "dummy" parameters (it doesn't matter what name you pick, as long as it's the same in the header and the body), functionality and interoperability are not affected by the choice of name.

For both method name and parameter names, the product-specific sections of these chapters will explain the naming convention for that product. All you have to do is realize the italic parts of the common code will be replaced by something else specific to a vendor in the vendor's generated method skeletons. The code in the chapters and on the floppy for each vendor has that vendor's naming convention replaced for the italicized part. The OMG server-side portability RFP is expected to define standards that will help make this part of your code more portable.

The functionality we're coding was determined by the A&D, which we presented in Chapter 19. We won't reprint it here, but you should refer to it continually in order to either write the code yourself, or to see why we're writing what we are.

Ready to code? Here we go.

24.3.1 Database Implementation for Depot and PNS

The **FindItemInfo** method on the **Depot** object is responsible for returning the price information of an item specified by its bar code. The item information is stored in a database. The Pseudo-Name Service also maintains a database of the name-object reference associations.

For simplicity and brevity, the databases for both the **Depot** and the **PseudoNameService** are based on an in-memory, singly linked, circular list. In addition to the pointer used to maintain the list, each element contains a pointer to a string representing the single key by which the list may be searched, a pointer to the arbitrary data associated with the key, and a pointer to a function that can be used to free the data.

Three functions provide an interface to the list: **db_init()** allocates storage for, and initializes, the head of a new list. A pointer to the new list is returned to the caller. **db_lookup()** takes as arguments a pointer to the list to search and a pointer to the key to search for. It returns either **NULL** if the key is not found, or a pointer to the data associated with the key.

db_insert() either adds a new item to the list or replaces an existing item. It takes as arguments a pointer to the head of the list, and pointers to the key, the data, and the free function associated with the item being added to the list. Should the key already be present in the list, the data associated with it is first freed using the free function specified when the item was inserted. A **NULL** free function is allowed, which represents that the associated data should not be freed. New items cause the allocation of a new list element that is inserted between the head and first element in the list. No means is provided to delete a list entry or the entire list, as these are not required by the example, although they would be trivial to add.

Here is the implementation of the simple database used for the depot and the nameserver. We first define a datatype called **DBEntry** that is used to manage the linked list in the database. The type **DbEntry** and **DbDB** are defined here.

```
typedef struct tagDbEntry
{
  struct tagDbEntry *nxt;        /* pointer to next
                                  * entry in list
                                  */
       void          *data;      /* pointer to data
                                  * associated with
                                  * this entry
                                  */
       char          *key;       /* key to search
                                  * for this entry
                                  */
```

```
DbFreeFN            free;       /* pointer to
                                 * function to
                                 * free data if
                                 * this entry
                                 * is replaced
                                 * (may be NULL)
                                 */

} DbEntry;
typedef DbEntry *DbDb; /* opaque type representing
                        * the data store
                        */
```

Here is the implementation of the **db_init** function. This function allocates space for the **DbEntry** structure and initializes the elements.

```
DbDb db_init(void)
{
  DbEntry *new;

  new       = malloc(sizeof(DbEntry));
  new->nxt  = new;
  new->data = NULL;
  new->key  = NULL;
  new->free = NULL;
  return new;
} /* end of db_init() */
```

The database also uses a utility function called **lookup**, which does a linear search for the key and returns the database entry if the key exists. Otherwise, it returns **NULL**. The implementation of lookup is shown next.

```
static DbEntry *lookup(char *key, DbDb db)
{
  DbEntry *ppp;

  ppp = db->nxt;
  while (ppp->key != NULL)
  {
    if (!strcmp(ppp->key, key))
    {
      return ppp;
    }
    ppp = ppp->nxt;
  }
```

```
    return NULL;
} /* end of lookup() */
```

Now we describe the implementation of the **db_insert** and **db_lookup** functions. The **db_insert** function first checks to see if the key already exists by invoking **lookup**. If the key exists, then the previous data associated with this key is released. If the key does not exist, then a new **DbEntry** stucture is created and inserted at the beginning of the list. The data that is passed into the **db_insert** function is associated with the key.

```
void db_insert(char *key, void *data, DbFreeFN free, DbDb db)
{
  DbEntry *ppp;

  ppp = lookup(key, db);
  if (ppp != NULL)
  {
      if (ppp->free != NULL)
      {
          ppp->free(ppp->data);
      }
  }
  else
  {
    ppp        = malloc(sizeof(DbEntry));
    ppp->key   = strdup(key);
    ppp->nxt   = db->nxt;
    db->nxt    = ppp;
  }
  ppp->data = data;
  ppp->free = free;

} /* End of db_insert() */
```

The **db_lookup** function returns the data associated with the specified key. It invokes **lookup** and returns the data member in the **DbEntry** structure if the key exists. **db_lookup** searches the database by invoking the **lookup** function.

```
void *db_lookup(char *key, DbDb db)
{
  DbEntry *ppp;
  ppp = lookup(key, db);
  return (ppp) ? ppp->data : NULL;
} /* end of db_lookup() */
```

24.3.2 PNS Methods Bind and Resolve

The Psuedo-Name Service supports two methods: **Bind** and **Resolve**. We looked at the C mapping in Section 24.2. The implementation of the **Bind** method is shown next. The **BindName** and **ResolveName** methods use two datatypes to manage the database. Here they are:

```
typedef   struct _item
{
  CORBA_Object   obj;
} item_s, *item_p;
typedef struct tagPNameState
{
  DbDb   db;
} PNameState;
void PseudoNameService_BindName (
                    CORBA_Object pNameServObject,
                    CORBA_Environment   *ev,
                    CORBA_string        ObjectName,
                    CORBA_Object        ObjectRef)
{
  PNameState    *ostate;
  item_p        anItem;

  /* product specific code to get the database
   * (ostate) could be obtained from an instance
   * variable, by querying the BOA or other means
   */
  anItem        = malloc (sizeof(item_s));

anItem->obj = CORBA_Object_duplicate(ObjectRef,
                                             ev);
  db_insert(ObjectName, anItem, free_item,
                                    ostate->db);
}
```

The **Resolve** method looks up the name (key) in the database. The data that is the object reference associated with the name is returned if it is registered with the name service. If the registration does not exist, then a **NULL** object reference is returned.

```
CORBA_Object PseudoNameService_ResolveName(
            CORBA_Object     pNameServObject,
            CORBA_Environment *ev,
            CORBA_char        *ObjectName)
```

```
{
  item_p          theItem;
  PNameState      *ostate;
  CORBA_Object    theObject;

  /* product specific code to get the database
   * (ostate) could be obtained from an instance
   * variable, by querying the BOA or other means
   */
  if (theItem = db_lookup((char *)ObjectName
                     ,ostate->db)) {
     theObject = theItem->obj;
  }
else {
     theObject = CORBA_OBJECT_NIL;
}
return theObject;
}
```

24.3.3 Depot Object FindItemInfo Method

The implementation of the **CentralOffice_Depot_FindItemInfo** method requires that the database be set up. The database is created by reading the depot.dat file (as specified in Section 24.1). The code for setting up the database is implemented by a utility function called **db_init**. The implementation uses the following datatypes:

```
typedef  struct _item
{
  char              barcode[MAX_STR_LENGTH];
  AStore_ItemTypes  itemType;
  float             cost;
  char              description[MAX_STR_LENGTH];
  long              quantity;
} item_s, *item_p;
typedef struct tagDepotState
{
  DbDb  db;

} DepotState;
typedef void *ObjectStatePtr;

ObjectStatePtr depot_init(void)
```

```c
{
  FILE               *fp;
  char               code[MAX_STR_LENGTH];
  char               desc[MAX_STR_LENGTH];
  char               itemType[MAX_STR_LENGTH];
  long               quantity;
  float              cost;
  item_p             anItem;
  CORBA_Environment  ev;
  CORBA_string       stringref;
  DepotState         *ostate;


/* create the database */
  ostate    = malloc(sizeof(DepotState));
  ostate->db = db_init();

  /*
   * Now open and read the depot data file.
   * Each "record" is saved in the data store.
   * The primary (only) key is the barcode.
   */

  fp = fopen (DEPOT_FILE, "r");
  while (fscanf (fp, "%s%s%d%f%s",
                 code, desc, &quantity,
                   &cost, itemType) == 5) {
    anItem = malloc (sizeof(item_s));
    if (anItem){
      strcpy(anItem->barcode, code);
      strcpy(anItem->description, desc);
      anItem->cost     = cost;
      anItem->quantity = quantity;

      if (!strcmp(itemType, "FOOD")){
        anItem->itemType = AStore_food;
      }else if (!strcmp(itemType, "CLOTHES")){
        anItem->itemType = AStore_clothes;
      }else if (!strcmp(itemType, "OTHER")){
        anItem->itemType = AStore_other;
      }
      db_insert(anItem->barcode, anItem, NULL,
                        ostate->db);
    }
  }
  fclose (fp);
```

```
        return (ObjectStatePtr)ostate;
    } /* end of depot_init() */
```

Once the database has been instantiated, the **FindItemInfo** method on
the **Depot** object will be able to look up the database and find pricing information for a given bar code. The implementation of the `find_item_info`
method is quite straightforward:

```
void CentralOffice_Depot_FindItemInfo(
                CentralOffice_Depot   DepotObj,
                CORBA_Environment     *ev,
                CentralOffice_AStoreId    store_id,
                POS_Barcode           Item,
                CORBA_long            Quantity,
                CentralOffice_ItemInfo      *IInfo)
{
  item_p            theItem;
  CentralOffice__ItemInfo  theItemInfo;
  DepotState        *ostate;

  /* The ostate is set here. This product
   * is product specific
   */

  if (theItem = db_lookup((char *)Item,
            ostate->db))
  {
     IInfo->Item     = theItem->barcode;
     IInfo->Itemtype = theItem->itemType;
     IInfo->Itemcost = theItem->cost;
     IInfo->Name     = theItem->description;
     IInfo->Quantity = theItem->quantity;


theItem->quantity -= Quantity;

return;
}
 else {
     /* raise exception */
     CORBA_BOA_set_exception(TheBoa,ev,
                CORBA_USER_EXCEPTION,
                ex_AStore_BarcodeNotFound,
                (void *)&Item);
     }
}
```

24.3.4 Implementation Summary

If you've been typing in the code as you went along, your depot and PNS code are nearly complete. You're ready to make just a few adjustments for your specific ORB, and prepare to run your Depot and PNS objects. Granted, you won't be able to test them until you've completed a few more chapters, but this does give you a chance to fire up a server for the first time.

24.4 CONNECTING TO THE ORB AND BOA, AND STARTING THE DEPOT OBJECT

The depot and PNS objects are servers, and the server-side connection to the ORB has not been standardized by OMG to the same extent as the client. The organization is taking care of this now, but until they finish up, we'll have to do a little more of the work ourselves in the form of ORB-specific code: names for functions, for the first two parameters, and possibly other items. That code is presented in the remainder of this chapter, along with product-specific procedures to create and fire up your objects.

At this point, go to the section in this chapter on your specific ORB product and follow its procedures to get your objects ready and running. After you've finished, go to Chapter 27 to code the Store object.

24.5 OBJECTBROKER

This section details the steps needed under ObjectBroker's C-binding to produce code for the Central Office's Depot server and for the Pseudo-Name Server.

As we start these first steps to creating our multiple client/server model using CORBA, it is worth stepping back to consider what we're about to do. For ObjectBroker, a CORBA server is one of three things: an independent process, a library, or a DLL; these all respond to requests from clients on one or more objects. (Any of these may also be a client to other servers, but that's almost trivial.) For this book, we'll use the simplest option, an independent process, started from the command line.

For our purposes, a server contains:

- a main C-program (written by you, the programmer, possibly with aid from the ObjectBroker QuickStart utility);
- an ORB (a library supplied by the vendor);
- a BOA (a library supplied by the vendor, possibly separate from the ORB);
- dispatch routines that work with the BOA to call on the methods (generated completely by ObjectBroker);

- method routines for the operations the operation performs (supplied by you, the user, with aid from ObjectBroker);
- subsidiary, convenience routines never seen outside the process (some supplied by the you, the user, some by ObjectBroker's QuickStart utility).

CORBA is currently not very prescriptive about how these elements fit together or even that these are the exact components needed; as a result, the level of portability is not the highest for the server-side (for any of the language bindings). (Work is proceeding in OMG to remedy that problem now) There is enough looseness in the CORBA specs to allow different vendors great latitude on how to implement these connections. That is why you will see a fair amount of difference in the server code, often in the main programs and in object initialization. Some vendors may choose to optimize for speed over flexibility; some took a different computer science course. (Many of the differences are hidden in the other language bindings that use language features that can inherit from low-level methods that do the hard work we'll have to do in C. Even so, ObjectBroker tries to shield you from as much as possible in the C-bindings, as well.)

In the issues of portability and bindings, the interesting parts of the connections are in *how* the processes get started, *how* options for this server are communicated to the ORB, *how* memory management occurs, and *how* to handle the case when the server is to be stopped externally (from a command line for instance). The examples for ObjectBroker show ObjectBroker's experience in dealing with these topics for several years, along with its ideas on how to do this. The one major issue we won't deal with much is memory management since it's not needed much for this example. When you start your own work, however, this will loom large in your learning curve.

24.5.1 Object State

One concept worth discussing now is the idea of object state, as it is used not only with PNS and Depot in this example, but with all other objects in the entire application. (Put another way, once you've got a good idea, beat it to death).

Each "interface" defined by OMG is "abstract." Whenever an object is created, it has some state that makes it different from every other object. For example, if there are several POS stations in a store, each has an object associated with it, and, depending on the configuration of the store's computers, it should be possible to run the same code, using different state, on the same computer. This is not a new idea; it goes back to the first days of "reentrant" code in the first days of time-sharing computers. The only difference is the mechanism.

The way we use state in the C-binding is common among the vendors; it uses a special feature of CORBA's object-creation feature. Whenever you create an object, you can specify that part of the object is "reference data." This reference data is stored by the ORB with the definition of the object and, more important, can be retrieved, used, and set by "shared" code to work on data different between instances of an object. Typically, we do not want the definition of an object to become large (for other reasons); thus the "reference data" is, as practiced here, an identifier, possibly the address of some heap-allocated storage that serves as the state data for the instance of the object.

Of course, each type of object has needs for widely varying state data. This example uses a technique that accommodates this need. This technique is on the edge of CORBA/non-CORBA, so we won't go into it much. You can read the the details about reference data—declaring it, creating it, retrieving it, and using it—in each main program (each server's main program) and in the files misc.h and misc.c, which contain a mix of useful local, vendor-independent routines and local, vendor-dependent routines.

24.5.2 Comparing Depot and PNS

The procedures for creating Depot and PNS servers are practically identical, with the only differences occurring in the initialization of the two objects and in the methods (or operation implementations) for each object.

The similarities of the PNS and the Depot are the following:

- The PNS is a pure server—that is, it never calls an object outside itself.

- The Central Office Depot server is almost a pure server. The only client-style call it makes is to the PNS BindName routine to identify itself as the Depot server so that other routines can find it. After that, the Depot server acts very much like the PNS.

- The Depot server uses the same method of storing information in memory—a linear list. It returns data from this list to its callers using the same linear search routine used for the PNS list of names and object references. Details are immaterial to the CORBA part of this book so we won't bother looking at the routine. Treat it like poison ivy—something that sits on the floppy distributed with the book, but that you don't really have to deal with.

- The structure of the main programs are the same. Indeed the structure of all the main programs for ObjectBroker are the same if you use the Quick-Start utility. (The QuickStart utility generates what ObjectBroker terms "dedicated servers," those that handle only CORBA requests. ObjectBroker also supports integration with a number of other popular event schemes

(Windows, X-windows) as well as the ability to easily integrate with custom schemes.)

Thus, we will first discuss the procedures to get PNS operational in ObjectBroker, and can then simply add a couple pieces to describe how to do the same for Depot.

24.5.3   Similarity to Other Vendors' Code

As mentioned, ObjectBroker has a QuickStart utility that makes it easy for you to start creating your client/server system. This utility not only performs all of the activities of Chapter 23 for you, but it also creates main program skeletons with client calls, main program skeletons setting up server processes, and libraries of useful routines, as well as the method skeletons that you might well expect. That is, it fills in many of the underdetermined methods of CORBA. You may then fill in the skeletons, change them, or throw them away and do something completely different.

This facility does, however, make it a little difficult to try to match ObjectBroker code produced by the QuickStart utility with code produced by (often similar) facilities of other vendors. We've compromised by using as much common code as possible in the methods, but the server main-programs and some of the utility programs are sometimes located in different modules or in a different order within a module.We'll explain some of the reasons for this shortly. As a result, you will not be able to easily lay together two pieces of code from different vendors to see the differences. Careful study, however, will convince you that the CORBA model being used is the same, with, at most, different names.

24.5.4   Pseudo-Name Service (Main)

In ObjectBroker, the main program for PNS was originally created by the QuickStart utility and then modified to match some of the structure of the other vendors. It is structured as follows:

- front matter, comprising: includes, globals, external prototypes, and forward references
- main
- routine RegisterPseudoNameServiceImpl
- routine pnamemain_clean_up

Front Matter   None of the front matter should be surprising to C programmers. The one different kind of include file that you will get used to seeing in ObjectBroker is:

```
#include "pnamesvc.imh"
```

The suffix .imh helps you remember that you are using an include file for the implementation rather than the client of the PNS. (You would include only the .h for the client.) Since all .imh files generated by ObjectBroker themselves include the corresponding .h files, you won't see includes of the .h files in the ObjectBroker-generated code modules.

The one, non-QuickStart-generated external prototype worth mentioning is that for Create_PseudoNameService_Object. Such a creation routine is not specified by CORBA nor generated as part of ObjectBroker. In this example, we have manually included its prototype in the main and manually included the code for it in the pnamesvc.c file, the file of methods for the services. ObjectBroker has plans to create stubs like this for you in the future.

Pseudo-Name Service Main   The PNS main (in file pname_m.c) first declares a CORBA-specified variable in which the ORB can present any errors:

```
CORBA_Environment ev;
```

Ignoring debugging output statements (printf...) and some comments, the remainder of main is:

```
TheOrb = CORBA_DEC_ORB_OBJECT;
TheBoa = CORBA_DEC_BOA_OBJECT;

if (!RegisterPseudoNameServiceImpl (&ev))
    {OBB_ORB_rundown(TheOrb,&ev,(CORBA_Flags) 0);
    IsException (&ev,(CORBA_string)
                "OBB_ORB_rundown failed \n");
    return(0);}

pname_ref= Create_PseudoNameService_Object
            (argc, argv, &ev );

OBB_BOA_main_loop(TheOrb,&ev,(CORBA_Flags)0);
pnamemain_clean_up(&ev);
```

Setting **TheOrb** and **TheBoa** variables from constants (obtained from one of the include files provided by ObjectBroker) allows the rest of this code to be the same as for those ORBs that have already implemented the recently approved Initialization service for CORBA. ObjectBroker, of course, will be implementing these new services as soon as possible while continuing commitments to current customers.

RegisterPseudoNameServiceImpl is a routine generated by the Quick-Start utility. It reaches into the right part of the other generated routines (pnsdsp.c) to tell the ORB that an implementation is available.

The call on **Create_PseudoNameService_Object** tells that routine in the pnamesvc.c module to create a PNS object, originally with no names and object references. We'll talk about this more in a moment.

After registering the implementation and creating the object, we make a vendor-specific call (as do all C-binding applications) to tell the ORB to start dispatching requests for service; in this case, on **OBB_BOA_main_loop**.

After returning from the ObjectBroker main loop, the main program cleans up by calling **pnamemain_clean_up**, then ends. How do you get out of the "main loop"? See the **pnamemain_clean_up** routine next for a discussion.

RegisterPseudoNameServiceImpl   Since this is generated by the Quick-Start utility, the exact code doesn't need to be listed here. You are allowed to change it, but you don't have to for this example. What we will mention is that CORBA specifies that implementations be registered in an Implementation Repository for access by an ORB and by the BOA. There are many options for the registration. The .iml file we produced in Chapter 23 specified our design decisions, and these were generated into the code produced in the module pnsdsp.c. Since we've already done the hard part, all we have to do is now call **RegisterPseudoNameServiceImpl**, which takes care of the details. This routine also performs the CORBA-specified action of "activating" the implementation that was just registered. Again, since this is a begin-ners guide, we won't tell you into which level of Dante's Inferno you would end up should you fail to do this. Aren't you glad ObjectBroker generates it for you?

pnamemain_clean_up   This subroutine is very like what the QuickStart utility produces, but is slightly modified to be similar to what the other vendors use. It is primarily for cleaning up after PNS when the PNS is terminated. Usually, the only way such a service is terminated (other than by system crash) is by call from a command line or by an explicit operation. Typically, in ObjectBroker, an operator issues the command:

```
> obbmsho
```

to display active implementations that could be stopped; the operator then issues the command:

```
> obbmstp nnnn
```

where **nnnn** is the management UUID of the implementation shown as the result of the **obbmsho** command. This method of stopping an implementation is far superior to merely using the operating system "process stop" since it allows the implementation to shut down cleanly: clean up any memory, close files, and generally act as a responsible citizen.

The specific code for **pnamemain_clean_up** is mercifully short:

```
DeactivateImpl(PseudoNameServiceImpl, ev);
UnregisterImpl(PseudoNameServiceImpl, ev);
CORBA_Object_release(
     (CORBA_Object)PseudoNameServiceImpl, ev);
OBB_ORB_rundown (TheOrb, ev, (CORBA_Flags) 0);
```

Just as **RegisterPseudoNameServiceImpl** registered and then activated the implementation, we must, in reverse order, deactivate and unregister it. (The actual routines that do this are in the misc.c module, as they work for all implementations given the correct parameters. Putting them in that module allows us to do some useful error checking without taking extra space in the code or in this explanation.) In addition, we release the implementation (which, interestingly, is itself an object, but that's a whole different story). Finally, we execute the final, vendor-specific, absolutely last, final, and definitive, end-of-the-world request to ObjectBroker—**OBB_ORB_rundown**.

24.5.5   Pseudo-Name Service (Methods)

When we first generated the method routine file pnamesvc.c from the PNS .idl file in Chapter 23, we generated a skeleton file that had in it essentially the following:

```
/* comments... */
#include "PNAMESVC.IMH"
/* OBB_PRESERVE_BEGIN(INCLUDES) */
....
/* OBB_PRESERVE_END(INCLUDES) */

/* ROUTINE NAME: PseudoNameServiceImpl__notify*/
CORBA_Status PseudoNameServiceImpl__notify (...)
{ ObjectBroker generated code }

/* ROUTINE NAME: PseudoNameServiceImpl_BindName*/
void PseudoNameServiceImpl_BindName
   (CORBA_Object object, CORBA_Environment * ev,
    CORBA_string ObjectName,
    CORBA_Object ObjectRef)
```

```
{
/* OBB_PRESERVE_BEGIN(PseudoNameServiceImpl_BindName) */
   ...
/* OBB_PRESERVE_END(PseudoNameServiceImpl_BindName) */
   return;
}

/*ROUTINE NAME: PseudoNameServiceImpl_ResolveName */
CORBA_Object PseudoNameServiceImpl_ResolveName
   (CORBA_Object object, CORBA_Environment * ev,
    CORBA_string ObjectName)
{
/* OBB_PRESERVE_BEGIN(PseudoNameServiceImpl_ResolveName) */
   ....
/* OBB_PRESERVE_END(PseudoNameServiceImpl_ResolveName) */
   return;
}
```

That is, pnamesvc.c starts out as a skeleton of three subroutines. The first routine, **PseudoNameServiceImpl_notify** is entirely generated by ObjectBroker, and simple applications never have to touch it. This routine is provided for you in case an operator at a console sends some kind of message to the implementation. (See the previous section for **pnamemain_clean_up** for further details.) This routine is especially valuable for advanced users.

The two other skeleton routines are the methods called when this implementation is chosen by ObjectBroker to service a client's request. As explained in Section 24.3 on common code, the names of these routines are not exactly the same as the names of the routines that you call when you issue a client request (which are discussed in Section 24.2) due to a nonportable aspect of CORBA under repair now. ObjectBroker (and every other vendor) has thus had to choose a name that would not conflict with the client name, which *is* detailed by CORBA. The preceding code fragment shows that ObjectBroker takes the interface name, appends Impl_, and then appends the name of the operation (method). You will see other names from other vendors, not only with the C-binding, but C++ as well. Also, as explained in the section on common code, the names of the first two parameters to every method, implicit parameters, are not specified by CORBA and may be different. The ObjectBroker-generated code uses the names object and ev. You can merely mentally replace them when you look at the common code section.

Each of the skeleton routines have comments containing the strings **OBB_PRESERVE_BEGIN()** and **OBB_PRESERVE_END()** with the name of the routine as the parameter, and a line of dots between the comments. You should delete the dots and fill in the body of the methods with the code needed to execute that method. In this case, you would merely fill in the body of the code from the common code for PseudoNameService's **BindName** and **ResolveName**.

There is another difference from Section 24.3's common code. Section 24.3 explains that the method of finding state is different for each vendor, and it has a comment in the common code stating where the difference is. For ObjectBroker, simply replace that comment with the single code line:

```
ostate = get_state_ptr(TheBoa, ev, object);
```

This calls the routine **get_state_ptr** (in module misc.c) that retrieves the state from the object reference itself.

If you need some other code to be included in the skeleton (such as **#include**, global storage, or even some service routines), you can put such code at the beginning, between the lines labelled:

```
/* OBB_PRESERVE_BEGIN(INCLUDES) */
....
/* OBB_PRESERVE_END(INCLUDES) */
```

Simply replace the dots with your own code. This is the place we manually put in data structures needed for the object, service routines, and initialization routines, both state and object.

Any code you put between the **OBB_PRESERVE** markers will be preserved the next time the method skeletons are generated if this file already exists. For example, if you add an operation (method) to an interface, an entirely new implementation subroutine is needed. Using the appropriate **obbgen -t** command given in Section 23.8, you will find that ObjectBroker saves all the code you have written and then adds the new routine skeleton. Even if you only change parameters to an existing operation or datatypes, Object-Broker will save the code you previously added for the operation—it is then your job to make the code match the new set of parameters. By the way, this advantage also applies to the code that ships on the floppy with this book. The method code is already written in this fashion; you can "regenerate" the methods for the PNS and end up with essentially the same file.

In the case of file pnamesvc.c, we took liberal advantage of the section at the beginning of the skeleton (**/*OBB_PRESERVE_BEGIN(INCLUDES)*/**) and added several **#include** files, some global references, some type declarations for describing the Pseudo-Name Service, in-memory database, and three subroutines.

The nonsubroutine code lines (ignoring comments) were:

```
#include "db.h"
#include "misc.h"
#include "common.h"
#include <stdlib.h>

CORBA_ImplementationDef PseudoNameServiceImpl;
CORBA_ORB               TheOrb;
CORBA_BOA               TheBoa;

typedef  struct _item
{CORBA_Object  obj;
} item_s, *item_p;

typedef struct tagPNameState
{DbDb   db;
} PNameState;
```

The three subroutines are all service routines for the Pseudo-Name Service. This technique allows us to keep together related routines in a single module and yet keep the advantages of being able to regenerate method code when the IDL changes (as we all know applications are wont to do). There are two little routines, **free_item** and **pname_init**, used by the larger routine, taken exactly from the common code presented earlier in this chapter.

Create_PseudoNameService_Object, which we discussed briefly already, also goes here. This routine creates an object that acts as the Pseudo-Name Service and initializes its value to be an empty list (that is, it has no knowledge of object references at the start). In addition, this particular creation routine writes out a "stringified" copy of its object reference to a file; this file can then be copied to any other computer hooking into this POS example. Thus, it is possible for those routines to get easy access to the PNS object and use it thereafter; only one such stringified file must be passed around. The code for this routine is actually not large. It is just different enough from the other vendors' code that we all thought it was worth listing separately since it makes reference to symbols generated by the vendors' IDL compiler.

```
CORBA_Object Create_PseudoNameService_Object
  (CORBA_long argc,
   CORBA_char **argv,
   CORBA_Environment *ev)
{
  CORBA_Object         obj;
  CORBA_ReferenceData  id;
```

```
FILE*                   fp;
ObjectStatePtr          objstate;

objstate = pname_init();
compose_refdata(&id, objstate);
obj = CORBA_BOA_create(TheBoa,
                       ev,
                       &id, /*reference data*/
                       PseudoNameService__OBJ,
                       PseudoNameServiceImpl);
if( ev->_major != CORBA_NO_EXCEPTION )
    {application_terminate(
        "Failed to create object",ev );;}

/* write object reference to a file */
ref_to_file(obj, ev, PNAME_REF);
return obj;
} /* end of Create_PseudoNameService_Object() */
```

The interesting parts are:

- The call on the common routine **pname_init**, which initializes state to **no name references** in variable **objstate**. This routine is in this same module and just sets a linked list to **null**.

- The call on **compose_refdata**, which puts the object's state in a form usable as **reference data** (as in variable **id**) when the object is created. The routine **compose_refdata** is in the misc.c file and is quite short, just allocating a buffer, setting its length, and setting a pointer.

- The call on (CORBA-specified routine) **CORBA_BOA_create** that actually creates the reference to the object, incorporating the **id** data as reference data. The name of the object being created (that is, the InterfaceDec object reference, **PseudoNameService__OBJ**) is provided by ObjectBroker in the pnamesvc.imh include file. The name of the implementation reference (that is, the ImplDef object reference, **PseudoNameServiceImpl**) is obtained from the global storage where it was put from the pname_m.c module's **RegisterPseudoNameServiceImpl** routine.

24.5.6 Pseudo-Name Service (Dispatch)

The last part of the PNS process (server) is its dispatch routines. These routines are generated by the **obbgen -d** command as in Section 23.8. The generated routines use the .IML and .MML files to configure our system as we want it. The dispatch routines never have to be touched, but they do have to be compiled and linked with the pname_m main module.

24.5.7 Pseudo-Name Service (Build)

To create a PNS executable image (or whatever you call it on your operating system), you have to compile the following files from the floppy with your favorite C compiler and hook up with the ORB library supplied with ObjectBroker.

pname_m.c—the main program

pnamesvc.c—the methods and supporting routines

pnsdsp.c—the routines that provide the link between BOA and methods

misc.c—a mixture of handwritten and vendor-supplied, convenience routines

linear.c—purely C language utility routines for handling in memory lists

After successful compilation, you link these with the ObjectBroker library, usually called something like obb.lib, but almost certainly different on every system. Check the documentation for the name and its location.

24.5.8 Depot

The Depot code is organized exactly as the PNS code, with only name differences in the main module depot_m.c and in the methods.

24.5.9 Depot (Main)

If you lay the two files pname_m.c and depot_m.c side by side, you will see a clear one-to-one correspondence, the only difference being in the replacement of the name PseudoNameService with Depot. This is not surprising since no object-specific work is intended to be done in the main files, but in the methods. (Hey, you understand something, why change it? Besides, it was mostly generated, remember?)

24.5.10 Depot (Methods)

The Depot methods, are, of course, different. Everything that we mentioned about method skeletons for PNS refers to the Depot (as well as any other generated method implementation). There is the completely ObjectBroker-generated utility routine, **DepotImpl__notify**, and only one method, **DepotImpl_FindItemInfo**. The code for **DepotImpl_FindItemInfo** is essentially the common code, subject to the comments listed under Pseudo-NameService about the function header and retrieving object state.

Code added at the **OBB_PRESERVE_XXX(INCLUDES)** at the beginning of the module consists of includes, globals, and two routines. The first is code to read from the grocery depot database routine **depot_init**; since this has nothing to do with CORBA, we will leave its understanding as an exercise for the student.

The second routine added at the beginning of the methods is similar to the routine in PNS. It is called (hold your breath) **Create_CentralOffice_Depot_Object**. (By the way, this name is over 31 characters long. Some operating systems don't allow linker names to be longer than 31 characters. Because of the name formation rules of CORBA's C-Binding, it is fairly easy to generate such long names. Whenever ObjectBroker comes across such a name, it creates a C macro with the first 31 characters of the name for the benefit of the linker. Several of the names in Chapter 23 had that property and, if you actually ran the commands, you saw messages from ObjectBroker's IDL compiler about creating the macros. For those systems without such restrictions, ObjectBroker optionally uses only the longer name.) In this case, the name was of our own devising, so we created our own 31-character macro, and the code should work on any of ObjectBroker's many platforms.

There are three differences between the Create_... routines of pnamesvc.c and central.c. The central.c version:

- Does not have to write its object reference to a file. That's one line fewer.
- Calls a service routine (from misc.c) to find a reference to the PNS (that's one line more, for a net of zero line change so far):

```
pname = NameService(ev);
```

This returns the reference to the PNS object.

- Calls the PNS to inform it that it is ready for business (one line extra now):

```
PseudoNameService_BindName(pname, ev,
                      DEPOT_REF, obj);
```

Anybody else can now query the PNS via **PseudoNameService_ResolveName** to discover the object reference to the central office's Depot.

24.5.11   Depot (Build)

The Depot server is built from almost the same kinds of files (with the exception of names) as the PNS. One extra file is needed:

depot_m.c—the main program

central.c—the methods and supporting routines

cendsp.c—the routines that provide the link between BOA and methods

misc.c—a mixture of handwritten and vendor-supplied, convenience routines

linear.c—purely C language utility routines for handling in memory lists

pnsstb.c—(extra) stub routines for PNS

The extra routine for Depot acts as a client to PNS, by calling on one of its methods. Because of this, we must provide the stub routines generated for PNS in Chapter 23.3. The ORB takes care, then, of transferring control from the stub to the appropriate PNS method—which is, after all, what this whole book is about.

24.6   SOMOBJECTS DEPOT AND PSEUDO-NAME SERVICE IMPLEMENTATIONS

This section describes the SOM-specific C code for implementing the Central-Office module and the Pseudo-NameService classes. Some general implementation characteristics are discussed before examination of the code.

24.6.1   Server Status Messages

Just about every method in objects on the servers contains a **printf** statement that prints information about server activities to the standard output. This was obviously very useful during implementation and debugging of the point-of-sale application code. However, the status information is also useful in monitoring the activities of the usually silent servers while running the example. If each of the servers is started in its own window, the person running the application can watch as an entry in the POSTerminal window causes methods calls to percolate through the servers.

24.6.2   Error and Exception Handling

In order to simplify the code presentation, very little error and exception handling is done in the example implementaton. The BarcodeNotFound exception is explicitly handled. Other error and exception conditions are noted, and program execution is terminated.

To check exceptions, this statement follows each CORBA method invocation:

```
    if(ev._major != CORBA_NO_EXCEPTION) handle_exception(&ev);
```

handle_exception is a function with the following implementation:

```
void handle_exception (Environment *ev)
{
    AStore_BarcodeNotFound *barcodeError;
    StExcep         *stex;
    char            *exid;

    switch(ev->_major)
    {
    case SYSTEM_EXCEPTION:
    /* print system exception value  */
        stex = somExceptionValue(ev);
        printf("System exception: code = %d "
                "status = %s\n", stex->minor,
                stex->completed);
        exit (1);

    case USER_EXCEPTION:
        /*  print user exception value  */
        if (strcmp((somExceptionId(ev)),
                        ex_BarcodeNotFound) == 0)
        {
            barcodeError = (BarcodeNotFound*)
                                somExceptionValue(ev);
            printf("User exception: Barcode not"
                        " found for item - %s\n",
                    barcodeError->item);
        }
        return;
         default:
                application_terminate("none of the"
                            " above", ev);
    }
}
```

24.6.3 Cleanup

In the point-of-sale example, objects are created but never explicitly destroyed. We assume that the objects will be destroyed when the server processes are terminated, in which case all memory allocated within the process will be freed. As a result, the default destructor routines generated by the SOM compiler are used for cleanup.

24.6.4   Utility Functions

A set of utility functions besides the **handle_exception** function is implemented in a file named util.c on the accompanying diskette. One such function, which was implicitly used in the implementation of the handle_exception function, is **application_terminate**. The other functions are only listed here. Refer to the diskette for the complete implementation of these functions.

```
void application_terminate (char  *message,
    Environment *ev):
```

This function prints the message on the screen and terminates the application:

```
void  ref_to_file (CORBA_Object   obj,
    CORBA_Environment *ev, CORBA_char *filename);
```

This function writes the string form an object reference into the file whose name is specified by the last parameter:

```
CORBA_Object  file_to_ref (CORBA_Environment *ev,
    CORBA_char *filename);
```

This function is the opposite of ref_to_file. It reads the string form of an object reference and returns an object reference:

```
void register_server (CORBA_Environment *ev,
    CORBA_Object server);
```

This function registers the server object with the PseudoNameService. The implementation of this object finds the nameserver and uses the **BindName** method on the PseudoNameService object as specified in Section 24.3 to register the server.

24.6.5   Implementing the PseudoNameService Class and the Depot Module

The PseudoNameService and Depot interfaces are defined in the PNS.idl and Central.idl files, respectively. As described in Section 23.9.2, the IDL files are processed by the IDL compiler, **sc**. Since, for this example, we are using C as the implementation language, **sc** is invoked with the **-s"h:ih:c"** flags. The following files are produced by **sc**, when the command here is executed.

```
sc -s"h:ih:c"  PNS.idl Central.idl
```

PNamesvc.h—the include file for C-usage bindings for interface in Pnamesvc.idl

PNamesvc.ih—the include file for C implementation for interface in Pnamesvc.idl

PNamesvc.c—the template file for C implementation of interface in Pnamesvc.idl

Central.h—the include file for C-usage bindings for interfaces in Central.idl

Central.ih—the include file for C implementation for interfaces in Central.idl

Central.c—the template file for C implementations of interfaces in Central.idl

The common code section describes the implementations for most of the methods. In this section, we will describe only the constructor methods for the Pseudo-Name Service and Depot classes. But before we look at the implementation of the constructor methods, we will look at excerpts of the idl files from Section 23.9 that contain SOM-specific extensions. The IDL definition for the PseudoNameService class follows:

```
#ifdef __SOMIDL__
#include <somdserv.idl>
interface PseudoNameService : SOMDServer
#else
interface PseudoNameService
#endif
{
   void BindName(in string ObjectName
#ifdef __SOMIDL__
          ,in SOMObject ObjectRef)

   SOMObject ResolveName(in string ObjectName);


#else
          ,in Object ObjectRef);

   Object ResolveName(in string ObjectName);
#endif
```

```
#ifdef __SOMIDL__
        implementation {
        releaseorder:BindName,
                ResolveName;
        override:somDefaultInit,
                somDestruct;
        somToken ostate;
        dllname = "dobjs.dll";
};
#endif
```

Note that the PseudoNameService interface is derived from the SOMD-Server object. This means that an instance of this interface is a server. Also, objects in a server's address space are not necessarily a subclass of the SOMDServer interface. In this example, since the nameserver supports only one interface, it is convenient to do so. In the implementation definition, the **ostate** instance variable, whose C type is **void ***, is a pointer to an instance of the **PNameState** structure.

Now we are ready to look at the implementation of the constructor method for the PseudoNameService interface. The template code automatically generated by the SOM compiler is depicted in the code listings in italics, and the code that the programmer adds is depicted in our standard code font. Constants used in the code appear in uppercase letters and are defined in a file called commons.h, which is included in the diskette. The default object constructor template generated by the SOM compiler is called **somDefaultInit**. The constructor method is called during creation of an object instance. A default constructor method accepts no arguments, but with a little additional work, the programmer can define a constructor routine that can accept arguments. This is shown in Section 27.6 for the StoreAccess class.

The constructor for the PseudoNameService class is shown next:

```
SOM_Scope void SOMLINK somDefaultInit(
                        PseudoNameService somSelf,
                        somInitCtrl* ctrl)
{
    CORBA_Environment ev;
    PNameState    *ostate;
    PseudoNameServiceData *somThis;
                                    /* set in BeginInitializer */
    somInitCtrl globalCtrl;
    somBooleanVector myMask;
```

```
          PseudoNameServiceMethodDebug("PseudoNameService",
                      "somDefaultInit");
          PseudoNameService_BeginInitializer_somDefaultInit;

          PseudoNameService_Init_SOMDServer_somDefaultInit(somSelf,
                                              ctrl);
          SOM_InitEnvironment(&ev);
          /*
           * Create and initialize the database
           */
     ostate          = SOMMalloc(sizeof(PNameState));
     ostate->db      = db_init();
     somThis->ostate = ostate;

     /* write object reference to a file  */

      ref_to_file(somSelf, &ev, PNAME_REF);

      SOM_UninitEnvironment(&ev);
      printf("PseudoNameService server initialized and ready\n");
}
```

The programmer-provided code in the function body simply calls the database initialization function and stores the return value in the state pointer.

The SOM extensions for the Depot object are similar to the extensions for the PseudoNameService object, as can be seen in Section 23.9. The constructor for the Depot class is shown next:

```
SOM_Scope void SOMLINK CentralOffice_DepotsomDefaultInit(
                      CentralOffice_Depot somSelf,
                      somInitCtrl* ctrl)
{
    FILE          *fp;
    CORBA_char    code[MAX_STR_LENGTH],
                  desc[MAX_STR_LENGTH],
                  itemType[MAX_STR_LENGTH];
    CORBA_long    quantity;
    CORBA_float   cost;
    item_p        anItem;
    CORBA_Environment  ev;
    DepotState    *ostate;

    CentralOffice_DepotData *somThis;
                              /* set in BeginInitializer */
```

```
    somInitCtrl globalCtrl;
    somBooleanVector myMask;
    CentralOffice_DepotMethodDebug("CentralOffice_Depot",
                                   "somDefaultInit");
    CentralOffice_Depot_BeginInitializer_somDefaultInit;
    CentralOffice_Depot_Init_SOMDServer_somDefaultInit(somSelf,
                                   ctrl);

/* initialize the CORBA_Environment structure */
SOM_InitEnvironment(&ev);
/*  Create and initialize the database    */
ostate    = SOMMalloc (sizeof(DepotState));
somThis->ostate    = ostate;
ostate->db  = db_init();

 /*
   *  Now open and read the depot data file.
   *  Each "record" is saved in the database. The primary
   *  (only) key is the barcode for the database operations.
   */

 fp = fopen (DEPOT_FILE, "r");

  if(!fp){
      printf("%s could not be opened\n", DEPOT_FILE);
      exit (1);
  }
  while (fscanf (fp, "%s%s%f%s%d", code, itemType,
                 &cost, desc, &quantity) == 5) {
      anItem = SOMMalloc (sizeof(item_s));
      if (anItem) {
          strcpy (anItem->barcode, code);
          strcpy (anItem->description, desc);
          anItem->cost = cost;
          anItem->quantity = quantity;
      if (!strcmp(itemType, "food"))
          anItem->itemType = AStore_food;
      else if (!strcmp(itemType, "clothes"))
          anItem->itemType = AStore_clothes;
      else if (!strcmp(itemType, "other"))
          anItem->itemType = AStore_other;
      db_insert (anItem->barcode, anItem, NULL, ostate->db);
      }
  }
  fclose (fp)
/* register with the PseudoNameService */
```

```
register_server(&ev,somSelf);
/*  clean up */
 SOM_UninitEnvironment(&ev);
 printf("Depot server initialized and ready\n");
}
```

The constructor for the Depot class initializes the database, reads the database information from depot.dat, inserts the information into the database, and registers with the PseudoNameService server.

Once the methods have been implemented in the PseudoNameService class and the CentralOffice module, the C code can be compiled and linked using the makefile included with the source code. The PseudoNameService and Depot servers are registered in the SOM Implementation Repository using **regimpl**, a utility for server registration. This tool can be used interactively with menu selection. The program also supports command-line options for server registration. The regimpl tool creates an implementation repository that is accessed by the SOMobjects runtime to find servers. Servers are identified by implementation aliases, which are user-friendly names. Servers also have implementation identifiers, which are UUIDs. Servers can be activated, found, and queried by their implementation ID also. The menu that is used in the interactive version of the regimpl tool is shown next.

```
DSOM IMPLEMENTATION REGISTRATION UTILITY
(C) Copyright IBM Corp. 1992,1994.  All rights reserved.
Implementation data being loaded from:
 /corba/book/example/impl_rep/
[ IMPLEMENTATION OPERATIONS ]
 1.Add   2.Delete  3.Change
 4.Show one  5.Show all  6.List aliases
[ CLASS OPERATIONS ]
 7.Add  8.Delete  9.Delete from all  10.List classes
[ SAVE & EXIT OPERATIONS ]
 11.Save data  12.Exit
```

The nameserver is registered with a **pnssvr** alias, and the server class is **PseudoNameService**. The server is started using the default server program somdsvr, which is part of the SOMobjects Toolkit. Since the Depot Object is also a server, it is registered as a server class for a server whose alias is centralsvr. The regimpl tool can also be used to query the server registrations. Here is a command-line query of the server registrations in the implementation repository.

```
regimpl -L
===========================================================
Implementation id.........: 306c4fdf-2d4f1e00-7f-00-10005ac958cc
Implementation alias......: centralsvr
Program name..............: somdsvr
Multithreaded.............: No
Server class..............: ::CentralOffice::Depot
Object reference file.....:
Object reference backup...:
Host name.................: localhost
===========================================================
Implementation id.........: 306c4fe2-0d78e500-7f-00-10005ac958cc
Implementation alias......: pnssvr
Program name..............: somdsvr
Multithreaded.............: No
Server class..............: PseudoNameService
Object reference file.....:
Object reference backup...:
Host name.................: localhost
```

Once registered, the Pseudo-NameService server can be activated using the command:

```
somdsvr -a pnssvr&
```

followed by the Depot server using the command:

```
somdsvr -a centralsvr&
```

24.7 DAIS SPECIFICS IN THE DEPOT

DAIS executables implement *capsules*, which, on a UNIX-like system, simply correspond to processes. We talk about capsules instead of processes because not all of the varied environments we provide implementations for have equivalents of UNIX processes, and we want to use the same terminology and code for them all.

All of the capsules in the example are similar in that they each create objects automatically when the executable is run from the command line. As a result, we have adopted a uniform structure for all the capsules. We'll describe that structure in detail here so you know what's going on, and we'll just mention the differences in the later chapters.

24.7.1 The main() Function

We have put the C **main()** function for the Central Office server in a file called depot_main.c. We first need to include some header files to give the server access to some externally defined facilities. For the depot this is as follows:

```
#include "orb.h"
#include "central.h"
#include "common.h"
```

The first file that we include is orb.h, which gives access to types and functions for directly accessing the ORB. All files containing code that makes use of ORB facilities will need to include this file (regardless of the application). We then include two files that are application-specific: central.h and common.h. The first is one of the files that we used **stubgen** to create in Chapter 23. We need this header file in any code file that makes use of types or methods defined in central.idl. Typically, this file will be included in the implementations of both clients and servers for interfaces defined in central.idl. Finally, we include common.h, which is a collection of definitions used in the whole application. Although these definitions are not necessarily related, we include them all in one file merely to keep the number of files down.

We next have a name mapping in the form of a **#define** and an external declaration:

```
#define new_CentralOffice_Depot \
Create_CentralOffice_Depot_Object

extern CORBA_Object
Create_CentralOffice_Depot_Object(
                         CORBA_long argc,
                         CORBA_char **argv,
                         CORBA_Environment *ev);
```

We use this name mapping as a form of null object factory. In DAIS, we would normally use the DAIS-specific facilities for object location and instantiation. However, we're staying as CORBA-conformant as possible and only creating objects in the same capsule, so this will do for the moment.

Next we have a few declarations for global variables:

```
static CentralOffice_Depot  depot_ref;
CORBA_ORB TheOrb;
CORBA_BOA TheBoa;
```

The first is a "permanent" reference to the Depot object that we're going to create. It's only used in this file, and only used here, so that we have a reference by which we can tidily dispose of the object when we've finished with it. The later two declarations are potentially used by all the files that make up the capsule; they allow easy access to the ORB and BOA once we have initialized them.

Now that we've got the framework in place we can get on with the capsule entry point, the C **main()** function:

```
int main(int argc, char **argv)
{
     CORBA_Environment  ev;
     int tmp_argc = argc;
     ev._major = CORBA_NO_EXCEPTION;

     TheOrb = CORBA_ORB_init(&tmp_argc,
                                   argv, argv[0], &ev);
     TerminateOnException("unable to access orb\n", &ev);
     TheBoa = CORBA_ORB_BOA_init(&tmp_argc,
                                   argv, argv[0], &ev);
     TerminateOnException("unable to access boa\n", &ev);

     depot_ref = new_CentralOffice_Depot(argc, argv, &ev);

     DAIS_capsule_set_terminator(depotmain_clean_up);

     DAIS_schedule();

} /* end of main() */
```

In this example, the role of the code in the C **main()** is to initialize the capsule by locating the ORB and creating the objects that are needed at startup. Obtaining a reference to the ORB and the BOA is performed through the standard initialization calls. After these calls, we check the **CORBA_Environment** to make sure that everything went okay. There are quite a few places in the example where a failure means we can't go on, so we have a function, **TerminateOnException()**, that terminates the capsule if an exception is detected. We don't need to examine this function too closely; it simply calls **DAIS_terminate()**, if necessary, to terminate the capsule, which closes the capsule down tidily and logs a message giving the exception condition and reason for the termination.

We then create the Depot object by calling a local **new** function. The **new** function takes the standard C main **argc** and **argv** arguments, which can be used to uniquely identify the new object and returns its object reference. We'll go into more detail for the **new** function a bit later.

We next come to a call, **DAIS_capsule_set_terminator()**, that does not yet have a CORBA equivalent, but we include it to show good practice. Other ORB vendors have mechanisms for achieving similar functionality. The call allows us to specify a clean-up function to be called when an attempt is made to terminate the capsule. We use it here to just inform the ORB that the objects have been destroyed using the standard CORBA functions, but it could be used for more complicated closedown procedures or even to reject the capsule termination request. We won't go into any more detail here; if you're interested, you can look at the code on the supplied example disk.

Finally, we make another DAIS-specific call, which passes control to the DAIS scheduler. This is the means by which we tell the ORB to start accepting requests for service; all C-binding implementations use a similar mechanism. As DAIS is an inherently multitasking environment, automatically providing multithreading in capsules on all platforms, this is called **DAIS_schedule()** rather than a name only referring to accepting requests.

This is the basic structure for the **main()** function for all the server capsules in the example; they differ only in the names and the number of objects that are created.

24.7.2 The Object Constructor

Each **new** function maps onto an object *constructor* whose job is to grab the resources needed by the new object (allocating memory, creating database records and so forth), initialize the state, and register the new object with the ORB. This is split up into two main sections; one that interfaces to the ORB for object creation and one that performs the application-specific initialization. The distinction is blurred somewhat between the two sections because some of the application-specific initialization involves obtaining object references for other objects, but the separation is valuable nonetheless. Although this code lies in the same file as the rest of the depot-specific code, we'll just look at the initialization functions for the moment and leave the rest of the contents of the file for later. We'll first have a look at the ORB-related initialization in the constructor and then go on to the application specifics.

As we mentioned earlier, we designed the object constructor to be invoked by the DAIS ORB for the creation of the object. In this example, we are not using this mechanism but we have retained the naming conventions and constructor pattern partly because it is a good way of doing things and partly because it makes it easier to modify the example to use the more advanced DAIS facilities if you wish. In order to use these facilities, we must give the function a specific name, and it must have the correct signature. The prototype for the Depot constructor is:

```
CORBA_Object
Create_CentralOffice_Depot_Object(CORBA_long argc,
                                  CORBA_char **argv,
                                  CORBA_Environment *ev)
```

In DAIS, the object constructor is called **Create_iname_Object()**, where **iname** is the scoped name of the interface. This allows the ORB to determine the name of the constructor to call when we want to create an object with a particular interface. The signature is relatively simple and mostly familiar; the arguments are those that you see for any C **main()** function with the addition of a pointer to a **CORBA_Environment** variable so that we can return exception information if we have problems. The return value is the object reference of the object that we are creating. All the object constructors in the example are declared in a similar way.

Inside the function we have a few variable declarations before we actually start the useful work. The first executable statement is a call to the application-specific initializer. We will look at this in more detail later; for now, we just need to know that the function returns a pointer to some memory to be associated with the object (the application's *object state*; see Section 24.5.1 for a little more detail on this). We then process the pointer to the object state to convert it to a form that the ORB can use to store with the object that we're about to create. The object will then be able to ask the ORB for this pointer whenever this instance of the object is invoked. We'll see this being done later on. The two lines that do this are as follows:

```
objstate = depot_init();
compose_refdata(&id, objstate);
```

Now we come to the most important part of the constructor, the creation of the object reference for the object itself:

```
obj = CORBA_BOA_create(TheBoa,
                       ev,
                       &id,
                       DAIS_CentralOffice_Depot_intf,
                       DAIS_CentralOffice_Depot_impl
                       );
TerminateOnException("unable to create depot", ev);
```

This is a standard call on the BOA with only a couple of points specific to DAIS. We have already gained a reference to the BOA using the standard

CORBA initialization call so we just use the global variable that we set up in the **main()** function. The definitions for the interface and implementation are provided in the central.h header file generated by **stubgen**. Their names are in a predefined format based on the scoped name of the interface, similar to the constructor names that we discussed earlier. The generic forms of the interface and implementation definitions are **DAIS_*iname*_intf** and **DAIS_*iname*_impl**, respectively. We use them directly here, although they could have been obtained from a repository.

The next few statements are involved with providing the other objects in the system with a way to get hold of the Depot object's reference using the Pseudo-Name Service:

```
pname = NameService(ev);
PseudoNameService_BindName(pname, ev, DEPOT_REF, obj);
TerminateOnException("unable to export offer", ev);
CORBA_Object_release(pname, ev);
```

The first statement uses "magic" to get hold of the object reference of the Pseudo-NameService (actually from a disk file; see Section 24.1.3 for more detail). The important thing to note here is that object references are allocated on the heap and need to be released after use.

We then make a remote invocation on the PNS using the object reference that we obtained to inform the PNS of the association between the name that we have given our new object and its object reference. As there is only one Depot object in the system, this is a *string literal*. For the other objects in the system, as we will see later, we create a name for the particular *instance* of the object because there is likely to be more than one object of the same type in the system. After checking for errors, we release the store associated with the object reference of the PNS, as promised.

Finally, we declare to the ORB that the *implementation* is ready to receive requests:

```
CORBA_BOA_impl_is_ready(TheBoa, ev,
DAIS_CentralOffice_Depot_impl);
TerminateOnException("Failed to set impl ready",ev );

return obj;
```

There are a couple of points to note here. In this example, the servers are examples of CORBA *persistent servers*, so the **CORBA_BOA_impl_is_ready()** call is used (other kinds of servers would use different calls). Also, the implementation that we pass in on the call is **DAIS_CentralOffice_Depot_impl**, which we have already discussed. Note that we don't invoke the DAIS scheduler at this point because we may want to create other objects as part of the initialization. Having checked for errors, we return the object reference of the new object (the Depot in this case) to the caller. This retains our approach of mapping onto a **new** operation for the object.

24.7.3 Application Initialization

Now that we've handled the initialization of the ORB and connected to it, we can have a quick look at the application-specific aspects of the initialization. As we have seen, the **main()** function calls an object-specific constructor which, in turn, calls an initialization routine for the application-specific part of the object. For the Depot object, there is no instance-specific information relating to the application, so for **depot_init()** we have the prototype:

```
ObjectStatePtr depot_init(void)
```

This aspect of **depot_init()** is rather simpler than some of the other application _init() routines, but it does demonstrate the allocation of application object state. At the top of the file we declare a structure, **DepotState**, that represents the application state of the depot:

```
typedef struct tagDepotState
{
   DbDb   db;
} DepotState;
```

As we will see, we define a state structure for all the other objects in the system with a similar name. State structures persist between object invocations—the ORB maintains an association between an object reference and the pointer or handle to its state. We allocate store for it as follows:

```
ostate       = malloc(sizeof(DepotState));
ostate->db = db_init();
```

Note that we are using the basic C **malloc()** routine, and we aren't checking for out-of-memory errors! For conciseness, we will use the approach throughout the example whenever we need to allocate some store that we can rely on to be available for the lifetime of the object. In this particular case, the only thing that we need to preserve is the handle to the depot database, which we obtain from a call to the vendor-independent **db_init()** routine.

The rest of **depot_init()** just reads the Depot database into store from the data file; it is described in Sections 24.3.1 and 24.3.3. Finally, we return the address of our DepotState structure to the caller as is required by our generic constructor pattern.

24.7.4 Depot Server Method Implementation

We have now covered the initialization and connection to the ORB aspects of the Depot server, so now all we have to do is describe the implementation of the one method that the Depot offers, **FindItemInfo()**, and the organization of the file that contains all this code. The IDL for the depot interface declares the method **FindItemInfo** as part of **interface Depot** in module CentralOffice. This is mapped by DAIS to a function prototype as follows:

```
void S_CentralOffice_Depot_FindItemInfo(
CentralOffice_Depot   _obj,
CORBA_Environment     *ev,
AStore_AStoreId       StoreId,
POS_Barcode           Item,
CORBA_long            Quantity,
AStore_ItemInfo       *IInfo)
```

We can see that the prototype is the same as that described in the Common Functionality section, 24.3, with two minor differences: in DAIS, within an object's method, the invoked object's reference is denoted _obj (similar to ***this** in C++), and the name of the method implementation function is prefixed with **S_** (to distinguish it from the function that is called in a client to invoke the method). The name _obj is just a convention, and you are free to change it if you wish.

In Chapter 23, we used **stubgen** not only to create the stubs and skeletons for the interfaces, but also to create empty templates for the methods within those interfaces. To create the implementation of the **FindItemInfo** method, we have merely taken the template from centralSrv.c, copied it into our implementation file, central.c, and filled in the implementation code.

The only difference in the implementation code itself is the way we obtain the application object state. We make a call from within the object's method to **get_state_ptr()**, which extracts the state pointer associated with the object reference where we put it earlier during initialization when the object reference was created. The implementations of **compose_refdata()** and **get_state_ptr()** are in the file misc.c. We won't look into them any deeper here as they use standard CORBA calls, and there are no DAIS-specific details.

The only DAIS-specific part of the Depot code that we haven't described are the header files that are included. These are shown here:

```
#include "orb.h"
#include "db.h"
#include "pnamesvc.h"
#include "misc.h"
```

```
#include "central.h"
#include "common.h"
```

orb.h gives access to the facilities offered by the ORB and must be present in all compilation units that make use of it. db.h, misc.h, and common.h contain structures, prototypes, and definitions that are shared with other parts of the system. central.h and pnamesvc.h contain the definitions that are required by both clients and servers for the interfaces defined in central.idl and pnamesvc.idl.

24.7.5 Building the Depot Capsule

Now that we have prepared all the code that makes up the capsule containing the Depot object, we need to compile it and build the final executable. Up to now, we haven't compiled up the shared application code, so we'll do that now. We're not introducing anything new here so we'll just go right ahead:

```
cc -c -I. -I$DAIS_ROOT/include misc.c
cc -c -I. -I$DAIS_ROOT/include linear.c
```

misc.c contains the shared miscellaneous functions for (de-)stringifying the object reference of the PNS, accessing the application object state, and exception handling. linear.c contains the linear list database implementation.

Similar commands are used to compile the code that is specific to the Depot object capsule:

```
cc -c -I. -I$DAIS_ROOT/include depot_main.c
cc -c -I. -I$DAIS_ROOT/include central.c
```

If all has gone well, we just need to combine the object files that we have just created into the final executable:

```
cc -o central depot_main.o central.o \
    misc.o linear.o c_pnamesvc.o \
    m_pnamesvc.o m_central.o s_central.o \
    -L$DAIS_ROOT/lib -ldais -lxti -lnsl
```

This needs just a little more explanation, although it should mostly be familiar to experienced C programmers. The **-o central** says that we want to create the final executable in a file called central. We next have the list of compiled application, stub, and skeleton code that we want linked. As the Depot capsule is a server for an interface in file central.idl, we need to include the corresponding server skeleton and optimized marshalling code. The Depot capsule is also a client of the Pseudo-Name Service so we need to include the stub and optimized marshalling code generated from pnamesvc.idl. Finally, we have the set of libraries containing the implementations of the ORB functions and the underlying communications support. As we mentioned in Chapter 23, we are assuming that the installation point for DAIS on your system is at $DAIS_ROOT. If all proceeds as planned, we have created the first capsule of our application.

24.7.6 Pseudo-Name Server

The Pseudo-Name Server capsule is very similar to the Depot capsule in that it contains an in-store database that, this time, holds the associations between object instance names and object references, and there is only one of them in the system. In fact, all the way down to the application initialization the two are practically identical except for the names. There are some differences, though, so we'll have a closer look.

In the PNS object constructor, instead of registering the object reference with the PNS (which would not be very useful!), we write the object reference to a file. This is all hidden inside the function **ref_to_file()**, which can be found in misc.c, if you are interested. The application initialization is also very slightly different because the PNS only needs to initialize an empty database.

When it comes to building the capsule, we have already compiled the shared code, so we don't need to do that again. We just need to compile the PNS-specific code:

```
cc -c -I. -I$DAIS_ROOT/include pname_main.c
cc -c -I. -I$DAIS_ROOT/include pnamesvc.c
```

and then link it all to make the PNS capsule:

```
cc -o PNS pname_main.o pnamesvc.o \
   misc.o linear.o s_pnamesvc.o \
   m_pnamesvc.o \
   -L$DAIS_ROOT/lib -ldais -lxti -lnsl
```

The PNS capsule is not a client of any interface so we just have to include the server skeleton and optimized marshalling code generated from pnamesvc.idl in the link.

We have now explored the DAIS specifics when connecting to the ORB and BOA; the creation of objects, including application state handling, server method implementation function signatures, and building of application capsules. We've done the hard part; the rest is just more of the same with a couple more fine details to cover.

CHAPTER 25

Coding the Depot in C++

25.1 C++ MAPPING COMPONENT

This section, and the one that follows, present C++ language code common to every C++ language ORB. If you're working the example in PowerBroker, Orbix, ORB Plus, or NEO, you need to read both of these sections before skipping to the section specific to your ORB. Don't try to skip this part; there's relatively little ORB-specific code, and all of the important stuff (like the interfaces and the functionality!) is worked in common code.

By the way, you should have just read the description of the language-independent functionality of the Depot in Section 24.1. If you didn't, turn back and read it now; it tells what we're going to do in this chapter. We summarized the OMG IDL-C++ language mapping in Chapter 8, and will take advantage of the material we presented there. We will also fill in some details that we skipped, when we need them here.

The IDL interfaces define, via the language mapping, the C++ language API for all of our objects. Your IDL compiler will produce the header files you need to bind to stubs and skeletons, but you still need to know the form of the declarations and invocations because they define the starting point for your coding project. That's what we'll cover in this section.

The declarations that we present here are probably in a file with a name like Depot.h (the exact name for your product was listed in its section of Chapter 23), produced by your IDL compiler so you won't have to type them in yourself. But you will need to be aware of their form (which is dictated by the standard OMG IDL C++ language mapping) when you connect with the stubs and skeletons. Here are the details you need to know.

456

25.1.1 C++ Generated from the Depot IDL Definitions

Recall the IDL definition of interface **Depot**:

```
module CentralOffice {
    interface Depot {
        void FindItemInfo(
            in AStore::AStoreId  StoreId,
            in POS::Barcode      Item,
            in long              Quantity,
            out AStore::ItemInfo IInfo)
            raises (AStore::BarcodeNotFound);
    };
};
```

This is translated by a standard IDL compiler into the following C++ definitions:

```
#include <CORBA.h>
namespace CentralOffice {
    class Depot : public CORBA::Object {
    public:
        virtual void FindItemInfo
                        (Store::AStoreId StoreId,
                         const char* Item,
                         CORBA::Long Quantity,
                         AStore::ItemInfo*& IInfo
                        )
    };
};
```

Because interface **Depot** is defined in a module called **CentralOffice**, the C++ class **Depot** is defined in a C++ *namespace* of the same name. (The **namespace** construct in C++ provides name scoping in much the same way as the **module** construct in IDL.) If the target C++ compiler does not support namespaces, a class of the same name is used instead (and all of the members of this class are made public). Class **Depot** defines the function(s) that a C++ client can invoke on an object of type **Depot**; it also defines the function(s) that must be implemented at the server-side.

Class **Depot** derives from the standard class **CORBA::Object**, from which it inherits CORBA support. The single IDL operation **FindItemInfo()** is translated into a single public member function of the same name. The first two parameters (**StoreId** and **Item**) are translated in a very straightforward manner. In C++, the type of parameter **Quantity** becomes **CORBA::Long**, which is a 32-bit quantity defined in the standard header file **CORBA.h**. The normal C++ type **long** is not used because its size varies from machine to machine.

The last parameter, **IInfo**, is defined as an IDL structure. Its C++ equivalent therefore is a (reference to a) pointer to a structure. The caller of the operation passes a pointer as the last parameter, and, once the call is completed, this pointer will point to the desired structure. The storage space for this structure will be allocated by the ORB.

25.1.2 C++ Generated from the Pseudo-Name Service IDL Definitions

The IDL definition of the Pseudo-Name Service:

```
interface PseudoNameService
{
    void  BindName(in string ObjectName,
                   in Object ObjectRef);
    Object ResolveName(in string ObjectName);
};
```

is translated into the following C++:

```
#include <CORBA.h>
class PseudoNameService:
                        public CORBA::Object {
public:
    virtual void BindName
                        (const char*        ObjectName,
                         CORBA::Object_ptr ObjectRef);
    virtual CORBA::Object_ptr ResolveName
                        (const char*        ObjectName);
};
```

Each of the two IDL operations is translated into a C++ public member function. The parameter types to **BindName()** are translated, respectively, into a simple C++ string type (**char***) and to the object reference type **CORBA::Object_ptr**. This reference type is defined in the standard header file **CORBA.h**. Variables of this type act like pointers in C++, and they can reference any instance of a class that derives from **CORBA::Object**; in a global sense, they can reference any CORBA object in the system.

The parameter type of operation **ResolveName()** is also translated into a **char***; and its return type is the C++ object reference type.

25.2 COMMON FUNCTIONALITY: DEPOT IMPLEMENTATION

Now we need to code the functionality of the Depot object and the Pseudo-Name Service object. There's almost nothing ORB-specific about this, so we'll do it all in this section. If you're working the example by hand, you'll need to type all of this code into your **.cc** files as we go along. At the end of this section, we'll send you off to the section on your specific ORB for final coding, compilation, and linking.

The IDL interface for the **Depot** was shown in Section 25.1.1. In this section, we'll implement this interface in C++.

Throughout the C++ code in this book, we have adopted the convention that interface I is implemented by C++ class **I_i**; hence, interface **Depot** will be implemented by class **Depot_i**. The code for the depot is given in the **Central** directory, and all filenames given here are relative to that directory. The IDL definition for **Depot** can be found in a file called Central.idl.

The overall system requires only one object of interface **Depot**. This is created in a server called **CentralSrv**, and the code for this is also given here.

The remainder of this section explains the code in the following order:

1. the code for the server **CentralSrv**,
2. the declaration and then implementation of class **Depot_i**.

25.2.1 The CentralSrv server

The actions of this **main()** routine are to:

- initialize the ORB by calling **ORB_init()** and **BOA_init()**;
- find the system's **PseudoNameService** object (line 17) using the **FindPNS()** function, which is explained in Section 25.3;
- create an instance of class **Depot_i**, passing it an object reference to the system's **PseudoNameService** object so that the **Depot_i** object can register itself with the Pseudo-Name Service (line 18);
- call the **impl_is_ready()** function on the BOA to inform it that the implementation is ready to accept incoming operation calls (line 19); in this case, operations calls on the **Depot_i** object. This function takes the server name as a parameter.

Here is the code (filename: Srv_Main.cc):

```
1    #include <iostream.h>
2    #include <stdio.h>
3    #include "Depot_i.h"
```

```
4      #include "../PNS/FindPNS.h"
5
6      int main(int argc, char* argv[]) {
7        CORBA::ORB_var orb =
8                  CORBA::ORB_init(argc,argv,"PRIMER_ORB");
9        CORBA::BOA_var boa =
10                 orb->BOA_init(argc,argv,"");
11
12
13       CentralOffice::Depot_var dep1;
14       PseudoNameService_var pns;
15
16       try {
17         pns=FindPNS(orb);
18         dep1 = new Depot_i(pns);
19         boa->impl_is_ready("CentralSrv");
20       }
21       catch(...) {
22         cerr << "ERROR Starting Depot Server"
23               << endl;
24         return 1;
25       }
26
27       return 0;
28     }
```

The actions of the **main()** function are coded within a **try** block, and the corresponding **catch** clause reports any exceptions that are raised.

25.2.2   Depot Implementation: Class Declaration

The class definition of **Depot_i** is shown in this subsection. The member function **FindItemInfo()** corresponds to the operation of the same name; its parameters and return type are dictated by the standard mapping from IDL to C++. In addition, class **Depot_i** adds other members required at the implementation level. Here, a member variable of type **DepotData** and a constructor are added. C++ type **DepotData** will be explained later in this chapter. In general, any number of member functions and variables can be added at this implementation stage.

```
// (filename: Depot_i.h)
1      #include "Central.hh"
2      #include "PNS.hh"
3      #include "DepotData.h"
```

```
4
5      class Depot_i :
6               public CentralOffice::DepotBOAImpl {
7        DepotData m_items;
8      public:
9        Depot_i(PseudoNameService_ptr PNS);
10        virtual void FindItemInfo
11               (AStore::AStoreId StoreId,
12               const char* Item,
13               CORBA::Long Quantity,
14               AStore::ItemInfo*& IInfo,
15        };
```

Other important details are:

▪ In line 6, **Depot_i** inherits from a BOA (Basic Object Adapter, explained in Section 5.6) class generated by the IDL compiler. This gives instances of class **Depot_i** the support they require to be CORBA objects. The name of the BOA class varies between the C++ ORBs; for example, it is **DepotBOAImpl** in Orbix and **Depot_base_impl** in PowerBroker. Only our servers (server **CentralSrv** here) are concerned with BOA classes; clients are not aware of them.

▪ In line 1, the file **Central.hh** is included; it contains the C++ definition of the IDL interface. It is automatically generated from the **Central.idl** file, which holds the definition of the **Depot** interface.

25.2.3 Depot Implementation: Class Implementation

The implementation of class **Depot_i** (filename Depot_i.cc) includes the following header files:

```
#include <fstream.h>
#include "Depot_i.h"
```

It also defines the following variables at the global level:

```
const int NITEMTYPES=3;
const char *depotdata_file = "depot.dat";
const char *itemTypesText[NITEMTYPES] =
                    {"FOOD","CLOTHES","OTHER"};
```

The last of these contains the string representation of the general classifications of the goods the **Depot** handles.

The constructor for class **Depot_i** is coded as follows. Its parameter is the object reference of the Pseudo-Name Service, with which it must register itself.

```
1    Depot_i::Depot_i(PseudoNameService_ptr PNS) {
2      AStore::ItemInfo loaditem;
3      loaditem.Item = new char[30];
4      loaditem.Name = new char[40];
5      char tempstring[30];
6      int i;
7      ifstream is(depotdata_file);
8      if (!is) {
9        cerr << "Could not open depot data file "
10              << depotdata_file << endl;
11       return;
12     }
13     while (!is.eof()) {
14       is >> loaditem.Item;
15       is >> loaditem.Name;
16       is >> loaditem.Quantity;
17       is >> loaditem.Itemcost;
18       // Read in the string containing the
19        // item type and convert it to an
20       // enumerated value
21       is >> tempstring;
22       i=0;
23       while (i < NITEMTYPES &&
24         strcmp(tempstring,itemTypesText[i]) != 0)
25         i++;
26       if (i < NITEMTYPES) {
27         loaditem.Itemtype=AStore::ItemTypes(i);
28         m_items.Insert(loaditem);
29       }
30     }
31     // Register the object with the name service
32     try {
33       PNS->BindName("Depot",this);
34     }
35     catch(...) {
36       cerr << "Trouble Binding the Depot" << endl;
37     }
38   }
```

The **Depot_i** object holds a search structure describing the items that it handles. This is held in its **m_items** member variable, which internally contains structures of type **AStore::ItemInfo**. The variable **m_items** is populated by reading lines from a data file (**depot.dat**).

The member variable **m_items** is of type **DepotData**, a C++ class that is used in the implementation of the Depot interface. **m_items** is used to store and then efficiently find descriptions of the items that the **Depot** stocks. Class **DepotData** is not directly related to any IDL definition since it does not need to be directly accessed by remote clients. It is explained later in this section.

Each line of **depot.dat** is read and handled in turn by the **Depot_i** constructor. Each item of a line is read into an object of type **Astore::Item-Info**, which can hold the description of one stock item. That **ItemInfo** object is then inserted into the **m_items** variable using the **insert()** function of class **DepotData**.

The code starts (lines 2 to 4) by creating and initializing a structure of type **AStore::ItemInfo**. It then opens the file depot.dat (line 7), and loops (line 13) until each line has been processed. Each line is read in the following order: item barcode, item name, stock level, item cost, and item type. The first four of these are easily read (lines 14 to 17). The item type is read as a string (line 21), and then converted into an enumerate value (of type **AStore::ItemTypes**). This conversion is done by comparing (line 24) the string read with each of the strings in the **itemTypesText** variable, which holds the strings **"FOOD"**, **"CLOTHES"**, and **"OTHER"**. If a match is found, then the index into the **itemTypesText** array is converted (line 27) into an enumerate constant of type **AStore::ItemTypes**.

By line 28, the structure has been fully read, and it is inserted into the **m_items** search structure. The final action of the constructor is to register the new object with the Pseudo-Name Service (line 33).

The code for the member function **FindItemInfo()** is shown next. The **in** parameters to this function include the **Barcode** of the item, and there is an **out** parameter (**IInfo**) of type **AStore::ItemInfo**. The function searches for the **Barcode** using the **m_items** member variable, using its **Locate()** function. This function returns a Boolean to indicate whether the item has been found. If the item has been found, the **IInfo** parameter will be updated to contain details of the found item. Otherwise, the **FindItemInfo()** function raises a **BarcodeNotFound** exception back to the client that called it.

```
1       void Depot_i::FindItemInfo
2                   ( AStore::AStoreId StoreId,
3                     const char* Item,
4                     CORBA::Long Quantity,
5                     AStore::ItemInfo*& IInfo) {
```

```
6              IInfo = new AStore::ItemInfo;
7              if (m_items.Locate(Item,*IInfo)) {
8              }
9              else {
10                 // Raise the exception here
11                 throw(AStore::BarcodeNotFound(Item));
12             }
13         }
```

On line 6, the **out** parameter **IInfo** is initialized to a new **AStore::ItemInfo** structure. The **in** parameter **Item** is then used to search for the required item in the **Depot**'s search structure (line 7). If the item is found, the **IInfo** parameter will have been updated, and the actions of the function are complete. If the item is not found, a new exception is created on line 11, and thrown to the caller.

Class **Depot_i** uses class **DepotData** as the type of its member variable **m_items**. Class **DepotData** is used as a transitory store and quick-search facility for the items known to the **Depot**. The remainder of this subsection shows the implementation of this class, which is declared as follows (filename DepotData.h):

```
#include "Central.hh"

// The depot stores all info about the products
// as a binary tree.
// This is the basic tree node:

class TreeNode {
public:
  TreeNode *m_left;
  TreeNode *m_right;
  AStore::ItemInfo m_item;

  TreeNode() : m_left(0), m_right(0) {}
};

class DepotData {
  TreeNode *m_root;
  virtual unsigned long LocateNode
                    (const char* bc,
                     TreeNode * &ret_node);
public:
  DepotData() : m_root(0) {}
  virtual unsigned long Locate
```

```
                   (const char* bc,
                    AStore::ItemInfo &i);
    virtual void Insert(const AStore::ItemInfo &i);
};
```

As well as a constructor, class **DepotData** defines member functions **Insert()** and **Locate()**. The former adds an item description, and the latter searches for an item and updates its second parameter to contain all of the information known about it. **Locate()** returns a Boolean to indicate the success or failure of the search.

To store its data, the **DepotData** class uses a binary search tree (member variable **m_root**), the nodes of which are of class **TreeNode** (another C++ class that is not directly related to the IDL definitions). **TreeData** is declared as follows:

```
class TreeNode {
public:
    TreeNode *m_left, *m_right;
    AStore::ItemInfo m_item;
    TreeNode() : m_left(0), m_right(0) {}
};
```

TreeData holds its left (**m_left**) and right (**m_right**) pointers and an item of type **AStore::ItemInfo**. It provides a simple a constructor to initialize its left and right pointers. For simplicity, the two pointers and the item pointer are public, but it would also have been easy to add access functions to set and get these values.

The code for **Locate()** and **Insert()** is in file DepotData.cc.

We will discuss the code for the function **DepotItem::Insert()** first. The first action of this function is to find the correct position for the new data in its binary search tree. This is done on line 7 using the private member function **LocateNode()**. This returns the Boolean value **false** if the item being inserted does not already exist in the binary tree. Line 7 also tests the return value of **LocateNode()**. If the item is not already present, line 8 creates a new node of the binary tree, and line 9 assigns it to its **m_item** member variable (the left and right pointers will be automatically set to zero by the constructor of **TreeNode**).

The next step is to attach the new node to the existing binary tree. If the tree is currently empty, line 11 makes the new node the root node. Otherwise, line 14 tests whether the new node should be added to the left or the right of the correct node position (the correct position is returned as the second (reference) parameter of **LocateNode()**). Line 15 attaches the new node to the left; line 17 attaches it to the right.

Finally, if **LocateNode()** indicates that the item is already recorded in the binary tree, line 20 replaces the old value with the new value:

```
1       #include <iostream.h>
2       #include "DepotData.h"
3
4       void DepotData::Insert
5                               (const AStore::ItemInfo &i) {
6         TreeNode *temp;
7         if (!LocateNode(i.Item,temp)) {
8           TreeNode *new_node = new TreeNode;
9           new_node->m_item = i;
10          if (m_root==0) {
11            m_root=new_node;
12            return;
13          }
14          if (strcmp(i.Item,temp->m_item.Item)<0)
15            temp->m_left=new_node;
16          else
17            temp->m_right=new_node;
18        }
19        else {
20          temp->m_item=i;
21        }
22      }
```

The private function **LocateNode()** performs the normal binary search algorithm, branching to the left if the sought-after position is less than the current node, and to the right if it is greater. The code, without further explanation, is as follows:

```
unsigned long DepotData::LocateNode
                    (const char* bc,
                     TreeNode * &ret_node) {
  int compare;
  ret_node=m_root;
  if (ret_node==0) return 0;
  compare=strcmp(bc,ret_node->m_item.Item);
  while (compare!=0) {
    if (compare<0) {
      if (ret_node->m_left==0)
        return 0;
      else
        ret_node=ret_node->m_left;
```

```
      }
    else {
      if (ret_node->m_right==0)
        return 0;
      else
        ret_node=ret_node->m_right;
    }
    compare=strcmp(bc,ret_node->m_item.Item);
  }
  return 1;
}
```

The **DepotData::Locate()** function is simply coded using the private function **LocateNode()**:

```
1      unsigned long DepotData::Locate(const char* bc,
2                               AStore::ItemInfo &i) {
3        TreeNode *t;
4        unsigned long status=LocateNode(bc,t);
5        if (status)
6          i=t->m_item;
7        return status;
8      }
```

Line 4 attempts to find the item in the binary tree; if it is present, the parameter **i** is updated to point to the **AStore::ItemInfo** structure found. The Boolean return value indicates whether the item was found.

25.3 PSEUDO-NAME SERVICE IMPLEMENTATION

The Pseudo-Name Service provides a shared facility for the components of the system, allowing them to register and find objects. This section tells how the PNS is implemented in C++, and also describes (in Section 25.3.4) the function **FindPNS()**, which is used by several of the objects in our system to find the PNS itself.

Interface **PseudoNameService** defines the IDL, and this is implemented by C++ class **pname_i**. (Our convention suggested that we should use the name **PseudoNameService_i** for this class, but we broke with the convention here to show that any C++ class name can be chosen.) An object of this type is created by a server called PNS. This subsection gives the code for server PNS, then for class **pname_i**, and, finally, for **FindPNS**.

The code for this server appears in the PNS subdirectory, and the filenames specified here are relative to that directory.

25.3.1 The PNS Server

The actions of this **main()** routine are to:

1. Initialize the ORB by calling **ORB_init()** and **BOA_init()**.
2. Create an instance of class **pname_i**.
3. Call the **impl_is_ready()** function on the BOA to inform it that this server is ready to accept incoming operation calls; in this case, operations call on the **pname_i** object.

This code is as follows (file name Srv_Main.cc):

```
1       #include <iostream.h>
2       #include <stdio.h>
3       #include "PNS_i.h"
4
5       int main(int argc, char* argv[])
6       {
7         CORBA::ORB_var orb =
8             CORBA::ORB_init(argc,argv,"PRIMER_ORB");
9         CORBA::BOA_var boa =
10            orb->BOA_init(argc,argv,"");
11
12        PseudoNameService_var PNS1;
13
14        try {
15          PNS1 = new pname_i(orb);
16          boa->impl_is_ready("PNSrv");
17        }
18        catch(...) {
19          cerr << "Error Starting Pseudo Nameserver"
20                  << endl;
21          return 1;
22        }
23
24        return 0;
25      }
```

You should reread the explanation of the **main()** function of the **CentralServer** server (which creates the object of interface **Depot**) if the structure of this code is not familiar to you. Lines 7 to 10 initialize the ORB; line 15 creates the object with interface **PNS**. Because the variable **PNS1** is of type **PseudoNameService_var**, the memory management of this object reference is handled automatically; in particular, the object reference is deleted once the variable **PNS1** goes out of scope. Line 16 calls the **impl_is_ready()** function.

25.3.2 Pseudo-Name Service Implementation: Class Declaration

Class **pname_i** is declared as follows (filename: pns_i.h):

```
#include "PNS.hh"
#include "PNSData.h"

class pname_i :
          public virtual PseudoNameServiceBOAImpl {
  PNData m_data;
public:
  pname_i(CORBA::ORB_ptr orb);
  virtual void BindName (const char* ObjectName,
                         CORBA::Object_ptr ObjectRef);
  virtual CORBA::Object_ptr ResolveName
                            (const char* ObjectName);
};
```

It declares a constructor and two member variables, **BindName()** and **ResolveName()**, both of which correspond to the IDL operations in interface **PseudoNameService**. It declares one member variable, **m_data**; this provides it with a search tree to store and find the object references that are registered with it.

25.3.3 PNS Implementation: Class Implementation

The constructor for **pname_i** is coded as follows (filename PNS_i.cc):

```
1      #include <iostream.h>
2      #include <fstream.h>
3      #include "PNS_i.h"
4
5      pname_i::pname_i(CORBA::ORB_ptr orb) {
6        ofstream os("PNS.dat");
7        if (os) {
8          char* refstring =
9                    orb->object_to_string(this);
10         os << refstring;
11         CORBA::string_free(refstring);
12       }
```

```
13          else {
14            cerr << "Error writing Pseudo Name-Service"
15                    << " object reference" << endl;
16          }
17       }
```

The clients and servers in the system must be able to find the Pseudo-Name Service, and we have decided to do this by giving each client and server a file (**PNS.dat**) that holds the stringified object reference for the **PseudoNameService** object within the **PNS** server. This file is output by the constructor of class **pname_i**; then this file needs to be copied to the clients and servers in the system. The function **object_to_string()** is called by the constructor (line 9) to find the stringified object reference of the **pname_i** object, and this is output to the file. Finally, on line 11, the string is freed using the standard **string_free()** function.

The **m_data** member variable of **pname_i** is a binary search tree (of type **PNData**); this maps from strings (registered names for objects) to object references. The code for class **PNData** is similar to that for class **DepotData** used by class **Depot_i**, and it is given in files **PNSData.h** and **PNSData.cc**.

The two classes **PNData** and **DepotData** differ from each other only in their internal datatypes. A better solution may have been to define a C++ template class that could have been the basis for the **DepotData** and **PNData** classes, but it was not safe to depend on the wide availability of the template facility in C++ when we wrote the code for this example.

Returning to the code for class **pname_i**, its **BindName()** function is passed a name (parameter **ObjectName**) and an object reference (parameter **ObjectRef**). It is coded simply by inserting the name to object reference mapping into the **m_data** member variable, which is of type **PNData** (filename PNS_i.cc):

```
1        void pname_i:: BindName (const char* ObjectName,
2                      CORBA::Object_ptr ObjectRef) {
3          m_data.Insert(ObjectName,
4                CORBA::Object::_duplicate(ObjectRef));
5          cout << "Registering object " << ObjectName
6                << endl;
7        }
```

The insertion into **m_data** is coded on line 3. The first parameter is the name under which the object is to be registered (the parameter **ObjectName**); the second parameter is the object reference (the parameter **ObjectRef**). Note that on line 4, the reference count of the object reference is increased, by calling **_duplicate()**, before it is inserted. The ORB rules state that this must be done. (The reference count of the **ObjectRef** object reference parameter is automatically incremented at the start of the function call, and it is automatically decremented at the end of the call. If the function wishes to retain a reference to the object, then it must call **_duplicate()**).

We now turn to the last function, **ResolveName()**. Its implementation uses the **Locate()** (line 6) function on the **m_data** member variable to search for the required object (specified by the **ObjectName** parameter) in the **m_data** member variable. If the object is found, the temporary variable **p** is updated to reference it. The **_duplicate()** function must be called (line 8) on the found object reference so that the **pname_i** object can continue to hold that object reference (otherwise, its reference count would fall to zero, and the reference would be deleted from the **pname_i** object's address space). If the object is not found, the **CORBA nil** object reference is returned (line 13).

The code is as follows (filename: PNS_i.cc):

```
1     CORBA::Object_ptr pname_i:: ResolveName
2                         (const char* ObjectName) {
3      cout << "Looking for object " << ObjectName
4           << endl;
5      CORBA::Object_ptr p;
6      if (m_data.Locate(ObjectName,p)) {
7       cout << "found it" << endl;
8       return CORBA::Object::_duplicate(p);
9      }
10      else
11      {
12        cout << "failed to find object" << endl;
13        return CORBA::Object::_nil();
14      }
15    }
```

25.3.4 FindPNS Definition and Implementation

Since many of the components of the system need to find the Pseudo-Name Service, we have provided a function **FindPNS()** that returns an object reference for it (filename FindPNS.h):

```
#include <CORBA.h>
#include "PNS.hh"

PseudoNameService_ptr FindPNS(CORBA::ORB_ptr orb);
```

The implementation of this function reads the stringified object reference of the Pseudo-Name Service from the file PNS.dat and converts it to an object reference. (Recall that the Pseudo-Name Service creates the file PNS.dat by taking the object reference of its **PseudoNameService** object and converting this to a string). The code for **FindPNS()** is as follows (filename FindPNS.cc):

```cpp
#include <iostream.h>
#include <fstream.h>
#include <CORBA.h>
#include "FindPNS.h"

PseudoNameService_ptr FindPNS(CORBA::ORB_ptr orb) {
  char refstring[1024];
  ifstream is("PNS.dat");
  if (is) {
    is.get(refstring,1023);
    return PseudoNameService::_narrow(
            orb->string_to_object(refstring));
  }
  else {
    cerr << "Error finding pseudo nameservice reference"
         << endl;
    return PseudoNameService::_nil();
  }
}
```

The function reads the contents of the file into the variable **refstring**, and then it calls the function **orb->string_to_object()** to convert the string to an object reference. The return value of **string_to_object()** is of type **CORBA::Object_ptr**, so this is narrowed to the type **PseudoNameService** by calling the static function **_narrow()**. If the file cannot be read, the nil object reference is returned.

25.4 EXCEPTION HANDLING

The standard C++ method of handling exceptions is new enough that some C++ compilers on the market still do not support it. As a result, the IDL C++ mapping specifies two methods of handling exceptions: standard and explicit. We've illustrated both in this book: ORB Plus uses explicit exception handling, while PowerBroker, Orbix, and NEO use C++ native exception handling.

The operation prototype used with the CentralOffice IDL module varies depending on whether standard C++ exceptions or explicit exception checking is used:

```
module CentralOffice {
    interface Depot {
        void FindItemInfo(
            in AStore::AStoreId    StoreId
            ,in POS::Barcode       Item
            ,in long               Quantity
            ,out AStore::ItemInfo  IInfo)
            raises (AStore::BarcodeNotFound);
    };
};
```

For standard C++ exceptions, the prototype is:

```
void Depot_i::FindItemInfo (AStore::AStoreId StoreId,
                            const char* Item,
                            CORBA::Long Quantity,
                            AStore::ItemInfo*& IInfo)
```

For explicit exception checking, the prototype is:

```
void Depot_i::FindItemInfo (AStore::AStoreId StoreId,
                            const char* Item,
                            CORBA::Long Quantity,
                            AStore::ItemInfo*& IInfo,
                            CORBA::Environment &IT_env)
```

The explicit exception handling prototype contains an additional parameter, **CORBA::Environment**, which is checked within a program to see if an exception occurred.

25.4.1 Standard C++ Exceptions

The standard C++ exception format is illustrated by its use in the function **FindItemInfo**. This function searches for the item that matches a bar code. If the item is found, the ItemInfo structure is returned to the caller. If the item is not found, an exception of the type **BarcodeNotFound** is thrown, as illustrated in this code:

```
void Depot_i::FindItemInfo (AStore::AStoreId StoreId,
                            const char* Item,
                            CORBA::Long Quantity,
                            AStore::ItemInfo*& IInfo){
    IInfo = new AStore::ItemInfo;
```

```
            if (m_items.Locate(Item,*IInfo)) {
            }
            else {
              // Raise the exception here
              throw(AStore::BarcodeNotFound(Item));
            }
    }
```

The exception is caught in the POSTerminal **SendBarcode** function, as shown next. This function has a catch for the **BarcodeNotFound** exception; it is a user exception that was defined in the IDL. There is also a catch specified for system exceptions.

```
void  POSTerminal_i:: SendBarcode (const char* Item){
  if (!LoggedIn())
    return;
   ...............................
  try {
    m_storeAccessRef->FindPrice(m_itemBarcode,
                        m_itemQuantity,
                          price,taxablePrice,ItemInf);
  }
  catch(const AStore::BarcodeNotFound& bcnf) {
    m_itemQuantity = 1;
    cerr << "Invalid Barcode Found" << endl;
    return;
  }
  catch (...) {
    m_itemQuantity = 1;
    cerr << "Error in find Price" << endl;
    return;
  }
   ...............................
}
```

25.4.2 Explicit C++ Exception Checking

In C++, CORBA exceptions can also be checked explicitly by use of the CORBA::Environment parameter. Explicit exception handling is illustrated next in the FindItemInfo function, which, if the item is not found, the BarCodeNotFound variable is allocated on the heap, and it is passed as a parameter to the exception operation of the IT_env instance of the environment object.

```
void Depot_i::FindItemInfo (AStore::AStoreId StoreId,
                            const char* Item,
                            CORBA::Long Quantity,
                            AStore::ItemInfo*& IInfo,
                            CORBA::Environment &IT_env) {
   IT_env.clear();
   IInfo = new AStore::ItemInfo;
   if (m_items.Locate(Item,*IInfo)) {
   }
   else {
      AStore::BarcodeNotFound *bcnf =
          new AStore::BarcodeNotFound;
      bcnf->item = Item;
      // Raise the exception here
      IT_env.exception(bcnf);
   }
}
```

The **SendBarcode** function invoked the **FindItemInfo** function. Before it can use the **ItemInfo** returned, it must first check to see whether an exception was returned. It does this by testing the environment object parameter to see if it contains an exception. The **IT_env.exception** function is invoked to return a pointer to the exception object. If the returned object pointer is **NULL**, then an exception did not occur. If an exception occurred, then the object pointer is checked to see what type of exception occurred. This is accomplished by attempting to narrow the pointer to the **AStore::BarcodeNotFound** object. If the narrowing succeeds, then it is this user exception; if the narrow fails, then it is a system exception.

```
void  POSTerminal_i:: SendBarcode (const POS::Barcode Item)
   {
            . . . . . . . . . . . . . . . . .

   m_storeAccessRef->FindPrice(m_itemBarcode,
         m_itemQuantity, price, taxablePrice,
         ItemInf, IT_env);
   if (IT_env.exception() != NULL)
      if (AStore::BarcodeNotFound::_narrow
         (IT_env.exception()) != NULL)
         {
            m_itemQuantity = 1;
            cout << "Invalid Barcode Found" << endl;
            IT_env.clear();
            return;
         }
```

```
        else
          {
            cout << "Error in find Price" << endl;
            return;
          }

              . . . . . . . . . . . . . . . . .
      }
```

25.4.3 Implementation Summary

If you've been typing in the code as you went along, your depot and PNS code are nearly complete. You're ready to make just a few adjustments for your specific ORB, and prepare to run your Depot and PNS objects. Granted, you won't be able to test them until you've completed a few more chapters, but this does give you a chance to fire up a server for the first time.

25.5 CONNECTING TO THE ORB AND BOA, AND STARTING THE DEPOT OBJECT

The Depot and PNS objects run in servers, and the server-side connection to the ORB has not been standardized by OMG to the same extent as the client. The organization is taking care of this now, but until they finish up, we'll have to do a little more of the work ourselves in the form of ORB-specific code. That code is presented in the remainder of this chapter, along with product-specific procedures that create and fire up your objects.

At this point, go to the section in this chapter on your specific ORB product and follow its procedures to get your objects ready and running. After you've finished, go to Section 27.1 to start coding the Store object.

25.6 THE POWERBROKER IMPLEMENTATION OF THE DEPOT

This section describes the PowerBroker implementation of the Depot and Pseudo-Name Service. The primary places where the Depot implementation differs from the references in Sections 25.2 and 25.3 are the base class names for **Depot_i** and the use of PowerBroker's Event service object.

The changes detailed in the following subsections must be made to complete the Depot and PseudoNameService implementations.

25.6.1 PowerBroker CORBA Include Files

In general, PowerBroker declarations of CORBA objects such as **BOA** and **ORB** are included for you by the generated source code files. For example, for the store IDL file Store.idl, the generated header store.h includes corba.h. The object implementation header file store_i.h must include Store.h.

Assuming PowerBroker has been installed according to the *PowerBroker Installation Guide*, the environment variable **PBHOME** should contain the installation directory. The following include statement allows application code to directly include PowerBroker include files:

```
// file store_i.h
#include <pbroker/corba/corba.h>
```

To instruct the C++ compiler or IDL compiler where to find this include file, use the -I option:

```
%idlc -I$PBHOME/include Store.idl

%CC -c -I$PBHOME/include store_i.C
```

25.6.2 Base Class Names

Idlc, the PowerBroker IDL compiler, generates a base implementation class for each IDL interface. Implementation classes, such as **Depot_i**, are derived from this base class. The naming convention followed by idlc is to append the string **_base_server** to the interface name. Thus, for the interface Depot, declare **Depot_i** as:

```
#include <Central.h>
class Depot_i : public CentralOffice::Depot_base_server
{
...
};
```

25.6.3 BOA::impl_is_ready

PowerBroker's implementation of the **ImplementationDef** interface is the class **XpsImplementationDef**. The CORBA 2.0 specification dictates that **impl_is_ready** take an **Implementationdef_ptr** as an argument; the call to **impl_is_ready** should be:

```
XpImplementationDef idef;
boa->impl_is_ready(&idef);
```

25.6.4 The PowerBroker Event Loop

The event loop allows the application process to detect and dispatch incoming requests such as method invocations from remote clients. Add the following code immediately after the "catch" block:

```
XpsEventService esvc;
esvc.mainloop();
```

25.6.5 Use of _out Classes for CORBA out and inout Arguments

For some IDL types, the C++ mapping defines a pointer-reference parameter type for the **inout** and **out** parameter passing modes. The C++ mapping requires that all operations support arguments of the IDL type's C++ type equivalent, as well as its **_var** counterpart. Unfortunately, many compilers do not support the pointer-reference return types required to support this behavior for **_vars**. To support **_var** behavior, PowerBroker defines an **_inout** or **_out** class type that is a "friend" of the **_var** class (which can have a side-effect on the **_var**'s internal pointer). Every time the C++ mapping defines a pointer-reference, idlc generates the **_inout** or **_out** type. This type can be treated as the expected pointer-reference type inside the application. For example, the signature of **FindItemInfo** is:

```
virtual void FindItemInfo(
     CORBA::Long          StoreId,
     const char           *Item,
     CORBA::Long          Quantity,
     AStore::ItemInfo_out  OutItemInfo);
```

but the implementation of **FindItemInfo** is the same as the described in the preceding Common Functionality section.

25.6.6 Compiling and Linking

Finally, you will need to compile and link the Depot and Pseudo-Name Service (PNS) programs. The object file for the main program should be linked with object files for all implementations that may be instantiated in your program. Additionally, because the Depot is a client of the Pseudo-Name Service, you need to link it with pnamesvc.o.

The directory $PBHOME/include must be searched for include files when you compile, and you must search the directory $PBHOME/lib for the library files libcorba.a and libpbroker.a when you link (actual library names are different when compiling under Windows NT).

The main functions for both programs are in files named Srv_Main.C. If you look on the diskette, notice that the Depot and PNS are in separate directories, but for simplicity, we'll ignore this issue here.

Type the following commands to compile the object implementation and the application mains for the depot:

```
% CC -c -I. -I$PBHOME/include depot_i.C Srv_Main.C
% CC -c -I. -I$PBHOME/include depot_i.C depotdata.C
```

To compile the Pseudo-Name Service, type:

```
% CC -c -I. -I$PBHOME/include Srv_Main.C PNS_i.C
% CC -c -I. -I$PBHOME/include Srv_Main.C PNSData.C
```

Type this command to link the Depot program:

```
% CC -o CentralSrv Srv_Main.o depot_i.o depotdata.o Central.o \
Central_s.o PNS.o pnsfind.o -L$PBHOME/lib -lpbcorba -lpbroker
```

Type this command to link the PNS program:

```
% CC -o PNS PNS_i.o PNSData.o Srv_Main.o PNS.o  PNS_s.o \
-L$PBHOME/lib -lpbcorba -lpbroker
```

25.7 DESCRIPTION OF THE ORBIX IMPLEMENTATION OF THE DEPOT AND PNS

This section explains how to compile and run the Depot and Pseudo-Name Service in Orbix. Since these are the first of the Orbix servers that we will discuss in depth, this explanation will give some background information that will not be repeated when the other servers are discussed later in the book.

25.7.1 Changes to the C++ Code for Orbix

Only one change needs to be made. The line written:

```
CORBA::ORB_var orb =
     CORBA::ORB_init(argc,argv,"PRIMER_ORB");
```

in the shared C++ code must be recoded to use the string **"Orbix"** instead of **"PRIMER_ORB"**.

Alternatively, the variable **CORBA::Orbix** can be used instead of finding Orbix using **ORB_init()** and **BOA_init()**. In fact, **ORB_init()** and

BOA_init() do not need to be called at all because initialization is handled automatically.

No other changes to the C++ code are required.

The Orbix code shown in this book uses the C++ exception handling mechanism. If your chosen C++ compiler does not support this feature, then Orbix will use the standard workaround; that is, it will add a **CORBA::Environment** variable as the last parameter to each C++ member function, as explained in Section 25.4.2.

25.7.2 Running Orbix

Orbix provides a daemon that allows clients to find servers in the system. In CORBA terms, this daemon implements the Implementation Repository. It must be run on each host that runs Orbix servers (but not necessarily on those that run just Orbix clients). It can be started by running the **orbixd** program provided in the Orbix **bin** directory. This can be done by the system administrator or by a programmer.

Before running the **orbixd** daemon, or running any client or utility command, the user should inform Orbix of the location of its configuration file. If this is in the file /etc/Orbix.cfg (on UNIX), then no further actions are required. Otherwise, the user must set the environment variable **IT_CONFIG_PATH** as follows (depending on whether the **csh** or **sh** are being used on UNIX):

```
# csh
setenv IT_CONFIG_PATH
              <pathname of the config. file>

# sh
IT_CONFIG_PATH=<pathname of the config. file>
export IT_CONFIG_PATH
```

25.7.3 Compiling Clients and Servers

Any of the popular C++ compilers can be used to compile the client and server code. Clients must be linked with the Orbix client-side library **ITclt**; servers must be linked with the Orbix server-side library **ITsrv**. These libraries are provided in the Orbix **lib** directory.

25.7.4 Registering Servers

Each Orbix server must be registered with Orbix, using the **putit** command. The server that creates the **Depot** object is called **CentralSrv**, and it can be registered as follows:

```
putit CentralSrv <full pathname of executable file
                      (CentralServer) for this server>
```

The server that creates the **PseudoNameService** object is called **PNSrv**, and it can be registered as follows:

```
putit PNSrv <full pathname of executable file
                 (PNSServer) for this server>
```

The benefit of registration with **putit** is that Orbix knows the name of the executable file that the server runs. Orbix can therefore launch the server if an invocation is made to one of its objects when the server is not currently running. Because clients are not launched by Orbix, they need not be registered.

The executable filename given to **putit** is specified as an absolute filename. It can be followed by any number of parameters for the executable code (this will be useful later when the store and output media servers are registered).

The **putit** command is one of a set of utility commands that help programmers and administrators to manage servers. Other commands include ones to list and remove servers, and to list the set of currently running servers. Each of these commands is implemented using an IDL interface to the Orbix Implementation Repository. This interface is published so that further commands can be added easily. On Windows and Windows NT, there is a graphical user interface to help manage servers. This tool uses the same IDL interface to communicate with the Orbix Implementation Repository.

Once registered, a server can be launched manually (for example, through the operating system's normal command line interpreter), or it will be started automatically when a client invokes an operation (or accesses an attribute) of one of the objects in the server. All of the CORBA *activation modes* are supported: shared, unshared, per-method-call and persistent, and some useful variations to these are provided.

25.7.5   Implementing an IDL Interface in Orbix

Each IDL interface must be implemented by a C++ class, which redefines each of the member functions that correspond to the attributes and operations of the IDL interface. (In some cases it may be useful to implement an interface a number of times within a single server; for example, to give different space/time trade-offs. This is supported in Orbix since more than one C++ implementation class can be written for any interface.) This class may inherit from the BOAImpl class generated by the IDL compiler. For example, to implement the interface **Depot**, the programmer would write a C++ class that inherits from class **DepotBOAImpl** (where BOA refers to the Basic Object Adapter, presented back in Section 5.6). By convention, the implementation class is called **Depot_i**:

```
class Depot_i : public DepotBOAImpl {
    // add member variables
public:
    // redefine all of the member functions that
    // correspond to IDL operations and attrs.
};
```

Instances of class **Depot_i** can be created by a server, and these automatically become CORBA objects. No special actions, other than the creation of an object, are required to make it a CORBA object:

```
Depot_i my_first_depot;
// constructor parameters are supported as normal.
```

Three C++ classes are associated with each IDL interface. For example, for interface **Depot**, the three classes are:

Class Name	Use
Depot	This gives the translation of IDL to C++. It is used mostly by the client. This class is a direct translation of the IDL interface; for example, there is one function for each operation.
DepotBOAImpl	The implementation class (by convention, **Depot_i**) may inherit from this class. This inheritance gives the implementation class all of the support it needs to instantiate CORBA objects. This class is used exclusively by the server side.
Depot_i	The implementation class, used exclusively by the server side. Any valid C++ class name can be chosen.

The client uses class **Depot**, and is not concerned with classes **Depot-BOAImpl** and **Depot_i**. This is just one example of the fact that the client is isolated from all implementation details, even to the extent of the chosen class name.

In some cases, programmers may not wish to have class **Depot_i** inherit from class **DepotBOAImpl**. This is supported because programmers can instead call the macro **DEF_TIE_Depot**, as follows:

```
class Depot_i {
    // add member variables
public:
    // define all of the member functions that
    // correspond to IDL operations and attrs.
};
DEF_TIE_Depot(Depot_i)
```

25.7.6 Makefile for the Depot and Pseudo-Name Service in Orbix

This section shows how to compile the PNS and Depot code. The PNS code should be compiled first (because this creates the file FindPNS.o, which is used by the other directories). On UNIX, typing **make** in each of the directories is all that is required to compile the code; and the procedure is equally straightforward on Windows.

Some of the makefile for the Pseudo-Name Service is shown here (directory PNS, file Makefile). Note that there are no special procedures: the code is simply compiled and linked with the server-side library. The full makefile includes rules for compiling PNSData.cc, PNS_i.cc, and Srv_Main.cc:

```
default:  PNSServer FindPNS.o

PNS_SERVER_OBJS = ../PNSS.o PNSData.o PNS_i.o \
                  Srv_Main.o

PNSServer: $(PNS_SERVER_OBJS)
    $(C++) $(C++FLAGS) -o PNSServer \
        $(PNS_SERVER_OBJS) $(LDFLAGS) -lITsrv
```

Here, $(C++) maps to the name of your chosen C++ compiler, and $(C++FLAGS) maps to the switches you may wish to add when calling this. $(LDFLAGS) maps to the linker's switches (normally just the pathname of the Orbix libraries). ITsrv is the name of the server-side library.

Some of the makefile for the depot follows (directory Central, file Makefile). The files Depot_i.cc, Srv_Main.cc, and DepotData.cc must be compiled as normal (the full makefile includes the rules for doing this):

```
default: CentralServer

Depot_SERVER_OBJS = ../CentralS.o ../StoreC.o \
                    ../PNSC.o \
                    Depot_i.o  Srv_Main.o \
                    DepotData.o ../PNS/FindPNS.o
```

```
CentralServer: $(Depot_SERVER_OBJS)
    $(C++) $(C++FLAGS) -o CentralServer  \
        $(Depot_SERVER_OBJS) $(LDFLAGS) -lITsrv
```

25.7.7 Binding to Orbix Objects

The Pseudo-Name Service is used in this book to help clients and servers to find the objects they must use in the system. As we described, this is a simple replacement for the CORBA Name Service, which we decided not to use in this version of the book (although it is provided by Orbix and some other ORBs). One remaining difficulty is that the clients and servers must find the Pseudo-Name Service itself, and we have enabled this by giving each client and server a file called PNS.dat that contains the stringified object reference of the **PseudoNameService** object (which runs in a server called **PNSrv**).

Orbix supports this approach; and it also supports the function **_bind()**, which sometimes simplifies the location of objects:

```
PseudoNameService_var the_pns;
// now find a PseudoNameService object in
// the PNSrv server:
the_pns = PseudoNameService::_bind(":PNSrv");
```

The **PNS.dat** file then is not required, and this may reduce your installation effort.

25.8 ORB PLUS

The basic steps in developing and running an ORB Plus application are:

1. Write the IDL interface for the object in the application.
2. Run the cidl compiler to translate the IDL interface into equivalent C++ code.
3. Write the declaration file (.h file) and the definition file (.cc file) for the C++ implementation class.
4. Write the **main()** for the server and link it with the object implementation.
5. Write one or more object clients.
6. Start the server process (in this example, the servers are started manually, but for persistent objects, the object locator can automatically start the servers).
7. Start the client(s).

The point-of-sale example is used to illustrate all these steps.

The ORB Plus code for the point-of-sale example is stored in the following subdirectories under the ORBPlus directory: Idl, Central, PNS, Store, POS. The system is built by issuing a **make** command in the ORB Plus directory. The **make** command generates four servers (Depot, Store, PseudoName, OutputMedia) and one client (point-of-sale client). All the servers are named Srv_Main. The client is named POSClt.

The ORB Plus code differs from the other C++ example code in the following ways:

- Explicit **CORBA::Environment** exception handling is used rather than standard C++ exceptions.
- The HPSOA object adapter is used rather than the BOA.

Explicit **CORBA::Environment** exception handling was described in Section 25.4.2. The example used in that section was from ORB Plus.

The HPSOA (HP Simplified Object Adapter) is written to provide better support for C++ implementation objects than the CORBA 2.0 BOA. The HPSOA provides the following functions:

HPSOA Functions

add_vs	Registers a name for the virtual server (VS) in which the object is executing.
run	Tells the HPSOA to start listening for requests.
shutdown	Tells the HPSOA to shut down all of its transports so that no more requests can be received by the process.

HPSOA VirtualServer Functions

register_impl	Registers a named object with a registered VS.
unregister_impl	Tells the VS to delete the registration for the given object.

There are two ways to register an object with the HPSOA:

- The **_this()** function of the object implementation, inherited from the base HPSOA::Object interface, dynamically generates an object reference for the object and registers it with the HPSOA. An object that always registers itself using **_this()** is considered *transient* since it is given different object references each time its server program is executed.
- The **VirtualServer::register_impl()** function allows an object to be registered with an identifier provided by the caller. As long as **HPSOA::add_vs()** is called every time with the same server name before

`register_impl()` is called, the registered object is considered to be persistent because it is given the same object reference every time its server program is executed.

The point-of-sale example uses only transient objects.

25.8.1 Writing Servers (Depot)

All the servers in this example have a similar structure, which is illustrated using Srv_Main.cc from Central directory. This is the server that represents the Depot.

```
#include <stdlib.h>
#include <iostream.h>
#include <stdio.h>
#include "Depot_i.h"
#include "../PNS/FindPNS.h"

int main(int argc, char* argv[]) {
```

Here are the steps to write a server in ORB Plus:

1. Create an instance of the **CORBA::Environment**.

    ```
    CORBA::Environment IT_env;
    ```

2. Initialize the ORB and return a reference to it. For ORB Plus, the identification used is **CORBA::HPORBid**.

    ```
    CORBA::ORB_var orb = CORBA::ORB_init(argc,
                            argv,CORBA::HPORBid, IT_env);
    ```

3. Check to see if an exception occurred when initializing the ORB.

    ```
    if (IT_env.exception()) {
       cerr << "ERROR Initializing ORB"<< endl;
       exit(EXIT_FAILURE);
    }
    ```

4. Initialize the HPSOA and return a reference to it.

    ```
    CORBA::HPSOA_var soa = orb->HPSOA_init(argc,
                            argv,CORBA::HPSOAid, IT_env);
    ```

5. Check to see if an exception occurred when initializing the HPSOA.

```
if (IT_env.exception()) {
    cerr << "ERROR Initializing HPSOA"<< endl;
    exit(EXIT_FAILURE);
}
```

6. Find the object reference for the PseudoNameServer.

```
PseudoNameService_var PNS=FindPNS(orb,IT_env);
```

7. Create an instance of the Depot_i C++ object. The CORBA object reference is created in the Depot_i constructor, in Depot_i.cc, using the _this() function.

```
Depot_i dep1(PNS, IT_env);
cout <<"central server up "<<endl;
```

8. The run method tells the HPSOA to start listening for requests.

```
    soa->run();
    return 0;
}
```

25.8.2 Writing Server Objects (Depot)

The first step in writing an object implementation, after running the cidl compiler, is to create a header file declaring the object implementation class. The cidl compiler produces an abstract base class from which the implementation class is derived. The following example (depot_i.h) illustrates a typical header file:

```
#ifndef depot_ih
#define depot_ih

#include "CentralServer.hh"
#include "PNSServer.hh"
#include "DepotData.h"
```

The Depot_i class is derived from the **HPSOA_CentralOffice::Depot** base class. The base class was generated by the cidl compiler for the Central.idl file:

```
class Depot_i : public HPSOA_CentralOffice::Depot {
  DepotData m_items;
public:
```

The constructor for the class:

```
Depot_i(PseudoNameService_ptr PNS,
        CORBA::Environment& IT_env);
```

The prototype of the **FindItemInfo** operation is shown next. This prototype must exactly match the prototype generated by the cidl compiler. Note the addition of the **CORBA::Environment** parameter.

```
virtual void FindItemInfo (AStore::AStoreId store_id,
                           const char* Item,
                           CORBA::Long Quantity,
                           AStore::ItemInfo*& IInfo,
                           CORBA::Environment &IT_env);
};


#endif
```

After the class has been properly declared, it must be implemented. The definition for the **Depot** constructor and **FindItemInfo** are found in **Depot_i.cc** file. Part of this file is shown here:

```
#include <fstream.h>
#include "Depot_i.h"

const int NITEMTYPES=3;

const char *depotdata_file = "depot.dat";

const char *itemTypesText[NITEMTYPES] =
    {"FOOD","CLOTHES","OTHER"};
```

The constructor for **Depot_i**:

```
Depot_i::Depot_i(PseudoNameService_ptr PNS,
CORBA::Environment& IT_env) {
    . . . . . . . . . . . . . . . . . . . . . . . . . .
```

Create the CORBA object reference using **_this()** to register it with the Pseudo-NameServer.

```
        // Register the object with the name service
        CentralOffice::Depot_var DepotObjRef = _this();
        PNS->BindName("Depot",DepotObjRef, IT_env);
    }
```

FindItemInfo receives a bar code and returns the item information. It uses explicit error checking, as was described in Section 25.4.2.

```
void Depot_i::FindItemInfo (AStore::AStoreId StoreId,
                            const char* Item,
                            CORBA::Long Quantity,
                            AStore::ItemInfo*& IInfo,
                            CORBA::Environment &IT_env) {
    IT_env.clear();
    IInfo = new AStore::ItemInfo;
    if (m_items.Locate(Item,*IInfo)) {
    }
    else {
        AStore::BarcodeNotFound *bcnf =
            new AStore::BarcodeNotFound;
        bcnf->item = Item;
        // Raise the exception here
        IT_env.exception(bcnf);
    }
}
```

25.8.3 PseudoNameService Coding Changes

The changes required for ORB Plus from the generic C++ code was described for the Depot in Sections 25.8.1 and 25.8.2. This section describes these changes for the Pseudo-NameService implementation. Refer to the Depot sections for a more detailed description of these changes.

Srv_Main changes are as follows:

1. Create an instance of CORBA::Environment.

    ```
    CORBA::Environment IT_env;
    ```

2. Initialize the ORB.

    ```
    CORBA::ORB_var orb =
            CORBA::ORB_init(argc,argv,CORBA::HPORBid,
                            IT_env);
    ```

```
if (IT_env.exception()) {
   cerr << "ERROR Initializing ORB" << endl;
   exit(EXIT_FAILURE);
}
```

3. Initialize the HPSOA.

```
CORBA::HPSOA_var soa = orb->HPSOA_init(argc,
                          argv,CORBA::HPSOA
                          IT_env);
if (IT_env.exception()) {
   cerr << "ERROR Initializing HPSOA" << endl;
   exit(EXIT_FAILURE);
}
```

4. Create an instance of the **pname_i** C++ object.

```
pname_i PNS1(orb);
```

5. Issue the HPSOA run command.

```
soa->run();
```

The header file PNS_i.h contains the following class descriptions: **pname_i** is derived from the **HPSOA_PseudoNameService** object, which was generated by the cidl compiler.

```
class pname_i : public virtual HPSOA_PseudoNameService {
```

The **BindName** and **ResolveName** parameters have the **CORBA:: Environment** parameter added.

The PNS_i.cc implementation file contains the following change: The constructor for the **pname_i** class uses the **_this()** function to construct a Pseudo-Name Server object reference:

```
pname_i::pname_i(CORBA::ORB_ptr orb) {
  ofstream os("PNS.dat");
  if (os) {
    PseudoNameService_var PNSObjRef= _this();
    char *refstring = orb->object_to_string(PNSObjRef);
    os << refstring;
    CORBA::string_free(refstring);
  }
```

```
  else {
    cerr << "Error writing Pseudo Name-Service object
    reference" << endl;
  }
}
```

25.9 SUNSOFT NEO

For NEO, we'll present the procedure for the Pseudo-Name Service first, and then the Depot object.

25.9.1 Coding the PseudoNameService (PNS)

Although NEO comes with a full-fledged CORBAservice-compliant Naming Service (NEOshare), for the purpose of this example, a pseudo-naming service was created from scratch.

Furthermore, all the platforms described in this book tried to follow a common development path in order to simplify comparisons by the reader. Although NEO easily lent itself to this exercise, the process used here to build a distributed object service is more complex than the normal NEO-works development process. (For a description of the typical development process used with NEOworks, please see the section entitled "Developing a Distributed Object Application with NEOworks" in Chapter 23.)

25.9.2 Imakefile: Generating a Makefile for the PNS

The first step is to have NEOworks generate a *dummy-server*. Later we will add application code to make it a complete Pseudo-Name Server. The simplest way to generate the dummy-server is to create a makefile that will contain rules for each step of the server development process. This makefile itself can be generated from a simple Imakefile, which specifies the name of server to build, and, optionally, additional object files and libraries.

```
#PNS/Imakefile

# preface this Imakefile with common
# information valid for each service
include ../Makefile.shared

# specify libraries needed by this server
SERVER_pname_LIBS = pnamesvc
```

```
#
SERVER_pname_LIBPATH = $(IDLSRC)
SERVER_pname_RUNPATH = $(IDLSRC)
SERVER_pname_OBJECTS = Srv_Main.o \
                            pname_i.o pndata.o
UserStartedServer(pname)
```

To generate the **Makefile** from the Imakefile, execute the utility **odfimake**:

```
% odfimake
```

25.9.3 pname.impl: NEOworks Hints to Generate the PNS Server Infrastructure

In addition, we need a trivial server implementation hints file **pname.impl**:

```
// PNS/pname.impl
import "pnamesvc.idl";

implementation pname_i : PseudoNameService {
    creator new_pname( CORBA::ORB_ptr id );
    timeout = 0;
};
```

This hints file contains all the information necessary for NEOworks to generate a sample implementation of interface **PseudoNameService** as defined in pnamesvc.idl. In a more complex example, the implementation record for **PseudoNameService** could contain more hints to specify how to provide persistence or how to handle special concurrency requirements. Here we simply specify that instances of this particular implementation will not be automatically deactivated, and that their constructor method should be called **new_pname()**.

One way to have NEOworks generate the dummy-server sample source code is to run **make** with no arguments:

```
% make
```

At this point we would normally copy the dummy-server's sample code into the local directory and fill in the body of the various methods. But since we are trying to stay as close as possible to the source code used by the other platform implementations presented in this book, we will instead write code similar to the other implementations (even using the same filenames). This means more manual work, but the result will be easier to compare with the other platform implementations.

25.9.4   pname_i.h

In order to remain as close as possible to the common code used by this example, we have defined a few macros in a file called compat.hh. By including this file, we will be able to use interchangeably the various typedefs used to represent object references to objects of interface Foo: Foo_ptr, Foo_var, and FooRef.

Then we declare the implementation class **pname_i**. Although not strictly required, we make **pname_i** inherit from the utility class **ODF::Servant**. This will allow any instance of pname_i to find out useful things such as its own object reference, its own reference data, and so on.

The creator function specified in pname.impl will be called when a new instance of **pname_i** is created. That creator function in turn will invoke **_initialize_new_pname()** to initialize the new instance.

The other two methods declared on class **pname_i** correspond to the two methods declared for **interface PseudoNameService**.

25.9.5   pname_i.cc

In order to benefit from the server infrastructure generated by NEOworks, we include odf_output/OdfpnameImpl.hh. This will pull in several other useful headers such as pname_i.h just described.

The implementation of the initialization method **_initialize_new_pname()** is similar to the regular class constructor except that the *stringification* of the objref for the current instance uses a real object reference to self (instead of the C++ pointer **this**). The real object reference is returned by invoking **servant_objref()**, a method inherited from **ODF::Servant**.

Note: Once more, in order to remain close to the common source code, some extraneous code (such as argc and argv initialization) was left in this version of the code, although it serves no purpose other than to help comparison by the reader.

25.9.6   Srv_Main.cc

There are two things to notice in this file: First, the ORB is initialized by invoking the routine **ODF::init()**, and a pointer to the ORB object can be obtained by calling **ODF::orb()**.

The second thing is more important. Because NEO is a fully multithreaded environment, it listens for requests, and executes requests onto objects implemented in this server in threads spawned from the main thread. As a result, **main()** does not lose control as the ORB starts to run. The flip side is that if **main()** exits, the entire server exits; therefore, we must have a blocking call, for example, **getchar()**, which will keep the Pseudo-Naming server from exiting until a key is pressed on its standard input.

The other source files do not need particular attention for NEO.

25.9.7 Building the PseudoNamingService

Now that the code has been written, it can be compiled and linked into an executable server by invoking make once more:

```
% make
```

The result will be an executable called **pname** in the current directory.

In a typical use of NEO, another makefile target knows how to package the server using standard UNIX packages. This way, the server and the necessary libraries and IFR data can be installed on any machine with a simple **pkgadd** command.

25.9.8 Coding the Depot in SunSoft NEO

Most of the notes presented for the PseudoNamingService implementation remain valid for the Depot's service implementation. In addition, a few remarks specific to the Depot are needed.

25.9.9 depot_i.cc, depotdata.cc

The mapping used in this version of the product requires members of complex IDL types, such as structs, to be manipulated through C++ *accessor* and *mutator* functions. Also, complex IDL types passed as out parameters are mapped as references to pointers to the complex type.

As a result, whereas some ORBs use references to the complex type instance, and thus use the dot notation to access the instance's members, in this implementation, a reference to a pointer and an arrow to an accessor function are used.

CHAPTER 26

Coding the Depot: Overview and Smalltalk Language Coding

26.1 GETTING STARTED

This chapter presents the implementation of the Depot in HP Distributed Smalltalk. Since there is no other Smalltalk implementation in the book, we weren't able to separate common code as precisely as the other languages, but we tried to maintain the distinction between OMG standard and ORB-specific components. So this discussion should be of value to you even if you're using a different Smalltalk-supporting ORB. We'll still separate the discussion of the IDL type and operations mapping from the implementation details.

You should have just read the description of the language-independent functionality of the Depot in Section 24.1. In it, we added implementation details to the problem-oriented A&D presented back in Chapter 19. If you didn't, turn back and read it now; it tells what we're going to do in this chapter.

This is the first time we enter Smalltalk code into our system. If you're planning to enter the methods by hand, open a system browser and add **OMG Primer Example** as a class category. All the classes described in this section should be added under this category. And, if you've read the example into the system from the floppy disk, open up a system browser on the **OMG Primer Example** class category to view the code as we discuss it.

26.2 SMALLTALK IMPLEMENTATION OF THE DEPOT

Recall the IDL definition of interface **Depot**:

```
module CentralOffice {

    interface Depot {
        #pragma selector FindItemInfo findItemInfo:barCode:quantity:itemInfo:
        void FindItemInfo (
                    in AStore::AStoreId     StoreId,
                    in POS::Barcode         Item,
                    in long                 Quantity,
                    out AStore::ItemInfo    IInfo)
                raises (AStore::BarcodeNotFound);
    };
};
```

Note that the selector pragma is HP Distributed Smalltalk-specific. Three Smalltalk classes, **Depot**, **ItemInfo**, and **ParseStoreDB** implement this interface. **Depot** implements the IDL operation **FindItemInfo**. **ItemInfo** is the Smalltalk representation of the IDL **struct ItemInfo** and is used both for argument passing as well as for the storage of data in the Store database. **ParseStoreDB** is a Smalltalk utility class used to read in the Store database from an ASCII file. Each one of these classes will be described in the following sections.

26.2.1 Smalltalk Implementation for Depot

The Smalltalk implementation class **Depot** is shown in the following code listing. The code discussion is organized according to protocol category, and any code references are by line number.

```
1     Class:   Depot
2
3     Superclass: Object
4     Category: OMG Primer Example
5     Instance variables:   storedb
6
7     Protocol: repository
8
9     CORBAName
10        ^#'::CentralOffice::Depot'
11
12    Protocol: Depot
13
```

```
14    findItemInfo: aStoreId barCode: aBarcode quantity: aCount
          itemInfo: info
15        | item |
16        item := storedb at: aBarcode ifAbsent:
              [^(CORBAConstants at:
              #'::AStore::BarcodeNotFound')
17        corbaRaiseWith: (Dictionary with: (Association key:
              #item value: aBarcode))].
18        item Quantity: item Quantity - aCount.
19        info value: item
20
21    Protocol: initialization
22
23    initialize
24        storedb := self readStoreDatabase: 'depot.dat'
              asFilename
25
26    Protocol: private
27
28    readStoreDatabase: fileName
29        | fileStream db |
30        fileName isReadable
31          ifTrue: [
32              [fileStream := fileName readStream.
33              db := ParseStoreDB new parse: fileStream]
34                  valueNowOrOnUnwindDo: [fileStream close]]
35          ifFalse: [db := nil].
36        ^db
```

- **Superclass** (line 3): **Depot** inherits from the Smalltalk class **Object**, which is the root of the Smalltalk inheritance tree.

- **Instance variables** (line 5): **storedb** holds a dictionary, which is keyed by bar code. This dictionary is created during **Depot** initialization from the ASCII file depot.dat. See the section on **ParseStoreDB** for details.

- **Protocol: repository** (lines 9–10): HP Distributed Smalltalk requires the **CORBAName** method to associate an IDL interface (in this case **Depot**) with its implementing Smalltalk class, also **Depot**.

- **Protocol: Depot** (lines 14–19): This protocol category is initial capitalized, indicating that all methods found in this category are implementations of IDL operations found in the corresponding IDL interface. Often, the mapping from an IDL operation to its Smalltalk implementation is made explicit by a selector pragma. In this case, the selector pragma maps the IDL operation **FindItemInfo** to the Smalltalk method **findItemInfo:barCode:quantity:itemInfo:**. Refer to the **CentralOffice** module for the corresponding IDL.

The **findItemInfo:barCode:quantity:itemInfo:** method implements two IDL-to-Smalltalk language binding features:

- First, raising an exception (lines 16–17): The **CORBAConstants** dictionary is populated with IDL exception objects, such as **::AStore::Barcode-NotFound**. In order to raise an IDL exception, the exception object is looked up in the **CORBAConstants** dictionary and sent the message **corbaRaiseWith:**.

- Second, passing back an out parameter (line 19). The last argument to the **findItemInfo:barCode:quantity:itemInfo:** method is defined in IDL as an **out** parameter. It is the caller's responsibility to pass **out** (and **in-out**) parameters via instances of a class conforming to the **CORBAParameter** protocol. This is accomplished by sending the **asCORBAParameter** message to the parameter to be passed. The receiving method computes a new parameter value and returns it to the caller by sending the **value:** message to parameter that was passed in.

  There is only one database for all stores, and thus the first parameter, **aStoreId** is ignored. Also, no check is done for allocating more items than are in the inventory (line 18).

- **Protocol: initialization** (lines 23–24): The method **initialize** is called to initialize a new instance of the Smalltalk class **Depot**. It calls the utility method, **readStoreDatabase:** with the hard-coded file name depot.dat. The result of this message send is stored in the instance variable **storedb**.

- **Protocol: private** (lines 28–36): The method **readStoreDatabase:** opens the file passed in as an argument and parses it as the Store database.

26.2.2 Smalltalk Implementation for ItemInfo

The **::AStore** module defines the IDL structure named **ItemInfo** shown next:

```
module AStore {
    #pragma class ItemInfo ItemInfo
    struct ItemInfo {
        POS::Barcode Item;
        ItemTypes Itemtype;
        float Itemcost;
        string Name;
        long Quantity;
    };
};
```

By default, the IDL struct **ItemInfo** would be mapped to an instance of the **Dictionary** class. The dictionary would have an entry for each field in the struct consisting of a key value pair where the key is the field name and the value is the value of the field. By using the HP Distributed Smalltalk class pragma, this behavior is overridden. The class pragma instructs the IDL compiler to associate the Smalltalk **ItemInfo** class with the IDL structure **ItemInfo**. This ensures that the IDL **ItemInfo** structure will always be represented as an **ItemInfo** class instance within Smalltalk.

The Smalltalk implementation of class **ItemInfo** is shown in the following code listing. The code discussion is organized according to protocol category, and any code references are by line number.

```
1    Class:       ItemInfo
2
3    Superclass: Object
4    Category:   OMG Primer Example
5    Instance variables: barCode name quantity itemCost taxType
6
7    Protocol: accessing
8
9    Item
10       ^barCode
11
12   Item: aBarCode
13       barCode := aBarCode
14
15   Itemcost
16       ^itemCost
17
18   Itemcost: aPrice
19       itemCost := aPrice
20
21   Itemtype
22       ^taxType
23
24   Itemtype: aType
25       taxType := aType
26
27   Name
28       ^name
29
30   Name: aName
31       name := aName
32
33   Quantity
```

```
34          ^quantity
35
36     Quantity: aCount
37          quantity := aCount
```

- **Superclass** (line 3): **ItemInfo** inherits from the Smalltalk class **Object**, which is the root of the Smalltalk inheritance tree.
- **Instance variables** (line 5): This class implements five instance variables, one for each of the IDL structure fields:

IDL Struct Field Name	Smalltalk Instance Variable
Item	barCode
ItemType	taxType
ItemCost	itemCost
Name	name
Quantity	quantity

- **Protocol: accessing** (lines 9–37): This protocol implements the accessors for the five instance variables. Since this class is mapped to an IDL structure (via a class pragma), all accessors are required to be defined (both set and get). At run time the appropriate accessors are called by the ORB: getters to marshall an **ItemInfo** instance as an IDL structure, and setters to unmarshall the IDL structure as an instance of **ItemInfo**.

Note that the method names begin with a capital letter, which violates the normal Smalltalk convention for selectors, because the field names of the IDL structure begin with a capital letter. If the IDL had been written with a Smalltalk mind-set, the field names would have begun with a lowercase letter.

26.2.3 Smalltalk Implementation for ParseStoreDB

The Smalltalk class **ParseStoreDB** is a utility class used by **Depot** to parse the Store database file. The database is stored as an ASCII file where each line in the file has the following format:

barcode description quantity itemcost taxtype

A line is terminated by a carriage return. For each line in the ASCII file, an instance of the class **ItemInfo** is created. These instances are associated with their corresponding bar codes and put into a dictionary.

The Smalltalk implementation of class **ParseStoreDB** is shown in the following code listing. The code discussion is organized according to protocol category, and any code references are by line number.

```
1    Class:       ParseStoreDB
2
3    Superclass: Scanner
4    Category:    OMG Primer Example
5
6    Protocol: scanning
7
8    scanLine: aString
9        | item |
10       item := ItemInfo new.
11       self scan: aString readStream.
12       item item: token asString.
13       self scanToken.
14       item name: token.
15       self scanToken.
16       item quantity: token.
17       self scanToken.
18       item itemcost: token.
19       self scanToken.
20       item itemtype: (self symbolToEnumerator: token
                asLowercase asSymbol).
21       ^item item -> item
22
23   symbolToEnumerator: aSymbol
24       | syms |
25       syms := CORBAConstants at: #'::AStore::ItemTypes'.
26       (syms includes: aSymbol)
27            ifTrue: [^CORBAConstants at:
                     #'::AStore::ItemTypes::' , aSymbol]
28
29   Protocol: parsing
30
31   parse: aStream
32       | db |
33       db := Dictionary new.
34       [aStream atEnd]
35            whileFalse: [db add: (self scanLine: (aStream upTo:
                Character cr))].
36       ^db
```

- **Superclass** (line 3): **ParseStoreDB** inherits from the Smalltalk class **Scanner**. This is the VisualWorks class from which lexical scanners are implemented.

- **Protocol: scanning** (lines 8–27): The **scanLine:** method is implemented by lines 8–21. This method takes a string as input and tokenizes it. The collected tokens are used to initialize an instance of the class **ItemInfo**. The method returns an association of the bar code and the **ItemInfo** instance.

- **symbolToEnumerator:** (lines 23–27): This method is called by the **scanLine:** method to convert the itemType from a Smalltalk symbol to its equivalent enumerator defined in **::AStore::ItemTypes**.

- **Protocol: parsing** (lines 31–36): The **parse:** method (lines 31–36) reads the input stream for the next line by calling **scanLine:**. Each parsed line is added to the **Dictionary** representing the database. The dictionary key is the bar code. The database is returned.

26.3 SMALLTALK IMPLEMENTATION OF THE PSEUDO-NAME SERVICE IDL DEFINITIONS

Since the CORBAServices Name Service is not yet implemented by all vendors, the primer example implements a subset called the Pseudo-Naming service (PNS). The PNS is implemented in Smalltalk by the **PseudoNameService** class. There are two IDL operations defined for the Pseudo-Name Service.

The Smalltalk implementation of class **PseudoNameService** is shown in the following code listing. The code discussion is organized according to protocol category, and any code references are by line number.

```
1     Class: PseudoNameService
2
3     Superclass: Object
4     Category:    OMG Primer Example
5     Instance variables: bindings
6
7     Protocol: repository
8
9     CORBAName
10        ^#'::PseudoNameService'
11
12    Protocol: PseudoNameService
13
14    bindName: objectName objectRef: reference
15        bindings isNil ifTrue: [bindings := Dictionary new: 10].
16        bindings at: objectName put: reference
17
18    resolveName: objectName
19        ^bindings at: objectName ifAbsent: [nil]
```

- **Superclass** (line 3): **PseudoNameService** inherits from the Smalltalk class **Object**, which is the root of the inheritance hierarchy.

- **Instance variables** (line 5): **bindings** is the instance variable that holds a dictionary of object name to object reference associations.

- **Protocol: repository** (lines 9–10): HP Distributed Smalltalk requires the **CORBAName** method to associate an IDL interface (in this case **PseudoNameService**) with its implementing Smalltalk class, also **PseudoNameService**.

- **Protocol: PseudoNameService** (lines 14–19): This protocol category is initial capitalized, indicating that all methods found in this category are implementations of IDL operations found in the corresponding IDL interface. Many times, the mapping from an IDL operation to its Smalltalk implementation is explicitly shown via the selector pragma. In this case, the default mapping is used (no selector pragmas specified). There are two IDL operations implemented in this protocol: First,

  ::PseudoNameService::BindName

  The Smalltalk method **bindName:objectRef:** (lines 14–16) implements this IDL operation. The bindings dictionary is lazily initialized. A new binding is created from the input arguments and added to the bindings dictionary. Second,

  ::PseudoNameService::ResolveName

  The the Smalltalk method **resolveName:** (lines 18–19) implements this IDL operation. The input argument is used as the key to look up the entry in the bindings dictionary. If found, the value associated with the key (the object reference) is returned. Otherwise **nil** is returned.

26.4 IMPLEMENTATION SUMMARY

If you've been typing code into your system as you worked your way through this chapter, or if you've read the code from the diskette, your Depot module implementation is complete. Now turn to Section 27.1 to start work on the Store object with an implementation overview.

CHAPTER 27

Coding the Store in C

27.1 LANGUAGE-INDEPENDENT OVERVIEW: STORE IMPLEMENTATION

Like Section 27.1 on the Depot, this section is for everyone, regardless of which programming language you're using. It adds implementation detail to the A&D for the Store, going as far as it can without getting language-specific—algorithms, file formats, data flow details. At the end of this section, we'll split into language-specific chapters.

To start, here's a list of CORBA features illustrated for the first time in the Store and StoreAccess objects:

- A single object (Store) acting as both client and server;
- **sequence**, **struct**, and **enum** IDL types;
- IDL **attributes**, including read-only; and
- a local CORBA object.

The Store, like the Depot, is implemented as a separate server executable. Unlike the Depot, though, there can be multiple Store objects in the system, so for identification purposes, each one is given a unique name that it registers with the name server on startup. This name is simply derived from an ID given on the command line.

One other value that a Store needs is the markup rate to be used for prices, which is given as the second parameter on the command line. For example, starting the Store using the command

```
store 10 26
```

will cause the markup rate to be 10 percent and the object to be named Store_26. (This will work fine in the example, but the low markup will probably result in financial failure for anything except a grocery store with one-day average turnover. For a more realistic demo, choose a markup between 50 and 100 percent. To simulate a commune or co-op with recruit volunteers and unpaid staff, try 5.)

The Tax object associated with the Store is also created at start-up time and initialized to the regional tax rate, which we've simply coded as a constant for simplicity.

Once started, a Store is able to accept login requests from POS terminals. When a terminal logs in, the terminal's details are recorded in the POSList, which is implemented here as a simple array. The login operation returns a reference to a dedicated StoreAccess object that the terminal will use on subsequent FindPrice requests.

The operations on the Store for updating and accessing the totals are implemented by searching and returning elements of the POSList or the POSList itself.

This concludes the language-independent discussion of the Store object implementation. If you're working the example in C, continue with the next section. If you're working in C++, skip to the start of Chapter 28. And if you're working in Smalltalk, skip to the start of Chapter 29.

27.2   C MAPPING COMPONENT

The organization of this chapter parallels Chapter 24: This section, and the one that follows, present C language code common to every C language ORB. If you're working the example in ObjectBroker, SOMObjects, or DAIS, you need to read both of these sections before skipping to the section specific to your ORB.

The function declarations that we present in this section are part of your next C language files. If you're working the example by typing it in yourself, you'll need to do so as you read along. If you plan on using the starter files produced by your ORB, grab them from the IDL compiler output—we listed the names in Chapter 23. They'll contain the declarations we present here, and possibly some additional code that your system will need later.

There are also global variables and structures in Store.idl, and there are three interfaces, some with multiple operations. As before, the vendors provide C declarations derived from the mapping for you in an .h file that you never have to touch (and, in fact, shouldn't). You might look at the .h file to see the mappings if you have doubts, but after a while you'll not even need to do that.

27.2.1   Store IDL Type Mappings

The IDL types are mapped to C datatypes as shown here. The IDL enum:

```
enum ItemTypes {food, clothes, other};
```

becomes:

```
typedef CORBA_unsigned_long AStore_ItemTypes;
#define AStore_food 1
#define AStore_clothes 2
#define AStore_other 3
```

You can declare something as type **AStore_ItemTypes**, then use the defines to refer to the value of the enumerations.

The IDL

typedef long AStoreId;

becomes

```
typedef CORBA_long AStore_AStoreId;
```

where CORBA_long is defined by your implementation, usually in some file like orb.h (a reference to which is often put into the include files generated by your vendor's code generator). All other primitive types in IDL are defined in this manner.

The IDL structure:

```
struct ItemInfo {
  POS::Barcode    Item;
  ItemTypes       Itemtype;
  float           Itemcost;
  string          Name;
  long            Quantity;
};
```

becomes a C structure declared as:

```
typedef struct AStore_ItemInfo {
        POS_Barcode     item;
        AStore_ItemTypes itemtype;
        CORBA_float     itemcost;
        CORBA_string    name;
        CORBA_long      quantity;
        } AStore_ItemInfo;
```

One thing you should be careful about is the definition of **CORBA_string**. It is defined as a pointer to a null-terminated array of characters. There are strict rules about using **CORBA_string**, and strict rules about who must allocate the memory and who must free it. You typically don't use the standard C **malloc** routines for this storage.

The IDL statement:

exception BarcodeNotFound { POS::Barcode item; };

gets mapped into:

```
typedef struct AStore_BarcodeNotFound {
        POS_Barcode item;
        } AStore_BarcodeNotFound;*/
#define ex_AStore_BarcodeNotFound <impl-unique>
```

where **<impl-unique>** is a number unique to the implementation. It might be, for example, the Interface Repository identifier for the exception. In any case, the vendor's generator would place this in your central.h file for you. The structure here is not used in this example; we use only the **ex_Astore_BarcodeNotFound** identifier for declaring our simple exception to the ORB. For more advanced uses and more complex exceptions, having more information becomes more useful to a server in returning information to the client about what went wrong.

The IDL structure:

```
POSInfo {
    POS::POSId    Id;
    StoreAccess   StoreAccessReference;
    float         TotalSales;
    float         TotalTaxes;
};
```

again maps simply into the C structure:

```
typedef struct AStore_POSInfo {
        POS_POSId          Id;
        AStore_StoreAccess StoreAccessReference;
        CORBA_float        TotalSales;
        CORBA_float        TotalTaxes;
        } AStore_POSInfo;
```

The real fun is in the IDL statement:

typedef sequence <POSInfo> POSList;

which maps into the C structure:

```
typedef struct {
        CORBA_unsigned_long _maximum;
        CORBA_unsigned_long _length;
        AStore_POSInfo      * _buffer;
        } CORBA_sequence_AStore_POSInfo;
typedef CORBA_sequence_AStore_POSInfo
        AStore_POSList;
```

You then declare something as **AStore_POSList** and get the structure defined above it. The point of CORBA sequences is that they are variable-length arrays of structures. The actual storage must be allocated by your program and pointed to by the **_buffer** pointer. You set the **_maximum** pointer to indicate the maximum number of elements of the array allowed, and you also set **_length** to indicate how many elements are currently being used. This structure is used in the Store to keep track of an arbitrarily large number of **POSInfo** structures; that is, structures keeping track of what each POS station is doing. In this simple example, the initialization code for the Store sets the maximum number of POS stations it wishes to deal with at run time; this could be arbitrarily large, but isn't for our simple example.

The last datatype declared in IDL is local to the Store interface:

```
struct StoreTotals {
   float    StoreTotal;
   float    StoreTaxTotal;
};
```

The mapping to C is:

```
typedef struct AStore_StoreTotals {
        CORBA_float StoreTotal;
        CORBA_float StoreTaxTotal;
        } AStore_StoreTotals;
```

Only two additional IDL datatypes need to be mapped for the Store to operate, and those come from the included file POS.idl, which contains the module POS.

```
typedef long POSId;
typedef string Barcode;
```

These are mapped to:

```
typedef CORBA_long    POS_POSId;
typedef CORBA_string POS_Barcode;
```

There are six operations explicitly defined in the three interfaces of the **AStore** module. In addition, since **AStore** has two read-only attributes, two additional operation signatures are automatically generated, corresponding to an operation that merely returns that attribute.

The eight operation signatures or C-function prototypes are listed next in the same order they appear in the Store.idl file. Again, your vendor will usually generate these automatically into an .h file that you can include in your client so that the C compiler can check that you are passing the right kind of parameters.

```
void AStore_StoreAccess_FindPrice(
    AStore_StoreAccess object,
    CORBA_Environment * ev,
    POS_Barcode        Item,
    CORBA_long         Quantity,
    CORBA_float        * ItemPrice,
    CORBA_float        * ItemTaxPrice,
    AStore_ItemInfo    * IInfo);

CORBA_float AStore_Tax_CalculateTax(
    AStore_Tax         object,
    CORBA_Environment * ev,
    CORBA_float        TaxableAmount);

CORBA_float AStore_Tax_FindTaxablePrice(
    AStore_Tax         object,
    CORBA_Environment * ev,
    CORBA_float        ItemPrice,
    AStore_ItemTypes  ItemType);

AStore_AStoreId AStore_Store__get_StoreId(
    AStore_Store       object,
    CORBA_Environment * ev);

AStore_Totals AStore_Store__get_Totals(
    AStore_Store       object,
    CORBA_Environment * ev);

CORBA_Object AStore_Store_Login (
    AStore_Store       object,
    CORBA_Environment * ev,
    POS_POSId          Id);
```

```
void AStore_Store_GetPOSTotals (
     AStore_Store          object,
     CORBA_Environment * ev,
     AStore_POSList      * POSData);

void AStore_Store_UpdateStoreTotals(
     AStore_Store          object,
     CORBA_Environment * ev,
     POS_POSId             Id,
     CORBA_float           Price,
     CORBA_float           Taxes);
```

This completes the C declarations generated by the IDL. Since the Store object is a server, we need to implement the functionality of these interfaces. We'll do that in the next section.

27.3 COMMON FUNCTIONALITY

Now we need to code the functionality of the Store object. There's almost nothing ORB-specific about this, so we'll do it all in this section. If you're working the example by hand, you'll need to type all of this code into your .c file as we go along. At the end of this section, we'll send you off to the section on your specific ORB for final coding, compilation, and linking.

As before, the methods for the objects have their function names and first two parameter names listed in *italics*. You remember why; we discussed this in Section 24.3. Just keep in mind that you'll have to substitute your ORB vendor's names here as well.

Since there are three different interfaces, we'll talk about the common functionality in three pieces, from the one with the fewest methods to the one with the most.

27.3.1 StoreAccess

StoreAccess has only a single method, but of course it needs to have its state initialized and objects created as well.

State Declaration   The state declaration is:

```
typedef struct tagStoreAccessState
{ CentralOffice_Depot   _depot_reference;
  AStore_Tax            _tax_reference;
  AStore_AStoreId       _store_id;
  CORBA_char            *tax_name;
  CORBA_float           markup;
} StoreAccessState;
```

This simply declares the information kept for every StoreAccess object created.

StoreAccess State Initialization   In order to initialize the state of a Store-Access object, we enter the following code, probably in the same module as the StoreAccess method, in order to keep similar routines together. (By the way, we have left out some debugging output you will find on the floppy. It's useful when you run the program to see where you are, but it only clutters up the text.)

```
ObjectStatePtr store_access_init(
                CORBA_long          argc,
                CORBA_char          **argv,
                CORBA_Environment   *ev)
{ PseudoNameService pname;
  StoreAccessState  *ostate;

  ostate = malloc(sizeof(StoreAccessState));

  if (argc != SA_ARGC)
      {application_terminate(
            "wrong number of arguments\n", ev);}

  if(1 != sscanf(argv[SA_MARKUP_ARG], SA_MARKUP_FMTSTR,
                &ostate->markup))
      {application_terminate("bad markup arg\n", ev);}

  if(1 != sscanf(argv[SA_ID_ARG], SA_ID_FMTSTR,
                &ostate->_store_id))
      {application_terminate("bad id arg\n", ev);}

  ostate->tax_name= malloc(sizeof(TAX_REF)+ID_LEN+1);
  sprintf(ostate->tax_name, "%s%d", TAX_REF,
          ostate->_store_id);

  pname = NameService(ev);
  ostate->_depot_reference =
   PseudoNameService_ResolveName(pname, ev, DEPOT_REF);
  ostate->_tax_reference   =
     PseudoNameService_ResolveName(pname, ev,
                                   ostate->tax_name);

  CORBA_Object_release(pname, ev);
  return ostate;
} /* end of store_access_init() */
```

This routine is called with the equivalent of two command-line arguments (as actually received by the Store startup command line). The first argument is expected to be the amount of markup for the Store, and the second is the Store's ID number. These values become part of the state of the StoreAccess object. The first executable statement (**ostate =**...) gets storage for the state. The lines down to the reference to **ostate->** make sure the right number of arguments got passed in, and then decode them into the state. Using the Store number, it then creates a name for the tax object for the Store (using the **sprintf** statement) of the form **tax_12**, for example, if this was executed for Store 12.

The routine then gets the reference to the PseudoNameService into **pname** by calling the common routine found in the misc.h file. Once it has that reference, it calls the PNS twice to get object references for the Depot and the tax reference it should use. (Clearly, the Store and the Depot must be started before the StoreAccess object, so that they can use the PNS to bind references to these objects.) These references are also stored in the state for StoreAccess.

StoreAccess Object Creation   Creating an object for the Store is ORB-dependent. Consult the individual product section for this.

StoreAccess FindPrice Method   The method is mostly common to the C bindings so we list it once here, showing the product-dependent part in italics so you can check the individual product sections for the last little details. As explained in Section 24.3, the method name and the names of the first two parameters are not specified yet by OMG, and there are slight differences among vendors—these items are shown in italics.

```
void AStore_StoreAccess_FindPrice(
     AStore_StoreAccess objectpar,
     CORBA_Environment   *ev,
     POS_Barcode         Item,
     CORBA_long          Quantity,
     CORBA_float         *ItemPrice,
     CORBA_float         *ItemTaxPrice,
     AStore_ItemInfo     *IInfo)
{
   StoreAccessState   *ostate;

   /* vendor dependent code to set variable ostate*/

   /* get the item_info structure from the depot */
   CentralOffice_Depot_FindItemInfo(
```

```
                    ostate->_depot_reference,
                    ev,
                    ostate->_store_id,
                    Item,
                    Quantity,
                    IInfo);

    switch (ev->_major)
      {
      case CORBA_USER_EXCEPTION:
         CORBA_exception_free(ev);
         CORBA_BOA_set_exception(
                    TheBoa,
                    ev,
                    CORBA_USER_EXCEPTION,
                    ex_AStore_BarcodeNotFound,
                    (void *)&Item);
         return;
         break;

      case CORBA_SYSTEM_EXCEPTION:
         return;
         break;
      }

    /* calculate the price based on cost + store specific
       markup percentage */
    *ItemPrice = IInfo->Itemcost +
                    (IInfo->Itemcost * ostate->markup);

    /* call the tax server to obtain taxable amount
       of price */

    *ItemTaxPrice = AStore_Tax_FindTaxablePrice(
                            ostate->_tax_reference,
                            ev,
                            *ItemPrice,
                            IInfo->Itemtype);

    return;
  } /* end of AStore_StoreAccess_FindPrice() */
```

Once this routine gets its state (vendor-dependent, marked in italics), it uses the Depot reference from the state to call on the Depot as a client, passing along parameter this routine received itself, as well as other parameters from the state. This routine shows one way of error checking after a method call. You should always do so, even though we don't always show it in this book to reduce size and confusion. (Do as I say...)

The Depot returns the raw (wholesale) cost of the object. This method then calculates the retail price by applying the markup from its state. Then it calls the tax reference (also from the object's state, set at **store_access_init** time) to find the amount of the price that is taxable. That's all.

27.3.2 Tax

The Tax object keeps its own state, gets initialized, and has two methods. This is kept in file tax.c.

Tax State   This routine carries on the grand tradition of simplification in our example, by hard coding the tax rate as part of its rather permanent state:

```
#define BASE_TAX_RATE 0.05
```

Of course, a more realistic example would do it differently. The remainder of the Tax state for all implementations is stored in the following structure:

```
typedef struct tagTaxState
{ AStore_AStoreId  _store_id;
  CORBA_float      rate;
  CORBA_char       *name;
} TaxState;
```

Tax State Initialization   The code for tax state initialization is called from the Tax object creation and is common.

```
ObjectStatePtr tax_init( CORBA_long         argc,
                         CORBA_char         **argv,
                         CORBA_Environment  *ev,
                         CORBA_char         **name)

{ TaxState  *ostate;
  ostate = malloc(sizeof(TaxState));

  if(1 != sscanf(argv[TAX_ID_ARG], TAX_ID_FMTSTR,
              &ostate->_store_id))
    {application_terminate("bad store id arg\n", ev);}
```

```
ostate->name = malloc(sizeof(TAX_REF)+ID_LEN+1);
sprintf(ostate->name, "%s%d", TAX_REF,
        ostate->_store_id);
*name = ostate->name;

ostate->rate = BASE_TAX_RATE;

return (ObjectStatePtr)ostate;
} /* end of tax_init() */
```

The routine first obtains memory for its state into pointer **ostate**. It is called with the parameters passed to the Store object main program when it is started (**argc** and **argv**). It uses one of these parameters to determine what the ID is of the Store it represents; if found correctly, it saves the Store's ID in its state. It then creates a name for itself of the form **tax_43**, for example, if the Store ID were 43; that name is also saved in the state (it will be used by Tax object creation in "binding" the tax object using the PNS). Finally, it saves the the tax rate in its state.

Tax Object Creation   This is more vendor-specific than common. See the upcoming sections.

Tax Method: FindTaxablePrice   The methods are mostly common to the C bindings so we list them once here, showing the product-dependent part in italics so you can check the individual product sections or code for the last little details. As explained in Section 24.3, the method name and the names of the first two parameters are not specified yet by OMG, and there are slight differences among vendors—these items are shown in italics. (By the way, we have left out some debugging output you will find on the floppy. It's useful when you run the program to see where you are, but it only clutters up the text.) The vendors usually provide you a skeleton (here in normal text), and you fill in the details (marked in bold).

```
CORBA_float AStore_Tax_FindTaxablePrice(
        AStore_Tax          objectpar,
        CORBA_Environment   *ev,
        CORBA_float         ItemPrice,
        AStore_ItemTypes    ItemType)
{
  /*if it is food or clothes then return zero, otherwise
    return ItemPrice */

  if (ItemType == AStore_other) return (ItemPrice);
  else return 0.0;

} /* end of AStore_Tax_FindTaxablePrice() */
```

This method is extremely simple and doesn't even need state. If the item type is "other," then the full price is returned as the taxable price; otherwise, there is no tax on this item, so it returns 0.

Tax Method: CalculateTax   The C code for calculating the tax is:

```
CORBA_float AStore_Tax_CalculateTax(
          AStore_Tax            objectpar,
          CORBA_Environment     *ev,
          CORBA_float           TaxableAmount)
{ TaxState            *ostate;

  /* vendor dependent code to set variable ostate*/

  return (TaxableAmount * ostate->rate);

} /* end of AStore_Tax_CalculateTax() */
```

This method is almost embarrassingly short. It first finds its object's state in a vendor-dependent fashion (hint: see the code; it's only one line). Once it has the state, it has the rate, and merely multiplies the input parameter by the rate to find the tax. The only way we could jazz it up would be to round it off.

27.3.3   Store

As with all the other objects, the Store object has state, a state initialization routine, an object creation routine, and method routines (in this case, five of them).

Store State   The Store is one of our more complex objects, and it has a correspondingly larger state than others in this section:

```
typedef struct tagStoreState
{ AStore_POSList          _poslist;
  AStore_POSInfo          _posarray[MAX_POSLIST_ENTRIES];
  AStore_Store_StoreTotals  _totals;
  CentralOffice_Depot     _depotReference;
  AStore_Tax              _taxReference;

  CORBA_float             _storeMarkup;
  AStore_AStoreId         _store_id;
```

```
        CORBA_char                  *store_name;
        CORBA_char                  *tax_name;
} StoreState;
```

This state keeps a list of what sales and taxes have been collected at each POS (_poslist and _posarray), and it keeps accumulated totals for the whole store (_totals). It keeps a reference to the Depot and the Tax objects for use by the Store (the two **xxxReference** entries). It keeps track of the markup and the ID for the Store, as well as the character representation of the Store's ID and the Tax object.

Store State Initialization   Initialization of the state of the Store is common.

```
ObjectStatePtr store_init(
            CORBA_long              argc,
            CORBA_char              **argv,
            CORBA_Environment       *ev,
            CORBA_char              **name)
{
  char                   reference[REF_MAX];
  FILE                   *fp;
  CORBA_string           stringref;
  StoreState             *ostate;
  PseudoNameService pname;

  ostate = malloc(sizeof(StoreState));

  /* associate the instance data poslist array with
     poslist sequence and initialize sequence */

  ostate->_poslist._buffer  = ostate->_posarray;
  ostate->_poslist._maximum = MAX_POSLIST_ENTRIES;
  ostate->_poslist._length  = 0;

  if (argc != S_ARGC)
     application_terminate("wrong number of args\n",
                              ev);

  if(1 != sscanf(argv[S_ID_ARG], S_ID_FMTSTR,
                 &ostate->_store_id))
     application_terminate("bad store id arg\n", ev);

  ostate->store_name = malloc(
                         sizeof(STORE_REF)+ID_LEN+1);
```

```
    sprintf(ostate->store_name, "%s%ld", STORE_REF,
            ostate->_store_id);

    ostate->tax_name = malloc(sizeof(TAX_REF)+ID_LEN+1);
    sprintf(ostate->tax_name, "%s%ld", TAX_REF,
            ostate->_store_id);

    *name  = ostate->store_name;
    pname  = NameService(ev);

    ostate->_depotReference  =
    PseudoNameService_ResolveName(pname, ev, DEPOT_REF);
    if( ev->_major != CORBA_NO_EXCEPTION )
     application_terminate("Failed to import depot",ev );

    ostate->_taxReference   =
      PseudoNameService_ResolveName(pname, ev,
                                    ostate->tax_name);
    if( ev->_major != CORBA_NO_EXCEPTION )
       application_terminate("Failed to import tax",ev );
    CORBA_Object_release(pname, ev);

    /* initialize StoreTotal = StoreTaxTotal = 0  */
    ostate->_totals.StoreTotal    = 0;
    ostate->_totals.StoreTaxTotal = 0;

    if (argc != S_ARGC)
       application_terminate(
            "wrong number of arguments\n", ev);

    if(1 != sscanf(argv[S_MARKUP_ARG], S_MARKUP_FMTSTR,
                   &ostate->_storeMarkup))
       application_terminate("bad markup arg\n", ev);

    if(1 != sscanf(argv[S_ID_ARG],       S_ID_FMTSTR,
                   &ostate->_store_id))
       application_terminate("bad id  arg\n", ev);

    printf("Store server is initialized and ready\n");
    return (ObjectStatePtr)ostate;
} /* end of store_init() */
```

Quite a piece of code, eh? Well, we've got a lot to initialize. Starting at the beginning, the initialization allocates memory for its state and sets its list of POSTerminals to null (that is, none have yet logged in). This is a little tricky if you've never dealt with an IDL mapped sequence before. The code first points the buffer part of the sequence to an array of POSInfo structures of a given size (most constant or size parameters are found in the common.h file). It then sets the sequence max to the size of that array and sets the current length to 0. When we look at processing of the POSList later, we'll see a little more how this works.

The code then checks the PseudoNameService for the Depot. If not found, it quits; if found, it saves the reference in the state.

The next item of interest results from how the Store main program gets started: from the command line, with two parameters, the first being the markup for this Store; and the second being the Store's ID number. For example, the startup command might be something like:

```
store 50 43
```

indicating a markup of 50 percent over cost and a store number of 43. The Store main program will use these parameters in creating a Tax object for the Store and then a Store object. The Store main program creates the Tax object first (passing these parameters to the Tax object creation routine); as a result, by the time control reaches this store initialization, the Tax object for the Store already exists and should be registered with the PNS.

When this Store initialization is called, it likewise gets the main program parameters, including the Store ID number. Checking that these parameters are present and converting them to internal form makes up a good part of the initialization and is probably familiar to most C programmers. Once the Store number is created, the initialization checks to see if the Tax object with that same ID number has been created, by calling the ResolveName method of the PNS.

As a result of the parsing, the markup is stored with the Store state (so it can be used to create a faked **argv** list later when the store login routine calls the create routine for a **StoreAccess** object).

Store State Object Creation   See the individual vendor's code for object creation. The object creation calls the state initialization for the major part of its work.

Store Method: __get_StoreId   The methods are mostly common to the C bindings so we list them once here, showing the product-dependent part in italics so you can check the individual product sections or code for the last little details. As explained in Section 24.3, the method name and the names of the first two parameters are not specified yet by OMG and there are slight differences among vendors—these items are shown in italics. (By the way, we have left out some debugging output you may find on the floppy, and the formatting may be a little different because of the different form factor for the book. The debugging output is useful when you run the program to see where you are, but it only clutters up the text. The form factor we just can't get around.)

For methods, the vendors usually provide you a skeleton (here in normal text), and you fill in the details (marked in bold). Bold italics show a (usually small) section of code that differs among vendors, so check the later sections or the floppy.

By the way, any IDL attribute generates at least one method. In this case, since the attribute was **readonly**, there is just one method, a **get**. You can always tell that the method was generated from an attribute because it has a double-underscore preceding the **get** to remind you.

The method **__get_StoreID** is quite simple since all it does it return the value of the IDL "read-only attribute" **StoreId**. The only trick is in getting the Store state, and that is vendor-specific. Look at the floppy; it's only a single line or so.

```
AStore_AStoreId AStore_Store__get_StoreId(
        AStore_Store         objectpar,
        CORBA_Environment   *ev)
{StoreState              *ostate;

  /* vendor dependent code to set variable ostate*/

  return ostate->_store_id;

} /* end of AStore_Store__get_StoreId() */
```

Store Method: __get_Totals   The method __get_Totals method is almost the same as __get_StoreId, with the only difference being that the value of the method is a structure with two components. That detail, however, is hidden from you by the C compiler, so it's almost the same.

```
AStore_Store_StoreTotals AStore_Store__get_Totals(
                AStore_Store         objectpar,
                CORBA_Environment   *ev)
{ StoreState *ostate;

  /* vendor dependent code to set variable ostate*/

  return ostate->_totals;

} /* end of AStore_Store__get_Totals() */
```

Store Method: Login The method for Login begins to be challenging. Begins? Wow!

```
AStore_StoreAccess AStore_Store_Login(
                   AStore_Store        objectpar,
                   CORBA_Environment   *ev,
                   POS_POSId           Id)
{ AStore_StoreAccess  store_access;
  int                 count = 0;
  int                 found = 0;
  CORBA_char**        argv;
  StoreState          *ostate;



  /* vendor dependent code to set variable ostate*/        .

  /* Check POSList to see if store_Id exists. If not,
   * add it to poslist, create a StoreAcess object
   *
   * If store_Id is already in the list, zero out totals
   * and return existing StoreAccess object
   *
   * As currently implemented, the POSList has room for
   * 50 POS entries If the table is full, additional
   * POSs trying to log in will receive a
   * NULL StoreAccess object */



  if (ostate->_poslist._length == MAX_POSLIST_ENTRIES)
      {
      printf("StoreAccess _poslist overflow\n");
      return NULL;
      }
  else
      {
      while ((count < ostate->_poslist._length) &&
            (!found))
          {
          if (ostate->_poslist._buffer[count].Id == Id)
              found = 1;
          count++;
          }
      }
```

```
if (!found)
    {/* if the POSid is not already in the poslist,
        add it, creating StoreAccess object */
    AStore_POSInfo   *new_pos;   /* temp pointer*/
    argv = malloc(sizeof(CORBA_char *) * SA_ARGC);
    argv[SA_MARKUP_ARG] = malloc(ARG_STR_LEN + 1);
    argv[SA_ID_ARG    ] = malloc(ARG_STR_LEN + 1);

    sprintf(argv[SA_MARKUP_ARG], SA_MARKUP_FMTSTR,
            ostate->_storeMarkup);
        sprintf(argv[SA_ID_ARG],      SA_ID_FMTSTR,
            ostate->_store_id);



        store_access = new_AStore_StoreAccess(
                        (CORBA_long)SA_ARGC,
                        argv,
                        ev);
    free(argv[SA_MARKUP_ARG]);
    free(argv[SA_ID_ARG]);
    free(argv);

    /* initialize the postlist entry */

    new_pos = & (ostate->_poslist._buffer
                    [ostate->_poslist._length]);

    new_pos->StoreAccessReference = store_access;
    new_pos->Id                   = Id;
    new_pos->TotalSales           = 0;
    new_pos->TotalTaxes           = 0;

    /* increment the length field of the POSList
        sequence */
    ostate->_poslist._length++;
    return store_access;
    }



else
    {
    /* reset POS totals */
    ostate->_poslist._buffer[count-1].TotalSales=0.0;
    ostate->_poslist._buffer[count-1].TotalTaxes=0.0;
```

```
        return ostate->_poslist._buffer[count-1].
                            StoreAccessReference;
    }
} /* end of AStore_Store_Login() */
```

This is one time we've left in the comments since the method is so long, and it's hard to key remarks here to the code. There are two main paths: where the POS with the given ID has already been used and where it hasn't. Where it has been used, it's simply a matter of a new cashier logging in; a StoreAccess object is already on file for the POS, in the POSList, and the only real work is to set the totals back to 0 and return the StoreAccess reference.

When the POS with the given ID it hasn't been used before, a new POS-Info structure has to be added to the POSList, and a new StoreAccess object has to be created. Our method here may be inelegant, but it's straightforward and it works: We actually re-create, from Store state, what the command line was that started the Store. We then pass that on to the create StoreAccess routine, which thinks it's getting the same thing the Store routine did, and then reparses the line to get the values out.

Store Method: GetPOSTotals   In spite of this method having a "Get" in its name, it wasn't generated from an attribute. It almost could be, but it wasn't for historical reasons in the design process: returning such a complex data structure as a value is okay for C and C++, but OMG will eventually have COBOL bindings, and COBOL doesn't currently deal with nonprimitive data structures. If you'll never deal with COBOL again, you won't have to worry about this choice.

```
void AStore_Store_GetPOSTotals(
        AStore_Store        objectpar,
        CORBA_Environment   *ev,
        AStore_POSList      *POSData)

{   StoreState  *ostate;

    /* vendor dependent code to set variable ostate*/

    *POSData = ostate->_poslist;

} /* end of AStore_Store_GetPOSTotals() */
```

In spite of the shortness of this method, you should be aware of the tremendous amount of work an ORB/BOA combination does behind the scenes to make it work. Recall that the **POSList** data structure is a sequence of structures, some of which contain strings. The ORB/BOA must do a complete copy of the entire variable-length structure and copy all the strings in it. Be careful—sometimes it's easy to write simple-looking code that turns out to be a real performance hog.

Store Method: UpdateStoreTotals   This method's interest is in finding which POS to update at the same time it updates the Store totals. The latter is just a matter of touching the Store state. The former is searching the array of **POSInfo** to find the correct POS to update also.

```
void AStore_Store_UpdateStoreTotals(
        AStore_Store         objectpar,
        CORBA_Environment    *ev,
        POS_POSId            Id,
        CORBA_float          Price,
        CORBA_float          Taxes)
{

    int         count = 0;
    int         found = 0;
    StoreState  *ostate;


    /* vendor dependent code to set variable ostate*/


    ostate->_totals.StoreTotal    += Price;
    ostate->_totals.StoreTaxTotal += Taxes;


    while ((count < ostate->_poslist._length) &&
          (!found))
      {
      if (ostate->_poslist._buffer[count].Id == Id)
          found = 1;
       count++;
      }


    if (!found)
    {
       printf("UpdateStoreTotals: serious problem!\n");
       return;
    }
```

```
        ostate->_poslist._buffer[count-1].TotalSales +=
                Price;
        ostate->_poslist._buffer[count-1].TotalTaxes +=
                Taxes;


    return;
} /* end of AStore_Store_UpdateStoreTotals() */
```

27.3.4 Implementation Summary

If you've been typing in the code as you went along, your Store code is nearly complete. You're ready to make just a few adjustments for your specific ORB, and prepare to run your Depot and PNS objects.

27.4 CONNECTING TO THE ORB AND BOA, AND STARTING THE STORE OBJECT

Following the pattern of previous chapters, we'll split now into ORB-specific sections. Turn to the section for your ORB for instructions on how to finish your Store object. When you're done, go to Chapter 30 to start coding the POSTerminal objects.

27.5 OBJECTBROKER

The primary new CORBA concept in the Store object is dealing with more than one interface (implementation) in the same process. The Store is more like the Depot of Chapter 24 than the Pseudo-Name Service because it acts both as a server—for requests on the Store interfaces—and as a client—for calls on the Pseudo-Name Service and on the Depot.

Recall from Chapter 24 that an ObjectBroker process like the Depot consists of a main, methods, dispatch, stubs, and user utility routines. For the Store, the specific files are:

store_m.c—the main program

store.c—the methods and supporting routines for the Store methods

store_ac.c—the methods and supporting routines for the StoreAccess methods

tax.c—the methods and supporting routines for the tax methods

stodsp.c—the routines that provide the link between BOA and the store methods misc.c—a mixture of handwritten and vendor-supplied, convenience routines

pnsstb.c—stub routines for PNS

depotstb.c—stub routines for the Depot

27.5.1   ObjectBroker Store Main

As with the previous sections, you could have had QuickStart generate a main program file for you. We've done that but made some modifications to it to remain similar to the other vendors so you can see the parallel nature of the code. The main program has four parts:

- global declarations, usually pointers to objects or implementations (not discussed further here);
- the **main()** itself;
- implementation registration routines;
- cleanup routines.

The main() Program   The main differs from the main of the PNS or the Depot only in that it recognizes that it is the main program of a server that contains three implementations.

```
CORBA_boolean main (int argc, char *argv[])
{
    CORBA_Environment      ev;


    /* convenience declarations, for similarity to other
       implementations */
    TheOrb = CORBA_DEC_ORB_OBJECT;
    TheBoa = CORBA_DEC_BOA_OBJECT;


    /* Register all */
    if (!RegisterAllmpls (&ev))
        {
        OBB_ORB_rundown (TheOrb, &ev, (CORBA_Flags) 0);
        IsException (&ev, (CORBA_string)
                    "OBB_ORB_rundown failed \n");
        return(0);
        }


    /*Create the two initial object references, register
      them with the name service*/
```

```
(void)Create_AStore_TaxObject(argc, argv,&ev );
(void)Create_AStore_Store_Object(argc, argv,&ev );

/* Jump into the main loop. */
OBB_BOA_main_loop (TheOrb, &ev, (CORBA_Flags)0 );


/*Finished -- clean up so we don't leave any memory
  or registration information*/
storermain_clean_up(&ev);
return(0);
}
```

You can see the only structural difference from depot_m.c (not counting the name difference) is the call on **RegisterAllImpls** (see next) instead of a call on a particular **RegisterXXXImpl** routine and calls on two object creation routines, the two "permanent" objects of the implementation since the StoreAccess create routine gets created on the fly by the Login operation of Store. As we'll see shortly, the **storemain_clean_up** routine parallels the **RegisterAllImpls** routine.

RegisterAllImpls   The **RegisterAllImpls** routine is a very simple routine that merely calls on the three **RegisterXXXImpl** routines for the three implementations of this process. QuickStart generates **RegisterAllImpls** as well as the three **Register...** routines, so we need not discuss these any further.

storemain_clean_up   The cleanup, instead of just cleaning up after a single implementation as in PNS and Depot, must properly clean up three implementations. Again, QuickStart generates this for you so you don't have to worry about it.

27.5.2 ObjectBroker Store Methods

There are three sets of methods and initializations to worry about, but these are all handled the same way as for the Pseudo-Name Service and the Depot. They are just the common code with the only three differences being as previously mentioned: implementation name, the first two default parameter names, and the method of getting state. The **CreateXXXObject** routine exactly parallels the previously described **Create** routines with only the names changing (since the xxx_init routines are common and they do the object-specific work).

27.5.3 ObjectBroker-Generated Files

The dispatch files (linkage between the BOA and the methods) for the Store are all generated into a single file, stodsp.c, by ObjectBroker. All you have to do is compile them and include them in the link step.

Since the Store methods and associated routines call as clients on the PNS and on the Depot, it must use the stubs for those services. These stubs were created as described in Chapter 23 and are called pnamestb.c and depstb.c. Again, all you have to do is compile and link them.

27.5.4 Miscellaneous Routines

The misc.c file was intended for use with all these servers. You've already compiled it for the previous processes, so you only need to remember to put it into the link list. The file linear.c was used by PNS and by Depot, but that was for their particular demands for a database. It is not used by the Store.

27.5.5 ObjectBroker Store (Build)

All you need to do now is link all the files just listed into an "executable" and start it at the command-line level, supplying the two parameters expected by the various Store creation routines mentioned in the common code: the markup percentage and the Store's ID number.

27.6 SOMOBJECTS: ASTORE MODULE IMPLEMENTATION

This section describes the SOM-specific C implementation for the AStore module. The implementation template for the AStore module (Store.c) was generated from the IDL file through the steps described in Section 29.2. In general, the methods in the AStore module are the common implementations described in Section 27.3. The implementations described should be inserted into the function stubs produced by the SOM compiler for each of the methods defined in the interfaces in the AStore module.

27.6.1 StoreAccess Object

The new SOM-specific extension in the definition of the StoreAccess interface is the constructor method for the StoreAccess object. In the SOM IDL file for the AStore module, a method called **storeInit** was defined in the **StoreAccess** interface and in the implementation definition section of the IDL; the method is qualified as an init method. When this IDL file is run through the SOM IDL compiler, the compiler generates a stub in the template for the storeInit method of the StoreAccess object. Excerpts from Store.idl relevant to the StoreAccess definition are reproduced here:

```
#ifdef __SOMIDL__
  interface StoreAccess : SOMObject {
#else
  interface StoreAccess {
#endif
     void    FindPrice(
             in POS::Barcode Item
             ,in long        Quantity
             ,out float      ItemPrice
             ,out float      ItemTaxPrice
             ,out ItemInfo IInfo)
         raises (BarcodeNotFound);
```

The StoreAccess object is derived from SOMObject, since all objects in the SOMobjects Toolkit have to be (directly or indirectly) derived from SOMObject.

```
#ifdef __SOMIDL__

     /* constructor for creating StoreAccess
      * instances with initialization parameters
      */
     void storeInit(
             inout somInitCtrl ctrl
             ,in SOMObject taxref
             ,in SOMObject depotref
             ,in float markup
             ,in long storeid);

     implementation {

         releaseorder: FindPrice, storeInit;
         storeInit: init;
         override: somDefaultInit, somDestruct;
         somToken ostate;
         dllname = "dobjs.dll";
     };
#endif

   };
```

As shown, the **StoreAccess** initialization method **storeInit** is defined. When this is qualified as an init method in the implementation part of the IDL definition, this becomes a nondefault constructor. **somDefaultInit** is the default constructor for all objects. Instances of interfaces, say **foo**, are created using a function **fooNew()** when C bindings are used. The semantics of this function are that it creates an uninitialized object and calls foo's **somDefaultInit** on the instance of the object. The initialized object is returned to the caller. Note that the user does not directly call **somDefaultInit**. **fooNew** is a function that is generated by the IDL compiler **sc**, and placed in the **foo.h** file for **foo.idl**. Similarly, when a nondefault constructor is specified, a user should be allowed to specify that initialization method. In the case of the **StoreAccess** interface, **StoreAccessNew** will call the default constructor. However, to create a new StoreAccess object using the storeInit constructor, the following function is generated by the IDL compiler for users:

```
AStore_StoreAccessNew_storeInit(ev,
          taxref, depotref, markup, storeid);
```

In our case, the Store object creates a StoreAccess object. The parameters that are passed to the **AStore_StoreAccessNew_storeInit** method are all part of the object state of the Store object.

We digress now, for the interested reader. The nondefault constructor as might be noted by the reader is like any other method defined in the IDL definition. Therefore, users can also call the nondefault constructors explicitly like other methods. However, if nondefault constructors are called on already initialized constructors, unpredictable results might happen—depending on what the constructors do. To solve this problem, SOM allows users to create uninitialized objects. A method on the class object called **somNewNoInit** is supported on all class objects. As mentioned in Section 20.3, all objects have a class object. By invoking **somNewNoInit** on the class object, an uninitialized **StoreAccess** object is first created. Then we invoke the **storeInit** method like any other method. The implementation of the function just given does this for the user. When C++ bindings are used, all nondefault SOM constructors can be used like C++ constructors.

The implementation for the storeInit constructor is shown next. Statements automatically generated by the SOM compiler appear in italics, while those added by the programmer appear in non-italics. As can be seen in the code, the method implementation simply assigns the input arguments to the appropriate elements in the object state structure for the StoreAccess object. The sharp-eyed reader might notice that the name and signature of the **AStore_StoreAccessNew_storeInit** are different from what is specified in the IDL file. The IDL compiler generates the **AStore_StoreAccessNew_storeInit** function as a convenience for the user.

This function calls the **AStore_StoreAccessstoreInit** function on an unini-tialized **StoreAccess** object.

```
/*
 * constructor for creating StoreAccess instances with
 * initialization parameters
 */
SOM_Scope void SOMLINK
     AStore_StoreAccessstoreInit(AStore_StoreAccess somSelf,
                                 Environment *ev,
                                 somInitCtrl* ctrl,
                                 SOMObject taxref,
                                 SOMObject depotref,
                                 float markup,
                                 long storeid)
{

    StoreAccessState   *ostate;
    AStore_StoreAccessData *somThis; /* set in
                                        BeginInitializer */
    somInitCtrl globalCtrl;
    somBooleanVector myMask;

    AStore_StoreAccessMethodDebug("AStore_StoreAccess",
                                  "storeInit");
    AStore_StoreAccess_BeginInitializer_storeInit;

    ostate = SOMMalloc (sizeof (StoreAccessState));
    somThis->ostate = ostate;
    ostate->_tax_reference = taxref;
    ostate->_depot_reference = depotref;
    ostate->markup = markup;
    ostate->_store_id = storeid;

    AStore_StoreAccess_Init_SOMObject_somDefaultInit(somSelf,
                                                     ctrl);

}
```

The implementation of the **FindPrice** method is similar to the one described in the common functionality section (Section 27.3).

27.6.2 Tax Object

The **Tax** object has the usual SOM extensions. The interface is shown here. The state information is kept in an object state structure, whose pointer is the **ostate** instance variable. The **Tax** object is derived from **SOMObject**.

```
#ifdef __SOMIDL__
  interface Tax : SOMObject {
#else
  interface Tax {
#endif

    float CalculateTax(in float          TaxableAmount);
    float FindTaxablePrice(in float      ItemPrice
                    ,in ItemTypes        ItemType);
#ifdef __SOMIDL__
      implementation {
          releaseorder: CalculateTax,
                 FindTaxablePrice;
          somToken    ostate;
          override:    somDefaultInit, somDestruct;
          dllname = "dobjs.dll";
      };
#endif
  };
};
```

The implementation of the somDefaultInit constructor for the Tax object is shown next. The IDL compiler-generated code is shown in *italics*. The constructor does not do much—it initializes the state of the Tax object. The constant tax rate is a constant defined in common.h. The implementations of FindTaxablePrice and CalculateTax methods are similar to the common code implementations described in Section 27.3.

```
SOM_Scope void SOMLINK AStore_TaxsomDefaultInit(
                    AStore_Tax somSelf,
                    somInitCtrl* ctrl)
{
    TaxState *ostate;
    AStore_TaxData *somThis; /* set in BeginInitializer */
    somInitCtrl globalCtrl;
    somBooleanVector myMask;

    CORBA_Environment ev;

    AStore_TaxMethodDebug("AStore_Tax","somDefaultInit");
    AStore_Tax_BeginInitializer_somDefaultInit;

    AStore_Tax_Init_SOMObject_somDefaultInit(somSelf, ctrl);
```

```
/* set the tax rate, this is hard wired for simplicity */
ostate          = SOMMalloc (sizeof(TaxState));
somThis->ostate = ostate;
ostate->rate    = BASE_TAX_RATE;
}
```

27.6.3 Store Object

The **Store** object has an interesting interface. It has two attributes, **StoreId** and **Totals**. Attributes have implicit methods to set and get their values. These methods are implicit in the sense that they do not have to be explicitly declared in the IDL file. However, users can invoke these methods and all CORBA implementations should support the invocation of the get and set methods. In the case of the **Store** interface, since the attributes **StoreId** and **Totals** are qualified as **readonly**, users cannot invoke the set method, but can only invoke the get method. In Section 27.3.3, the implementation of the **get_StoreId** and **get_Totals** were given. In SOMobjects Toolkit, these methods need not be implemented; these methods are generated by the IDL compiler. Since the attributes are also part of the state information of the object, they can be accessed by the somThis pointer as you have been seeing so far. The SOMobjects Toolkit has an underlying object model that makes this possible. However, for the example in this book, we have been using an explicit object state structure (**ostate**). The SOMobjects implementation has to do the extra work of maintaining consistent values in the **StoreState** structure and the state of the SOM object itself, as will be seen in the implementation of methods. This is the only difference, therefore, these methods will not be shown in the text; the reader is referred to the accompanying diskette.The SOMobjects Toolkit provides the flexibility of specifying the implementation of the get and set methods. However, for simplicity and brevity, it is not done here. The interface for the Store object with SOM extensions is shown next:

```
#ifdef __SOMIDL__
  interface Store : SOMDServer {
#else
  interface Store {
#endif
    struct StoreTotals {
      float  StoreTotal;
      float  StoreTaxTotal;
    };
    readonly attribute AStoreId StoreId;
    readonly attribute StoreTotals Totals;
```

```
        StoreAccess Login(in POS::POSId Id);
        void    GetPOSTotals(out POSList POSData);
        void    UpdateStoreTotals(
                in POS::POSId Id
                ,in float Price
                ,in float Taxes);
#ifdef __SOMIDL__
    implementation {
        releaseorder: Login, GetPOSTotals, UpdateStoreTotals,
                _get_StoreId, _get_Totals;
        override: somDefaultInit, somDestruct;
        somToken ostate;
        dllname = "dobjs.dll";
    };
#endif
    };
```

Note that the **Store** object is derived from the **SOMDServer** object. When the server process is activated, it has a Store object. The implementation of the **somDefaultInit** method is shown next. The compiler-generated code is in italics.

```
SOM_Scope void SOMLINK
    AStore_StoresomDefaultInit(
                            AStore_Store somSelf,
                            somInitCtrl* ctrl)
{
    AStore_StoreData *somThis; /* set in BeginInitializer */
    somInitCtrl globalCtrl;
    somBooleanVector myMask;
    SOMDObject sdo;
    PseudoNameService pnsRef;
    CORBA_Environment ev;
    StoreState        *ostate;

    AStore_StoreMethodDebug("AStore_Store",
                            "somDefaultInit");
    AStore_Store_BeginInitializer_somDefaultInit;
    AStore_Store_Init_SOMDServer_somDefaultInit(somSelf, ctrl);

    SOM_InitEnvironment(&ev);

    /* associate the instance data poslist
     * array with poslist sequence
```

```
 * and initialize sequence
 */
ostate = SOMMalloc (sizeof(StoreState));
somThis->ostate  = ostate;
ostate->_poslist._buffer = ostate->_posarray;
ostate->_poslist._maximum =
                         MAX_POSLIST_ENTRIES;
ostate->_poslist._length = 0;

/* get an object reference to the
 * PseudoNameService
 */

pnsRef = file_to_ref(&ev, PNAME_REF);
if (ev._major != CORBA_NO_EXCEPTION)
           handle_error(&ev);

/* get depot reference from a well known
 * place - the PNS
 */
ostate->_depotReference =
       PseudoNameService_ResolveName(pnsRef,
                            &ev, DEPOT_NAME);
if (ev._major != CORBA_NO_EXCEPTION)
                    handle_error(&ev);

/* create the Tax object locally */

ostate->_taxReference = AStore_TaxNew();

/* build an object reference for the
 * tax object
 */

sdo = SOMDServer_somdRefFromSOMObj(somSelf,
           &ev, ostate->_taxReference);
if(ev._major != CORBA_NO_EXCEPTION)
           handle_error(&ev);


/* register the Tax object with the
 * PseudoNameServer
 */

PseudoNameService_BindName(pnsRef, &ev,
                                 "tax", sdo);
```

```
if(ev._major != CORBA_NO_EXCEPTION)
                            handle_error(&ev);

/* release the Tax object reference */
CORBA_Object_release(sdo,&ev);
if(ev._major != CORBA_NO_EXCEPTION)
                        handle_error(&ev);

/* register server with the
 * PseudoNameService
 */

register_server(&ev,somSelf);
if (ev._major != CORBA_NO_EXCEPTION)
            handle_error(&ev);

 /* release the PNS object reference */
 CORBA_Object_release(pnsRef, &ev);
 if(ev._major != CORBA_NO_EXCEPTION)
                            handle_error(&ev);

 /*  initialize Totals 0  */

 somThis->Totals.StoreTotal = 0;
 somThis->Totals.StoreTaxTotal = 0;


/*  get storeid and markup instance data
 *  - hardwired for simplicity
 */

 somThis->StoreId = STOREID;
 ostate->_store_id = somThis->StoreId;
 ostate->_totals = somThis->Totals;
 ostate->_storeMarkup = MARKUP;

 /* clean up */
 SOM_UninitEnvironment(&ev);
 printf("Store server is initialized "
        "and ready\n");
}
```

Most of the code does simple initialization. The interesting piece is the creation of the **Tax** object. Since SOMobjects has an underlying object model, all objects are instances of **SOMObject**. In order to create an object reference, the method **somdRefFromSOMObj**, which is supported on a **SOMDServer** object, is invoked. This produces an object reference that can be exported. Since Store is a **SOMDServer** object, this method is invoked on the **Store** object instance. Note that object references can be produced only for instances of **SOMObject** in server processes. Once the object reference for the **Tax** object is created, the **Tax** object and the **Store** object are both registered with the nameserver.

Once the methods have been implemented in the **AStore** module, the C code can be compiled and linked using the makefile included with the source code. The Store server is registered in the SOM Implementation Repository using the regimpl utility. The server is registered with the server alias of **storesvr_1**. Once registered, the Store server can be activated using the following command:

```
somdsvr -a storesvr_1&
```

27.7 DAIS SPECIFICS IN THE STORE OBJECT

Since we've covered a lot of the issues on this topic in Chapter 24, we won't go into a lot of detail here. But there are a few new issues that deserve a mention. We'll cover the differences in the same order as we did for the Depot and PNS: **main()** and capsule startup, then object constructors followed by method implementations.

27.7.1 main()

The capsule start-up code is held in store_main.c. The first thing to note is that we are creating two static objects in the capsule. By static, we mean objects that are started automatically when the capsule is started, as opposed to objects that are created on demand (which we will also see happen in this chapter).

We use the same approach for creating the static objects in the store capsule as we do for both the Depot and the PNS. As a result, there are no complications at the **main()** level, and we can just call the constructors for the two objects and save their object references for later cleanup:

```
tax_ref   = new_AStore_Tax(argc, argv, &ev);
store_ref = new_AStore_Store(argc, argv, &ev);
```

We must start them in the order specified because the store constructor will fail if it can't locate its associated Tax object. It can only locate the Tax object by asking the PNS, but the PNS only knows about the Tax object after the Tax object has told it, so we have to have started the Tax object before the Store object.

In this simplified example, objects try to locate the other objects only once; if an object cannot be located, the capsule fails; clearly, the order in which we start up objects and, to a lesser extent the timing of the startup, is crucial. In a real system, we would have at least a pause and retry, or possibly a more complex mechanism that would use other services to locate an alternative (in DAIS, this can be an automatic process). To keep the example simple, however, we just try once.

The other main difference in store_main.c is in the capsule terminator. We have started two static objects so we should really tidy up both. This requires calling the CORBA functions twice with the appropriate arguments:

```
CORBA_BOA_deactivate_impl(TheBoa, &local_ev,
    DAIS_AStore_Store_impl);
CORBA_BOA_dispose(TheBoa, &local_ev, (CORBA_Object)
    store_ref);
CORBA_BOA_deactivate_impl(TheBoa, &local_ev,
    DAIS_AStore_Tax_impl);
CORBA_BOA_dispose(TheBoa, &local_ev, (CORBA_Object)
    tax_ref);
```

Now that we've sorted out the startup and shutdown, we can have a look at the Store object specifics, which are held in store.c.

27.7.2 Object Constructor: Store

The object constructor for the Store object is very similar to that of the Depot object. The main issue we are introducing here is that we are expecting to have multiple instances of the Store object in the system, which means that the name that we export to the PNS must be instance-specific. We leave the choice of this name to the application-specific initialization and pass a pointer to a string into the _init() routines so that it can let us know what choice has been made:

```
ostate = store_init(argc, argv, ev, &name);
```

We subsequently use this name in our **BindName** call on the PNS. Although the name is actually accessible from the object state, the object state is considered opaque at this level so we can't get at it that way.

There are no DAIS specifics in the application initialization so we can now have a look at the method implementations.

27.7.3   Method Implementations: Store

This section covers not only the method implementations but also the rest of the file for the Store object. Again, there are not many DAIS specifics.

The header files that must be included are as follows:

```
#include "orb.h"
#include "central.h"
#include "store.h"
#include "common.h"
#include "pnamesvc.h"
#include "misc.h"
```

These are mainly familiar by now: orb.h to give access to the ORB facilities, common.h and misc.h for shared facilities and definitions for the application, and then the include files corresponding to the IDL files for any interface definitions, in this case, central.h, store.h, and pnamesvc.h.

We also need a means for dynamically creating a StoreAccess object. We achieve this in the same way as for static objects, by creating a mapping representing a null factory using a **#define**.

```
#define new_AStore_StoreAccess \
Create_AStore_StoreAccess_Object

extern CORBA_Object
Create_AStore_StoreAccess_Object(CORBA_long argc,
                                 CORBA_char **argv,
                                 CORBA_Environment *ev);
```

Once again, in DAIS, we would normally use DAIS facilities (the DAIS Trader, Node Manager and Factory) for locating and instantiating an instance of the StoreAccess object. It would then be a system administration issue if the StoreAccess and store objects were colocated in the same capsule or node. The structure that we have adopted allows us to replace the **new** call with a call on the Trader and have the constructor called by the Factory.

As we saw earlier, the function names for the server method implementations are the same as the scoped name of the method prefixed by **s_**. The object reference of the invoked object is again **_obj** by convention. We list them all here for clarity:

```
AStore_StoreAccess
S_AStore_Store_Login(AStore_Store       _obj,
                     CORBA_Environment  *ev,
                     POS_POSId          Id)
    void
```

```
S_AStore_Store_GetPOSTotals(AStore_Store      _obj,
                            CORBA_Environment  *ev,
                            AStore_POSList     *POSData)
AStore_AStoreId
S_AStore_Store__get_StoreId(AStore_Store      _obj,
                            CORBA_Environment  *ev)
AStore_Store_StoreTotals
S_AStore_Store__get_Totals(AStore_Store       _obj,
                           CORBA_Environment   *ev)
void
S_AStore_Store_UpdateStoreTotals(AStore_Store      _obj,
                                 CORBA_Environment  *ev,
                                 POS_POSId          Id,
                                 CORBA_float        Price,
                                 CORBA_float        Taxes)
```

In all the methods apart from login, the only area that was likely to have been vendor-specific was the access to the object state, but, as we discussed in Chapter 24 for the DAIS implementation, we access the state in a CORBA-conformant fashion.

The creation of the StoreAccess object in the Login method is achieved by a call on the object constructor as we have done in the **main()** function for all the other objects, so although this is DAIS specific, we aren't introducing anything that we haven't seen before. This similarity is the reason for the slightly clumsy building of the constructor arguments in the Login method.

27.7.4 The Tax Object

The Tax object is implemented in its own file, tax.c. This is mainly done so that we can easily build it into a capsule separate from the Store and StoreAccess objects, should we wish. There are no new concepts introduced here so the only DAIS specifics are the include files:

```
#include "orb.h"
#include "store.h"
#include "pnamesvc.h"
#include "misc.h"
#include "common.h"
```

the server method implementations:

```
S_AStore_Tax_CalculateTax(AStore_Tax        _obj,
                          CORBA_Environment  *ev,
                          CORBA_float        TaxableAmount)
```

```
CORBA_float
S_AStore_Tax_FindTaxablePrice(AStore_Tax        _obj,
                              CORBA_Environment  *ev,
                              CORBA_float        ItemPrice,
                              AStore_ItemTypes   ItemType)
```

and the object constructor that is the same as that of the Store object, with the exception of its name, the name of the application initialization function, and the interface and implementation names used in the **create()** and **impl_is_ready()** calls. If you are typing in the example as you go, you can probably just cut and paste from store.c into tax.c on the diskette and modify the names appropriately.

27.7.5 StoreAccess Object

The implementation of the StoreAccess object is in file store_access.c for the same reasons that the Tax object is implemented in tax.c; we may at some stage want to have the Tax object in another capsule. There are no new issues relating to object creation and initialization in the StoreAccess object. Again, if you are typing in the example, you can just cut and paste from tax.c into store_access.c on the diskette and modify the names appropriately.

The include files in store_access.c are as follows:

```
#include "orb.h"
#include "central.h"
#include "pnamesvc.h"
#include "misc.h"
#include "common.h"
```

The StoreAccess object has only one method, **FindPrice**. For DAIS, the corresponding server method implementation is:

```
void S_AStore_StoreAccess_FindPrice(
                    AStore_StoreAccess _obj,
                    CORBA_Environment  *ev,
                    POS_Barcode        item,
                    CORBA_long         quantity,
                    CORBA_float        *ItemPrice,
                    CORBA_float        *item_tax_price,
                    AStore_ItemInfo    *item_info)
```

There is one further aspect that is ORB-vendor specific in **FindPrice**, and it slips by almost without being noticed. This relates to the allocation of the output arguments and return results on the server side. There the storage for the **item_info** structure is passed back to the object that invoked the FindPrice method. As implemented in DAIS, there is no problem, because the store was allocated by the ORB, and it will be deallocated by the ORB when the **FindPrice** method returns. This is an area that is not yet covered by the OMG standardization effort (although it is being addressed now) and hence may differ between different vendors' ORBs.

The problem may be seen more clearly with a different example. If we had a method that concatenated two strings passed as arguments, we would need to allocate storage in which to compose the concatenated string before passing it back to the caller. The problem lies in the fact that we can't deallocate this storage before returning because the ORB needs the storage to pass the string back to the caller. We can't deallocate *after* we have returned because we don't do *any* processing after we have returned. Hence, we would have a memory leak. This problem is solved by using a DAIS ORB-specific memory allocation routine to allocate the storage for the concatenated string. In this case, as the storage has been allocated by the ORB, it knows that it can (must) deallocate the storage when the method returns.

This concludes the coding for all the objects in the Store capsule; all that is left is to build it.

27.7.6 Build: Store, Tax, and StoreAccess Capsule

No new issues arise when building the Store capsule. We simply compile the capsule-specific code and combine it with the shared code and libraries as we have done for the PNS and Depot capsules:

```
cc -c -I. -I$DAIS_ROOT/include store_main.c
cc -c -I. -I$DAIS_ROOT/include store.c
cc -c -I. -I$DAIS_ROOT/include tax.c
cc -c -I. -I$DAIS_ROOT/include store_access.c
```

and then link everything to make the Store capsule. We don't need the database this time so the only shared code is in misc.o:

```
cc -o store store_main.o store.o \
    tax.o store_access.o misc.o c_pnamesvc.o \
    m_pnamesvc.o c_central.o m_central.o \
    c_store.o m_store.o s_store.o \
    -L$DAIS_ROOT/lib -ldais -lxti -lnsl
```

The Store capsule is a client of the PNS and Depot, and both a client *and* server for interfaces defined in store.idl. So we include the appropriate client stub, server skeleton, and optimized marshalling code.

At the end of this section we see that we can have multiple object types in a capsule and dynamically create objects. We have looked briefly at some issues relating to the ease with which we can move objects about if we code them correctly; we have also discussed some memory management issues.

## CHAPTER 28

Coding the Store in C++

28.1 C++ MAPPING OF STORE INTERFACES

This section, and the one that follows, present C++ language code for the Store module that is common to every C++ language ORB.

The declarations that we present here are probably in a file with a name like Store.h (the exact name for your product was listed in its section of Chapter 23), produced by your IDL compiler so you won't have to type them in yourself. But you will need to be aware of their form (which is dictated by the standard OMG IDL-C++ language mapping) when you connect with the stubs and skeletons.

When we finish coding the common functionality, we'll split into ORB-specific sections as before.

The Store is composed of several datatypes and three classes that implement the IDL interfaces Tax, Store, and StoreAccess. They are discussed in the analysis and design and declared in the IDL file Store.idl. The classes are **Tax_i**, **Store_i**, and **StoreAccess_i**; note the suffix **_i** is used to distinguish the implementation class from the corresponding stub class (generated by the IDL compiler). Each implementation class is derived from a base class generated by the IDL compiler.

Several key items to note about the C++ mapping for these classes are:

- The CORBA operations translate to C++ virtual functions, which we will reimplement in the **_i** classes.
- IDL built-in types such as **float** translate to types declared in the class CORBA.
- The base classes are generated by the IDL compiler, and their names vary between ORBs so they are not presented here.
- CORBA modules are mapped to C++ classes or namespaces.

Because the store IDL is defined within the CORBA module AStore, references to ItemTypes, AStoreId, and ItemInfo in the implementation classes are prefixed by the scope name AStore::.

We begin by presenting the IDL for the module AStore:

```
module AStore {

    enum ItemTypes {food, clothes, other};
    typedef long AStoreId;

    struct ItemInfo {
        POS::Barcode    Item;
        ItemTypes       Itemtype;
        float           Itemcost;
        string          Name;
        long            Quantity;
    };

    exception BarcodeNotFound {POS::Barcode item;};

    interface StoreAccess; // /forward reference

    struct POSInfo {
        POS::POSId      Id;
        StoreAccess     StoreAccessReference;
        float           TotalSales;
        float           TotalTaxes;
    };

    typedef sequence <POSInfo> POSList;

    interface Tax {

        float CalculateTax(in float TaxableAmount);

        float FindTaxablePrice(
                in float        ItemPrice,
                in ItemTypes    ItemType);

    };

    interface Store {
```

```
struct StoreTotals {
    float    StoreTotal;
    float    StoreTaxTotal;
};

readonly attribute AStoreId StoreId;

readonly attribute StoreTotals Totals;

StoreAccess Login(in POS::POSId Id);
void    GetPOSTotals(out POSList POSData);
void    UpdateStoreTotals(
            in POS::POSId    Id,
            in float         Price,
            in float         Taxes);
};

interface StoreAccess {

    void    FindPrice(
        in              POS::Barcode Item,
        in long         Quantity,
        out float       ItemPrice,
        out float       ItemTaxPrice,
        out ItemInfo    IInfo)
    raises (BarcodeNotFound);

    };
};
```

Now let's look at the C++ mapping for ItemTypes, AStoreId, and Item-Info.

```
enum ItemTypes {
    food,
    clothes,
    other,
    _ItemTypes = CORBA::enum32};

typedef CORBA::Long AStoreId;

struct  ItemInfo {
    CORBA::String_var  Item;
```

```
      AStore::ItemTypes   Itemtype;
      CORBA::Float        Itemcost;
      CORBA::String_var   Name;
      CORBA::Long         Quantity;
   };
```

The translation for these types is fairly straightforward. The fields **Item** and **Name**, of **ItemInfo**, defined as type **string** in the IDL, are mapped to the C++ type **CORBA::String_var**. CORBA does not require this mapping, only that it must behave as a **char ***.

The _var is used because these fields are variable-length and the _var class manages the memory of the string. A second point of interest is the last element of the enumerated list: _ItemTypes. This element is required (although the name may vary between ORBs) to ensure that enums are 32-bit types.

Here is the C++ mapping for the **Tax_i**, **Store_i**, and **StoreAccess_i** classes.

```
   class Store_i // base class omitted intentionally
   {
   public:
      virtual AStore::AStoreId StoreId();

      virtual AStore::Store::StoreTotals Totals();

      virtual AStore::StoreAccess_ptr Login(
          POS::POSId          Id);

      virtual void GetPOSTotals(
          AStore::POSList    *&POSData);

      virtual void UpdateStoreTotals(
          POS::POSId          Id,
          CORBA::Float        Price,
          CORBA::Float        Taxes);

   };

   class StoreAccess_i
   {
   public:
      virtual void FindPrice(
             const char          *Item,
             CORBA::Long          Quantity,
             CORBA::Float&        ItemPrice,
```

```
              CORBA::Float&          ItemTaxPrice,
              AStore::ItemInfo          *&IIInfo);
};


class Tax_i
{
public:
   virtual CORBA::Float CalculateTax(
     CORBA::Float TaxableAmount);

     virtual CORBA::Float FindTaxablePrice(
     CORBA::Float          ItemPrice,
     AStore::ItemTypes    Itemtype);
};
```

In the next section, we cover implementing these classes. This, of course, includes adding data members and additional functionality such as constructors that are required to support the functionality dictated by the A&D presented in Chapter 19.

28.2   COMMON FUNCTIONALITY

Now we need to code the functionality of the Store classes. There's almost nothing ORB-specific about this, so we'll do it all in this section. If you're working the example by hand, you'll need to type all of this code into your program files as we go along. At the end of this section, we'll send you off to the section on your specific ORB for final coding, compilation, and linking.

28.2.1   Introduction

The source code for the store has been partitioned into the following files:

Filename	Contents
Store_i.h	class definitions
Store_i.cc	class implementations
Srv_Main.cc	main program control

In our implementation, each Store executes a single instance of the **Store_i** and **Tax_i** classes. The **Store_i** object constructs a separate instance of **StoreAccess_i** for each point-of-sale (POS) terminal. For simplicity, all **Store_i**, **Tax_i**, and **StoreAccess_i** object instances execute within a single process.

The following sections describe the logic of the three classes and the **main()** program function.

28.2.2   Tax_i Class

Tax_i is the implementation of the IDL interface **Tax** defined in Store.idl. It is derived from a base class generated by the IDL compiler, and contains members and member functions called out in the A&D. To support the A&D requirements, we will take the declaration shown in Section 28.1 and add a private data member and a constructor.

To implement **Tax_i** we start with the following observations:

- **Tax_i** needs a data member that corresponds to the state variable **Rate** in the A&D:

```
CORBA::Float      m_regionRate;
```

m_regionRate will be a "private" data member of **Tax_i**.

- The state variable **taxTotal** called out in the A&D is actually calculated by **CalculateTax** each time it is invoked. Because there is no need to keep this value across calls, it was implemented as an automatic variable of CalculateTax.

- We know from the A&D that the StoreAccess object will use the Tax object to calculate item prices. The requirement for this is derived from the statement in the A&D for the StoreAccess object:

Call FindTaxablePrice operation on taxReference object with input arguments ItemPrice and itemTaxType, receiving back output argument item_tax_Price.

To support this requirement, **Tax_i** will use the PseudoNameService object to name itself so clients (such as StoreAccess) can connect to it.

Based on these observations, the completed declaration for the **Tax_i** class is:

```
class Tax_i
{
private:
    CORBA::Float        m_regionRate;
public:
    Tax_i(PseudoNameService_ptr pns,
        AStore::AStoreId      StoreID);
```

```
virtual CORBA::Float CalculateTax(
    CORBA::Float        TaxableAmount);

virtual CORBA::Float FindTaxablePrice(
    CORBA::Float        ItemPrice,
    AStore::ItemTypes   Itemtype);
};
```

Constructor   The **Tax_i** constructor accepts two arguments: a reference to the Name service object and the Store ID:

```
Tax_i::Tax_i(PseudoNameService_ptr pns,
             AStore::AStoreId        storeID)
```

The constructor uses the PseudoNameService method **BindName** to associate a "name" (that is, a string) to the instance being constructed. The call to **BindName** is bracketed by a **try** block. This is how we can detect errors such as **CORBA::COM_FAILURE**, which would indicate a communications failure.

To allow multiple store programs to run within the same "namespace", the **Tax_i** instance's name is the concatenation of **Tax_** and the Store ID. This works because each instance of Tax is used by exactly one Store object.

The constructor then sets the tax rate to 5 percent. To keep the code simple, we initialize the tax rate member **m_regionRate** from the C++ const **region_rate** defined in store_i.cc.

The complete implementation of the constructor is:

```
Tax_i::Tax_i(PseudoNameService_ptr pns,
             AStore::AStoreId storeID)
{
    // Register the object with the name server
    char regstr[255];
    sprintf(regstr,"Tax_%ld",storeID);
    try {
        pns->BindName(regstr,this);
    }
    catch(...) {
        cerr << "Trouble Binding Tax server" << endl;
    }

    // set tax rate applied to taxable goods
    m_regionRate = region_rate;
}
```

CalculateTax   The virtual member function **CalculateTax** computes the tax from **m_regionRate** and the input argument **TaxableAmount**. It then returns the tax amount.

```
CORBA::Float Tax_i::CalculateTax(
    CORBA::Float          TaxableAmount)
{
    return TaxableAmount* m_regionRate;
}
```

FindTaxablePrice   **FindTaxablePrice** encapsulates the algorithm for computing the taxable price of an item. In our implementation, the whole price of items of type "other" is taxed; all other item types are not taxed. Therefore, **FindTaxablePrice** returns either the value of the input argument price for item type "other" or 0.0 for all other item types:

```
CORBA::Float Tax_i::FindTaxablePrice(
                CORBA::Float          Price,
                AStore::ItemType      Itemtype)
{
    CORBA::Float taxprice;

    if (Itemtype == AStore::other)
        taxprice = Price;
    else
        taxprice = 0.0;
    return taxprice;
}
```

28.2.3 Store_i Class

The **Store_i** class is more sophisticated than the tax class in that it services all POSTerminals in the Store and keeps track of sales information for the Store. POS objects "log in" to the store to activate a session with a **StoreAccess_i** instance. **Store_i** also contains methods for obtaining sales information.

To implement **Store_i**, we first add private data members as specified in the A&D:

```
AStore::AStoreId            m_storeID;
CORBA::Float                m_storeTotal;
CORBA::Float                m_storeTaxTotal;
CORBA::Float                m_storeMarkup;
AStore::POSList             m_POSTerminals;
PseudoNameService_var       m_pns;
```

Store_i uses **m_pns** (which is a reference to the Pseudo-Name Service object) to "name" itself.

There are several places within **Store_i** where we will need to locate a particular POS in the **m_POSTerminals** list. To reduce the amount of redundant code and minimize coding errors, we will encapsulate this algorithm in a private function that accepts a POSId as an argument and returns an index into **m_POSTerminals**.

```
CORBA::ULong LocatePOSEntry(CORBA::Long);
```

The methods **StoreId**, **StoreTotal**, and **StoreTaxTotal** simply return the current values of **m_storeID**, **m_storeTotal**, and **m_storeTaxTotal** respectively. They are accessor methods that correspond to the readonly attributes defined in the IDL (in the file Store.idl):

```
readonly attribute AStore    StoreID;
readonly attribute float     StoreTotal;
readonly attribute float     StoreTaxTotal;
```

The following sections provide a detailed look at the implementation of the constructor and remaining member functions.

Constructor   **Store_i**'s constructor implements the processing defined as the operation Initialize in the Store Analysis and Design. The constructor names the instance using the PseudoNameService method **BindName**. As with the **Tax_i** constructor, the name is the concatenation of **Store_** and the Store ID. Finally, the instance members **m_storeTotal** and **m_storeTaxTotal** are set to **0**, and **m_storeID** and **m_storeMarkup** values are set from the in parameters. The **Store_i** constructor begins:

```
Store_i(
    PseudoNameService_ptr      pns,
    AStore::AStoreId           storeID,
    CORBA::Float               storeMarkup)
{
    // Register the object with the name server
    char refstring[1024];
    sprintf(refstring,"Store_%ld",storeID);
    m_pns = PseudoNameService::_duplicate(pns);
    try {
        pns->BindName(refstring,this);
    }
```

```
catch(...) {
    cerr << "Trouble Binding " << refstring
        << endl;
}

m_storeTotal    = 0;
m_storeTaxTotal = 0;
m_storeMarkup   = storeMarkup;
m_storeID       = storeID;
// ...
}
```

The last activity of the constructor is to initialize the sequence **m_POSTerminals**. Note that **m_POSTerminals** was defined in the IDL to be an unbounded (dynamic) sequence of **POSInfo** structs:

typedef sequence <POSInfo> POSList;

POSList is mapped to a C++ class that provides the ability to get and set the length and iterate over the elements using the **[]** operator (that is, the operator **[]** has been overloaded to return a C++ reference to the **POSInfo** object at the specified index location in the sequence). The POSList class has the following form:

```
class  POSList {
public:
    ...
    CORBA::ULong length() const;
    AStore::POSInfo& operator[](CORBA::ULong index)
    ...
private:
    AStore::POSInfo * data;
    ...
};
```

Refer to Chapter 8 and to your ORB vendor's documentation for a discussion of sequences and their mapping in C++.

The member function length and the **[]** operator allow us to initialize **m_POSTerminals** using the loop shown next. **StoreAccessReference** is initialized by calling **AStore::Store::_nil()**. As just mentioned, **_nil()** enables different ORBs to represent a "nil" **Store_ptr** or nil object reference differently. The remainder of **Store_i**'s constructor is:

```
CORBA::ULong len      = m_POSTerminals.length();
for (CORBA::ULong i = 0; i < len; i++)
{
    // EMPTY is '#define -1'
    m_POSTerminals[i].Id = EMPTY;
    m_POSTerminals[i].StoreAccessReference =
        AStore::Store::_nil();
}
```

Login   Login assigns a **StoreAccess_i** object to the POS and resets
the POS totals to 0. Login first calls the private member function
LocatePOSEntry to obtain a "slot" in the **m_POSTerminals** sequence.
It then initializes the Id, TotalSales, and TotalTaxes fields:

```
CORBA::ULong loc = LocatePOSEntry(Id);

m_POSTerminals[loc].Id         = Id;
m_POSTerminals[loc].TotalSales = 0;
m_POSTerminals[loc].TotalTaxes = 0;
```

Login next checks to see if a StoreAccess object exists, and, if needed,
constructs a new instance. It returns a reference to the StoreAccess object by
calling the StoreAccess class method **_duplicate** because the return value
will be deleted by the ORB as dictated by the C++ language mapping.

```
// check to see of a StoreAccess object exists for
// this m_POSTerminal allocate new one if needed.
if (CORBA::is_nil((AStore::StoreAccess_ptr
    )m_POSTerminals[loc].StoreAccessReference))
{
    // create a local instance of the
    // StoreAccess Object
    m_POSTerminals[loc].StoreAccessReference =
        new StoreAccess_i(
             m_pns
            ,this
            ,m_storeMarkup);
    if (CORBA::is_nil((AStore::StoreAccess_ptr )
        m_POSTerminals[loc].StoreAccessReference))
        cerr << "Store_i::Login: Unable to create
            StoreAccess object for POS Login" << endl;
}
return AStore::StoreAccess::_duplicate
    (m_POSTerminals[loc].StoreAccessReference);
```

LocatePOSEntry This private method encapsulates the details of searching the **m_POSTerminals** sequence for an available entry. It detects when an entry for the specified POS ID exists and reuses that slot, which prevents creation of a new StoreAccess reference when one already exists.

GetPOSTotals This method returns the **m_POSTerminals** sequence to the caller. Note that the argument is an out parameter; the semantics of CORBA remote method invocations requires that we allocate and return a copy of **m_POSTerminals**. Allocating memory is necessary for return values and out arguments that are variable-length types such as strings, object references, and sequences.

```
void Store_i::GetPOSTotals(
        AStore::POSList *&POSData)
{
    POSData = new AStore::POSList(m_POSTerminals);
}
```

UpdateStoreTotals **UpdateStoreTotals** is called to update the running totals for the POS terminal specified by the input parameter ID. It calls **LocatePOSEntry** to locate the entry in **m_POSTerminals**, then updates both the POS totals and the store totals:

```
void Store_i::UpdateStoreTotals(
                        CORBA::Long  Id,
                        CORBA::Float Price,
                        CORBA::Float Taxes)
{
    CORBA::ULong i = LocatePOSEntry(Id);
    if (i != EMPTY)
    {
        m_POSTerminals[i].TotalSales += Price;
        m_POSTerminals[i].TotalTaxes += Taxes;
        m_storeTotal              += Price;
        m_storeTaxTotal           += Taxes;
    }

    else
        cerr << "Store_i::UpdateStoreTotals: Could not locate
            POS Terminal " << Id << endl;
}
```

28.2.4 StoreAccess_i Class

StoreAccess provides a mechanism for managing POS sessions, and it is the intermediary between the POS and the central depot concerning access to the grocery item database.

Constructor The **StoreAccess_i** constructor sets the StoreAccess state variables from the input parameters. This includes setting **m_store**. We will call **_duplicate** to assign a copy of the input argument store. For example:

```
m_store =
    AStore::Store::_duplicate(store);
```

The issues here are similar to those just discussed for GetPOSTotals; Store is "owned" by the ORB and will be deallocated after the constructor returns. By calling **_duplicate**, we ensure that **m_store** will not "go out of scope." The complete implementation of the constructor is:

```
StoreAccess_i::StoreAccess_i(
    PseudoNameService_ptr pns,
    AStore::Store_var      store,
    CORBA::Float           markup)
{
    m_storeMarkup = markup;
    try
    {
        char refstr[255];
        AStore::AStoreId id = pStore->StoreId();
        sprintf(refstr,"Tax_%ld",id);
        m_tax= AStore::Tax::_narrow(pns->
            ResolveName(refstr));
        m_depot=
            CentralOffice::Depot::_narrow(pns->
                ResolveName("Depot"));
        m_store =
            AStore::Store::_duplicate(store);
    }
    catch(...) {
        cerr << "Trouble finding tax, store, or depot "
            << endl;
    }
}
```

FindPrice FindPrice computes the price and taxable price for the quantity of the item specified by the bar code. It also returns an **ItemInfo** struct, which it retrieves from the central depot. The price (**ItemPrice**) is computed as the cost times markup percent as required in the A&D:

Calculate ItemPrice as item's cost times storeMarkup.

The A&D and IDL specify that FindPrice should raise a **BarcodeNot-Found** exception if the input bar code is not known to the Depot. Because **Depot_i::FindItemInfo** itself raises this exception, we simply let the exception propogate to the caller.

```
void StoreAccess_i::FindPrice(
        const char          *Item,
        CORBA::Long         Quantity,
        CORBA::Float&       ItemPrice,
        CORBA::Float&       ItemTaxPrice,
        AStore::ItemInfo    *&IInfo)
{

    if (!CORBA::is_nil((const
    CentralOffice::Depot_ptr)m_depot))
    {
        AStore::ItemInfo *i2;
        m_depot->FindItemInfo(
                m_store->StoreId(),
                Item,
                Quantity,
                i2);

        IInfo       = new AStore::ItemInfo;
        *IInfo      = *i2;
        ItemPrice
            m_storeMarkup * IInfo->Itemcost;
        ItemTaxPrice = m_tax->FindTaxablePrice(
        ItemPrice,
        ((AStore::ItemInfo *) IInfo)->Itemtype);
    }
}
```

28.2.5 Srv_Main.c

The Store program expects the user to supply a store number and markup percent as command-line parameters. main first validates that the correct number of arguments were supplied, and then initializes the ORB

and BOA. main initializes the ORB and BOA by calling the methods
CORBA::ORB_init and **BOA_init**. This is typically the first activity of
a CORBA application.

```
if (argc<3) {
    cerr << "usage: " << argv[0] << "<Store Number>
        <Markup>" << endl;
    return 1;
}

CORBA::ORB_ptr orb  = CORBA::ORB_init(argc, argv);
CORBA::BOA_ptr boa  =
    orb->BOA_init(argc, argv, "");
```

main then constructs local (within the current address space) instances
of the **Tax_i** and **Store_i** classes. Note that this may be accomplished differently by each ORB. After the two objects are constructed, all application-
related activity is initiated by clients.

The three local CORBA objects **tax1**, **store1**, and **pns** are declared as
follows:

```
AStore::Tax_var          tax1;
AStore::Store_var        store1;
PseudoNameService_var    pns;
```

Note that each of these CORBA objects has been declared as a **_var** type.
The var classes manage the allocation and deallocation of stub and implementation instances, simplifying the application code. **Tax1** and **store1** will
"own" instances of the implementation class, and **pns** will hold an instance
of a stub (returned by **FindPNS**).

Tax_i and **Store_i** both take a PseudoNameService reference as an
argument. We will call **FindPNS** to obtain a reference to the name server.
Note that this processing is done within a C++ **try** block (shown shortly) to
allow us to catch any exceptions raised by **FindPNS** or the constructors. If
an exception is raised, then control jumps to the C++ **catch** block.

We verify that **FindPNS** was successful by ensuring that the return value
is non-nil. The Boolean method **CORBA::is_nil** operates on an object reference and returns **TRUE** if the reference is nil as defined by the ORB. The
local implementation instances of **Tax_i** and **Store_i** are instantiated by
invoking the C++ allocator **new** (this may vary between ORB implementations):

```
try
{
    pns=FindPNS(orb);
    if (CORBA::is_nil(pns))
    {
        cerr << "Unable to get a reference to the name
            service" << endl;
        return 1;
    }


    tax1 = new Tax_i(pns,atof(argv[1]));
    store1 = new
        Store_i(pns,atof(argv[1]),atol(argv[2]));
}
catch(...)
{
    cerr << "ERROR Starting Server" << endl;
    return 1;
}
```

Finally, main must enter an event loop, which detects and dispatches requests from (possibly remote) clients. This activity is specific to individual operating systems and ORBs, and is discussed in the upcoming ORB-specific sections.

28.2.6 Implementation Summary

If you've been typing in the code as you went along, your Store code is nearly complete. You're ready to make just a few adjustments for your specific ORB, and prepare to run your Store objects. Once more, you won't be able to test them until you've completed a few more chapters, but this does represent additional progress.

28.3 CONNECTING TO THE ORB AND BOA, AND STARTING THE STORE OBJECT

Once more, we have a few ORB-specific adjustments to make before our objects are complete. That code is presented in the remainder of this chapter, along with reminders of product-specific procedures to create and fire up your objects.

Next you need to go to the section in this chapter on your specific ORB product and follow its procedures to get your objects ready and running. After you've finished, go to Chapter 30 to start coding the POS objects.

28.4 POWERBROKER

The PowerBroker implementation of the store interfaces is very similar to the common functionality implementation. The PowerBroker-specific implementation issues are:

PowerBroker include files

base class names

BOA::impl_is_ready

the PowerBroker event loop

use of **_out** classes for CORBA **out** and **inout** arguments

Each of these issues was already described in detail in Section 25.6, The PowerBroker Implementation of the Depot.

To compile and link the store, follow these steps:

1. Type this command to compile the Store code:

```
% CC -c -I. -I$PBHOME/include store_i.C Srv_Main.C
```

2. Type this command to link the store program:

```
% CC -o store Srv_Main.o store_i.o Store.o Store_s.o
    Central.o \
PNS.o FindPNS.o -L$PBHOME/lib -lcorba -lpbroker
```

28.5 THE ORBIX IMPLEMENTATION OF THE STORE

Background information on how to code and run Orbix clients and servers is given in Section 25.7, and you should remind yourself of the material in that section before continuing.

28.5.1 Changes to the C++ Code

The lines written:

```
CORBA::ORB_var orb =
    CORBA::ORB_init(argc,argv,"PRIMER_ORB");
CORBA::BOA_var boa = orb->BOA_init(argc,argv);
```

in the shared C++ code must be recoded to use the string **Orbix** instead of **PRIMER_ORB**.

Alternatively, the variable **CORBA::Orbix** can be used to find Orbix instead of using **ORB_init()** and **BOA_init()**. In fact, **ORB_init()** and **BOA_init()** do not need to be called at all because initialization is handled automatically.

No other changes to the C++ code are required.

28.5.2 Registering the Server

The server that creates the Store object is called **StoreSrv**, and it can be registered by the following command (the line breaks shown here should not be included in the command; the individual parts of the command should be separated by spaces or tabs):

```
putit StoreSrv
        <full pathname of the executable file
                        (StoreServer) for this server>
        <Store_Number>
        <Markup>
```

Once registered, a server can be started manually (through the operating system's normal command-line interpreter), or it will be started automatically when a client invokes an operation (or accesses an attribute) of one of the objects in the server. The command-line arguments to the server have been specified to putit so that they will be passed to the server each time it is automatically launched.

28.5.3 Makefile for the Store in Orbix

Some of the makefile for the Store is shown here (directory Store, file Makefile). The full makefile includes rules for compiling the files Store_i.cc and Srv_Main.cc:

```
default: StoreServer

Store_SERVER_OBJS = ../StoreS.o ../CentralC.o \
                    ../PNSC.o \
                    ../PNS/FindPNS.o Store_i.o \
                    Srv_Main.o

StoreServer: $(Store_SERVER_OBJS)
    $(C++) $(C++FLAGS) -o StoreServer \
        $(Store_SERVER_OBJS) $(LDFLAGS) -lITsrv
```

28.6 ORB PLUS

The types of changes required for ORB Plus from the generic C++ code were described in detail for the Depot, in Section 25.8. This section describes these changes for the Store implementation. Refer to the Depot chapter for a more detailed description of these changes.

28.6.1 Srv_Main.cc

The changes for the Store Srv_Main are as follows:

1. Create an instance of **CORBA::Environment**.

```
CORBA::Environment IT_env;
```

2. Initialize the ORB.

```
CORBA::ORB_var orb =
        CORBA::ORB_init(argc,argv,CORBA::HPORBid,
                            IT_env);
if (IT_env.exception()) {
   cerr << "ERROR Initializing ORB" << endl;
   exit(EXIT_FAILURE);
}
```

3. Initialize the **HPSOA**.

```
CORBA::HPSOA_var soa = orb->HPSOA_init(argc,
                            argv,CORBA::HPSOA,
                            IT_env);
if (IT_env.exception()) {
   cerr << "ERROR Initializing HPSOA" << endl;
   exit(EXIT_FAILURE);
}
```

4. Create an instance of the **Tax_i** C++ object.

```
Tax_i  tax1(pns,atol(argv[1]), IT_env);
```

5. Create an instance of the **Store_i** C++ object.

```
CORBA::Float markup;
   istrstream s(argv[2]);
   s >> markup;
   Store_i store1(pns,atol(argv[1]), markup, IT_env);
```

6. Issue the HPSOA run command.

```
soa->run();
```

28.6.2 Store_i

The header file Store_i.h contains the following class descriptions:

- Tax_i is derived from the **HPSOA_AStore::Tax** object, which was generated by the cidl compiler.

```
class Tax_i: public virtual HPSOA_AStore::Tax {
```

- **Store_i** is derived from the **HPSOA_AStore** object.

```
class Store_i : public virtual HPSOA_AStore::Store {
```

- The operations (**CalculateTax, FindTaxablePrice, StoreId, StoreTotals, Login, GetPOSTotals, UpdateStoreTotals, FindPrice**) have the **CORBA::Environment** parameter added.

The implementation file Store_i.cc contains the following changes from the generic C++ code:

- The Tax_i and Store_i constructors use the **_this()** function to obtain the object reference.

```
// Register the Tax object with the name server
  char regstr[255];
  sprintf(regstr,"Tax_%ld",StoreId);
  AStore::Tax_var TaxObjRef = _this();
  pns->BindName(regstr,TaxObjRef, IT_env);

// Register the Store object with the name server
  char refstring[512];
  sprintf(refstring,"Store_%ld",StoreId);
  m_pns            = pns;
  AStore::Store_var StoreObjRef = _this();
  m_pns->BindName(refstring, StoreObjRef, IT_env);
```

For all operations, explicit exception checking is used instead of standard C++ exceptions.

28.7   SUNSOFT NEO

Most of the notes presented for the PseudoNamingService implementation (Coding the PseudoNameService (PNS), Section 25.9.1) remain valid for the Store's implementation. However, a few remarks specific to the Store are needed.

28.7.1   store.impl

Unlike the Depot and the PseudoNameService, which both had only one interface defined for the server, the Store server must implement several interfaces: **AStore::Tax**, **AStore::Store**, and **AStore::StoreAccess**.

Therefore, the store.impl file needs to contain implementation directives for each of the three interfaces. For example, the implementation record for **AStore::Tax** directs ODF to generate a C++ class called **Tax_i** with an initialization method called **_initialize_new_Tax()** and with no timeout; the object will remain activated until the server exits.

28.7.2   Srv_Main.cc

This is where the Tax and Store objects are created. This is done by invoking the appropriate creator method as specified in store.impl. For example, a new Tax object can be created by calling:

```
OdfTax_i::new_Tax( pns );
```

The class **OdfTax_i** is an infrastructure class generated by NEOworks to support the actual implementation class **Tax_i**. The static method **new_Tax()** is defined on **OdfTax_i**. It creates a new object reference (with interface **AStore::Tax**) and an instance of the implementation class (*servant*); in this case, an instance of **Tax_I**. Finally, **new_Tax()** calls **_initialize_new_Tax()** on the new instance of **Tax_I** and returns the new object reference.

The same mechanism is used to create the new Store object.

28.7.3   store_i.cc

In the initialization method, **Store_I::_initialize_new_Store()** creates the **m_POSTerminals.buffer** sequence by invoking:

```
AStore::POSInfo::_new_bracket( 10 );
```

This call is similar to **new AStore::POSInfo[10]**, but is used to allocate sequence buffers.

CHAPTER 29

Coding the Store
in Smalltalk

29.1 GETTING STARTED ON THE STORE

This chapter presents the implementation of the Store module in HP Distributed Smalltalk. As we did in Chapter 26, we'll try to keep the standard IDL and Smalltalk components separate from the HP implementation details. You should have just read the description of the language-independent implementation details for the Store in Section 27.1. If you didn't, turn back and read it now; it tells what we're going to do in this chapter.

As before, this Smalltalk code must be entered into your system. If you're typing it in by hand as you work the example, open up a system browser and view the **OMG Primer Example** class category. All classes discussed in this section should be added to this class category. And, if you read everything in from the floppy disk, open up a system browser on the **OMG Primer Example** class category to view the code as we discuss it. In either case, when you reach the end of the chapter, your Store implementation will be complete.

The requirements for the Store objects were fixed in our A&D in Sections 19.1.4, 19.1.5, and 19.1.6; implementation details were added in Section 27.1. You'll need to refer to those sections in order to follow us as we code the Smalltalk that implements them.

29.2 SMALLTALK IMPLEMENTATION OF THE STORE IDL

Three IDL interfaces (**Store**, **StoreAccess**, and **Tax**) and a data structure (**POSInfo**) are associated with the Store, as seen in the partial IDL listing here. As always, the class pragma on **POSInfo** is specific to HP Distributed Smalltalk. Of particular interest is the **Store** interface, which illustrates the use of read-only attributes and structure-valued attributes. Four Smalltalk classes provide the implementation for the store: **Store**, **StoreAccess**, **Tax**, and **POSInfo**.

```
module AStore {

    enum ItemTypes {food, clothes, other};

    typedef long AStoreId;

    #pragma class ItemInfo ItemInfo
    struct ItemInfo {
        POS::Barcode Item;
        ItemTypes Itemtype;
        float Itemcost;
        string Name;
        long Quantity;
    };

    exception BarcodeNotFound {POS::Barcode item; };
    interface StoreAccess;

    #pragma class POSInfo POSInfo
    struct POSInfo {
        POS::POSId Id;
        StoreAccess StoreAccessReference;
        float TotalSales;
        float TotalTaxes;
    };

    typedef sequence<POSInfo> POSList;

    interface Tax {
        float CalculateTax (in float TaxableAmount);
        float FindTaxablePrice (in float ItemPrice, in ItemTypes ItemType);
    };

    interface Store {
        struct StoreTotals {float StoreTotal; float StoreTaxTotal; };

        readonly attribute AStoreId StoreId;
        readonly attribute StoreTotals Totals;
        StoreAccess Login (in POS::POSId Id);
```

```
        void GetPOSTotals (out POSList POSData);
        void UpdateStoreTotals (in POS::POSId Id, in float Price,
        in float Taxes);
};

interface StoreAccess {
    void FindPrice (
                    in POS::Barcode Item,
                    in long Quantity,
                    out float ItemPrice,
                    out float ItemTaxPrice,
                    out ItemInfo IInfo)
                raises (BarcodeNotFound);
    };
};
```

29.2.1 Smalltalk Implementation for Store

The Smalltalk implementation of **Store** is shown in the following code listing. The code discussion is organized according to protocol category, and any code references are by line number.

```
1     Class:      Store
2
3     Superclass: Object
4     Category:   OMG Primer Example
5     Instance variables:storeTotal storeTaxTotal POSTerminals
6                        storeMarkup storeId
7     Class variables:SA
8
9     Protocol: repository
10
11    CORBAName
12        ^#'::AStore::Store'
13
14    Protocol: Store
15
16    getPOSTotals: list
17        list value: POSTerminals copy
18
19    login: aPOSId
20        | pos |
21        pos := POSTerminals detect: [:t | t Id = aPOSId]
22                        ifNone: [nil].
23        pos isNil
```

```
24              ifTrue:
25                  [pos := POSInfo new: aPOSId.
26                   SA := StoreAccess new initialize: storeId
                            markup: storeMarkup.
27                   pos StoreAccessReference: SA.
28                   POSTerminals add: pos]
29              ifFalse: [pos reset].
30          ^pos StoreAccessReference
31
32      StoreId
33          ^storeId
34
35      Totals
36          ^Dictionary with: #StoreTotal -> storeTotal with:
                #StoreTaxTotal -> storeTaxTotal
37
38      updateStoreTotals: posId price: sales taxes: taxes
39          | pos |
40          pos := POSTerminals detect: [:t | t Id = posId]
41                          ifNone: [self error: 'POS not found
                                in list.'].
42          pos addToSales: sales.
43          pos addToTaxes: taxes.
44          storeTotal := storeTotal + sales.
45          storeTaxTotal := storeTaxTotal + taxes
46
47      Protocol: initialization
48
49      initialize: theStoreId markup: theMarkup
50          storeId := theStoreId.
51          storeMarkup := theMarkup.
52          storeTotal := 0.0.
53          storeTaxTotal := 0.0.
54          POSTerminals := OrderedCollection new
```

▪ **Superclass** (line 3): **Store** inherits from the Smalltalk class **Object**, which is the root of the Smalltalk inheritance tree.

▪ **Instance variables** (lines 5–6): **storeTotal**, **storeTaxTotal**, **POSTerminals**, **storeMarkup**, and **storeId** are the instance variables that hold the running Store totals and tax totals, the list of logged-in POS terminals, the store markup, and the Store ID respectively.

▪ **Class variables** (line 7): **SA** is used to hold an instance of the **StoreAccess** class. An instance of the **StoreAccess** class is created by the Store and passed out (as an object reference) to the POS terminal. Maintaining a reference to the **StoreAccess** instance ensures that it will not be garbage collected, which must not happen if a reference is passed outside the image. The HP Distributed Smalltalk preferred technique would be to use the CORBAservices Lifecyle service, but this example explicitly does not use the CORBAservices.

▪   **Protocol: repository** (lines 11–12): HP Distributed Smalltalk requires the **CORBAName** method to associate an IDL interface (in this case **Store**) with its implementing Smalltalk class, **Store**.

▪   **Protocol: Store** (lines 16–45): This protocol category is initial capitalized, which indicates that all methods found in this category are implementations of IDL operations found in the corresponding IDL interface. Many times, the mapping from an IDL operation to its Smalltalk implementation is explicitly shown via the selector pragma. In this case, the default mapping is used (no selector pragmas specified). There are three IDL operations implemented in this protocol:

::AStore::Store::GetPOSTotals

This IDL operation is implemented by the **getPOSTotals:** method. A copy of the collection of registered (logged-in) POS terminals for this Store is returned. Here again is an example of a CORBA **out** parameter implemented in Smalltalk via the Smalltalk language bindings. The caller of **getPOSTotals:** sets up the **out** parameter using the **asCORBAParameter** method. In order for **getPOSTotals:** to return its result as an **out** parameter, it sends **value:** to its argument, **list**, with a copy of the collection of POS terminals.

::AStore::Store::Login

This IDL operation is implemented by the **Login:** method. A check is done to see if the terminal requesting login is already logged in. If so, the corresponding **StoreAccess** reference is returned. Otherwise, a new **POSInfo** instance is created and initialized with the Store Access object, Store ID, and markup. The **POSInfo** instance is added to the collection of logged-in POS terminals for this store. The Store Access object reference is returned.

This method demonstrates the passing out of an object reference. It creates a local **StoreAccess** object and returns it to the caller (possibly remote). A reference to the **StoreAccess** object is kept in the class variable SA so that a garbage collection will not mistakenly collect this object, invalidating the returned reference.

::AStore::Store::UpdateStoreTotals

This IDL operation is implemented by the **updateStoreTotals: price:taxes:** method.

It increments the sales and tax totals for the given POS terminal. The running Store totals are also updated.

There are also two IDL operations on attributes implemented in this protocol:

::AStore::Store::StoreId

StoreId is a read-only attribute that is implemented by the **StoreId** method. The value of the **storeId** instance variable is returned. Since this attribute is read-only, there is no set method.

::AStore::Store::Totals

Totals is a read-only attribute that holds a structure that contains the **storeTotal** and **storeTaxTotal** values. This is an example of how a default binding for a structure works. This attribute is implemented by the **Totals** method. The two values are stored as instance variables of the **Store** class. When the **Totals** method is called, a **Dictionary** is created with entries keyed by the IDL struct field names. The corresponding values are the values of the respective instance variables.

29.2.2 Smalltalk Implementation for Tax

The Smalltalk implementation **Tax** is shown in the following code listing. The code discussion is organized according to protocol category, and any code references are by line number.

```
1       Class: Tax
2
3       Superclass:       Object
4       Category:         OMG Primer Example
5       Class variables:  RegionRate
6
7       Protocol: repository
8
9       CORBAName
10          ^#'::AStore::Tax'
11
12      Protocol: Tax
13
14      calculateTax: amount
15          ^amount * RegionRate
16
17      findTaxablePrice: itemPrice itemType: taxType
18          taxType = (CORBAConstants at:
```

```
                    #'::AStore::ItemTypes::other')
19                  ifTrue: [^itemPrice]
20                  ifFalse: [^0.0]
21
22     MetaClass Protocol: class initialization
23
24     initialize
25         RegionRate := 0.05
```

- **Superclass** (line 3): **Tax** inherits from the Smalltalk class **Object**, which is the root of the Smalltalk inheritance tree.

- **Class variables** (line 5): **RegionRate** is a class variable that is set to the flat tax rate, 5 percent for this example, at the time the **Tax** class is initialized.

- **Protocol: repository** (lines 9–10): HP Distributed Smalltalk requires the **CORBAName** method to associate an IDL interface (in this case **Tax**) with its implementing Smalltalk class, **Tax**.

- **Protocol: Tax** (lines 14–20): This protocol category is initial capitalized, which indicates that all methods found in this category are implementations of IDL operations found in the corresponding IDL interface. Many times, the mapping from an IDL operation to its Smalltalk implementation is explicitly shown via the selector pragma. In this case, the default mapping is used (no selector pragmas specified). There are two IDL operations implemented in this protocol:

    ::AStore::Tax::CalculateTax

    This IDL operation is implemented by the **calculateTax:** method (lines 14–15). The input amount is multiplied by the tax rate, and the result is returned.

    ::AStore::Tax::FindTaxablePrice

    This IDL operation is implemented by the **findTaxablePrice: itemType:** method (lines 17–20). This method determines how much, if any, of the item price is taxable. If the item tax type is food or clothes, then the item is not taxable, (0 is returned); otherwise, the item is taxable.

    This method shows the use of enumerations as the tax type (second argument) is compared to see if it is 'other' (line 18).

    MetaClass Protocol: class initialization (line 22): The initialize method (lines 24–25) is classed when the **Tax** class is initialized (loaded). The **RegionRate** class variable is set to the 5 percent flat tax rate.

29.2.3 Smalltalk Implementation for StoreAccess

The Smalltalk implementation class **StoreAccess** is shown in the following code listing. The code discussion is organized according to protocol category, and any code references are by line number.

```
1       Class:          StoreAccess
2
3       Superclass: Object
4       Category:   OMG Primer Example
5       Instance variables: storeId storeMarkup tax depot
6
7       Protocol: repository
8
9       CORBAName
10          ^#'::AStore::StoreAccess'
11
12      Protocol: StoreAccess
13
14      findPrice: aBarcode quantity: aCount itemPrice: aPrice
            itemTaxPrice: aTaxPrice iInfo: item
15          | itemInfo cost |
16          (CORBAConstants at: '::AStore::BarcodeNotFound')
17              corbaHandle: [:ev | ^(CORBAConstants at:
                    #'::AStore::BarcodeNotFound')
18                      corbaRaiseWith: (Dictionary with:
                        (Association key: #item value:
                        aBarcode))]
19              do:
20                  [depot
21                      findItemInfo: storeId
22                      barCode: aBarcode
23                      quantity: aCount
24                      itemInfo: (itemInfo := nil
                        asCORBAParameter).
25                  cost := itemInfo value Itemcost.
26                  cost := cost + (cost * storeMarkup).
27                  aPrice value: cost.
28                  aTaxPrice value: (tax findTaxablePrice:
                    cost itemType: itemInfo value Itemtype).
29                  item value: itemInfo value]
30
31      Protocol: accessing
32
33      StoreId
34          ^storeId
35
```

```
36     StoreId: anId
37          storeId := anId
38
39     Protocol: initialization
40
41     initialize: theStoreId markup: theMarkup
42          | pns |
43          storeId := theStoreId.
44          storeMarkup := theMarkup.
45          pns := ORBObject pseudoNameService.
46          depot := pns resolveName: 'Depot'.
47          tax := pns resolveName: 'Tax_' , storeId asString
```

▪ **Superclass** (line 3): **StoreAccess** inherits from the Smalltalk class **Object**, which is the root of the Smalltalk inheritance tree.

▪ **Instance variables** (line 5): **storeId**, **storeMarkup**, **tax**, and **depot** hold the Store ID, the Store markup percentage, and references to the Tax and Depot objects respectively.

▪ **Protocol: repository** (lines 9–10): HP Distributed Smalltalk requires the **CORBAName** method to associate an IDL interface (in this case **StoreAccess**) with its implementing Smalltalk class, **StoreAccess**.

▪ **Protocol: StoreAccess** (lines 14–29): This protocol category is initial capitalized, which indicates that all methods found in this category are implementations of IDL operations found in the corresponding IDL interface. Many times, the mapping from an IDL operation to its Smalltalk implementation is explicitly shown via the selector pragma. In this case, the default mapping is used (no selector pragmas specified). There is one IDL operation implemented in this protocol:

::AStore::StoreAccess::FindPrice

This IDL operation is implemented by the **findPrice:quantity: itemPrice:itemTaxPrice:iInfo:** method (lines 14–29).

This method retrieves item cost and tax type from the Depot. Before the Depot call is made, an exception handler is set up for the **::AStore::BarcodeNotFound** exception (lines 16–18). The **corbaHandle:** block is called if the exception is raised while executing the **do:** block. If the exception is raised, it is passed on with illegal bar code (line 18).

The call is made to the Depot. The item price is increased by the markup (lines 25–26) and returned as the value of an **out** parameter (line 27). The Tax object is consulted to compute the tax amount (line 28) and the result is passed back as an **out** parameter (line 28).

Finally, the **ItemInfo** structure is passed back as an **out** parameter (line 29).

Note the use of **asCORBAParameter** to set up the call to the Depot (line 24).

- **Protocol: accessing** (lines 33–37): The methods in this protocol implement the setting and getting of the **StoreId** attribute.

- **Protocol: initialize** (lines 41–47): The **initialize** method is called to initialize a new instance of a **StoreAccess** object. The storeId and markup are set from the input arguments. The object references to the **Tax** and **Depot** objects are obtained from the **PseudoNameService**.

29.2.4 Smalltalk Implementation for POSInfo

The IDL structure **::AStore::POSInfo** is implemented by the Smalltalk class **POSInfo**. By default, an IDL struct is mapped to an instance of the **Dictionary** class. The Dictionary will have an entry for each field in the struct consisting of a key-value pair where the key is the field name and the value is the value of the field. By using the class pragma, this behavior is overridden.

The class pragma instructs the IDL compiler to associate the Smalltalk **POSInfo** class with the IDL structure **POSInfo**. This ensures that the IDL **ItemInfo** structure will always be represented as an **ItemInfo** class instance within Smalltalk.

The Smalltalk implementation of **POSInfo** is shown in the following code listing. The code discussion is organized according to protocol category, and any code references are by line number.

```
1      Class: POSInfo
2
3      Superclass: Object
4      Category:   OMG Primer Example
5      Instance variables: id totalSales totalTaxes
6                          storeAccessReference
7
8      Protocol: repository
9
10     CORBAType
11         ^ORBObject lookupMetaId: #'::AStore::POSInfo'
12
13     Protocol: operations
14
15     addToSales: amount
```

```
16          totalSales := totalSales + amount
17
18     addToTaxes: amount
19          totalTaxes := totalTaxes + amount
20
21     reset
22          totalSales := 0.0.
23          totalTaxes := 0.0
24
25     Protocol: accessing
26
27     Id
28          ^id
29
30     Id: newId
31          id := newId
32
33     StoreAccessReference
34          ^storeAccessReference
35
36     StoreAccessReference: anAccessObject
37          storeAccessReference := anAccessObject
38
39     TotalSales
40          ^totalSales
41
42     TotalSales: sales
43          totalSales := sales
44
45     TotalTaxes
46          ^totalTaxes
47
48     TotalTaxes: taxes
49          totalTaxes := taxes
50
51     Protocol: initialization
52
53     initialize: aPOSId
54          id := aPOSId.
55          totalSales := 0.0.
56          totalTaxes := 0.0
57
58     MetaClass protocol: initialize-release
59
60     new: aPOSId
61          ^self basicNew initialize: aPOSId
```

- **Superclass** (line 3): **POSInfo** inherits from the Smalltalk class **Object**, which is the root of the Smalltalk inheritance tree.

- **Instance variables** (lines 5–6): **id**, **totalSales**, **totalTaxes**, and **storeAccessReference** hold the POS terminal's running sales and tax totals and the object reference to the Store Access object respectively.

- **Protocol: repository** (lines 10–11): HP Distributed Smalltalk requires the **CORBAName** method to associate an IDL interface (in this case **POSInfo**) with its implementing Smalltalk class, **POSInfo**.

- **Protocol: operations** (lines 15–23): The methods **addToSales:** and **addToTaxes:** both take an amount argument, and add the amount to the **totalSales** and **totalTaxes** respectively. The **reset** method sets the totals to 0.

- **Protocol: accessing** (lines 27–49): This protocol implements the accessors for the four instance variables. Since this class is mapped to an IDL structure (via a class pragma), all accessors are required to be defined (both set and get). At run time, the appropriate accessors are called by the ORB: getters to marshall a **POSInfo** instance as an IDL structure, and setters to unmarshall the IDL structure as an instance of **POSInfo**. Note that the method names begin with a capital letter, which violates the normal Smalltalk convention for selectors, because the field names of the IDL structure begin with a capital letter. If the IDL had been written with a Smalltalk mind-set, the field names would have begun with a lowercase letter.

- **Protocol: initialization** (lines 53–56): The **initialize** method is called when a new **POSInfo** instance is created to zero the totals and set the ID.

- **MetaClass Protocol: initialize-release** (lines 58–61): The **new** method is redefined to call the **initialize** method.

29.3 IMPLEMENTATION SUMMARY

If you've been typing code into your system as you worked your way through this chapter, or if you've read the code in from the diskette, your Store module implementation is complete. Now turn to Section 30.1 for the implementation overview of the last module containing the POS objects.

CHAPTER 30

Coding the POS in C

30.1 OVERVIEW

This is the last module—the physical points-of-sale (POS) terminals in each store. Once more, this section is for everyone, regardless of which programming language you're using. It adds implementation detail to the A&D for the POS, going as far as it can without becoming language-specific—algorithms, file formats, data flow details. At the end of this section, we'll split into language-specific chapters.

Here are the CORBA features used for the first time (well, almost) in this module:

- CORBA objects with a user interface, making CORBA calls in response to user input;
- a CORBA object with only client interfaces—no BOA linkage; and
- local CORBA objects (okay, okay, not for the first time).

We avoided use of a graphical user interface (GUI) for simplicity (well, not completely), even though we believe that this is the best way to access most applications, including ones based on CORBA. If you're looking for a programming exercise (after you finish modifying this example to use the standard Naming CORBAservice), try modifying your POS module to use a GUI. This will make a more impressive looking demo, even though it doesn't have much to do with CORBA. It will, at least, demonstrate that CORBA and the GUI that you choose can run together in the same module.

There is one POS for each sales position in the store, and each POS is used by one salesperson. Its inputs come from a bar-code reader and from a keypad, and it outputs printed receipts for the customers of the store.

An implementation of the POS must handle these two inputs, communicate as required with the **Store** object local to its store, print receipts, and record brief sales statistics. In this book, the POS is implemented as a CORBA client called **posclt** and a server called **outsrv**. This client and server form a unit, and this pair should be run on each physical point-of-sale terminal.

The **outsrv** server contains a single object of interface **OutputMedia** that prints receipts. It has one operation defined as follows:

boolean OutputText (in string StringToPrint);

The implementation of the **OutputMedia** object is therefore very straight-forward, and in particular it does not interpret the strings that it prints.

Internally, the **posclt** client contains two CORBA objects, one each of interfaces **POSTerminal** and **InputMedia**. The **POSTerminal** object implements the main functionality of the point-of-sale terminal; in particular, it communicates with the **Store** object to find prices, records statistics, and prints receipts by invoking the **OutputText()** operation on the **OutputMedia** object in the **outsrv** server.

The **InputMedia** object in **posclt** handles the inputs. It has two operations, one to accept inputs from the bar-code reader and the other to accept inputs from the keypad. Since our development machines are not equipped with these special input devices, the code in this book uses a simple input reader. This reads lines of input from a normal computer keyboard and passes them to the **InputMedia** object using one of its two operations, shown in the following list. Strings of digits are interpreted as bar codes, and are passed to the **InputMedia** object using the **BarcodeInput()** operation; other input is passed, uninterpreted, using the **KeypadInput()** operation.

The relationship between the components on each point-of-sale terminal is shown in Figure 30.1.

Interface **InputMedia** defines two operations, which are called by the input reader code.

Operation	Meaning
BarcodeInput()	Simulate input of a bar-code reader.
KeypadInput()	Simulate input from the keypad.

The **POSclt** process creates the **POSTerminal** and **InputMedia** objects—and gives the **InputMedia** object a reference to the **POSTerminal** object so that it can make operation calls on it. These two objects are therefore always collocated in this example, showing how CORBA supports distribution transparency; objects are used in the same way whether they are local or remote.

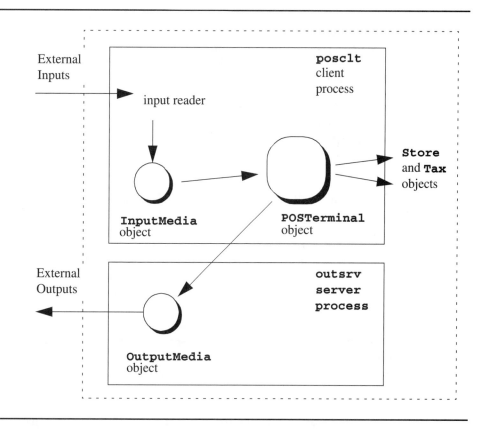

Figure 30.1. Components of each POSTerminal and their relationships.

The **OutputMedia** object is in a separate server that runs on the same machine as the POS. Once it is created, the **OutputMedia** object registers itself with the Pseudo-Name Service. The **POSTerminal** object uses the Pseudo-Name Service (actually its **ResolveName()** operation) to find the **OutputMedia**, **Store**, and **Tax** objects it needs to use (it uses one of each of these three types). These three objects are named as follows within the Pseudo-Name Service:

Store object	**Store_** appended with the store identifier (decimal number)
Tax object	**Tax_** appended with the store identifier (decimal number)
OutputMedia object	**OutputMedia_** appended with the point-of-sale identifier (decimal number)

Each Store is given a unique identifier in the system, and each POS is given an identifier unique within its Store.

The **POSTerminal** interface defines six operations:

```
void Login();
void PrintPOSSalesSummary();
void PrintStoreSalesSummary();
void SendBarcode(in Barcode Item);
void ItemQuantity(in long Quantity);
void EndOfSale();
```

Each of these is invoked by the **InputMedia** object collocated with the **POSTerminal** object. Therefore, the **InputMedia** object sends bar codes to the **POSTerminal** object using the **SendBarcode()** operation. Keypad input is parsed by the **InputMedia** object and sent to the **POSTerminal** object using one of the five other operations.

The implementation of **Login()** requires the **POSTerminal** object to invoke the **Login()** operation on its **Store** object. In order to be able to implement the **PrintPOSSalesSummary()** operation, the **POSTerminal** object must record its own sales and tax totals; the implementation of this operation outputs these values using the **OutputMedia** object.

The implementation of the **PrintStoreSalesSummary()** operation communicates with the local **Store** object to find the store's sales and tax totals and also the sales and tax figures for each **POSTerminal** connected to the store. This data is then formatted and output, again via the **OutputMedia** object.

The **ItemQuantity()** operation is called by the **InputMedia** object when the salesperson uses the keypad to indicate that more than one instance of an item is being purchased. The **POSTerminal** must remember this value (the **Quantity** parameter), and use it on the next invocation of the **SendBarcode()** operation. It then communicates with the **Store** object to find information about the item being purchased, and in particular its price. A line describing the purchase is then output via the **OutputMedia** object.

The **EndOfSale()** operation communicates with the **Tax** object to calculate the tax due on the overall sale, and then it outputs a sales summary, via the **OutputMedia** object, at the end of the receipt.

It is also important that the **POSTerminal** object knows whether it is currently logged on to the **Store** object. It should ignore all other operation calls until the **Login()** operation has been called.

30.1.1 Command-Line Arguments

Each physical point-of-sale terminal contains one **posclt** client and one **outsrv** server. Each one needs to know its unique *POS number* so that it can distinguish itself from the other point-of-sale terminals. Therefore, these two programs take a POS number as a command-line argument. In addition, the **POSTerminal** object in the **POSclt** must know which **Store** object to communicate with, and hence the **POSclt** program also takes a **Store** number as a command-line argument. The **POSTerminal** object appends this **Store** number to the string `Store_` when searching for the correct storing using the Pseudo-Name Service. The command-line arguments are shown here:

`posclt` Store_number and POS_number

`outsrv` POS_number

This concludes the language-independent discussion of the POS implementation. If you're working the example in C, continue with the next section. If you're working in C++, skip to the start of Chapter 31. And if you're working in Smalltalk, skip to the start of Chapter 32.

30.2 C MAPPING COMPONENT

Like Chapters 24 and 27, this section, and the one that follows, present C language code common to every C language ORB. If you're working the example in ObjectBroker, SOMObjects, or DAIS, read both of these sections before skipping to the section specific to your ORB.

The function declarations that we present in this section are part of your next C language file. If you're working the example by typing it in yourself, you'll need to type them in as you read along. If you plan on using the starter files produced by your ORB, grab them from the IDL compiler output—we listed the names in Chapter 23. They contain the declarations we present here, and possibly some additional code that your system will need later.

The C mappings for the definitions of the POS module in the pos.idl file are derived using the rules described in Chapter 7 and Section 24.2. The IDL types are mapped to C datatypes as shown here:

IDL Type	C Type
POS::POSId	`POS_POSId`
POS::Barcode	`POS_Barcode`
POS::InputMedia::OperatorCmd	`POS_InputMedia_OperatorCmd`

Three interfaces—InputMedia, OutputMedia, and POSTerminal—are defined in the POS module in addition to the types. The interaction between these objects was shown in Figure 30.1. The C mapping for the InputMedia methods is shown in the following code:

```
void POS_InputMedia_BarcodeInput (
        POS_InputMedia inputObj,
        CORBA_Environment *ev,
        POS_Barcode Item);

void POS_InputMedia_KeypadInput (
        POS_InputMedia inputObj,
        CORBA_Environment *ev,
        POS_InputMedia_OperatorCmd Cmd);
```

The OutputMedia interface supports one method, whose C mapping is shown next:

```
CORBA_boolean POS_OutputMedia_OutputText (
        POS_OutputMedia    outputObject,
        CORBA_Environment *ev,
        CORBA_string       StringToPrint);
```

The POSTerminal interface supports six methods to perform various operations. The C mapping of each of the seven methods is shown next. A description of the functionality of the methods is given in the following section.

```
void POS_POSTerminal_Login (
        POS_POSTerminal    POSObject,
        CORBA_Environment *ev);

void POS_POSTerminal_PrintPOSSalesSummary (
        POS_POSTerminal    POSObject,
        CORBA_Environment *ev);

void POS_POSTerminal_PrintStoreSalesSummary (
        POS_POSTerminal    POSObject,
        CORBA_Environment *ev);

void POS_POSTerminal_SendBarcode (
        POS_POSTerminal    POSObject,
        CORBA_Environment *ev,
        POS_BarCode        Item);

void POS_POSTerminal_ItemQuantity (
        POS_POSTerminal    POSObject,
        CORBA_Environment *ev,
        CORBA_long         Quantity);
```

```
void POS_POSTerminal_EndOfSale (
        POS_POSTerminal    POSObject,
        CORBA_Environment *ev);
```

In each of these methods, there are two arguments in the C function proto-type that were implicit in the IDL operation declaration. They are the target object and the Environment.

This completes the C declarations generated by the IDL. Now we need to implement the functionality of these interfaces. We'll do that in the next section.

30.3   COMMON FUNCTIONALITY

Next we'll code the functionality of the three POS objects. There's almost nothing ORB-specific about this, so we'll do it all in this section. If you're working the example by hand, type all of this code into your .c file as we go along. At the end of this section, we'll send you off to the section on your specific ORB for final coding, compilation, and linking. Since this is the last module (Hooray!), the only thing left to do after this is run it; that's in Chapter 33.

As before, the methods for the objects have their function names and first two parameter names listed in *italics*. You remember why; we discussed this in Section 24.3. Just keep in mind that you'll have to substitute your ORB vendor's names here as well.

The **InputMedia** object supports two methods. The **BarcodeInput** method accepts a **POS_Barcode** parameter and invokes the **SendBarcode** method on the **POSTerminal** object. The **KeypadInput** method takes a command en-tered via a keyboard of type **POS_InputMedia_OperatorCmd** (a string) and invokes the appropriate method on the **POSTerminal** object. The **OutputText** method on the **OutputMedia** object just prints the string passed to it. The various methods of the **POSTerminal** object support operations such as login to POSTerminal, logoff from a POSTerminal, printing sales summary, and so on. Product-specific parts of the implementation are shown in italics.

30.3.1   The InputMedia Methods

State Declaration   The state declaration is:

```
typedef struct tagImState
{
  POS_POSTerminal    _posreference;
  POS_POSId          _id;
  CORBA_char         *pos_name;
} ImState;
```

This simply declares the information for every InputMedia object created. We initialize it using the following function:

```
ObjectStatePtr
im_init(CORBA_long          argc,
        CORBA_char          **argv,
        CORBA_Environment   *ev,
        CORBA_char          **name)
{
  ImState  *ostate;
  PseudoNameService  pname;

  ostate = malloc(sizeof(ImState));

  if(1 != sscanf(argv[IM_ID_ARG], IM_ID_FMTSTR,
              &ostate->_id))
          application_terminate("bad pos id arg\n", ev);

  ostate->pos_name = malloc(sizeof(POSTERM_REF) +
                              ID_LEN+1);
  sprintf(ostate->pos_name, "%s%d", POSTERM_REF,
          ostate->_id);

  pname = NameService(ev);
  ostate->_posreference =
    PseudoNameService_ResolveName(pname, ev,
    ostate->pos_name);
  if( ev->_major != CORBA_NO_EXCEPTION )
    application_terminate("unable to import pos",ev );

  CORBA_Object_release(pname, ev);

  *name = "input_media";

  return ostate;

} /* end of im_init() */
```

This initializes the InputMedia's object state in a similar way to that of the store_access object in Chapter 27. There is a detailed description there if you are uncertain about anything in this function.

InputMedia Object Creation   Creating an object for the InputMedia is not common. Consult the individual product section for this.

BarcodeInput Method   The **BarcodeInput** method has a very simple implementation. It invokes the **SendBarcode** method on the **POSTerminal** object. The **POSTerminal** object is a state variable of the **InputMedia** object. The code for this method is mostly common. The function prototype and object state access mechanism are vendor-specific, as usual.

```
void  POS_InputMedia_BarcodeInput(
                  POS_InputMedia InputMediaObj,
                  CORBA_Environment *ev,
                  POS_Barcode Item)
{
    ImStat *ostate;
   /* ostate is part of the state
    * information of the input media object. This
    * information is obtained in a product
    * specific way.
    */
    POS_POSTerminal_sendBarcode(ostate->_posreference,
                              ev, Item);
    handle_error("Error sending barcode", ev);
}
```

The **handle_error** routine is a utility routine that checks for exceptions and performs the appropriate exception handling.

KeypadInput Method   The **KeypadInput** method on the **InputMedia** object has a simple switch statement. It invokes the appropriate method on the POSTerminal object based on what the keypad input is.

```
void  POS_InputMedia_KeypadInput(
            POS_InputMedia InputMediaObj,
            CORBA_Environment *ev,
            POS_InputMedia_OperatorCmd Cmd)
{
    ImStat *ostate;
   /* ostate is part of the state
    * information of the input media object. This
    * information is obtained in a product
    * specific way.
    */
    switch (toupper(Cmd[0]))
    {
    case 'L':
    POS_POSTerminal_Login(ostate->_posreference,ev);
```

```
      handle_error("Error on login", ev);
      break;
case 'P':
 POS_POSTerminal_PrintPOSSalesSummary(
            ostate->_posreference, ev);
  handle_error("Error on POS sales summary", ev);
  break;
case 'S':
 POS_POSTerminal_PrintStoreSalesSummary(
            ostate->_posreference, ev);
  handle_error("Error on store sales summary", ev);
  break;
case 'T':
 POS_POSTerminal_EndOfSale(ostate->_posreference,
                            ev);
  handle_error("Error at end of sale", ev);
  break;
case 'Q':
 POS_POSTerminal_ItemQuantity(
                          ostate->_posreference,
                          ev, atol(++Cmd));
  handle_error("Error setting item quantity", ev);
  break;
default: printf("input ignored\n"); /*
                                   ignore */
  }
  return;
}
```

30.3.2   The OutputMedia Object

State Declaration   The object state for the OutputMedia object is actually null, but we have one anyway for debugging purposes and to keep things similar to the other objects.

```
typedef struct tagOmState
{
  char *name;
  CORBA_long id;
} OmState;
```

State Initialization   The debugging information in the state is initialized in much the same way as for the InputMedia object. We won't list it here as it makes little difference if you code it or not because the state is not used in our example.

OutputText Method   The implementation of the OutputText method is trivial in this example. In the real world, this method would actually print the price on a store register tape. It is one of the few (possibly the only) stateless method in the example.

```
CORBA_boolean POS_OutputMedia_output_text(
          POS_OutputMedia OutputMediaObj,
          CORBA_Environment *ev,
          CORBA_string StringToPrint)
{
      return(printf("%s", StringToPrint));
}
```

30.3.3   The POSTerminal Object

The methods of the **POSTerminal** object perform all the actual processing of inputs to the system that are collected by the the **InputMedia** object.

State Declaration   There is a fair bit of state associated with the POS-Terminal object. It invokes methods on the Store, StoreAccess, and Output-Media objects, so it needs to hold their object references and PNS names (it needs the names initially and retains them for debugging purposes). It also holds state relating to the current sale, if one is in progress.

```
typedef struct tagPOSTermState
{
  CORBA_float            _saleSubtotal;
  CORBA_long             _quantity;
  POS_POSId              _posid;
  AStore_AStoreId        _store_id;
  CORBA_float            _saleTaxableSubtotal;
  AStore_StoreAccess     _accessreference;
  AStore_Store           _storereference;
  POS_OutputMedia        _outputreference;
  AStore_Tax             _taxreference;
  CORBA_char             *store_name;
  CORBA_char             *om_name;
  CORBA_char             *tax_name;
  CORBA_char             *pos_name;

} POSTermState;
```

State Initialization   With all that state, the initialization is also quite lengthy. We have seen similar code elsewhere, though, so we we can just type it in without explaining further:

```
ObjectStatePtr
posterm_init(CORBA_long          argc,
             CORBA_char          **argv,
             CORBA_Environment    *ev,
             CORBA_char          **name
                 )
{
  POSTermState         *ostate;
  PseudoNameService   pname;

  ostate = malloc(sizeof(POSTermState));

  if (argc != POS_ARGC)
    application_terminate("wrong number of args\n",
                          ev);

  if(1 != sscanf(argv[POS_ID_ARG], POS_ID_FMTSTR,
                 &ostate->_posid))
    application_terminate("bad pos id arg\n", ev);

  if(1 != sscanf(argv[POS_STORE_ARG], POS_STORE_FMTSTR,
                 &ostate->_store_id))
    application_terminate("bad store id arg\n", ev);

  ostate->pos_name = malloc(sizeof(POSTERM_REF)
                            + ID_LEN+1);
  sprintf(ostate->pos_name, "%s%d", POSTERM_REF,
                          ostate->_posid);
  *name = ostate->pos_name;

  ostate->store_name = malloc(sizeof(STORE_REF)
                              + ID_LEN+1);
  sprintf(ostate->store_name, "%s%d", STORE_REF,
              ostate->_store_id);

  ostate->om_name = malloc(sizeof(OUTPUTMEDIA_REF)
                           +ID_LEN+1);
  sprintf(ostate->om_name, "%s%d", OUTPUTMEDIA_REF,
                        ostate->_posid);

  ostate->tax_name = malloc(sizeof(TAX_REF)+ID_LEN+1);
  sprintf(ostate->tax_name, "%s%d", TAX_REF,
                                ostate->_store_id);

  pname                   = NameService(ev);
  ostate->_storereference =
```

```
                        PseudoNameService_ResolveName(
                                    pname,
                                    ev,
                                    ostate->store_name);
        handle_error("Failed to import store",ev );

        ostate->_taxreference      =
                        PseudoNameService_ResolveName(
                                    pname,
                                    ev,
          handle_error("Failed to create tax object",ev );

        ostate->_outputreference =
                        PseudoNameService_ResolveName(
                                    pname,
                                    ev,
                                    ostate->om_name);
        handle_error("Failed to create output media",ev );

        CORBA_Object_release(pname, ev);

        ostate->_quantity          = 1;
        ostate->_accessreference =
                    (AStore_StoreAccess)CORBA_OBJECT_NIL;


        return ostate;

    } /* end of posterm_init() */
```

POSTerminal_Login Method   The **Login** method logs in to the Store using the reference that it has in its state. The **Store** object returns a **StoreAccess** object. See Chapter 27 for details of the **Store** object.

```
    void POS_POSTerminalLogin(
            POS_POSTerminal POSObject,
                CORBA_Environment *ev)

    {
        POSTermState *ostate;
        /* NOTE: ostate contains the POSTerm
         * state information. The values are
         * obtained in a product-specific manner
         * which is not illustrated here in the
         * common functionality section
         */
```

```
        /* check to see if we are in the middle of
         * a sale
         */

        if (ostate->_saleSubtotal != 0
                    || ostate->_quantity != 1) {
          printf("POSTerminal_login - login ignored"
                 " sale in progress\n");
            return;
        }
        else{
          /* log in to the Store and get StoreAccess
           * object
           */
          ostate->_accessReference = AStore_Store_Login(
                         ostate->_storeReference,
                         ev,ostate->_posId);
          handle_error("Error logging into store", ev);
          printf("POS::login - logged into Store\n");
        }
    }
```

PrintPOSSalesSummary Method   The **PrintPOSSalesSummary** method prints out the sales summary. This method gets the **POSList** from the Store object and looks for its **POSid** in the list. Instead of getting the **POSList**, we could have queried the **Store** object for the sales summary of just a specific **POSTerminal**. However, we need a method that returns the sales summary for all **POSTerminal** objects, to get the sales summary for the entire store in the **PrintStoreSalesSummary** method. We use **GetPOSTotals** method in both cases.

```
    void POS_POSterminal_PrintPOSSalesSummary(
                    POS_POSTerminal POSObject,
                    CORBA_Environment *ev)
  {
    CORBA_char outstring[STR_MAX];
    AStore_POSList poslist;
    CORBA_short count = 0;
    CORBA_short found = 0;
    POSTermState *ostate;
     /* NOTE: ostate contains the POSTerm
      * state information. The values are
      * obtained in a product-specific manner
      * which is not illustrated here in the
      * common functionality section
      */
```

```
/* check to see if we are in the
 * middle of a sale
 */
if ((ostate->_saleSubtotal != 0 ) ||
    (ostate->_quantity != 1))
{
 printf("POS_POSTerminal_PrintPOSSalesSummary"
        "- ignored sale in progress\n");
 return;
}

/*  get poslist from store */
    AStore_Store_GetPOSTotals(ostate->_storeReference,
            ev,&poslist);
  handle_error("Error getting POS totals", ev);

/* look for POSId in poslist */

while ((count < poslist._length) && (!found)){
    if (poslist._buffer[count].Id ==
                ostate->_posId) found = 1;
    count++;
}

/*  if it is not there, we have a problem  */
/*  otherwise, print out the totals */

if (!found) {
 printf("POS_POSTerminal_PrintPOSSalesSummary"
        " POS not found\n");
    CORBA_free(&poslist);
    return;
}
else {
    sprintf(outstring,"Total POS sales = %.2f "
        "  Total POS taxes = %.2f\n",
        poslist._buffer[count-1].TotalSales,
        poslist._buffer[count-1].TotalTaxes);
        POS_OutputMedia_OutputText(
                        ostate->_outputReference,
                        ev,outstring);
    CORBA_free(&poslist);
    return;
}
}
```

POSTerminal_PrintStoreSalesSummary The **PrintStoreSalesSummary** prints the sales summary on the **OutputMedia** object for all the **POSTerminal** objects in the store. The implementation gets the **POSList** and prints the summary for each **POSId** in the list. The implementation of the **PrintStore-SalesSummary** is as follows.

```c
void POS_POSTerminalPrintStoreSalesSummary(
        POS_POSTerminal POSObject,
        CORBA_Environment *ev)
{
    CORBA_char outstring[STR_MAX];
    AStore_POSList poslist;
    AStore_Store_StoreTotals storetotals;
    CORBA_short count;

    POSTermState *ostate;
     /* NOTE: ostate contains the POSTerm
      * state information. The values are
      * obtained in a product-specific manner
      * which is not illustrated here in the
      * common functionality section
      */
    /*  check to see if we are in the
      * middle of a sale
      */

    if ((ostate->_saleSubtotal != 0 ) ||
        (ostate->_quantity  != 1)) {
      printf("POSTerminal_PrintStoreSalesSummary"
             " - ignored, sale in progress\n");
     return;
    }
      printf("POS::print_POS_sales_summary -\n");
    /*  get and print the totals for the Store  */

    storetotals = AStore_Store__get_Totals(
          ostate->_storeReference,ev);
    handle_error("Error getting Totals", ev);

    sprintf(outstring, "Store total = %.2f "
      " Store tax = %.2f\n",
      storetotals.StoreTotal,
      storetotals.StoreTaxTotal);

    POS_OutputMedia_OutputText(
                       ostate->_outputReference,
```

```
                                  ev,outstring);
        handle_error("Error outputting text", ev);

        /*  get the poslist from the Store object  */

        AStore_Store_GetPOSTotals(ostate->_storeReference,
                                  ev,
                                  &poslist);
        handle_error("Error getting POS totals", ev);

        /*  run through the list, printing out
         * the totals
         */

        for (count = 0; count < poslist._length;
             count++){
         sprintf(outstring," POSID = %d  "
                " POSTotal =  %.2f "
                   POSTaxTotal = %.2f\n",
                   poslist._buffer[count].Id,
                   poslist._buffer[count].TotalSales,
                   poslist._buffer[count].TotalTaxes);

            POS_OutputMedia_OutputText(
                                 ostate->_outputReference,
                                 ev,outstring);
         handle_error("Error outputting text", ev);
        }

        /*  free returned memory  */

        CORBA_free(&poslist);
        return;
    }
```

POSTerminal_SendBarcode Method   The next method, **SendBarcode**,
takes as input the bar code of the item and prints the price of the item
on the **OutputMedia** object. This method also keeps a running total of the
sales and identifies which items are taxable. The implementation follows:

```
    void POS_POSTerminal_SendBarcode(
            POS_POSTerminal POSObject,
                CORBA_Environment *ev,
                POS_Barcode Item)
        {
```

```
CORBA_char outstring[STR_MAX];
CORBA_float    itemprice,itemtaxprice;
AStore_ItemInfo iteminfo;

POSTermState *ostate;
 /* NOTE: ostate contains the POSTerm
  * state information. The values are
  * obtained in a product-specific manner
  * which is not illustrated here in the
  * common functionality section
  */
printf("POS::send_barcode - \n");

/*  call FindPrice on the StoreAccess object
 */

    AStore_StoreAccess_FindPrice(
      ostate->_accessReference, ev, Item,
      ostate->_quantity, &itemprice, &itemtaxprice,
      &iteminfo);

/*  check for and handle exception  */

if (ev->_major != NO_EXCEPTION)
{
 handle_error("Error on finding price", ev);
 ostate->_quantity = 1;
 return;
}

/*  accumulate totals for the current sale  */

ostate->_saleSubtotal += itemprice
                       * ostate->_quantity;
ostate->_saleTaxableSubtotal += itemtaxprice
                       * ostate->_quantity;

/* print out information with format depending
 * upon whether item is taxable or not
 */
if (itemtaxprice)
   sprintf(outstring,"%s*  %s  %d   %.2f"
                     " %.2f\n",
        iteminfo.Item, iteminfo.Name,
        ostate->_quantity,itemprice,
        itemprice * ostate->_quantity);
```

```
    else
     sprintf(outstring,"%s   %s   %d     %.2f"
                          "    %.2f\n",
            iteminfo.Item, iteminfo.Name,
          ostate->_quantity,itemprice,
          itemprice * ostate->_quantity);


    POS_OutputMedia_OutputText(
                 ostate->_outputReference,ev,outstring);
    handle_error("Error outputting text", ev);

    /* free memory and reset quantity
      * instance variable
      */

    CORBA_free(&iteminfo);
    ostate->_quantity = 1;

    return;
}
```

POSTerminal_ItemQuantity Method   The implementation of the **ItemQuantity** is shown next. The quantity information is used in the **SendBarCode** method to compute the total price of sale of multiple items of the same kind.

```
void   POS_POSTerminal_ItemQuantity(
          POS_POSTerminal POSObject,
               CORBA_Environment *ev,
               long Quantity)
{
    POSTermState *ostate;
     /* NOTE: ostate contains the POSTerm
       * state information. The values are
       * obtained in a product-specific manner
       * which is not illustrated here in the
       * common functionality section
       */

    ostate->_quantity = Quantity;
}
```

POSTerminal_EndOfSale Method   The implementation of the **EndOfSale** method is given next. This method prints the subtotal before tax, the tax,

and the total of the complete sales transaction. The method also updates the
total for the **POSTerminal** in the **Store** object.

```
void POS_POSTerminalEndOfSale(
          POS_POSTerminal POSObject,
          CORBA_Environment *ev)
{
    CORBA_float tax;
    CORBA_char  outstring[STR_MAX];
    POSTermState *ostate;
     /* NOTE: ostate contains the POSTerm
      * state information. The values are
      * obtained in a product-specific manner
      * which is not illustrated here in the
      * common functionality section
      */

    /* make sure we are in a sale */
    /* total should not be zero */
     if (ostate->_saleSubtotal == 0){
     printf("EndOfSale ignored, there is no "
             " sale in progress\n");
        return;
     }


/* quantity should be 1 */
    if (ostate->_quantity != 1){
        printf("EndOfSale ignored, "
                "transaction in progress\n");
     return;
     }
 /* get tax */

    tax =  AStore_Tax_CalculateTax(
                        ostate->_taxReference,
                        ev,
                        ostate->_saleTaxableSubtotal);
    /* update store total */
    AStore_Store_UpdateStoreTotals(
                        ostate->_storeReference,
                        ev,
                        ostate->_posId,
                        ostate->_saleSubtotal,
```

```
                                        tax);
      handle_error("Cannot update store totals", ev);

         /* format string and send text to
          * OutputMedia
          */

         sprintf(outstring," Subtotal   %7.2f\n Tax"
                    "            %7.2f\n Total        %7.2f\n",
                       ostate->_saleSubtotal,
                    tax, ostate->_saleSubtotal + tax);

         POS_OutputMedia_OutputText(
                          ostate->_outputReference,
                          ev,outstring);

         /* zero out subtotal accumulators and
          * reset quantity
          */

         ostate->_saleSubtotal = 0.0;
         ostate->_saleTaxableSubtotal = 0.0;
         ostate->_quantity = 1;
      }
```

30.3.4 Implementation Summary

If you've been typing in the code as you went along, your POS code is nearly complete. You're ready to make just a few adjustments for your specific ORB, and compile and link your POS objects.

30.4 CONNECTING TO THE ORB AND BOA, AND STARTING THE STORE OBJECT

Following the pattern of previous chapters, we'll split now into ORB-specific sections. Turn to the section for your ORB for instructions on how to finish your Store object. When you're done, go to Chapter 33 to fire up your objects and run your system!

30.5 OBJECTBROKER

The common design for the POS specifies two processes: one with just the OutputMedia object and one with the POSTerminal object and the Input-Media object.

30.5.1 OutputMedia Object

The OutputMedia server is a pure server, which is structured exactly like the Pseudo-Name Server. The only difference is that it has a much simpler state and a single method that is practically trivial. There is nothing new to learn about CORBA or ObjectBroker from by examining this code. The ObjectBroker implementation uses the common code discussed previously with the usual three caveats on method names, parameter names, and getting state. You can examine the code on the floppy. The process contains files, as before, for the main, the method and associated routines, the dispatcher, and a utilities routine file:

om_m.c—the main program

om.c—the method and supporting routines for the OutputMedia methods

omdsp.c—the routines that provide the link between BOA and the OutputMedia method

misc.c—a mixture of handwritten and vendor-supplied, convenience routines

30.5.2 POSTerminal and InputMedia Objects

There are two important points about ObjectBroker that are illustrated by the process containing these two objects, although the user-supplied code for all but the main program is identical to what we've seen before. There are two interfaces in this process, consequently it is organized similar to the Store (which had three) with respect to how registration and cleanup happen. The process contains files, as before, for the main, the methods and associated routines, the dispatchers, stubs for its client usage, and a utilities routine file:

pos_m.c—the main program

posterm.c—the methods and supporting routines for the POSTerminal methods

im.c—the methods and supporting routines for the InputMedia methods

postidsp.c—the routines that provide the link between BOA and the POS methods for these two interfaces

misc.c—a mixture of handwritten and vendor-supplied, convenience routines

pnsstb.c—stub routines for PNS methods

stostb.c—stub routines for the Store methods

imstb.c—stub routines for the InputMedia methods

omstb.c—stub routines for the OutputMedia methods

Since this is the third chapter in which we've seen a similar structure, we'll mention only the two new points, concerning the main program and the fact that the POS methods are local.

Main Program Structure   In previous versions of the main program, we've always called the vendor-supplied subroutine **OBB_BOA_main_loop** to turn control over to ObjectBroker to service calls on methods in this process. There are two methods in the process, but they are local and are not called by any other routine (see the next section for a description of what this means). This means that the process acts entirely as a client, and the main program takes care of itself. It creates its own loop, reading from the input device.

Given this structure, the main program part that is the one line **main_loop** call is replaced with a call on an internal subroutine, **process_input()** (which could just as well have been in-line code). Object-Broker doesn't have to deal with events so the subroutine just processes in that routine until it returns and calls the clean-up routine. If a different structure of the process had been part of the design, ObjectBroker could have dealt with that structure as easily.

The subroutine that handles input is the following. It reads a line of input from the keyboard and dispatches by calling one of two methods, KeyboardInput or BarcodeInput. These methods then call the appropriate POSTerminal methods, which may call Store or StoreAccess methods. (The program ends by reading an "x," not specified in the design, but it's always nice to end gracefully.) A similar function is also used by the DAIS implementation.

```
void process_input(void)
{
  CORBA_Environment   ev;
  char                instring[STR_MAX+1];

  while (1)
      {
      printf("input: \n");
      fscanf(stdin, "%20s", instring);
      /* if first chararacter is a number, call barcode
         else call keypad */
```

```
        if (instring[0] == 'x')
          {printf("exit selected");
           return;
          }

        if (isdigit(instring[0]))
            {
            POS_InputMedia_BarcodeInput(
                        im_ref,&ev,instring);
            (void)IsException(&ev,"Failed barcode");
            }
        else
            {
            POS_InputMedia_KeypadInput(
                        im_ref,&ev,instring);
            (void)IsException(&ev,"Failed keycode");
            }
        }

   } /* end of process_input() */
```

Local or Built-In Methods   In Chapter 23, we had configured the POSTerminal and InputMedia implementations to be *local*, or *built-in*, methods; that is, these methods are located in the same address space as their client, which just happens to be the main program of this process. This design decision was carried out by changing one line in the .IML files for these two interfaces. We don't have to worry about anything else. This design decision was carried through into the dispatch routines we asked ObjectBroker to generate. These are routines we never modify manually; if we change our minds about the configuration, we merely change the .IML file and regenerate the dispatch routines.

The client doesn't call these operations different in any way from how it would call an operation in a different process or different computer. It is only the .IML and the generated, never-touched routines that contain the configuration information, thereby achieving the CORBA goal of location-independent code.

30.6   SOMOBJECTS POS MODULE IMPLEMENTATION

30.6.1   SOMobjects POS Module Implementation

This section describes the SOM-specific implementation of the POS module. In general, the SOM implementation uses the common implementation code for its methods. This code is placed in the implementation template generated by the SOM compiler from the POS.idl file.

The state information for the InputMedia, OutputMedia, and the POS-Terminal objects are accessed through the **ostate** instance variable in the corresponding SOMObject, which is defined in the SOM-specific extension section in the Pos.idl file. Also, since the OutputMedia object is located in a server process, as previously shown in Figure 30.1, it is derived from SOMD-Server object. This means an instance of the OutputMedia object is a server object. InputMedia and POSTerminal objects are both derived from SOMObject, since they are both in the client address space. It is important to note here that it is not always necessary for objects in a server's address space to be derived from the SOMDServer interface. Any SOMObjects server can support multiple interfaces. A client could then ask the server object to create an instance of an interface the server supports. In this example, since, the outsrv server process supports only one interface, it is convenient to make the OutputMedia object a subclass of the SOMDServer interface. When the server process is created, then, we already have an OutputMedia object.

30.6.2 OutputMedia Object

The SOM-specific extensions for the OutputMedia object definitions in POS.idl are shown next. Note that the OutputMedia object is derived from the SOMDServer object. Then, in the implementation section, note that the **somDefaultInit** method is overridden. As stated earlier, **somDefaultInit** is the default constructor method for all objects.

```
#ifdef __SOMIDL__
  interface OutputMedia : SOMDServer {
#else
  interface OutputMedia {
#endif
    boolean    OutputText(in string StringToPrint);

#ifdef __SOMIDL__
    implementation {
        releaseorder : OutputText;
        override:   somDefaultInit, somDestruct;
        somToken      ostate;
        dllname = "dobjs.dll";
    };
#endif
  };
```

Even though **OutputText** is the only method supported by this interface, is still mentioned in the release order for reasons of release-to-release binary compatibility. Finally, the implementation of this interface in POS.c is packaged in the dobjs.dll file with implementations of other interfaces. The implementation of the **OutputText** method is similar to the implementation in Section 30.3. The implementation of the **SOMDefaultInit** method is shown here.

```
SOM_Scope void SOMLINK
    POS_OutputMediasomDefaultInit (
                    POS_OutputMedia somSelf,
                    somInitCtrl* ctrl) {

POS_OutputMediaData *somThis; /* set in
                                BeginInitializer */
somInitCtrl globalCtrl;
somBooleanVector myMask;

CORBA_Environment ev;
POS_OutputMediaMethodDebug("POS_OutputMedia",
                            "somDefaultInit");

POS_OutputMedia_BeginInitializer_somDefaultInit;
POS_OutputMedia_Init_SOMDServer_somDefaultInit(
                    somSelf, ctrl);

SOM_InitEnvironment(&ev);

register_server(&ev,somSelf);
/* clean up */
SOM_UninitEnvironment(&ev);
printf("OutputMedia server initialized "
        "and ready\n");
return;
}
```

The main function of the constructor is to register the server (**Output-Media** object) with the nameserver; `register_server` is a utility function that was described in Section 24.6.

30.6.3   The InputMedia Object

The SOM extensions to the definition of the **InputMedia** interface are shown next. The interface is derived from **SOMObject**, because all objects must be (directly or indirectly) derived from **SOMObject**.

```
#ifdef __SOMIDL__
  interface InputMedia : SOMObject {
#else
  interface InputMedia {
#endif

    typedef string OperatorCmd;

    void    BarcodeInput(in Barcode Item);
    void    KeypadInput(in OperatorCmd Cmd);


#ifdef __SOMIDL__
      implementation {
        releaseorder:  BarcodeInput, KeypadInput;
        override:      somDefaultInit,
                       somDestruct;
        somToken       ostate;

      dllname = "dobjs.dll";
    };
#endif


  };
```

The SOM extension in the implementation definition section specifies the release order and the methods that are overridden—somDefaultInit and somDestruct. The ostate instance variable is a pointer to an instance of the ImState structure defined in Section 30.3. The implementation of the somDefaultInit, which is the default constructor for the **InputMedia** object, is shown next.

```
SOM_Scope void SOMLINK
          POS_InputMediasomDefaultInit(
                               POS_InputMedia somSelf,
                          somInitCtrl* ctrl)
{
  POS_InputMediaData *somThis; /* set in
                            BeginInitializer */
  somInitCtrl globalCtrl;
  somBooleanVector myMask;
  ImState *ostate;
```

```
    POS_InputMediaMethodDebug("POS_InputMedia",
                              "somDefaultInit");
    POS_InputMedia_BeginInitializer_somDefaultInit;
    POS_InputMedia_Init_SOMObject_somDefaultInit(
                        somSelf, ctrl);

  /*
   * create the POSTerminal object and store
   * it in the ostate
   * structure  instance variable
   */

    ostate = SOMMalloc (sizeof(ImState));
    ostate->_posreference = POS_POSTerminalNew();
    somThis->ostate = ostate;
    return;
}
```

As described in Section 30.1, the **InputMedia** object has a reference to the **POSTerminal** object. The `somDefaultInit` method is the appropriate place for the **InputMedia** object to create and keep a reference to the **POSTerminal** object.

30.6.4   The POSTerminal Object

The SOM extensions of the **POSTerminal** object interface definitions are similar to those of the **InputMedia** object and are shown here.

```
ifdef __SOMIDL__
  interface POSTerminal : SOMObject {
#else
  interface POSTerminal {
#endif

    void Login();
    void PrintPOSSalesSummary();
    void PrintStoreSalesSummary();
    void SendBarcode(in Barcode Item);
    void ItemQuantity (in long Qty);
    void EndOfSale();

#ifdef __SOMIDL__
    implementation {
        releaseorder: Login, PrintPOSSalesSummary,
```

```
        PrintStoreSalesSummary,
        SendBarcode, ItemQuantity,
        EndOfSale;
     override:somDefaultInit, somDestruct;
     somToken ostate;
     dllname = "dobjs.dll";
  };
#endif
 };
```

In the implementation section, the **ostate** instance variable is a pointer
to an instance of the **POSTermState** structure defined in Section 30.3. As
with other interfaces, the implementation of all the methods is similar to
the common code described in Section 30.3. The **somDefaultInit** method is
the interesting exception. The POSTerminal object needs to interact with
the Store, Tax, and OutputMedia objects. These objects can be found from
the nameserver. In **somDefaultInit**, we first get an object reference for the
nameserver object. Then we query the nameserver for the various objects.
These object references are stored in the object state structure. The implementation of the somDefaultInit method is shown here.

```
SOM_Scope void SOMLINK
        POS_POSTerminalsomDefaultInit(
                POS_POSTerminal somSelf,
                somInitCtrl* ctrl)
{
   POS_POSTerminalData *somThis; /* set in
                              BeginInitializer */
   somInitCtrl globalCtrl;
   somBooleanVector myMask;
   POSTermState       *ostate;

PseudoNameService pnsRef;
CORBA_Environment ev;
CORBA_char         namestr[STR_MAX];

POS_POSTerminalMethodDebug("POS_POSTerminal",
              "somDefaultInit");

POS_POSTerminal_BeginInitializer_somDefaultInit;

POS_POSTerminal_Init_SOMObject_somDefaultInit(
                somSelf, ctrl);
```

```c
/* initialize the CORBA_Environment  structure */
SOM_InitEnvironment(&ev);

/* set the posid. posid is a global variable */
ostate =  SOMMalloc(sizeof(POSTermState));
somThis->ostate = ostate;
ostate->_posid = atol(posid);

printf("POSID = %d\n",ostate->_posid);
/* get an object reference to the
 * PseudoNameService
 */

pnsRef = file_to_ref(&ev,PNAME_REF);
if(ev._major != CORBA_NO_EXCEPTION)
          handle_error(&ev);


/* get the Store object reference from the PNS */
sprintf (namestr, "%s%s", "storesvr_" ,posid);
ostate->_storereference = PseudoNameService_ResolveName(pnsRef,
                                        &ev, namestr);
if(ev._major != CORBA_NO_EXCEPTION)
          handle_exception (&ev);
 if(CORBA_Object_is_nil(
          ostate>_storereference,&ev))
 {
    printf("cannot find: %s\n", namestr);
    exit(1);
  }


  /* get the Tax object reference from the PNS */

ostate->_taxreference = PseudoNameService_ResolveName(pnsRef,
                              &ev, "tax");
if(ev._major != CORBA_NO_EXCEPTION)
          handle_exception (&ev);

if(CORBA_Object_is_nil(
          ostate->_taxreference,&ev))
{
    printf("cannot find tax Object: %s\n",
                                        namestr);
    exit(1);
 }
```

```
/* get the OutputMedia object reference from
 *the PNS
 */

sprintf (namestr, "%s%s", "outputsvr_" ,storeid);
ostate->_outputreference =
           PseudoNameService_ResolveName(pnsRef,
                                        &ev, namestr);
    if(ev._major != CORBA_NO_EXCEPTION)
           handle_exception (&ev);

    if(CORBA_Object_is_nil(
          ostate->_outputreference,&ev))
    {
     printf("cannot find media object : %s\n",
                                    namestr);
     exit(1);
    }

    /* free the PNS object reference */

    CORBA_Object_release(pnsRef, &ev);
    if(ev._major != CORBA_NO_EXCEPTION)
                          handle_exception (&ev);

    /* clean up */

    SOM_UninitEnvironment(&ev);

    ostate->_quantity = 1;
    return;
}
```

30.6.5 The POS Client Program

Most of the interfaces that we have discussed so far are instantiated in server processes. We pointed out in Section 30.1 that the InputMedia object and POSTerminal objects are created in a pure client program. The command-processing loop of the client program follows. The InputMedia object is created first. As shown in the code for somDefaultInit method of the InputMedia object, the POSTerminal object is created by the InputMedia object. The first operation that is performed on the POSTerminal object is the login operation. After login, input is processed either as a bar-code input or as a keypad input. The user terminates the application by typing **x**.

```
main(int arg c, char x*argv)
{
    POS_InputMedia inputmedia
    /* create the inputmedia object */
    inputmedia = POS_InputMediaNew();

    /* Let the user login first */
    printf("Please log in:  ");

    /* fall into a loop, reading from the
     * keyboard and calling barcode_input
     * or keypad_input as appropriate on the
     * InputMedia object until the user
     * shuts down the system by entering  X
     */
    while (1) {
        scanf("%s",instring);
        if ((toupper(instring[0]) == 'X')) {
            SOMD_Uninit(&ev);
            SOM_UninitEnvironment(&ev);
            application_terminate ("exit selected",
                                        &ev);
        }
        else if (isdigit(instring[0]))
            POS_InputMedia_BarcodeInput(
                    inputmedia,&ev,instring);
        else
            POS_InputMedia_KeypadInput(
                        inputmedia,&ev,instring);
            if (ev._major != CORBA_NO_EXCEPTION)
                handle_exception (&ev);
            CORBA_exception_free (&ev);
    }
}
```

Once the methods have been implemented in the POS module, the C
code can be compiled and linked using the makefile included with the source
code. The POS application can be invoked using the following command:

```
posclt -posid n -storeid m
```

where the numbers following the -posid and -storeid arguments refer to
the POSId of the POSTerminal and the StoreId of the Store to which the
POSTerminal should connect. For purposes of the example in the book, two
OutputMedia servers, with aliases **outputsvr_1** and **outputsvr_2**, are
registered.

30.7 DAIS SPECIFICS IN THE POS OBJECT

The impact on a DAIS implementation of the new concepts that we introduce in this chapter is relatively minor. As we mentioned at the beginning of the chapter, the new concepts are: objects that only make client use of interfaces (the object is not a server), objects with a user interface, and objects that are completely local.

With an object that only makes use of the client side of interfaces, it is not strictly necessary to initialize the BOA, just the ORB. In actual fact, in this example, there are also objects that are servers so we have to initialize the BOA in the capsule anyway. The principle still stands, though.

The completely local objects in DAIS are more of a system administration issue than a build issue. In DAIS, the ORB detects whether an invocation is local or remote, and optimizes it if appropriate. Of course, for a local invocation, the code for the object must also be local but the decision as to whether to use the local object is a *late* one; it is actually made at run time. This is not normally a significant overhead because the object location is determined when the client obtains the object reference, not at every method invocation. It is at run time that you normally constrain the object selection to be local if you wish. Be that as it may, if you neither want nor need this flexibility, you can bypass the selection mechanism by fixing the object location as we are showing here for the InputMedia object, and the DAIS ORB will optimize the call because it is local.

POS Capsule main() The `main()` routine for the POS capsule starts up the POSTerm and InputMedia objects. It is, however, slightly different from that of the other capsules; it has an extra call just before starting the scheduler:

```
DAIS_spawn(process_input, NULL, &ev);
```

This call prepares a thread to be run when we finally call `DAIS_schedule()`. This thread is used for handling the user input, and it is implemented in the function `process_input()`, passed in the preceding call. The reason is that DAIS provides multithreading facilities across all platforms, which requires that the scheduler have control of the capsule so that it can perform the task switching. The only constraint that this places on us is that the input processing must be implemented as a callable function rather than as in-line code in the main function. We probably would have done this anyway as part of the functional decomposition of our implementation. The benefits that this approach offers include the ability to run multiple application tasks and to implement applications that use asynchronous calls, although we aren't making use of them in this example.

Otherwise, the function is similar to all the other main() functions that we have coded already, with minor name changes dependent on the objects that we are starting.

InputMedia Object   There is one point about the construction of the Input-Media object that is unusual. To demonstrate the use of completely local objects, we are not exporting a name for the particular instance of the Input-Media object to the PNS; we just leave its object reference in a global variable for other objects in the capsule to pick up. Otherwise, the constructor and application initialization are very similar to all the other objects in the system. The whole of the InputMedia object is implemented in file im.c.

process_input()   This is the routine that handles user input. It is almost the same as that used for the ObjectBroker implementation, and we won't show it again here. The only difference is in the error-handling routine that is called; you can substitute a call to **handle_error()** here with no problems.

We can see in the implementation of **process_input()** that we don't make a call on the PNS to determine the object reference of the InputMedia object. This is because we made the decision to fix the InputMedia object in the same capsule. As a result, we just pick the object reference from a global variable to demonstrate completely local objects.

OutputMedia Capsule   From the viewpoint of object creation and connection to the ORB, the OutputMedia capsule is very similar to the PNS with just a change of names. In fact, it is so similar that we won't list it here. If you have problems, look at or copy the code on the diskette. It is implemented in two files: om.c and om_main.c (again so that we can easily link the Output-Media code into other capsules if we decide to reorganize the distribution or want to build generic capsules).

Build of POSTerm and OutputMedia Capsules   Again, we see nothing new in the building of the two final capsules. We have already compiled all the stub, skeleton, marshalling, and shared code, so we just have to compile the capsule-specific code:

```
cc -c -I. -I$DAIS_ROOT/include pos_main.c
cc -c -I. -I$DAIS_ROOT/include posterm.c
cc -c -I. -I$DAIS_ROOT/include im.c
cc -c -I. -I$DAIS_ROOT/include om_main.c
cc -c -I. -I$DAIS_ROOT/include om.c
```

and then link to create the two capsules:

```
cc -o pos pos_main.o posterm.o \
    im.o misc.o c_pnamesvc.o \
    m_pnamesvc.o \
    c_store.o m_store.o \
    c_pos.o m_pos.o s_pos.o \
    -L$DAIS_ROOT/lib -ldais -lxti -lnsl
```

The pos capsule makes client use of interfaces defined in pos.idl, pnamesvc.idl, and store.idl, and implements a server for pos.idl so we include the appropriate generated code.

```
cc -o om om_main.o \
    om.o misc.o c_pnamesvc.o \
    m_pnamesvc.o \
    m_pos.o s_pos.o \
    -L$DAIS_ROOT/lib -ldais -lxti -lnsl
```

The OutputMedia capsule makes client use of interfaces defined in pnamesvc.idl and implements a server for pos.idl.

At this point, we have seen how to implement capsules that contain totally local objects and a user interface. We have also seen how, using DAIS, we can implement multithreaded applications. This concludes the C coding exercise. You will find the instructions on how to run the application in Chapter 33.

CHAPTER 31

Coding the POS in C++

31.1 C++ GENERATED FROM THE POS IDL DEFINITIONS

This section, and the one that follows, present C++ language code for the Store module that is common to every C++ language ORB.

The declarations we present here are probably in a file with a name like POS.h (the exact name for your product was listed in its section of Chapter 23), produced by your IDL compiler so you won't have to type them in yourself. But you will need to be aware of their form (which is dictated by the standard OMG IDL C++ language mapping) when you connect with the stubs and skeletons. This section contains the details you need to know.

When we finish coding the common functionality, we'll split into ORB-specific sections as before.

Recall that the POS components of the example are defined in an IDL module called POS:

```
module POS {

    typedef long POSId;
    typedef string Barcode;

    interface InputMedia {
        typedef string OperatorCmd;
        void      BarcodeInput (in Barcode Item);
        void      KeypadInput (in OperatorCmd Cmd);
    };
```

```
interface OutputMedia {
    boolean    OutputText (in string StringToPrint );
};

interface POSTerminal {
    void Login();
    void PrintPOSSalesSummary();
    void PrintStoreSalesSummary();
    void SendBarcode (in Barcode Item);
    void ItemQuantity (in long Quantity);
    void EndOfSale();
};
};
```

This is translated into the following C++ definitions:

```
namespace POS { // or class POS

    typedef CORBA::Long    POSId;
    typedef char* Barcode;

    class InputMedia : public CORBA::Object{
        // shown later
    };

    class OutputMedia : public CORBA::Object{
        // shown later
    };

    class POSTerminal : public CORBA::Object {
        // shown later
    };

};
```

The two **typedef** definitions are translated into C++ equivalents of the same name. The types become **CORBA::Long** (a 32-bit type) and **char***, respectively. Each of the three IDL interfaces, **InputMedia**, **OutputMedia**, and **POSTerminal** are translated into C++ class. These will be discussed in turn in the remainder of this subsection.

31.1.1 InputMedia

Interface InputMedia is defined as:

```
interface InputMedia {
    typedef string OperatorCmd;
    void BarcodeInput(in Barcode Item);
    void KeypadInput(in OperatorCmd Cmd);
};
```

It is translated into the following C++:

```
class InputMedia :public CORBA::Object {
public:
    virtual void BarcodeInput
                        (const char* Item);
    virtual void KeypadInput
                        (const char* Cmd);
};
```

Since **interface InputMedia** defines a new type (**OperatorCmd**), this **typedef** is translated into its equivalent in C++. Each of the two operations (**BarcodeInput()** and **KeypadInput()**) are translated into public member functions. The C++ parameter types are straightforward translations of their IDL counterparts.

31.1.2 OutputMedia

Interface OutputMedia is defined as:

```
interface OutputMedia {
    boolean OutputText (in string StringToPrint);
};
```

It is translated into the following C++:

```
class OutputMedia : public CORBA::Object {
public:
    virtual CORBA::Boolean OutputText
                    (const char* StringToPrint);
};
```

As usual, the operation (**OutputText()**) is translated into a public member function of the same name. The return type becomes **CORBA::Boolean**, which is defined in the header file **CORBA.h**.

31.1.3 POSTerminal

Interface POSTerminal is defined as:

```
interface POSTerminal {
    void Login();
    void PrintPOSSalesSummary();
    void PrintStoreSalesSummary();
    void SendBarcode (in Barcode Item);
    void ItemQuantity (in long Quantity);
    void EndOfSale();
};
```

It is translated into the following in C++:

```
class POSTerminal : public CORBA::Object {
public:
    virtual void Login ();
    virtual void PrintPOSSalesSummary ();
    virtual void PrintStoreSalesSummary ();
    virtual void SendBarcode
                    (const char* Item);
    virtual void ItemQuantity
                    (CORBA::Long Quantity);
    virtual void EndOfSale ();
};
```

Each of the IDL operations is translated into a public member function. The parameter to operation **SendBarcode()** translates to the simple string type in C++, which is **char***. The parameter to function **ItemQuantity()** is the 32-bit type **CORBA::Long**.

This completes the presentation of the C++ declarations generated by the IDL compiler. Now we need to implement the functionality of these interfaces. We'll do that in the next section.

31.2 COMMON POS IMPLEMENTATION IN C++

There's almost nothing ORB-specific about the functionality, so we'll do it all in this section. If you're working the example by hand, type this code into your code files as we go along. At the end of this section, we'll send you off to the section on your specific ORB for final coding, compilation, and linking. Since this is the last module (Hooray!), the only thing left to do after this is to run it; that's in Chapter 33.

The point-of-sale terminal is made up of the following components: **POSTerminal**, **InputMedia**, and **OutputMedia**). Each of these IDL interfaces is implemented by a C++ class (respectively, **POSTerminal_i**, **InputMedia_i**, **OutputMedia_i**), and an instance of each is created.

Two separate processes are created. The first is a client: it holds one object of type **POSTerminal** and one object of type **InputMedia**. The latter accepts input from the user and communicates it to the **POSTerminal** object. This is an example of a local call (within a single address space) between two CORBA objects. The second process is a server, called **outsrv**, which holds a single object of type **OutputMedia**. This object is invoked by the **POSTerminal** object when it wishes to output a line of the sales receipt.

This section explains the implementation of the components of the point-of-sale terminal in the following order:

1. the point-of-sale client (**POSclient**)
2. the output media server (**OutputSrv**)
3. the declarations and then implementations of each of the IDL interfaces, in turn,

   - InputMedia
   - POSTerminal
   - OutputMedia

The code for these is given in the **POS** directory, and the filenames given in this section are relative to that directory.

31.2.1 Implementation of the POS Client

Here is the code for the POS client, based on the requirements we set down in the Analysis & Design in Chapter 19:

```
1    #include <iostream.h>
2    #include <stdlib.h>
3    #include "POS_IM.h"
4    #include "POS_Ter.h"
5    #include "../PNS/FindPNS.h"
6
7    int main(int argc, char **argv)
8    {
9      if (argc<3) {
10       cerr << "usage: " << argv[0]
11             << "<Store Number> <POS Number>"
12             << endl;
13       return 1;
14     }
```

```
15
16      CORBA::ORB_var orb =
17         CORBA::ORB_init(argc,argv,"PRIMER_ORB");
18      CORBA::BOA_var boa =
19          orb->BOA_init(argc,argv,"");
20
21      POS::POSTerminal_var Ter;
22      PseudoNameService_var pns;
23
24      try {
25        pns=FindPNS(orb);
26        Ter = new POSTerminal_i
27               (pns,atol(argv[1]),atol(argv[2]));
28      }
29      catch(...) {
30        cerr << "ERROR Starting POS Terminal"
31             << endl;
32        return 1;
33      }
34
35      POS::InputMedia_var InPut;
36      char caBuff[255];
37
38      try {
39        InPut = new InputMedia_i(Ter);
40      }
41      catch(...) {
42        cerr << "Error starting InputMedia"
43             << endl;
44        return 1;
45      }
46
47      cout << "Command Summary :" << endl;
48      cout << "L : Login   P : POS Sales Summary"
49           " S : Store Sales Summary" << endl;
50      cout << "T : Total   Q : Quantity"
51           " X : Exit" << endl << endl;
52      do {
53        cout << "Enter code, command (L,P,Q,S,T)"
54             << " or X to exit : ";
55        try {
56          cin.getline(caBuff,250);
57          if ((caBuff[0] >= '0')
58                     && (caBuff[0] <= '9'))
59            InPut->BarcodeInput(caBuff);
60          else
```

```
61                 InPut->KeypadInput(caBuff);
62           }
63           catch(...) {
64             cerr << "ERROR using Input Media"
65                     << endl;
66             return 1;
67           }
68         }while (caBuff[0] != 'x'
69                          && caBuff[0] != 'X');
70
71         return 0;
72     }
```

The main function of the **POSclt** client process starts by initializing the ORB (lines 16 to 19). It then calls the **FindPNS()** function to locate the Pseudo-Name Service, and the **pns** variable is updated to reference it. On line 26, a CORBA object of type **POSTerminal** is created (by creating a C++ object of class **POSTerminal_i**). The constructor arguments to this are the reference to the Pseudo-Name Service (this is necessary because the **POSTerminal_i** object needs to communicate with the Pseudo-Name Service), the Store identifier number, and the POS identifier number. Any errors in finding the Pseudo-Name Service or creating the **POSTerminal_i** object are tested for on line 29.

On line 39, the main function creates its **InputMedia** object, giving it an object reference for the **POSTerminal** object. In a real implementation of the system, the **InputMedia** object would receive input events from the POS's special hardware (the bar-code reader and the keypad); but in our simple implementation the main function reads the input from the normal keyboard and passes it to the **InputMedia** object. A menu is first output to the user (lines 47 to 51), and the main function enters a loop on line 52. Once the prompt is written (line 53), a line of input is read on line 56. Each such line is tested, and if it begins with a decimal digit (the test is made on lines 57 and 58) the input is treated as a bar code, and is forwarded to the **InputMedia** object (on line 59) by calling its **BarcodeInput()** operation. Otherwise, it is treated as a keypad input and passed without interpretation to **InputMedia** object by calling its **KeypadInput()** operation. Errors during input are tested on line 63. The exit condition (character **x** or **X**) is tested on lines 68–69.

31.2.2 Implementation of the Output Media Server (outsrv)

The main function of this server simply creates an object of type **OutputMedia_i**, and then calls the standard **impl_is_ready()** function to inform the ORB that this server is ready to accept incoming operation calls to its objects (in this case, calls to the **OutputMedia_i** object):

```
1      #include <iostream.h>
2      #include <stdlib.h>
3      #include <stdio.h>
4      #include "POS_OM.h"
5      #include "../PNS/FindPNS.h"
6
7      int main(int argc, char* argv[]) {
8        if (argc<2) {
9          cerr << "usage: " << argv[0]
10               << "<POS Number>" << endl;
11         return 1;
12       }
13
14       CORBA::ORB_var orb =
15               CORBA::ORB_init(argc,argv,"PRIMER_ORB");
16       CORBA::BOA_var boa =
17               orb->BOA_init(argc,argv,"");
18
19       POS::OutputMedia_var OutPut;
20       PseudoNameService_var pns;
21
22
23       try {
24         pns=FindPNS(orb);
25         OutPut = new OutputMedia_i
26                             (pns,atol(argv[1]));
27         boa->impl_is_ready("OutputSrv");
28       }
29       catch(...) {
30         cerr << "ERROR Starting OutputMedia
31               << " Server" << endl;
32         return 1;
33       }
34
35       return 0;
36     }
```

The ORB is initialized on lines 14 to 17. The **FindPNS()** function is used to find the Pseudo-Name Service because this is needed by the **OutputMedia** object, so that it can register itself. The **OutputMedia** object is created on line 25; the constructor parameters are the reference to the Pseudo-Name Service and the POS identifier number. The **impl_is_ready()** function is passed the server name (line 27); and the server is then ready to accept operation invocations on its objects.

31.2.3   InputMedia Implementation: Class Declaration

Interface **InputMedia** is implemented by the C++ class **InputMedia_i**. The sole member variable is a pointer to the **POSTerminal** object that is to be used; this variable is initialized by the constructor. The two member functions correspond to the two operations of the **InputMedia** IDL interface:

```
#include "POS.hh"

class InputMedia_i
            public virtual POS::InputMediaBOAImpl
{
     POS::POSTerminal_ptr m_pTerminal;
public:
     InputMedia_i(POS::POSTerminal_ptr pTer);
     virtual void BarcodeInput (const char* Item);
     virtual void KeypadInput (const char* Cmd)
};
```

31.2.4   InputMedia Implementation: Class Implementation

The constructor of **InputMedia_i** is coded simply by initializing the **m_pTerminal** member variable to the value passed as a parameter. The parameter is duplicated because the destructor of the **m_pTerminal** object reference will automatically release (reduce the reference count by one) the object that it references.

```
#include <iostream.h>
#include <stdlib.h>
#include <ctype.h>
#include "POS_IM.h"

InputMedia_i::InputMedia_i
                     (POS::POSTerminal_ptr pTer) {
   // we will communicate with the POS terminal later:
   m_POSTerminalRef =
              POS::POSTerminal::duplicate(pTer);
}
```

The **BarcodeInput()** operation is coded simply by calling the **SendBarcode()** operation on the **POSTerminal** object, and then checking for any errors:

```
void   InputMedia_i:: BarcodeInput
                                (const char* Item) {
  try {
    m_POSTerminalRef->SendBarcode(Item);
  }
  catch(...) {
    cerr << "Error in Sending barcode" << endl;
  }
}
```

The `KeypadInput()` function is passed a command (defined to be of type `POS::InputMedia::OperatorCmd`, which is a string). It tests the first character and uses the following list to recognize the command to be executed. The `InputMedia` object itself does not process commands; instead, it simply calls the correct operation on the `POSTerminal` object.

Characters	Meaning	Function to Call on the POSTerminal object
l or L	login	Login()
p or P	print POS sales summary for this POS	PrintPOSSalesSummary()
s or S	print store sales summary for the whole store	PrintStoreSalesSummary()
t or T	end the sale of items to this customer	EndOfSale()
q or Q	set the quantity of the item being purchased	ItemQuantity()

The characters q and Q are followed by the actual quantity setting, as a string of digits. These digits are converted to an integer value before calling the `ItemQuantity()` operation on the `POSTerminal` object. The other commands are not followed by any input values.

The `KeypadInput()` function has therefore been coded as follows:

```
void  InputMedia_i:: KeypadInput (const char* Cmd) {
  char* pStr = Cmd;
  try {
    long lTot = 0;
    switch(toupper(*pStr)) {
      default : cerr << "Invalid entry" << endl;
                break;
      case 'X': break;
      case 'L': m_POSTerminalRef->Login();
```

```
                        break;
            case 'P': m_POSTerminalRef->
                                PrintPOSSalesSummary();
                        break;
            case 'S': m_POSTerminalRef->
                                PrintStoreSalesSummary();
                        break;
            case 'T': m_POSTerminalRef->EndOfSale();
                        break;
            case 'Q': while(*(++pStr) == ' ');
                lTot = atol(pStr);
                m_POSTerminalRef->ItemQuantity(lTot);
                break;
            }
        }
        catch(...) {
            cerr << "Error in transmitting command" << endl;
        }
    }
```

Note that, in order to simplify the **switch** statement, the function
toupper() is used to convert the first input character to uppercase. The
switch condition for **Q** converts the rest of the input line to an integer value,
and then passes this to the **ItemQuantity()** operation.

31.2.5   POSTerminal Implementation: Class Declaration

The code for the **POSTerminal** interface is shown next. Its member functions
correspond to the IDL operations defined in its interface, with the addition
of a constructor. Its member variables will be explained shortly.

```
#include "POS.hh"
#include "Store.hh"
#include "PNS.hh"


//-----------POS Terminal -------------
    class POSTerminal_i :
            public virtual POS::POSTerminalBOAImpl
    {
    private:
        POS::Barcode   m_itemBarcode;
        CORBA::Long     m_itemQuantity;
        AStore::Tax_var       m_taxRef;
        AStore::Store_var   m_storeRef;
        AStore::StoreAccess_va   m_storeAccessRef;
        POS::OutputMedia_var      m_outputMediaRef;
```

```
   CORBA::Float   m_saleSubTotal;
   CORBA::Float   m_saleTaxableSubTotal;
   CORBA::Float   m_POSTotal;
   CORBA::Float   m_POSTaxTotal;
   POS::POSId     m_id;
   unsigned char LoggedIn();
            // returns Boolean

public:
   POSTerminal_i(PseudoNameService_ptr pns,
                 CORBA::Long StoreId,
                 POS::POSId id);

   virtual void Login ();
   virtual void PrintPOSSalesSummary ();
   virtual void PrintStoreSalesSummary ();
   virtual void SendBarcode (const char* Item);
   virtual void ItemQuantity (CORBA::Long Quantity);
   virtual void EndOfSale ();
};
```

The member variables of class **POSTerminal_i** are explained in the following table:

Name	Description
m_itemBarcode	The current bar code (identifying the item currently being purchased at this point-of-sale terminal).
m_itemQuantity	This is the number of items of a given type that are currently being purchased. This variable is initialized to 1, and it is changed by the **ItemQuantity()** operation. The **SendBarcode()** operation, which signals to the **POSTerminal** that an item is being purchased, assesses this variable to determine how many of this item are being purchased. The variable is then reset to value 1.
m_taxRef	The object reference of the **Tax** object. This is initialized in the constructor of the **POSTerminal** object, by searching for the correct **Tax** object using the Pseudo-Name Service.
M_storeRef	The object reference of the **Store** object. This is initialized in the constructor of the **POSTerminal** object, by searching for the cor-

rect **Store** object using the Pseudo-Name Service.

m_storeAccessRef	The object reference of the **StoreAccess** object. The **Login()** operation on the **POSTerminal** logs the point-of-sale terminal into the **Store** object. The Store object returns an object reference to a newly created **StoreAccess** object, through which the **POSTerminal** subsequently accesses the store information.
m_outputMediaRef	The object reference of the **OutputMedia** object to which to print receipts and reports. This is initialized in the constructor of the **POSTerminal** object, by searching for the correct **OutputMedia** object using the Pseudo-Name Service.
m_saleSubTotal	The sales total so far for the sale to the current customer.
m_saleTaxableSubTotal	The sales tax so far for the sale to the current customer.
m_POSTotal	This POS's total sales since power up.
m_POSTaxTotal	This POS's total tax since power up.
m_id	This POS's identifier (a unique number within the Store that the POS uses). This is passed to the process as a command-line argument.

31.2.6 POSTerminal Implementation: Class Implementation

The main actions of each of the member functions are as follows. The description of each function is followed by the C++ code to implement it:

POSTerminal_i() This constructor initializes the **m_taxRef**, **m_storeRef**, and **m_outputMediaRef** member variables by binding to the correct **Tax**, **Store**, and **OutputMedia** objects, respectively. It uses the Pseudo-Name Service to find each object, using the following strings, respectively: "Tax_"<Store_identifier>, "Store_"<Store_identifier>, "OutputMedia_" <POS_identifier>. Finally, it initializes the other member variables.

```
#include <iostream.h>
#include <stdio.h>
#include "POS_Ter.h"
```

```
POSTerminal_i::POSTerminal_i
                       (PseudoNameService_ptr pns,
                        CORBA::Long StoreId,
                        POS::POSId Id)
    : m_itemBarcode(0),m_id(Id),m_POSTaxTotal(0.0),
      m_POSTotal(0.0),m_saleTaxableSubTotal(0.0),
      m_saleSubTotal(0.0),
      m_storeAccessRef
    (AStore::StoreAccess::_nil())  {
// use the PNS to find our Tax,
// Store and OutputMedia objects:
char caStr[255];
try {
  sprintf(caStr,"Tax_%ld",StoreId);
  m_taxRef = AStore::Tax::_narrow
                          (pns->ResolveName(caStr));
  sprintf(caStr,"Store_%ld",StoreId);
  m_storeRef = AStore::Store::_narrow
                          (pns->ResolveName(caStr));
  sprintf(caStr,"OutputMedia_%ld",Id);
  m_outputMediaRef =
            POS::OutputMedia::_narrow
                          (pns->ResolveName(caStr));
}
catch(...) {
  cerr << "Trouble finding tax, store,
        << " or outputmedia " << endl;
}
}
```

Login()   This function calls the **Login()** operation on the Store object, tests for errors, and then initializes the member variables to their correct state for the start of a sales session for a customer. The return value of the **Login()** operation is assigned to the **m_StoreAccessRef** member variable. The **Login()** operation on the store is called, and this returns a reference to a **StoreAccess** object, which is used when the **POSTerminal** subsequently needs to find the price of a item. The first few lines ensure that the **Login()** function has no effect if the POS is already logged in.

```
void  POSTerminal_i:: Login () {
  if (!CORBA::is_nil(m_storeAccessRef)) {
    cerr << "Can't log in twice" << endl;
    return;
  }
  // Get a reference to the StoreAccess object
  // for this POS
```

```
try {
  m_storeAccessRef = m_storeRef->Login(m_id);
}
catch(...) {
  cerr << "Error in Login" << endl;
  return;
}
m_saleSubTotal = m_POSTotal =
                            m_POSTaxTotal = 0.0;
m_itemQuantity = 1;
}
```

PrintPOSSalesSummary()   The result of calling this function is the writing of a single line to the receipt containing the POS total sales and the POS total tax. The output is constructed using the **sprintf()** library function, and output using the **OutputText()** operation of the **OutputMedia** object.

Note that this function returns immediately without doing any work if the **POSTerminal** is currently handling a sale. That is, we do not allow the sales totals to be printed while a customer's items are being rung up. The function determines whether it is handling a sale by testing the **m_itemBarcode** and **m_saleSubTotal** member variables. If either of these is nonzero, then the terminal must be handling a sale.

```
void  POSTerminal_i:: PrintPOSSalesSummary () {
  if (!LoggedIn())
    return;
  if ((m_itemBarcode != 0) ||
                        (m_saleSubTotal != 0.0))
    return;
  char caOpStr[255];
  sprintf(caOpStr,"%25s %8.2f\n%25s %8.2f\n"
          "Point of Sale Total : ", m_POSTotal,
          "    Tax Total : ", m_POSTaxTotal);
  try {
    m_outputMediaRef->OutputText(caOpStr);
  }
  catch(...) {
    cerr << "Error in Sales Summary" << endl;
  }
}
```

PrintStoreSalesSummary()   This function communicates with the **POSTerminal**'s **Store** object (calling **StoreTotal()** and **StoreTaxTotal()**) to find the **Store**'s sales totals, and it then outputs these using the

OutputText() operation on the **OutputMedia** object (again, it uses the standard **sprintf()** function to construct the string to output).

It then calls the **Store**'s **GetPOSTotals()** operation to find the sales totals for each of the **POSTerminal** objects connected to the **Store**. Once this operation call returns, the function iterates (using a **for** statement) through the sequence returned in the operation's parameter. To process the sequence, the function determines its length using the **length()** function, and then it constructs a string to output for each entry. There will be one entry for each **POSTerminal** connected to the **Store**.

Note that the function also returns immediately if the **POSTerminal** is currently handling a sale.

```cpp
void  POSTerminal_i:: PrintStoreSalesSummary () {
  if (!LoggedIn())
    return;
  if ((m_itemBarcode != 0) ||
                        (m_saleSubTotal != 0.0))
    return;
  char caOpStr[255];

  // Find and output the total sales and
  // tax for the store

  AStore::Store::StoreTotals tots;
  try {
    tots = m_storeRef->Totals();
  }
  catch(...) {
    cerr << "Error finding store totals" << endl;
    return;
  }
  sprintf(caOpStr,"%s %7.2f\n%s %7.2f\n",
          "Total Sales :=",tots.StoreTotal,
          "Total Tax   :=",tots.StoreTaxTotal);
  try {
    m_outputMediaRef->OutputText("STORE TOTALS");
    m_outputMediaRef->OutputText(caOpStr);
  }
  catch(...) {
    cerr << "Error with Output Media" << endl;
    return;
  }

  // Output the totals for each POS in turn
```

```
AStore::POSList_var PL;
try {
  m_storeRef->GetPOSTotals(PL);
}
catch(...) {
  cerr << "Error Getting Store Totals" << endl;
  return;
}

for (CORBA::ULong i = 0; i < PL->length(); i++) {
  if (PL[i].Id>0) {
    sprintf(caOpStr,
        "%15s %ld\n%15s %9.2f\n%15s %9.2f\n",
        "POS    I.D. : ", PL[i].Id,
        "Total Sales : ", PL[i].TotalSales,
        "Total Tax : ", PL[i].TotalTaxes);
    try {
      m_outputMediaRef->OutputText(caOpStr);
    }
    catch(...) {
      cerr << "Error with Output Media" << endl;
      return;
    }
  }
} // end for
}
```

SendBarcode()   This function handles the purchasing of one or more items of a given type by the current customer. The parameter to the function specifies the bar code of the item being purchased. The number of these items that are being purchased is determined by the object's **m_itemQuantity** member variable. This defaults to 1, but it may have been changed by a preceding call to the **ItemQuantity()** operation.

The function's first action is to find the price and other information of the item described by the bar code (using the **FindPrice()** operation on the **StoreAccess** object). If any error occurs (the user-defined **BarcodeNotFound** exception or a system exception is raised when calling the **FindPrice()** operation) this is reported on the standard error output (and the purchase quantity is reset to the default of **1**).

If all goes well, the **price** variable passed to the call to **FindPrice()** will have been updated to be the price of the item. This is multiplied by the quantity and assigned to the **itemExt** variable, which in turn is used to update the **m_salesSubTotal** member variable (which is the record of the amount being spent by the current customer). Then a line is output to summarize the item sale. **sprintf()** is once again used to construct this output line, which is output using the **OutputText()** operation on the **OutputMedia** object. The output line gives the item quantity, item bar code, item name, item cost, and total cost (that is, the item cost multiplied by the item quantity). Note that taxable items are marked with an asterisk on the output lines of the receipt.

Finally, the tax subtotal (**m_saleTaxableSubTotal**) is updated to reflect the purchase by this customer. The **taxablePrice** variable (updated as an out parameter by the **FindPrice()** operation) is multiplied by the quantity of the current item being purchased, and then added to the **m_saleTaxableSubTotal** member variable).

```cpp
void  POSTerminal_i:: SendBarcode (const char* Item) {
  if (!LoggedIn())
    return;
  AStore::ItemInfo_var ItemInf;
  CORBA::Float price;
  CORBA::Float taxablePrice;
  delete[] m_itemBarcode;
  m_itemBarcode = new char[strlen(Item) + 1];
  strcpy(m_itemBarcode,Item);

  try {
    m_storeAccessRef->
          FindPrice(m_itemBarcode,m_itemQuantity,
                    price,taxablePrice,ItemInf);
  }
  catch(const AStore::BarcodeNotFound& bcnf) {
    m_itemQuantity = 1;
    cerr << "Invalid Barcode Found" << endl;
    return;
  }
  catch (...) {
    m_itemQuantity = 1;
    cerr << "Error in find Price" << endl;
    return;
  }

  CORBA::Float itemExt = (CORBA::Float)
                              (m_itemQuantity * price);

  m_saleSubTotal += itemExt;

  char caOpStr[255];
  char* szFmtStr = "%3d %10s %20s %7.2f %7.2f %s";
```

```
      sprintf(caOpStr,
                    szFmtStr,m_itemQuantity,
                    m_itemBarcode,ItemInf->Name,
                    ItemInf->Itemcost,itemExt,
                    ((taxablePrice > 0.0)?" *","") );

      try {
        m_outputMediaRef->OutputText(caOpStr);
      }
      catch(...) {
        cerr << "Error with Output Media" << endl;
        return;
      }
      m_saleTaxableSubTotal += taxablePrice *
                                        m_itemQuantity;
      m_itemQuantity = 1;
   }
```

ItemQuantity()   This function simply changes the `m_itemQuantity` member variable, which is used by the next call to the `SendBarcode()` function.

```
   void  POSTerminal_i:: ItemQuantity
                          (CORBA::Long Quantity) {
     if (!LoggedIn())
        return;
     if (Quantity > 0)
        m_itemQuantity = Quantity;
   }
```

EndOfSale()   This function signals that all of the purchases for the current customer have been rung up. It outputs (via the `OutputMedia` object) the total taxable sales made on this occasion, and then it uses the `CalculateTax()` operation of the `Tax` object to determine the corresponding tax. This value is then output, also using the `OutputMedia` object.

The tax value returned by the `CalculateTax()` operation is also used by the `EndOfSale()` function to determine the overall tax total of this sale (`m_saleTax + m_saleSubTotal`).

The function next outputs the total sale value, followed by a "Thank You" banner (naturally, it uses the Gaelic version of this saying: "Go raibh maith agat"). Once this is finished, the POS can inform the store of the total sale value and total price of this sale, using the `Store`'s `UpdateStoreTotal()` operation. Finally, the member variables are reset to initial values.

```
void  POSTerminal_i:: EndOfSale () {
  char caOpStr[255];
  if (!LoggedIn())
    return;

  sprintf(caOpStr, "Taxable Sub-Total :  %8.2f"
                 ,m_saleTaxableSubTotal);
  m_outputMediaRef->OutputText(caOpStr);
  CORBA::Float saleTax = m_taxRef->
              CalculateTax(m_saleTaxableSubTotal);
  sprintf(caOpStr,"Taxes : %8.2f",saleTax);
  m_outputMediaRef->OutputText(caOpStr);

  CORBA::Float saleTotal = saleTax + m_saleSubTotal;
  sprintf(caOpStr,"Total : %8.2f", saleTotal);
  m_outputMediaRef->OutputText(caOpStr);

  m_outputMediaRef->OutputText
                        ("\nGo raibh maith agat\n");
  m_POSTotal += saleTotal;
  m_POSTaxTotal += saleTax;

  try {
    m_storeRef->UpdateStoreTotals
                            (m_id,saleTotal,saleTax);
  }
  catch(...) {
    cerr << "Error Ending sale" << endl ;
  }

  m_saleSubTotal = m_saleTaxableSubTotal = 0;
  m_itemQuantity = 1;
  if (m_itemBarcode) {
    delete[] m_itemBarcode;
    m_itemBarcode = 0;
  }
  return;
}
```

Class **POSTerminal_i** also declares a private function **LoggedIn()**. This returns a Boolean indication of whether the **Login()** operation has been called. Since the effect of the **Login()** operation is to set the **m_storeAccessRef** member variable, the return value of **LoggedIn()** can be determined by whether the **m_storeAccessRef** object reference is nil. The code is as follows:

```
unsigned char POSTerminal_i::LoggedIn() {
  if (CORBA::is_nil(m_storeAccessRef)) {
    cerr << "Need to log in first" << endl;
    return 0;
  }
  else
    return 1;
}
```

31.2.7 OutputMedia Implementation: Class Declaration

Interface **OutputMedia** is implemented by class **OutputMedia_i**, as shown
here:

```
class OutputMedia_i :
               public virtual POS::OutputMediaBOAImpl {
    POS::POSId m_id;
public:
    OutputMedia_i(PseudoNameService_ptr pns,
                    POS::POSId Id);
    virtual CORBA::Boolean OutputText
                    (const char* StringToPrint);
};
```

Its single member function, **OutputText()**, corresponds to the operation
in the IDL interface definition. The constructor's parameters take the object reference of the Pseudo-Name Service (this is needed because the
OutputMedia_i object must register itself), and the POS identifier number.

31.2.8 OutputMedia Implementation: Class Implementation

The constructor of **OutputMedia_i** is coded as follows:

```
#include <iostream.h>
#include <stdio.h>
#include "POS_OM.h"

OutputMedia_i::OutputMedia_i
          (PseudoNameService_ptr pns, POS::POSId Id)
{
  m_id=Id;
  // Register the object with the name service
  char refstring[1024];
  sprintf(refstring, "OutputMedia_%ld",m_id);
```

```
try {
  pns->BindName(refstring,this);
}
catch(...) {
  cerr << "Trouble Binding " << refstring << endl;
}
}
```

The implementation of the **OutputText()** function simply prints a single message on standard output:

```
CORBA::Boolean OutputMedia_i:: OutputText
                        (const char* StringToPrint)
{
    if (StringToPrint)
        cout << StringToPrint << endl;
    return 1;
}
```

31.2.9 Implementation Summary

If you've been typing in the code as you went along, your POS code is nearly complete. You're ready to make just a few adjustments for your specific ORB, and compile and link your POS objects.

31.3 CONNECTING TO THE ORB AND BOA, AND STARTING THE POS OBJECTS

Following the pattern of previous chapters, we'll split now into ORB-specific sections. Turn to the section for your ORB for instructions on how to finish up your POS objects. When you're done, go to Chapter 33 to fire up your objects and run your system!

31.4 POWERBROKER

The PowerBroker implementation of the POS interfaces is very similar to the common functionality implementation. The PowerBroker specific implementation issues are:

PowerBroker include files

base class names

BOA::impl_is_ready

the PowerBroker event loop

use of _out classes for CORBA **out** and **inout** arguments.

Each of these issues was described in detail in section Section 25.6, The PowerBroker Implementation of the Depot.

To compile and link the POS programs, type the following commands:

```
% CC -c -I$PBHOME/include POS_Ter.C POS_IM.C POS_OM.C
% CC -c -I$PBHOME/include Srv_Main.C
% CC -o POSClt POS_Ter.o POS_IM.o POS.o POS_s.o FindPNS.o \
-L$PBHOME/lib -lcorba -lpbroker
% CC -o outsrv POS_OM.o POS.o POS_s.o FindPNS.o \
-L$PBHOME/lib -lpbcorba -lpbroker
```

31.5   DESCRIPTION OF THE ORBIX IMPLEMENTATION OF THE POS

Background information on how to run Orbix clients and servers was given in Section 25.7, and you should remind yourself of the material in that section before continuing with the C++ code.

In C++, the point-of-sale terminal itself consists of one client and one server. The server, **OutputSrv**, contains the **OutputMedia** object, and the client contains the **InputMedia** and **POSTerminal** objects. The compilation and running of both of these are discussed in this section. Note also that it would be straightforward to run the client and the server code in the one process (with or without the Orbix support for lightweight threads); these were kept separate simply to show that a single machine can run multiple clients and servers.

31.5.1   Changes to the C++ Code

The only change required to the C++ code is that the lines written:

```
CORBA::ORB_var orb =
                 CORBA::ORB_init(argc,argv,"PRIMER_ORB");
CORBA::BOA_var boa = orb->BOA_init(argc,argv);
```

must be recoded to use the string "**Orbix**" instead of "**PRIMER_ORB**".

Alternatively, the **CORBA::Orbix** can be used to find Orbix instead of using **ORB_init()** and **BOA_init()**. In fact, **ORB_init()** and **BOA_init()** do not need to be called at all because initialization is handled automatically.

No other changes to the C++ code are required.

31.5.2 Registering the Server

The server that creates the **OutputMedia** object is called **OutputSrv**, and it can be registered with the following one-line command:

```
putit OutputSrv
          <full pathname of executable
               file (OutputServer) for this server>
          <POS_number>
```

Once registered, a server can be started manually (through the operating system's normal command-line interpreter), or it will be started automatically when a client invokes an operation (or accesses an attribute) of one of the objects in the server. The command-line argument to the server has been specified to **putit** so that it will be passed to the server each time it is automatically launched.

The client (executable file **POSclient**) is not registered with **putit**. It can be started from any command-line interpreter or by any other means. It takes two command-line arguments: the Store number and the POS number.

31.5.3 Makefile for the Server OutputSrv and Client POSClient in Orbix

A single makefile is shared between the server **OutputSrv** and the client **POSclient** (directory **POS**, file **Makefile**). The target **OutputSrv** makes the server, and the target **POSclient** makes the client. Some of that makefile is shown here. The full makefile includes rules for compiling the files Srv_Main.cc, POS_IM.cc, POS_OM.cc, POS_Ter.cc, and POSClt.cc:

```
default: POSClient OutputServer

OUTMED_OBJS = ../POSS.o ../PNSC.o POS_OM.o Srv_Main.o\
               ../PNS/FindPNS.o \
POSCLT_OBJS = ../POSC.o ../CentralC.cc ../StoreC.o \
               ../PNSC.o POS_Ter.o POS_IM.o \
               POSClt.o ../PNS/FindPNS.o

OutputServer: $(OUTMED_OBJS)
     $(C++) $(C++FLAGS) -o OutputServer \
          $(OUTMED_OBJS) $(LDFLAGS) -lITsrv

POSClient: $(POSCLT_OBJS)
     $(C++) $(C++FLAGS) -o POSClient \
          $(POSCLT_OBJS) $(LDFLAGS) -lITsrv
```

Section 21.3.3 contains a pointer to information about a Visual Basic GUI for this programming example.

31.6   ORB PLUS

The changes required for ORB Plus from the generic C++ code was described in detail for the Depot in Section 25.8. This section describes these changes for the POS implementation. Refer to the Depot chapter for a more detailed description of these changes.

31.6.1   Srv_Main

The changes for the OutputMedia **Srv_Main** are as follows:

1. Create an instance of CORBA::Environment.

    ```
    CORBA::Environment IT_env;
    ```

2. Initialize the ORB.

    ```
    CORBA::ORB_var orb = CORBA::ORB_init(argc,
                         argv,CORBA::HPORBid,
                         IT_env);
       if (IT_env.exception()) {
          cerr << "ERROR Initializing ORB" << endl;
          exit(EXIT_FAILURE);
       }
    ```

3. Initialize the **HPSOA**.

    ```
    CORBA::HPSOA_var soa = orb->HPSOA_init(argc,
                           argv,CORBA::HPSOAid,
                           IT_env);
       if (IT_env.exception()) {
          cerr << "ERROR Initializing HPSOA" << endl;
          exit(EXIT_FAILURE);
       }
    ```

4. Create an instance of the **OutputMedia_i** C++ object.

    ```
    OutputMedia_i OutPut( pns,atol(argv[1]), IT_env);
    ```

5. Issue the HPSOA run command.

```
soa->run();
```

31.6.2 POSClt

The changes to the POS client POSClt are as follows:

1. Create an instance of CORBA::Environment.

```
CORBA::Environment IT_env;
```

2. Initialize the ORB.

```
CORBA::ORB_var orb = CORBA::ORB_init(argc,argv,CORBA::HPORBid,
                                     IT_env);
if (IT_env.exception()) {
   cerr << "ERROR Initializing ORB" << endl;
   exit(EXIT_FAILURE);
}
```

3. Initialize the HPSOA.

```
CORBA::HPSOA_var soa = orb->HPSOA_init(argc,
                          argv,CORBA::HPSOAid,
                                     IT_env);
if (IT_env.exception()) {
   cerr << "ERROR Initializing HPSOA" << endl;
   exit(EXIT_FAILURE);
}
```

4. Create the POSTerminal_i C++ object.

```
POSTerminal_i* Ter = new POSTerminal_i(pns,
                          atol(argv[1]),atol(argv[2]),
                          IT_env);
```

5. Create the POSTerminal CORBA object reference.

```
POS::POSTerminal_var TerObj = Ter->_this();
```

6. Create the InputMedia C++ object.

```
char caBuff[255];
InputMedia_i* InPut = new InputMedia_i(TerObj);
```

31.6.3 POS_IM

Changes to the POS_IM.h declarations are:

- The **InputMedia_i** object inherits from the **HPSOA_POS::InputMedia** base class, which is generated by the cidl compiler.

```
class InputMedia_i :public virtual HPSOA_POS::InputMedia
```

- The BarcodeInput and KeypadInput operations have the **CORBA:: Environment** parameter added.

The only change to the POS_IM.cc implementation is the explicit checking of errors.

31.6.4 POS_OM

Changes to the POS_OM.h declarations are:

- The **OutputMedia_i** object inherits from **HPSOA_POS::OutputMedia**.

```
class OutputMedia_i : public virtual HPSOA_POS::OutputMedia {
```

- The OutputText operation has the **CORBA::Environment** parameter added.

The only change to the POS_OM.cc implementation is the explicit checking of errors.

31.6.5 POS_Ter

Changes to the POS_Ter.h declarations are:

- The **POSTerminal_i** object inherits from the **HPSOA_POS::POS-Terminals** base class.

```
POSTerminal_i : public virtual HPSOA_POS::POSTerminals
```

- The **POSTerminal_i** operations have the **CORBA::Environment** parameter added.

The only change to the POS_Ter.cc implementation is the explicit checking of errors.

31.7 NEO

Most of the notes presented for the PseudoNamingService implementation (Coding the **PseudoNameService** (PNS) in Section 25.9.1) remain valid for the POS's implementation.

31.7.1 Two Separate Servers

The common code used for this example implements the POS in two separate servers: the POS input service (InputMedia and POSTerminal in directory *POS.ter*) and the POS output service (OutputMedia in directory *POS.out*).

The multithreaded architecture of SolarisNEO allows all three objects to be implemented in the same server. But in order to remain as close as possible to the common implementation code required by single-threaded servers, two separate servers are built.

## CHAPTER 32

Coding the POS in Smalltalk

32.1 GETTING STARTED ON THE POS

This chapter presents the implementation of the POS module in HP Distributed Smalltalk. As we did in the previous Smalltalk chapters, we'll try to keep the standard IDL and Smalltalk components separate from the HP implementation details.

You should have just read the description of the language-independent implementation details of the POS in Section 30.1. If you didn't, turn back and read it now; it tells what we're going to do in this chapter.

As before, but now for the final time, this Smalltalk code must be entered into your system. If you're typing it in by hand as you work the example, open a system browser and view the **OMG Primer Example** class category. If you read everything in from the floppy disk, open a system browser on the **OMG Primer Example** class category to view the code as we discuss it. In either case, when you reach the end of this chapter, the IS system for your retail empire will be complete and ready to run!

The requirements for the POS object and its various associated objects were fixed in our A&D in Sections 19.1.1, 19.1.2, and 19.1.3; implementation details were added in Section 30.1. Refer to those sections in order to follow as we code the Smalltalk that implements them.

32.2   SMALLTALK IMPLEMENTATION OF THE POSTERMINAL IDL

We begin the POSTerminal discussion with the IDL:

```
module POS {

    typedef long POSId;

    typedef string Barcode;

    interface InputMedia {
        typedef string OperatorCmd;

        void BarcodeInput (in Barcode Item);
        void KeypadInput (in OperatorCmd Cmd);
    };

    interface OutputMedia {
        boolean OutputText (in string StringToPrint);
    };

    interface POSTerminal {
        void Login ();
        void PrintPOSSalesSummary ();
        void PrintStoreSalesSummary ();
        void SendBarcode (in Barcode Item);
        void ItemQuantity (in long Quantity);
        void EndOfSale ();
    };
};
```

The POS terminal handles the interactions between the media devices (keypad, bar-code scanner, and sales tape). The state of a sales transaction is maintained by the POS terminal. Sales report generation is handled by the POS terminal, both for the terminal as well as the store.

The POS module is implemented by the following Smalltalk classes:

`POSTerminal`

`InputMedia`

`OutputMedia`

This chapter will also describe the **OMGPrimerExample** class, which is used to generate a running example.

32.2.1   Smalltalk Implementation for POSTerminal

The Smalltalk implementation class **POSTerminal** is shown in the following code listing. The code discussion is organized according to protocol category, and any code references are by line number.

```
1      Class:      POSTerminal
2
3      Superclass: Object
4      Category:   OMG Primer Example
5      Instance variables: itemBarcode itemQuantity item
6                          taxReference storeReference
7                          storeAccessReference
8                          outputMediaReference itemExtension
9                          saleSubtotal saleTaxableSubtotal
10                         saleTotal saleTax POSTotal
11                         POSTaxTotal POSid
12
13     Protocol: repository
14
15     CORBAName
16         ^#'::POS::POSTerminal'
17
18     Protocol: POSTerminal
19
20     endOfSale
21         | msg |
22         self checkForLogin.
23         msg := String new writeStream.
24         msg nextPutAll: 'Taxable subtotal: '; nextPutAll:
                 (self format: saleTaxableSubtotal); nextPut:
                 Character space.
25         outputMediaReference outputText: msg contents.
26         saleTax := taxReference calculateTax:
                 saleTaxableSubtotal.
27         saleTotal := saleSubtotal + saleTax.
28         msg reset.
29         msg nextPutAll: 'Total: '; nextPutAll: (self format:
                 saleTotal).
30         outputMediaReference outputText: msg contents.
31         POSTotal := POSTotal + saleTotal.
32         POSTaxTotal := POSTaxTotal + saleTax.
33         storeReference
34             updateStoreTotals: POSid
35             price: saleTotal
36             taxes: saleTax.
```

```
37          itemBarcode := nil.
38          saleSubtotal := saleTaxableSubtotal := 0.0.
39          itemQuantity := 1
40
41     itemQuantity: quantity
42          self checkForLogin.
43          itemQuantity := quantity
44
45     login
46          storeAccessReference isNil ifFalse: [self error:
                'Cannot login in twice!'].
47          itemQuantity := 1.
48          saleSubtotal := saleTaxableSubtotal := saleTotal :=
                saleTax := POSTotal := POSTaxTotal := 0.0.
49          storeAccessReference := storeReference login: POSId
50
51     printPOSSalesSummary
52          | msg |
53          self checkForLogin.
54          itemBarcode isNil ifFalse: [^self].
55          saleSubtotal isZero ifFalse: [^self].
56          msg := String new writeStream.
57          msg nextPutAll: 'Totals for POS terminal ';
                nextPutAll: POSid printString.
58          outputMediaReference outputText: msg contents.
59          msg reset.
60          msg tab; nextPutAll: 'Total Sales: '; nextPutAll:
                (self format: POSTotal).
61          outputMediaReference outputText: msg contents.
62          msg reset.
63          msg tab; nextPutAll: 'Total Taxes: '; nextPutAll:
                (self format: POSTaxTotal).
64          outputMediaReference outputText: msg contents
65
66     printStoreSalesSummary
67          | msg aList totals |
68          self checkForLogin.
69          itemBarcode isNil ifFalse: [^self].
70          saleSubtotal isZero ifFalse: [^self].
71          msg := String new writeStream.
72          msg nextPutAll: 'Totals for store '; nextPutAll:
                storeReference StoreId printString.
73          outputMediaReference outputText: msg contents.
74          msg reset.
75          totals := storeReference Totals.
76          msg tab; nextPutAll: 'Total Store Sales: $';
```

```
                          nextPutAll: (self format: (totals at:
                             #StoreTotal)).
77        outputMediaReference outputText: msg contents.
78        msg reset.
79        msg tab; nextPutAll: 'Total Store Taxes: $';
              nextPutAll: (self format: (totals at:
                 #StoreTaxTotal)).
80        outputMediaReference outputText: msg contents.
81        msg reset.
82        storeReference getPOSTotals: (aList := nil
              asCORBAParameter).
83        aList value
84            do:
85                  [:t |
86                  msg tab; nextPutAll: 'Totals for POS
                         terminal '; nextPutAll: t Id
                         printString.
87                  outputMediaReference outputText: msg
                         contents.
88                  msg reset.
89                  msg tab; tab; nextPutAll: 'Total Sales: ';
                         nextPutAll: (self format:
                         t TotalSales).
90                  outputMediaReference outputText: msg
                         contents.
91                  msg reset.
92                  msg tab; tab; nextPutAll: 'Total Taxes: ';
                         nextPutAll: (self format:
                             t TotalTaxes).
93                  outputMediaReference outputText: msg
                         contents]
94
95     sendBarcode: barcodeString
96          | price tax msg itemInfo|
97          self checkForLogin.
98          price := nil asCORBAParameter.
99          tax := nil asCORBAParameter.
100         itemInfo := nil asCORBAParameter.
101         itemBarcode := barcodeString.
102         (CORBAConstants at: '::AStore::BarcodeNotFound')
103             corbaHandle:
104                  [:ev |
105                  itemBarcode := nil.
106                  itemQuantity := 1.
107                  ^nil]
108             do:
```

```
109                        [storeAccessReference
110                             findPrice: itemBarcode
111                             quantity: itemQuantity
112                             itemPrice: price
113                             itemTaxPrice: tax
114                             iInfo: itemInfo.
115                        saleSubtotal := saleSubtotal + (price
                               value * itemQuantity).
116                        saleTaxableSubtotal := saleTaxableSubtotal
                               + (tax value * itemQuantity).
117                        msg := String new writeStream.
118                        msg nextPutAll: itemBarcode.
119                        tax value isZero ifFalse: [msg
                               nextPutAll: '*   ']
120                             ifTrue: [msg nextPutAll: '    '].
121                        msg nextPutAll: itemInfo value Name; space;
                               nextPutAll: itemQuantity printString;
                               space; nextPutAll: (self format: price
                               value); space; nextPutAll: (self
                               format: price value * itemQuantity).
122                        outputMediaReference outputText: msg
                               contents.
123                        itemQuantity := 1]
124
125   sendBarcodeAndQuantity: barCodeString quantity: aCount
126        self itemQuantity: aCount.
127        self sendBarcode: barCodeString
128
129
130   Protocol: initialization
131
132   initialize: aStoreId posId: anId
133        | pns |
134        pns := ORBObject pseudoNameService.
135        taxReference := pns resolveName: 'Tax_' , aStoreId
                asString.
136        storeReference := pns resolveName: 'Store_' ,
                aStoreId asString.
137        outputMediaReference := pns resolveName:
                'OutputMedia_' , anId asString.
138        itemBarcode := nil.
139        POSid := anId.
140        POSTotal := POSTaxTotal := 0.0.
141        saleSubtotal := saleTaxableSubtotal := 0.0
142
143   Protocol: private
```

```
144
145   checkForLogin
146        storeAccessReference isNil ifTrue: [self error:
                'Need to login in first!']
147
148   format: amount
149        "Format amount as a dollar amount"
150
151        ^PrintConverter print: amount formattedBy:
                '$######.##'
```

- **Superclass** (line 3): **POSTerminal** inherits from the Smalltalk class **Object**, which is the base of the Smalltalk inheritance tree.

- **Protocol: repository** (lines 15–16): HP Distributed Smalltalk requires the **CORBAName** method to associate an IDL interface (in this case **POSTerminal**) with its implementing Smalltalk class, **POSTerminal**.

- **Protocol: POSTerminal** (lines 20–127): This protocol category is initial capitalized, which indicates that all methods found in this category are implementations of IDL operations found in the corresponding IDL interface. Many times, the mapping from an IDL operation to its Smalltalk implementation is explicitly shown via the selector pragma. In this case, the default mapping is used (no selector pragmas specified). There are six IDL operations implemented in this protocol:

   ::POS::POSTerminal::Login

   This IDL operation is implemented by the **login** method (lines 45–49).

   This message is sent by the keypad when the L command is entered and indicates that a new cashier is logging in. If the **StoreAccess** reference is not nil (already logged in) then report an error. Otherwise reset the sales totals and use the **Store** reference to get the **StoreAccess** reference.

   ::POS::POSTerminal::PrintPOSSalesSummary

   This IDL operation is implemented by the **printPOSSalesSummary** method (lines 51–64).

   Print the sales total (sales and taxes) since the last login. This message is sent by the keypad when the P command is entered. Ignore this message (do nothing) if a cashier is not logged in or the **itemBarCode** and the **saleSubTotal** is nonzero (the POS terminal is in the middle of a sale). The totals are formatted and sent as strings to the **OutputMedia** object for printing (lines 58, 61, 64).

::POS::POSTerminal::PrintStoreSalesSummary

This IDL operation is implemented by the **printStoreSales-Summary** method (lines 66–93).

Print the totals (sales and taxes) for the Store since the store computer was last initialized. Also print the totals (sales and taxes) for each POS terminal that is logged in. This message is sent by the keypad when the S command is entered. Ignore this message (do nothing) if not logged in and if **itemBarcode** or **saleSubTotal** is nonzero since the POS terminal is in the middle of a sale. The totals are formatted and sent as strings to the **OutputMedia** object for printing (lines 73, 77, 80, 87, 90, 93).

::POS::POSTerminal::SendBarcode

This IDL operation is implemented by the **sendBarcode:** method (lines 95–123).

Called from the bar-code scanner when an item has been scanned. A cashier must be logged in. A call to the **Store** object via the **StoreAccess** reference is set up. This involves setting up three **out** parameters (lines 98–100). Also, the **BarcodeNotFound** exception is caught. If the call on the **Store** object succeeds, then the sale subtotals are updated (lines 115–116). The data for the scanned item is formatted and output to the **OutputMedia** object (lines 117–122).

::POS::POSTerminal::EndOfSale

This IDL operation is implemented by the **endOfSale** method (lines 20–39).

A cashier must be logged in. The sale is completed by calculating the tax and completing the printing of the sales slip (lines 23–30). The POS terminal totals are updated (lines 31–32) and the Store object's running totals are updated via a call through the Store reference. The sale totals are reset, preparing for a new sales transaction.

::POS::POSTerminal::ItemQuantity

This IDL operation is implemented by the **itemQuantity:** method (lines 41–43). Set the quantity to be applied to an individual bar-code scan. Successive calls simply overwrite the previous quantity. The quantity is reset to 1 after bar-code processing is complete so that the next bar code will be processed with quantity 1.

32.2.2 Smalltalk Implementation for InputMedia

InputMedia simulates a keypad and bar-code scanner for demo purposes. The keypad is simulated by pushbuttons. The following keys are defined:

L—a login request by a new cashier. Send the **login** message to the **POSTerminal** associated with this keypad.

P—a print all sales since last login request. Send the **printPOSSales-Summary** message to the **POSTerminal** associated with this keypad.

S—a sum of all store sales request. Send the **printStoreSales-Summary** message to the **POSTerminal** associated with this keypad.

Q—an item quantity request. Send the **itemQuantity:** message to the **POSTerminal** associated with this keypad, with the entered quantity as an argument.

T—an end of sales request. Send the **endOfSale** message to the **POSTerminal** associated with this keypad.

The Smalltalk implementation class **InputMedia** is shown in the following code listing. The code discussion is organized according to protocol category, and any code references are by line number.

```
1       Class:      InputMedia
2
3       Superclass: ApplicationModel
4       Category:   OMG Primer Example
5       Instance variables: barcode POSReference quantity
6
7       Protocol: repository
8
9       CORBAName
10          ^#'::POS::InputMedia'
11
12      Protocol: aspects
13
14      barcode
15          ^barcode isNil
16              ifTrue: [barcode := String new asValue]
17              ifFalse: [barcode]
18
19      quantity
20          ^quantity isNil
21              ifTrue: [quantity := 1 asValue]
22              ifFalse: [quantity]
```

```
23
24      Protocol: actions
25
26      barcodeInput
27          POSReference sendBarcode: self barcode value
28
29      cashierLogin
30          POSReference login
31
32      endOfSale
33          POSReference endOfSale
34
35      itemQuantity
36          POSReference itemQuantity: self quantity value
37
38      printPOSSalesSummary
39          POSReference printPOSSalesSummary
40
41      printStoreSalesSummary
42          POSReference printStoreSalesSummary
43
44      Protocol: initialization
45
46      initialize: aPOSTerminal
47          POSReference := aPOSTerminal.
48          self open
49
50      MetaClass Protocol: Iinterface specs
51
52      windowSpec
53          <resource: #canvas>
54          ^#(#FullSpec
55              #window:
56              #(#WindowSpec
57                  #label: 'OMG Primer Example'
58                  #min: #(#Point 272 215 )
59                  #max: #(#Point 272 215 )
60                  #bounds: #(#Rectangle 355 343 627 558 )
61                  #menu: #menuBar )
62              #component:
63              #(#SpecCollection
64                  #collection: #(
65                      #(#LabelSpec
66                          #layout: #(#Point 31 18 )
67                          #label: 'Barcode Scanner' )
68                      #(#LabelSpec
```

```
69                          #layout: #(#Point 58 83 )
70                          #label: 'Keypad' )
71          #(#InputFieldSpec
72                          #layout: #(#Rectangle 15 46
                                149 70 )
73                          #model: #barcode
74                          #alignment: #right
75                          #type: #string )
76          #(#ActionButtonSpec
77                          #layout: #(#Rectangle 179 42
                                234 72 )
78                          #model: #barcodeInput
79                          #label: 'Scan'
80                          #defaultable: true )
81          #(#ActionButtonSpec
82                          #layout: #(#Rectangle 20 114
                                72 139 )
83                          #model: #cashierLogin
84                          #label: 'L'
85                          #defaultable: true )
86          #(#ActionButtonSpec
87                          #layout: #(#Rectangle 91 115
                                143 140 )
88                          #model: #printPOSSalesSummary
89                          #label: 'P'
90                          #defaultable: true )
91          #(#ActionButtonSpec
92                          #layout: #(#Rectangle 20 147
                                72 172 )
93                          #model: #printStoreSalesSummary
94                          #label: 'S'
95                          #defaultable: true )
96          #(#ActionButtonSpec
97                          #layout: #(#Rectangle 92 148
                                144 173 )
98                          #model: #endOfSale
99                          #label: 'T'
100                         #defaultable: true )
101         #(#ActionButtonSpec
102                         #layout: #(#Rectangle 92 182
                                144 207 )
103                         #model: #itemQuantity
104                         #label: 'Q'
105                         #defaultable: true )
106         #(#InputFieldSpec
```

```
107                          #layout: #(#Rectangle 21 181
                                69 206 )
108                          #model: #quantity
109                          #alignment: #right
110                          #type: #number ) ) ) )
```

- **Superclass** (line 3): **InputMedia** inherits from the Smalltalk class **ApplicationModel**, which is the point of inheritance for all (most) Smalltalk applications whose user interface is generated by the VisualWorks builder.

- **Instance variables** (line 5): The **InputMedia** object keeps track of the current bar code and quantity. An object reference to the associated POS terminal is stored in **POSReference**.

- **Protocol: repository** (lines 9–10): HP Distributed Smalltalk requires the **CORBAName** method to associate an IDL interface (in this case **InputMedia**) with its implementing Smalltalk class, **InputMedia**.

- **Protocol: aspects** (lines 14–22): This protocol category contains the methods associated with the input fields in the user interface. There are two such fields, one for the bar code and one for the quantity.

- **Protocol: actions** (lines 26–42): This protocol category contains the methods called from the user interface. These methods forward the request to the associated POS terminal through the POSTerminal object reference stored in POSReference. Arguments for the various calls are collected from the two aspect variables **barcode** and **quantity**.

- **Protocol: initialization** (lines 46–48): The **initialize** method is called when a new **InputMedia** object is created. It sets the **POSReference** to the associated **POSTerminal** object reference and opens the user interface.

- **MetaClass Protocol: interface specs** (lines 52–110): The **windowSpec** method was generated by the VisualWorks user interface generator. Its screen appearance is shown in Figure 32.1.

32.2.3 Smalltalk Implementation for OutputMedia

OutputMedia simulates a sales tape printer showing the current status of a transaction. It is simulated by a **TextCollector** and an associated **TextCollectorView**.

The Smalltalk implementation class **OutputMedia** is shown in the following code listing. The code discussion is organized according to protocol category, and any code references are by line number.

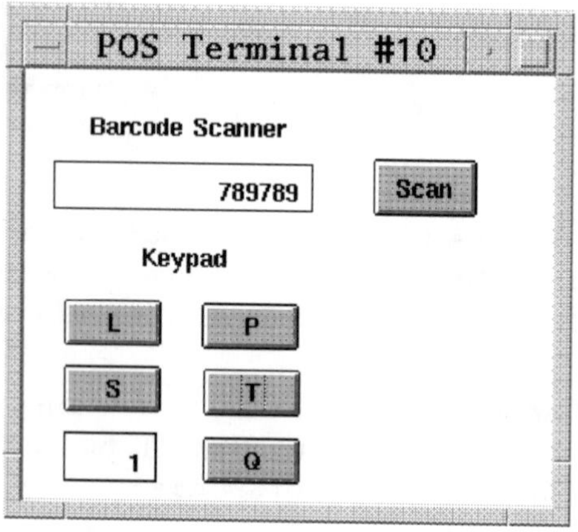

Figure 32.1. `WindowSpec` method screen appearance.

```
1    Class: OutputMedia
2
3    Superclass: Object
4    Category:    OMG Primer Example
5    Instance variables: transcript view
6
7    Protocol: repository
8
9    CORBAName
10        ^#'::POS::OutputMedia'
11
12   Protocol: OutputMedia
13
14   outputText: aString
15        transcript show: aString; cr.
16        ^true
17
18   Protocol: accessing
19
20   transcript
21        ^transcript
22
23   transcript: newTranscript
24        transcript := newTranscript
25
26   view
27        ^view
```

```
28
29    view: newView
30        view := newView
31
32    Protocol: initialize
33
34    initialize: aPOSId
35        self transcript: TextCollector new.
36        self view: (TextCollectorView createOn: self
                   transcript label: 'Sales Tape Printer for POS
                   Terminal #', aPOSId asString).
37        self view minimumSize: 500 @ 150.
38        self view maximumSize: 500 @ 150.
39        self view open.
40        ^self
41
```

- **Superclass** (line 3): **OutputMedia** inherits from the Smalltalk class **Object**, which is the base of the Smalltalk inheritance tree.

- **Instance variables** (line 5): **transcript** holds the instance of **TextCollector**, and **view** holds the associated **TextCollectorView** instance.

- **Protocol: repository** (lines 9–10): HP Distributed Smalltalk requires the **CORBAName** method to associate an IDL interface (in this case, **OutputMedia**) with its implementing Smalltalk class, **OutputMedia**.

- **Protocol: OutputMedia** (lines 14–16): This protocol category is initial capitalized, which indicates that all methods found in this category are implementations of IDL operations found in the corresponding IDL interface. Many times, the mapping from an IDL operation to its Smalltalk implementation is explicitly shown via the selector pragma. In this case, the default mapping is used (no selector pragmas specified). There is one IDL operation implemented in this protocol:

  ::POS::OutputMedia::OutputText

  This IDL operation is implemented by the **outputText:** method (lines 14–16).

  The parameter, a string, is simply written on the text collector with a trailing carriage return.

- **Protocol: accessing** (lines 20–30): This protocol category implements the setters and getters of the two instance variables **transcript** and **view**.

- **Protocol: initialize** (lines 34–40): The **initialize** method is called to initialize a new instance of **OutputMedia**. A new **TextCollector**

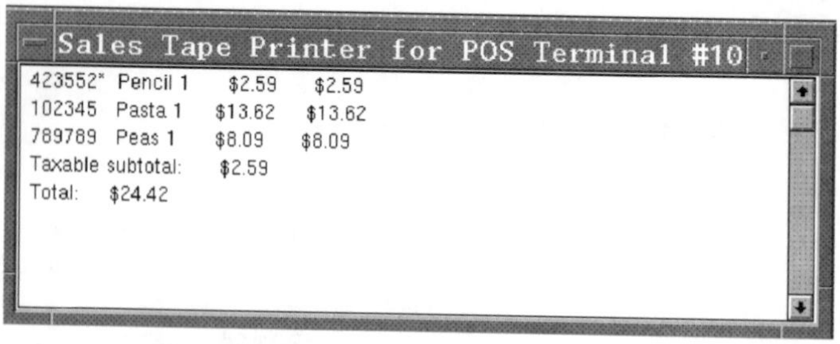

Figure 32.2. `TextCollectorView` screen appearance.

is created, and the associated **TextCollectorView** is created and opened. The screen appearance is shown in Figure 32.2.

32.3 THE OMGPRIMEREXAMPLE SMALLTALK CLASS

The HP Distributed Smalltalk version of the POS example is controlled by the class, **OMGPrimerExample**. The purpose of this class is to make it easy to set up and run the POS example. It is within this class that all of the distributed objects are initially created. This is much like the object server processes of the C++ implementation. The code follows:

```
1     Class: OMGPrimerExample
2
3     Superclass: ApplicationModel
4     Category:   OMG Primer Example
5     Class variables: DEPOT OM PNS POS STORE TAX
6
7     MetaClass Protocol: startup
8
9     createDepot
10        | pns |
11        DEPOT := Depot new initialize.
12        pns := ORBObject pseudoNameService.
13        pns bindName: 'Depot' objectRef: DEPOT
14
15    createOutputMedia: posId
16        | pns |
17        OM := OutputMedia new initialize: posId.
18        pns := ORBObject pseudoNameService.
19        pns bindName: 'OutputMedia_' , posId asString
              objectRef: OM
```

```
20
21    createPNS
22        PNS := PseudoNameService new.
23        ORBObject referenceToFile: 'pns.dat' object: PNS
24
25    createPOSTerminal: aPOSId store: aStoreId
26        | im|
27        POS := POSTerminal new initialize: aStoreId posId:
              aPOSId.
28        im := InputMedia new initialize: POS.
29        im builder window label: 'POS Terminal #', aPOSId
              asString.
30
31    createStore: storeId markup: percentage
32        | pns |
33        pns := ORBObject pseudoNameService.
34        STORE := Store new initialize: storeId markup:
              percentage.
35        pns bindName: 'Store_' , storeId asString objectRef:
              STORE.
36        TAX := Tax new.
37        pns bindName: 'Tax_' , storeId asString objectRef:
              TAX
38
39    localRPCDemo
40        self createPNS.
41        self createDepot.
42        self createOutputMedia: 10.
43        self createStore: 42 markup: 0.1.
44        self createPOSTerminal: 10 store: 42
```

- **Superclass** (line 3): **OMGPrimerExample** inherits from the Smalltalk class **Object**, which is the base of the Smalltalk inheritance tree.

- **Class variables** (line 5): **DEPOT**, **OM**, **PNS**, **POS**, **STORE**, and **TAX** are class variables used to reference created instances of **Depot**, **OutputMedia**, **PseudoNameService**, **POSTerminal**, **Store**, and **Tax**, respectively. This reference prevents the objects from being garbage collected. This technique is used instead of the Lifecycle service.

- **MetaClass Protocol: startup** (lines 9–44): There are six methods in this category:

createDepot

This method creates a **Depot** object and registers it with the Pseudo-Name Service. A reference is also stored in the **DEPOT** class variable.

createOutputMedia

This method creates an **OutputMedia** object (sales tape printer) associated with the POSTerminal identified by **posId**. The reference is bound into the Pseudo-Name Service as well as the **OM** class variable.

createPNS

This method creates a **PseudoNameService** (PNS) object that will act as the server of the PNS for the demo. The reference to the PNS object is written to the file pns.dat as a stringified object reference. Other images can unstringify the reference, thus connecting to the PNS.

createPOSTerminal:store

This method will create a **POSTerminal** with the given ID and associated with the given store. It also creates an **InputMedia** object (bar-code scanner and keypad) which is associated with the POS terminal.

createStore:markup

This method is used to create a **Store** and **Tax** object. The Store and Tax references are then added to the Pseudo-Name Service under the name Store_n and Tax_n respectively, where n is the Store ID number.

localRPCDemo

This method starts up the OMG primer example in a single HP DST image. The Store ID is 42 and the POSTerminal is terminal 10.

32.4 IMPLEMENTATION SUMMARY

If you've been typing code into your system as you worked your way through this chapter, or if you've read the code in from the diskette, your POS module implementation is finished and your example implementation is complete. Now turn to Chapter 33 for instructions on how to run the IS system for your retail empire.

CHAPTER 33

Running the Example

33.1 RUNNING THE EXAMPLE

Congratulations! You have finished coding and compiling the example. Now it's time to fire up the objects and run the software side of your retailing empire. All the information you need to do this is in an individual section for your ORB, since system-dependent aspects such as command lines are not part of any OMG specification.

While not nearly complete enough to run a real warehouse and store, the example still includes enough objects and functionality to demonstrate how an enterprise could run its operations on a base of distributed objects.

Go ahead and exercise your new application. After you've run it for a while, there are a couple of things you could do next:

- You could adopt the example to use an OMG-standard Naming Service, if one comes with your ORB.
- You could write a graphical user interface (GUI) for POS input and output.
- You could demo the distributed objects to your boss or the other people in your company who need to know about this technology.
- You could use your new skills in a distributed object development project to build something else your company can use.

Now, let's run the example.

33.2   RUNNING THE EXAMPLE IN OBJECTBROKER

33.2.1   Specific Command Lines

For the sake of this book, the following commands can be thought of as being run from five separate terminals or five windows or whatever means you have in your operating system for starting five processes.

It is important to start these processes in a particular order, since they all depend on the Pseudo-Name Service being available, and those closer to the clerk at the POS station expect the others to be available when they start.

1. Starting the Pseudo-Name Service is a simple command line since there is only one in the system:

    > `PNS`

2. Starting the Depot is a simple command line for the same reason:

    > `CentralSrv`

3. Starting the Store requires you to supply a store ID number and a markup value as parameters on the command line:

    > `store 26 10`

    specifying `store_26` to the Pseudo-Name Service with a markup of 10 times cost.

4. We start the OutputMedia server next, with a parameter telling its POS ID number. For example, to specify the printer for POS station `pos_12`, enter:

    > `outsrv 12`

5. Finally, we start our pure client, where everything starts—the POS station, with the first parameter specifying the POS ID first and then the Store ID. To match the preceding lines, we'd enter:

    > `posclt 12 26`

    That is, this process identifies `pos_12` connecting to `store_26`.

After this, you can start entering data at this last started process. Quick! Buy out the store—there's a hurricane (Gulf Coast)/blizzard (Upper Midwest)/tornado (Central Midwest)/earthquake (California Coast)/Fog (UK)/Guinness shortage (Dublin) coming!

33.3 RUNNING THE EXAMPLE IN SOMOBJECTS

To recap the programming excercise in this book, we defined the following interfaces: **PseudoNameService**, **CentralOffice::Depot**, **POS::Input-Media**, **POS::OutputMedia**, **POS::POSTerminal**, **AStore::Store-Access**, **AStore::Tax**, and **AStore::Store**.

The interfaces have been partitioned among the servers to achieve the functionality of the point-of-sale example. There are four server types (but 5 instances) defined. The servers and the classes they serve are shown here:

pnssvr	PseudoNameService
centralsvr	CentralOffic::Depot
storesvr	AStore::Store, AStore::Tax, AStore::StoreAccess
outputsvr	POS::OutputTerminal

There is one client **posclt** that takes command-line arguments that specify the POSId and the StoreId. To simplify the implementation, we have registered one Store server whose alias is **storesvr_1** and two Output-Media servers whose aliases are **outputsvr_1** and **outputsvr_2**. The **posclt** itself creates the following objects:

posclt	POS::InputMedia and POS::POSTerminal

33.3.1 Running the Example

Until now, we have not had the opportunity to mention somdd, the important daemon used in SOMObjects. somdd is used for server activation, server location and binding, and other services. It serves as a server port-mapper for clients. Clients always connect and talk to somdd before they can get a binding to the actual server. So, in order to run the example, we start somdd daemon first as shown here. (Assume a UNIX-like environment where jobs can be started in the background with an ampersand (&).) Alternatively, they could each be started in a separate window. A dollar sign, $, is the command prompt of the operating system.

```
$ somdd &
```

Then we start the servers in the sequence. The sequence is important, because when a server comes up, it expects the other server to be active. For example, when the **centralsvr** (Depot server) comes up, it expects **pnssvr** (nameserver) to exist so that it can register itself. Therefore, the servers are started in the following sequence:

1. First start the PNS server:

   ```
   $ somdsvr -a pnssvr &
   ```

2. Now start the Depot server:

   ```
   $ somdsvr -a centralsvr &
   ```

3. Now, we are ready to start the OutputMedia servers:

   ```
   $ somdsvr -a outputsvr_1 &
   $ somdsvr -a outputsvr_2 &
   ```

4. Finally, we start the Store server as:

   ```
   $ somdsvr -a storesvr_1 &
   ```

Note that the POSId, 1 or 2, is implicit in the alias of the OutputMedia servers. Similarly, for reasons of simplicity and without loss of generality, we use a Store server with StoreId 1. Our Store ID and Markup are hard-coded in the Store (but *not* in the POS), because we are using the generic *somdsvr* program.

Now, we can start the posclt by specifying the StoreId and POSId as command-line arguments as shown:

```
$ posclt -storeid 1 -posid 2
```

At this point, the posclt is waiting to accept input. The first operation has to be a login. Type **L** or **1**. The subsequent input can be a bar code or other commands. Bar-code inputs are processed by **BarcodeInput**, and other commands are processed by **KeypadInput** method on the InputMedia object. Platform-specific script files are also provided on the diskette for convenience. Please see the README file.

33.4 RUNNING THE EXAMPLE IN DAIS

There are a number of options available for starting and running DAIS applications. For the purposes of this example, we have kept things in common across ORB vendors, resulting in a command-line approach where every capsule has to be started explicitly. A far more desirable approach is for the application to specify its requirements for the services that it needs and for the system to locate services to match those requirements, starting new services as required. This is the basis on which DAIS applications would normally be designed.

As we mentioned before, this example does not retry if it can't locate a service that it requires on startup, so we have to ensure that the startup sequence is correct and give sufficient time for the capsules to start up before starting the next capsule. The timing is not normally critical if you are entering the start-up commands by hand, but may become relevant if you create a script to perform the startup.

These instructions assume that you have DAIS installed on your system and that it has been configured correctly. In general, configuration merely involves running an interactive script to set up your user environment. We also assume that each capsule is being run on a different terminal or in a different xterm session; as described and provided on disk, the capsules generate diagnostic output that would be confusing if all the capsules were to be run in the background from the same terminal session. Alternatively you could redirect the output from the capsules to a file, and run them in background from the same terminal session.

We have generated all the capsules in the same directory, so, with that directory as our current working directory, we just type:

```
pns
```

which starts the Pseudo-NameService capsule. The PNS is a pure server and not dependent on any other services; therefore it may be started first. This is not true for all the other capsules because they are all dependent on the PNS.

We have the choice now of starting either the OutputMedia or Depot capsules as they are both pure servers apart from a dependence on the PNS. We will start the Depot first:

```
depot
```

followed by the OutputMedia capsule. Note that we have to make a decision on the ID of our POS here because the OutputMedia is associated at startup with a particular POS. We choose a POS ID of 123 here:

```
om id=123
```

In fact, we could start the OutputMedia after the Store if we wanted; the only constraint is that we must have started it before the corresponding POS. The POS is dependent on the Store, so it's the Store that we have to start next:

```
store store=99
```

We arbitrarily assign a store ID of 99. Finally, we start the POS and associate it with the OutputMedia and Store that we have already started:

```
pos id=123 store=99
```

From here on, you can log in to the Store, enter bar codes and end and total sales as per the A&D. You can also start up as many stores as you wish and up to 50 POSs for each store. When you start up a POS, don't forget that you have to start up a corresponding OutputMedia capsule first.

As a further exercise, if you have DAIS configured on a number of systems, you can try a distributed test. For this, all you have to do is copy the pns.ref file to each system after the PNS has been started. You can then start up the capsules as just shown and everything will still work as if they were on the same system.

33.5 RUNNING THE EXAMPLE IN POWERBROKER

Our example system runs as five separate programs. If you have been following along through Chapters 25, 28, and 31, recall that we compiled and linked our programs. These programs are:

Program	Objects
PNS	PseudoNameService
store	Store, Tax, StoreAcess
CentralSrv	Depot
POSClt	POSTerminal, InputMedia
OutSrv	OutputMedia

Running the system under PowerBroker is straightforward; each program should be started in a separate window (for example, xterm window) as follows. Because there are dependencies between the objects in our system, the order in which we start the programs is important. The Pseudo-NameService is used by all of the other objects so we must start it first. Next we can start the OutputMedia and Depot programs, followed by the store, and finally we start the POS, which is a client to objects in each of the other programs. The specific UNIX commands are shown here.

1. Type the following command to start the PNS program:

```
% PNS
```

2. Start the OutputMedia and supply a POS ID as a command-line argument:

    ```
    % OutSrv 1
    ```

3. Start the Depot:

    ```
    % CentralSrv
    ```

4. Type this command to start the Store, supplying a store number and markup value as arguments:

    ```
    % store 26 10
    ```

5. The POSTerminal/InputMedia program is started as follows. It expects a Store ID and POS ID as arguments:

    ```
    % POS 26 1
    ```

6. At last, we can begin entering commands to the POS program.

33.6 RUNNING THE EXAMPLE IN ORBIX

This section gives an overview of running the example on Orbix. You should get the latest code and instructions for different platforms from IONA. Some of the explanation that follows is specific to UNIX, but we have tried to be as general as we can.

The Orbix code directory is structured as follows:

- Uppermost directory: This contains the IDL files (Central.idl, Store.idl, POS.idl, and PNS.idl), and the overall Makefile.
- Directory Central: This contains the code for the Depot (files Srv_Main.cc, Depot_i.h, Depot_i.cc, DepotData.h, DepotData.cc, depot.dat, and Makefile).
- Directory Store: This contains the code for the Store (files Srv_Main.cc, Store_i.h, Store_i.cc, and Makefile).
- Directory POS: This contains the code for the POSTerminal (files Srv_Main.cc, POSClt.cc, POS_IM.h, POS_IM.cc, POS_OM.h, POS_OM.cc, POS_Ter.h, POS_Ter.cc, and Makefile).
- Directory PNS: This contains the code for the Pseudo-Name Service (files Srv_Main.cc, PNS_i.h, PNS_i.cc, PNSData.h, PNSData.cc, FindPNS.h, FindPNS.cc, and Makefile).

- Directory Launcher: This directory will be explained later in this section (files: Launcher.cc and Makefile).

The code can be compiled using the Makefile in the uppermost directory. This uses the Makefiles in each of the subdirectories (it is important that this starts with the PNS directory because the file FindPNS.o is used by each of the other subdirectories).

The following executables are created (Windows users, substitute a backslash \ for the forward slash / in these names):

- PNS/PNSServer: This creates the **PseudoNameService** objects.
- Central/CentralServer: This creates the **Depot** object.
- Store/StoreServer: This creates the **Store** object.
- POS/OutputServerv: This creates the **OutputMedia** object.
- POS/POSClient: This client provides a simple interface to the POS terminal.
- Launcher/Launcherv: This is explained later in this section.

To run the code, first ensure that you are in the uppermost directory and that you have carried out the normal Orbix set-up procedure. That is, you have set up the **IT_CONFIG_PATH** environment variable on UNIX if you wish to use a configuration file other than /etc/Orbix.cfg; and you have to run the Orbix daemon, **orbixd**, on any machine that runs server code. You should then register each of the servers. Recall the **putit** commands shown in each of the C++ chapters of this book:

```
putit CentralSrv <full pathname of the executable file
                      (CentralServer) for this server>
putit StoreSrv
    <full pathname of the executable file
                      (StoreServer) for this server>
    <Store_number, e.g. 1>
    <Markup, e.g. 0.20>
putit OutputSrv
          <full pathname of the executable
              file (OutputServer) for this server>
          <POS_number, e.g. 1>
putit PNSSrv <full pathname of the executable file
                (PNSServer) for this server>
```

The Store and POS numbers are simple integers, and the markup is a floating point number.

After this, run the executable code. Run the PNS server first, followed by the executables **CentralServer**, **StoreServer**, and **OutputServer**. Finally, run the client (**POSClient**) or the Visual Basic version of this (in which case, you should *not* run **OutputServer**, because the Visual Basic code incorporates this functionality).

The order of execution is important for a number of reasons. First, the PNS outputs a file PNS.dat (containing an object reference) that the other executables use to find the **PseudoNameService** object. Therefore it must be run first. (The Orbix **_bind()** function can be used to find any object in the system, making it unnecessary to use the file PNS.dat. To do this, replace the code in the **FindPNS()** function in **FindPNS.cc** with the following:

```
return PseudoNameService::_bind(":PNSrv",<hostname>)
```

The host name can be replaced with the empty string if the Orbix *locator* has been configured, or if the PNS is local.) Second, the **Depot** registers itself with the PNS, and this must occur before the **Store** tries to find it. The same applies for the **OutputMedia** object: It must register itself before the **POSTerminal** object tries to find it.

Neither of these problems would arise in a real system, but they arise here because of our collective decision to use a Pseudo-Name Service rather than the CORBAservices Naming Service. The important difference is that the CORBAservice Naming Service would always be available, and each ORB would provide a simple way for clients to find it. This means that the file PNS.dat would not be required and the PNS would not need to be powered up first. The Naming Service would be an integral part of many applications.

The CORBAservice Naming Service would also remove the other ordering restriction. Its advantage is that it stores its data in a persistent store, so once an object is registered with it, clients can find that object whether or not that object's server is currently running. For example, the Store could ask the Naming Service for a reference to the Depot object, and once the Store uses this reference, the Depot would be automatically powered up (if it were not running already). The ordering restriction would therefore be removed.

To help you to launch the demonstration system in the correct order, we have written a simple Orbix client that binds to each of the objects in the system, launching them if they are not already running. Although it is not necessary to use this launcher, it is worthwhile to present its code here (file: Launcher/Launcher.cc):

```
#include "../PNS.hh"
#include "../POS.hh"
#include "../Central.hh"
```

```
#include "../Store.hh"
#include <iostream.h>
#include <unistd.h>

main() {
  try {
    PseudoNameService::_bind(":PNSrv","");
    cout << "PNS Started" << endl;

    CentralOffice::Depot::_bind
                              (":CentralSrv","");
    cout << "CentralSrv Started" << endl;

    AStore::Store::_bind(":StoreSrv","");
    cout << "StoreSrv started" << endl;

    POS::OutputMedia::_bind(":OutputSrv","");
    cout << "All started" << endl;
  }
  catch(...) {
    cerr << "Error starting a server" << endl;
    return -1;
  }
  ENDTRY
  return 0;
}
```

This **main()** routine makes four calls to the **_bind()** function provided by Orbix. These calls will find the required objects (respectively, the **PseudoNameService** object, the **Depot** object, the **Store** object, and the **OutputMedia** object), and hence start their servers.

33.7 RUNNING THE EXAMPLE IN ORB PLUS

The directories in which the example resides are:

PNS—Contains the Pseudo-Name Server.

POS—Contains the point-of-sales servers and clients.

Central—Contains the Depot server.

Idl—Contains the IDL. ORB Plus does not require any modification of the standard IDL.

Store—Contains the Store server.

The example is compiled and linked by issuing a **make** in the parent directory. The example is executed as follows:

1. Start the Pseudo-Name server:

    `./PNS/Srv_Main&`

2. Start the Depot server:

    `./Central/Srv_Main&`

3. Start the Store server (storeid 10, markup *2):

    `./Store/Srv_Main 10 2&`

4. Start the output media server (POSId 30):

    `./POS/Srv_Main 30&`

5. Invoke the POS client (Storeid 10, POS 30):

    `./POS/posclt 10 30`

33.8 RUNNING THE EXAMPLE WITH SOLARISNEO

In order to see the output of each server, the example requires five windows to be opened, one for each of the following: the Pseudo-Name Service, the Depot, the Store, the POS OutputMedia and the POS Input/Terminal.

Once again we try to follow the generic example. As a result, many operations have to be done by hand, such as launching the servers. In a regular SolarisNEO environment, the servers would be registered with the ORB once at installation time, and thereafter would be automatically launched by the ORB daemon as needed. Not having to monitor the servers and the ability of servers to come back up automatically after deactivation or system failure could be significant factors in lowering the administration cost of a distributed computing environment.

Here is the output of the five windows shown interleaved. Each input or output line is preceded by the name of the window in which it appears, and user input is in **bold**. We've inserted some comments, shown in *italic*.

Window   **Display (user input in boldface)**

First we need to launch the Pseudo-Name Service. From the PNS directory:

PNS	example/PNS% **pname**
PNS	Pseudo Name Server running. Press <Return> to terminate.

Now we can start the Depot server from the "central" directory:

DEPOT	example/central% **depot**
PNS	Registering object Depot
DEPOT	Depot server running. Press <Return> to terminate.

And we start the Store server from the store directory (101 and 1.05 are the store ID and markup respectively):

STORE	example/store% **store 101 1.05**
PNS	Registering object Tax
PNS	Registering object Store_101
STORE	Store server running. Press <Return> to terminate.

We start the Output Media server from the POS.out directory (25 is the POS ID):

POS.OUTPUT	example/POS.out% **outsrv 25**
PNS	Registering object OutputMedia_25
POS.OUTPUT	OutputMedia Server running. Press <Return> to terminate.

Finally, we start the Input/Terminal server from POS.ter (101 and 25 are the Store and POS ID respectively):

POS>INPUT	example/POS.ter% **posclt 101 25**
PNS	Looking for object Tax
PNS	Looking for object Store_101
PNS	Looking for object OutputMedia_25
PNS	Looking for object Tax

```
PNS            Looking for object Depot
POS>INPUT      Command Summary :-
POS>INPUT      L : Login  P : POS Sales Summary  S : Store
               Sales Summary
POS>INPUT      T : Total  Q : Quantity    X : Exit
POS>INPUT
```

Before anything else, we must log in the POS:

```
POS>INPUT      Enter code, command (L,P,Q,S,T) or X to exit
               : l
```

Let's ring up the first sale (3 pencils, some pasta, and 5 units of parsley):

```
POS>INPUT      Enter code, command (L,P,Q,S,T) or X to exit
               : q 3
POS>INPUT      Enter code, command (L,P,Q,S,T) or X to exit
               : 423552
POS.OUTPUT     3  423552    Pencil  2.35  7.05 *
POS>INPUT      Enter code, command (L,P,Q,S,T) or X to exit
               : 102345
POS.OUTPUT     1  102345    Pasta  12.38  12.38
POS>INPUT      Enter code, command (L,P,Q,S,T) or X to exit
               : q 5
POS>INPUT      Enter code, command (L,P,Q,S,T) or X to exit
               : 923988
POS.OUTPUT     5  923988    Persil  12.34  61.70
POS>INPUT      Enter code, command (L,P,Q,S,T) or X to exit
               : t
POS.OUTPUT     Taxable Sub-Total :=  7.05
POS.OUTPUT     Taxes     :=  0.35
POS.OUTPUT     Total     :=  81.48
POS.OUTPUT
POS.OUTPUT     Go raibh maith agat
POS.OUTPUT
```

And another simple sale (1 pen):

```
POS>INPUT      Enter code, command (L,P,Q,S,T) or X to exit
               : 234234
```

```
POS.OUTPUT    1  234234     Pen  8.31  8.31  *
POS>INPUT     Enter code, command (L,P,Q,S,T) or X to exit
              : t
POS.OUTPUT    Taxable Sub-Total := 8.31
POS.OUTPUT    Taxes     := 0.42
POS.OUTPUT    Total     := 8.73
POS.OUTPUT
POS.OUTPUT    Go raibh maith agat
POS.OUTPUT
```

We ask for the current total for this store:

```
POS>INPUT     Enter code, command (L,P,Q,S,T) or X to exit
              : p
POS.OUTPUT     Point of Sale Total := 90.21
POS.OUTPUT        Tax Total := 0.77
POS.OUTPUT
```

Finally, we exit the POS terminal/InputMedia:

```
POS>INPUT     Enter code, command (L,P,Q,S,T) or X to exit
              : x
```

We also terminate all the other servers by pressing <CR> in each one.

Have a good day! 'twas a pleasure to serve you!

33.9 RUNNING THE HP DISTRIBUTED SMALLTALK POS EXAMPLE

The HP Distributed Smalltalk version of the POS example can be run in two different scenarios. The first takes advantage of the local RPC mechanism of HP Distributed Smalltalk. With local RPC testing enabled, it is possible to run the POS example in a single HP Distributed Smalltalk image and have the POS example objects behave as if they are fully distributed. This is the easiest way to run this example.

The second way to run the example is in a fully distributed fashion with multiple images on multiple machines. This is more complex than the previous scenario, but it is more realistic.

Both scenarios are started with the aid of the **OMGPrimerExample** class. This class makes it easy to set up and run the POS example. This class is described in Chapter 32.

33.9.1 Scenario 1: Running as a Single Image with Local RPC Testing

Do the following:

1. Start up your image on your local machine.
2. File in the code file, omg.ch, in each image.
3. Save out the image.
4. Start the ORB and enable local RPC testing. Using local RPC testing simulates running in a distributed environment. Execute the following statement in the transcript:

    ```
    OMGPrimerExample localRPCDemo
    ```

    Note that the Store ID will default to 42 and the POS terminal will default to 10. Now the user interface for the POS terminal comes up, and you can exercise the example.

33.9.2 Scenario 2: Running with Multiple Remote Images

In this scenario, we will run in a fully distributed fashion with multiple machines and images. For this scenario do the following:

1. Start up your images on your local machine and the machines in your network setup.
2. File in the code file, omg.ch, in each image.
3. Save out the image(s).

In this case you will run run the example in the configuration shown in Figure 33.1.

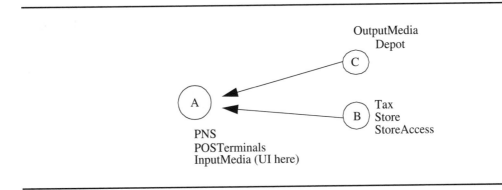

Figure 33.1. Smalltalk multimachine configuration.

4. Designate machine A as the location of the Pseudo-Naming Service (PNS). Start the image and the ORB, then execute:

    ```
    OMGPrimerExample createPNS
    ```

    This will create the file pns.dat that contains the object reference to the PNS on machine A.

5. Copy the pns.dat file created in step 1 to machine B and machine C. It should be placed in the directory where the image is located.

6. Copy the depot.dat file to machine C. It should be placed in the directory where the image is located.

7. On machine C, bring up the image and start the ORB. Execute:

    ```
    OMGPrimerExample createDepot
    OMGPrimerExample createOutputMedia: posId
    ```

    For *posId*, you must specify a positive integer value; for example, 1.

8. On machine B, bring up the image and start the ORB. Execute:

    ```
    OMGPrimerExample createStore: storeId markup: percentage
    ```

    For *storeId*, specifiy an integer value; for example, 42. For *percentage*, you must specify a floating value; for example, 0.1.

9. On machine A, bring up the image and start the ORB. Execute:

    ```
    OMGPrimerExample createPOSTerminal: posId store: storeId
    ```

    Make sure the *posId* and the *storeId* are the same as specified in steps 5 and 7 respectively.

Now the primer example user interface will display and be ready for execution.

Contacts and References

A.1 ORGANIZATIONS AND CONTACTS

A.1.1 The Object Management Group

The mailing address of the Object Management Group is:

Object Management Group
492 Old Connecticut Path
Framingham, MA 01701 USA
Phone: 508-820-4300
Fax: 508-820-4303
Email: *info@omg.org* or *request@omg.org*. Or to the author at
siegel@omg.org.
URL: http://www.omg.org.

Material available from OMG includes a free membership information kit, a
free CORBA products directory, and a publication order form listing available
publications and their prices. Publication information is also available on the
OMG Web page cited here.

A.1.2 Digital Equipment Corporation

For information on ObjectBroker, contact:

Digital Equipment Corporation
ObjectBroker Product Management
ZKO2-2/R80
110 Spit Brook Road
Nashua, NH 03062

Phone: 1-800-DIGITAL
Fax: 1-603-881-0120; give name ObjectBroker Product
Management/R80
URL: http://www.digital.com/info/objectbroker
Email: For email and up-to-date contact information, check the Web
page.

A.1.3 Expersoft Corporation:

For information on PowerBroker, contact:

Expersoft Corporation
6620 Mesa Ridge Road
San Diego, CA 92121
Phone: (619) 546-4100
Fax: (619) 450-0644
Email: mktg@expersoft.com
URL: http://www.expersoft.com

A.1.4 Hewlett-Packard

For information on Distributed Smalltalk, contact:

ParcPlace–Digitalk, Inc
999 East Arques Avenue
Sunnyvale, CA 94086-4593
Phone: 800-759-7272
Phone: 408-481-9090
Fax: 408-481-9095
URL: http://www.parcplace.com

For information on ORB Plus, contact:

Hewlett-Packard Company
Paul Rafter/MS 42UNC
19111 Pruneridge Avenue
Cupertino, CA 95014-9807
Phone: 408-447-5761
Fax: 408-447-0872
Email: prafter@cup.hp.com
URL: http//www.hp.com

A.1.5 IBM

For information on SOM and DSOM, contact:

IBM Direct
4111 North Side Parkway
Atlanta, GA 30321
Phone: 1-800-426-2255
Fax: 1-800-242-6329
URL: http://www.software.ibm.com/objects/somobjects

A.1.6 ICL

For information on DAIS, contact:

In the United Kingdom:
ICL Object Software Labs
Wenlock Way
West Gorton
Manchester, M12 5DR, UK
Phone: (+44) 161 223 1301 x3771
Fax: (+44) 161 263 0482

In the United States:
ICL
Commerce Park Drive
Reston, VA 22091, USA
Phone: (+1) 703-648-3300
Fax: (+1) 703-648-3326
Email: dais@wg.icl.co.uk
URL: http://www.icl.com/products/dais/ home.html

A.1.7 IONA Technologies

IONA Technologies, based in Dublin, Ireland, also maintains offices in the United States. Here is information for both sites:

Main office:
IONA Technologies
8-10 Lower Pembroke Street
Dublin 2, Ireland

Phone: + 353 1 6625255
Fax: + 353 1 6625244

United States office:
IONA Technologies
201 Broadway, Suite 25, 3rd floor
Cambridge, MA 02139-1955
Phone: 800-orbix4u (800-672-4948) or 617-679-0900
Fax: 508-679-0910

Either site:
Email: info@iona.com
URL: http://www.iona.com

A.1.8   SunSoft

For information on NEO, contact:

SunSoft, Inc.
2550 Garcia Avenue
Mountain View, CA 94043-1100 USA
Phone: (512)345-2412 or 1-800-SUNSOFT
URL: http://www.sun.com/sunsoft/ or
http://www.Sun.COM/sunsoft/DOE

A.2   REFERENCES

A.2.1   Chapter 1

Guttman, Michael and Matthews, Jason, *The Object Technology Revolution*: John Wiley & Sons, Inc., New York, 1995.

Mowbray, Thomas J. and Zahavi, Ron, *The Essential CORBA*: John Wiley & Sons, Inc., New York, 1995.

A.2.2   Chapter 3

The Common Object Request Broker Architecture and Specification; Revision 2.0: Object Management Group, Inc., Framingham, MA., July 1995.

A.2.3   Chapter 6

AES/Distributed Computing—Remote Procedure Call, Revision B: Open Software Foundation, Cambridge, MA., 1993.

This document may be downloaded from the OSF DCE Web page at no charge: http://www.osf.org/dce.

A.2.4 Chapter 10

CORBAservices: Common Object Services Specification, Revised Edition: Object Management Group, Inc., Framingham, MA., March 1995.

A.2.5 Chapter 11

R.G.G. Cattell, T. Atwood, J. Duhl, G. Ferran, M. Loomis, and D. Wade, *The Object Database Standard: ODMG-93 v1.2*. San Mateo, CA: Morgan Kaufman, 1993.

A.2.6 Chapter 12

ISO/IEC JTC1/SC21 Working Group 7 (Open Distributed Processing), *The RM-ODP Trader Standard*.

This document is not yet published officially, but may be downloaded from the ODP-information Web site at http://www.dstc.edu.au/AU/research_news/odp/ref_model/ref_model.html. Selecting *RM-ODP Standards* brings up a Web page that allows downloading of the Trader document.

A.2.7 Chapter 14

The OMG Transaction Service is defined in *CORBAservices: Common Object Services Specification, Revised Edition*: Object Management Group, Inc., Framingham, MA., March 1995.

Additional TP standards and specifications are defined in *Distributed Transaction Processing: the TxRPC Specification*. X/Open Document P305, X/Open Company Ltd., Reading, UK.

Distributed Transaction Processing: the XA Specification. X/Open Document C193, X/Open Company Ltd., Reading, UK.

Distributed Transaction Processing: the XATMI Specification. X/Open Document P306, X/Open Company Ltd., Reading, UK.

For an introduction to transaction processing, read Jim Gray and Andreas Reuter, *Transaction Processing: Concepts and Techniques*. San Francisco, Morgan Kaufman, 1992.

Finally, Ed Cobb's original article "Objects and Transactions: Together at Last," *Object Magazine*, January 1995, SIGS Publications, New York.

A.2.8   Chapter 15

The OMG Query Service is defined in *CORBAservices: Common Object Services Specification, Revised Edition*: Object Management Group, Inc., Framingham, MA., March 1995.

SQL-92 Query, the subset of SQL-92 that deals directly with query, is defined in *Database Language—SQL*, American National Standard x3.135-1992, ANSI, January 1992.

OQL-93 is defined by the Object Database Management Group in R.G.G. Cattell, T. Atwood, J. Duhl, G. Ferran, M. Loomis, and D. Wade, *The Object Database Standard: ODMG-93 v1.2*. San Mateo, CA: Morgan Kaufman, 1993.

A.2.9   Chapter 16

OMG White Paper on Security. Framingham, MA: Object Management Group, document number 94-4-16, April, 1994. This document is available from OMG without charge.

A.2.10   Chapter 17

OpenDoc information, and the OpenDoc specification itself, are available from either Component Integration Laboratories, San Francisco, CA (http://www.cil.org) or from OMG. OpenDoc was expected to become the OMG Compound Document CORBAfacility as this book goes to press; once adoption is complete, the OpenDoc specification will be available in the OMG CORBAfacilities Specification publication.

A.2.11   Chapter 20

Danforth, Scott, Paul Koenen, and Bruce Tate, *Objects for OS/2*, New York: Van Nostrand Reinhold, 1994.

IBM Publication, *SOMobjects Developer Toolkit, Users Guide*, SC23-2680-01.

Lau, Christina, *Object-Oriented Programming Using SOM and DSOM*, New York: Van Nostrand Reinhold, 1994.

A.2.12   Chapter 21

PowerBroker User's Guide, Expersoft Corporation, San Diego, 1995.

PowerBroker Reference Manual, Expersoft Corporation, San Diego, 1995.

Margaret A. Ellis and Bjarne Stroustup, *The Annotated C++ Reference Manual*. Reading, MA: Addison-Wesley, 1994.

Orbix Programming Guide, IONA Technologies Ltd., Dublin, 1995.

Orbix Reference Guide, IONA Technologies Ltd., Dublin, 1995.

Orbix-OLE Programming Guide, IONA Technologies Ltd., Dublin, 1995.

The Orbix Architecture, IONA Technologies Ltd., Dublin, 1995.

Annrai O'Toole, "Distributing Objects with Orbix," *AIXpert Magazine*, May 1995, pp. 18–26.

John V. Tisaranni, "Product Review: IONA's Orbix Object Request Broker," *Object Magazine*, July/August 1995, pp. 82–87.

Mark Betz, "Building a CORBA Object Server," *Software Development Magazine*, October 1995, pp. 53–61.

Robert Orfali, Dan Harkey, and Jeri Edwards, *The Essential Distributed Objects Survival Guide*, John Wiley & Sons, Inc., New York, 1995.

Technology Audit: Orbix, Butler Group, Hull, England, November 1994.

A.2.13 Chapter 23

IBM Publication, *SOMobjects Developer Toolkit, Users Guide*, SC23-2680-01.

IDL Types

B.1 BASIC IDL TYPES

This information on IDL types is summarized from the OMG CORBA core specification. For more details, refer to the original specification or the documentation that came with your ORB product.

B.1.1 Integer Types

IDL supports **long** and **short** signed and **unsigned** integer datatypes. **long** represents the range $-2^{31}..2^{31} - 1$ while **unsigned long** represents the range $0..2^{32} - 1$. **short** represents the range $-2^{15}..2^{15} - 1$, while **unsigned short** represents the range $0..2^{16} - 1$.

B.1.2 Floating-Point Types

IDL floating-point types are **float** and **double**. The **float** type represents IEEE single-precision floating point numbers; the **double** type represents IEEE double-precision floating point numbers. The IEEE floating point standard specification (*IEEE Standard for Binary Floating-Point Arithmetic*, ANSI/IEEE Std 754-1985) should be consulted for more information on the precision afforded by these types.

B.1.3 Char Type

The **char** datatype consists of 8-bit quantities, defined by the ISO Latin-1 (8859.1) character set standard for all possible graphic characters, and the ASCII (ISO 646) standard for null and formatting characters.

B.1.4 Boolean Type

The **boolean** datatype is used to denote a data item that can only take one of the values TRUE and FALSE.

B.1.5 Octet Type

The **octet** type is an 8-bit quantity that is guaranteed not to undergo any conversion when transmitted by the communication system.

B.1.6 Any Type

The **any** type permits the specification of values that can express any OMG IDL type.

B.2 CONSTRUCTED TYPES

The constructed types consist of structs, unions, and enumerated types.

B.2.1 Structures

The structure syntax is:

```
<struct_type>     ::= "struct" <identifier> "{" <member_list> "}"
<member_list>     ::= <member> +
<member>          ::= <type_spec> <declarators> ";"
```

The **<identifier>** in **<struct_type>** defines a new legal type. Structure types may also be named using a **typedef** declaration.

Name scoping rules require that the member declarators in a particular structure be unique. The value of a **struct** is the value of all of its members.

B.2.2 Discriminated Unions

The discriminated **union** syntax is:

```
<union_type>        ::= "union" <identifier> "switch" "(" <switch_type_spec> ")"
                            "{" <switch_body> "}"
<switch_type_spec>  ::= <integer_type>
                      |  <char_type>
                      |  <boolean_type>
                      |  <enum_type>
```

	<scoped_name>
\<switch_body\>	::= \<case\>$^+$
\<case\>	::= \<case_label\>$^+$ \<element_spec\> ";"
\<case_label\>	::= "case" \<const_exp\> ":"
	"default" ":"
\<element_spec\>	::= \<type_spec\> \<declarator\>

OMG IDL unions are a cross between the C **union** and **switch** statements. IDL unions must be discriminated; that is, the union header must specify a typed tag field that determines which union member to use for the current instance of a call. The **\<identifier\>** following the **union** keyword defines a new legal type. Union types may also be named using a **type-def** declaration. The **\<const_exp\>** in a **\<case_label\>** must be consistent with the **\<switch_type_spec\>**. A **default** case can appear at most once. The **\<scoped_name\>** in the **\<switch_type_spec\>** production must be a previously defined **integer**, **char**, **boolean**, or **enum** type.

Case labels must match or be automatically castable to the defined type of the discriminator. The complete set of case label matching rules are shown in the following list:

Discriminator Type	Matched By
long	any integer value in the value range of long
short	any integer value in the value range of short
unsigned long	any integer value in the value range of unsigned long
unsigned short	any integer value in the value range of unsigned short
char	char
boolean	TRUE or FALSE
enum	any enumerator for the discriminator enum type

Name scoping rules require that the element declarators in a particular union be unique. If the **\<switch_type_spec\>** is an **\<enum_type\>**, the identifier for the enumeration is in the scope of the union; as a result, it must be distinct from the element declarators.

It is not required that all possible values of the union discriminator be listed in the **\<switch_body\>**. The value of a union is the value of the discriminator, together with one of the following:

- If the discriminator value was explicitly listed in a **case** statement, the value of the element associated with that **case** statement.

- If a default **case** label was specified, the value of the element associated with the default **case** label.
- No additional value.

Access to the discriminator and the related element is language-mapping dependent.

B.2.3 Enumerations

Enumerated types consist of ordered lists of identifiers. The syntax is:

```
<enum_type>      ::= "enum" <identifier> "{" <enumerator> { ","
<enumerator> }* "}"
<enumerator>     ::= <identifier>
```

A maximum of 2^{32} identifiers may be specified in an enumeration; as such, the enumerated names must be mapped to a native datatype capable of representing a maximally sized enumeration. The order in which the identifiers are named in the specification of an enumeration defines the relative order of the identifiers. Any language mapping that permits two enumerators to be compared or defines successor/predecessor functions on enumerators must conform to this ordering relation. The **<identifier>** following the **enum** keyword defines a new legal type. Enumerated types may also be named using a **typedef** declaration.

B.2.4 Template Types

The template types are:

```
<template_type_spec>::= <sequence_type>
                     |   <string_type>
```

B.2.5 Sequences

IDL defines the sequence type **sequence**. A sequence is a one-dimensional array with two characteristics: a maximum size (which is fixed at compile time) and a length (which is determined at run time).
The syntax is:

```
<sequence_type>      ::= "sequence" "<" <simple_type_spec> ","
<positive_int_const> ">"
                     |   "sequence" "<" <simple_type_spec> ">"
```

The second parameter in a sequence declaration indicates the maximum size of the sequence. If a positive integer constant is specified for the maximum size, the sequence is termed a bounded sequence. Prior to passing a bounded sequence as a function argument (or as a field in a structure or union), the length of the sequence must be set in a language-mapping dependent manner. After receiving a sequence result from an operation invocation, the length of the returned sequence will have been set; this value may be obtained in a language-mapping dependent manner.

If no maximum size is specified, the size of the sequence is unspecified (unbounded). Prior to passing such a sequence as a function argument (or as a field in a structure or union), the length of the sequence, the maximum size of the sequence, and the address of a buffer to hold the sequence must be set in a language-mapping dependent manner. After receiving such a sequence result from an operation invocation, the length of the returned sequence will have been set; this value may be obtained in a language-mapping dependent manner.

A sequence type may be used as the type parameter for another sequence type. For example, the following:

typedef sequence< sequence<long> > Fred;

declares Fred to be of type "unbounded sequence of unbounded sequence of long". Note that for nested sequence declarations, white space must be used to separate the two ">" tokens ending the declaration so they are not parsed as a single ">>" token.

B.2.6 Strings

IDL defines the string type **string** consisting of all possible 8-bit quantities except null. A string is similar to a sequence of char. As with sequences of any type, prior to passing a string as a function argument (or as a field in a structure or union), the length of the string must be set in a language-mapping dependent manner. The syntax is:

<string_type>   ::= "string" "<" <positive_int_const> ">"
** | "string"**

The argument to the string declaration is the maximum size of the string. If a positive integer maximum size is specified, the string is termed a bounded string; if no maximum size is specified, the string is termed an unbounded string.

Strings are singled out as a separate type because many languages have special built-in functions or standard library functions for string manipulation. A separate string type may permit substantial optimization in the handling of strings compared to what can be done with sequences of general types.

B.3 COMPLEX DECLARATOR

B.3.1 Arrays

OMG IDL defines multidimensional, fixed-size arrays. An array includes explicit sizes for each dimension.

The syntax for arrays is:

```
<array_declarator>    ::= <identifier> <fixed_array_size>⁺
<fixed_array_size>    ::= "[" <positive? _int_const> "]"
```

The array size (in each dimension) is fixed at compile time. When an array is passed as a parameter in an operation invocation, all elements of the array are transmitted.

The implementation of array indices is language mapping-specific; passing an array index as a parameter may yield incorrect results.

Index

687